VISUAL QUICKPRO GUIDE

PHP 6
AND MySQL 5

FOR DYNAMIC WEB SITES

Larry Ullman

 Peachpit Press

Visual QuickPro Guide

PHP 6 and MySQL 5 for Dynamic Web Sites

Larry Ullman

Peachpit Press

1249 Eighth Street
Berkeley, CA 94710
510/524-2178
510/524-2221 (fax)
Find us on the Web at: www.peachpit.com
To report errors, please send a note to: errata@peachpit.com
Peachpit Press is a division of Pearson Education.

Editor: Rebecca Gulick
Copy Editor: Bob Campbell
Production Coordinator: Becky Winter
Compositors: Myrna Vladic, Jerry Ballew, and Rick Gordon
Indexer: Rebecca Plunkett
Cover Production: Louisa Adair
Technical Reviewer: Arpad Ray

ISBN-13: 978-0-321-52599-4
ISBN-10: 0-321-52599-X

9 8 7 6 5 4 3 2 1

Printed and bound in the United States of America

Dedication

Dedicated to the fine faculty at my alma
mater, Northeast Missouri State University.
In particular, I would like to thank: Dr. Monica
Barron, Dr. Dennis Leavens, Dr. Ed Tyler, and
Dr. Cole Woodcox, whom I also have the
pleasure of calling my friend. I would not be
who I am as a writer, as a student, as a
teacher, or as a person if it were not for the
magnanimous, affecting, and brilliant
instruction I received from these educators.

Special Thanks to:

My heartfelt thanks to everyone at Peachpit Press, as always.

My gratitude to editor extraordinaire Rebecca Gulick, who makes my job so much easier. And thanks to Bob Campbell for his hard work, helpful suggestions, and impressive attention to detail. Thanks also to Rebecca Plunkett for indexing and Becky Winter, Myrna Vladic, Jerry Ballew, and Rick Gordon for laying out the book, and thanks to Arpad Ray for his technical review.

Kudos to the good people working on PHP, MySQL, Apache, phpMyAdmin, and XAMPP, among other great projects. And a hearty "cheers" to the denizens of the various newsgroups, mailing lists, support forums, etc., who offer assistance and advice to those in need.

Thanks, as always, to the readers, whose support gives my job relevance. An extra helping of thanks to those who provided the translations in Chapter 15, "Example—Message Board," and who offered up recommendations as to what they'd like to see in this edition.

Thanks to Nicole and Christina for entertaining and taking care of the kids so that I could get some work done.

Finally, I would not be able to get through a single book if it weren't for the love and support of my wife, Jessica. And a special shout out to Zoe and Sam, who give me reasons to, and not to, write books!

TABLE OF CONTENTS

TABLE OF CONTENTS

INTRODUCTION

Today's Web users expect exciting pages that are updated frequently and provide a customized experience. For them, Web sites are more like communities, to which they'll return time and again. At the same time, Web site administrators want sites that are easier to update and maintain, understanding that's the only real way to keep up with visitors' expectations. For these reasons and more, PHP and MySQL have become the de facto standards for creating dynamic, database-driven Web sites.

This book represents the culmination of my many years of Web development experience coupled with the value of having written several previous books on the technologies discussed herein. The focus of this book is on covering the most important knowledge in the most efficient manner. It will teach you how to begin developing dynamic Web sites and give you plenty of example code to get you started. All you need to provide is an eagerness to learn.

Well, that and a computer.

What Are Dynamic Web Sites?

Dynamic Web sites are flexible and potent creatures, more accurately described as *applications* than merely sites. Dynamic Web sites

◆ Respond to different parameters (for example, the time of day or the version of the visitor's Web browser)

◆ Have a "memory," allowing for user registration and login, e-commerce, and similar processes

◆ Almost always have HTML forms, so that people can perform searches, provide feedback, and so forth

◆ Often have interfaces where administrators can manage the site's content

◆ Are easier to maintain, upgrade, and build upon than statically made sites

There are many technologies available for creating dynamic Web sites. The most common are ASP.NET (Active Server Pages, a Microsoft construct), JSP (Java Server Pages), ColdFusion, Ruby on Rails, and PHP. Dynamic Web sites don't always rely on a database, but more and more of them do, particularly as excellent database applications like MySQL are available at little to no cost.

Figure i.1 The home page for PHP.

What is PHP?

PHP originally stood for "Personal Home Page" as it was created in 1994 by Rasmus Lerdorf to track the visitors to his online résumé. As its usefulness and capabilities grew (and as it started being used in more professional situations), it came to mean "PHP: Hypertext Preprocessor."

According to the official PHP Web site, found at www.php.net (**Figure i.1**), PHP is a "widely-used general-purpose scripting language that is especially suited for Web development and can be embedded into HTML." It's a long but descriptive definition, whose meaning I'll explain.

Starting at the end of that statement, to say that PHP can be embedded into HTML means that you can take a standard HTML page, drop in some PHP wherever you need it, and end up with a dynamic result. This attribute makes PHP very approachable for anyone that's done even a little bit of HTML work.

Also, PHP is a scripting language, as opposed to a programming language: PHP was designed to write Web scripts, not stand-alone applications (although, with some extra effort, you can now create applications in PHP). PHP scripts run only after an event occurs—for example, when a user submits a form or goes to a URL.

I should add to this definition that PHP is a *server-side, cross-platform* technology, both descriptions being important. Server-side refers to the fact that everything PHP does occurs on the server. A Web server application, like Apache or Microsoft's IIS (Internet Information Services), is required and all PHP scripts must be accessed through a URL (http://-something). Its cross-platform nature means that PHP runs on most operating systems, including Windows, Unix (and its many variants), and Macintosh. More important, the PHP scripts written on one server will normally work on another with little or no modification.

At the time the book was written, PHP was at version 5.2.4, with version 4.4.7 still being maintained. Support for version 4 is being dropped, though, and it's recommended that everyone use at least version 5 of PHP. This edition of this book actually focuses on version 6 of PHP, to be released in late 2007 or in 2008. If you're still using version 4, you really should upgrade. If that's not in your plans, then please grab the second edition of this book instead. If you're using PHP 5, either the second or this edition of the book will work for you. In this edition, I will make it clear which features and functions are PHP 6–specific.

What's new in PHP 6

Because of the planned extinction of PHP 4, many users and Web hosting companies will likely make a quick transition from PHP 4 to PHP 5 to PHP 6. To discuss what's new in PHP 6, I'll start with the even bigger differences between PHP 4 and 5.

PHP 5, like PHP 4 before it, is a major new development of this popular programming language. The most critical changes in PHP 5 involve object-oriented programming (OOP).Those changes don't really impact this book, as OOP isn't covered (I do so in my book *PHP 5 Advanced: Visual QuickPro Guide*). With respect to this book, the biggest change in PHP 5 is the addition of the Improved MySQL Extension, which is used to communicate with MySQL. The Improved MySQL Extension offers many benefits over the older MySQL extension and will be used exclusively.

The big change in PHP 6 is support for Unicode, which is to say that PHP can now handle characters in every language in the world. This is huge, and it's also one of the reasons it's taken a while to release PHP 6. What this means in terms of programming is covered in Chapter 14, "Making Universal Sites." The information in that chapter is also used in Chapter 15, "Example—Message Board." Beyond Unicode support, PHP 6 cleans up a lot of garbage that was left in PHP 5 even though the recommendation was not to use such things. The two biggest removals are the "Magic Quotes" and "register globals" features.

Why use PHP?

Put simply, when it comes to developing dynamic Web sites, PHP is better, faster, and easier to learn than the alternatives. What you get with PHP is excellent performance, a tight integration with nearly every database available, stability, portability, and a nearly limitless feature set due to its extendibility. All of this comes at no cost (PHP is open source) and with a very manageable learning curve. PHP is one of the best marriages I've ever seen between the ease with which beginning programmers can start using it and the ability for more advanced programmers to do everything they require.

Finally, the proof is in the pudding: PHP has seen an exponential growth in use since its inception, overtaking ASP as the most popular scripting language being used today. It's the most requested module for Apache (the most-used Web server), and by the time this book hits the shelves, PHP will be on nearly 25 million domains.

Of course, you might assume that I, as the author of a book on PHP (several, actually), have a biased opinion. Although not nearly to the same extent as PHP, I've also developed sites using Java Server Pages (JSP), Ruby on Rails (RoR), and ASP.NET. Each has its pluses and minuses, but PHP is the technology I always return to. You might hear that it doesn't perform or scale as well as other technologies, but Yahoo! handles over 3.5 billion hits per day using PHP (yes, *billion*). You might also wonder how secure PHP is. But security isn't in the language; it's in how that language is used. Rest assured that a complete and up-to-date discussion of all the relevant security concerns is provided by this book!

How PHP works

As previously stated, PHP is a server-side language. This means that the code you write in PHP sits on a host computer called a *server*. The server sends Web pages to the requesting visitors (you, the client, with your Web browser).

When a visitor goes to a Web site written in PHP, the server reads the PHP code and then processes it according to its scripted directions. In the example shown in **Figure i.2**, the PHP code tells the server to send the appropriate data—HTML code—to the Web browser, which treats the received code as it would a standard HTML page.

This differs from a static HTML site where, when a request is made, the server merely sends the HTML data to the Web browser and there is no server-side interpretation occurring (**Figure i.3**). Because no server-side action is required, you can run HTML pages in your Web browser without using a server at all.

To the end user and their Web browser there is no perceptible difference between what home.html and home.php may look like, but how that page's content was created will be significantly different.

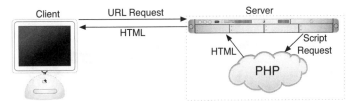

Figure i.2 How PHP fits into the client/server model when a user requests a Web page.

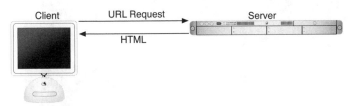

Figure i.3 The client/server process when a request for a static HTML page is made.

What is MySQL?

MySQL (www.mysql.com, **Figure i.4**) is the world's most popular open-source database. In fact, today MySQL is a viable competitor to the pricey goliaths such as Oracle and Microsoft's SQL Server. Like PHP, MySQL offers excellent performance, portability, and reliability, with a moderate learning curve and little to no cost.

MySQL is a database management system (DBMS) for relational databases (therefore, MySQL is an RDBMS). A database, in the simplest terms, is a collection of interrelated data, be it text, numbers, or binary files, that are stored and kept organized by the DBMS.

There are many types of databases, from the simple flat-file to relational and object-oriented. A relational database uses multiple tables to store information in its most discernable parts. While relational databases may involve more thought in the design and programming stages, they offer an improvement to reliability and data integrity that more than makes up for the extra effort required. Further, relational databases are more searchable and allow for concurrent users.

By incorporating a database into a Web application, some of the data generated by PHP can be retrieved from MySQL (**Figure i.5**). This further moves the site's content from a static (hard-coded) basis to a flexible one, flexibility being the key to a dynamic Web site.

MySQL is an open-source application, like PHP, meaning that it is free to use or even modify (the source code itself is downloadable). There are occasions in which you should pay for a MySQL license, especially if you are making money from the sales or incorporation of the MySQL product. Check MySQL's licensing policy for more information on this.

Figure i.4 The home page for the MySQL database application.

The MySQL software consists of several pieces, including the MySQL server (*mysqld*, which runs and manages the databases), the MySQL client (*mysql*, which gives you an interface to the server), and numerous utilities for maintenance and other purposes. PHP has always had good support for MySQL, and that is even more true in the most recent versions of the language.

MySQL has been known to handle databases as large as 60,000 tables with more than five billion rows. MySQL can work with tables as large as eight million terabytes on some operating systems, generally a healthy 4 GB otherwise. MySQL is used by NASA and the United States Census Bureau, among many others.

At the time of this writing, MySQL is on version 5.0.45, with versions 5.1 and 6.0 in development. The version of MySQL you have affects what features you can use, so it's important that you know what you're working with. For this book, MySQL 5.0.45 was used, although you should be able to do everything in this book as long as you're using a version of MySQL greater than 4.1. (My book *MySQL: Visual QuickStart Guide* goes into the more advanced and newer features of MySQL 5 that aren't used in this book.)

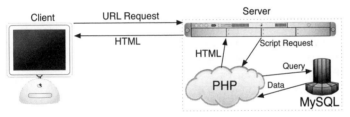

Figure i.5 How most of the dynamic Web applications in this book will work, using both PHP and MySQL.

Pronunciation Guide

Trivial as it may be, I should clarify up front that MySQL is technically pronounced "My Ess Que Ell," just as SQL should be said "Ess Que Ell." This is a question many people have when first working with these technologies. While not a critical issue, it's always best to pronounce acronyms correctly.

What You'll Need

To follow the examples in this book, you'll need the following tools:

- A Web server application (for example, Apache, Abyss, or IIS)

- PHP

- MySQL

- A Web browser (Microsoft's Internet Explorer, Mozilla's Firefox, Apple's Safari, etc.)

- A text editor, PHP-capable WYSIWYG application (Adobe's Dreamweaver qualifies), or IDE (integrated development environment)

- An FTP application, if using a remote server

One of the great things about developing dynamic Web sites with PHP and MySQL is that all of the requirements can be met at no cost whatsoever, regardless of your operating system! Apache, PHP, and MySQL are each free; most Web browsers can be had without cost; and many good text editors are available for nothing.

The appendix discusses the installation process on the Windows and Mac OS X operating systems. If you have a computer, you are only a couple of downloads away from being able to create dynamic Web sites (in that case, your computer would represent both the client and the server in Figures i.2 and i.5). Conversely, you could purchase Web hosting for only dollars per month that will provide you with a PHP- and MySQL-enabled environment already online.

About This Book

This book teaches how to develop dynamic Web sites with PHP and MySQL, covering the knowledge that most developers might require. In keeping with the format of the Visual QuickPro series, the information is discussed using a step-by-step approach with corresponding images. The focus has been kept on real-world, practical examples, avoiding "here's something you could do but never would" scenarios. As a practicing Web developer myself, I wrote about the information that I use and avoided those topics immaterial to the task at hand. As a practicing writer, I made certain to include topics and techniques that I know readers are asking about.

The structure of the book is linear, and the intention is that you'll read it in order. It begins with three chapters covering the fundamentals of PHP (by the second chapter, you will have already developed your first dynamic Web page). After that, there are three chapters on SQL (Structured Query Language, which is used to interact with all databases) and MySQL. They teach the basics of SQL, database design, and the MySQL application in particular. Then there's one chapter on debugging and error management, information everyone needs. This is followed by a chapter introducing how to use PHP and MySQL together, a remarkably easy thing to do.

The following five chapters teach more application techniques to round out your knowledge. Security, in particular, is repeatedly addressed in those pages. Chapter 14, "Making Universal Sites," is entirely new to this edition of the book, showing you how to broaden the reach of your sites. Finally, I've included three example chapters, in which the heart of different Web applications are developed, with instructions.

Is this book for you?

This book was written for a wide range of people within the beginner-to-intermediate range. The book makes use of XHTML for future compatibility, so solid experience with XHTML, or its forebear HTML, is a must. Although this book covers many things, it does not formally teach HTML or Web page design. Some CSS is sprinkled about these pages but also not taught.

Second, this book expects that you have one of the following:

◆ The drive and ability to learn without much hand holding, or...

◆ Familiarity with another programming language (even solid JavaScript skills would qualify), or...

◆ A cursory knowledge of PHP

Make no mistake: This book covers PHP and MySQL from A to Z, teaching everything you'll need to know to develop real-world Web sites, but particularly the early chapters cover PHP at a quick pace. For this reason I recommend either some programming experience or a curious and independent spirit when it comes to learning new things. If you find that the material goes too quickly, you should probably start off with the latest edition of my book *PHP for the World Wide Web: Visual QuickStart Guide*, which goes at a more tempered pace.

No database experience is required, since SQL and MySQL are discussed starting at a more basic level.

What's new in this edition

The first two editions of this book have been very popular, and I've received a lot of positive feedback on them (thanks!). In writing this new edition, I wanted to do more than just update the material for the latest versions of PHP and MySQL, although that is an overriding consideration throughout the book. Other new features you'll find are:

◆ New examples demonstrating techniques frequently requested by readers

◆ Some additional advanced MySQL and SQL examples

◆ A dedicated chapter on thwarting common Web site abuses and attacks

◆ A brand-new chapter on working with multiple languages and time zones

◆ A brand-new example chapter on creating a message board (or forum)

◆ Expanded and updated installation and configuration instructions

◆ Removal of outdated content (e.g., things used in older versions of PHP or not applicable to PHP 6)

For those of you that also own the first and/or second edition (thanks, thanks, thanks!), I believe that these new features will also make this edition a required fixture on your desk or bookshelf.

How this book compares to my other books

This is my fourth PHP and/or MySQL title, after (in order)

◆ *PHP for the World Wide Web: Visual QuickStart Guide*

◆ *PHP 5 Advanced for the World Wide Web: Visual QuickPro Guide*

◆ *MySQL: Visual QuickStart Guide*

I hope this résumé implies a certain level of qualification to write this book, but how do you, as a reader standing in a bookstore, decide which title is for you? Of course, you are more than welcome to splurge and buy the whole set, earning my eternal gratitude, but...

The *PHP for the World Wide Web: Visual QuickStart Guide* book is very much a beginner's guide to PHP. This title overlaps it some, mostly in the first three chapters, but uses new examples so as not to be redundant. For novices, this book acts as a follow-up to that one. The advanced book is really a sequel to this one, as it assumes a fair amount of knowledge and builds upon many things taught here. The MySQL book focuses almost exclusively on MySQL (there are but two chapters that use PHP).

With that in mind, read the section "Is this book for you?" and see if the requirements apply. If you have no programming experience at all and would prefer to be taught PHP more gingerly, my first book would be better. If you are already very comfortable with PHP and want to learn more of its advanced capabilities, pick up the second. If you are most interested in MySQL and are not concerned with learning much about PHP, check out the third.

That being said, if you want to learn everything you need to know to begin developing dynamic Web sites with PHP and MySQL today, then this is the book for you! It references the most current versions of both technologies, uses techniques not previously discussed in other books, and contains its own unique examples.

And whatever book you do choose, make sure you're getting the most recent edition or, barring that, the edition that best matches the versions of the technologies you'll be using.

Companion Web Site

I have developed a companion Web site specifically for this book, which you may reach at www.DMCinsights.com/phpmysql3/ (**Figure i.6**). There you will find every script from this book, a text file containing lengthy SQL commands, and a list of errata that occurred during publication. (If you have problem with a command or script, and you are following the book exactly, check the errata to ensure there is not a printing error before driving yourself absolutely mad.) At this Web site you will also find useful Web links, a highly popular forum where readers can ask and answer each other's questions (I answer many of them myself), and more!

Questions, comments, or suggestions?

If you have any questions on PHP or MySQL, you can turn to one of the many Web sites, mailing lists, newsgroups, and FAQ repositories already in existence. A quick search online will turn up virtually unlimited resources. For that matter, if you need an immediate answer, those sources or a quick Web search will most assuredly serve your needs (in all likelihood, someone else has already seen and solved your exact problem).

You can also direct your questions, comments, and suggestions to me. You'll get the fastest reply using the book's corresponding forum (I always answer those questions first). If you'd rather email me, my contact information is available on the Web site. I do try to answer every email I receive, although I cannot guarantee a quick reply.

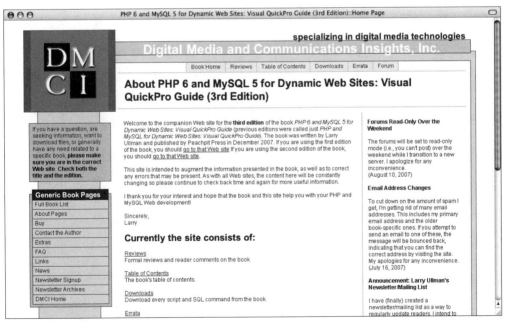

Figure i.6 The companion Web site for this book.

INTRODUCTION TO PHP

To use an old chestnut, every journey starts with one small step, and the first step in developing dynamic Web applications with PHP and MySQL is to learn the fundamentals of the scripting language itself.

Although this book focuses on using MySQL and PHP in combination, you'll do a vast majority of your legwork using PHP alone. In this and the following chapter, you'll learn its basics, from syntax to variables, operators, and language constructs (conditionals, loops, and whatnot). At the same time you are picking up these fundamentals, you'll also begin developing usable code that you'll integrate into larger applications later in the book.

This introductory chapter will cruise through most of the basics of the PHP language. You'll learn the syntax for coding PHP, how to send data to the Web browser, and how to use two kinds of variables (strings and numbers) plus constants. Some of the examples may seem inconsequential, but they'll demonstrate ideas you'll have to master in order to write more advanced scripts further down the line.

Basic Syntax

As stated in the book's introduction, PHP is an *HTML-embedded* scripting language. This means that you can intermingle PHP and HTML code within the same file. So to begin programming with PHP, start with a simple Web page. **Script 1.1** gives an example of a no-frills, no-content XHTML Transitional document, which will be used as the foundation for every Web page in the book (this book does not formally discuss [X]HTML; see a resource dedicated to the topic for more information).

To add PHP code to a page, place it within PHP tags:

```
<?php

?>
```

Anything placed within these tags will be treated by the Web server as PHP (meaning the PHP interpreter will process the code). Any text outside of the PHP tags is immediately sent to the Web browser as regular HTML.

Along with placing PHP code within PHP tags, your PHP files must have a proper extension. The extension tells the server to treat the script in a special way, namely, as a PHP page. Most Web servers will use .html or .htm for standard HTML pages, and normally, .php is preferred for your PHP files.

To make a basic PHP script:

1. Create a new document in your text editor or Integrated Development Environment (**Script 1.2**).

   It generally does not matter what application you use, be it Dreamweaver (a fancy IDE), BBEdit (a great and popular Macintosh plain-text editor), or vi (a plain-text Unix editor, lacking a graphical interface). Still, some text editors and

Script 1.1 A basic XHTML 1.o Transitional Web page.

```
1    <!DOCTYPE html PUBLIC "-//W3C//DTD XHTML
     1.0 Transitional//EN" "http://www.w3.org/
     TR/xhtml1/DTD/xhtml1-transitional.dtd">

2    <html xmlns="http://www.w3.org/1999/
     xhtml" xml:lang="en" lang="en">

3    <head>

4      <meta http-equiv="content-type" content=
       "text/html; charset=iso-8859-1" />

5      <title>Page Title</title>

6    </head>

7    <body>

8    </body>

9    </html>
```

Script 1.2 This first PHP script doesn't do anything, per se, but does demonstrate how a PHP script is written. It'll also be used as a test, prior to getting into elaborate PHP code.

```
1   <!DOCTYPE html PUBLIC "-//W3C//DTD XHTML
    1.0 Transitional//EN" "http://www.w3.org/
    TR/xhtml1/DTD/xhtml1-transitional.dtd">

2   <html xmlns="http://www.w3.org/1999/xhtml"
    xml:lang="en" lang="en">

3   <head>

4     <meta http-equiv="content-type" content=
      "text/html; charset=iso-8859-1" />

5     <title>Basic PHP Page</title>

6   </head>

7   <body>

8   <p>This is standard HTML.</p>

9   <?php

10  ?>

11  </body>

12  </html>
```

IDEs make typing and debugging HTML and PHP easier (conversely, Notepad on Windows does some things that makes coding harder). If you don't already have an application you're attached to, search the Web or use the book's corresponding forum (www.DMCInsights.com/phorum/) to find one.

2. Start a basic HTML document.

```
<!DOCTYPE html PUBLIC "-//W3C//
→ DTD XHTML 1.0 Transitional//EN""
→ http://www.w3.org/TR/xhtml1/DTD/
→ xhtml1-transitional.dtd">

<html xmlns="http://www.w3.org/1999/
→ xhtml" xml:lang="en" lang="en">

<head>

  <meta http-equiv="content-type"
  → content="text/html; charset=
  → iso-8859-1" />

  <title>Basic PHP Page</title>

</head>

<body>

<p>This is standard HTML.</p>

</body>

</html>
```

Although this is the syntax being used throughout the book, you can change the HTML to match whichever standard you intend to use (e.g., HTML 4.0 Strict). Again, see a dedicated (X)HTML resource if you're unfamiliar with this HTML code (see the first tip).

continues on next page

BASIC SYNTAX

3

3. Before the closing body tag, insert your PHP tags.

```
<?php

?>
```

These are the formal PHP tags, also known as XML-style tags. Although PHP supports other tag types (see the second tip), I recommend that you use the formal type, and I will do so throughout this book.

4. Save the file as first.php.

Remember that if you don't save the file using an appropriate PHP extension, the script will not execute properly.

5. Place the file in the proper directory of your Web server.

If you are running PHP on your own computer (presumably after following the installation directions in Appendix A, "Installation"), you just need to move, copy, or save the file to a specific folder on your computer. Check the documentation for your particular Web server to identify the correct directory, if you don't already know what it is.

If you are running PHP on a hosted server (i.e., on a remote computer), you'll need to use an FTP application to upload the file to the proper directory. Your hosting company will provide you with access and the other necessary information.

6. Run first.php in your Web browser (**Figure 1.1**).

Because PHP scripts need to be parsed by the server, you *absolutely must* access them via the URL. You cannot simply open them in your Web browser as you would a file in other applications.

If you are running PHP on your own computer, you'll need to go to something like http://localhost/first.php, http://127.0.0.1/first.php, or

http://localhost/~*<user>*/first.php (on Mac OS X, using your actual username for *<user>*). If you are using a Web host, you'll need to use http://*your-domain-name*/first.php (e. g., http://www.example.com/first.php).

Figure 1.1 While it seems like any other (simple) HTML page, this is in fact a PHP script and the basis for the rest of the examples in the book.

7. If you don't see results like those in Figure 1.1, start debugging.

Part of learning any programming language is mastering debugging. It's a sometimes-painful but absolutely necessary process. With this first example, if you don't see a simple, but perfectly valid, Web page, follow these steps:

1. Confirm that you have a working PHP installation (see Appendix A for testing instructions).

2. Make sure that you are running the script through a URL. The address in the Web browser must begin with http://. If it starts with file://, that's the problem (**Figure 1.2**).

3. If you get a file not found (or similar) error, you've likely put the file in the wrong directory or mistyped the file's name (either when saving it or in your Web browser).

If you've gone through all this and are still having problems, turn to the book's corresponding forum (www.DMCInsights.com/phorum/list.php?20).

✔ Tips

■ To find more information about HTML and XHTML, check out Elizabeth Castro's excellent book *HTML, XHTML, and CSS, Sixth Edition: Visual QuickStart Guide*, (Peachpit Press, 2006) or search the Web.

■ There are actually three different pairs of PHP tags. Besides the formal (<?php and ?>), there are the short tags (<? and ?>), and the script style (<script language="php"> and </script>). This last style is rarely used, and the formal style is recommended.

■ Because I am running PHP on my own computer, you will sometimes see URLs like http://127.0.0.1:8000/first.php in this book's figures. The important thing is that I'm running these scripts via http://; don't let the rest of the URL confuse you.

■ You can embed multiple sections of PHP code within a single HTML document (i.e., you can go in and out of the two languages). You'll see examples of this throughout the book.

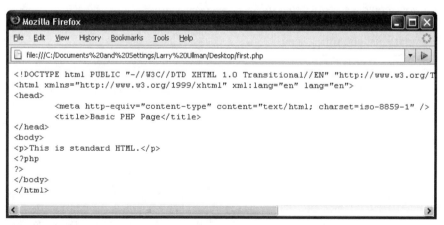

Figure 1.2 If you see the actual PHP code (in this case, the tags) in the Web browser, this means that the PHP Web server is not running the code for one reason or another.

Sending Data to the Web Browser

To create dynamic Web sites with PHP, you must know how to send data to the Web browser. PHP has a number of built-in functions for this purpose, the most common being echo() and print(). I personally tend to favor echo():

```
echo 'Hello, world!';

echo "What's new?";
```

You could use print() instead, if you prefer:

```
print "Hello, world!";

print "What's new?";
```

As you can see from these examples, you can use either single or double quotation marks (but there is a distinction between the two types of quotation marks, which will be made clear by the chapter's end). The first quotation mark after the function name indicates the start of the message to be printed. The next matching quotation mark (i.e., the next quotation mark of the same kind as the opening mark) indicates the end of the message to be printed.

Along with learning how to send data to the Web browser, you should also notice that in PHP all statements (a line of executed code, in layman's terms) must end with a semi-colon. Also, PHP is case-insensitive when it comes to function names, so ECHO(), echo(), eCHo(), and so forth will all work. The all-lowercase version is easiest to type, of course.

Needing an Escape

As you might discover, one of the complications with sending data to the Web involves printing single and double quotation marks. Either of the following will cause errors:

```
echo "She said, "How are you?"";

echo 'I'm just ducky.';
```

There are two solutions to this problem. First, use single quotation marks when printing a double quotation mark and vice versa:

```
echo 'She said, "How are you?"';

echo "I'm just ducky.";
```

Or, you can *escape* the problematic character by preceding it with a backslash:

```
echo "She said, \"How are you?\"";

print 'I\'m just ducky.';
```

As escaped quotation mark will merely be printed like any other character. Understanding how to use the backslash to escape a character is an important concept, and one that will be covered in more depth at the end of the chapter.

Script 1.3 Using print() or echo(), PHP can send data to the Web browser (see Figure 1.3).

```
      ┌─────────────────────────────────────┐
      │ ⬤ ⬤ ⬤            📄 Script           │
      ├─────────────────────────────────────┤
1     <!DOCTYPE html PUBLIC "-//W3C//DTD XHTML
      1.0 Transitional//EN" "http://www.w3.org/
      TR/xhtml1/DTD/xhtml1-transitional.dtd">

2     <html xmlns="http://www.w3.org/1999/xhtml"
      xml:lang="en" lang="en">

3     <head>

4       <meta http-equiv="content-type" content=
      "text/html; charset=iso-8859-1" />

5       <title>Using Echo()</title>

6     </head>

7     <body>

8     <p>This is standard HTML.</p>

9     <?php

10    echo 'This was generated using PHP!';

11    ?>

12    </body>

13    </html>
```

Figure 1.3 The results still aren't glamorous, but this page was in part dynamically generated by PHP.

```
┌─────────────────────────────────────┐
│ ⬤ ⬤ ⬤      Mozilla Firefox      ⬭   │
├─────────────────────────────────────┤
│ 🌐 http://127.0.0.1:8000/second.php ▼ ▷ │
├─────────────────────────────────────┤
│                                     │
│ Parse error: syntax error, unexpected │
│ T_STRING, expecting ',' or ';' in    │
│ /Applications/Abyss Web              │
│ Server/htdocs/second.php on line 10  │
│                                     │
├─────────────────────────────────────┤
│ Done                        ⬤  ⦿  / │
└─────────────────────────────────────┘
```

Figure 1.4 This may be the first of many parse errors you see as a PHP programmer (this one is caused by an un-escaped quotation mark).

To send data to the Web browser:

1. Open first.php (refer to Script 1.2) in your text editor or IDE.

2. Between the PHP tags (lines 9 and 10), add a simple message (**Script 1.3**).

   ```
   echo 'This was generated using
   → PHP!';
   ```

   It truly doesn't matter what message you type here, which function you use (echo() or print()), or which quotation marks, for that matter—just be careful if you are printing a single or double quotation mark as part of your message (see the sidebar "Needing an Escape").

3. If you want, change the page title to better describe this page (line 5).

   ```
   <title>Using Echo()</title>
   ```

   This change only affects the browser window's title bar.

4. Save the file as second.php, place it in your Web directory, and test it in your Web browser (**Figure 1.3**).

5. If necessary, debug the script.

   If you see a parse error instead of your message (see **Figure 1.4**), check that you have both opened and closed your quotation marks and escaped any problematic characters (see the sidebar). Also be certain to conclude each statement with a semicolon.

   continues on next page

SENDING DATA TO THE WEB BROWSER

If you see an entirely blank page, this is probably for one of two reasons:

▲ There is a problem with your HTML. Test this by viewing the source of your page and looking for HTML problems there (**Figure 1.5**).

▲ An error occurred, but *display_errors* is turned off in your PHP configuration, so nothing is shown. In this case, see the section in Appendix A on how to configure PHP so that you can turn *display_errors* back on.

Figure 1.5 One possible cause of a blank PHP page is a simple HTML error, like the closing title tag here (it's missing the slash).

✔ Tips

■ Technically, echo() and print() are language constructs, not functions. That being said, don't be flummoxed as I continue to call them "functions" for convenience. Also, I include the parentheses when referring to functions—say echo(), not just echo—to help distinguish them from variables and other parts of PHP. This is just my own little convention.

■ You can, and often will, use echo() and print() to send HTML code to the Web browser, like so (**Figure 1.6**):

```
echo '<p>Hello, <b>world</b>!</p>';
```

■ Echo() and print() can both be used to print text over multiple lines:

```
echo 'This sentence is

printed over two lines.';
```

What happens in this case is that the return (created by pressing Enter or Return) becomes part of the printed message, which isn't terminated until the closing single quotation mark. The net result will be the "printing" of the return in the HTML source code (**Figure 1.7**). This will not have an effect on the generated page (**Figure 1.8**). For more on this, see the sidebar "Understanding White Space."

Figure 1.6 PHP can send HTML code (like the formatting here) as well as simple text (see Figure 1.3) to the Web browser.

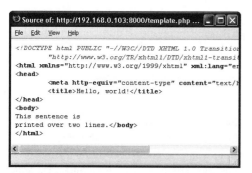

Figure 1.7 Printing text and HTML over multiple PHP lines will generate HTML source code that also extends over multiple lines. Note that extraneous white spacing in the HTML source will not affect the look of a page (see Figure 1.8) but can make the source easier to review.

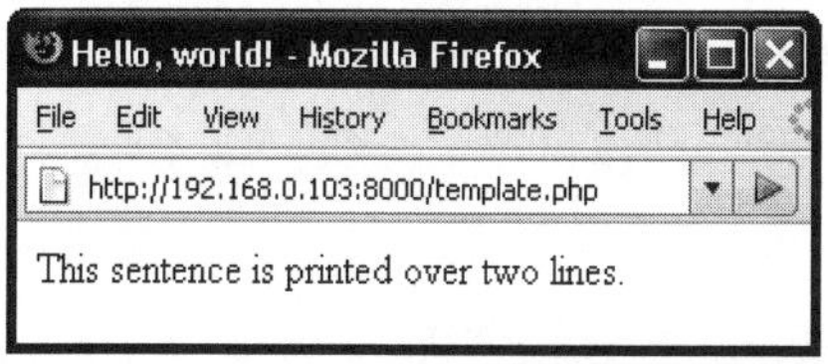

Figure 1.8 The return in the HTML source (Figure 1.7) has no effect on the rendered result. The only way to alter the spacing of a displayed Web page is to use HTML tags (like ‹br /› and ‹p›‹/p›).

Understanding White Space

With PHP you send data (like HTML tags and text) to the Web browser, which will, in turn, render that data as the Web page the end user sees. Thus, what you are doing with PHP is creating the *HTML source* of a Web page. With this in mind, there are three areas of notable *white space* (extra spaces, tabs, and blank lines): in your PHP scripts, in your HTML source, and in the rendered Web page.

PHP is generally white space insensitive, meaning that you can space out your code however you want to make your scripts more legible. HTML is also generally white space insensitive. Specifically, the only white space in HTML that affects the rendered page is a single space (multiple spaces still get rendered as one). If your HTML source has text on multiple lines, that doesn't mean it'll appear on multiple lines in the rendered page (see Figures 1.7 and 1.8).

To alter the spacing in a rendered Web page, use the HTML tags **
** (line break, **
** in older HTML standards) and **<p></p>** (paragraph). To alter the spacing of the HTML source created with PHP, you can

◆ Use echo() or print() over the course of several lines.

or

◆ Print the newline character (\n) within double quotation marks.

Writing Comments

Creating executable PHP code is only a part of the programming process (admittedly, it's the most important part). A secondary but still crucial aspect to any programming endeavor involves documenting your code.

In HTML you can add comments using special tags:

```
<!-- Comment goes here. -->
```

HTML comments are viewable in the source (**Figure 1.9**) but do not appear in the rendered page.

PHP comments are different in that they aren't sent to the Web browser at all, meaning they won't be viewable to the end user, even when looking at the HTML source.

PHP supports three comment types. The first uses the pound or number symbol (#):

```
# This is a comment.
```

The second uses two slashes:

```
// This is also a comment.
```

Both of these cause PHP to ignore everything that follows until the end of the line (when you press Return or Enter). Thus, these two comments are for single lines only. They are also often used to place a comment on the same line as some PHP code:

```
print 'Hello!'; // Say hello.
```

A third style allows comments to run over multiple lines:

```
/* This is a longer comment

that spans two lines. */
```

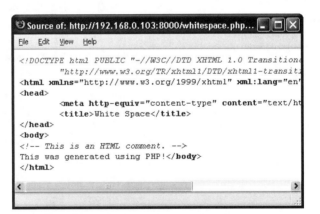

Figure 1.9 HTML comments appear in the browser's source code but not in the rendered Web page.

Script 1.4 These basic comments demonstrate the three syntaxes you can use in PHP.

```
1   <!DOCTYPE html PUBLIC "-//W3C//DTD XHTML
    1.0 Transitional//EN" "http://www.w3.org/
    TR/xhtml1/DTD/xhtml1-transitional.dtd">

2   <html xmlns="http://www.w3.org/1999/
    xhtml" xml:lang="en" lang="en">

3   <head>

4     <meta http-equiv="content-type" content=
      "text/html; charset=iso-8859-1" />

5     <title>Comments</title>

6   </head>

7   <body>

8   <?php

9

10  # Created August 27, 2007

11  # Created by Larry E. Ullman

12  # This script does nothing much.

13

14  echo '<p>This is a line of text.<br />This
    is another line of text.</p>';

15

16  /*

17  echo 'This line will not be executed.';

18  */

19

20  echo "<p>Now I'm done.</p>"; // End of PHP
    code.

21

22  ?>

23  </body>

24  </html>
```

To comment your scripts:

1. Begin a new PHP document in your text editor or IDE, starting with the initial HTML (**Script 1.4**).

   ```
   <!DOCTYPE html PUBLIC "-//W3C//
   → DTD XHTML 1.0 Transitional//EN"
   → "http://www.w3.org/TR/xhtml1/DTD/
   → xhtml1-transitional.dtd">

   <html xmlns="http://www.w3.org/1999/
   → xhtml" xml:lang="en" lang="en">

   <head>

     <meta http-equiv="content-type"
     content="text/html; charset=iso-
     8859-1" />

     <title>Comments</title>

   </head>

   <body>
   ```

2. Add the initial PHP tag and write your first comments.

   ```
   <?php

   # Created August 26, 2007

   # Created by Larry E. Ullman

   # This script does nothing much.
   ```

   One of the first comments each script should contain is an introductory block that lists creation date, modification date, creator, creator's contact information, purpose of the script, and so on. Some people suggest that the shell-style comments (#) stand out more in a script and are therefore best for this kind of notation.

3. Send some HTML to the Web browser.

   ```
   echo '<p>This is a line of text.
   → <br />This is another line of
   → text.</p>';
   ```

continues on next page

It doesn't matter what you do here, just so the Web browser has something to display. For the sake of variety, I'll have the echo() statement print some HTML tags, including a line break (<br />) to add some spacing to the generated HTML page.

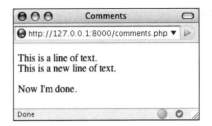

Figure 1.10 The PHP comments in Script 1.4 don't appear in the Web page or the HTML source (Figure 1.11).

4. Use the multiline comments to comment out a second echo() statement.

```
/*
echo 'This line will not be
→ executed.';
*/
```

By surrounding any block of PHP code with /* and */, you can render that code inert without having to delete it from your script. By later removing the comment tags, you can reactivate that section of PHP code.

5. Add a final comment after a third echo() statement.

```
echo "<p>Now I'm done.</p>"; // End
→ of PHP code.
```

This last (superfluous) comment shows how to place one at the end of a line, a common practice. Note that I used double quotation marks to surround the message, as single quotation marks would conflict with the apostrophe (see the "Needing an Escape" sidebar, earlier in the chapter).

6. Close the PHP section and complete the HTML page.

```
?>
</body>
</html>
```

7. Save the file as comments.php, place it in your Web directory, and test it in your Web browser (**Figure 1.10**).

8. If you're the curious type, check the source code in your Web browser to confirm that the PHP comments do not appear there (**Figure 1.11**).

✔ Tips

■ You shouldn't nest (place one inside another) multiline comments (/* */). Doing so will cause problems.

■ Any of the PHP comments can be used at the end of a line (say, after a function call):

```
echo 'Howdy'; /* Say 'Howdy' */
```

Although this is allowed, it's far less common.

■ It's nearly impossible to over-comment your scripts. Always err on the side of writing too many comments as you code. That being said, in the interest of saving space, the scripts in this book will not be as well documented as I would suggest they should be.

■ It's also important that as you change a script you keep the comments up-to-date and accurate. There's nothing more confusing than a comment that says one thing when the code really does something else.

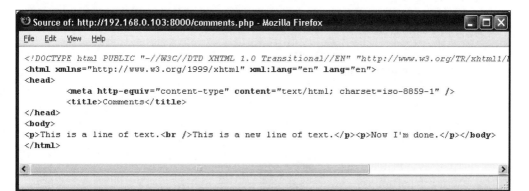

```
Source of: http://192.168.0.103:8000/comments.php - Mozilla Firefox
File  Edit  View  Help

<!DOCTYPE html PUBLIC "-//W3C//DTD XHTML 1.0 Transitional//EN" "http://www.w3.org/TR/xhtml1/
<html xmlns="http://www.w3.org/1999/xhtml" xml:lang="en" lang="en">
<head>
        <meta http-equiv="content-type" content="text/html; charset=iso-8859-1" />
        <title>Comments</title>
</head>
<body>
<p>This is a line of text.<br />This is a new line of text.</p><p>Now I'm done.</p></body>
</html>
```

Figure 1.11 The PHP comments from Script 1.4 are nowhere to be seen in the client's browser.

What Are Variables?

Variables are containers used to temporarily store values. These values can be numbers, text, or much more complex data. PHP has eight types of variables. These include four scalar (single-valued) types—*Boolean* (`TRUE` or `FALSE`), *integer*, *floating point* (decimals), and *strings* (characters); two nonscalar (multivalued)—*arrays* and *objects*; plus *resources* (which you'll see when interacting with databases) and *NULL* (which is a special type that has no value).

Regardless of what type you are creating, all variables in PHP follow certain syntactical rules:

◆ A variable's name—also called its *identifier*—must start with a dollar sign ($), for example, `$name`.

◆ The variable's name can contain a combination of strings, numbers, and the underscore, for example, `$my_report1`.

◆ The first character after the dollar sign must be either a letter or an underscore (it cannot be a number).

◆ Variable names in PHP are case-sensitive. This is a *very* important rule. It means that `$name` and `$Name` are entirely different variables.

To begin working with variables, let's make use of several predefined variables whose values are automatically established when a PHP script is run. Before getting into this script, there are two more things you should know. First, variables can be assigned values using the equals sign (=), also called the *assignment operator*. Second, variables can be printed without quotation marks:

```
print $some_var;
```

Script 1.5 This script prints three of PHP's many predefined variables.

```
000                    Script
1    <!DOCTYPE html PUBLIC "-//W3C//DTD XHTML
     1.0 Transitional//EN" "http://www.w3.org/
     TR/xhtml1/DTD/xhtml1-transitional.dtd">

2    <html xmlns="http://www.w3.org/1999/xhtml"
     xml:lang="en" lang="en">

3    <head>

4      <meta http-equiv="content-type" content=
       "text/html; charset=iso-8859-1" />

5      <title>Predefined Variables</title>

6    </head>

7    <body>

8    <?php # Script 1.5 - predefined.php

9

10   // Create a shorthand version of the
     variable names:

11   $file = $_SERVER['SCRIPT_FILENAME'];

12   $user = $_SERVER['HTTP_USER_AGENT'];

13   $server = $_SERVER['SERVER_
     SOFTWARE'];

14

15   // Print the name of this script:

16   echo "<p>You are running the file:<br
     /><b>$file</b>.</p>\n";

17

18   // Print the user's information:

19   echo "<p>You are viewing this page using:
     <br /><b>$user</b></p>\n";

20

21   // Print the server's information:

22   echo "<p>This server is running:<br /><b>
     $server</b>.</p>\n";

23

24   ?>

25   </body>

26   </html>
```

Or variables can be printed within double quotation marks:

```
print "Hello, $name";
```

You cannot print variables within single quotation marks:

```
print 'Hello, $name'; // Won't work!
```

To use variables:

1. Begin a new PHP document in your text editor or IDE, starting with the initial HTML (**Script 1.5**).

```
<!DOCTYPE html PUBLIC "-//W3C//
   DTD XHTML 1.0 Transitional//EN"
"http://www.w3.org/TR/xhtml1/DTD/
   xhtml1-transitional.dtd">
<html xmlns="http://www.w3.org/1999/
   xhtml" xml:lang="en" lang="en">
<head>
   <meta http-equiv="content-type"
   → content="text/html; charset=
   → iso-8859-1" />
   <title>Predefined Variables</
   → title>
</head>
<body>
```

2. Add your opening PHP tag and your first comment.

```
<?php # Script 1.5 - predefined.php
```

From here on out, my scripts will no longer comment on the creator, creation date, and so forth, although you should continue to document your scripts thoroughly. I will, however, make a comment listing the script number and filename for ease of cross-referencing (both in

continues on next page

the book and when you download them from the book's supporting Web site, www.DMCInsights.com/phpmysql3/).

3. Create a shorthand version of the first variable to be used in this script.

```
$file = $_SERVER['SCRIPT_FILENAME'];
```

This script will use three variables, each of which comes from the larger and pre-defined $_SERVER variable. $_SERVER refers to a mass of server-related information. The first variable the script uses is $_SERVER['SCRIPT_FILENAME']. This variable stores the full path and name of the script being run (for example, C:\Program Files\Apache\htdocs\predefined.php).

The value stored in $_SERVER['SCRIPT_FILENAME'] will be assigned to the new variable $file. Creating new variables with shorter names and then assigning them values from $_SERVER will make it easier to refer to the variables when printing them. (It also gets around some other issues you'll learn about in due time.)

4. Create a shorthand version of the other two variables.

```
$user = $_SERVER['HTTP_USER_AGENT'];
```
```
$server = $_SERVER['SERVER_
→ SOFTWARE'];
```

$_SERVER['HTTP_USER_AGENT'] represents the Web browser and operating system of the user accessing the script. This value is assigned to $user.

$_SERVER['SERVER_SOFTWARE'] represents the Web application on the server that's

running PHP (e.g., Apache, Abyss, Xitami, IIS). This is the program that must be installed (see Appendix A) in order to run PHP scripts on that computer.

5. Print out the name of the script being run.

```
echo "<p>You are running the file:
→ <br /><b>$file</b>.</p>\n";
```

The first variable to be printed is $file. Notice that this variable must be printed out within double quotation marks and that I also make use of the PHP newline (\n), which will add a line break in the generated HTML source. Some basic HTML tags—paragraph and bold—are added to give the generated page some flair.

6. Print out the information of the user accessing the script.

```
echo "<p>You are viewing this page
→ using:<br /><b>$user</b></p>\n";
```

This line prints the second variable, $user. To repeat what's said in the fourth step, $user correlates to $_SERVER['HTTP_USER_AGENT'] and refers to the operating system, browser type, and browser version being used to access the Web page.

7. Print out the server information.

```
echo "<p>This server is running:<br
→ /><b>$server</b>.</p>\n";
```

8. Complete the HTML and PHP code.

```
?>
</body>
</html>
```

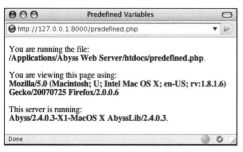

Figure 1.12 The predefined.php script reports back to the viewer information about the script, the Web browser being used to view it, and the server itself.

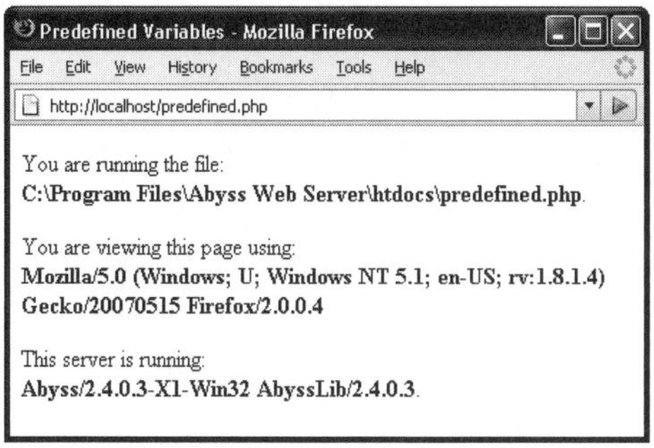

Figure 1.13 This is the book's first truly dynamic script, in that the Web page changes depending upon the server running it and the Web browser viewing it (compare with Figure 1.12).

9. Save your file as `predefined.php`, place it in your Web directory, and test it in your Web browser (**Figure 1.12**).

✔ Tips

- If you have problems with this, or any other script, turn to the book's corresponding Web forum (`www.DMCInsights.com/phorum/`) for assistance.

- If possible, run this script using a different Web browser and/or on another server (**Figure 1.13**).

- The most important consideration when creating variables is to use a consistent naming scheme. In this book you'll see that I use all-lowercase letters for my variable names, with underscores separating words (`$first_name`). Some programmers prefer to use capitalization instead: `$FirstName`.

- PHP is very casual in how it treats variables, meaning that you don't need to initialize them (set an immediate value) or declare them (set a specific type), and you can convert a variable among the many types without problem.

Introducing Strings

The first variable type to delve into is *strings*. A string is merely a quoted chunk of characters: letters, numbers, spaces, punctuation, and so forth. These are all strings:

◆ 'Tobias'

◆ "In watermelon sugar"

◆ '100'

◆ 'August 2, 2006'

To make a string variable, assign a string value to a valid variable name:

```
$first_name = 'Tobias';
```

```
$today = 'August 2, 2006';
```

When creating strings, you can use either single or double quotation marks to encapsulate the characters, just as you would when printing text. Likewise, you must use the same type of quotation mark for the beginning and the end of the string. If that same mark appears within the string, it must be escaped:

```
$var = "Define \"platitude\", please.";
```

To print out the value of a string, use either

```
echo() or print():
```

```
echo $first_name;
```

To print the value of string within a context, use double quotation marks:

```
echo "Hello, $first_name";
```

You've already worked with strings once—when using the predefined variables in the preceding section. In this next example, you'll create and use new strings.

Script 1.6 String variables are created and their values sent to the Web browser in this introductory script.

```
1   <!DOCTYPE html PUBLIC "-//W3C//DTD XHTML
    1.0 Transitional//EN" "http://www.w3.org/
    TR/xhtml1/DTD/xhtml1-transitional.dtd">
2   <html xmlns="http://www.w3.org/1999/
    xhtml" xml:lang="en" lang="en">
3   <head>
4     <meta http-equiv="content-type" content=
      "text/html; charset=iso-8859-1" />
5     <title>Strings</title>
6   </head>
7   <body>
8   <?php # Script 1.6 - strings.php
9
10  // Create the variables:
11  $first_name = 'Haruki';
12  $last_name = 'Murakami';
13  $book = 'Kafka on the Shore';
14
15  //Print the values:
16  echo "<p>The book <em>$book</em> was
    written by $first_name $last_name.</p>";
17
18  ?>
19  </body>
20  </html>
```

To use strings:

1. Begin a new PHP document in your text editor or IDE, starting with the initial HTML and including the opening PHP tag (**Script 1.6**).

   ```
   <!DOCTYPE html PUBLIC "-//W3C//
   → DTD XHTML 1.0 Transitional//EN"
   → "http://www.w3.org/TR/xhtml1/DTD/
   → xhtml1-transitional.dtd">
   <html xmlns="http://www.w3.org/1999/
     → xhtml" xml:lang="en" lang="en">
   <head>
     <meta http-equiv="content-type"
     → content="text/html; charset=
     → iso-8859-1" />
     <title>Strings</title>
   </head>
   <body>
   <?php # Script 1.6 - strings.php
   ```

2. Within the PHP tags, create three variables.

   ```
   $first_name = 'Haruki';
   $last_name = 'Murakami';
   $book = 'Kafka on the Shore';
   ```

   This rudimentary example creates $first_name, $last_name, and $book variables that will then be printed out in a message.

3. Add an echo() statement.

   ```
   echo "<p>The book <em>$book</em>
   → was written by $first_name
   → $last_name.</p>";
   ```

   continues on next page

INTRODUCING STRINGS

19

All this script does is print a statement of authorship based upon three established variables. A little HTML formatting (the emphasis on the book's title) is thrown in to make it more attractive. Remember to use double quotation marks here for the variable values to be printed out appropriately (more on the importance of double quotation marks at the chapter's end).

4. Complete the HTML and PHP code.

```
?>

</body>

</html>
```

5. Save the file as strings.php, place it in your Web directory, and test it in your Web browser (**Figure 1.14**).

6. If desired, change the values of the three variables, save the file, and run the script again (**Figure 1.15**).

✔ Tips

■ If you assign another value to an existing variable (say $book), the new value will overwrite the old one. For example:

```
$book = 'High Fidelity';

$book = 'The Corrections';

/* $book now has a value of

'The Corrections'. */
```

■ PHP has no set limits on how big a string can be. It's theoretically possible that you'll be limited by the resources of the server, but it's doubtful that you'll ever encounter such a problem.

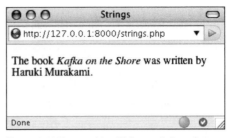

Figure 1.14 The resulting Web page is based upon printing out the values of three variables.

Figure 1.15 The output of the script is changed by altering the variables in it.

Script 1.7 Concatenation gives you the ability to easily manipulate strings, like creating an author's name from the combination of their first and last names.

```
 ⊖ ⊙ ⊙                    📄 Script
1    <!DOCTYPE html PUBLIC "-//W3C//DTD XHTML
     1.0 Transitional//EN" "http://www.w3.org/
     TR/xhtml1/DTD/xhtml1-transitional.dtd">

2    <html
     xmlns="http://www.w3.org/1999/xhtml"
     xml:lang="en" lang="en">

3    <head>

4      <meta http-equiv="content-type" content=
       "text/html; charset=iso-8859-1" />

5      <title>Concatenation</title>

6    </head>

7    <body>

8    <?php # Script 1.7 - concat.php

9

10   // Create the variables:

11   $first_name = 'Melissa';

12   $last_name = 'Bank';

13   $author = $first_name . ' ' . $last_name;

14

15   $book = 'The Girls\' Guide to Hunting and
     Fishing';

16

17   //Print the values:

18   echo "<p>The book <em>$book</em> was
     written by $author.</p>";

19

20   ?>

21   </body>

22   </html>
```

Concatenating Strings

Concatenation is like addition for strings, whereby characters are added to the end of the string. It's performed using the *concatenation operator*, which is the period (.):

```
$city= 'Seattle';
```

```
$state = 'Washington';
```

```
$address = $city . $state;
```

The $address variable now has the value *SeattleWashington*, which almost achieves the desired result (*Seattle, Washington*). To improve upon this, you could write

```
$address = $city . ', ' . $state;
```

so that a comma and a space are added to the mix.

Concatenation works with strings or numbers. Either of these statements will produce the same result (*Seattle, Washington 98101*):

```
$address = $city . ', ' . $state .
 ' 98101';
```

```
$address = $city . ', ' . $state .
 ' ' . 98101;
```

Let's modify strings.php to use this new operator.

To use concatenation:

1. Open strings.php (refer to Script 1.6) in your text editor or IDE.

2. After you've established the $first_name and $last_name variables (lines 11 and 12), add this line (**Script 1.7**):

   ```
   $author = $first_name . ' ' .
    $last_name;
   ```

continues on next page

As a demonstration of concatenation, a new variable—$author—will be created as the concatenation of two existing strings and a space in between.

3. Change the echo() statement to use this new variable.

```
echo "<p>The book <em>$book</em> was
→ written by $author.</p>";
```

Since the two variables have been turned into one, the echo() statement should be altered accordingly.

4. If desired, change the HTML page title and the values of the first name, last name, and book variables.

5. Save the file as concat.php, place it in your Web directory, and test it in your Web browser (**Figure 1.16**).

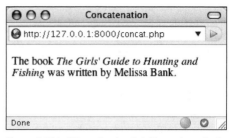

Figure 1.16 In this revised script, the end result of concatenation is not apparent to the user (compare with Figures 1.14 and 1.15).

✔ Tips

■ PHP has a slew of useful string-specific functions, which you'll see over the course of this book. For example, to calculate how long a string is (how many characters it contains), use strlen():

```
$num = strlen('some string');
```

■ You can have PHP convert the case of strings with: strtolower(), which makes it entirely lowercase; strtoupper(), which makes it entirely uppercase; ucfirst(), which capitalizes the first character; and ucwords(), which capitalizes the first character of every word.

■ If you are merely concatenating one value to another, you can use the *concatenation assignment operator* (.=). The following are equivalent:

```
$title = $title . $subtitle;
$title .= $subtitle;
```

■ The initial example in this section could be rewritten using either

```
$address = "$city, $state";
```

or

```
$address = $city;
$address .= ', ';
$address .= $state;
```

CONCATENATING STRINGS

Introducing Numbers

In introducing variables, I was explicit in stating that PHP has both integer and floating-point (decimal) number types. In my experience, though, these two types can be classified under the generic title *numbers* without losing any valuable distinction (for the most part). Valid number-type variables in PHP can be anything like

◆ 8

◆ 3.14

◆ 10980843985

◆ -4.2398508

◆ 4.4e2

Notice that these values are never quoted—in which case they'd be strings with numeric values—nor do they include commas to indicate thousands. Also, a number is assumed to be positive unless it is preceded by the minus sign (-).

Along with the standard arithmetic operators you can use on numbers (**Table 1.1**), there are dozens of functions. Two common ones are round() and number_format().

The former rounds a decimal to the nearest integer:

```
$n = 3.14;
$n = round ($n); // 3
```

It can also round to a specified number of decimal places:

```
$n = 3.142857;
$n = round ($n, 3); // 3.143
```

The number_format() function turns a number into the more commonly written version, grouped into thousands using commas:

```
$n = 20943;
$n = number_format ($n); // 20,943
```

This function can also set a specified number of decimal points:

```
$n = 20943;
$n = number_format ($n, 2); // 20,943.00
```

To practice with numbers, let's write a mock-up script that performs the calculations one might use in an e-commerce shopping cart.

TABLE 1.1 The standard mathematical operators.

Arithmetic Operators	
OPERATOR	MEANING
+	Addition
-	Subtraction
*	Multiplication
/	Division
%	Modulus
++	Increment
--	Decrement

To use numbers:

1. Begin a new PHP document in your text editor or IDE (**Script 1.8**).

```
<!DOCTYPE html PUBLIC "-//W3C//
DTD XHTML 1.0 Transitional//EN"
"http://www.w3.org/TR/xhtml1/DTD/
xhtml1-transitional.dtd">
<html xmlns="http://www.w3.org/1999/
xhtml" xml:lang="en" lang="en">
<head>
  <meta http-equiv="content-type"
  → content="text/html; charset=
  → iso-8859-1" />
  <title>Numbers</title>
</head>
<body>
<?php # Script 1.8 - numbers.php
```

2. Establish the requisite variables.

```
$quantity = 30;
$price = 119.95;
$taxrate = .05;
```

This script will use three hard-coded variables upon which calculations will be made. Later in the book, you'll see how these values can be dynamically determined (i.e., by user interaction with an HTML form).

3. Perform the calculations.

```
$total = $quantity * $price;
$total = $total + ($total * $taxrate);
```

The first line establishes the order total as the number of widgets purchased multiplied by the price of each widget.

Script 1.8 The numbers.php script demonstrates basic mathematical calculations, like those used in an e-commerce application.

```
1   <!DOCTYPE html PUBLIC "-//W3C//DTD XHTML
    1.0 Transitional//EN" "http://www.w3.org/
    TR/xhtml1/DTD/xhtml1-transitional.dtd">
2   <html xmlns="http://www.w3.org/1999/xhtml"
    xml:lang="en" lang="en">
3   <head>
4     <meta http-equiv="content-type" content=
      "text/html; charset=iso-8859-1" />
5     <title>Numbers</title>
6   </head>
7   <body>
8   <?php # Script 1.8 - numbers.php
9
10  // Set the variables:
11  $quantity = 30; // Buying 30 widgets.
12  $price = 119.95;
13  $taxrate = .05; // 5% sales tax.
14
15  // Calculate the total:
16  $total = $quantity * $price;
17  $total = $total + ($total * $taxrate); //
    Calculate and add the tax.
18
19  // Format the total:
20  $total = number_format ($total, 2);
21
22  // Print the results:
23  echo '<p>You are purchasing <b>' .
    $quantity . '</b> widget(s) at a cost
    of <b>$' . $price . '</b> each. With
    tax, the total comes to <b>$' . $total .
    '</b>.</p>';
24
25  ?>
26  </body>
27  </html>
```

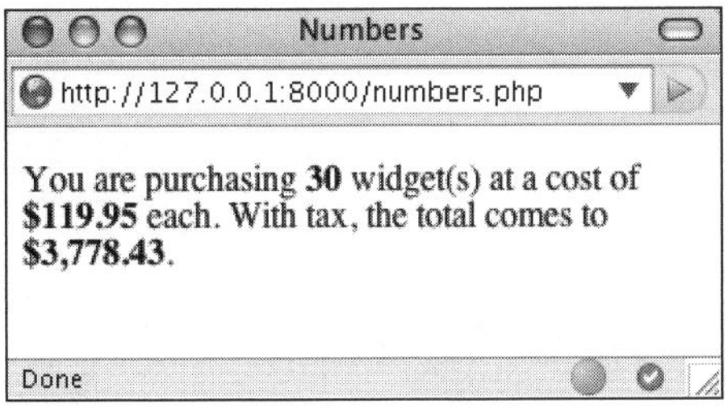

Figure 1.17 The numbers PHP page (Script 1.8) performs calculations based upon set values.

Figure 1.18 To change the generated Web page, alter any or all of the three variables (compare with Figure 1.17).

The second line then adds the amount of tax to the total (calculated by multiplying the tax rate by the total).

4. Format the total.

```
$total = number_format ($total, 2);
```

The `number_format()` function will group the total into thousands and round it to two decimal places. This will make the display more appropriate to the end user.

5. Print the results.

```
echo '<p>You are purchasing <b>' .
→$quantity . '</b> widget(s) at a cost
→of <b>$' . $price . '</b> each. With
→ tax, the total comes to <b>$' .
→ $total . '</b>.</p>';
```

The last step in the script is to print out the results. To use a combination of HTML, printed dollar signs, and variables, the `echo()` statement uses both single-quoted text and concatenated variables.

You could also put this all within a double-quoted string (as in previous examples), but when PHP encounters, for example, `at a cost of $$price` in the `echo()` statement, the double dollar sign would cause problems. You'll see an alternative solution in the last example of this chapter.

6. Complete the PHP code and the HTML page.

```
?>
</body>
</html>
```

7. Save the file as `numbers.php`, place it in your Web directory, and test it in your Web browser (**Figure 1.17**).

8. If desired, change the initial three variables and rerun the script (**Figure 1.18**).

continues on next page

✔ Tips

- PHP supports a maximum integer of around two billion on most platforms. With numbers larger than that, PHP will automatically use a floating-point type.

- When dealing with arithmetic, the issue of precedence arises (the order in which complex calculations are made). While the PHP manual and other sources tend to list out the hierarchy of precedence, I find programming to be safer and more legible when I group clauses in parentheses to force the execution order (see line 17 of Script 1.8).

- Computers are notoriously poor at dealing with decimals. For example, the number *2.0* may actually be stored as *1.99999*. Most of the time this won't be a problem, but in cases where mathematical precision is paramount, rely on integers, not decimals. The PHP manual has information on this subject, as well as alternative functions for improving computational accuracy.

- Many of the mathematical operators also have a corresponding assignment operator, letting you create a shorthand for assigning values. This line,

  `$total = $total + ($total * $taxrate);`

  could be rewritten as

  `$total += ($total * $taxrate);`

- If you set a `$price` value without using two decimals (e.g., *119.9* or *34*), you would want to apply `number_format()` to `$price` before printing it.

Introducing Constants

Constants, like variables, are used to temporarily store a value, but otherwise, constants and variables differ in many ways. For starters, to create a constant, you use the `define()` function instead of the assignment operator (`=`):

```
define ('NAME', 'value');
```

Notice that, as a rule of thumb, constants are named using all capitals, although this is not required. Most importantly, constants do not use the initial dollar sign as variables do (because constants are not variables).

A constant can only be assigned a scalar value, like a string or a number. And unlike variables, a constant's value cannot be changed.

To access a constant's value, like when you want to print it, you cannot put the constant within quotation marks:

```
echo "Hello, USERNAME"; // Won't work!
```

With that code, PHP would literally print *Hello, USERNAME* and not the value of the USERNAME constant (because there's no indication that USERNAME is anything other than literal text). Instead, either print the constant by itself:

```
echo 'Hello, ';
```

```
echo USERNAME;
```

or use the concatenation operator:

```
echo 'Hello, ' . USERNAME;
```

PHP runs with several predefined constants, much like the predefined variables used earlier in the chapter. These include PHP_VERSION (the version of PHP running) and PHP_OS (the operating system of the server).

To use constants:

1. Begin a new PHP document in your text editor or IDE (**Script 1.9**).

   ```
   <!DOCTYPE html PUBLIC "-//W3C//DTD
   → XHTML 1.0 Transitional//EN"
   → "http://www.w3.org/TR/xhtml1/
   → DTD/xhtml1-transitional.dtd">

   <html xmlns="http://www.w3.org/1999/
   → xhtml" xml:lang="en" lang="en">

   <head>

     <meta http-equiv="content-type"
   → content="text/html; charset=
   → iso-8859-1" />

     <title>Constants</title>

   </head>

   <body>

   <?php # Script 1.9 - constants.php
   ```

2. Create a new date constant.

   ```
   define ('TODAY', August 28, 2007');
   ```

   An admittedly trivial use of constants, but this example will illustrate the point. In Chapter 8, "Using PHP with MySQL," you'll see how to use constants to store your database access information.

3. Print out the date, the PHP version, and operating system information.

   ```
   echo '<p>Today is ' . TODAY . '.<br
   → />This server is running version
   → <b>' . PHP_VERSION . '</b> of PHP
   → on the <b>' . PHP_OS . '</b>
   → operating system.</p>';
   ```

   Since constants cannot be printed within quotation marks, use the concatenation operator to create the echo() statement.

Script 1.9 Constants are another temporary storage tool you can use in PHP, distinct from variables.

```
1    <!DOCTYPE html PUBLIC "-//W3C//DTD XHTML
     1.0 Transitional//EN" "http://www.w3.org/
     TR/xhtml1/DTD/xhtml1-transitional.dtd">

2    <html xmlns="http://www.w3.org/1999/xhtml"
     xml:lang="en" lang="en">

3    <head>

4      <meta http-equiv="content-type" content=
       "text/html; charset=iso-8859-1" />

5      <title>Constants</title>

6    </head>

7    <body>

8    <?php # Script 1.9 - constants.php

9

10   // Set today's date as a constant:

11   define ('TODAY', 'August 28, 2007');

12

13   // Print a message, using predefined
     constants and the TODAY constant:

14   echo '<p>Today is ' . TODAY . '.<br />This
     server is running version <b>' . PHP_
     VERSION . '</b> of PHP on the <b>' . PHP_
     OS . '</b> operating system.</p>';

15

16   ?>

17   </body>

18   </html>
```

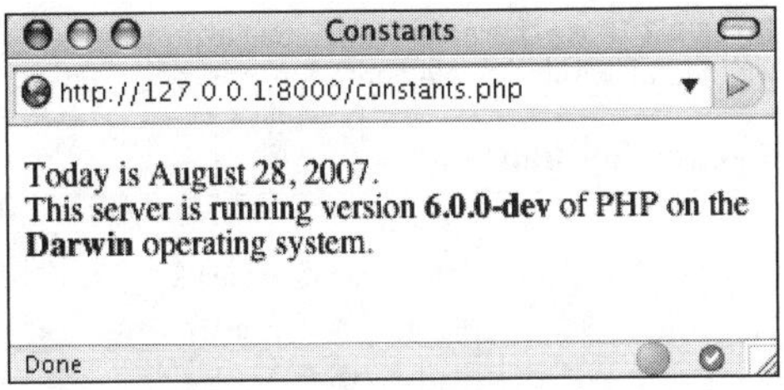

Figure 1.19 By making use of PHP's constants, you can learn more about your PHP setup.

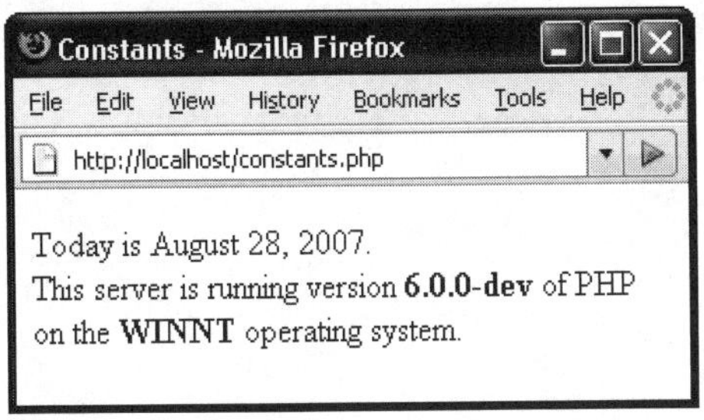

Figure 1.20 Running the same script (refer to Script 1.9) on different servers garners different results.

4. Complete the PHP code and the HTML page.

   ?>

   </body>

   </html>

5. Save the file as `constants.php`, place it in your Web directory, and test it in your Web browser (**Figure 1.19**).

✔ Tips

- If possible, run this script on another PHP-enabled server (**Figure 1.20**).

- In Chapter 11, "Cookies and Sessions," you'll learn about another constant, SID (which stands for *session ID*).

Single vs. Double Quotation Marks

In PHP it's important to understand how single quotation marks differ from double quotation marks. With echo() and print(), or when assigning values to strings, you can use either, as in the examples uses so far. But there is a key difference between the two types of quotation marks and when you should use which. I've introduced this difference already, but it's an important enough concept to merit more discussion.

In PHP, values enclosed within single quotation marks will be treated literally, whereas those within double quotation marks will be interpreted. In other words, placing variables and special characters (**Table 1.2**) within double quotes will result in their represented values printed, not their literal values. For example, assume that you have

```
$var = 'test';
```

The code echo "var is equal to $var"; will print out *var is equal to test*, whereas the code echo 'var is equal to $var'; will print out *var is equal to $var*. Using an escaped dollar sign, the code echo "\$var is equal to $var"; will print out *$var is equal to test*, whereas the code echo '\$var is equal to $var'; will print out *\$var is equal to $var*.

As these examples should illustrate, double quotation marks will replace a variable's name (**$var**) with its value (*test*) and a special character's code (**\$**) with its represented value (*$*). Single quotes will always display exactly what you type, except for the escaped single quote (\') and the escaped backslash (\\), which are printed as a single quotation mark and a single backslash, respectively.

As another example of how the two quotation marks differ, let's modify the numbers.php script as an experiment.

TABLE 1.2 These characters have special meanings when used within double quotation marks.

Escape Sequences	
CODE	**MEANING**
\"	Double quotation mark
\'	Single quotation mark
\\	Backslash
\n	Newline
\r	Carriage return
\t	Tab
\$	Dollar sign

Script 1.10 This, the final script in the chapter, demonstrates the differences between using single and double quotation marks.

```
⊖ ◯ ⊖              📄 Script
1   <!DOCTYPE html PUBLIC "-//W3C//DTD XHTML
    1.0 Transitional//EN" "http://www.w3.org/
    TR/xhtml1/DTD/xhtml1-transitional.dtd">

2   <html xmlns="http://www.w3.org/1999/xhtml"
    xml:lang="en" lang="en">

3   <head>

4     <meta http-equiv="content-type" content=
      "text/html; charset=iso-8859-1" />

5     <title>Quotation Marks</title>

6   </head>

7   <body>

8   <?php # Script 1.10 - quotes.php

9

10  // Set the variables:

11  $quantity = 30; // Buying 30 widgets.

12  $price = 119.95;

13  $taxrate = .05; // 5% sales tax.

14

15  // Calculate the total.

16  $total = $quantity * $price;

17  $total = $total + ($total * $taxrate); //
    Calculate and add the tax.

18

19  // Format the total:

20  $total = number_format ($total, 2);

21

22  // Print the results using double quotation
    marks:

23  echo '<h3>Using double quotation
    marks:</h3>';

24  echo "<p>You are purchasing <b>$quantity
    </b> widget(s) at a cost of <b>\$$price</b>
    each. With tax, the total comes to <b>\
    $$total</b>.</p>\n";

25

26  // Print the results using single quotation
    marks:

27  echo '<h3>Using single quotation
    marks:</h3>';
                              (script continues)
```

To use single and double quotation marks:

1. Open numbers.php (refer to Script 1.8) in your text editor or IDE.

2. Delete the existing echo() statement (**Script 1.10**).

3. Print a caption and then rewrite the original echo() statement using double quotation marks.

   ```
   echo '<h3>Using double quotation
   → marks:</h3>';
   ```

   ```
   echo "<p>You are purchasing <b>$
   → quantity</b> widget(s) at a cost
   → of <b>\$$price</b> each. With tax,
   →  the total comes to <b>\$$total</
   → b>.</p>\n";
   ```

   In the original script, the results were printed using single quotation marks and concatenation. The same result can be achieved using double quotation marks. When using double quotation marks, the variables can be placed within the string.

   There is one catch, though: trying to print a dollar amount as *$12.34* (where *12.34* comes from a variable) would suggest that you would code $$var. That will not work; instead, escape the initial dollar sign, resulting in \$$var, as you see

continues on next page

Script 1.10 *continued*

```
⊖ ◯ ⊖              📄 Script
28  echo '<p>You are purchasing <b>$quantity
    </b> widget(s) at a cost of <b>\$$price</b>
    each. With tax, the total comes to
    <b>\$$total</b>.</p>\n';

29

30  ?>

31  </body>

32  </html>
```

SINGLE VS. DOUBLE QUOTATION MARKS

twice in this code. The first dollar sign will be printed, and the second becomes the start of the variable name.

4. Repeat the echo() statements, this time using single quotation marks.

```
echo '<h3>Using single quotation
marks:</h3>';

echo '<p>You are purchasing <b>$
→ quantity</b> widget(s) at a cost
→ of <b>\$$price</b> each. With tax,
→  the total comes to <b>\$$total
→ </b>.</p>\n';
```

This echo() statement is used to highlight the difference between using single or double quotation marks. It will not work as desired, and the resulting page will show you exactly what does happen instead.

5. If you want, change the page's title.

6. Save the file as quotes.php, place it in your Web directory, and test it in your Web browser (**Figure 1.21**).

7. View the source of the Web page to see how using the newline character (\n) within each quotation mark type also differs.

You should see that when you place the newline character within double quotation marks it creates a newline in the HTML source. When placed within single quotation marks, the literal characters \ and n are printed instead.

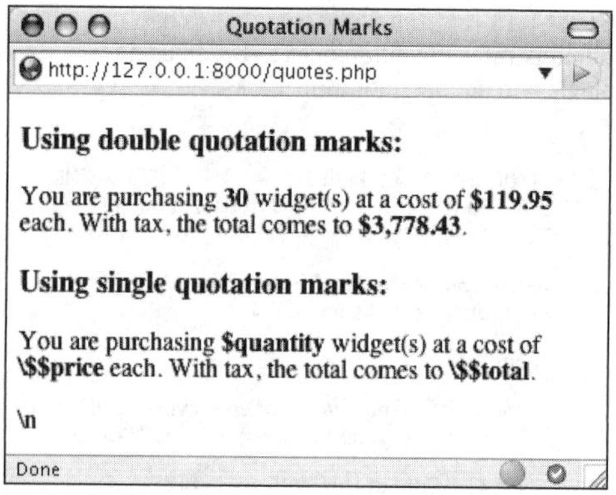

Figure 1.21 These results demonstrate when and how you'd use one type of quotation mark as opposed to the other. If you're still unclear as to the difference between the types, use double quotation marks and you're less likely to have problems.

✔ Tips

■ Because PHP will attempt to find variables within double quotation marks, using single quotation marks is theoretically faster. If you need to print the value of a variable, though, you *must* use double quotation marks.

■ As valid HTML often includes a lot of double-quoted attributes, it's often easiest to use single quotation marks when printing HTML with PHP:

```
echo '<table width="80%" border="0"
→ cellspacing="2" cellpadding="3"
→ align="center">';
```

If you were to print out this HTML using double quotation marks, you would have to escape all of the double quotation marks in the string:

```
echo "<table width=\"80%\" border=\
→ "0\" cellspacing=\"2\" cellpadding
→ =\"3\" align=\"center\">";
```

Programming with PHP

Now that you have the fundamentals of the PHP scripting language down, it's time to build on those basics and start truly programming. In this chapter you'll begin creating more elaborate scripts while still learning some of the standard constructs, functions, and syntax of the language.

You'll begin by creating an HTML form, then learning how you can use PHP to handle the submitted values. From there, the chapter covers conditionals and the remaining operators (Chapter 1, "Introduction to PHP," presented the assignment, concatenation, and mathematical operators), arrays (another variable type), and one last language construct, loops.

Creating an HTML Form

Handling an HTML form with PHP is perhaps the most important process in any dynamic Web site. Two steps are involved: first you create the HTML form itself, and then you create the corresponding PHP script that will receive and process the form data.

It would be outside the realm of this book to go into HTML forms in any detail, but I will lead you through one quick example so that it may be used throughout the chapter. If you're unfamiliar with the basics of an HTML form, including the various types of elements, see an HTML resource for more information.

An HTML form is created using the form tags and various elements for taking input. The form tags look like

```
<form action="script.php" method="post">
</form>
```

In terms of PHP, the most important attribute of your form tag is action, which dictates to which page the form data will be sent. The second attribute—method—has its own issues (see the "Choosing a Method" sidebar), but post is the value you'll use most frequently.

The different inputs—be they text boxes, radio buttons, select menus, check boxes, etc.—are placed within the opening and closing form tags. As you'll see in the next section, what kinds of inputs your form has makes little difference to the PHP script handling it. You should, however, pay attention to the names you give your form inputs, as they'll be of critical importance when it comes to your PHP code.

Choosing a Method

The method attribute of a form dictates how the data is sent to the handling page. The two options—get and post—refer to the HTTP (Hypertext Transfer Protocol) method to be used. The get method sends the submitted data to the receiving page as a series of *name-value* pairs appended to the URL. For example,

```
http://www.example.com/script. php?
→ name=Homer&gender=M&age=35
```

The benefit of using the get method is that the resulting page can be bookmarked in the user's Web browser (since it's a URL). For that matter, you can also click Back in your Web browser to return to a get page, or reload it without problems (none of which is true for post). But there is a limit in how much data can be transmitted via get, and this method is less secure (since the data is visible).

Generally speaking, get is used for requesting information, like a particular record from a database or the results of a search (searches almost always use get). The post method is used when an action is required, as when a database record will be updated or an email should be sent. For these reasons I will primarily use post throughout this book, with noted exceptions.

Script 2.1 This simple HTML form will be used for several of the examples in this chapter.

```
● ● ●                    📄 Script
1    <!DOCTYPE html PUBLIC "-//W3C//DTD XHTML
     1.0 Transitional//EN" "http://www.w3.org/
     TR/xhtml1/DTD/xhtml1-transitional.dtd">

2    <html xmlns="http://www.w3.org/1999/xhtml"
     xml:lang="en" lang="en">

3    <head>

4        <meta http-equiv="content-type" con-
         tent="text/html; charset=iso-8859-1" />

5        <title>Simple HTML Form</title>

6    </head>

7    <body>

8    <!-- Script 2.1 - form.html -->

9

10   <form action="handle_form.php"
     method="post">

11

12       <fieldset><legend>Enter your
         information in the form below:</legend>

13

14       <p><b>Name:</b> <input type="text"
         name="name" size="20" maxlength="40"
         /></p>

15

16       <p><b>Email Address:</b> <input
         type="text" name="email" size="40"
         maxlength="60" /></p>

17

18       <p><b>Gender:</b> <input type="radio"
         name="gender" value="M" /> Male <input
         type="radio" name="gender" value="F" />
         Female</p>

19

20       <p><b>Age:</b></p>

21       <select name="age">

22           <option value="0-29">Under
             30</option>

23           <option value="30-60">Between 30 and
             60</option>
```

(script continues on next page)

To create an HTML form:

1. Begin a new HTML document in your text editor (**Script 2.1**).

   ```
   <!DOCTYPE html PUBLIC "-//W3C//
   → DTD XHTML 1.0 Transitional//EN"
   → "http://www.w3.org/TR/xhtml1/DTD/
   → xhtml1-transitional.dtd">
   <html xmlns="http://www.w3.org/1999/
   → xhtml" xml:lang="en" lang="en">
   <head>
     <meta http-equiv="content-type"
   → content="text/html; charset=
   → iso-8859-1" />
     <title>Simple HTML Form</title>
   </head>
   <body>
   <!-- Script 2.1 - form.html -->
   ```

   There's nothing significantly new here. The document still uses the same basic syntax for an HTML page as in the previous chapter. An HTML comment indicates the file's name and number.

2. Add the initial form tag.

   ```
   <form action="handle_form.php"
   → method="post">
   ```

   Since the action attribute dictates to which script the form data will go, you should give it an appropriate name (*handle_form* to correspond with this script: form.html) and the .php extension (since a PHP page will handle this form's data).

3. Begin the HTML form.

   ```
   <fieldset><legend>Enter your
   → information in the form
   → below:</legend>
   ```

   continues on next page

I'm using the `fieldset` and `legend` HTML tags because I like the way they make the HTML form look (they add a box around the form with a title at top). This isn't pertinent to the form itself, though.

4. Add two text inputs.

   ```
   <p><b>Name:</b> <input type="text"
   → name="name" size="20" maxlength=
   → "40" /></p>
   ```

   ```
   <p><b>Email Address:</b> <input
   → type="text" name="email" size="40"
   → maxlength="60" /></p>
   ```

   These are just simple text inputs, allowing the user to enter their name and email address (**Figure 2.1**). In case you are wondering, the extra space and slash at the end of each input's tag are required for valid XHTML. With standard HTML, these tags would conclude, for instance, with `maxlength="40">` or `maxlength="60">` instead.

5. Add a pair of radio buttons.

   ```
   <p><b>Gender:</b> <input type=
   → "radio" name="gender" value=
   → "M" /> Male <input type=
   → "radio" name="gender" value=
   → "F" /> Female</p>
   ```

   The radio buttons (**Figure 2.2**) both have the same name, meaning that only one of the two can be selected. They have different values, though.

6. Add a pull-down menu.

   ```
   <p><b>Age:</b>
   ```

   ```
   <select name="age">
   ```

   ```
     <option value="0-29">Under 30</
   → option>
   ```

   ```
     <option value="30-60">Between 30
   → and 60</option>
   ```

Script 2.1 *continued*

```
  ⊝ ⊝ ⊝                         Script
24        <option value="60+">Over 60</option>
25    </select></p>
26
27    <p><b>Comments:</b> <textarea
      name="comments" rows="3"
      cols="40"></textarea></p>
28
29    </fieldset>
30
31    <div align="center"><input type=
      "submit" name="submit" value=
      "Submit My Information" /></div>
32
33  </form>
34
35  </body>
36  </html>
```

Figure 2.1 Two text inputs.

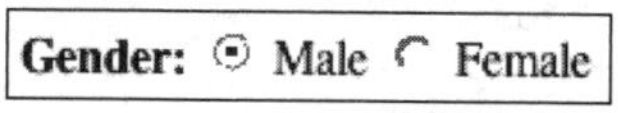

Figure 2.2 If multiple radio buttons have the same name, only one can be chosen by the user.

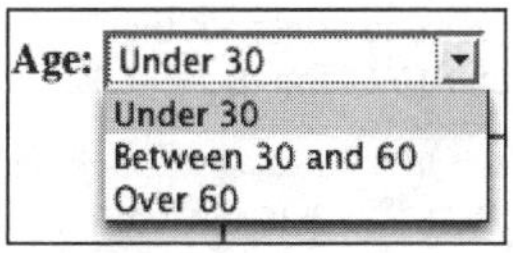

Figure 2.3 The pull-down menu offers three options, of which only one can be selected (in this example).

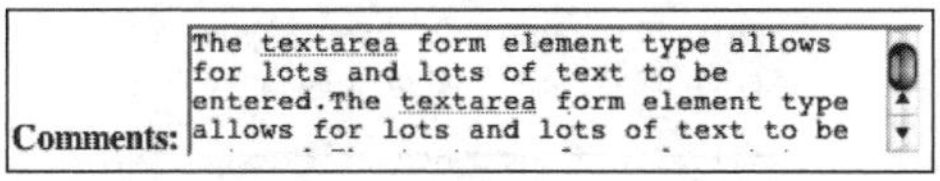

Figure 2.4 The textarea form element type allows for lots and lots of text to be entered.

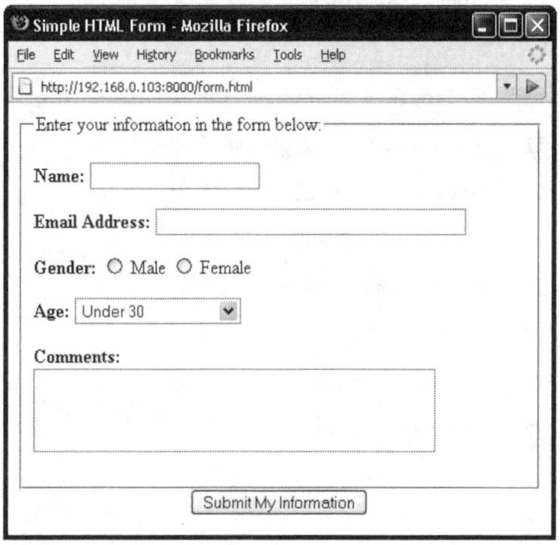

Figure 2.5 The complete form, which requests some basic information from the user.

```
<option value="60+">Over 60</
→ option>

</select></p>
```

The select tag starts the pull-down menu, and then each option tag will create another line in the list of choices (**Figure 2.3**).

7. Add a text box for comments.

```
<p><b>Comments:</b> <textarea name=
→ "comments" rows="3" cols="40"></
→ textarea></p>
```

Textareas are different from text inputs; they are presented as a box (**Figure 2.4**), not as a single line. They allow for much more information to be typed and are useful for taking user comments.

8. Complete the form.

```
</fieldset>

<div align="center"><input type=
→ "submit" name="submit" value=
→ "Submit My Information" /></div>

</form>
```

The first tag closes the fieldset that was opened in Step 3. Then a submit button is created and centered using a div tag. Finally the form is closed.

9. Complete the HTML page.

```
</body>

</html>
```

10. Save the file as form.html, place it in your Web directory, and view it in your Web browser (**Figure 2.5**).

✔ Tip

■ Since this page contains just HTML, it uses an .html extension. It could instead use a .php extension without harm (since code outside of the PHP tags is treated as HTML).

Handling an HTML Form

Now that the HTML form has been created, it's time to write a bare-bones PHP script to handle it. To say that this script will be *handling* the form means that the PHP page will do something with the data it receives (which is the data the user entered into the form). In this chapter, the scripts will simply print the data back to the Web browser. In later examples, form data will be stored in a MySQL database, compared against previously stored values, sent in emails, and more.

The beauty of PHP—and what makes it so easy to learn and use—is how well it interacts with HTML forms. PHP scripts store the received information in special variables. For example, say you have a form with an input defined like so:

```
<input type="text" name="city" />
```

Whatever the user types into that element will be accessible via a PHP variable named `$_REQUEST['city']`. It is very important that the spelling and capitalization match *exactly*! PHP is case-sensitive when it comes to variable names, so `$_REQUEST['city']` will work, but `$_Request['city']` or `$_REQUEST['City']` will have no value.

This next example will be a PHP script that handles the already-created HTML form (Script 2.1). This script will assign the form data to new variables (to be used as shorthand, just like in Script 1.5, `predefined.php`). The script will then print the received values.

To handle an HTML form:

1. Create a new PHP document in your text editor or IDE, beginning with the HTML (**Script 2.2**).

```
<!DOCTYPE html PUBLIC "-//W3C//
→ DTD XHTML 1.0 Transitional//EN"
→ "http://www.w3.org/TR/xhtml1/DTD/
```

Script 2.2 This script receives and prints out the information entered into an HTML form (Script 2.1).

```
1   <!DOCTYPE html PUBLIC "-//W3C//DTD XHTML
    1.0 Transitional//EN" "http://www.w3.org/
    TR/xhtml1/DTD/xhtml1-transitional.dtd">
2   <html xmlns="http://www.w3.org/1999/xhtml"
    xml:lang="en" lang="en">
3   <head>
4       <meta http-equiv="content-type" con-
        tent="text/html; charset=iso-8859-1" />
5       <title>Form Feedback</title>
6   </head>
7   <body>
8   <?php # Script 2.2 - handle_form.php
9
10  // Create a shorthand for the form data:
11  $name = $_REQUEST['name'];
12  $email = $_REQUEST['email'];
13  $comments = $_REQUEST['comments'];
14  /* Not used:
15  $_REQUEST['age']
16  $_REQUEST['gender']
17  $_REQUEST['submit']
18  */
19
20  // Print the submitted information:
21  echo "<p>Thank you, <b>$name</b>, for the
    following comments:<br />
22  <tt>$comments</tt></p>
23  <p>We will reply to you at
    <i>$email</i>.</p>\n";
24
25  ?>
26  </body>
27  </html>
```

Table 2.1 The HTML form elements and their corresponding PHP variables.

Form Elements to PHP Variables

ELEMENT NAME	VARIABLE NAME
name	$_REQUEST['name']
email	$_REQUEST['email']
comments	$_REQUEST['comments']
age	$_REQUEST['age']
gender	$_REQUEST['gender']
submit	$_REQUEST['submit']

```
→ xhtml1-transitional.dtd">

<html xmlns="http://www.w3.org/1999/

→ xhtml" xml:lang="en" lang="en">

<head>

  <meta http-equiv="content-type"

→ content="text/html; charset=

→ iso-8859-1" />

  <title>Form Feedback</title>

</head>

<body>
```

2. Add the opening PHP tag and create a shorthand version of the form data variables.

```
<?php # Script 2.2 - handle_form.php

$name = $_REQUEST['name'];

$email = $_REQUEST['email'];

$comments = $_REQUEST['comments'];
```

Following the rules outlined before, the data entered into the first form input, which is called *name*, will be accessible through the variable $_REQUEST['name'] (**Table 2.1**). The data entered into the email form input, which has a name value of *email*, will be accessible through $_REQUEST['email']. The same applies to the comments data. Again, the spelling and capitalization of your variables here must exactly match the corresponding name values in the HTML form.

3. Print out the received name, email, and comments values.

```
echo "<p>Thank you, <b>$name</b>,

→ for the following comments:<br />

<tt>$comments</tt></p>

<p>We will reply to you at <i>

→ $email</i>.</p>\n";
```

continues on next page

The submitted values are simply printed out using the echo() statement, double quotation marks, and a wee bit of HTML formatting.

4. Complete the HTML page.

?>

</body>

</html>

5. Save the file as handle_form.php and place it in the same Web directory as form.html.

6. Test both documents in your Web browser by loading form.html through a URL and then filling out and submitting the form (**Figures 2.6** and **2.7**).

Because the PHP script must be run through a URL (see Chapter 1), the form must also be run through a URL. Otherwise, when you go to submit the form, you'll see PHP code (**Figure 2.8**) instead of the proper result (Figure 2.7).

✔ Tips

- $_REQUEST is a special variable type, known as a *superglobal*. It stores all of the data sent to a PHP page through either the GET or POST method, as well as data accessible in cookies. Superglobals will be discussed later in the chapter.

- If you have any problems with this script, apply the debugging techniques suggested in Chapter 1. If those don't solve the problem, check out the extended debugging techniques listed in Chapter 7, "Error Handling and Debugging." If you're still stymied, turn to the book's supporting forum for assistance (www.DMCInsights. com/phorum/).

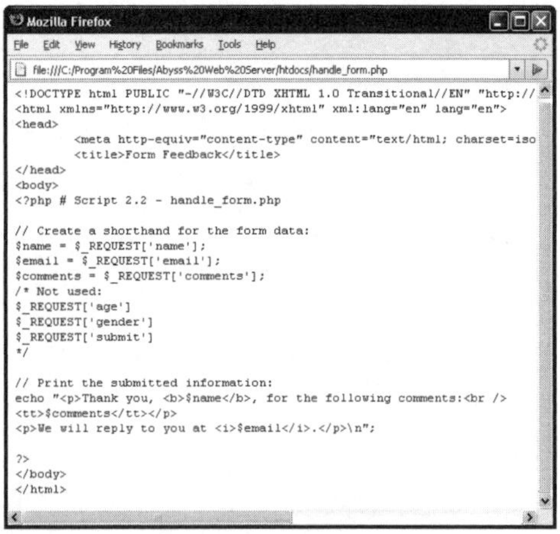

Figure 2.6 To test handle_form.php, you must load the form through a URL, then fill it out and submit it.

Figure 2.7 Your script should display results like this.

Figure 2.8 If you see the PHP code itself after submitting the form, the problem is likely that you did not access the form through a URL.

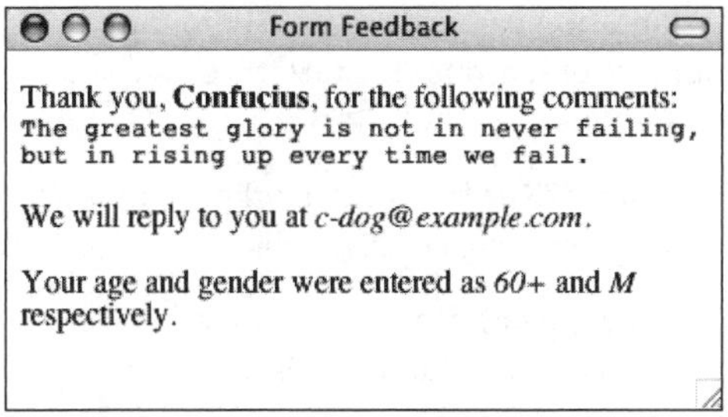

Figure 2.9 The values of *gender* and *age* correspond to those defined in the form's HTML.

- If the PHP script shows blank spaces where a variable's value should have been printed, it means that the variable has no value. The two most likely causes are: you failed to enter a value in the form; or you misspelled or mis-capitalized the variable's name.

- If you see any *Undefined variable: variablename* errors, this is because the variables you refer to have no value and PHP is set on the highest level of error reporting. The previous tip provides suggestions as to why a variable wouldn't have a value. Chapter 7 discusses error reporting in detail.

- For a comparison of how PHP handles the different form input types, print out the $_REQUEST['age'] and $_REQUEST ['gender'] values (**Figure 2.9**).

Magic Quotes

Earlier versions of PHP had a feature called *Magic Quotes*, which was removed in PHP 6. Magic Quotes—when enabled—automatically escapes single and double quotation marks found in submitted form data (there were actually three kinds of Magic Quotes, but this one kind is most important here). So the string *I'm going out* would be turned into *I\'m going out*.

The escaping of potentially problematic characters can be useful and even necessary in some situations. But if Magic Quotes are enabled on your PHP installation (which means you're using a pre–PHP 6 version), you'll see these backslashes when the PHP script prints out the form data. You can undo its effect using the stripslashes() function:

```
$var = stripslashes($var);
```

This function will remove any backslashes found in $var. This will have the effect of turning an escaped submitted string back to its original, non-escaped value.

To use this in handle_form.php (Script 2.2), you would write:

```
$name = stripslashes($_REQUEST['name']);
```

If you're using PHP 6 or later, you no longer need to worry about this, as Magic Quotes has been removed (for several good reasons).

Conditionals and Operators

PHP's three primary terms for creating conditionals are if, else, and elseif (which can also be written as two words, else if).

Every conditional begins with an if clause:

```
if (condition) {
    // Do something!
}
```

An if can also have an else clause:

```
if (condition) {
    // Do something!
} else {
    // Do something else!
}
```

An elseif clause allows you to add more conditions:

```
if (condition1) {
    // Do something!
} elseif (condition2) {
    // Do something else!
} else {
    // Do something different!
}
```

If a condition is true, the code in the following curly braces ({}) will be executed. If not, PHP will continue on. If there is a second condition (after an elseif), that will be checked for truth. The process will continue—you can use as many elseif clauses as you want—until PHP hits an else, which will be automatically executed at that point, or until the conditional terminates without an else. For this reason, it's important that the else always come last and be treated as the default action unless specific criteria (the conditions) are met.

A condition can be true in PHP for any number of reasons. To start, these are true conditions:

◆ $var, if $var has a value other than 0, an empty string, FALSE, or NULL

◆ isset($var), if $var has any value other than NULL, including 0, FALSE, or an empty string

◆ TRUE, true, True, etc.

In the second example, a new function, isset(), is introduced. This function checks if a variable is set, meaning that it has a value other than NULL (as a reminder, NULL is a special type in PHP, representing no set value). You can also use the comparative and logical operators (**Table 2.2**) in conjunction with parentheses to make more complicated expressions.

TABLE 2.2 These operators are frequently used when writing conditionals.

Comparative and Logical Operators			
SYMBOL	MEANING	TYPE	EXAMPLE
==	is equal to	comparison	$x == $y
!=	is not equal to	comparison	$x != $y
<	less than	comparison	$x < $y
>	greater than	comparison	$x > $y
<=	less than or equal to	comparison	$x <= $y
>=	greater than or equal to	comparison	$x >= $y
!	not	logical	!$x
&&	and	logical	$x && $y
||	or	logical	$x || $y
XOR	and not	logical	$x XOR $y

Script 2.3 Conditionals allow a script to modify behavior according to specific criteria. In this remade version of handle_form.php, two conditionals are used to validate the gender radio buttons.

```
1    <!DOCTYPE html PUBLIC "-//W3C//DTD XHTML
     1.0 Transitional//EN"

2        "http://www.w3.org/TR/xhtml1/DTD/
         xhtml1-transitional.dtd">

3    <html xmlns="http://www.w3.org/1999/xhtml"
     xml:lang="en" lang="en">

4    <head>

5      <meta http-equiv="content-type" con-
       tent=
       "text/html; charset=iso-8859-1" />

6      <title>Form Feedback</title>

7    </head>

8    <body>

9    <?php # Script 2.3 - handle_form.php #2

10

11   // Create a shorthand for the form data:

12   $name = $_REQUEST['name'];

13   $email = $_REQUEST['email'];

14   $comments = $_REQUEST['comments'];

15

16   // Create the $gender variable:

17   if (isset($_REQUEST['gender'])) {

18     $gender = $_REQUEST['gender'];

19   } else {

20     $gender = NULL;

21   }

22

23   // Print the submitted information:

24   echo "<p>Thank you, <b>$name</b>, for the
       following comments:<br />

25   <tt>$comments</tt></p>

26   <p>We will reply to you at <i>$email</i>.
       </p>\n";
```

(script continues on next page)

To use conditionals:

1. Open handle_form.php (refer to Script 2.2) in your text editor or IDE.

2. Before the echo() statement, add a conditional that creates a $gender variable (**Script 2.3**).

   ```
   if (isset($_REQUEST['gender'])) {

       $gender = $_REQUEST['gender'];

   } else {

       $gender = NULL;

   }
   ```

   This is a simple and effective way to validate a form input (particularly a radio button, check box, or select). If the user checks either gender radio button, then $_REQUEST['gender'] will have a value, meaning that the condition isset($_REQUEST['gender']) is true. In such a case, the shorthand version of this variable—$gender—is assigned the value of $_REQUEST['gender'], repeating the technique used with $name, $email, and $comments. If the user does not click one of the radio buttons, then this condition is not true, and $gender is assigned the value of NULL, indicating that it has no value. Notice that NULL is not in quotes.

continues on next page

3. After the echo() statement, add another conditional that prints a message based upon $gender's value.

```
if ($gender == 'M') {
    echo '<p><b>Good day, Sir!</b>
    → </p>';
} elseif ($gender == 'F') {
    echo '<p><b>Good day, Madam!</b>
    → </p>';
} else {
    echo '<p><b>You forgot to enter
    → your gender!</b></p>';
}
```

This if-elseif-else conditional looks at the value of the $gender variable and prints a different message for each possibility. It's very important to remember that the double equals sign (==) means equals, whereas a single equals sign (=) assigns a value. The distinction is important because the condition $gender == 'M' may or may not be true, but $gender = 'M' will always be true.

Also, the values used here—*M* and *F*—must be exactly the same as those in the HTML form (the values for each radio button). Equality is a case-sensitive comparison with strings, so *m* will not equal *M*.

4. Save the file, place it in your Web directory, and test it in your Web browser (**Figures 2.10**, **2.11**, and **2.12**).

Script 2.3 *continued*

```
27
28   // Print a message based upon the gender
     value:
29   if ($gender == 'M') {
30       echo '<p><b>Good day, Sir!</b></p>';
31   } elseif ($gender == 'F') {
32       echo '<p><b>Good day, Madam!</b></p>';
33   } else { // No gender selected.
34       echo '<p><b>You forgot to enter your
         gender!</b></p>';
35   }
36
37   ?>
38   </body>
39   </html>
```

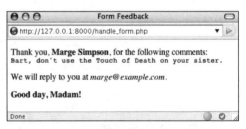

Figure 2.10 The gender-based conditional prints a different message for each choice in the form.

Figure 2.11 The same script will produce different salutations (compare with Figure 2.10) when the gender values change.

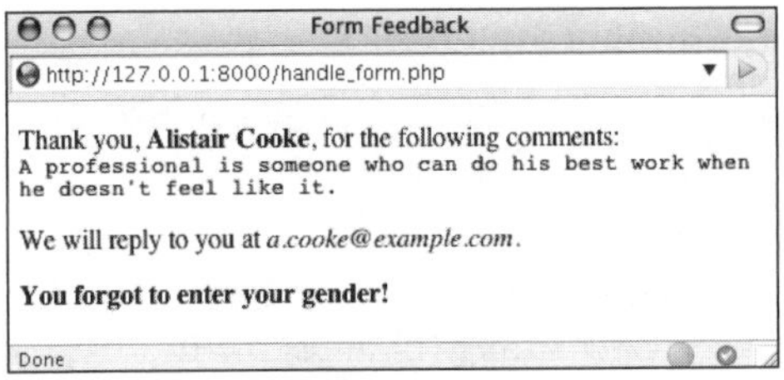

Figure 2.12 If no gender was selected, a message is printed indicating to the user their oversight.

Switch

PHP has another type of conditional, called the switch, best used in place of a long if-elseif-else conditional. The syntax of switch is

```
switch ($variable) {
  case 'value1':
    // Do this.
    break;
  case 'value2':
    // Do this instead.
    break;
  default:
    // Do this then.
    break;
}
```

The switch conditional compares the value of $variable to the different *cases*. When it finds a match, the following code is executed, up until the break. If no match is found, the *default* is executed, assuming it exists (it's optional). The switch conditional is limited in its usage in that it can only check a variable's value for equality against certain cases; more complex conditions cannot be easily checked.

✔ Tips

■ Although PHP has no strict formatting rules, it's standard procedure and good programming form to make it clear when one block of code is a subset of a conditional. Indenting the block is the norm.

■ You can—and frequently will—nest conditionals (place one inside another).

■ The first conditional in this script (the isset()) is a perfect example of how to use a default value. The assumption (the else) is that $gender has a NULL value unless the one condition is met: that $_REQUEST['gender'] is set.

■ The curly braces used to indicate the beginning and end of a conditional are not required if you are executing only one statement. I would recommend that you almost always use them, though, as a matter of clarity.

Validating Form Data

A critical concept related to handling HTML forms is that of validating form data. In terms of both error management and security, you should absolutely never trust the data being entered in an HTML form. Whether erroneous data is purposefully malicious or just unintentionally inappropriate, it's up to you—the Web architect—to test it against expectations.

Validating form data requires the use of conditionals and any number of functions, operators, and expressions. One standard function to be used is isset(), which tests if a variable has a value (including *0*, FALSE, or an empty string, but not NULL). You saw an example of this in the preceding script.

One issue with the isset() function is that an empty string tests as TRUE, meaning that isset() is not an effective way to validate text inputs and text boxes from an HTML form. To check that a user typed something into textual elements, you can use the empty() function. It checks if a variable has an *empty* value: an empty string, *0*, NULL, or FALSE.

The first aim of form validation is seeing if *something* was entered or selected in form elements. The second goal is to ensure that submitted data is of the right type (numeric, string, etc.), of the right format (like an email address), or a specific acceptable value (like *$gender* being equal to either *M* or *F*). As handling forms is a main use of PHP, validating form data is a point that will be re-emphasized time and again in subsequent chapters. But first, let's create a new handle_form.php to make sure variables have values before they're referenced (there will be enough changes in this version that simply updating Script 2.3 doesn't make sense).

To validate your forms:

1. Begin a new PHP script in your text editor or IDE (**Script 2.4**).

   ```
   <!DOCTYPE html PUBLIC "-//W3C//DTD
   → XHTML 1.0 Transitional//EN" "http:
   → //www.w3.org/TR/xhtml1/DTD/
   → xhtml1-transitional.dtd">

   <html xmlns="http://www.w3.org/1999/
   → xhtml" xml:lang="en" lang="en">

   <head>

     <meta http-equiv="content-type"
   → content="text/html; charset=
   → iso-8859-1" />

     <title>Form Feedback</title>

   </head>

   <body>

   <?php # Script 2.4 - handle_
   → form.php #3
   ```

2. Within the HTML head, add some CSS (Cascading Style Sheets) code.

   ```
   <style type="text/css" title="text/
   → css" media="all">

   .error {

     font-weight: bold;

     color: #C00

   }

   </style>
   ```

   CSS is the preferred way to handle many formatting and layout issues in an HTML page. You'll see a little bit of CSS here and there in this book; if you're not familiar with the subject, check out a dedicated CSS reference.

   continues on page 49

Script 2.4 Validating HTML form data before you use it is critical to Web security and achieving professional results. Here, conditionals check that every referenced form element has a value.

```
1   <!DOCTYPE html PUBLIC "-//W3C//DTD XHTML 1.0 Transitional//EN" "http://www.w3.org/TR/xhtml1/DTD/
    → xhtml1-transitional.dtd">
2   <html xmlns="http://www.w3.org/1999/xhtml" xml:lang="en" lang="en">
3   <head>
4     <meta http-equiv="content-type" content="text/html; charset=iso-8859-1" />
5     <title>Form Feedback</title>
6     <style type="text/css" title="text/css" media="all">
7     .error {
8       font-weight: bold;
9       color: #C00
10    }
11    </style>
12  </head>
13  <body>
14  <?php # Script 2.4 - handle_form.php #3
15
16  // Validate the name:
17  if (!empty($_REQUEST['name'])) {
18     $name = $_REQUEST['name'];
19  } else {
20     $name = NULL;
21     echo '<p class="error">You forgot to enter your name!</p>';
22  }
23
24  // Validate the email:
25  if (!empty($_REQUEST['email'])) {
26     $email = $_REQUEST['email'];
27  } else {
28     $email = NULL;
29     echo '<p class="error">You forgot to enter your email address!</p>';
30  }
31
32  // Validate the comments:
33  if (!empty($_REQUEST['comments'])) {
34     $comments = $_REQUEST['comments'];
35  } else {
36     $comments = NULL;
```

(script continues on next page)

Script 2.4 *continued*

```
37    echo '<p class="error">You forgot to enter your comments!</p>';
38    }
39
40    // Validate the gender:
41    if (isset($_REQUEST['gender'])) {
42
43      $gender = $_REQUEST['gender'];
44
45      if ($gender == 'M') {
46        echo '<p><b>Good day, Sir!</b></p>';
47      } elseif ($gender == 'F') {
48        echo '<p><b>Good day, Madam!</b></p>';
49      } else { // Unacceptable value.
50        $gender = NULL;
51        echo '<p class="error">Gender should be either "M" or "F"!</p>';
52      }
53
54    } else { // $_REQUEST['gender'] is not set.
55      $gender = NULL;
56      echo '<p class="error">You forgot to select your gender!</p>';
57    }
58
59    // If everything is OK, print the message:
60    if ($name && $email && $gender && $comments) {
61
62      echo "<p>Thank you, <b>$name</b>, for the following comments:<br />
63      <tt>$comments</tt></p>
64      <p>We will reply to you at <i>$email</i>.</p>\n";
65
66    } else { // Missing form value.
67      echo '<p class="error">Please go back and fill out the form again.</p>';
68    }
69
70    ?>
71    </body>
72    </html>
```

In this script I'm defining one CSS class, called *error*. Any HTML element that has this class name will be formatted in a bold, red color (which will be more apparent in your Web browser than in this black-and-white book).

3. Check if the name was entered.

```
if (!empty($_REQUEST['name'])) {

   $name = $_REQUEST['name'];

} else {

   $name = NULL;

   echo '<p class="error">You forgot
→ to enter your name!</p>';

}
```

A simple way to check that a form text input was filled out is to use the empty() function. If $_REQUEST['name'] has a value other than an empty string, *0*, NULL, or FALSE, assume that their name was entered and a shorthand variable is assigned that value. If $_REQUEST['name'] is empty, the $name variable is set to NULL and an error message printed. This error message uses the CSS class.

4. Repeat the same process for the email address and comments.

```
if (!empty($_REQUEST['email'])) {

   $email = $_REQUEST['email'];

} else {

   $email = NULL;

   echo '<p class="error">You forgot
to enter your email address!</p>';

}

if (!empty($_REQUEST['comments'])) {

   $comments = $_REQUEST['comments'];

} else {

   $comments = NULL;
```

```
   echo '<p class="error">You forgot
→ to enter your comments!</p>';

}
```

Both variables receive the same treatment as $_REQUEST['name'] in Step 3.

5. Begin validating the gender variable.

```
if (isset($_REQUEST['gender'])) {

   $gender = $_REQUEST['gender'];
```

The validation of the gender is a two-step process. First, check if it has a value or not, using isset(). This starts the main if-else conditional, which otherwise behaves like those for the name, email address, and comments.

6. Check $gender against specific values.

```
if ($gender == 'M') {

   echo '<p><b>Good day, Sir!</b>
→ </p>';

} elseif ($gender == 'F') {

   echo '<p><b>Good day, Madam!</b>
→ </p>';

} else {

   $gender = NULL;

   echo '<p class="error">Gender
→ should be either "M" or "F"!
→ </p>';

}
```

Within the gender if clause is a nested if-elseif-else conditional that tests the variable's value against what's acceptable. This is the second part of the two-step gender validation.

continues on next page

The conditions themselves are the same as those in the last script. If gender does not end up being equal to either *M* or *F*, a problem occurred and an error message is printed. The `$gender` variable is also set to `NULL` in such cases, because it has an unacceptable value.

If `$gender` does have a valid value, a gender-specific message is printed.

7. Complete the main gender `if-else` conditional.

```
} else {

  $gender = NULL;

  echo '<p class="error">You forgot
  → to select your gender!</p>';

}
```

This `else` clause applies if `$_REQUEST['gender']` is not set. The complete, nested conditionals (see lines 41–57 of Script 2.4) successfully check every possibility:

▲ `$_REQUEST['gender']` is not set

▲ `$_REQUEST['gender']` has a value of *M*

▲ `$_REQUEST['gender']` has a value of *F*

▲ `$_REQUEST['gender']` has some other value

You may wonder how this last case may be possible, considering the values are established in the HTML form. If a malicious user creates their own form that gets submitted to your `handle_form.php` script (which is very easy to do), they could give `$_REQUEST['gender']` any value they want.

8. Print the message if all of the tests have been passed.

```
if ($name && $email && $gender &&
→ $comments) {

  echo "<p>Thank you, <b>$name</b>,
  → for the following comments:
  → <br />

  <tt>$comments</tt></p>

  <p>We will reply to you at <i>$
  → email</i>.</p>\n";

} else { // Missing form value.

  echo '<p class="error">Please go
  → back and fill out the form
  → again.</p>';

}
```

This main condition is true if every listed variable has a true value. Each variable will have a value if it passed its test but have a value of `NULL` if it didn't. If every variable has a value, the form was completed, so the *Thank you* message will be printed. If any of the variables are `NULL`, the second message will be printed (**Figures 2.13** and **2.14**).

9. Close the PHP section and complete the HTML code.

```
?>

</body>

</html>
```

10. Save the file as `handle_form.php`, place it in the same Web directory as `form.html`, and test it in your Web browser (Figures 2.13 and 2.14).

Fill out the form to different levels of completeness to test the new script (**Figure 2.15**).

Figure 2.13 The script now checks that every form element was filled out (except the age) and reports on those that weren't.

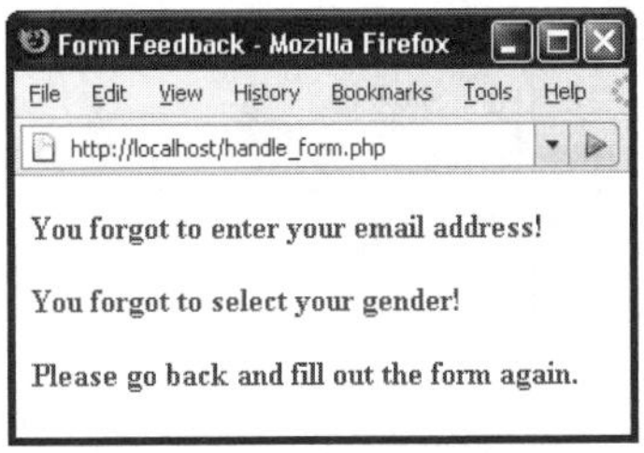

Figure 2.14 If even one or two fields were skipped, the *Thank you* message is not printed...

Figure 2.15 ...but if everything was entered properly, the script behaves as it previously had (although the gender-specific message now appears at the top of the results).

✔ Tips

■ To test if a submitted value is a number, use the is_numeric() function.

■ In Chapter 13, "Perl-Compatible Regular Expressions," you'll see how to validate form data using regular expressions.

■ The $age variable is still not used or validated for the sake of saving book space. To validate it, repeat the $gender validation routine, referring to $_REQUEST['age'] instead. To test $age's specific value, use an if-elseif-elseif-else, checking against the corresponding pull-down options (*0-29, 30-60, 60+*).

■ It's considered good form (pun intended) to let a user know which fields are required when they're filling out the form, and where applicable, the format of that field (like a date or a phone number).

VALIDATING FORM DATA

Introducing Arrays

The final variable type covered in this book is the array. Unlike strings and numbers (which are scalar variables, meaning they can store only a single value at a time), an *array* can hold multiple, separate pieces of information. An array is therefore like a list of values, each value being a string or a number or even another array.

Arrays are structured as a series of *key-value* pairs, where one pair is an item or *element* of that array. For each item in the list, there is a *key* (or *index*) associated with it (**Table 2.3**).

PHP supports two kinds of arrays: *indexed*, which use numbers as the keys (as in Table 2.3), and *associative*, which use strings as keys (**Table 2.4**). As in most programming languages, with indexed arrays, your arrays will begin with the first index at 0, unless you specify the keys explicitly.

An array follows the same naming rules as any other variable. So offhand, you might not be able to tell that $var is an array as opposed to a string or number. The important syntactical difference arises when accessing individual array elements.

To refer to a specific value in an array, start with the array variable name, followed by the key in square brackets:

echo $artists[2]; // Wilco

echo $states['MD']; // Maryland

You can see that the array keys are used like other values in PHP: numbers (e.g., *2*) are never quoted, whereas strings (*MD*) must be.

Table 2.3 The $artists array uses numbers for its keys.

Array Example 1: $artists	
KEY	VALUE
0	Death Cab for Cutie
1	Postal Service
2	Wilco
3	Damien Rice
4	White Stripes

Table 2.4 The $states array uses strings (specifically the state abbreviation) for its keys.

Array Example 2: $states	
KEY	VALUE
MD	Maryland
PA	Pennsylvania
IL	Illinois
MO	Missouri
IA	Iowa

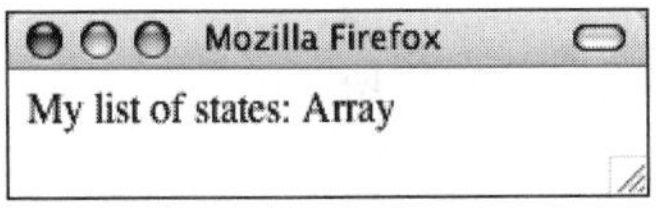

Figure 2.16 Attempting to print an array by just referring to the array name results in the word *Array* being printed instead.

Superglobal Arrays

PHP includes several predefined arrays called the *superglobal* variables. They are: $_GET, $_POST, $_REQUEST, $_SERVER, $_ENV, $_SESSION, and $_COOKIE.

The $_GET variable is where PHP stores all of the values sent to a PHP script via the get method (possibly but not necessarily from an HTML form). $_POST stores all of the data sent to a PHP script from an HTML form that uses the post method. Both of these—along with $_COOKIE—are subsets of $_REQUEST, which you've been using.

$_SERVER, which was used in Chapter 1, stores information about the server PHP is running on, as does $_ENV. $_SESSION and $_COOKIE will both be discussed in Chapter 11, "Cookies and Sessions."

One aspect of good security and programming is to be precise when referring to a variable. This means that, although you can use $_REQUEST to access form data submitted through the post method, $_POST would be more accurate.

Because arrays use a different syntax than other variables, printing them can be trickier. First, since an array can contain multiple values, you cannot easily print them (**Figure 2.16**):

```
echo "My list of states: $states";
```

However, printing an individual element's value is simple if it uses indexed (numeric) keys:

```
echo "The first artist is $artists[0].";
```

But if the array uses strings for the keys, the quotes used to surround the key will muddle the syntax. The following code will cause a parse error:

```
echo "IL is $states['IL'].";  // BAD!
```

To fix this, wrap the array name and key in curly braces when an array uses strings for its keys:

```
echo "IL is {$states['IL']}.";
```

If arrays seem slightly familiar to you already, that's because you've already worked with two: $_SERVER (in Chapter 1) and $_REQUEST (in this chapter). To acquaint you with another array and how to print array values directly, one final basic version of the handle_form.php page will be created using the more specific $_POST array (see the sidebar on "Superglobal Arrays").

INTRODUCING ARRAYS

To use arrays:

1. Begin a new PHP script in your text editor (**Script 2.5**).

```
<!DOCTYPE html PUBLIC "-//W3C//DTD
→ XHTML 1.0 Transitional//EN"
→ "http://www.w3.org/TR/xhtml1/
→ DTD/xhtml1-transitional.dtd">

<html xmlns="http://www.w3.org/1999/
→ xhtml" xml:lang="en" lang="en">

<head>

  <meta http-equiv="content-type"
→ content="text/html; charset=
→ iso-8859-1" />

  <title>Form Feedback</title>

  <style type="text/css" title=
→ "text/css" media="all">

  .error {

    font-weight: bold;

    color: #C00

  }

  </style>

</head>

<body>

<?php # Script 2.5 - handle_
→ form.php #4
```

As with the previous handle_form.php (Script 2.4), this one defines a CSS class.

2. Perform some basic form validation.

```
if ( !empty($_POST['name']) &&
→ !empty($_POST['comments']) &&
→ !empty($_POST['email']) ) {
```

In the previous version of this script, the values are accessed by referring to the $_REQUEST array. But since these variables come from a form that uses the **post** method (see Script 2.1), **$_POST** would be a more exact, and therefore more secure, reference (see the sidebar).

Script 2.5 The superglobal variables, like $_POST here, are just one type of array you'll use in PHP.

```
1   <!DOCTYPE html PUBLIC "-//W3C//DTD XHTML
    1.0 Transitional//EN" "http://www.w3.
    org/TR/xhtml1/DTD/xhtml1-transitional.
    dtd">
2   <html xmlns="http://www.w3.org/1999/xhtml"
    xml:lang="en" lang="en">
3   <head>
4      <meta http-equiv="content-type"
       content="text/html; charset=
       iso-8859-1" />
5      <title>Form Feedback</title>
6      <style type="text/css" title="text/css"
       media="all">
7      .error {
8         font-weight: bold;
9         color: #C00
10     }
11     </style>
12  </head>
13  <body>
14  <?php # Script 2.5 - handle_form.php #4
15
16  // Print the submitted information:
17  if ( !empty($_POST['name']) && !empty
    ($_POST['comments']) && !empty($_POST
    ['email']) ) {
18     echo "<p>Thank you, <b>{$_POST['name']}
       </b>, for the following comments:
       <br />
19  <tt>{$_POST['comments']}</tt></p>
20  <p>We will reply to you at <i>
    {$_POST ['email']}</i>.</p>\n";
21  } else { // Missing form value.
22     echo '<p class="error">Please go back
       and fill out the form again.</p>';
23  }
24  ?>
25  </body>
26  </html>
```

This conditional checks that these three text inputs are all not empty. Using the *and* operator (&&), the entire conditional is only true if each of the three subconditionals is true.

3. Print the message.

```
echo "<p>Thank you, <b>{$_POST
→ ['name']}</b>, for the following
→ comments:<br />

<tt>{$_POST['comments']}</tt></p>

<p>We will reply to you at <i>{$_
→ POST['email']}</i>.</p>\n";
```

After you comprehend the *concept* of an array, you still need to master the syntax involved in printing one. When printing an array element that uses a string for its key, use the curly braces (as in {$_POST['name']} here) to avoid parse errors.

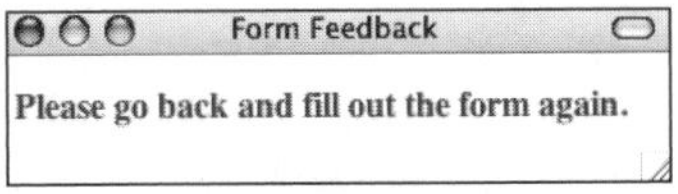

4. Complete the conditional begun in Step 2.

```
} else {
  echo '<p class="error">Please go
  → back and fill out the form
  → again.</p>';
}
```

If any of the three subconditionals in Step 2 is not true (which is to say, if any of the variables has an empty value), then this else clause applies and an error message is printed (**Figure 2.17**).

5. Complete the PHP and HTML code.

```
?>

</body>

</html>
```

6. Save the file, place it in the same Web directory as form.html, and test it in your Web browser (**Figure 2.18**).

✔ Tips

- Because PHP is lax with its variable structures, an array can even use a combination of numbers and strings as its keys. The only important rule is that the keys of an array must each be unique.

- If you find the syntax of accessing superglobal arrays directly to be confusing (e.g., $_POST['name']), you can use the shorthand technique at the top of your scripts as you have been:

  ```
  $name = $_POST['name'];
  ```

  In this script, you would then need to change the conditional and the echo() statement to refer to $name et al.

Figure 2.17 If any of the three tested form inputs is empty, this generic error message is printed.

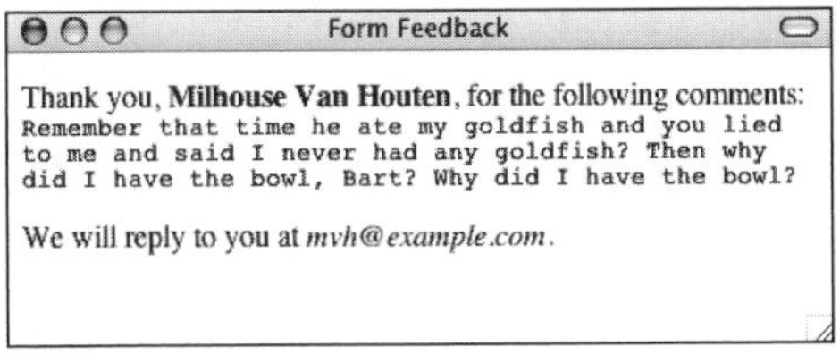

Figure 2.18 The fact that the script now uses the $_POST array has no effect on the visible result.

Creating arrays

The preceding example uses a PHP-generated array, but there will frequently be times when you want to create your own. There are two primary ways to define your own array. First, you could add an element at a time to build one:

```
$band[] = 'Jemaine';

$band[] = 'Bret';

$band[] = 'Murray';
```

Now $band[0] has a value of *Jemaine*; $band[1], *Bret*, and $band[2], *Murray* (because arrays are indexed starting at 0).

Alternatively, you can specify the key when adding an element. But it's important to understand that if you specify a key and a value already exists indexed with that same key, the new value will overwrite the existing one.

```
$band['fan'] = 'Mel';

$band['fan'] = 'Dave'; // New value

$array[2] = 'apple';

$array[2] = 'orange'; // New value
```

Instead of adding one element at a time, you can use the array() function to build an entire array in one step:

```
$states = array ('IA' => 'Iowa', 'MD' =>
→ 'Maryland');
```

This function can be used whether or not you explicitly set the key:

```
$artists = array ('Clem Snide', 'Shins',
→ 'Eels');
```

Or, if you set the first numeric key value, the added values will be keyed incrementally thereafter:

```
$days = array (1 => 'Sun', 'Mon', 'Tue');
echo $days[3]; // Tue
```

Figure 2.19 These pull-down menus will be created using arrays and the foreach loop.

The array() function is also used to initialize an array, prior to referencing it:

```
$tv = array();
```

```
$tv[] = 'Flight of the Conchords';
```

Initializing an array (or any variable) in PHP isn't required, but it makes for clearer code and can help avoid errors.

Finally, if you want to create an array of sequential numbers, you can use the range() function:

```
$ten = range (1, 10);
```

Accessing arrays

You've already seen how to access individual array elements using its keys (e.g., $_POST['email']). This works when you know exactly what the keys are or if you want to refer to only a single element. To access every array element, use the foreach loop:

```
foreach ($array as $value) {
    // Do something with $value.
}
```

The foreach loop will iterate through every element in $array, assigning each element's value to the $value variable. To access both the keys and values, use

```
foreach ($array as $key => $value) {
    echo "The value at $key is $value.";
}
```

(You can use any valid variable name in place of $key and $value, like just $k and $v, if you'd like.)

Using arrays, I'll show how easy it is to make a set of form pull-down menus for selecting a date (**Figure 2.19**).

To create and access arrays:

1. Create a new PHP document in your text editor or IDE (**Script 2.6**).

```
<!DOCTYPE html PUBLIC "-//W3C//
→ DTD XHTML 1.0 Transitional//EN"
→ "http://www.w3.org/TR/xhtml1/DTD/
→ xhtml1-transitional.dtd">
<html xmlns="http://www.w3.org/1999/
→ xhtml" xml:lang="en" lang="en">
<head>
  <meta http-equiv="content-type"
  → content="text/html; charset=
  → iso-8859-1" />
  <title>Calendar</title>
</head>
<body>
<form action="calendar.php"
 method="post">
<?php # Script 2.6 - calendar.php
```

One thing to note here is that even though the page won't contain a complete HTML form, the form tags are still required to create the pull-down menus.

Script 2.6 Arrays are used to dynamically create three pull-down menus (see Figure 2.19).

```
1   <!DOCTYPE html PUBLIC "-//W3C//DTD
    XHTML 1.0 Transitional//EN"
    "http://www.w3.org/TR/xhtml1/DTD/
    xhtml1-transitional.dtd">
2   <html xmlns="http://www.w3.org/1999/xhtml"
    xml:lang="en" lang="en">
3   <head>
4     <meta http-equiv="content-type"
      content="text/html; charset=
      iso-8859-1" />
5     <title>Calendar</title>
6   </head>
7   <body>
8   <form action="calendar.php" method="post">
9   <?php # Script 2.6 - calendar.php
10
11  // This script makes three pull-down
    menus
12  // for an HTML form: months, days, years.
13
14  // Make the months array:
15  $months = array (1 => 'January',
    'February', 'March', 'April', 'May',
    'June', 'July', 'August', 'September',
    'October', 'November', 'December');
16
17  // Make the days and years arrays:
18  $days = range (1, 31);
19  $years = range (2008, 2018);
20
21  // Make the months pull-down menu:
22  echo '<select name="month">';
23  foreach ($months as $key => $value) {
24    echo "<option value=\"$key\">$value
      </option>\n";
25  }
26  echo '</select>';
27
```

(script continues on next page)

Script 2.6 *continued*

```
     📄 Script
28   // Make the days pull-down menu:
29   echo '<select name="day">';
30   foreach ($days as $value) {
31     echo "<option value=\"$value\">$value
       </option>\n";
32   }
33   echo '</select>';
34
35   // Make the years pull-down menu:
36   echo '<select name="year">';
37   foreach ($years as $value) {
38     echo "<option value=\"$value\">$value
       </option>\n";
39   }
40   echo '</select>';
41
42   ?>
43   </form>
44   </body>
45   </html>
```

2. Create an array for the months.

```
$months = array (1 => 'January',
→ 'February', 'March', 'April',
→ 'May', 'June', 'July', 'August',
→ 'September', 'October',
→ 'November', 'December');
```

This first array will use numbers for the keys, from 1 to 12. Since the value of the first key is specified, the following values will be indexed incrementally (in other words, the 1 => code creates an array indexed from 1 to 12, instead of from 0 to 11).

3. Create the arrays for the days of the month and the years.

```
$days = range (1, 31);
```

```
$years = range (2008, 2018);
```

Using the range() function, you can easily make an array of numbers.

4. Generate the month pull-down menu.

```
echo '<select name="month">';
foreach ($months as $key => $value) {
  echo "<option value=\"$key\">
  → $value</option>\n";
}
echo '</select>';
```

continues on next page

The foreach loop can quickly generate all of the HTML code for the month pull-down menu. Each execution of the loop will create a line of code like `<option value="1">January</option>` (**Figure 2.20**).

5. Generate the day and year pull-down menus.

```
echo '<select name="day">';

foreach ($days as $value) {

  echo "<option value=\"$value\">
  → $value</option>\n";

}

echo '</select>';

echo '<select name="year">';

foreach ($years as $value) {

  echo "<option value=\"$value\">
  → $value</option>\n";

}

echo '</select>';
```

Unlike the month example, both the day and year pull-down menus will use the same thing for the option's value and label (a number, Figure 2.20).

6. Close the PHP, the form tag, and the HTML page.

```
?>

</form>

</body>

</html>
```

7. Save the file as `calendar.php`, place it in your Web directory, and test it in your Web browser.

Figure 2.20 Most of the HTML source was generated by just a few lines of PHP.

✔ Tips

- To determine the number of elements in an array, use the count()function.

  `$num = count($array);`

- The range() function can also create an array of sequential letters:

  `$alphabet = range ('a', 'z');`

- An array's key can be multiple-worded strings, such as *first name* or *phone number*.

- The is_array() function confirms that a variable is of the array type.

- If you see an *Invalid argument supplied for foreach()* error message, that means you are trying to use a foreach loop on a variable that is not an array.

Multidimensional arrays

When introducing arrays, I mentioned that an array's values could be any combination of numbers, strings, and even other arrays. This last option—an array consisting of other arrays—creates a *multidimensional array*.

Multidimensional arrays are much more common than you might expect but remarkably easy to work with. As an example, start with an array of prime numbers:

```
$primes = array(2, 3, 5, 7, …);
```

Then create an array of sphenic numbers (don't worry: I had no idea what a sphenic number was either; I had to look it up):

```
$sphenic = array(30, 42, 66, 70, …);
```

These two arrays could be combined into one multidimensional array like so:

```
$numbers = array ('Primes' => $primes,
→ 'Sphenic' => $sphenic);
```

Now, $numbers is a multidimensional array. To access the prime numbers sub-array, refer to $numbers['Primes']. To access the prime number 5, use $numbers['Primes'][2] (it's the third element in the array, but the array starts indexing at 0). To print out one of these values, surround the whole construct in curly braces:

```
echo "The first prime number is
→ {$numbers['Prime'][0]}.";
```

Of course, you can also access multidimensional arrays using the foreach loop, nesting one inside another if necessary. This next example will do just that.

To use multidimensional arrays:

1. Create a new PHP document in your text editor (**Script 2.7**).

continues on next page

Script 2.7 The multidimensional array is created by using other arrays for its values. Two foreach loops, one nested inside of the other, can access every array element.

```
1   <!DOCTYPE html PUBLIC "-//W3C//DTD XHTML
    1.0 Transitional//EN" "http://www.w3.
    org/TR/xhtml1/DTD/xhtml1-transitional.
    dtd">

2   <html xmlns="http://www.w3.org/1999/xhtml"
    xml:lang="en" lang="en">

3   <head>

4       <meta http-equiv="content-type"
        content="text/html; charset=
        iso-8859-1" />

5       <title>Multidimensional Arrays</title>

6   </head>

7   <body>

8   <p>Some North American States, Provinces,
    and Territories:</p>

9   <?php # Script 2.7 - multi.php

10

11  // Create one array:

12  $mexico = array(

13  'YU' => 'Yucatan',

14  'BC' => 'Baja California',

15  'OA' => 'Oaxaca'

16  );

17

18  // Create another array:

19  $us = array (

20  'MD' => 'Maryland',

21  'IL' => 'Illinois',

22  'PA' => 'Pennsylvania',

23  'IA' => 'Iowa'

24  );

25

26  // Create a third array:

27  $canada = array (

28  'QC' => 'Quebec',
```

(script continues on next page)

```
<!DOCTYPE html PUBLIC "-//W3C//DTD
→ XHTML 1.0 Transitional//EN" "http:
→ //www.w3.org/TR/xhtml1/DTD/
→ xhtml1-transitional.dtd">

<html xmlns="http://www.w3.org/
→ 1999/xhtml" xml:lang="en"
→ lang="en">

<head>

  <meta http-equiv="content-type"
  → content="text/html; charset=
  → iso-8859-1" />

  <title>Multidimensional Arrays
  → </title>

</head>

<body>

<p>Some North American States,
→ Provinces, and Territories:</p>

<?php # Script 2.7 - multi.php
```

This PHP page will print out some of the states, provinces, and territories found in the three North American countries (Mexico, the United States, and Canada, **Figure 2.21**).

2. Create an array of Mexican states.

```
$mexico = array(
'YU' => 'Yucatan',
'BC' => 'Baja California',
'OA' => 'Oaxaca'
);
```

This is an associative array, using the state's postal abbreviation as its key. The state's full name is the element's value. This is obviously an incomplete list, just used to demonstrate the concept.

Because PHP is generally whitespace-insensitive, the creation of the array can be written over multiple lines, which makes it easier to read.

Script 2.7 *continued*

```
29   'AB' => 'Alberta',
30   'NT' => 'Northwest Territories',
31   'YT' => 'Yukon',
32   'PE' => 'Prince Edward Island'
33   );
34
35   // Combine the arrays:
36   $n_america = array(
37   'Mexico' => $mexico,
38   'United States' => $us,
39   'Canada' => $canada
40   );
41
42   // Loop through the countries:
43   foreach ($n_america as $country => $list)
     {
44
45     // Print a heading:
46     echo "<h2>$country</h2><ul>";
47
48     // Print each state, province, or
       territory:
49     foreach ($list as $k => $v) {
50       echo "<li>$k - $v</li>\n";
51     }
52
53     // Close the list:
54     echo '</ul>';
55
56   } // End of main FOREACH.
57
58   ?>
59   </body>
60   </html>
```

3. Create the second and third arrays.

```
$us = array (
'MD' => 'Maryland',
'IL' => 'Illinois',
'PA' => 'Pennsylvania',
'IA' => 'Iowa'
);
$canada = array (
'QC' => 'Quebec',
'AB' => 'Alberta',
'NT' => 'Northwest Territories',
'YT' => 'Yukon',
'PE' => 'Prince Edward Island'
);
```

Figure 2.21 The end result of running this PHP page (Script 2.7), where each country is printed, followed by an abbreviated list of its states, provinces, and territories.

4. Combine all of the arrays into one.

```
$n_america = array(
'Mexico' => $mexico,
'United States' => $us,
'Canada' => $canada
);
```

You don't have to create three arrays and then assign them to a fourth in order to make the desired multidimensional array. But I think it's easier to read and understand this way (defining a multidimensional array in one step makes for some ugly code).

The $n_america array now contains three elements. The key for each element is a string, which is the country's name. The value for each element is the list of states, provinces, and territories found within that country.

5. Begin the primary foreach loop.

```
foreach ($n_america as $country =>
→ $list) {
    echo "<h2>$country</h2><ul>";
```

Following the syntax outlined earlier, this loop will access every element of $n_america. This means that this loop will run three times. Within each iteration of the loop, the $country variable will store the $n_america array's key (*Mexico*, *Canada*, or *United States*). Also within each iteration of the loop, the $list variable will store the element's value (the equivalent of $mexico, $us, and $canada).

To print out the results, the loop begins by printing the country's name within H2 tags. Because the states and so forth should be displayed as an HTML list, the initial unordered list tag (<ul>) is printed as well.

continues on next page

INTRODUCING ARRAYS

6. Create a second foreach loop.

```
foreach ($list as $k => $v) {
    echo "<li>$k - $v</li>\n";
}
```

This loop will run through each sub-array (first $mexico, then $us, and then $canada). With each iteration of this loop, $k will store the abbreviation and $v the full name. Both are printed out within HTML list tags. The newline character is also used, to better format the HTML source code.

7. Complete the outer foreach loop.

```
    echo '</ul>';
} // End of main FOREACH.
```

After the inner foreach loop is done, the outer foreach loop has to close the unordered list begun in Step 5.

8. Complete the PHP and HTML.

```
?>
</body>
</html>
```

9. Save the file as multi.php, place it in your Web directory, and test it in your Web browser (Figure 2.21).

10. If you want, check out the HTML source code to see what PHP created.

✔ Tips

■ Multidimensional arrays can also come from an HTML form. For example, if a form has a series of checkboxes with the name *interests[]*—

```
<input type="checkbox" name=
→ "interests[]" value="Music"
→ /> Music

<input type="checkbox" name=
→ "interests[]" value="Movies"
→ /> Movies

<input type="checkbox" name=
→ "interests[]" value="Books"
→ /> Books
```

—the $_POST variable in the receiving PHP page will be multidimensional. $_POST['interests'] will be an array, with $_POST['interests'][0] storing the value of the *first checked box* (e.g., *Movies*), $_POST['interests'][1] storing the second (*Books*), etc. Note that only the checked boxes will get passed to the PHP page.

■ You can also end up with a multidimensional array if an HTML form's select menu allows for multiple selections:

```
<select name="interests[]" multiple=
→ "multiple">
    <option value="Music">Music
→ </option>
    <option value="Movies">Movies
→ </option>
    <option value="Books">Books
→ </option>
    <option value="Napping">Napping
→ </option>
</select>
```

Again, only the selected values will be passed to the PHP page.

Sorting arrays

One of the many advantages arrays have over the other variable types is the ability to sort them. PHP includes several functions you can use for sorting arrays, all simple in syntax:

```
$names = array ('Moe', 'Larry',
→ 'Curly');

sort($names);
```

The sorting functions perform three kinds of sorts. First, you can sort an array by value, discarding the original keys, using sort(). It's important to understand that the array's keys will be reset after the sorting process, so if the key-value relationship is important, you *should not* use this function.

Second, you can sort an array by value while maintaining the keys, using asort(). Third, you can sort an array by key, using ksort(). Each of these can sort in reverse order if you change them to rsort(), arsort(), and krsort() respectively.

To demonstrate the effect sorting arrays will have, I'll create an array of movie titles and ratings (how much I liked them on a scale of 1 to 10) and then display this list in different ways.

Arrays and Strings

Because arrays and strings are so commonly used, PHP has two functions for converting between them.

```
$array = explode (separator,
→ $string);

$string = implode (glue, $array);
```

The key to using and understanding these two functions is the *separator* and *glue* relationships. When turning an array into a string, you set the glue—the characters or code that will be inserted between the array values in the generated string. Conversely, when turning a string into an array, you specify the separator, which is the token that marks what should become separate array elements. For example, start with a string:

```
$s1 = 'Mon-Tue-Wed-Thu-Fri';

$days_array = explode ('-', $s1);
```

The $days_array variable is now a five-element array, with *Mon* indexed at 0, *Tue* indexed at 1, etc.

```
$s2 = implode (', ', $days_array);
```

The $string2 variable is now a comma-separated list of days: *Mon, Tue, Wed, Thu, Fri.*

To sort arrays:

1. Create a new PHP document in your text editor or IDE (**Script 2.8**).

```
<!DOCTYPE html PUBLIC "-//W3C//DTD
→ XHTML 1.0 Transitional//EN" "http:
→ //www.w3.org/TR/xhtml1/DTD/
→ xhtml1-transitional.dtd">

<html xmlns="http://www.w3.
→ org/1999/xhtml" xml:lang="en"
→ lang="en">

<head>

  <meta http-equiv="content-type"
  → content="text/html; charset=
  → iso-8859-1" />

  <title>Sorting Arrays</title>

</head>

<body>
```

2. Create an HTML table.

```
<table border="0" cellspacing="3"
→ cellpadding="3" align="center">

  <tr>

    <td><h2>Rating</h2></td>

    <td><h2>Title</h2></td>

  </tr>
```

To make the ordered list easier to read, it'll be printed within an HTML table. The table is begun here.

Script 2.8 An array is defined, then sorted in two different ways: first by value, then by key (in reverse order).

```
1    <!DOCTYPE html PUBLIC "-//W3C//DTD XHTML
     1.0 Transitional//EN" "http://www.w3.org/
     TR/xhtml1/DTD/xhtml1-transitional.dtd">

2    <html xmlns="http://www.w3.org/1999/xhtml"
     xml:lang="en" lang="en">

3    <head>

4      <meta http-equiv="content-type"
       content="text/html; charset=
       iso-8859-1" />

5      <title>Sorting Arrays</title>

6    </head>

7    <body>

8    <table border="0" cellspacing="3"
     cellpadding="3" align="center">

9      <tr>

10       <td><h2>Rating</h2></td>

11       <td><h2>Title</h2></td>

12     </tr>

13   <?php # Script 2.8 - sorting.php

14

15   // Create the array:

16   $movies = array (

17   10 => 'Casablanca',

18   9 => 'To Kill a Mockingbird',

19   2 => 'The English Patient',

20   8 => 'Stranger Than Fiction',

21   5 => 'Story of the Weeping Camel',

22   7 => 'Donnie Darko'

23   );

24

25   // Display the movies in their original
     order:

26   echo '<tr><td colspan="2"><b>In their
     original order:</b></td></tr>';
```

(script continues on next page)

Script 2.8 *continued*

```
⊖ ○ ⊖                    Script
27   foreach ($movies as $key => $value) {
28       echo "<tr><td>$key</td>
29       <td>$value</td></tr>\n";
30   }
31
32   // Display the movies sorted by title:
33   asort($movies);
34   echo '<tr><td colspan="2"><b>Sorted by
     title:</b></td></tr>';
35   foreach ($movies as $key => $value) {
36       echo "<tr><td>$key</td>
37       <td>$value</td></tr>\n";
38   }
39
40   // Display the movies sorted by rating:
41   krsort($movies);
42   echo '<tr><td colspan="2"><b>Sorted by
     rating:</b></td></tr>';
43   foreach ($movies as $key => $value) {
44       echo "<tr><td>$key</td>
45       <td>$value</td></tr>\n";
46   }
47
48   ?>
49   </table>
50   </body>
51   </html>
```

3. Add the opening PHP tag and create a new array.

```
<?php
$movies = array (
10 => 'Casablanca',
9 => 'To Kill a Mockingbird',
2 => 'The English Patient',
8 => 'Stranger Than Fiction',
5 => 'Story of the Weeping Camel',
7 => 'Donnie Darko'
);
```

This array uses movie titles as the values and their respective ratings as their key. This structure will open up several possibilities for sorting the whole list. Feel free to change the movie listings and rankings as you see fit (just don't chastise me for my taste in films).

4. Print out the array as is.

```
echo '<tr><td colspan="2"><b>In
→ their original order:</b></td>
→ </tr>';
foreach ($movies as $key => $value)
→ {
    echo "<tr><td>$key</td>
    <td>$value</td></tr>\n";
}
```

At this point in the script, the array is in the same order as it was defined. To verify this, print it out. A caption is first printed across both table columns. Then, within the **foreach** loop, the key is printed in the first column and the value in the second. A newline is also printed to improve the readability of the HTML source code.

continues on next page

INTRODUCING ARRAYS

5. Sort the array alphabetically by title and print it again.

```
asort($movies);

echo '<tr><td colspan="2"><b>Sorted
→ by title:</b></td></tr>';

foreach ($movies as $key => $value)
→ {

  echo "<tr><td>$key</td>

  <td>$value</td></tr>\n";

}
```

The asort() function sorts an array by value while maintaining the key-value relationship. The rest of the code is a repetition of Step 4.

6. Sort the array numerically by descending rating and print again.

```
krsort($movies);

echo '<tr><td colspan="2"><b>Sorted
→ by rating:</b></td></tr>';

foreach ($movies as $key => $value)
→ {

  echo "<tr><td>$key</td>

  <td>$value</td></tr>\n";

}
```

The ksort() function will sort an array by key, but in ascending order. Since the highest-ranking films should be listed first, the order must be reversed, using krsort(). This function, like asort(), maintains the key-value relationships.

INTRODUCING ARRAYS

Rating Title

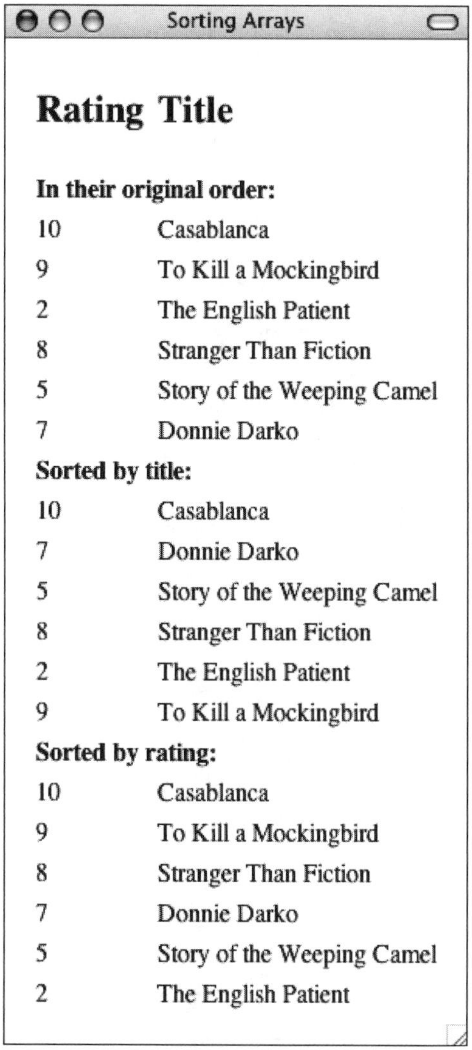

In their original order:

10	Casablanca
9	To Kill a Mockingbird
2	The English Patient
8	Stranger Than Fiction
5	Story of the Weeping Camel
7	Donnie Darko

Sorted by title:

10	Casablanca
7	Donnie Darko
5	Story of the Weeping Camel
8	Stranger Than Fiction
2	The English Patient
9	To Kill a Mockingbird

Sorted by rating:

10	Casablanca
9	To Kill a Mockingbird
8	Stranger Than Fiction
7	Donnie Darko
5	Story of the Weeping Camel
2	The English Patient

Figure 2.22 This page demonstrates the different ways arrays can be sorted.

7. Complete the PHP, the table, and the HTML.

```
?>
</table>
</body>
</html>
```

8. Save the file as `sorting.php`, place it in your Web directory, and test it in your Web browser (**Figure 2.22**).

✔ Tips

- If you want to use decimal ratings for the movies, the rating numbers must be quoted or else PHP would drop the decimal points (numeric keys are always integers).

- To randomize the order of an array, use `shuffle()`.

- PHP's `natsort()` function can be used to sort arrays in a more natural order (primarily handling numbers in strings better).

- Multidimensional arrays can be sorted in PHP with a little effort. See the PHP manual for more information on the `usort()` function or check out my *PHP 5 Advanced: Visual QuickPro Guide* book.

- PHP will sort arrays as if they were in English by default. If you need to sort an array in another language, use PHP's `setlocale()` function to change the language setting. Chapter 14, "Making Universal Sites," goes into using different languages.

INTRODUCING ARRAYS

69

For and While Loops

The last language construct to discuss in this chapter is loops. You've already used one, `foreach`, to access every element in an array. The next two types of loops you'll use are `for` and `while`.

The `while` loop looks like this:

```
while (condition) {

    // Do something.

}
```

As long as the *condition* part of the loop is true, the loop will be executed. Once it becomes false, the loop is stopped (**Figure 2.23**). If the condition is never true, the loop will never be executed. The `while` loop will most frequently be used when retrieving results from a database, as you'll see in Chapter 8, "Using PHP with MySQL."

The `for` loop has a more complicated syntax:

```
for (initial expression; condition;

 closing expression) {

    // Do something.

}
```

Upon first executing the loop, the initial expression is run. Then the condition is checked and, if true, the contents of the loop are executed. After execution, the closing expression is run and the condition is checked again. This process continues until the condition is false (**Figure 2.24**). As an example,

```
for ($i = 1; $i <= 10; $i++) {

    echo $i;

}
```

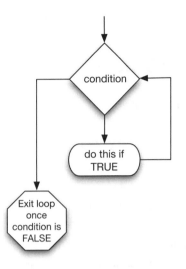

Figure 2.23 A flowchart representation of how PHP handles a `while` loop.

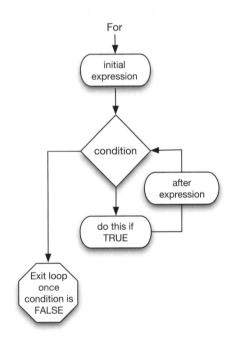

Figure 2.24 A flowchart representation of how PHP handles the more complex `for` loop.

Script 2.9 Loops are often used in conjunction with or in lieu of an array. Here, two for loops replace the arrays and foreach loops used in the script previously.

```
000                    Script
1    <!DOCTYPE html PUBLIC "-//W3C//DTD XHTML
     1.0 Transitional//EN"
2              "http://www.w3.org/TR/xhtml1/
               DTD/xhtml1-transitional.dtd">
3    <html xmlns="http://www.w3.org/1999/xhtml"
     xml:lang="en" lang="en">
4    <head>
5      <meta http-equiv="content-type"
       content="text/html; charset=
       iso-8859-1" />
6      <title>Calendar</title>
7    </head>
8    <body>
9    <form action="calendar.php" method="post">
10   <?php # Script 2.9 - calendar.php #2
11
12   // This script makes three pull-down menus
13   // for an HTML form: months, days, years.
14
15   // Make the months array:
16   $months = array (1 => 'January',
     'February', 'March', 'April', 'May',
     'June', 'July', 'August', 'September',
     'October', 'November', 'December');
17
18   // Make the months pull-down menu:
19   echo '<select name="month">';
20   foreach ($months as $key => $value) {
21     echo "<option value=\"$key\">$value</
       option>\n";
22   }
23   echo '</select>';
24
25   // Make the days pull-down menu:
26   echo '<select name="day">';
```

(script continues on next page)

The first time this loop is run, the $i variable is set to the value of *1*. Then the condition is checked (*is 1 less than or equal to 10?*). Since this is true, *1* is printed out (echo $i). Then, $i is incremented to *2* ($i++), the condition is checked, and so forth. The result of this script will be the numbers 1 through 10 printed out.

The functionality of both loops is similar enough that for and while can often be used interchangeably. Still, experience will reveal that the for loop is a better choice for doing something *a known number of times*, whereas while is used when a condition will be true an *unknown number of times*.

In this chapter's last example, the calendar script created earlier will be rewritten using for loops in place of two of the foreach loops.

To use loops:

1. Open calendar.php (refer to Script 2.6) in your text editor or IDE.

2. Delete the creation of the $days and $years arrays (lines 18–19).

   Using loops, the same result of the two pull-down menus can be achieved without the extra code and memory overhead involved with an array. So these two arrays will be deleted, while still keeping the $months array.

3. Rewrite the $days foreach loop as a for loop (**Script 2.9**).

   ```
   for ($day = 1; $day <= 31; $day++) {
     echo "<option value=\"$day\">$day
     → </option>\n";
   }
   ```

   continues on next page

This standard for loop begins by initializing the $day variable as *1*. It will continue the loop until $day is greater than 31, and upon each iteration, $day will be incremented by 1. The content of the loop itself (which is executed 31 times) is an echo() statement.

4. Rewrite the $years foreach loop as a for loop.

```
for ($year = 2008; $year <= 2018;
→ $year++) {

    echo "<option value=\"$year\">$year
    → </option>\n";

}
```

The structure of this loop is fundamentally the same as the previous for loop, but the $year variable is initially set to *2008* instead of *1*. As long as $year is less than or equal to 2018, the loop will be executed. Within the loop, the echo() statement is run.

5. Save the file, place it in your Web directory, and test it in your Web browser (**Figure 2.25**).

✔ Tips

- PHP also has a do…while loop with a slightly different syntax (check the manual). This loop will always be executed at least once.

- When using loops, watch your parameters and conditions to avoid the dreaded infinite loop, which occurs when a loop's condition is never going to be false.

Script 2.9 *continued*

```
27   for ($day = 1; $day <= 31; $day++) {
28       echo "<option value=\"$day\">$day</
         option>\n";
29   }
30   echo '</select>';
31
32   // Make the years pull-down menu:
33   echo '<select name="year">';
34   for ($year = 2008; $year <= 2018;
     $year++) {
35       echo "<option value=\"$year\">$year</
         option>\n";
36   }
37   echo '</select>';
38
39   ?>
40   </form>
41   </body>
42   </html>
```

Figure 2.25 The calendar form looks quite the same as it had previously (see Figure 2.19) but was created with two fewer arrays (compare Script 2.9 with Script 2.6).

CREATING DYNAMIC WEB SITES

With the fundamentals of PHP under your belt, it's time to begin building truly dynamic Web sites. Dynamic Web sites, as opposed to the static ones on which the Web was first built, are easier to maintain, are more responsive to users, and can alter their content in response to differing situations. This chapter introduces three new ideas, all commonly used to create more sophisticated Web applications (Chapter 10, "Web Application Development," covers another handful of topics along these same lines).

The first subject involves using external files. This is an important concept, as more complex sites often demand compartmentalizing some HTML or PHP code. Then the chapter returns to the subject of handling HTML forms. You'll learn some new variations on this standard process. Finally, you'll learn how to define and use your own functions.

Including Multiple Files

To this point, every script in the book has consisted of a single file that contains all of the required HTML and PHP code. But as you develop more complex Web sites, you'll see that this methodology has many limitations. PHP can readily make use of external files, a capability that allows you to divide your scripts and Web sites into distinct parts. Frequently you will use external files to extract your HTML from your PHP or to separate out commonly used processes.

PHP has four functions for using external files: `include()`, `include_once()`, `require()`, and `require_once()`. To use them, your PHP script would have a line like

```
include_once('filename.php');

require('/path/to/filename.html');
```

Using any one of these functions has the end result of taking all the content of the included file and dropping it in the parent script (the one calling the function) at that juncture. An important consideration with included files is that PHP will treat the included code as HTML (i.e., send it directly to the browser) unless the file contains code within the PHP tags.

In terms of functionality, it also doesn't matter what extension the included file uses, be it `.php` or `.html`. However, by giving the file a symbolic name, it helps to convey its purpose (e.g., an included file of HTML might use `.inc.html`). Also note that you can use either absolute or relative paths to the included file (see the sidebar for more).

Absolute vs. Relative Paths

When referencing any external item, be it an included file in PHP, a CSS document in HTML, or an image, you have the choice of using either an absolute or a relative path. An absolute path says where a file is starting from the root directory of the computer. Such paths are always correct, no matter the location of the referencing (parent) file. For example, a PHP script can include a file using

```
include ('C:/php/includes/file.php');

include('/usr/xyz/includes/file.php');
```

Assuming `file.php` exists in the named location, the inclusion will work (barring any permissions issues). The second example, in case you're not familiar with the syntax, would be a Unix (and Mac OS X) absolute path. Absolute paths always start with something like `C:/` or `/`.

A relative path uses the referencing (parent) file as the starting point. To move up one folder, use two periods together. To move into a folder, use its name followed by a slash. So assuming the current script is in the www/ex1 folder and you want to include something in www/ex2, the code would be:

```
include('../ex2/file.php');
```

A relative path will remain accurate, even if moved to another server, as long as the files keep their current relationship.

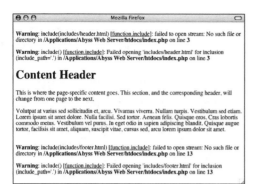

Figure 3.1 Two failed `include()` calls generate these four error messages (assuming that PHP is configured to display errors), but the rest of the page continues to execute.

Figure 3.2 The failure of a `require()` function call will print an error and terminate the execution of the script. If PHP is not configured to display errors, then the script will terminate without printing the problem first (i.e., it'd be a blank page).

The `include()` and `require()` functions are exactly the same when working properly but behave differently when they fail. If an `include()` function doesn't work (it cannot include the file for some reason), a warning will be printed to the Web browser (**Figure 3.1**), but the script will continue to run. If `require()` fails, an error is printed and the script is halted (**Figure 3.2**).

Both functions also have a `*_once()` version, which guarantees that the file in question is included only once regardless of how many times a script may (presumably inadvertently) attempt to include it.

```
require_once('filename.php');

include_once('filename.php');
```

In this next example, included files will separate the primary HTML formatting from any PHP code. Then, the rest of the examples in this chapter will be able to have the same appearance—as if they are all part of the same Web site—without the need to rewrite the HTML every time. This technique creates a template system, an easy way to make large applications consistent and manageable. The focus in these examples is on the PHP code itself; you should also read the sidebar later in the chapter on "Site Structure" so that you understand the organizational scheme on the server. If you have any questions about the CSS (Cascading Style Sheets) or (X)HTML used in the example, see a dedicated resource on those topics.

To include multiple files:

1. Design an HTML page in your text or WYSIWYG editor (**Script 3.1** and **Figure 3.3**).

   To start creating a template for a Web site, design the layout like a standard HTML page, independent of any PHP code. For this chapter's example, I'm using a slightly modified version of the "Plain and Simple" template created by Christopher Robinson (www.edg3.co.uk) and used with his kind permission.

2. Mark where any page-specific content goes.

   Almost every Web site has several common elements on each page—header, navigation, advertising, footer, etc.—and one or more page-specific sections. In the HTML page (Script 3.1), enclose the section of the layout that will change from page to page within HTML comments to indicate its status.

   continues on page 78

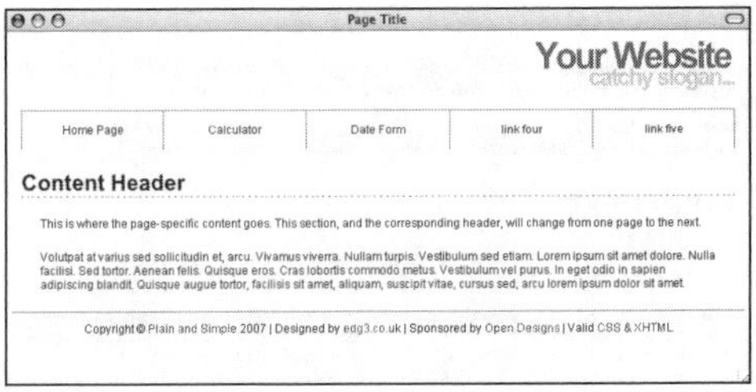

Figure 3.3 The HTML and CSS design as it appears in the Web browser (without using any PHP).

Script 3.1 The HTML template for this chapter's Web pages. Download the style.css file it uses from the book's supporting Web site (www.DMCInsights.com/phpmysql3/).

```
1   <!DOCTYPE html PUBLIC "-//W3C//DTD XHTML 1.0 Strict//EN" "http://www.w3.org/TR/xhtml1/DTD/
    xhtml1-strict.dtd">

2   <html xmlns="http://www.w3.org/1999/xhtml">

3   <head>

4     <title>Page Title</title>

5     <link rel="stylesheet" href="includes/style.css" type="text/css" media="screen" />

6     <meta http-equiv="content-type" content="text/html; charset=utf-8" />

7   </head>

8   <body>

9     <div id="header">

10        <h1>Your Website</h1>

11        <h2>catchy slogan...</h2>

12    </div>

13    <div id="navigation">
```

(script continues on next page)

Script 3.1 *continued*

```
14        <ul>
15          <li><a href="index.php">Home Page</a></li>
16          <li><a href="calculator.php">Calculator</a></li>
17          <li><a href="dateform.php">Date Form</a></li>
18          <li><a href="#">link four</a></li>
19          <li><a href="#">link five</a></li>
20        </ul>
21      </div>
22      <div id="content"><!-- Start of the page-specific content. -->
23        <h1>Content Header</h1>
24
25        <p>This is where the page-specific content goes. This section, and the corresponding
           header, will change from one page to the next.</p>
26
27        <p>Volutpat at varius sed sollicitudin et, arcu. Vivamus viverra. Nullam turpis. Vestibulum
           sed etiam. Lorem ipsum sit amet dolore. Nulla facilisi. Sed tortor. Aenean felis.
           Quisque eros. Cras lobortis commodo metus. Vestibulum vel purus. In eget odio in sapien
           adipiscing blandit. Quisque augue tortor, facilisis sit amet, aliquam, suscipit vitae,
           cursus sed, arcu lorem ipsum dolor sit amet.</p>
28
29      <!-- End of the page-specific content. --></div>
30
31      <div id="footer">
32        <p>Copyright &copy; <a href="#">Plain and Simple</a> 2007 | Designed by <a href="http://
           www.edg3.co.uk/">edg3.co.uk</a> | Sponsored by <a href="http://www.opendesigns.org/">Open
           Designs</a> | Valid <a href="http://jigsaw.w3.org/css-validator/">CSS</a> &amp; <a
           href="http://validator.w3.org/">XHTML</a></p>
33      </div>
34    </body>
35  </html>
```

INCLUDING MULTIPLE FILES

3. Copy everything from the first line of the layout's HTML source to just before the page-specific content and paste it in a new document (**Script 3.2**).

```
<!DOCTYPE html PUBLIC "-//W3C//DTD
→ XHTML 1.0 Strict//EN" "http://
→ www.w3.org/TR/xhtml1/DTD/
→ xhtml1-strict.dtd">

<html xmlns="http://www.w3.org/
→ 1999/xhtml">

<head>

  <title>Page Title</title>

  <link rel="stylesheet" href=
→ "includes/style.css" type="text/
→ css" media="screen" />

  <meta http-equiv="content-type"
→ content="text/html; charset=utf-8"
/>

</head>

<body>

  <div id="header">

    <h1>Your Website</h1>

    <h2>catchy slogan...</h2>

  </div>

  <div id="navigation">

    <ul>

      <li><a href="index.php">Home
→ Page</a></li>

      <li><a href="calculator.php">
→ Calculator</a></li>

      <li><a href="dateform.php">
→ Date Form</a></li>

      <li><a href="#">link four</a>
→ </li>

      <li><a href="#">link
five</a></li>
```

Script 3.2 The initial HTML for each Web page is stored in a header file.

```
1    <!DOCTYPE html PUBLIC "-//W3C//DTD XHTML
     1.0 Strict//EN" "http://www.w3.org/TR/
     xhtml1/DTD/xhtml1-strict.dtd">

2    <html xmlns="http://www.w3.org/1999/
     xhtml">

3    <head>

4      <title><?php echo $page_title; ?>
       </title>

5      <link rel="stylesheet" href="includes/
       style.css" type="text/css" media=
       "screen" />

6      <meta http-equiv="content-type"
       content="text/html; charset=utf-8" />

7    </head>

8    <body>

9      <div id="header">

10         <h1>Your Website</h1>

11         <h2>catchy slogan...</h2>

12     </div>

13     <div id="navigation">

14       <ul>

15         <li><a href="index.php">Home Page
           </a></li>

16         <li><a href="calculator.php">
           Calculator</a></li>

17         <li><a href="dateform.php">Date
           Form</a></li>

18         <li><a href="#">link four</a></li>

19         <li><a href="#">link five</a></li>

20       </ul>

21     </div>

22     <div id="content"><!-- Start of the
       page-specific content. -->

23   <!-- Script 3.2 - header.html -->
```

Script 3.3 The concluding HTML for each Web page is stored in this footer file.

```
         Script
1    <!-- Script 3.3 - footer.html -->
2    <!-- End of the page-specific
     >content. --></div>
3
4    <div id="footer">
5        <p>Copyright &copy; <a href="#">Plain
         and Simple</a> 2007 | Designed by
         <a href="http://www.edg3.co.uk/
         ">edg3.co.uk</a> | Sponsored by <a
         href="http://www.opendesigns.org/
         ">Open Designs</a> | Valid <a
         href="http://jigsaw.w3.org/
         css-validator/">CSS</a> &amp; <a
         href="http://validator.w3.org/">
         XHTML</a></p>
6    </div>
7    </body>
8    </html>
```

```
    </ul>
  </div>
  <div id="content"><!-- Start of the
→ page-specific content. -->
```

<!-- Script 3.2 - header.html -->

This first file will contain the initial HTML tags (from DOCTYPE through the head and into the beginning of the page body). It also has the code that makes the Web site name and slogan, plus the horizontal bar of links across the top (see Figure 3.3). Finally, as each page's content goes within a DIV whose id value is *content*, this file includes that code as well.

4. Change the page's title line to read

   ```
   <title><?php echo $page_title; ?>
   → </title>
   ```

   The page title (which appears at the top of the Web browser; see Figure 3.3) should be changeable on a page-by-page basis. For that to be possible, this value will be based upon a PHP variable, which will then be printed out. You'll see how this plays out shortly.

5. Save the file as header.html.

   As stated already, included files can use just about any extension for the filename. So this file is called header.html, indicating that it is the template's header file and that it contains (primarily) HTML.

6. Copy everything in the original template from the end of the page-specific content to the end of the page and paste it in a new file (**Script 3.3**).

   ```
   <!-- Script 3.3 - footer.html -->
     <!-- End of the page-specific
   → content. --></div>
   ```

continues on next page

INCLUDING MULTIPLE FILES

```
<div id="footer">

    <p>Copyright &copy; <a href=
  → "#">Plain and Simple</a> 2007
  → | Designed by <a href="http://
  → www.edg3.co.uk/">edg3.co.uk
  → </a> | Sponsored by <a href=
  → "http://www.opendesigns.org/">
  → Open Designs</a> | Valid <a
  → href="http://jigsaw.w3.org/
  → css-validator/">CSS</a> &amp;
  → <a href="http://validator.
  → w3.org/">XHTML</a></p>

  </div>

</body>

</html>
```

The footer file starts by closing the content DIV opened in the header file (see Step 3). Then the footer is added, which will be the same for every page on the site, and the HTML document itself is completed.

7. Save the file as footer.html.

8. Begin a new PHP document in your text editor or IDE (**Script 3.4**).

```
<?php # Script 3.4 - index.php
```

Since this script will use the included files for most of its HTML, it can begin and end with the PHP tags.

9. Set the $page_title variable and include the HTML header.

```
$page_title = 'Welcome to this
→ Site!';
```

```
include ('includes/header.html');
```

The $page_title variable will store the value that appears in the top of the browser window (and therefore, is also the default value when a person bookmarks the page). This variable is printed

Script 3.4 This script generates a complete Web page by including a template stored in two external files.

```
1   <?php # Script 3.4 - index.php

2   $page_title = 'Welcome to this Site!';

3   include ('includes/header.html');

4   ?>

5

6   <h1>Content Header</h1>

7

8       <p>This is where the page-specific
        content goes. This section, and the
        corresponding header, will change
        from one page to the next.</p>

9

10      <p>Volutpat at varius sed sollicitudin
        et, arcu. Vivamus viverra. Nullam
        turpis. Vestibulum sed etiam. Lorem
        ipsum sit amet dolore. Nulla
        facilisi. Sed tortor. Aenean felis.
        Quisque eros. Cras lobortis commodo
        metus. Vestibulum vel purus. In eget
        odio in sapien adipiscing blandit.
        Quisque augue tortor, facilisis sit
        amet, aliquam, suscipit vitae, cursus
        sed, arcu lorem ipsum dolor sit
        amet.</p>

11

12  <?php

13  include ('includes/footer.html');

14  ?>
```

in `header.html` (see Script 3.2). By defining the variable prior to including the header file, the header file will have access to that variable. Remember that this `include()` line has the effect of dropping the contents of the included file into this page at this spot.

The `include()` function call uses a relative path to `header.html` (see the sidebar, "Absolute vs. Relative Paths"). The syntax states that in the same folder as this file is a folder called `includes` and in that folder is a file named `header.html`.

10. Close the PHP tags and add the page-specific content.

```
?>
<h1>Content Header</h1>
  <p>This is where the page-specific
  → content goes. This section, and
  → the corresponding header, will
  → change from one page to the
  → next.</p>

  <p>Volutpat at varius sed
  → sollicitudin et, arcu. Vivamus
  → viverra. Nullam turpis.
  → Vestibulum sed etiam. Lorem
  → ipsum sit amet dolore. Nulla
  → facilisi. Sed tortor. Aenean
  → felis. Quisque eros. Cras
  → lobortis commodo metus.
  → Vestibulum vel purus. In eget
  → odio in sapien adipiscing
  → blandit. Quisque augue tortor,
  → facilisis sit amet, aliquam,
  → suscipit vitae, cursus sed, arcu
  → lorem ipsum dolor sit amet.</p>
```

For most pages, PHP will generate this content, instead of having static text. This information could be sent to the browser using `echo()`, but since there's no dynamic content here, it's easier and more efficient to exit the PHP tags temporarily.

11. Create a final PHP section and include the footer file.

```
<?php
include ('includes/footer.html');
?>
```

12. Save the file as `index.php`, and place it in your Web directory.

13. Create an `includes` directory in the same folder as `index.php`. Then place `header.html`, `footer.html`, and `style.css` (downloaded from www.DMCInsights.com/phpmysql3/), into this `includes` directory.

Note: in order to save space, the CSS file for this example (which controls the layout) is not included in the book. You can download the file through the book's supporting Web site (see the Extras page) or do without it (the template will still work, it just won't look as nice).

continues on next page

14. Test the template system by going to the `index.php` page in your Web browser (**Figure 3.4**).

The `index.php` page is the end result of the template system. You do not need to access any of the included files directly, as `index.php` will take care of incorporating their contents. As this is a PHP page, you still need to access it through a URL.

15. If desired, view the HTML source of the page (**Figure 3.5**).

Figure 3.4 Now the same layout (see Figure 3.3) has been created using external files in PHP.

```
<!DOCTYPE html PUBLIC "-//W3C//DTD XHTML 1.0 Strict//EN" "http://www.w3.org/TR/xhtm
<html xmlns="http://www.w3.org/1999/xhtml">
<head>
        <title>Welcome to this Site!</title>
        <link rel="stylesheet" href="includes/style.css" type="text/css" media="scr
        <meta http-equiv="content-type" content="text/html; charset=utf-8" />
</head>
<body>
        <div id="header">
                <h1>Your Website</h1>
                <h2>catchy slogan...</h2>
        </div>
        <div id="navigation">
                <ul>
                        <li><a href="index.php">Home Page</a></li>
                        <li><a href="calculator.php">Calculator</a></li>
                        <li><a href="dateform.php">Date Form</a></li>
                        <li><a href="#">link four</a></li>
                        <li><a href="#">link five</a></li>
                </ul>
        </div>
        <div id="content"><!-- Start of the page-specific content. -->
<!-- Script 3.2 - header.html -->

<h1>Content Header</h1>

        <p>This is where the page-specific content goes. This section, and the corr

        <p>Volutpat at varius sed sollicitudin et, arcu. Vivamus viverra. Nullam tu

<!-- Script 3.3 - footer.html -->
        <!-- End of the page-specific content. --></div>

        <div id="footer">
                <p>Copyright &copy; <a href="#">Plain and Simple</a> 2007 | Designe
        </div>
</body>
</html>
```

Figure 3.5 The generated HTML source of the Web page should replicate the code in the original template (refer to Script 3.1).

✔ Tips

■ In the `php.ini` configuration file, you can adjust the `include_path` setting, which dictates where PHP is and is not allowed to retrieve included files.

Figure 3.6 This is the same HTML page without using the corresponding CSS file (compare with Figure 3.4).

■ As you'll see in Chapter 8, "Using PHP with MySQL," any included file that contains sensitive information (like database access) should be stored outside of the Web document directory so it can't be viewed within a Web browser.

■ Since `require()` has more impact on a script when it fails, it's recommended for mission-critical includes (like those that connect to a database). The `include()` function would be used for less important inclusions. The `*_once()` versions provide for nice redundancy checking in complex applications, but they may be unnecessary in simple sites.

■ Because of the way CSS works, if you don't use the CSS file or if the browser doesn't read the CSS, the generated result is still functional, just not aesthetically as pleasing (see **Figure 3.6**).

Site Structure

When you begin using multiple files in your Web applications, the overall site structure becomes more important. When laying out your site, there are three considerations:

◆ Ease of maintenance

◆ Security

◆ Ease of user navigation

Using external files for holding standard procedures (i.e., PHP code), CSS, JavaScript, and the HTML design will greatly improve the ease of maintaining your site because commonly edited code is placed in one central location. I'll frequently make an `includes` or `templates` directory to store these files apart from the main scripts (the ones that are accessed directly in the Web browser).

I recommend using the `.inc` or `.html` file extension for documents where security is not an issue (such as HTML templates) and `.php` for files that contain more sensitive data (such as database access information). You can also use both `.inc` and `.html` or `.php` so that a file is clearly indicated as an include of a certain type: `db.inc.php` or `header.inc.html`.

Finally, try to structure your sites so that they are easy for your users to navigate, both by clicking links and by manually typing a URL. Try to avoid creating too many nested folders or using hard-to-type directory names and filenames containing both upper- and lowercase letters.

Handling HTML Forms, Revisited

A good portion of Chapter 2, "Programming with PHP," involves handling HTML forms with PHP. All of those examples use two separate files: one that displays the form and another that receives it. While there's certainly nothing wrong with this method, there are advantages to putting the entire process into one script.

To have one page both display and handle a form, a conditional must check which action (display or handle) should be taken:

```
if (/* form has been submitted */) {
    // Handle it.
} else {
    // Display it.
}
```

To determine if the form has been submitted, check if a $_POST variable is set (assuming that the form uses the POST method, of course). For example, create a hidden form input with a name of *submitted* and any value:

```
<input type="hidden" name="submitted"
→ value="1" />
```

Then the condition testing for form submission would be (**Figure 3.7**)

```
if (isset($_POST['submitted'])) {
    // Handle it.
} else {
    // Display it.
}
```

If you want a page to handle a form and then display it again (e.g., to add a record to a database and then give an option to add another), lose the else clause:

```
if (isset($_POST['submitted'])) {
    // Handle it.
}
// Display the form.
```

Using that code, a script will handle a form if it has been submitted and display the form every time the page is loaded.

To demonstrate this important technique (of having the same page both display and handle a form), let's create a simple sales calculator.

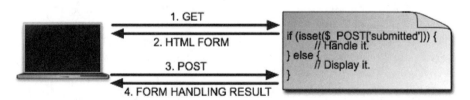

Figure 3.7 The interactions between the user and this PHP script on the server involves the user making two requests of this script. The first is a standard request (a GET request); where the form has not been submitted, $_POST is therefore empty, and so the script displays the form. When the form is submitted, the same script is requested again (a POST request this time), $_POST['submitted'] has a value, and so the form is handled.

Script 3.5 The `calculator.php` script both displays a simple form and handles the form data: performing some calculations and reporting upon the results.

```
                    Script
1   <?php # Script 3.5 - calculator.php
2
3   $page_title = 'Widget Cost Calculator';
4   include ('includes/header.html');
5
6   // Check for form submission:
7   if (isset($_POST['submitted'])) {
8
9       // Minimal form validation:
10      if ( is_numeric($_POST['quantity']) &&
        is_numeric($_POST['price']) &&
        is_numeric($_POST['tax']) ) {
11
12          // Calculate the results:
13          $total = ($_POST['quantity'] *
            $_POST['price']);
14          $taxrate = ($_POST['tax'] / 100); //
            Turn 5% into .05.
15          $total += ($total * $taxrate); // Add
            the tax.
16
17          // Print the results:
18          echo '<h1>Total Cost</h1>
19  <p>The total cost of purchasing ' .
            $_POST['quantity'] . ' widget(s) at $' .
            number_format ($_POST['price'], 2) . '
            each, including a tax rate of ' .
            $_POST['tax'] . '%, is $' .
            number_format ($total, 2) . '.</p>';
20
21      } else { // Invalid submitted values.
22          echo '<h1>Error!</h1>
23          <p class="error">Please enter a valid
            quantity, price, and tax.</p>';
24      }
25
26  } // End of main isset() IF.
```

(script continues on next page)

To handle HTML forms:

1. Create a new PHP document in your text editor or IDE (**Script 3.5**).

    ```
    <?php # Script 3.5 - calculator.php
    $page_title = 'Widget Cost
    Calculator';
    include ('includes/header.html');
    ```

    This, and all the remaining examples in the chapter, will use the same template system as `index.php` (Script 3.4). The beginning syntax of each page will therefore be the same, but the page titles will differ.

2. Write the conditional for handling the form.

    ```
    if (isset($_POST['submitted'])) {
    ```

    As suggested already, checking if a form element, like `$_POST['submitted']`, is set can test if the form has been submitted. This variable will be correlate to a hidden input in the form.

3. Validate the form.

    ```
    if ( is_numeric($_POST['quantity'])
    → && is_numeric($_POST['price']) &&
    → is_numeric($_POST['tax']) ) {
    ```

    The validation here is very simple: it merely checks that three submitted variables are all numeric types. You can certainly elaborate on this, perhaps checking that the quantity is an integer and that all values are positive (in fact, Chapter 12, "Security Methods," has a variation on this script that does just that).

    If the validation passes all of the tests, the calculations will be made; otherwise, the user will be asked to try again.

    continues on next page

4. Perform the calculations.

```
$total = ($_POST['quantity'] *
→ $_POST['price']);

$taxrate = ($_POST['tax'] / 100);

$total += ($total * $taxrate);
```

The first line calculates the before-tax total as the quantity times the price. The second line changes the tax value from a percentage (say, 5%) to a decimal (.05), which will be needed in the subsequent calculation. The third line adds to the total the amount of tax, calculated by multiplying the total by the tax rate. The addition assignment operator (+=) makes the code a bit shorter. Alternatively you could write

```
$total = $total + ($total *
→ $taxrate);
```

5. Print the results.

```
echo '<h1>Total Cost</h1>

<p>The total cost of purchasing ' .
→ $_POST['quantity'] . ' widget(s)
→ at $' . number_format ($_POST
→ ['price'], 2) . ' each, including
→ a tax rate of ' . $_POST['tax'] .
→ '%, is $' . number_format ($total,
→ 2) . '.</p>';
```

All of the values are printed out, formatting the price and total with the number_format() function. Using the concatenation operator (the period) allows the formatted numeric values to be appended to the printed message.

Script 3.5 *continued*

```
27
28    // Leave the PHP section and create the
      HTML form:
29    ?>
30    <h1>Widget Cost Calculator</h1>
31    <form action="calculator.php" method=
      "post">
32      <p>Quantity: <input type="text" name=
        "quantity" size="5" maxlength="5" /></p>
33      <p>Price: <input type="text" name=
        "price" size="5" maxlength="10" /></p>
34      <p>Tax (%): <input type="text" name=
        "tax" size="5" maxlength="5" /></p>
35      <p><input type="submit" name="submit"
        value="Calculate!" /></p>
36      <input type="hidden" name="submitted"
        value="1" />
37    </form>
38    <?php // Include the footer:
39    include ('includes/footer.html');
40    ?>
```

6. Complete the conditionals and close the PHP tag.

```
    } else {

      echo '<h1>Error!</h1>

      <p class="error">Please enter
→ a valid quantity, price, and
→ tax.</p>';

    }

  }

?>
```

The else clause completes the validation conditional (Step 3), printing an error if the three submitted values aren't all numeric. The final closing curly brace closes the isset($_POST['submitted']) conditional. Finally, the PHP section is closed so that the form can be created without using echo() (see Step 7).

7. Display the HTML form.

```
<h1>Widget Cost Calculator</h1>

<form action="calculator.php"
→ method="post">

    <p>Quantity: <input type="text"
→ name="quantity" size="5"
→ maxlength=→ "5" /></p>

    <p>Price: <input type="text" name=
→ "price" size="5" maxlength="10"
→ /></p>

    <p>Tax (%): <input type="text"
→ name="tax" size="5" maxlength="5"
→ /></p>

    <p><input type="submit" name=
→ "submit" value="Calculate!"
→ /></p>

    <input type="hidden" name=
→ "submitted" value="1" />

</form>
```

The form itself is fairly obvious, containing only two new tricks. First, the action attribute uses this script's name, so that the form submits back to this page instead of to another. Second, there is a hidden input called *submitted* with a value of *1*. This is the flag variable whose existence will be checked to determine whether or not to handle the form (see the main conditional in Step 2 or on line 7). Because this is just a flag variable, it can be given any value (I'll normally use either *1* or *TRUE*).

8. Include the footer file.

```
<?php

include ('includes/footer.html');

?>
```

9. Save the file as `calculator.php`, place it in your Web directory, and test it in your Web browser (**Figures 3.8**, **3.9**, and **3.10**).

✔ Tips

■ Another common method for checking if a form has been submitted is to see if the submit button's variable—`$_POST['submit']` here—is set. The only downside to this method is that it won't work in some browsers if the user submits the form by pressing Return or Enter.

■ If you use an image for your submit button, you'll also want to use a hidden input to test for the form's submission.

■ You can also have a form submit back to itself by using no value for the `action` attribute:

```
<form action="" method="post">
```

By doing so, the form will always submit back to this same page, even if you later change the name of the script.

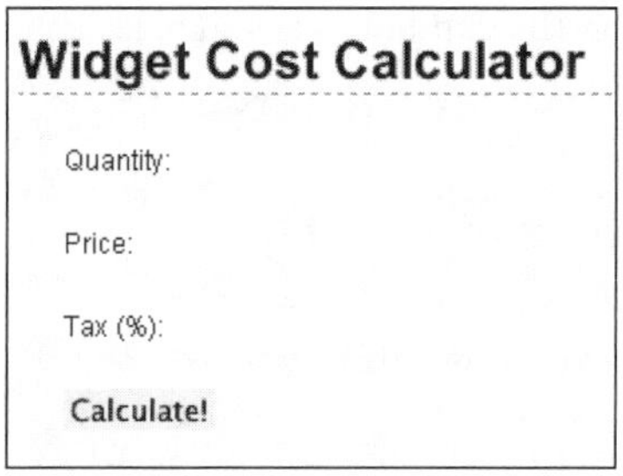

Figure 3.8 The HTML form, upon first viewing it in the Web browser. The CSS style sheet gives the inputs and the submit button a more subtle appearance (in Firefox, at least). To save space, I've captured only the form and not the page header or footer.

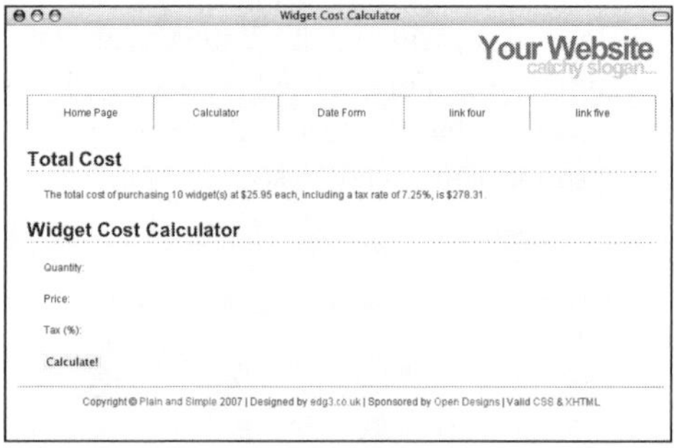

Figure 3.9 The page performs the calculations, reports on the results, and then redisplays the form.

Figure 3.10 If any of the submitted values is not numeric, an error message is displayed.

Making Sticky Forms

A *sticky form* is simply a standard HTML form that remembers how you filled it out. This is a particularly nice feature for end users, especially if you are requiring them to resubmit a form after filling it out incorrectly in the first place, as in Figure 3.10. (Some Web browsers will also remember values entered into forms for you; this is a separate but potentially overlapping issue from using PHP to accomplish this.)

To preset what's entered in a text box, use its `value` attribute:

```
<input type="text" name="city" size="20"
→ value="Innsbruck" />
```

To have PHP preset that value, print the appropriate variable (this assumes that the referenced variable exists):

```
<input type="text" name="city" size="20"
→ value="<?php echo $city; ?>" />
```

(This is also a nice example of the benefit of PHP's HTML-embedded nature: you can place PHP code anywhere, including within form elements.)

To preset the status of radio buttons or check boxes (i.e., to precheck them), add the code `checked="checked"` to their input tag. Using PHP, you might write:

```
<input type="radio" name="gender" value=
→ "F" <?php if ($gender == 'F')) {
  echo 'checked="checked"';
} ?>/>
```

To preset the value of a `textarea`, place the value between the `textarea` tags:

```
<textarea name="comments" rows="10"
→ cols="50"><?php echo $comments;
→ ?></textarea>
```

Note hear that the `textarea` tag does not have a `value` attribute like the standard `text` input.

To preselect a pull-down menu, add `selected="selected"` to the appropriate option. This is really easy if you also use PHP to generate the menu:

```
echo '<select name="year">';
for ($y = 2008; $y <= 2018; $y++) {
  echo "<option value=\"$y\"";
  if ($year == $y) {
    echo ' selected="selected"';
  }
  echo ">$y</option>\n";
}
echo '</select>';
```

With this new information in mind, let's rewrite `calculator.php` so that it's sticky.

To make a sticky form:

1. Open calculator.php (refer to Script 3.5) in your text editor or IDE.

2. Change the quantity input to read (**Script 3.6**)

   ```
   <p>Quantity: <input type="text"
   → name="quantity" size="5"
   → maxlength="5" value="<?php if
   → (isset($_POST['quantity'])) echo
   → $_POST['quantity']; ?>" /></p>
   ```

   The first change is to add the value attribute to the input. Then, print out the value of the submitted quantity variable ($_POST['quantity']). Since the first time the page is loaded, $_POST['quantity'] has no value, a conditional ensures that the variable is set before attempting to print it. The end result for setting the input's value is the PHP code

   ```
   <?php
   if (isset($_POST['quantity'])) {
     echo $_POST['quantity'];
   }
   ?>
   ```

   This can be condensed to the more minimal form used in the script (you can omit the curly braces if you have only one statement within a conditional block, although I very rarely recommend that you do so).

3. Repeat the process for the price and tax.

   ```
   <p>Price: <input type="text" name=
   → "price" size="5" maxlength="10"
   → value="<?php if (isset($_POST
   → ['price'])) echo $_POST['price'];
   → ?>" /></p>
   ```

Script 3.6 The calculator's form now recalls the previously entered values (creating a *sticky form*).

```
1    <?php # Script 3.6 - calculator.php #2
2
3    $page_title = 'Widget Cost Calculator';
4    include ('includes/header.html');
5
6    // Check for form submission:
7    if (isset($_POST['submitted'])) {
8
9        // Minimal form validation:
10       if ( is_numeric($_POST['quantity']) &&
         is_numeric($_POST['price']) &&
         is_numeric($_POST['tax']) ) {
11
12           // Calculate the results:
13           $total = ($_POST['quantity'] *
             $_POST['price']);
14           $taxrate = ($_POST['tax'] / 100); //
             Turn 5% into .05.
15           $total += ($total * $taxrate); // Add
             the tax.
16
17           // Print the results:
18           echo '<h1>Total Cost</h1>';
19       <p>The total cost of purchasing ' .
         $_POST['quantity'] . ' widget(s) at $' .
         number_format ($_POST['price'], 2) . '
         each, including a tax rate of ' .
         $_POST['tax'] . '%, is $' .
         number_format ($total, 2) . '.</p>';
20
21       } else { // Invalid submitted values.
22           echo '<h1>Error!</h1>
23           <p class="error">Please enter a valid
             quantity, price, and tax.';
24       }
25
26   } // End of main isset() IF.
27
```

(script continues on next page)

Script 3.6 *continued*

```
       🖹 Script
28   // Leave the PHP section and create the
     HTML form:

29   ?>

30   <h1>Widget Cost Calculator</h1>

31   <form action="calculator.php"
     method="post">

32   <p>Quantity: <input type="text" name=
     "quantity" size="5" maxlength="5"
     value="<?php if (isset($_POST['quantity']
     )) echo $_POST['quantity']; ?>" /></p>

33   <p>Price: <input type="text" name="price"
     size="5" maxlength="10" value="<?php if
     (isset($_POST['price'])) echo $_POST
     ['price']; ?>" /></p>

34   <p>Tax (%): <input type="text" name="tax"
     size="5" maxlength="5" value="<?php if
     (isset($_POST['tax'])) echo $_POST
     ['tax']; ?>" /></p>

35     <p><input type="submit" name="submit"
       value="Calculate!" /></p>

36     <input type="hidden" name="submitted"
       value="TRUE" />

37   </form>

38   <?php // Include the footer:

39   include ('includes/footer.html');

40   ?>
```

```
<p>Tax (%): <input type="text"
→ name="tax" size="5" maxlength="5"
→ value="<?php if (isset($_POST
→ ['tax'])) echo $_POST['tax']; ?>"
→ /></p>
```

4. Save the file as calculator.php, place it in your Web directory, and test it in your Web browser (**Figures 3.11** and **3.12**).

✔ Tips

■ Because some PHP code in this example exists inside of the HTML form value attributes, error messages may not be obvious. If problems occur, check the HTML source of the page to see if PHP errors are printed within the value attributes.

■ You should always double-quote HTML attributes, particularly the value attribute of a form input. If you don't, multi-word values like *Elliott Smith* will appear as just *Elliott* in the Web browser.

■ On account of a limitation in how HTML works, you cannot preset the value of a password input type.

Total Cost

The total cost of purchasing 5 widget(s) at $122.00 each, including a tax rate of 6%, is $646.60.

Widget Cost Calculator

Quantity: 5

Price: 122.00

Tax (%): 6

Calculate!

Figure 3.11 The form now recalls the previously submitted values...

Error!

Please enter a valid quantity, price, and tax.

Widget Cost Calculator

Quantity:

Price: 34.50

Tax (%): 3.25

Calculate!

Figure 3.12 ...whether or not the form was completely filled out.

Creating Your Own Functions

PHP has a lot of built-in functions, addressing almost every need you might have. More importantly, though, PHP has the capability for you to define and use your own functions for whatever purpose. The syntax for making your own function is

```
function function_name () {
    // Function code.
}
```

The name of your function can be any combination of letters, numbers, and the underscore, but it must begin with either a letter or the underscore. You also cannot use an existing function name for your function (*print*, *echo*, *isset*, and so on). One perfectly valid function definition is

```
function do_nothing() {
    // Do nothing.
}
```

In PHP, as mentioned in the first chapter, function names are case-insensitive (unlike variable names), so you could call that function using do_Nothing() or DO_NOTHING() or Do_Nothing(), etc (but not donothing() or DoNothing()).

The code within the function can do nearly anything, from generating HTML to performing calculations. This chapter runs through a couple of examples and you'll see some others throughout the rest of the book.

Script 3.7 This user-defined function creates a series of pull-down menus (see Figure 3.13).

```
1    <?php # Script 3.7 - dateform.php
2
3    $page_title = 'Calendar Form';
4    include ('includes/header.html');
5
6    // This function makes three pull-down
     menus
7    // for selecting a month, day, and year.
8    function make_calendar_pulldowns() {
9
10      // Make the months array:
11      $months = array (1 => 'January',
        'February', 'March', 'April', 'May',
        'June', 'July', 'August', 'September',
        'October', 'November', 'December');
12
13      // Make the months pull-down menu:
14      echo '<select name="month">';
15      foreach ($months as $key => $value) {
16          echo "<option value=\"$key\">
            $value</option>\n";
17      }
18      echo '</select>';
19
20      // Make the days pull-down menu:
21      echo '<select name="day">';
22      for ($day = 1; $day <= 31; $day++) {
23          echo "<option value=\"$day\">$day
            </option>\n";
24      }
25      echo '</select>';
26
27      // Make the years pull-down menu:
28      echo '<select name="year">';
29      for ($year = 2008; $year <= 2018;
        $year++) {
```

(script continues on next page)

Script 3.7 *continued*

```
○ ○ ○                    Script
30        echo "<option value=\"$year\">
          $year</option>\n";

31      }

32      echo '</select>';

33

34  } // End of the function definition.

35

36    // Create the form tags:

37    echo '<h1>Select a Date:</h1>

38    <form action="dateform.php" method=
      "post">';

39

40    // Call the function.

41    make_calendar_pulldowns();

42

43    echo '</form>';

44

45    include ('includes/footer.html');

46    ?>
```

To create your own function:

1. Create a new PHP document in your text editor or IDE (**Script 3.7**).

   ```php
   <?php # Script 3.7 - dateform.php
   $page_title = 'Calendar Form';
   include ('includes/header.html');
   ```

   This page will use the same HTML template as the previous two.

2. Begin defining a new function.

   ```php
   function make_calendar_pulldowns() {
   ```

   The function to be written here will generate the form pull-down menus necessary for selecting a month, day, and a year, just like calendar.php (refer to Script 2.9). The function's name clearly states its purpose.

   Although not required, it's conventional to place a function definition near the very top of a script or in a separate file.

3. Generate the pull-down menus.

   ```php
   $months = array (1 => 'January',
   → 'February', 'March', 'April',
   → 'May', 'June', 'July', 'August',
   → 'September', 'October', 'November',
   → 'December');
   echo '<select name="month">';
   foreach ($months as $key => $value) {
      echo "<option value=\"$key\">$value
      → </option>\n";
   }
   ```

continues on next page

```
echo '</select>';

echo '<select name="day">';

for ($day = 1; $day <= 31; $day++) {

  echo "<option value=\"$day\">$day
  → </option>\n";

}

echo '</select>';

echo '<select name="year">';

for ($year = 2008; $year <= 2018;
→ $year++) {

  echo "<option value=\"$year\">$year
  → </option>\n";

}

echo '</select>';
```

This code is exactly as it was in the original script, only it's now placed within a function definition.

4. Close the function definition.

```
} // End of the function definition.
```

It's helpful to place a comment at the end of a function definition so that you know where a definition starts and stops.

5. Create the form and call the function.

```
echo '<h1>Select a Date:</h1>

<form action="dateform.php"
→ method="post">';

make_calendar_pulldowns();

echo '</form>';
```

This code will create a header tag, plus the tags for the form. The call to the make_calendar_pulldowns() function will have the end result of creating the code for the three pull-down menus.

6. Complete the PHP script by including the HTML footer.

```
include ('includes/footer.html');

?>
```

7. Save the file as dateform.php, place it in your Web directory (in the same folder as index.php), and test it in your Web browser (**Figure 3.13**).

✔ Tips

■ If you ever see a *call to undefined function function_name* error, this means that you are calling a function that hasn't been defined. This can happen if you misspell the function's name (either when defining or calling it) or if you fail to include the file where the function is defined.

■ Because a user-defined function takes up some memory, you should be prudent about when to use one. As a general rule, functions are best used for chunks of code that may be executed in several places in a script or Web site.

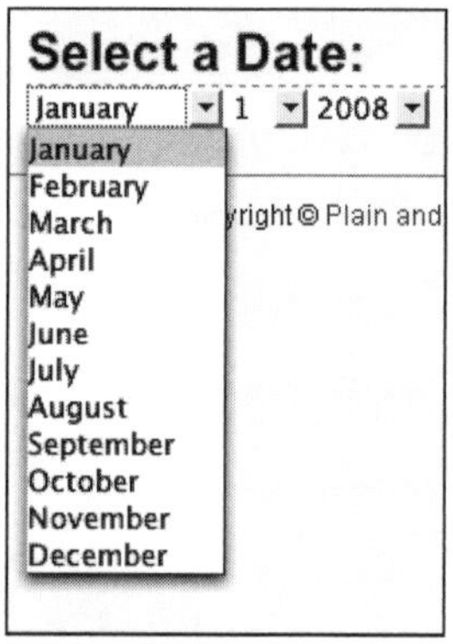

Figure 3.13 These pull-down menus are generated by a user-defined function.

Creating a function that takes arguments

Just like PHP's built-in functions, those you write can take *arguments* (also called *parameters*). For example, the `isset()` function takes as an argument the name of a variable to be tested. The `strlen()` function takes as an argument the string whose character length will be determined.

A function can take any number of arguments, but the order in which you list them is critical. To allow for arguments, add variables to a function's definition:

```
function print_hello ($first, $last) {

    // Function code.

}
```

The variable names you use for your arguments are irrelevant to the rest of the script (more on this in the "Variable Scope" sidebar toward the end of this chapter), but try to use valid, meaningful names.

Once the function is defined, you can then call it as you would any other function in PHP, sending literal values or variables to it:

```
print_hello ('Jimmy', 'Stewart');

$surname = 'Stewart';

print_hello ('Jimmy', $surname);
```

As with any function in PHP, failure to send the right number of arguments results in an error (**Figure 3.14**).

To demonstrate this concept, let's rewrite the calculator process as a function.

Warning: Missing argument 3 for calculate_total(), called in /Applications/Abyss Web Server/htdocs/calculator.php on line 30 and defined in **/Applications/Abyss Web Server/htdocs/calculator.php** on line **8**

Figure 3.14 Failure to send a function the proper number (and sometimes type) of arguments creates an error.

To define functions that take arguments:

1. Open calculator.php (Script 3.6) in your text editor or IDE.

2. After including the header file, define the calculate_total() function (**Script 3.8**).

   ```
   function calculate_total ($qty,
   → $cost, $tax) {
     $total = ($qty * $cost);
     $taxrate = ($tax / 100);
     $total += ($total * $taxrate);
     echo '<p>The total cost of
   → purchasing ' . $qty . ' widget(s)
   → at $' . number_format ($cost, 2)
   → . ' each, including a tax rate of
   → ' . $tax . '%, is $' . number_
   → format ($total, 2) . '.</p>';
   }
   ```

   This function performs the same calculations as it did before and then prints out the result. It takes three arguments: the quantity being ordered, the price, and the tax rate. Notice that the variables used as arguments are not $_POST['quantity'], $_POST['price'], and $_POST['tax']. The function's argument variables are particular to this function and have their own names. Notice as well that the calculations, and the printed result, use these function-specific variables, not those in $_POST (which will actually be sent to this function when it's called).

3. Change the contents of the validation conditional (where the calculations were previously made) to read

   ```
   echo '<h1>Total Cost</h1>';
   calculate_total ($_POST['quantity'],
   → $_POST['price'], $_POST['tax']);
   ```

Script 3.8 The calculator.php script now uses a function to perform its calculations. Unlike the make_calendar_pulldowns() user-defined function, this one takes arguments.

```
1    <?php # Script 3.8 - calculator.php #3
2
3    $page_title = 'Widget Cost Calculator';
4    include ('includes/header.html');
5
6    /* This function calculates a total
7    and then prints the results. */
8    function calculate_total ($qty, $cost,
     $tax) {
9
10     $total = ($qty * $cost);
11     $taxrate = ($tax / 100); // Turn 5%
       into .05.
12     $total += ($total * $taxrate); //
       Add the tax.
13
14     // Print the results:
15     echo '<p>The total cost of purchasing '
       . $qty . ' widget(s) at $' . number_
       format ($cost, 2) . ' each, including a
       tax rate of ' . $tax . '%, is $' .
       number_format ($total, 2) . '.</p>';
16
17   } // End of function.
18
19   // Check for form submission:
20   if (isset($_POST['submitted'])) {
21
22     // Minimal form validation:
23     if ( is_numeric($_POST['quantity']) &&
       is_numeric($_POST['price']) &&
       is_numeric($_POST['tax']) ) {
24
25       // Print the heading:
26       echo '<h1>Total Cost</h1>';
```

(script continues on next page)

CREATING YOUR OWN FUNCTIONS

Script 3.8 *continued*

```
27
28      // Call the function:
29      calculate_total ($_POST['quantity'],
        $_POST['price'], $_POST['tax']);

30
31    } else { // Invalid submitted values.
32      echo '<h1>Error!</h1>
33      <p class="error">Please enter a valid
        quantity, price, and tax.</p>';
34    }

35
36  } // End of main isset() IF.

37
38  // Leave the PHP section and create the
    HTML form:
39  ?>
40  <h1>Widget Cost Calculator</h1>
41  <form action="calculator.php" method=
    "post">
42      <p>Quantity: <input type="text" name=
        "quantity" size="5" maxlength="5" value=
        "<?php if (isset($_POST['quantity']))
        echo $_POST['quantity']; ?>" /></p>
43      <p>Price: <input type="text" name=
        "price" size="5" maxlength="10" value=
        "<?php if (isset($_POST['price'])) echo
        $_POST['price']; ?>" /></p>
44      <p>Tax (%): <input type="text" name=
        "tax" size="5" maxlength="5" value=
        "<?php if (isset($_POST['tax'])) echo
        $_POST['tax']; ?>" /></p>
45      <p><input type="submit" name="submit"
        value="Calculate!" /></p>
46      <input type="hidden" name="submitted"
        value="TRUE" />
47  </form>
48  <?php // Include the footer:
49  include ('includes/footer.html');
50  ?>
```

Again, this is just a minor rewrite of the way the script worked before. Assuming that all of the submitted values are numeric, a heading is printed (this is not done within the function) and the function is called (which will calculate and print the total).

When calling the function, three arguments are passed to it, each of which is a $_POST variable. The value of $_POST['quantity'] will be assigned to the function's $qty variable; the value of $_POST['price'] will be assigned to the function's $cost variable; and the value of $_POST['tax'] will be assigned to the function's $tax variable.

4. Save the file as calculator.php, place it in your Web directory, and test it in your Web browser (**Figure 3.15**).

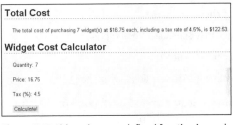

Figure 3.15 Although a user-defined function is used to perform the calculations (see Script 3.8), the end result is no different to the user (see Figure 3.11).

Setting default argument values

Another variant on defining your own functions is to preset an argument's value. To do so, assign the argument a value in the function's definition:

```
function greet ($name, $msg = 'Hello') {

    echo "$msg, $name!";

}
```

The end result of setting a default argument value is that that particular argument becomes optional when calling the function. If a value is passed to it, the passed value is used; otherwise, the default value is used.

You can set default values for as many of the arguments as you want, as long as those arguments come last in the function definition. In other words, the required arguments should always be listed first.

With the example function just defined, any of these will work:

```
greet ($surname, $message);

greet ('Zoe');

greet ('Sam', 'Good evening');
```

However, just greet() will not work. Also, there's no way to pass $greeting a value without passing one to $name as well (argument values must be passed in order, and you can't skip a required argument).

To set default argument values:

1. Open calculator.php (refer to Script 3.8) in your text editor or IDE.

2. Change the function definition line (line 9) so that only the quantity and cost are required (**Script 3.9**).

```
function calculate_total ($qty,
→ $cost, $tax = 5) {
```

continues on page 100

Script 3.9 The calculate_total() function now assumes a set tax rate unless one is specified when the function is called.

```
1    <?php # Script 3.9 - calculator.php #4

2

3    $page_title = 'Widget Cost Calculator';

4    include ('includes/header.html');

5

6    /* This function calculates a total

7    and then prints the results.

8    The $tax argument is optional (it has a
     default value). */

9    function calculate_total ($qty, $cost, $tax
     = 5) {

10

11    $total = ($qty * $cost);

12    $taxrate = ($tax / 100); // Turn 5% into
      .05.

13    $total += ($total * $taxrate); // Add
      the tax.

14

15    // Print the results:

16    echo '<p>The total cost of purchasing '
      . $qty . ' widget(s) at $' . number_
      format ($cost, 2) . ' each, including a
      tax rate of ' . $tax . '%, is $' .
      number_format ($total, 2) . '.</p>';

17

18    } // End of function.

19

20    // Check for form submission:

21    if (isset($_POST['submitted'])) {

22

23      // Minimal form validation:

24      if ( is_numeric($_POST['quantity']) &&
        is_numeric($_POST['price']) ) {

25

26        // Print the heading:
```

(script continues on next page)

Script 3.9 *continued*

```
27        echo '<h1>Total Cost</h1>';

28

29        // Call the function, with or without tax:

30        if (is_numeric($_POST['tax'])) {

31           calculate_total ($_POST['quantity'], $_POST['price'], $_POST['tax']);

32        } else {

33           calculate_total ($_POST['quantity'], $_POST['price']);

34        }

35

36     } else { // Invalid submitted values.

37        echo '<h1>Error!</h1>

38        <p class="error">Please enter a valid quantity and price.</p>';

39     }

40

41  } // End of main isset() IF.

42

43  // Leave the PHP section and create the HTML form:

44  ?>

45  <h1>Widget Cost Calculator</h1>

46  <form action="calculator.php" method="post">

47     <p>Quantity: <input type="text" name="quantity" size="5" maxlength="5" value="<?php if
       (isset($_POST['quantity'])) echo $_POST['quantity']; ?>" /></p>

48     <p>Price: <input type="text" name="price" size="5" maxlength="10" value="<?php if
       (isset($_POST['price'])) echo $_POST['price']; ?>" /></p>

49     <p>Tax (%): <input type="text" name="tax" size="5" maxlength="5" value="<?php if
       (isset($_POST['tax'])) echo $_POST['tax']; ?>" /> (optional)</p>

50     <p><input type="submit" name="submit" value="Calculate!" /></p>

51     <input type="hidden" name="submitted" value="TRUE" />

52  </form>

53  <?php // Include the footer:

54  include ('includes/footer.html');

55  ?>
```

The value of the $tax variable is now hard-coded in the function definition, making it optional.

3. Change the form validation to read

```
if (is_numeric($_POST['quantity'])
 && is_numeric($_POST['price'])) {
```

Because the tax value will be optional, only the other two variables are required and need to be validated.

4. Change the function call line to

```
if (is_numeric($_POST['tax'])) {
  calculate_total ($_POST
  → ['quantity'], $_POST
  → ['price'], $_POST['tax']);
} else {
  calculate_total ($_POST
  → ['quantity'], $_POST['price']);
}
```

If the tax value has also been submitted (and is numeric), then the function will be called as before, providing the user-submitted tax rate. Otherwise, the function is called providing just the two arguments, in which case the default value will be used for the tax rate.

5. Change the error message to only report on the quantity and price.

```
echo '<h1>Error!</h1>
<p class="error">Please enter a valid
→ quantity and price.</p>';
```

Since the tax will now be optional, the error message is changed accordingly.

6. If you want, mark the tax value in the form as optional.

```
<p>Tax (%): <input type="text"
name="tax" size="5" maxlength="5"
value="<?php if (isset($_POST
['tax'])) echo $_POST['tax']; ?>"
/> (optional)</p>
```

A parenthetical is added to the tax input, indicating to the user that this value is optional.

7. Save the file, place it in your Web directory, and test it in your Web browser (**Figures 3.16** and **3.17**).

✔ Tips

- To pass a function no value for an argument, use either an empty string (' '), NULL, or FALSE.

- In the PHP manual, square brackets ([]) are used to indicate a function's optional parameters (**Figure 3.18**).

Total Cost

The total cost of purchasing 4 widget(s) at $1.99 each, including a tax rate of 5%, is $8.36.

Widget Cost Calculator

Quantity: 4

Price: **1.99**

Tax (%):   (optional)

Calculate!

Figure 3.16 If no tax value is entered, the default value of 5% will be used in the calculation.

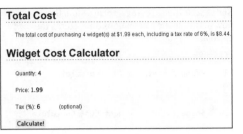

Figure 3.17 If the user enters a tax value, it will be used instead of the default value.

Returning values from a function

The final attribute of a user-defined function to discuss is that of returning values. Some, but not all, functions do this. For example, print() will return either a *1* or a *0* indicating its success, whereas echo() will not. As another example, the strlen() function returns a number correlating to the number of characters in a string.

To have a function return a value, use the return statement.

```
function find_sign ($month, $day) {
    // Function code.
    return $sign;
}
```

A function can return a value (say a string or a number) or a variable whose value has been created by the function. When calling a function that returns a value, you can assign the function result to a variable:

```
$my_sign = find_sign ('October', 23);
```

or use it as an argument when calling another function:

```
print find_sign ('October', 23);
```

Let's update the calculate_total() function one last time so that it returns the calculated total instead of printing it.

continues on next page

CREATING YOUR OWN FUNCTIONS

```
string number_format ( float $number [, int $decimals [, string $dec_point, string $thousands_sep]] )
```

Figure 3.18 The PHP manual's description of the number_format() function shows that only the first argument is required.

To have a function return a value:

1. Open calculator.php (refer to Script 3.9) in your text editor or IDE.

2. Remove the echo() statement from the function definition and replace it with a return statement (**Script 3.10**)

   ```
   return number_format($total, 2);
   ```

   This version of the function will not print the results. Instead it will return just the calculated total, formatted to two decimal places.

3. Change the function call lines to

   ```
   if (is_numeric($_POST['tax'])) {
     $sum = calculate_total ($_POST
     → ['quantity'], $_POST['price'],
     → $_POST['tax']);
   } else {
     $sum = calculate_total ($_POST
     → ['quantity'], $_POST['price']);
   }
   ```

   Since the function now returns instead of prints the calculation results, the invocation of the function needs to be assigned to a variable so that the total can be printed later in the script.

continues on page 104

Script 3.10 The calculate_total() function now performs the calculations and returns the calculated result.

```
1   <?php # Script 3.10 - calculator.php #5
2
3   $page_title = 'Widget Cost Calculator';
4   include ('includes/header.html');
5
6   /* This function calculates a total
7   and then returns the results.
8   The $tax argument is optional (it has a
    default value). */
9   function calculate_total ($qty, $cost,
    $tax = 5) {
10
11    $total = ($qty * $cost);
12    $taxrate = ($tax / 100); // Turn 5% into
      .05.
13    $total += ($total * $taxrate); // Add
      the tax.
14
15    return number_format($total, 2);
16
17  } // End of function.
18
19  // Check for form submission:
20  if (isset($_POST['submitted'])) {
21
22    // Minimal form validation:
23    if ( is_numeric($_POST['quantity']) &&
      is_numeric($_POST['price']) ) {
24
25      // Print the heading:
26      echo '<h1>Total Cost</h1>';
27
28      // Call the function, with or without
        tax:
29      if (is_numeric($_POST['tax'])) {
```

(script continues on next page)

Script 3.10 *continued*

```
 30        $sum = calculate_total ($_POST['quantity'], $_POST['price'], $_POST['tax']);
 31     } else {
 32        $sum = calculate_total ($_POST['quantity'], $_POST['price']);
 33     }
 34
 35     // Print the results:
 36     echo '<p>The total cost of purchasing ' . $_POST['quantity'] . ' widget(s) at $' . number_
        format ($_POST['price'], 2) . ' each, with tax, is $' . $sum . '.</p>';
 37
 38   } else { // Invalid submitted values.
 39        echo '<h1>Error!</h1>
 40        <p class="error">Please enter a valid quantity and price.</p>';
 41   }
 42
 43 } // End of main isset() IF.
 44
 45 // Leave the PHP section and create the HTML form:
 46 ?>
 47 <h1>Widget Cost Calculator</h1>
 48 <form action="calculator.php" method="post">
 49   <p>Quantity: <input type="text" name="quantity" size="5" maxlength="5" value="<?php if
      (isset($_POST['quantity'])) echo $_POST['quantity']; ?>" /></p>
 50   <p>Price: <input type="text" name="price" size="5" maxlength="10" value="<?php if
      (isset($_POST['price'])) echo $_POST['price']; ?>" /></p>
 51   <p>Tax (%): <input type="text" name="tax" size="5" maxlength="5" value="<?php if
      (isset($_POST['tax'])) echo $_POST['tax']; ?>" /> (optional)</p>
 52   <p><input type="submit" name="submit" value="Calculate!" /></p>
 53   <input type="hidden" name="submitted" value="TRUE" />
 54 </form>
 55 <?php // Include the footer:
 56 include ('includes/footer.html');
 57 ?>
```

4. Add a new echo() statement that prints the results.

```
echo '<p>The total cost of
→ purchasing ' . $_POST['quantity']
→ . ' widget(s) at $' . number_
→ format ($_POST['price'], 2) . '
→ each, with tax, is $' . $sum .
→ '.</p>';
```

Since the function just returns a value, a new echo() statement must be added to the main code. This statement uses the quantity and price from the form (both found in $_POST) and the total returned by the function (assigned to $sum). It does not, however, report on the tax rate used (see the final tip).

5. Save the file, place it in your Web directory, and test it in your Web browser (**Figure 3.19**).

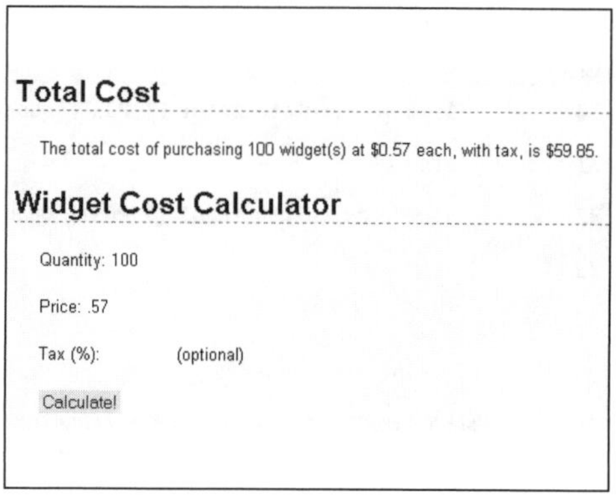

✔ Tips

- Although this last example may seem more complex (with the function performing a calculation and the main code printing the results), it actually demonstrates better programming style. Ideally, functions should perform universal, obvious tasks (like a calculation) and be independent of page-specific factors like HTML formatting.

- The return statement terminates the code execution at that point, so any code within a function after an executed return will never run.

Total Cost

The total cost of purchasing 100 widget(s) at $0.57 each, with tax, is $59.85.

Widget Cost Calculator

Quantity: 100

Price: .57

Tax (%):   (optional)

Calculate!

Figure 3.19 The calculator's user-defined function now returns, instead of prints, the results, but this change has little impact on what the user sees.

■ A function can have multiple `return` statements (e.g., in a `switch` statement or conditional) but only one, at most, will ever be invoked. For example, functions commonly do something like this:

```
function some_function () {

    if (/* condition */) {

            return TRUE;

    } else {

            return FALSE;

    }

}
```

■ To have a function return multiple values, use the `array()` function to return an array. By changing the return line in Script 3.10 to

```
return array ($total, $tax);
```

the function could return both the total of the calculation and the tax rate used (which could be the default value or a user-supplied one).

■ When calling a function that returns an array, use the `list()` function to assign the array elements to individual variables:

```
list ($sum, $taxrate) = calculate_
→ total ($_POST['quantity'],
→ $_POST['price'], $_POST['tax']);
```

Variable Scope

Every variable in PHP has a *scope* to it, which is to say a realm in which the variable (and therefore its value) can be accessed. For starters, variables have the scope of the page in which they reside. So if you define $var, the rest of the page can access $var, but other pages generally cannot (unless you use special variables).

Since included files act as if they were part of the original (including) script, variables defined before an include() line are available to the included file (as you've already seen with $page_title and header.html). Further, variables defined within the included file are available to the parent (including) script *after* the include() line.

User-defined functions have their own scope: variables defined within a function are not available outside of it, and variables defined outside of a function are not available within it. For this reason, a variable inside of a function can have the same name as one outside of it but still be an entirely different variable with a different value. This is a confusing concept for many beginning programmers.

To alter the variable scope within a function, you can use the global statement.

```
function function_name() {

    global $var;

}
$var = 20;

function_name(); // Function call.
```

In this example, $var inside of the function is now the same as $var outside of it. This means that the function $var already has a value of *20*, and if that value changes inside of the function, the external $var's value will also change.

Another option for circumventing variable scope is to make use of the superglobals: $_GET, $_POST, $_REQUEST, etc. These variables are automatically accessible within your functions (hence, they are *super*global). You can also add elements to the $GLOBALS array to make them available within a function.

All of that being said, it's almost always best not to use global variables within a function. Functions should be designed so that they receive every value they need as arguments and return whatever value (or values) need to be returned. Relying upon global variables within a function makes them more context-dependent, and consequently less useful.

INTRODUCTION TO MYSQL

Because this book discusses how to integrate several technologies (primarily PHP, SQL, and MySQL), a solid understanding of each individually is important before you begin writing PHP scripts that use SQL to interact with MySQL. This chapter is a departure from its predecessors in that it temporarily leaves PHP behind to delve into MySQL.

MySQL is the world's most popular open-source database application (according to MySQL's Web site, www.mysql.com) and is commonly used with PHP. The MySQL software comes with the database server (which stores the actual data), different client applications (for interacting with the database server), and several utilities. In this chapter you'll see how to define a simple table using MySQL's allowed data types and other properties. Then you'll learn how to interact with the MySQL server using two different client applications. All of this information will be the foundation for the SQL taught in the next two chapters.

This chapter assumes you have access to a running MySQL server. If you are working on your own computer, see Appendix A, "Installation," for instructions on installing MySQL, starting MySQL, and creating MySQL users (all of which must already be done in order to finish this chapter). If you are using a hosted server, your Web host should provide you with the database access.

Naming Database Elements

Before you start working with databases, you have to identify your needs. The purpose of the application (or Web site, in this case) dictates how the database should be designed. With that in mind, the examples in this chapter and the next will use a database that stores some user registration information.

When creating databases and tables, you should come up with names (formally called *identifiers*) that are clear, meaningful, and easy to type. Also, identifiers

- Should only contain letters, numbers, and the underscore (no spaces)

- Should not be the same as an existing keyword (like an SQL term or a function name)

- Should be treated as case-sensitive

- Cannot be longer than 64 characters (approximately)

- Must be unique within its realm

This last rule means that a table cannot have two columns with the same name and a database cannot have two tables with the same name. You can, however, use the same column name in two different tables in the same database (in fact, you often will do this). As for the first three rules, I use the word *should*, as these are good policies more than exact requirements. Exceptions can be made to these rules, but the syntax for doing so can be complicated. Abiding by these suggestions is a reasonable limitation and will help avoid complications.

To name a database's elements:

1. Determine the database's name.

   This is the easiest and, arguably, least important step. Just make sure that the database name is unique for that MySQL server. If you're using a hosted server, your Web host will likely provide a database name that may or may not include your account or domain name.

   For this first example, the database will be called *sitename*, as the information and techniques could apply to any generic site.

2. Determine the table names.

   The table names just need to be unique within this database, which shouldn't be a problem. For this example, which stores user registration information, the only table will be called *users*.

3. Determine the column names for each table.

   The *users* table will have columns to store a user ID, a first name, a last name, an email address, a password, and the registration date. **Table 4.1** shows these columns, with sample data, using proper identifiers. As MySQL has a function called *password*, I've changed the name of that column to just *pass*. This isn't strictly necessary but is really a good idea.

✔ Tips

- Chapter 6, "Advanced SQL and MySQL," discusses database design in more detail, using a more complex example.

- To be precise, the length limit for the names of databases, tables, and columns is actually 64 *bytes*, not characters. While most characters in many languages require one byte apiece, it's possible to use a multi-byte character in an identifier. But 64 bytes is still a lot of space, so this probably won't be an issue for you.

- Whether or not an identifier in MySQL is case-sensitive actually depends upon many things. On Windows and normally on Mac OS X, database and table names are generally case-insensitive. On Unix and some Mac OS X setups, they are case-sensitive. Column names are always case-insensitive. It's really best, in my opinion, to always use all lowercase letters and work as if case-sensitivity applied.

Table 4.1 The *users* table will have these six columns, to store records like the sample data here.

users Table	
COLUMN NAME	EXAMPLE
user_id	834
first_name	Larry
last_name	David
email	ld@example.com
pass	emily07
registration_date	2007-12-31 19:21:03

Choosing Your Column Types

Once you have identified all of the tables and columns that the database will need, you should determine each column's data type. When creating a table, MySQL requires that you explicitly state what sort of information each column will contain. There are three primary types, which is true for almost every database application:

◆ Text (aka *strings*)

◆ Numbers

◆ Dates and times

Within each of these, there are a number of variants—some of which are MySQL-specific—you can use. Choosing your column types correctly not only dictates what information can be stored and how but also affects the database's overall performance. **Table 4.2** lists most of the available types for MySQL, how much space they take up, and brief descriptions of each type.

Table 4.2 The common MySQL data types you can use for defining columns. Note: some of these limits may change in different versions of MySQL, and the character set may also impact the size of the text types.

MySQL Data Types		
Type	Size	Description
CHAR[Length]	*Length* bytes	A fixed-length field from 0 to 255 characters long
VARCHAR[Length]	String length + 1 or 2 bytes	A variable-length field from 0 to 65,535 characters long
TINYTEXT	String length + 1 bytes	A string with a maximum length of 255 characters
TEXT	String length + 2 bytes	A string with a maximum length of 65,535 characters
MEDIUMTEXT	String length + 3 bytes	A string with a maximum length of 16,777,215 characters
LONGTEXT	String length + 4 bytes	A string with a maximum length of 4,294,967,295 characters
TINYINT[Length]	1 byte	Range of –128 to 127 or 0 to 255 unsigned
SMALLINT[Length]	2 bytes	Range of –32,768 to 32,767 or 0 to 65,535 unsigned
MEDIUMINT[Length]	3 bytes	Range of –8,388,608 to 8,388,607 or 0 to 16,777,215 unsigned
INT[Length]	4 bytes	Range of –2,147,483,648 to 2,147,483,647 or 0 to 4,294,967,295 unsigned
BIGINT[Length]	8 bytes	Range of –9,223,372,036,854,775,808 to 9,223,372,036,854,775,807 or 0 to 18,446,744,073,709,551,615 unsigned
FLOAT[Length, Decimals]	4 bytes	A small number with a floating decimal point
DOUBLE[Length, Decimals]	8 bytes	A large number with a floating decimal point
DECIMAL[Length, Decimals]	Length + 1 or 2 bytes	A DOUBLE stored as a string, allowing for a fixed decimal point
DATE	3 bytes	In the format of YYYY-MM-DD
DATETIME	8 bytes	In the format of YYYY-MM-DD HH:MM:SS
TIMESTAMP	4 bytes	In the format of YYYYMMDDHHMMSS; acceptable range ends in the year 2037
TIME	3 bytes	In the format of HH:MM:SS
ENUM	1 or 2 bytes	Short for *enumeration*, which means that each column can have one of several possible values
SET	1, 2, 3, 4, or 8 bytes	Like ENUM except that each column can have more than one of several possible values

Many of the types can take an optional *Length* attribute, limiting their size. (The square brackets, [ ], indicate an optional parameter to be put in parentheses.) For performance purposes, you should place some restrictions on how much data can be stored in any column. But understand that attempting to insert a string five characters long into a CHAR(2) column will result in truncation of the final three characters (only the first two characters would be stored; the rest would be lost forever). This is true for any field in which the size is set (CHAR, VARCHAR, INT, etc.). So your length should always correspond to the maximum possible value (as a number) or longest possible string (as text) that might be stored.

The various date types have all sorts of unique behaviors, which are documented in the MySQL manual. You'll use the DATE and TIME fields primarily without modification, so you need not worry too much about their intricacies.

There are also two special types—ENUM and SET—that allow you to define a series of acceptable values for that column. An ENUM column can have only one value of a possible several thousand, while SET allows for several of up to 64 possible values. These are available in MySQL but aren't present in every database application.

To select the column types:

1. Identify whether a column should be a text, number, or date/time type (**Table 4.3**).

   This is normally an easy and obvious step, but you want to be as specific as possible. For example, the date *2006-08-02* (MySQL format) could be stored as a string—*August 2, 2006*. But if you use the proper date format, you'll have a more useful database (and, as you'll see, there are functions that can turn *2006-08-02* into *August 2, 2006*).

2. Choose the most appropriate subtype for each column (**Table 4.4**).

   For this example, the *user_id* is set as a MEDIUMINT, allowing for up to nearly 17 million values (as an *unsigned*, or non-negative, number). The *registration_date* will be a DATETIME. It can store both the date and the specific time a user registered. When deciding among the date types, consider whether or not you'll want to access just the date, the time, or possibly both. If unsure, err on the side of storing too much information.

   The other fields will be mostly VARCHAR, since their lengths will differ from record to record. The only exception is the password column, which will be a fixed-length CHAR (you'll see why when inserting records in the next chapter). See the sidebar "CHAR vs. VARCHAR" for more information on these two types.

Table 4.3 The *users* table with assigned generic data types.

users Table	
COLUMN NAME	TYPE
user_id	number
first_name	text
last_name	text
email	text
pass	text
registration_date	date/time

Table 4.4 The *users* table with more specific data types.

users Table	
COLUMN NAME	TYPE
user_id	MEDIUMINT
first_name	VARCHAR
last_name	VARCHAR
email	VARCHAR
pass	CHAR
registration_date	DATETIME

Table 4.5 The *users* table with set length attributes.

users Table	
COLUMN NAME	TYPE
user_id	MEDIUMINT
first_name	VARCHAR(20)
last_name	VARCHAR(40)
email	VARCHAR(60)
pass	CHAR(40)
registration_date	DATETIME

CHAR vs. VARCHAR

Both of these types store strings and can be set with a maximum length. One primary difference between the two is that anything stored as a CHAR will always be stored as a string the length of the column (using spaces to pad it; these spaces will be removed when you retrieve the stored value from the database). Conversely, strings stored in a VARCHAR column will require only as much space as the string itself. So the word *cat* in a VARCHAR(10) column requires four bytes of space (the length of the string plus 1), but in a CHAR(10) column, that same word requires 10 bytes of space. So, generally speaking, VARCHAR columns tend to take up less disk space than CHAR columns.

However, databases are normally faster when working with fixed-size columns, which is an argument in favor of CHAR. And that same three-letter word—*cat*—in a CHAR(3) only uses 3 bytes but in a VARCHAR(10) requires 4. So how do you decide which to use?

If a string field will *always* be of a set length (e.g., a state abbreviation), use CHAR; otherwise, use VARCHAR. You may notice, though, that in some cases MySQL defines a column as the one type (like CHAR) even though you created it as the other (VARCHAR). This is perfectly normal and is MySQL's way of improving performance.

3. Set the maximum length for text columns (**Table 4.5**).

The size of any field should be restricted to the smallest possible value, based upon the largest possible input. For example, if a column is storing a state abbreviation, it would be defined as a CHAR(2). Other times you might have to guess somewhat: I can't think of any first names longer than about 10 characters, but just to be safe I'll allow for up to 20.

✔ Tips

■ The length attribute for numeric types does not affect the range of values that can be stored in the column. Columns defined as TINYINT(1) or TINYINT(20) can store the exact same values. Instead, for integers, the length dictates the display width; for decimals, the length is the total number of digits that can be stored.

■ Many of the data types have synonymous names: INT and INTEGER, DEC and DECIMAL, etc.

■ The TIMESTAMP field type is automatically set as the current date and time when an INSERT or UPDATE occurs, even if no value is specified for that particular field. If a table has multiple TIMESTAMP columns, only the first one will be updated when an INSERT or UPDATE is performed.

■ MySQL also has several variants on the text types that allow for storing binary data. These types are BINARY, VARBINARY, TINYBLOB, MEDIUMBLOB, and LONGBLOB. Such types are used for storing files or encrypted data.

CHOOSING YOUR COLUMN TYPES

Choosing Other Column Properties

Besides deciding what data types and sizes you should use for your columns, you should consider a handful of other properties.

First, every column, regardless of type, can be defined as NOT NULL. The NULL value, in databases and programming, is equivalent to saying that the field has no value. Ideally, in a properly designed database, every column of every row in every table should have a value, but that isn't always the case. To force a field to have a value, add the NOT NULL description to its column type. For example, a required dollar amount can be described as

```
cost DECIMAL(5,2) NOT NULL
```

When creating a table, you can also specify a default value for any column, regardless of type. In cases where a majority of the records will have the same value for a column, presetting a default will save you from having to specify a value when inserting new rows (unless that row's value for that column is different from the norm).

```
gender ENUM('M', 'F') default 'F'
```

With the *gender* column, if no value is specified when adding a record, the default will be used.

If a column does not have a default value and one is not specified for a new record, that field will be given a NULL value. However, if no value is specified and the column is defined as NOT NULL, an error will occur.

The number types can be marked as UNSIGNED, which limits the stored data to positive numbers and zero. This also effectively doubles the range of positive numbers that can be stored (because no negative numbers will be kept, see Table 4.2). You can also flag the number types as ZEROFILL, which means that

any extra room will be padded with zeros (ZEROFILLs are also automatically UNSIGNED).

Finally, when designing a database, you'll need to consider creating indexes, adding keys, and using the AUTO_INCREMENT property. Chapter 6 discusses these concepts in greater detail, but in the meantime, check out the sidebar "Indexes, Keys, and AUTO_INCREMENT" to learn how they affect the *users* table.

To finish defining your columns:

1. Identify your primary key.

   The primary key is quixotically both arbitrary and critically important. Almost always a number value, the primary key is a unique way to refer to a particular record. For example, your phone number has no inherent value but is unique to you (your home or mobile phone).

   In the *users* table, the *user_id* will be the primary key: an arbitrary number used to refer to a row of data. Again, Chapter 6 will go into the concept of primary keys in more detail.

2. Identify which columns cannot have a NULL value.

   In this example, every field is required (cannot be NULL). If you stored peoples' addresses, by contrast, you might have *address_line1* and *address_line2*, with the latter one being optional (it could have a NULL value). In general, tables that have a lot of NULL values suggest a poor design (more on this in...you guessed it...Chapter 6).

3. Make any numeric type UNSIGNED if it won't ever store negative numbers.

   The *user_id*, which will be a number, should be UNSIGNED so that it's always positive. Other examples of UNSIGNED numbers would be the price of items in an e-commerce example, a telephone extension for a business, or a zip code.

Table 4.6 The final description of the *users* table. The *user_id* will also be defined as an auto-incremented primary key.

users Table

COLUMN NAME	TYPE
user_id	MEDIUMINT UNSIGNED NOT NULL
first_name	VARCHAR(20) NOT NULL
last_name	VARCHAR(40) NOT NULL
email	VARCHAR(60) NOT NULL
pass	CHAR(40) NOT NULL
registration_date	DATETIME NOT NULL

4. Establish the default value for any column.

None of the columns here logically implies a default value.

5. Confirm the final column definitions (**Table 4.6**).

Before creating the tables, you should revisit the type and range of data you'll store to make sure that your database effectively accounts for everything.

✔ Tip

- Text columns can also have defined *character sets* and *collations*. This will mean more once you start working with multiple languages (see Chapter 14, "Making Universal Sites").

Indexes, Keys, and AUTO_INCREMENT

Two concepts closely related to database design are indexes and keys. An *index* in a database is a way of requesting that the database keep an eye on the values of a specific column or combination of columns (loosely stated). The end result of this is improved performance when retrieving records but marginally hindered performance when inserting records or updating them.

A *key* in a database table is integral to the normalization process used for designing more complicated databases (see Chapter 6). There are two types of keys: *primary* and *foreign*. Each table should have one primary key, and the primary key in one table is often linked as a foreign key in another.

A table's primary key is an artificial way to refer to a record and should abide by three rules:

1. It must always have a value.

2. That value must never change.

3. That value must be unique for each record in the table.

In the *users* table, the *user_id* will be designated as a PRIMARY KEY, which is both a description of the column and a directive to MySQL to index it. Since the *user_id* is a number (which primary keys almost always will be), also add the AUTO_INCREMENT description to the column, which tells MySQL to use the next-highest number as the *user_id* value for each added record. You'll see what this means in practice when you begin inserting records.

Accessing MySQL

In order to create tables, add records, and request information from a database, some sort of *client* is necessary to communicate with the MySQL server. Later in the book, PHP scripts will act in this role, but being able to use another interface is necessary. Although there are oodles of client applications available, I'll focus on two: the *mysql client* (or *mysql monitor*, as it is also called) and the Web-based phpMyAdmin. A third option, the MySQL Query Browser, is not discussed in this book but can be found at the MySQL Web site (www.mysql.com), should you not be satisfied with these two choices.

Using the mysql Client

The mysql client is normally installed with the rest of the MySQL software. Although the mysql client does not have a pretty graphical interface, it's a reliable, standard tool that's easy to use and behaves consistently on many different operating systems.

The mysql client is accessed from a command-line interface, be it the Terminal application in Linux or Mac OS X (**Figure 4.1**), or a DOS prompt in Windows (**Figure 4.2**). If you're not comfortable with command-line interactions, you might find this interface to be challenging, but it becomes easy to use in no time.

To start an application from the command line, type its name and press Return or Enter:

```
mysql
```

When invoking this application, you can add arguments to affect how it runs. The most common arguments are the username, password, and hostname (computer name or URL) you want to connect using. You establish these arguments like so:

```
mysql -u username -p -h hostname
```

The -p option will cause the client to prompt you for the password. You can also specify the password on this line if you prefer—by typing it directly after the -p prompt—but it will be visible, which is insecure. The -h hostname argument is optional, and you can leave it off unless you cannot connect to the MySQL server without it.

Within the mysql client, every statement (SQL command) needs to be terminated by a semicolon. These semicolons are an indication to the client that the query is complete and should be run. The semicolons are not part of the SQL itself (this is a common point of confusion). What this also means is that you can continue the same SQL statement over several lines within the mysql client, which makes it easier to read and to edit, should that be necessary.

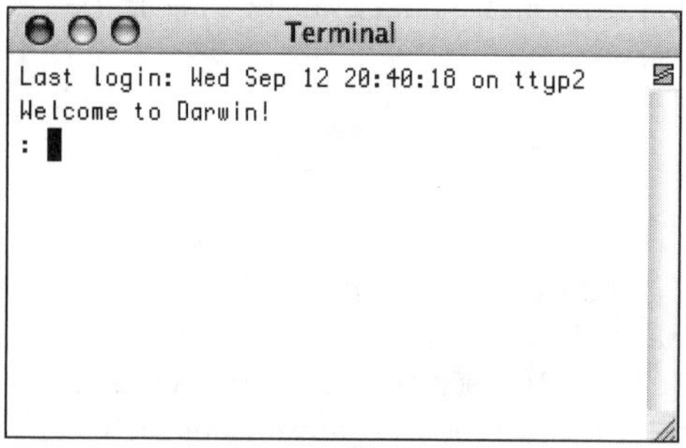

Figure 4.1 A Terminal window in Mac OS X.

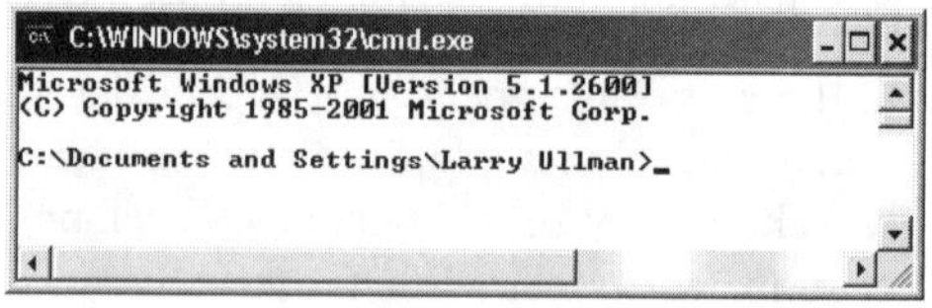

Figure 4.2 A Windows DOS prompt or console (although the default is for white text on a black background).

As a quick demonstration of accessing and using the mysql client, these next steps will show you how to start the mysql client, select a database to use, and quit the client. Before following these steps,

◆ The MySQL server must be running.

◆ You must have a username and password with proper access.

Both of these ideas are explained in Appendix A.

As a side note, in the following steps and throughout the rest of the book, I will continue to provide images using the mysql client on both Windows and Mac OS X. While the appearance differs, the steps and results will be identical. So in short, don't be concerned about why one image shows the DOS prompt and the next a Terminal.

To use the mysql client:

1. Access your system from a command-line interface.

   On Unix systems and Mac OS X, this is just a matter of bringing up the Terminal or a similar application.

   If you are using Windows and followed the instructions in Appendix A, you can choose Start > Programs > MySQL > MySQL Server *X.X* > MySQL Command Line Client (**Figure 4.3**). Then you can skip to Step 3. If you don't have a MySQL Command Line Client option available, you'll need to choose Run from the Start menu, type cmd in the window, and press Enter to bring up a DOS prompt (then follow the instructions in the next step).

   continues on next page

Figure 4.3 The MySQL Windows installer creates a link in your Start menu so that you can easily get into the mysql client.

2. Invoke the mysql client, using the appropriate command (**Figure 4.4**).

/path/to/mysql/bin/mysql -u *username* -p

The */path/to/mysql* part of this step will be largely dictated by the operating system you are running and where MySQL was installed. This might therefore be

▲ /usr/local/mysql/bin/mysql - u
  → *username* -p (on Mac OS X and Unix)

or

▲ C:\mysql\bin\mysql -u *username* -p
  (on Windows)

The basic premise is that you are running the mysql client, connecting as *username*, and requesting to be prompted for the password. Not to overstate the point, but the username and password values that you use must already be established in MySQL as a valid user (see Appendix A).

3. Enter the password at the prompt and press Return/Enter.

The password you use here should be for the user you specified in the preceding step. If you used the MySQL Command Line Client link on Windows (Figure 4.3), the user is *root*, so you should use that password (probably established during installation and configuration, see Appendix A).

If you used the proper username/password combination (i.e., someone with valid access), you should be greeted as shown in **Figure 4.5**. If access is denied, you're probably not using the correct values (see Appendix A for instructions on creating users).

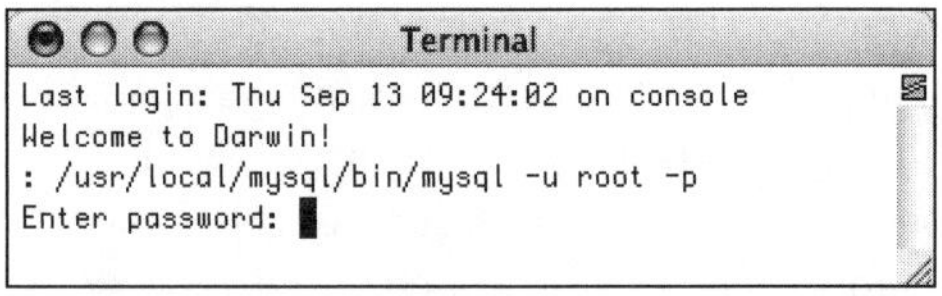

Figure 4.4 Access the mysql client by entering the full path to the utility, along with the proper arguments.

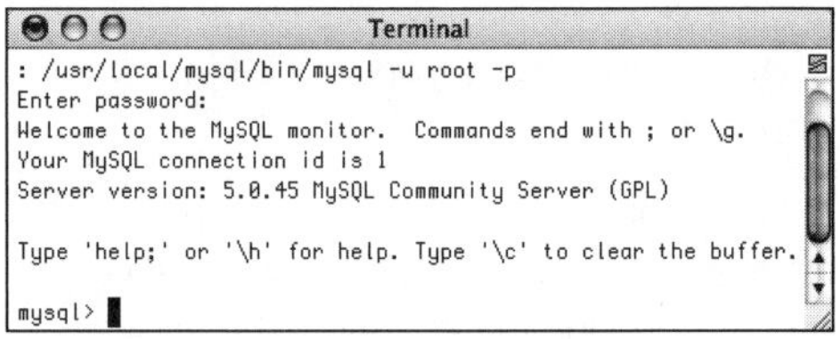

Figure 4.5 If you are successfully able to log in, you'll see a welcome message like this.

ACCESSING MYSQL

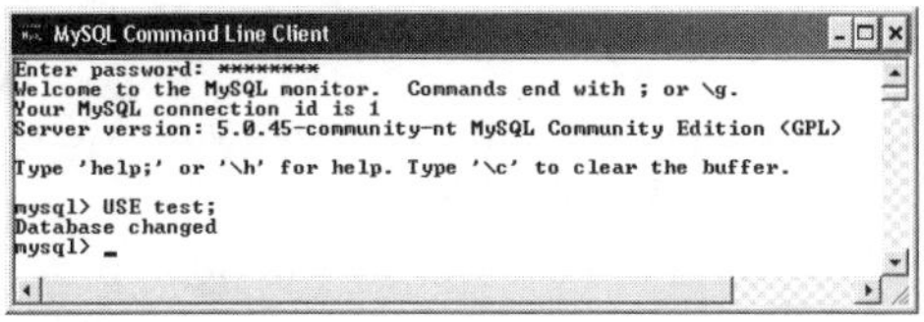

Figure 4.6 After getting into the mysql client, run a USE command to choose the database with which you want to work.

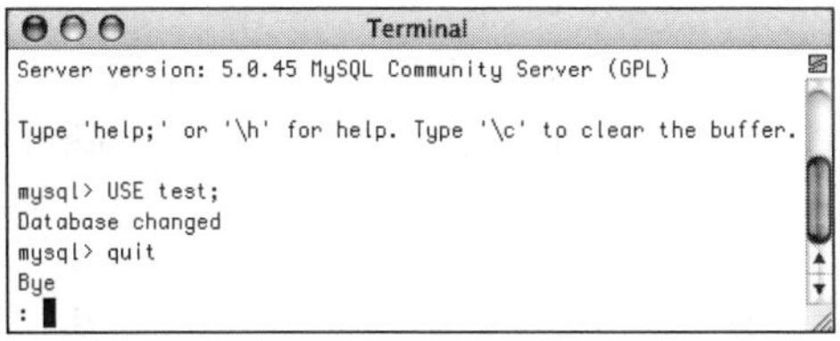

Figure 4.7 Type either exit or quit to terminate your session and leave the mysql client.

4. Select the database you want to use (**Figure 4.6**).

   USE test;

   The USE command selects the database to be used for every subsequent command. The *test* database is one that MySQL installs by default. Assuming it exists on your server, all users should be able to access it.

5. Quit out of mysql (**Figure 4.7**).

   quit

   You can also use the command exit to leave the client. This step—unlike most other commands you enter in the mysql client—does not require a semicolon at the end.

   If you used the MySQL Command Line Client, this will also close the DOS prompt window.

✔ Tips

- If you know in advance which database you will want to use, you can simplify matters by starting mysql with

  */path/to/mysql/bin/*mysql -u *username*
  → -p *databasename*

- To see what else you can do with the mysql client, type

  */path/to/mysql/bin/*mysql --help

- The mysql client on most systems allows you to use the up and down arrows to scroll through previously entered commands. If you make a mistake in typing a query, you can scroll up to find it, and then correct the error.

- If you are in a long statement and make a mistake, cancel the current operation by typing c and pressing Return or Enter. If mysql thinks a closing single or double quotation mark is missing (as indicated by the '> and "> prompts), you'll need to enter the appropriate quotation mark first.

ACCESSING MySQL

Using phpMyAdmin

phpMyAdmin (www.phpmyadmin.net) is one of the best and most popular applications written in PHP. Its sole purpose is to provide an interface to a MySQL server. It's somewhat easier and more natural to use than the mysql client but requires a PHP installation and must be accessed through a Web browser. If you're running MySQL on your own computer, you might find that using the mysql client makes more sense, as installing and configuring phpMyAdmin constitutes unnecessary extra work (although all-in-one PHP and MySQL installers may do this for you). If using a hosted server, your Web host is virtually guaranteed to provide phpMyAdmin as the primary way to work with MySQL and the mysql client may not be an option.

Using phpMyAdmin isn't hard, but the next steps run through the basics so that you'll know what to do in the following chapters.

To use phpMyAdmin:

1. Access phpMyAdmin through your Web browser (**Figure 4.8**).

   The URL you use will depend upon your situation. If running on your own computer, this might be http://localhost/phpMyAdmin/. If running on a hosted site, your Web host will provide you with the proper URL. In all likelihood, phpMyAdmin would be available through the site's control panel (should one exist).

   Note that phpMyAdmin will only work if it's been properly configured to connect to MySQL with a valid username/password/hostname combination. If you see a message like the one in **Figure 4.9**, you're probably not using the correct values (see Appendix A for instructions on creating users).

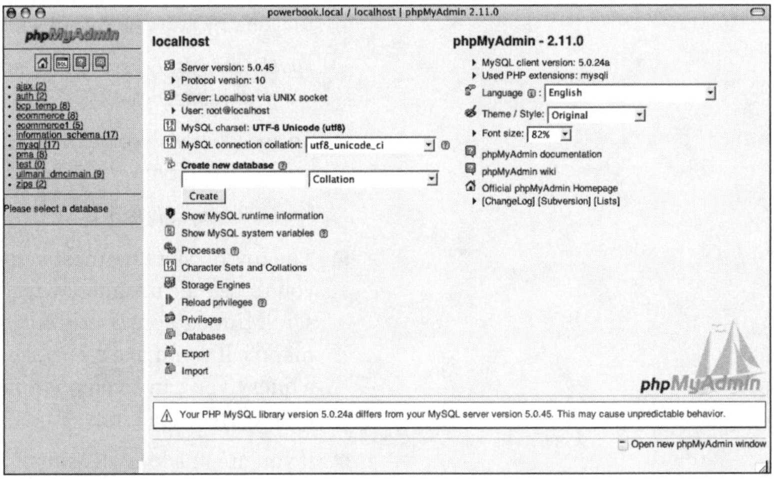

Figure 4.8 The first phpMyAdmin page (when connected as a MySQL user that can access multiple databases).

2. If possible and necessary, use the menu on the left to select a database to use (**Figure 4.10**).

What options you have here will vary depending upon what MySQL user phpMyAdmin is connecting as. That user might have access to one database, several databases, or every database. On a hosted site where you have just one database, that database will probably already be selected for you (**Figure 4.11**). On your own computer, with phpMyAdmin connecting as the MySQL root user, you would see a pull-down menu (Figure 4.10) or a simple list of available databases (Figure 4.8).

continues on next page

Figure 4.9 Every client application requires a proper username/password/hostname combination in order to interact with the MySQL server.

Figure 4.10 Use the list of databases on the left side of the window to choose with which database you want to work. This is the equivalent of running a USE *databasename* query within the mysql client (see Figure 4.6).

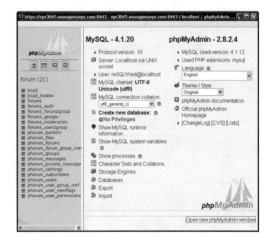

Figure 4.11 If phpMyAdmin only has access to one database, it'll likely already be selected when you load the page.

ACCESSING MySQL

3. Use the SQL tab (**Figure 4.12**) or the SQL query window (**Figure 4.13**) to enter SQL commands.

The next two chapters, and the occasional one later in the book, will provide SQL commands that must be run to create, populate, or alter tables. These might look like

```
INSERT INTO tablename (col1, col2)
→ VALUES (x, y)
```

These commands can be run using the mysql client, phpMyAdmin, or any other interface. To run them within phpMyAdmin, just type them into one of the SQL prompts and click *Go*.

✔ Tips

■ There's a lot more that can be done with phpMyAdmin, but full coverage would require a chapter in its own right (and a long chapter at that). The information presented here will be enough for you to follow any of the examples in the book, should you not want to use the mysql client.

■ phpMyAdmin can be configured to use a special database that will record your query history, allow you to bookmark queries, and more.

■ One of the best reasons to use phpMyAdmin is to transfer a database from one computer to another. Use the Export tab in phpMyAdmin connected to the source computer to create a file of data. Then, on the destination computer, use the Import tab in phpMyAdmin (connected to that MySQL server) to complete the transfer.

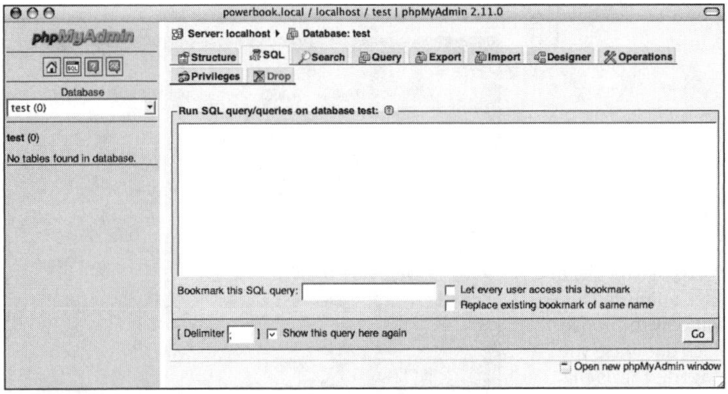

Figure 4.12 The SQL tab, in the main part of the window, can be used to run any SQL command.

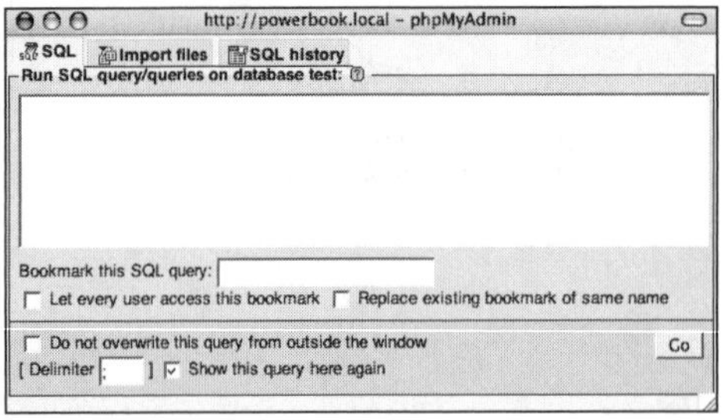

Figure 4.13 The SQL window can also be used to run commands. It pops up after clicking the SQL icon at the top of the left side of the browser (see the second icon from the left in Figure 4.10).

INTRODUCTION TO SQL

The preceding chapter provides a quick introduction to MySQL. The focus there is on two topics: using MySQL's rules and data types to define a database, and how to interact with the MySQL server. This chapter moves on to the *lingua franca* of databases: SQL.

SQL, short for Structured Query Language, is a group of special words used exclusively for interacting with databases. Every major database uses SQL, and MySQL is no exception. There are multiple versions of SQL and MySQL has its own variations on the SQL standards, but SQL is still surprisingly easy to learn and use. In fact, the hardest thing to do in SQL is use it to its full potential!

In this chapter you'll learn all the SQL you need to know to create tables, populate them, and run other basic queries. The examples will all use the *users* table discussed in the preceding chapter. Also, as with that other chapter, this chapter assumes you have access to a running MySQL server and know how to use a client application to interact with it.

Creating Databases and Tables

The first logical use of SQL will be to create a database. The syntax for creating a new database is simply

```
CREATE DATABASE databasename
```

That's all there is to it (as I said, SQL is easy to learn)!

The CREATE term is also used for making tables:

```
CREATE TABLE tablename (

column1name description,

column2name description

...)
```

As you can see from this syntax, after naming the table, you define each column within parentheses. Each column-description pair should be separated from the next by a comma. Should you choose to create indexes at this time, you can add those at the end of the creation statement, but you can add indexes at a later time as well. (Indexes are more formally discussed in Chapter 6, "Advanced SQL and MySQL," but Chapter 4, "Introduction to MySQL," introduced the topic.)

In case you were wondering, SQL is case-insensitive. However, I strongly recommend making it a habit to capitalize the SQL keywords as in the preceding example syntax and the following steps. Doing so helps to contrast the SQL terms from the database, table, and column names.

To create databases and tables:

1. Access MySQL using whichever client you prefer.

   Chapter 4 shows how to use two of the most common interfaces—the mysql client and phpMyAdmin—to communicate with a MySQL server. Using the steps in the last chapter, you should now connect to MySQL.

   Throughout the rest of this chapter, most of the SQL examples will be entered using the mysql client, but they will work just the same in phpMyAdmin or any other client tool.

2. Create and select the new database (**Figure 5.1**).

   ```
   CREATE DATABASE sitename;

   USE sitename;
   ```

   This first line creates the database (assuming that you are connected to MySQL as a user with permission to create new databases). The second line tells MySQL that you want to work within this database from here on out. Remember that within the mysql client, you must terminate every SQL command with a semicolon, although these semicolons aren't technically part of SQL itself. If executing multiple queries at once within phpMyAdmin, they should also be separated by semicolons (**Figure 5.2**). If running only a single query within phpMyAdmin, no semicolons are necessary.

   If you are using a hosting company's MySQL, they will probably create the database for you. In that case, just connect to MySQL and select the database.

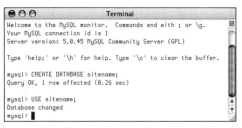

Figure 5.1 A new database, called *sitename*, is created in MySQL. It is then selected for future queries.

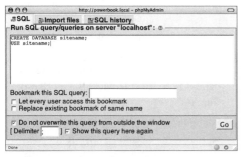

Figure 5.2 The same commands for creating and selecting a database can be run within phpMyAdmin's SQL window.

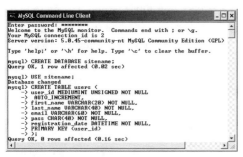

Figure 5.3 This CREATE SQL command will make the *users* table.

3. Create the *users* table (**Figure 5.3**).

```
CREATE TABLE users (
user_id MEDIUMINT UNSIGNED NOT NULL
AUTO_INCREMENT,
first_name VARCHAR(20) NOT NULL,
last_name VARCHAR(40) NOT NULL,
email VARCHAR(60) NOT NULL,
pass CHAR(40) NOT NULL,
registration_date DATETIME NOT NULL,
PRIMARY KEY (user_id)
);
```

The design for the *users* table is developed in Chapter 4. There, the names, types, and attributes of each column in the table are determined based upon a number of criteria (see that chapter for more information). Here, that information is placed within the CREATE table syntax to actually make the table in the database.

Because the mysql client will not run a query until it encounters a semicolon, you can enter statements over multiple lines as in Figure 5.3 (by pressing Return or Enter at the end of each line). This often makes a query easier to read and debug. In phpMyAdmin, you can also run queries over multiple lines, although they will not be run until you click Go.

continues on next page

4. Confirm the existence of the table (**Figure 5.4**).

```
SHOW TABLES;
```

```
SHOW COLUMNS FROM users;
```

The SHOW command reveals the tables in a database or the column names and types in a table.

Also, you might notice in Figure 5.4 that the default value for *user_id* is NULL, even though this column was defined as NOT NULL. This is actually correct and has to do with *user_id* being an automatically incremented primary key. MySQL will often make minor changes to a column's definition for better performance or other reasons.

In phpMyAdmin, a database's tables are listed on the left side of the browser window, under the database's name (**Figure 5.5**). Click a table's name to view its columns (**Figure 5.6**).

✔ Tips

■ The rest of this chapter assumes that you are using the mysql client or comparable tool and have already selected the *sitename* database with USE.

■ The order you list the columns when creating a table has no functional impact, but there are stylistic suggestions for how to order them. I normally list the primary-key column first, followed by any foreign-key columns (more on this subject in the next chapter), followed by the rest of the columns, concluding with any date columns.

■ When creating a table, you have the option of specifying its type. MySQL supports many table types, each with its own strengths and weaknesses. If you do not specify a table type, MySQL will automatically create the table using the default type for that MySQL installation. Chapter 6 discusses this in more detail.

■ When creating tables and text columns, you have the option to specify its *collation* and *character set*. Both come into play when using multiple languages or languages not native to the MySQL server. Chapter 14, "Making Universal Sites," covers these subjects.

■ DESCRIBE *tablename* is the same statement as SHOW COLUMNS FROM *tablename*.

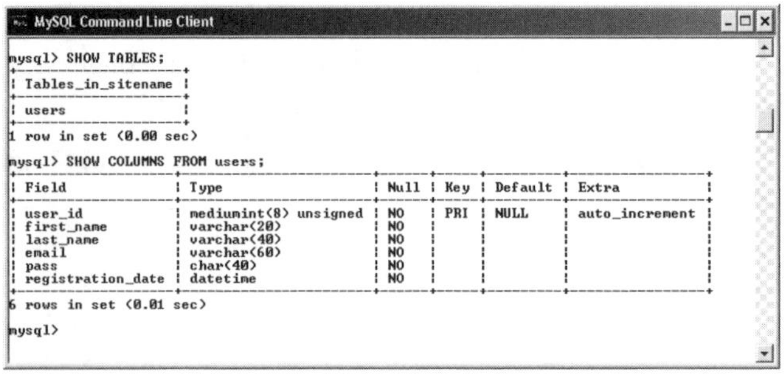

Figure 5.4 Confirm the existence of, and columns in, a table using the SHOW command.

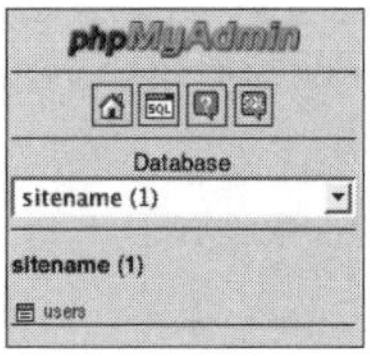

Figure 5.5 phpMyAdmin shows that the *sitename* database contains one table, named *users*.

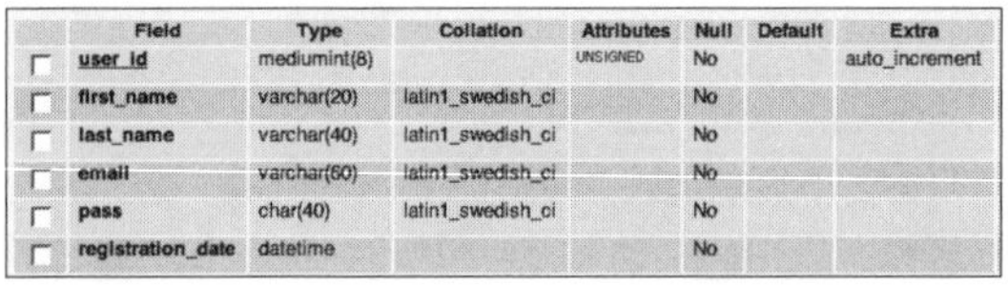

Figure 5.6 phpMyAdmin shows a table's definition on this screen (accessed by clicking the table's name in the left-hand column).

Inserting Records

After a database and its table(s) have been created, you can start populating them using the INSERT command. There are two ways that an INSERT query can be written. With the first method, you name the columns to be populated:

```
INSERT INTO tablename (column1, column2
→ …) VALUES (value1, value2 …)
```

```
INSERT INTO tablename (column4, column8)
→ VALUES (valueX, valueY)
```

Using this structure, you can add rows of records, populating only the columns that matter. The result will be that any columns not given a value will be treated as NULL (or given a default value, if one was defined). Note that if a column cannot have a NULL value (it was defined as NOT NULL) and does not have a default value, not specifying a value will cause an error.

The second format for inserting records is not to specify any columns at all but to include values for every one:

```
INSERT INTO tablename VALUES (value1,
→ NULL, value2, value3, …)
```

If you use this second method, you must specify a value, even if it's NULL, for every column. If there are six columns in the table, you must list six values. Failure to match the number of values to the number of columns will cause an error. For this and other reasons, the first format of inserting records is generally preferable.

continues on next page

Quotes in Queries

In every SQL command:

- Numeric values shouldn't be quoted.

- String values (for CHAR, VARCHAR, and TEXT column types) must always be quoted.

- Date and time values must always be quoted.

- Functions cannot be quoted.

- The word NULL must not be quoted.

Unnecessarily quoting a numeric value normally won't cause problems (although you still shouldn't do it), but misusing quotation marks in the other situations will almost always mess things up. Also, it does not matter if you use single or double quotation marks, so long as you consistently pair them (an opening mark with a matching closing one).

And, as with PHP, if you need to use a quotation mark in a value, either use the other quotation mark type to encapsulate it or escape the mark by preceding it with a backslash:

```
INSERT INTO tablename (last_name)
→ VALUES ('O\'Toole')
```

MySQL also allows you to insert multiple rows at one time, separating each record by a comma.

INSERT INTO *tablename* (*column1, column4*)
→ VALUES (*valueA, valueB*),

(*valueC, valueD*),

(*valueE, valueF*)

While you can do this with MySQL, it is not acceptable within the SQL standard and is therefore not supported by all database applications.

Note that in all of these examples, placeholders are used for the actual table names, column names, and values. Furthermore, the examples forgo quotation marks. In real queries, you must abide by certain rules to avoid errors (see the "Quotes in Queries" sidebar).

To insert data into a table:

1. Insert one row of data into the *users* table, naming the columns to be populated (**Figure 5.7**).

   INSERT INTO users

   (first_name, last_name, email, pass,
   → registration_date)

   VALUES ('Larry', 'Ullman',
   → 'email@example.com',
   → SHA1('mypass'), NOW());

   Again, this syntax (where the specific columns are named) is more foolproof but not always the most convenient. For the first name, last name, and email columns, simple strings are used for the values (and strings must always be quoted).

   For the password and registration date columns, two functions are being used to generate the values (see the sidebar "Two MySQL Functions"). The SHA1() function will encrypt the password (*mypass* in this example). The NOW() function will set the *registration_date* as this moment.

When using any function in an SQL statement, do not place it within quotation marks. You also must not have any spaces between the function's name and the following parenthesis (so NOW() not NOW ()).

2. Insert one row of data into the *users* table, without naming the columns (**Figure 5.8**).

   INSERT INTO users VALUES

   (NULL, 'Zoe', 'Isabella',
   → 'email2@example.com',
   → SHA1('mojito'), NOW());

   In this second syntactical example, every column must be provided with a value. The *user_id* column is given a NULL value, which will cause MySQL to use the next logical number, per its AUTO_INCREMENT description. In other words, the first record will be assigned a *user_id* of 1, the second, 2, and so on.

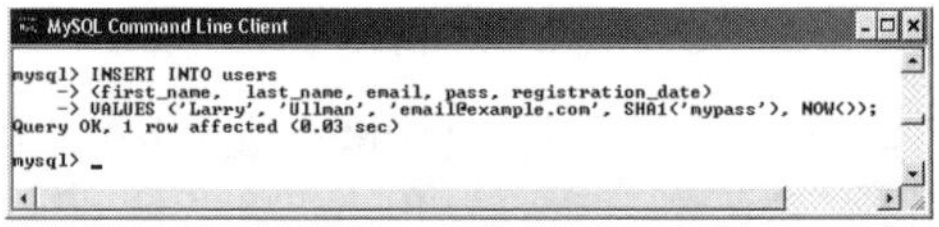

Figure 5.7 This query inserts a single record into the *users* table. The *1 row affected* message indicates the success of the insertion.

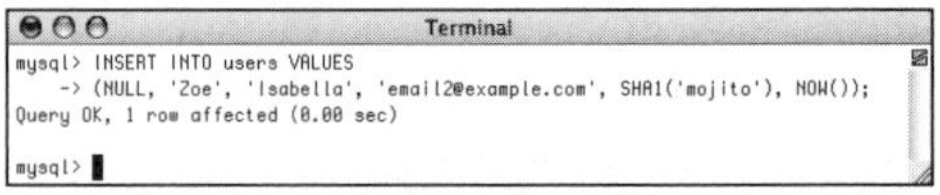

Figure 5.8 Another record is inserted into the table, this time by providing a value for every column in the table.

3. Insert several values into the *users* table (**Figure 5.9**).

```
INSERT INTO users (first_name,
→ last_name, email, pass,
→ registration_date) VALUES
('John', 'Lennon',
→ 'john@beatles.com',
→ SHA1('Happin3ss'), NOW()),
('Paul', 'McCartney',
→ 'paul@beatles.com',
→ SHA1('letITbe'), NOW()),
('George', 'Harrison',
→ 'george@beatles.com',
→ SHA1('something'), NOW()),
('Ringo', 'Starr',
→ 'ringo@beatles.com',
→ SHA1('thisboy'), NOW());
```

Since MySQL allows you to insert multiple values at once, you can take advantage of this and fill up the table with records.

continues on next page

Figure 5.9 This one query—which MySQL allows but other databases will not—inserts several records into the table at once.

Two MySQL Functions

Although functions are discussed in more detail later in this chapter, two need to be introduced at this time: SHA1() and NOW().

The SHA1() function is one way to encrypt data. This function creates an encrypted string that is always exactly 40 characters long (which is why the *users* table's *pass* column is defined as CHAR(40)). SHA1() is a one-way encryption technique, meaning that it cannot be reversed. It's useful for storing sensitive data that need not be viewed in an unencrypted form again, but it's obviously not a good choice for sensitive data that should be protected but later seen (like credit card numbers). SHA1() is available as of MySQL 5.0.2; if you are using an earlier version, you can use the MD5() function instead. This function does the same task, using a different algorithm, and returns a 32-character long string (if using MD5(), your *pass* column could be defined as a CHAR(32) instead).

The NOW() function is handy for date, time, and timestamp columns, since it will insert the current date and time (on the server) for that field.

4. Continue Steps 1 and 2 until you've thoroughly populated the *users* table.

Throughout the rest of this chapter I will be performing queries based upon the records I entered into my database. Should your database not have the same specific records as mine, change the particulars accordingly. The fundamental thinking behind the following queries should still apply regardless of the data, since the *sitename* database has a set column and table structure.

✔ Tips

■ On the downloads page of the book's supporting Web site (www.DMCInsights. com/phpmysql3/), you can download all of the SQL commands for the book. Using some of these commands, you can populate your *users* table exactly as I have.

■ The term INTO in INSERT statements is optional in current versions of MySQL.

■ phpMyAdmin's INSERT tab allows you to insert records using an HTML form (**Figure 5.10**).

Field	Type	Function	Null	Value
user_id	mediumint(8) unsigned	▾		
first_name	varchar(20)	▾		Larry
last_name	varchar(40)	▾		Ullman
email	varchar(60)	▾		email@example.com
pass	char(40)	SHA1 ▾		mypass
registration_date	datetime	NOW ▾		

Go

Figure 5.10 phpMyAdmin's INSERT form shows a table's columns and provides text boxes for entering values. The pull-down menu lists functions that can be used, like SHA1() for the password or NOW() for the registration date.

INSERTING RECORDS

Selecting Data

Now that the database has some records in it, you can retrieve the stored information with the most used of all SQL terms, `SELECT`. A `SELECT` query returns rows of records using the syntax

`SELECT which_columns FROM which_table`

The simplest `SELECT` query is

`SELECT * FROM tablename`

The asterisk means that you want to view every column. The alternative would be to specify the columns to be returned, with each separated from the next by a comma:

`SELECT column1, column3 FROM tablename`

There are a few benefits to being explicit about which columns are selected. The first is performance: There's no reason to fetch columns you will not be using. The second is order: You can return columns in an order other than their layout in the table. Third—and you'll see this later in the chapter—naming the columns allows you to manipulate the values in those columns using functions.

To select data from a table:

1. Retrieve all the data from the *users* table (**Figure 5.11**).

   `SELECT * FROM users;`

   This very basic SQL command will retrieve every column of every row stored within that table.

continues on next page

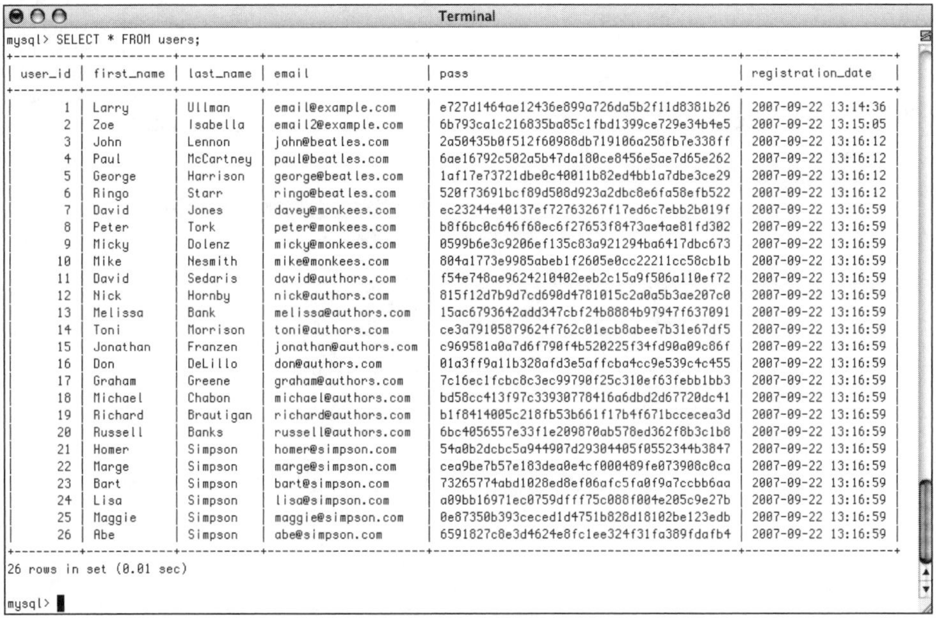

```
mysql> SELECT * FROM users;
+---------+------------+-----------+----------------------+------------------------------------------+---------------------+
| user_id | first_name | last_name | email                | pass                                     | registration_date   |
+---------+------------+-----------+----------------------+------------------------------------------+---------------------+
|       1 | Larry      | Ullman    | email@example.com    | e727d1464ae12436e899a726da5b2f11d8381b26 | 2007-09-22 13:14:36 |
|       2 | Zoe        | Isabella  | email2@example.com   | 6b793ca1c216835ba85c1fbd1399ce729e34b4e5 | 2007-09-22 13:15:05 |
|       3 | John       | Lennon    | john@beatles.com     | 2a50435b0f512f60988db719106a258fb7e338ff | 2007-09-22 13:16:12 |
|       4 | Paul       | McCartney | paul@beatles.com     | 6ae16792c502a5b47da180ce8456e5ae7d65e262 | 2007-09-22 13:16:12 |
|       5 | George     | Harrison  | george@beatles.com   | 1af17e73721dbe0c40011b82ed4bb1a7dbe3ce29 | 2007-09-22 13:16:12 |
|       6 | Ringo      | Starr     | ringo@beatles.com    | 520f73691bcf89d508d923a2dbc8e6fa58efb522 | 2007-09-22 13:16:12 |
|       7 | David      | Jones     | davey@monkees.com    | ec23244e40137ef72763267f17ed6c7ebb2b019f | 2007-09-22 13:16:59 |
|       8 | Peter      | Tork      | peter@monkees.com    | b8f6bc0c646f68ec6f27653f8473ae4ae81fd302 | 2007-09-22 13:16:59 |
|       9 | Micky      | Dolenz    | micky@monkees.com    | 0599b6e3c9206ef135c83a921294ba6417dbc673 | 2007-09-22 13:16:59 |
|      10 | Mike       | Nesmith   | mike@monkees.com     | 804a1773e9985abeb1f2605e0cc22211cc58cb1b | 2007-09-22 13:16:59 |
|      11 | David      | Sedaris   | david@authors.com    | f54e748ae9624210402eeb2c15a9f506a110ef72 | 2007-09-22 13:16:59 |
|      12 | Nick       | Hornby    | nick@authors.com     | 815f12d7b9d7cd690d4781015c2a0a5b3ae207c0 | 2007-09-22 13:16:59 |
|      13 | Melissa    | Bank      | melissa@authors.com  | 15ac6793642add347cbf24b8884b97947f637091 | 2007-09-22 13:16:59 |
|      14 | Toni       | Morrison  | toni@authors.com     | ce3a79105879624f762c01ecb8abee7b31e67df5 | 2007-09-22 13:16:59 |
|      15 | Jonathan   | Franzen   | jonathan@authors.com | c969581a0a7d6f790f4b520225f34fd90a09c86f | 2007-09-22 13:16:59 |
|      16 | Don        | DeLillo   | don@authors.com      | 01a3ff9a11b328afd3e5affcba4cc9e539c4c455 | 2007-09-22 13:16:59 |
|      17 | Graham     | Greene    | graham@authors.com   | 7c16ec1fcbc8c3ec99790f25c310ef63febb1bb3 | 2007-09-22 13:16:59 |
|      18 | Michael    | Chabon    | michael@authors.com  | bd58cc413f97c33930778416a6dbd2d67720dc41 | 2007-09-22 13:16:59 |
|      19 | Richard    | Brautigan | richard@authors.com  | b1f8414005c218fb53b661f17b4f671bccecea3d | 2007-09-22 13:16:59 |
|      20 | Russell    | Banks     | russell@authors.com  | 6bc4056557e33f1e209870ab578ed362f8b3c1b8 | 2007-09-22 13:16:59 |
|      21 | Homer      | Simpson   | homer@simpson.com    | 54a0b2dcbc5a944907d29304405f0552344b3847 | 2007-09-22 13:16:59 |
|      22 | Marge      | Simpson   | marge@simpson.com    | cea9be7b57e183dea0e4cf000489fe073908c0ca | 2007-09-22 13:16:59 |
|      23 | Bart       | Simpson   | bart@simpson.com     | 73265774abd1028ed8ef06afc5fa0f9a7ccbb6aa | 2007-09-22 13:16:59 |
|      24 | Lisa       | Simpson   | lisa@simpson.com     | a09bb16971ec0759dfff75c088f004e205c9e27b | 2007-09-22 13:16:59 |
|      25 | Maggie     | Simpson   | maggie@simpson.com   | 0e87350b393ceced1d4751b828d18102be123edb | 2007-09-22 13:16:59 |
|      26 | Abe        | Simpson   | abe@simpson.com      | 6591827c8e3d4624e8fc1ee324f31fa389fdafb4 | 2007-09-22 13:16:59 |
+---------+------------+-----------+----------------------+------------------------------------------+---------------------+
26 rows in set (0.01 sec)

mysql>
```

Figure 5.11 The `SELECT * FROM tablename` query returns every column for every record stored in the table.

2. Retrieve just the first and last names from *users* (**Figure 5.12**).

```
SELECT first_name, last_name
FROM users;
```

Instead of showing the data from every column in the *users* table, you can use the SELECT statement to limit the results to only the fields you need.

✔ Tips

- In phpMyAdmin, the Browse tab runs a simple SELECT query.

- You can actually use SELECT without naming tables or columns. For example, SELECT NOW(); (**Figure 5.13**).

- The order in which you list columns in your SELECT statement dictates the order in which the values are presented (compare Figure 5.12 with **Figure 5.14**).

- With SELECT queries, you can even retrieve the same column multiple times, a feature that enables you to manipulate the column's data in many different ways.

Figure 5.12 Only two of the columns for every record in the table are returned by this query.

Figure 5.13 Many queries can be run without specifying a database or table. This query selects the result of calling the NOW() function, which returns the current date and time (according to MySQL).

Figure 5.14 If a SELECT query specifies the columns to be returned, they'll be displayed in that order.

Table 5.1 These MySQL operators are frequently (but not exclusively) used with WHERE expressions.

MySQL Operators

OPERATOR	MEANING
=	Equals
<	Less than
>	Greater than
<=	Less than or equal to
>=	Greater than or equal to
!= (also < >)	Not equal to
IS NOT NULL	Has a value
IS NULL	Does not have a value
BETWEEN	Within a range
NOT BETWEEN	Outside of a range
IN	Found within a list of values
OR (also ||)	Where one of two conditionals is true
AND (also &&)	Where both conditionals are true
NOT (also !)	Where the condition is not true

Using Conditionals

The SELECT query as used thus far will always retrieve every record from a table. But often you'll want to limit what rows are returned, based upon certain criteria. This can be accomplished by adding conditionals to SELECT queries. These conditionals use the SQL term WHERE and are written much as you'd write a conditional in PHP.

```
SELECT which_columns FROM which_table
→ WHERE condition(s)
```

Table 5.1 lists the most common operators you would use within a conditional. For example, a simple equality check:

```
SELECT name FROM people WHERE
birth_date = '2008-01-26'
```

The operators can be used together, along with parentheses, to create more complex expressions:

```
SELECT * FROM items WHERE
(price BETWEEN 10.00 AND 20.00) AND
(quantity > 0)
SELECT * FROM cities WHERE
(zip_code = 90210) OR (zip_code = 90211)
```

To demonstrate using conditionals, let's run some more SELECT queries on the *sitename* database. The examples that follow will be just a few of the nearly limitless possibilities. Over the course of this chapter and the entire book you will see how conditionals are used in all types of queries.

To use conditionals:

1. Select all of the users whose last name is *Simpson* (**Figure 5.15**).

   ```
   SELECT * FROM users
   WHERE last_name = 'Simpson';
   ```

   This simple query returns every column of every row whose *last_name* value is *Simpson*.

2. Select just the first names of users whose last name is *Simpson* (**Figure 5.16**).

   ```
   SELECT first_name FROM users
   WHERE last_name = 'Simpson';
   ```

   Here only one column (*first_name*) is being returned for each row. Although it may seem strange, you do not have to select a column on which you are performing

a WHERE. The reason for this is that the columns listed after SELECT dictate only what columns to return and the columns listed in a WHERE dictate which rows to return.

3. Select every column from every record in the *users* table that does not have an email address (**Figure 5.17**).

   ```
   SELECT * FROM users
   WHERE email IS NULL;
   ```

   The IS NULL conditional is the same as saying *does not have a value*. Keep in mind that an empty string is different than NULL and therefore would not match this condition. Such a case would, however, match

   ```
   SELECT * FROM users WHERE email='';
   ```

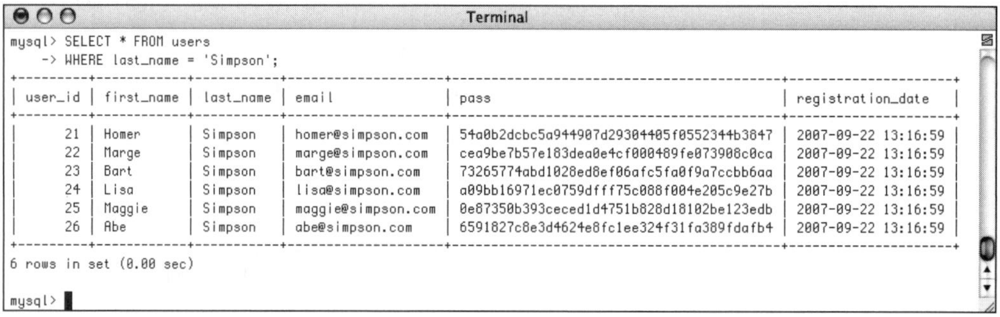

Figure 5.15 All of the Simpsons who have registered.

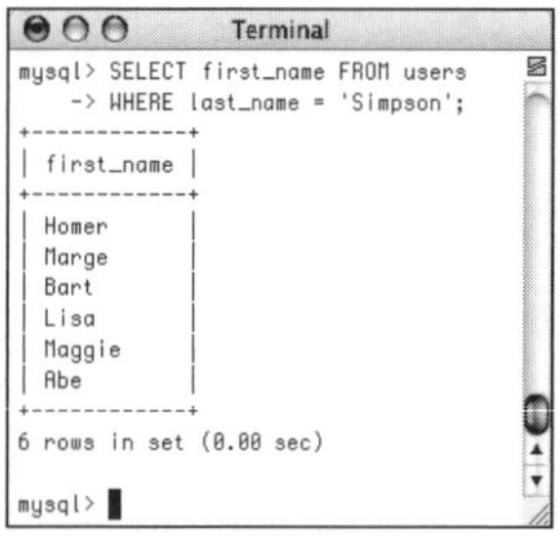

Figure 5.16 Just the first names of all of the Simpsons who have registered.

Figure 5.17 No records are returned by this query because the email column cannot have a NULL value. So this query did work; it just had no matching records.

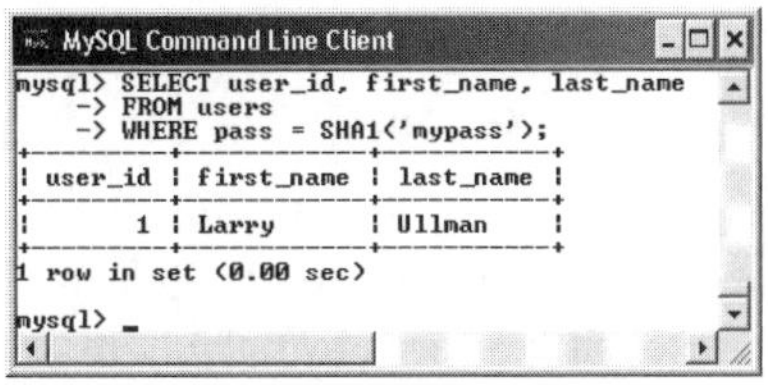

Figure 5.18 Conditionals can make use of functions, like SHA1() here.

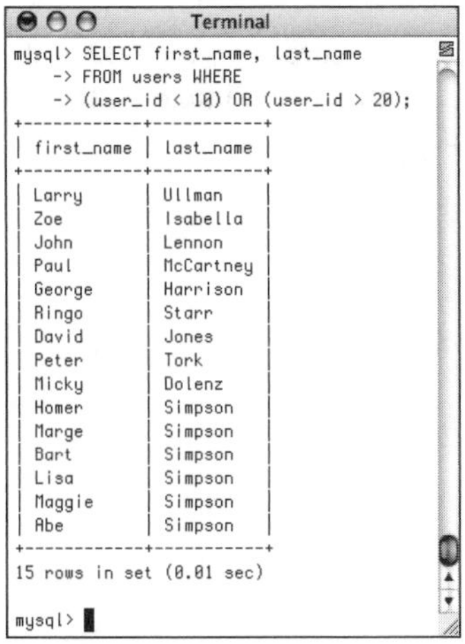

Figure 5.19 This query uses two conditions and the OR operator.

4. Select the user ID, first name, and last name of all records in which the password is *mypass* (**Figure 5.18**).

```
SELECT user_id, first_name, last_name
FROM users
WHERE pass = SHA1('mypass');
```

Since the stored passwords were encrypted with the SHA1() function, you can match it by using that same encryption function in a conditional. SHA1() is case-sensitive, so this query will work only if the passwords (stored vs. queried) match exactly.

5. Select the user names whose user ID is less than 10 or greater than 20 (**Figure 5.19**).

```
SELECT first_name, last_name
FROM users WHERE
(user_id < 10) OR (user_id > 20);
```

This same query could also be written as

```
SELECT first_name, last_name FROM
users WHERE user_id
NOT BETWEEN 10 and 20;
```

or even

```
SELECT first_name, last_name FROM
users WHERE user_id NOT IN
(10, 11, 12, 13, 14, 15, 16, 17, 18,
→ 19, 20);
```

✔ Tip

■ You can perform mathematical calculations within your queries using the mathematic addition (+), subtraction (-), multiplication (*), and division (/) characters.

USING CONDITIONALS

Using LIKE and NOT LIKE

Using numbers, dates, and NULLs in conditionals is a straightforward process, but strings can be trickier. You can check for string equality with a query such as

```
SELECT * FROM users
WHERE last_name = 'Simpson'
```

However, comparing strings in a more liberal manner requires extra operators and characters. If, for example, you wanted to match a person's last name that could be *Smith* or *Smiths* or *Smithson*, you would need a more flexible conditional. This is where the LIKE and NOT LIKE terms come in. These are used—primarily with strings—in conjunction with two wildcard characters: the underscore (_), which matches a single character, and the percentage sign (%), which matches zero or more characters. In the last-name example, the query would be

```
SELECT * FROM users
WHERE last_name LIKE 'Smith%'
```

This query will return all rows whose *last_name* value begins with *Smith*. Because it's a case-insensitive search by default, it would also apply to names that begin with *smith*.

To use LIKE:

1. Select all of the records in which the last name starts with *Bank* (**Figure 5.20**).

    ```
    SELECT * FROM users
    WHERE last_name LIKE 'Bank%';
    ```

```
mysql> SELECT * FROM users
    -> WHERE last_name LIKE 'Bank%';
+---------+------------+-----------+---------------------+------------------------------------------+---------------------+
| user_id | first_name | last_name | email               | pass                                     | registration_date   |
+---------+------------+-----------+---------------------+------------------------------------------+---------------------+
|      13 | Melissa    | Bank      | melissa@authors.com | 15ac6793642add347cbf24b8884b97947f637091 | 2007-09-22 13:16:59 |
|      20 | Russell    | Banks     | russell@authors.com | 6bc4056557e33f1e209870ab578ed362f8b3c1b8 | 2007-09-22 13:16:59 |
+---------+------------+-----------+---------------------+------------------------------------------+---------------------+
2 rows in set (0.00 sec)

mysql>
```

Figure 5.20 The LIKE SQL term adds flexibility to your conditionals. This query matches any record where the last name value begins with *Bank*.

Figure 5.21 A NOT LIKE conditional returns records based upon what a value does not contain.

2. Select the name for every record whose email address is not of the form *something@authors.com* (**Figure 5.21**).

SELECT first_name, last_name

FROM users WHERE

email NOT LIKE '%@authors.com';

To rule out the presence of values in a string, use NOT LIKE with the wildcard.

✔ Tips

- Queries with a LIKE conditional are generally slower because they can't take advantage of indexes, so use this format only if you absolutely have to.

- The wildcard characters can be used at the front and/or back of a string in your queries.

  SELECT * FROM users

  WHERE user_name LIKE '_smith%'

- Although LIKE and NOT LIKE are normally used with strings, they can also be applied to numeric columns.

- To use either the literal underscore or the percentage sign in a LIKE or NOT LIKE query, you will need to escape it (by preceding the character with a backslash) so that it is not confused with a wildcard.

- The underscore can be used in combination with itself; as an example, LIKE '__' would find any two-letter combination.

- In the next chapter you'll learn about FULLTEXT searches, which can be better than LIKE searches.

Sorting Query Results

By default, a SELECT query's results will be returned in a meaningless order. To sort them in a meaningful way, use an ORDER BY clause.

SELECT * FROM *tablename* ORDER BY *column*

SELECT * FROM orders ORDER BY total

The default order when using ORDER BY is ascending (abbreviated ASC), meaning that numbers increase from small to large, dates go from older to most recent, and text is sorted alphabetically. You can reverse this by specifying a descending order (abbreviated DESC).

SELECT * FROM *tablename*

ORDER BY *column* DESC

You can even order the returned values by multiple columns:

SELECT * FROM tablename

ORDER BY column1, column2

You can, and frequently will, use ORDER BY with WHERE or other clauses. When doing so, place the ORDER BY after the conditions:

SELECT * FROM *tablename* WHERE *conditions*

ORDER BY *column*

To sort data:

1. Select all of the users in alphabetical order by last name (**Figure 5.22**).

   SELECT first_name, last_name FROM

   users ORDER BY last_name;

   If you compare these results with those in Figure 5.12, you'll see the benefits of using ORDER BY.

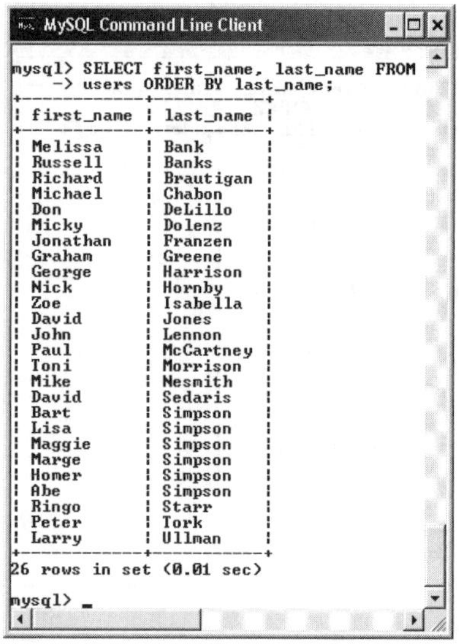

Figure 5.22 The records in alphabetical order by last name.

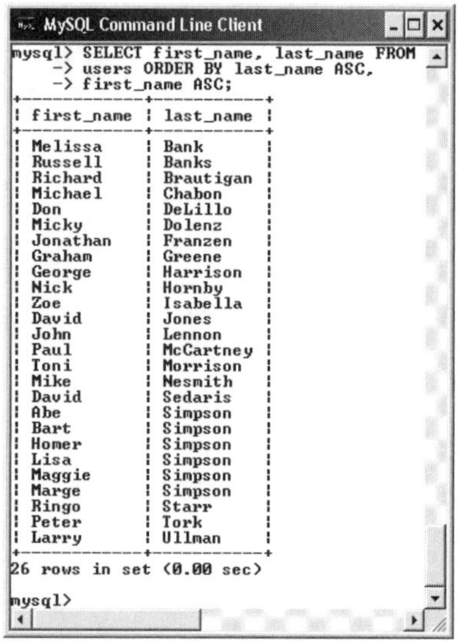

Figure 5.23 The records in alphabetical order, first by last name, and then by first name within that.

2. Display all of the users in alphabetical order by last name and then first name (**Figure 5.23**).

```
SELECT first_name, last_name FROM
users ORDER BY last_name ASC,
first_name ASC;
```

In this query, the effect would be that every row is returned, first ordered by the *last_name*, and then by *first_name* within the *last_name*s. The effect is most evident among the Simpsons.

3. Show all of the non-Simpson users by date registered (**Figure 5.24**).

```
SELECT * FROM users
WHERE last_name != 'Simpson'
ORDER BY registration_date DESC;
```

You can use an ORDER BY on any column type, including numbers and dates. The clause can also be used in a query with a conditional, placing the ORDER BY after the WHERE.

✔ Tips

- Because MySQL works naturally with any number of languages, the ORDER BY will be based upon the collation being used (see Chapter 14).

- If the column that you choose to sort on contains NULL values, those will appear first, both in ascending and descending order.

```
⊙⊙⊙                              Terminal
mysql> SELECT * FROM users
    -> WHERE last_name != 'Simpson'
    -> ORDER BY registration_date DESC;
+---------+------------+------------+--------------------+----------------------------------+---------------------+
| user_id | first_name | last_name  | email              | pass                             | registration_date   |
+---------+------------+------------+--------------------+----------------------------------+---------------------+
|      20 | Russell    | Banks      | russell@authors.com| 6bc4056557e33f1e209870ab578ed362f8b3c1b8 | 2007-09-22 13:16:59 |
|      12 | Nick       | Hornby     | nick@authors.com   | 815f12d7b9d7cd690d4781015c2a0a5b3ae207c0 | 2007-09-22 13:16:59 |
|      13 | Melissa    | Bank       | melissa@authors.com| 15ac6793642add347cbf24b8884b97947f637091 | 2007-09-22 13:16:59 |
|      14 | Toni       | Morrison   | toni@authors.com   | ce3a79105879624f762c01ecb8abee7b31e67df5 | 2007-09-22 13:16:59 |
|      15 | Jonathan   | Franzen    | jonathan@authors.com | c969581a0a7d6f790f4b520225f34fd90a09c86f | 2007-09-22 13:16:59 |
|      16 | Don        | DeLillo    | don@authors.com    | 01a3ff9a11b328afd3e5affcba4cc9e539c4c455 | 2007-09-22 13:16:59 |
|      17 | Graham     | Greene     | graham@authors.com | 7c16ec1fcbc8c3ec99790f25c310ef63febb1bb3 | 2007-09-22 13:16:59 |
|      18 | Michael    | Chabon     | michael@authors.com| bd58cc413f97c33930778416a6dbd2d67720dc41 | 2007-09-22 13:16:59 |
|      19 | Richard    | Brautigan  | richard@authors.com| b1f8414005c218fb53b661f17b4f671bccecea3d | 2007-09-22 13:16:59 |
|      11 | David      | Sedaris    | david@authors.com  | f54e748ae9624210402eeb2c15a9f506a110ef72 | 2007-09-22 13:16:59 |
|      10 | Mike       | Nesmith    | mike@monkees.com   | 804a1773e9985abeb1f2605e0cc22211cc58cb1b | 2007-09-22 13:16:59 |
|       9 | Micky      | Dolenz     | micky@monkees.com  | 0599b6a3c9206ef135c83a921294ba6417dbc673 | 2007-09-22 13:16:59 |
|       8 | Peter      | Tork       | peter@monkees.com  | b8f6bc0c646f68ec6f27653f8473ae4ae81fd302 | 2007-09-22 13:16:59 |
|       7 | David      | Jones      | davey@monkees.com  | ec23244e0137ef72763267f17ed6c7ebb2b019f | 2007-09-22 13:16:59 |
|       3 | John       | Lennon     | john@beatles.com   | 2a50435b0f512f60988db719106a258fb7e338ff | 2007-09-22 13:16:12 |
|       4 | Paul       | McCartney  | paul@beatles.com   | 6ae16792c502a5b47da180ce8456e5ae7d65e262 | 2007-09-22 13:16:12 |
|       5 | George     | Harrison   | george@beatles.com | 1af17e73721dbe0c40011b82ed4bb1a7dbe3ce29 | 2007-09-22 13:16:12 |
|       6 | Ringo      | Starr      | ringo@beatles.com  | 520f73691bcf89d508d923a2dbc8e6fa58efb522 | 2007-09-22 13:16:12 |
|       2 | Zoe        | Isabella   | email2@example.com | 6b793ca1c216835ba85c1fbd1399ce729e34b4e5 | 2007-09-22 13:15:05 |
|       1 | Larry      | Ullman     | email@example.com  | e727d1464ae12436e899a726da5b2f11d8381b26 | 2007-09-22 13:14:36 |
+---------+------------+------------+--------------------+----------------------------------+---------------------+
20 rows in set (0.01 sec)

mysql> ▮
```

Figure 5.24 All of the users not named *Simpson*, displayed by date registered, with the most recent listed first.

Limiting Query Results

Another SQL clause that can be added to most queries is LIMIT. In a SELECT query, WHERE dictates which records to return, and ORDER BY decides how those records are sorted, but LIMIT states how many records to return. It is used like so:

SELECT * FROM *tablename* LIMIT *x*

In such queries, only the initial *x* records from the query result will be returned. To return only three matching records, use:

SELECT * FROM *tablename* LIMIT 3

Using this format

SELECT * FROM *tablename* LIMIT *x*, *y*

you can have *y* records returned, starting at *x*. To have records 11 through 20 returned, you would write

SELECT * FROM *tablename* LIMIT 10, 10

Like arrays in PHP, result sets begin at 0 when it comes to LIMITs, so 10 is the 11th record.

You can use LIMIT with WHERE and/or ORDER BY clauses, always placing LIMIT last.

SELECT *which_columns* FROM *tablename* WHERE

conditions ORDER BY *column* LIMIT *x*

To limit the amount of data returned:

1. Select the last five registered users (**Figure 5.25**).

   SELECT first_name, last_name

   FROM users ORDER BY

   registration_date DESC LIMIT 5;

   To return the latest of anything, sort the data by date, in descending order. Then, to see just the most recent five, add LIMIT 5 to the query.

Figure 5.25 Using the LIMIT clause, a query can return a specific number of records.

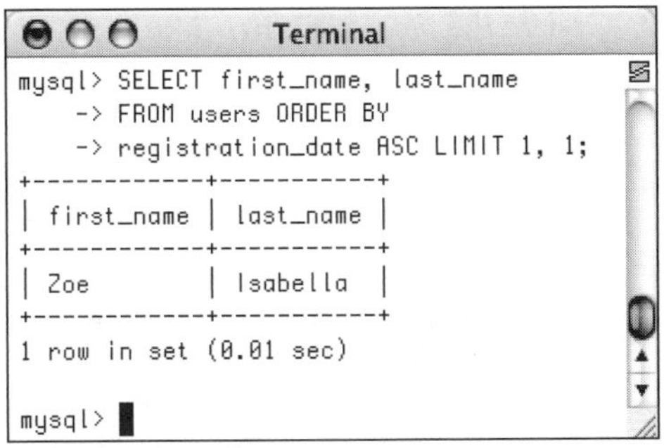

```
●○○          Terminal
mysql> SELECT first_name, last_name
    -> FROM users ORDER BY
    -> registration_date ASC LIMIT 1, 1;
+------------+-----------+
| first_name | last_name |
+------------+-----------+
| Zoe        | Isabella  |
+------------+-----------+
1 row in set (0.01 sec)

mysql> ▊
```

Figure 5.26 Thanks to the LIMIT clause, a query can even return records from the middle of a group, using the LIMIT *x*, *y* format.

2. Select the second person to register (**Figure 5.26**).

    SELECT first_name, last_name

    FROM users ORDER BY

    registration_date ASC LIMIT 1, 1;

    This may look strange, but it's just a good application of the information learned so far. First, order all of the records by *registration_date* ascending, so the first people to register would be returned first. Then, limit the returned results to start at 1 (which is the second row) and to return just one record.

✔ Tips

- The LIMIT *x*, *y* clause is most frequently used when paginating query results (showing them in blocks over multiple pages). You'll see this in Chapter 9, "Common Programming Techniques."

- A LIMIT clause does not improve the execution speed of a query, since MySQL still has to assemble the entire result and then truncate the list. But a LIMIT clause will minimize the amount of data to handle when it comes to the mysql client or your PHP scripts.

- The LIMIT term is not part of the SQL standard and is therefore (sadly) not available on all databases.

- The LIMIT clause can be used with most types of queries, not just SELECTs.

LIMITING QUERY RESULTS

Updating Data

Once tables contain some data, you have the potential need to edit those existing records. This might be necessary if information was entered incorrectly or if the data changes (such as a last name or email address). The syntax for updating records is

UPDATE *tablename* SET *column=value*

You can alter multiple columns at a single time, separating each from the next by a comma.

UPDATE *tablename* SET *column1=valueA,*

column5=valueB…

You will almost always want to use a WHERE clause to specify what rows should be updated; otherwise, the change would be applied to every record.

UPDATE *tablename* SET *column2=value*

WHERE *column5=value*

Updates, along with deletions, are one of the most important reasons to use a primary key. This value—which should never change—can be a reference point in WHERE clauses, even if every other field needs to be altered.

To update a record:

1. Find the primary key for the record to be updated (**Figure 5.27**).

   SELECT user_id FROM users

   WHERE first_name = 'Michael'

   AND last_name='Chabon';

   In this example, I'll change the email for this author's record. To do so, I must first find that record's primary key, which this query accomplishes.

2. Update the record (**Figure 5.28**).

   UPDATE users

   SET email='mike@authors.com'

   WHERE user_id = 18;

   To change the email address, I use an UPDATE query, using the primary key (*user_id*) to specify to which record the update should apply. MySQL will report upon the success of the query and how many rows were affected.

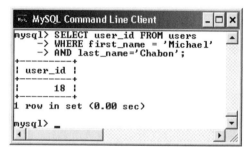

Figure 5.27 Before updating a record, determine which primary key to use in the UPDATE's WHERE clause.

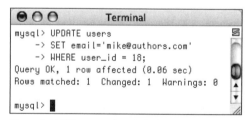

Figure 5.28 This query altered the value of one column in just one row.

3. Confirm that the change was made (**Figure 5.29**).

```
SELECT * FROM users
WHERE user_id=18;
```

Although MySQL already indicated the update was successful (see Figure 5.28), it can't hurt to select the record again to confirm that the proper changes occurred.

✔ Tips

■ Be extra certain to use a WHERE conditional whenever you use UPDATE unless you want the changes to affect every row.

■ If you run an update query that doesn't actually change any values (like UPDATE users SET first_name='mike' WHERE first_name='mike'), you won't see any errors but no rows will be affected. More recent versions of MySQL would show that X rows matched the query but that 0 rows were changed.

■ To protect yourself against accidentally updating too many rows, apply a LIMIT clause to your UPDATEs:

```
UPDATE users SET
email='mike@authors.com'
WHERE user_id = 18 LIMIT 1
```

■ You should never perform an UPDATE on a primary-key column, because this value should never change. Altering the value of a primary key could have serious repercussions.

■ To update a record in phpMyAdmin, you can run an UPDATE query using the SQL window or tab. Alternatively, run a SELECT query to find the record you want to update, and then click the pencil next to the record (**Figure 5.30**). This will bring up a form similar to Figure 5.10, where you can edit the record's current values.

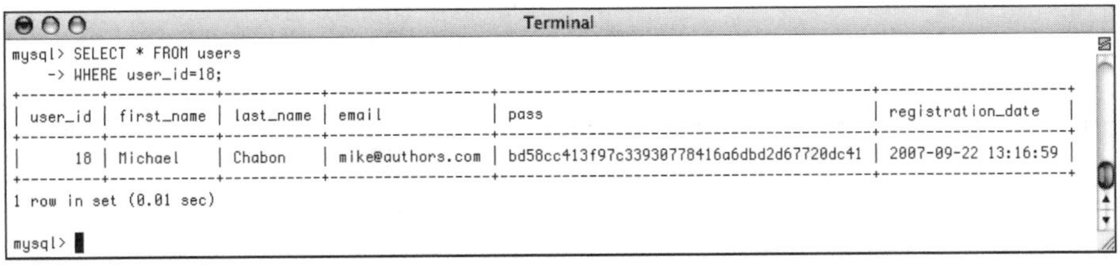

Figure 5.29 As a final step, you can confirm the update by selecting the record again.

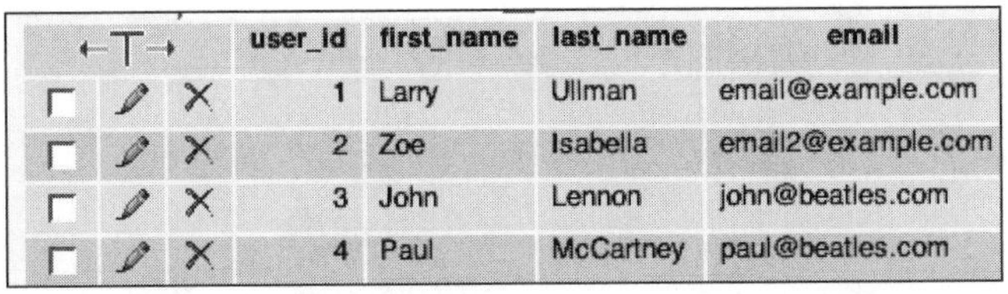

←⊤→	user_id	first_name	last_name	email
□ ✏ ✕	1	Larry	Ullman	email@example.com
□ ✏ ✕	2	Zoe	Isabella	email2@example.com
□ ✏ ✕	3	John	Lennon	john@beatles.com
□ ✏ ✕	4	Paul	McCartney	paul@beatles.com

Figure 5.30 A partial view of browsing records in phpMyAdmin. Click the pencil to edit a record; click the X to delete it.

UPDATING DATA

Deleting Data

Along with updating existing records, another step you might need to take is to entirely remove a record from the database. To do this, you use the DELETE command.

DELETE FROM *tablename*

That command as written will delete every record in a table, making it empty again. Once you have deleted a record, there is no way of retrieving it.

In most cases you'll want to delete individual rows, not all of them. To do so, use a WHERE clause

DELETE FROM *tablename* WHERE *condition*

To delete a record:

1. Find the primary key for the record to be deleted (**Figure 5.31**).

   SELECT user_id FROM users

   WHERE first_name='Peter'

   AND last_name='Tork';

   Just as in the UPDATE example, I first need to determine which primary key to use for the delete.

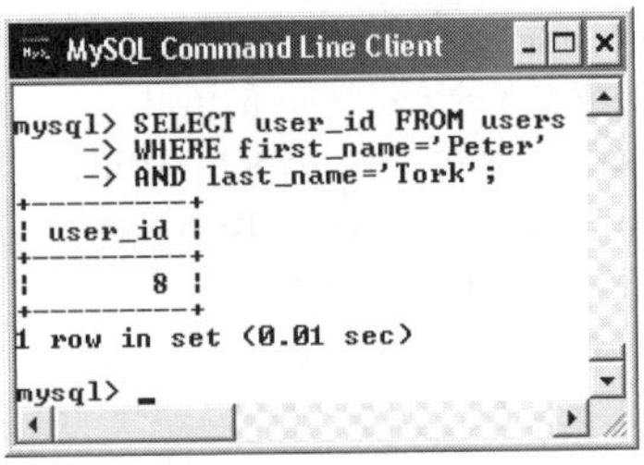

Figure 5.31 The *user_id* will be used to refer to this record in a DELETE query.

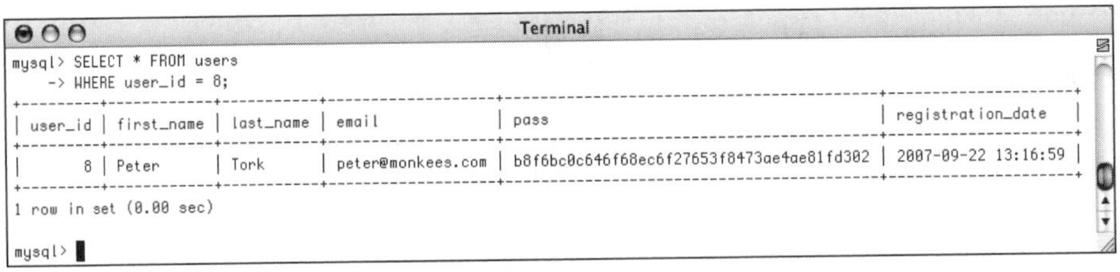

Figure 5.32 To preview the effect of a DELETE query, first run a syntactically similar SELECT query.

2. Preview what will happen when the delete is made (**Figure 5.32**).

```
SELECT * FROM users
WHERE user_id = 8;
```

A really good trick for safeguarding against errant deletions is to first run the query using SELECT * instead of DELETE. The results of this query will represent which row(s) will be affected by the deletion.

3. Delete the record (**Figure 5.33**).

```
DELETE FROM users
WHERE user_id = 8 LIMIT 1;
```

As with the update, MySQL will report on the successful execution of the query and how many rows were affected. At this point, there is no way of reinstating the deleted records unless you backed up the database beforehand.

Even though the SELECT query (Step 2 and Figure 5.32) only returned the one row, just to be extra careful, a LIMIT 1 clause is added to the DELETE query.

4. Confirm that the change was made (**Figure 5.34**).

```
SELECT user_id, first_name, last_name
FROM users ORDER BY user_id ASC;
```

You could also confirm the change by running the query in Step 1.

✔ Tips

■ The preferred way to empty a table is to use TRUNCATE:

```
TRUNCATE TABLE tablename
```

■ To delete all of the data in a table, as well as the table itself, use DROP TABLE:

```
DROP TABLE tablename
```

■ To delete an entire database, including every table therein and all of its data, use

```
DROP DATABASE databasename
```

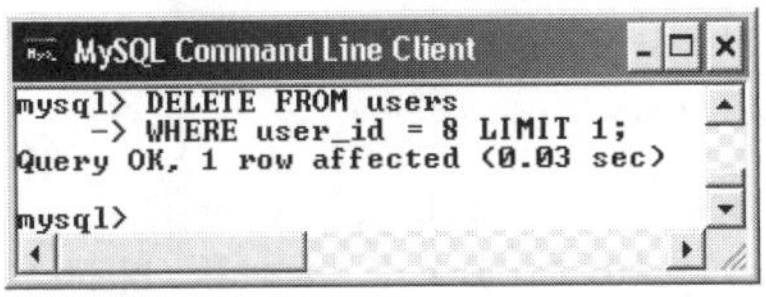

Figure 5.33 Deleting one record from the table.

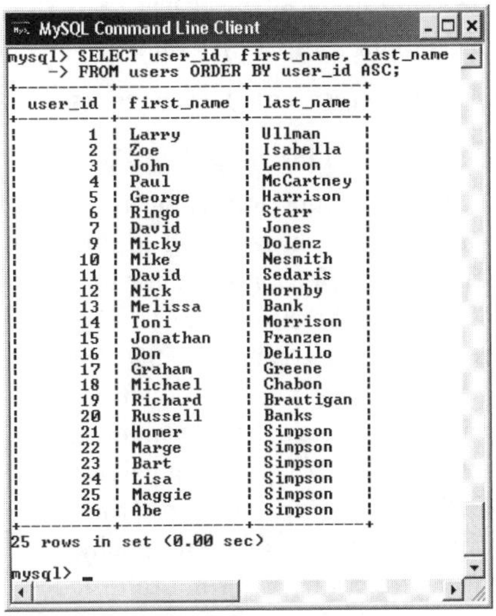

Figure 5.34 The record whose *user_id* was 8 is no longer part of this table.

DELETING DATA

Using Functions

To wrap up this chapter, you'll learn about a number of functions that you can use in your MySQL queries. You have already seen two—NOW() and SHA1()—but those are just the tip of the iceberg. Most of the functions you'll see here are used with SELECT queries to format and alter the returned data, but you may use MySQL functions other types of queries as well.

To apply a function to a column's values, the query would look like

```
SELECT FUNCTION(column) FROM tablename
```

To apply a function to one column's values while also selecting some other columns, you can write a query like either of these:

- ```
  SELECT *, FUNCTION(column) FROM
  → tablename
  ```

- ```
  SELECT column1, FUNCTION(column2),
  → column3 FROM tablename
  ```

Before getting to the actual functions, make note of a couple more things. First, functions are often applied to stored data (i.e., columns) but can also be applied to literal values. Either of these applications of the UPPER() function (which capitalizes a string) is valid:

```
SELECT UPPER(first_name) FROM users
```

```
SELECT UPPER('this string')
```

Second, while the function names themselves are case-insensitive, I will continue to write them in an all-capitalized format, to help distinguish them from table and column names (as I also capitalize SQL terms). Third, an important rule with functions is that you cannot have spaces between the function name and the opening parenthesis in MySQL, although spaces within the parentheses are acceptable. And finally, when using functions to format returned data, you'll often want to make uses of *aliases*, a concept discussed in the sidebar.

Aliases

An *alias* is merely a symbolic renaming of a thing in a query. Normally applied to tables, columns, or function calls, aliases provide a shortcut for referring to something. Aliases are created using the term AS:

```
SELECT registration_date AS reg
```

```
FROM users
```

Aliases are case-sensitive strings composed of numbers, letters, and the underscore but are normally kept to a very short length. As you'll see in the following examples, aliases are often reflected in the headings of the returned results. For the preceding sample, the query results returned will contain one column of data, named *reg*.

If you've defined an alias on a table or a column, the entire query must consistently use that same alias rather than the original name. For example,

```
SELECT first_name AS name FROM users
→ WHERE name='Sam'
```

This differs from standard SQL, which doesn't support the use of aliases in WHERE conditionals.

Text functions

The first group of functions to demonstrate are those meant for manipulating text. The most common of the functions in this category are listed in **Table 5.2**.

CONCAT(), perhaps the most useful of the text functions, deserves special attention. The CONCAT() function accomplishes concatenation, for which PHP uses the period (see Chapter 1, "Introduction to PHP"). The syntax for concatenation requires you to place, within parentheses, the various values you want assembled, in order and separated by commas:

```
SELECT CONCAT(t1, t2) FROM tablename
```

While you can—and normally will—apply CONCAT() to columns, you can also incorporate strings, entered within quotation marks. For example, to format a person's name as *First<SPACE>Last*, you would use

```
SELECT CONCAT(first_name, ' ', last_name)
FROM users
```

Because concatenation normally returns values in a new format, it's an excellent time to use an alias (see the sidebar):

```
SELECT CONCAT(first_name, ' ', last_name)
AS Name FROM users
```

Table 5.2 Some of MySQL's functions for working with text. As with most functions, these can be applied to either columns or literal values (both represented by *t*, *t1*, *t2*, etc).

Text Functions		
FUNCTION	USAGE	RETURNS
CONCAT()	CONCAT(t1, t2, ...)	A new string of the form *t1t2*.
CONCAT_WS()	CONCAT(S, t1, t2, ...)	A new string of the form *t1St2S...*
LENGTH()	LENGTH(t)	The number of characters in *t*.
LEFT()	LEFT(t, y)	The leftmost *y* characters from *t*.
RIGHT()	RIGHT(t, x)	The rightmost *x* characters from *t*.
TRIM()	TRIM(t)	*t* with excess spaces from the beginning and end removed.
UPPER()	UPPER(t)	*t* capitalized.
LOWER()	LOWER(t)	*t* in all-lowercase format.
SUBSTRING()	SUBSTRING(t, x, y)	*y* characters from *t* beginning with *x* (indexed from 0).

To format text:

1. Concatenate the names *without* using an alias (**Figure 5.35**).

```
SELECT CONCAT(last_name, ', ',
→ first_name) FROM users;
```

This query will demonstrate two things. First, the users' last names, a comma and a space, plus their first names are concatenated together to make one string (in the format of *Last, First*). Second, as the figure shows, if you don't use an alias, the returned data's column heading will be the function call. In the mysql client or phpMyAdmin, this is just unsightly; when using PHP to connect to MySQL, this will likely be a problem.

2. Concatenate the names while using an alias (**Figure 5.36**).

```
SELECT CONCAT(last_name, ', ',
→ first_name)

AS Name FROM users ORDER BY Name;
```

To use an alias, just add `AS` *aliasname* after the item to be renamed. The alias will be the new title for the returned data. To make the query a little more interesting, the same alias is also used in the `ORDER BY` clause.

Figure 5.35 This simple concatenation returns every registered user's full name. Notice how the column heading is the use of the CONCAT() function.

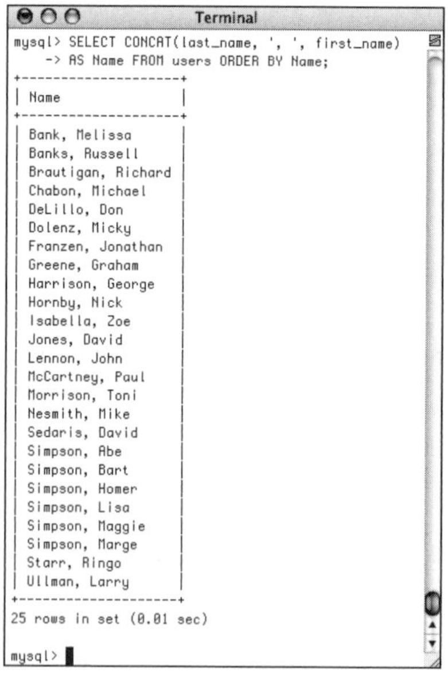

Figure 5.36 By using an alias, the returned data is under the column heading of *Name* (compare with Figure 5.35).

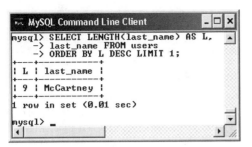

Figure 5.37 By using the LENGTH() function, an alias, an ORDER BY clause, and a LIMIT clause, this query returns the length and value of the longest stored name.

3. Find the longest last name (**Figure 5.37**).

```
SELECT LENGTH(last_name) AS L,
last_name FROM users
ORDER BY L DESC LIMIT 1;
```

To determine which registered user's last name is the longest (has the most characters in it), use the LENGTH() function. To find the name, select both the last name value and the calculated length, which is given an alias of *L*. To then find the longest name, order all of the results by *L*, in descending order, but only return the first record.

✔ Tips

- A query like that in Step 3 (also Figure 5.37) may be useful for helping to fine-tune your column lengths once your database has some records in it.

- MySQL has two functions for performing regular expression searches on text: REGEXP() and NOT REGEXP(). Chapter 13, "Perl-Compatible Regular Expressions," introduces regular expressions using PHP.

- CONCAT() has a corollary function called CONCAT_WS(), which stands for *with separator*. The syntax is CONCAT_WS(*separator*, *t1*, *t2*, ...). The separator will be inserted between each of the listed columns or values. For example, to format a person's full name as *First<SPACE>Middle<SPACE> Last*, you would write

  ```
  SELECT CONCAT_WS(' ', first, middle,
  → last) AS Name FROM tablename
  ```

  CONCAT_WS() has an added advantage over CONCAT() in that it will ignore columns with NULL values. So that query might return *Joe Banks* from one record but *Jane Sojourner Adams* from another.

Numeric functions

Besides the standard math operators that MySQL uses (for addition, subtraction, multiplication, and division), there are a couple dozen functions for formatting and performing calculations on numeric values. **Table 5.3** lists the most common of these, some of which will be demonstrated shortly.

I want to specifically highlight three of these functions: FORMAT(), ROUND(), and RAND(). The first—which is not technically number-specific—turns any number into a more conventionally formatted layout. For example, if you stored the cost of a car as *20198.20*, FORMAT(car_cost, 2) would turn that number into the more common *20,198.20*.

ROUND() will take one value, presumably from a column, and round that to a specified number of decimal places. If no decimal places are indicated, it will round the number to the nearest integer. If more decimal places are indicated than exist in the original number, the remaining spaces are padded with zeros (to the right of the decimal point).

The RAND() function, as you might infer, is used for returning random numbers (**Figure 5.38**).

SELECT RAND()

A further benefit to the RAND() function is that it can be used with your queries to return the results in a random order.

SELECT * FROM *tablename* ORDER BY RAND()

Table 5.3 Some of MySQL's functions for working with numbers. As with most functions, these can be applied to either columns or literal values (both represented by *n*, *n1*, *n2*, etc.).

Numeric Functions		
FUNCTION	USAGE	RETURNS
ABS()	ABS(n)	The absolute value of *n*.
CEILING()	CEILING(n)	The next-highest integer based upon the value of *n*.
FLOOR()	FLOOR(n)	The integer value of *n*.
FORMAT()	FORMAT(n1, n2)	*n1* formatted as a number with *n2* decimal places and commas inserted every three spaces.
MOD()	MOD(n1, n2)	The remainder of dividing *n1* by *n2*.
POW()	POW(n1, n2)	*n1* to the *n2* power.
RAND()	RAND()	A random number between 0 and 1.0.
ROUND()	ROUND(n1, n2)	*n1* rounded to *n2* decimal places.
SQRT()	SQRT(n)	The square root of *n*.

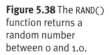

Figure 5.38 The RAND() function returns a random number between 0 and 1.0.

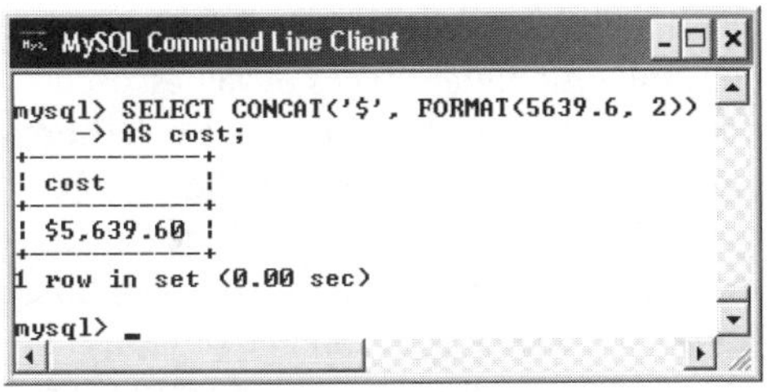

Figure 5.39 Using an arbitrary example, this query shows how the FORMAT() function works.

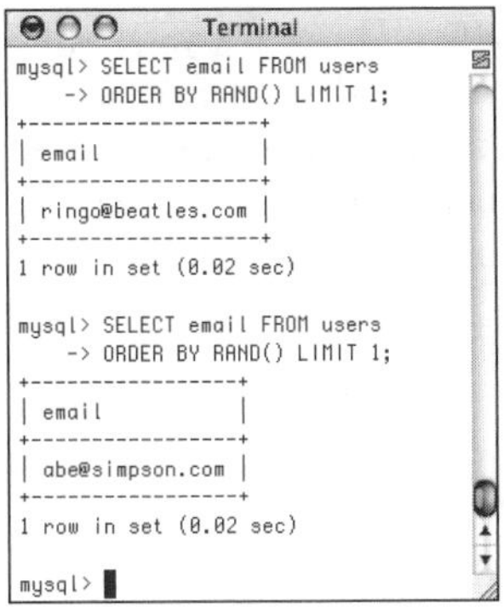

Figure 5.40 Subsequent executions of the same query return different random results.

To use numeric functions:

1. Display a number, formatting the amount as dollars (**Figure 5.39**).

   ```
   SELECT CONCAT('$', FORMAT(5639.6, 2))
   AS cost;
   ```

   Using the FORMAT() function, as just described, with CONCAT(), you can turn any number into a currency format as you might display it in a Web page.

2. Retrieve a random email address from the table (**Figure 5.40**).

   ```
   SELECT email FROM users
   ORDER BY RAND() LIMIT 1;
   ```

   What happens with this query is: All of the email addresses are selected; the order they are in is shuffled (ORDER BY RAND()); and then the first one is returned. Running this same query multiple times will produce different random results. Notice that you do not specify a column to which RAND() is applied.

✔ Tips

■ Along with the mathematical functions listed here, there are several trigonometric, exponential, and other types of numeric functions available.

■ The MOD() function is the same as using the percent sign:

   ```
   SELECT MOD(9,2)
   SELECT 9%2
   ```

   It returns the remainder of a division (*1* in these examples).

USING FUNCTIONS

Date and time functions

The date and time column types in MySQL are particularly flexible and useful. But because many database users are not familiar with all of the available date and time functions, these options are frequently underused. Whether you want to make calculations based upon a date or return only the month name from a value, MySQL has a function for that purpose. **Table 5.4** lists most of these; see the MySQL manual for a complete list.

MySQL supports two data types that store both a date and a time (DATETIME and TIMESTAMP), one type that stores just the date (DATE), one that stores just the time (TIME),

and one that stores just a year (YEAR). Besides allowing for different types of values, each data type also has its own unique behaviors (again, I'd recommend reading the MySQL manual's pages on this for all of the details). But MySQL is very flexible as to which functions you can use with which type. You can apply a date function to any value that contains a date (i.e., DATETIME, TIMESTAMP, and DATE), or you can apply an hour function to any value that contains the time (i.e., DATETIME, TIMESTAMP, and TIME). MySQL will use the part of the value that it needs and ignore the rest. What you cannot do, however, is apply a date function to a TIME value or a time function to a DATE or YEAR value.

Table 5.4 Some of MySQL's functions for working with dates and times. As with most functions, these can be applied to either columns or literal values (both represented by *dt*, short for *datetime*).

Date and Time Functions

FUNCTION	USAGE	RETURNS
HOUR()	HOUR(dt)	The hour value of *dt*.
MINUTE()	MINUTE(dt)	The minute value of *dt*.
SECOND()	SECOND(dt)	The second value of *dt*.
DAYNAME()	DAYNAME(dt)	The name of the day for *dt*.
DAYOFMONTH()	DAYOFMONTH(dt)	The numerical day value of *dt*.
MONTHNAME()	MONTHNAME(dt)	The name of the month of *dt*.
MONTH()	MONTH(dt)	The numerical month value of *dt*.
YEAR()	YEAR(column)	The year value of *dt*.
CURDATE()	CURDATE()	The current date.
CURTIME()	CURTIME()	The current time.
NOW()	NOW()	The current date and time.
UNIX_TIMESTAMP()	UNIX_TIMESTAMP(*dt*)	The number of seconds since the epoch until the current moment or until the date specified.

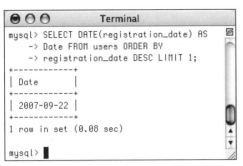

Figure 5.41 The date functions can be used to extract information from stored values.

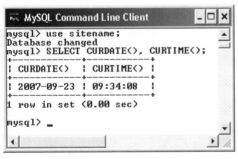

Figure 5.42 This query returns the name of the day that a given date represents.

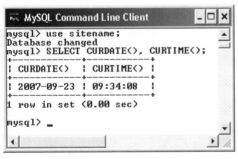

Figure 5.43 This query, not run on any particular table, returns the current date and time on the MySQL server.

To use date and time functions:

1. Display the date that the last user registered (**Figure 5.41**).

   SELECT DATE(registration_date) AS

   Date FROM users ORDER BY

   registration_date DESC LIMIT 1;

   The DATE() function returns the date part of a value. To see the date that the last person registered, an ORDER BY clause lists the users starting with the most recently registered and this result is limited to just one record.

2. Display the day of the week that the first user registered (**Figure 5.42**).

   SELECT DAYNAME(registration_date) AS

   Weekday FROM users ORDER BY

   registration_date ASC LIMIT 1;

   This is similar to the query in Step 1 but the results are returned in ascending order and the DAYNAME() function is applied to the *registration_date* column. This function returns *Sunday*, *Monday*, *Tuesday*, etc., for a given date.

3. Show the current date and time, according to MySQL (**Figure 5.43**).

   SELECT CURDATE(), CURTIME();

   To show what date and time MySQL currently thinks it is, you can select the CURDATE() and CURTIME() functions, which return these values. This is another example of a query that can be run without referring to a particular table name.

continues on next page

USING FUNCTIONS

4. Show the last day of the current month (**Figure 5.44**).

```
SELECT LAST_DAY(CURDATE()),
MONTHNAME(CURDATE());
```

As the last query showed, `CURDATE()` returns the current date on the server. This value can be used as an argument to the `LAST_DAY()` function, which returns the last date in the month for a given date. The `MONTHNAME()` function returns the name of the current month.

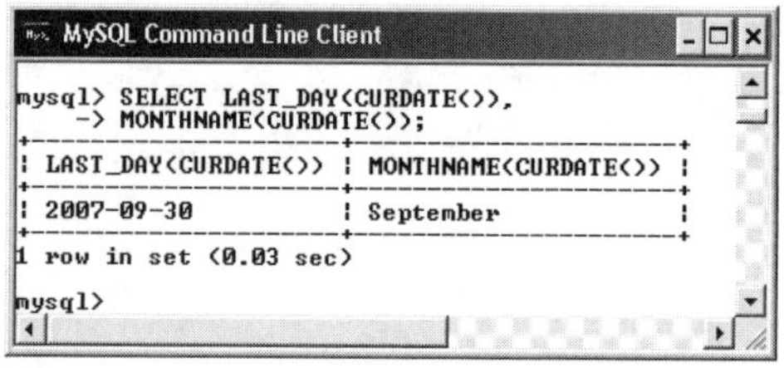

Figure 5.44 Among the many things MySQL can do with date and time types is determine the last date in a month or the name value of a given date.

✔ Tips

- The date and time returned by MySQL's date and time functions correspond to those on the server, not on the client accessing the database.

- Not mentioned in this section or in Table 5.4 are `ADDDATE()`, `SUBDATE()`, `ADDTIME()`, and `SUBTIME()`. Each can be used to perform arithmetic on date and time values. These can be very useful (for example, to find everyone registered within the past week) but their syntax is cumbersome. As always, see the MySQL manual for more information.

- As of MySQL 5.0.2, the server will also prevent invalid dates (e.g., February 31, 2009) from being inserted into a date or date/time column.

USING FUNCTIONS

Table 5.5 Use these parameters with the DATE_FORMAT() and TIME_FORMAT() functions.

*_FORMAT() Parameters		
TERM	**USAGE**	**EXAMPLE**
%e	Day of the month	1-31
%d	Day of the month, two digit	01-31
%D	Day with suffix	1st-31st
%W	Weekday name	Sunday-Saturday
%a	Abbreviated	Sun-Sat weekday name
%c	Month number	1-12
%m	Month number, two digit	01-12
%M	Month name	January-December
%b	Month name, abbreviated	Jan-Dec
%Y	Year	2002
%y	Year	02
%l	Hour (lowercase L)	1-12
%h	Hour, two digit	01-12
%k	Hour, 24-hour clock	0-23
%H	Hour, 24-hour clock, two digit	00-23
%i	Minutes	00-59
%S	Seconds	00-59
%r	Time	8:17:02 PM
%T	Time, 24-hour clock	20:17:02
%p	AM or PM	AM or PM

Formatting the date and time

There are two additional date and time functions that you might find yourself using more than all of the others combined: DATE_FORMAT() and TIME_FORMAT(). There is some overlap between the two and when you would use one or the other.

DATE_FORMAT() can be used to format both the date and time if a value contains both (e.g., *YYYY-MM-DD HH:MM:SS*). Comparatively, TIME_FORMAT() can format only the time value and must be used if only the time value is being stored (e.g., *HH:MM:SS*). The syntax is

```
SELECT DATE_FORMAT(datetime, formatting)
```

The *formatting* relies upon combinations of key codes and the percent sign to indicate what values you want returned. **Table 5.5** lists the available date- and time-formatting parameters. You can use these in any combination, along with literal characters, such as punctuation, to return a date and time in a more presentable form.

Assuming that a column called *the_date* has the date and time of *1996-04-20 11:07:45* stored in it, common formatting tasks and results would be

◆ Time (11:07:45 AM)

```
TIME_FORMAT(the_date, '%r')
```

◆ Time without seconds (11:07 AM)

```
TIME_FORMAT(the_date, '%l:%i %p')
```

◆ Date (April 20th, 1996)

```
DATE_FORMAT(the_date, '%M %D, %Y')
```

To format the date and time:

1. Return the current date and time as *Month DD, YYYY - HH:MM* (**Figure 5.45**).

SELECT DATE_FORMAT(NOW(),'%M %e, %Y
→ - %l:%i');

Using the NOW() function, which returns the current date and time, you can practice formatting to see what results are returned.

2. Display the current time, using 24-hour notation (**Figure 5.46**).

SELECT TIME_FORMAT(CURTIME(), '%T');

3. Select the email address and date registered, ordered by date registered, formatting the date as *Weekday (abbreviated) Month (abbreviated) Day Year*, for the last five registered users (**Figure 5.47**).

SELECT email,
→ DATE_FORMAT(registration_date,
→ '%a %b %e %Y')

AS Date FROM users

ORDER BY registration_date DESC

LIMIT 5;

This is just one more example of how you can use these formatting functions to alter the output of an SQL query.

✔ Tips

■ In your Web applications, you should almost always use MySQL functions to format any dates coming from the database.

■ The only way to access the date or time on the client (the user's machine) is to use JavaScript. It cannot be done with PHP or MySQL.

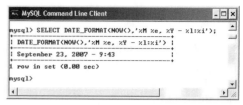

Figure 5.45 The current date and time, formatted.

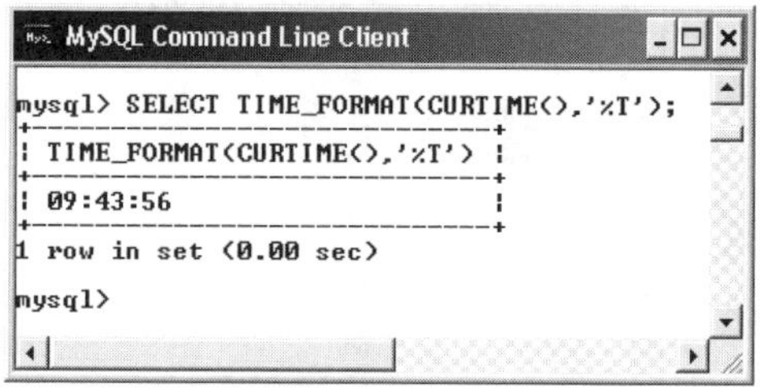

Figure 5.46 The current time, in a 24-hour format.

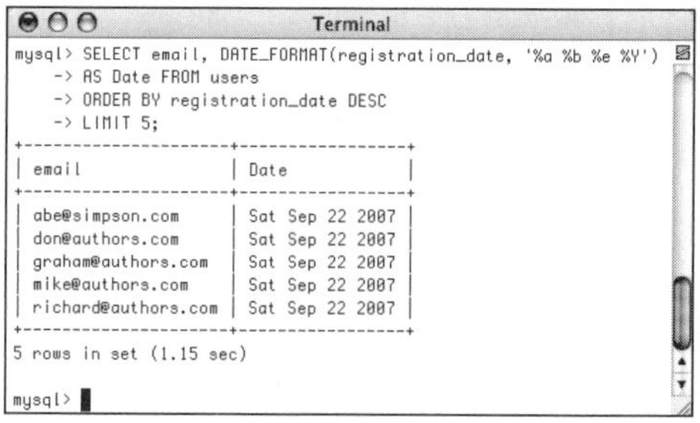

Figure 5.47 The DATE_FORMAT() function is used to pre-format the registration date when selecting records from the *users* table.

ADVANCED SQL AND MYSQL

This chapter picks up where its predecessor left off, discussing more advanced SQL and MySQL topics. While the basics of both technologies will certainly get you by, it's these more complex ideas that make sophisticated applications possible.

The chapter begins by discussing database design in greater detail, using a message board as the example. More elaborate databases like a forum require SQL queries called *joins*, so that subject will follow. From there, the chapter introduces a category of functions that are specifically used when grouping query results.

After that, the subjects turn to advanced MySQL concepts: indexes, changing the structure of existing tables, and table types. The chapter concludes with two more MySQL features: performing full text searches and transactions.

Database Design

Whenever you are working with a relational database management system such as MySQL, the first step in creating and using a database is to establish the database's structure (also called the database *schema*). Database design, aka *data modeling*, is crucial for successful long-term management of information. Using a process called *normalization*, you carefully eliminate redundancies and other problems that will undermine the integrity of your database.

The techniques you will learn over the next few pages will help to ensure the viability, usefulness, and reliability of your databases. The specific example to be discussed—a forum where users can post messages—will be more explicitly used in Chapter 15, "Example—Message Board," but the principles of normalization apply to any database you might create. (The *sitename* example as created in the past two chapters was properly normalized, even though that was never discussed.)

Normalization

Normalization was developed by an IBM researcher named E.F. Codd in the early 1970s (he also invented the relational database). A relational database is merely a collection of data, organized in a particular manner, and Dr. Codd created a series of rules called *normal forms* that help define that organization. In this chapter I will discuss the first three of the normal forms, which are sufficient for most database designs.

Before you begin normalizing your database, you must define the role of the application being developed. Whether it means that you thoroughly discuss the subject with a client or figure it out for yourself, understanding how the information will be accessed dictates the modeling. Thus, this process will require paper and pen rather than the MySQL software itself (although database design is applicable to any relational database, not just MySQL).

In this example I want to create a message board where users can post messages and other users can reply. I imagine that users will need to register, then log in with a username/password combination, in order to post messages. I also expect that there could be multiple forums for different subjects. I have listed a sample row of data in **Table 6.1**. The database itself will be called *forum*.

✔ Tips

■ One of the best ways to determine what information should be stored in a database is to think about what questions will be asked of the database and what data would be included in the answers.

■ Normalization can be hard to learn if you fixate on the little things. Each of the normal forms is defined in a very cryptic way; even when put into layman's terms, they can still be confounding. My best advice is to focus on the big picture as you follow along. Once you've gone through normalization and see the end result, the overall process should be clear enough.

Table 6.1 Representative data for the kind of information to be stored in the database.

Sample Forum Data	
ITEM	EXAMPLE
username	troutster
password	mypass
actual name	Larry Ullman
user email	email@example.com
forum	MySQL
message subject	Question about normalization.
message body	I have a question about...
message date	February 2, 2008 12:20 AM

Keys

As briefly mentioned in Chapter 4, "Introduction to MySQL," keys are integral to normalized databases. There are two types of keys: *primary* and *foreign*. A primary key is a unique identifier that has to abide by certain rules. They must

◆ Always have a value (they cannot be NULL)

◆ Have a value that remains the same (never changes)

◆ Have a unique value for each record in a table

The best real-world example of a primary key is the U.S. Social Security number: each individual has a unique Social Security number, and that number never changes. Just as the Social Security number is an artificial construct used to identify people, you'll frequently find creating an arbitrary primary key for each table to be the best design practice.

The second type of key is a foreign key. Foreign keys are the representation in Table B of the primary key from Table A. If you have a *cinema* database with a *movies* table and a *directors* table, the primary key from *directors* would be linked as a foreign key in *movies*. You'll see better how this works as the normalization process continues.

Table 6.2 A primary key is added to the table as an easy way to reference the records.

Sample Forum Data	
ITEM	EXAMPLE
message ID	325
username	troutster
password	mypass
actual name	Larry Ullman
user email	email@example.com
forum	MySQL
message subject	Question about normalization.
message body	I have a question about…
message date	February 2, 2008 12:20 AM

The *forum* database is just a simple table as it stands (Table 6.1), but before beginning the normalization process, identify at least one primary key (the foreign keys will come in later steps).

To assign a primary key:

1. Look for any fields that meet the three tests for a primary key.

In this example (Table 6.1), no column really fits all of the criteria for a primary key. The username and email address will be unique for each forum user but will not be unique for each record in the database (because the same user could post multiple messages). The same subject could be used multiple times as well. The message body will likely be unique for each message but could change (if edited), violating one of the rules of primary keys.

2. If no logical primary key exists, invent one (**Table 6.2**).

Frequently, you will need to create a primary key because no good solution presents itself. In this example, a *message ID* is manufactured. When you create a primary key that has no other meaning or purpose, it's called a *surrogate* primary key.

✔ Tips

■ As a rule of thumb, I name my primary keys using at least part of the table's name (e.g., *message*) and the word *id*. Some database developers like to add the abbreviation *pk* to the name as well.

■ MySQL allows for only one primary key per table, although you can base a primary key on multiple columns (this means the combination of those columns must be unique and never change).

■ Ideally, your primary key should always be an integer, which results in better MySQL performance.

Relationships

Database relationships refer to how the data in one table relates to the data in another. There are three types of relationships between any two tables: *one-to-one*, *one-to-many*, or *many-to-many*. (Two tables in a database may also be unrelated.)

A relationship is one-to-one if one and only one item in Table A applies to one and only one item in Table B. For example, each U.S. citizen has only one Social Security number, and each Social Security number applies to only one U.S. citizen; no citizen can have two Social Security numbers, and no Social Security number can refer to two citizens.

A relationship is one-to-many if one item in Table A can apply to multiple items in Table B. The terms *female* and *male* will apply to many people, but each person can be only one or the other (in theory). A one-to-many relationship is the most common one between tables in normalized databases.

Finally, a relationship is many-to-many if multiple items in Table A can apply to multiple items in Table B. A record album can contain songs by multiple artists, and artists can make multiple albums. *You should try to avoid many-to-many relationships in your design* because they lead to data redundancy and integrity problems. Instead of having many-to-many relationships, properly designed databases use *intermediary tables* that break down one many-to-many relationship into two one-to-many relationships.

Relationships and keys work together in that a key in one table will normally relate to a key in another, as mentioned earlier.

✔ Tips

■ Database modeling uses certain conventions to represent the structure of the database, which I'll follow through a series of images in this chapter. The symbols for the three types of relationships are shown in **Figure 6.1**.

■ The process of database design results in an *ERD* (entity-relationship diagram) or *ERM* (entity-relationship model). This graphical representation of a database uses boxes for tables, ovals for columns, and the symbols from Figure 6.1 to represent the relationships.

■ There are many programs available to help create a database schema, including MySQL Workbench (www.mysql.com), which is in alpha release at the time of this writing.

■ The term "relational" in RDBMS actually stems from the tables, which are technically called *relations*.

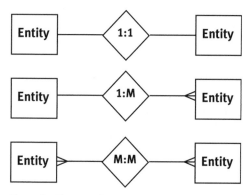

Figure 6.1 These symbols, or variations on them, are commonly used to represent relationships in database modeling schemes.

First Normal Form

As already stated, normalizing a database is the process of adjusting the database's structure according to several rules, called *forms*. Your database should adhere to each rule exactly, and the forms must be followed in order.

Every table in a database must have the following two qualities in order to be in First Normal Form (1NF):

◆ Each column must contain only one value (this is sometimes described as being *atomic* or *indivisible*).

◆ No table can have repeating groups of related data.

Table 6.3 The *actual name* column has been broken in two to store data more atomically.

Forum Database, Atomic	
Item	Example
message ID	325
username	troutster
password	mypass
first name	Larry
last name	Ullman
user email	email@example.com
forum	MySQL
message subject	Question about normalization.
message body	I have a question about...
message date	February 2, 2008 12:20 AM

A table containing one field for a person's entire address (street, city, state, zip code, country) would *not* be 1NF compliant, because it has multiple values in one column, violating the first property above. As for the second, a *movies* table that had columns such as *actor1*, *actor2*, *actor3*, and so on would fail to be 1NF compliant because of the repeating columns all listing the exact same kind of information.

I'll begin the normalization process by checking the existing structure (Table 6.2) for 1NF compliance. Any columns that are not atomic will be broken into multiple columns. If a table has repeating similar columns, then those will be turned into their own, separate table.

To make a database 1NF compliant:

1. Identify any field that contains multiple pieces of information.

   Looking at Table 6.2, one field is not 1NF compliant: *actual name*. The example record contained both the first name and the last name in this one column.

   The *message date* field contains a day, a month, and a year, plus a time, but subdividing past that level of specificity is really not warranted. And, as the end of the last chapter shows, MySQL can handle dates and times quite nicely using the `DATETIME` type.

   Other examples of problems would be if a table used just one column for multiple phone numbers (mobile, home, work), or stored a person's multiple interests (cooking, dancing, skiing, etc.) in a single column.

2. Break up any fields found in Step 1 into distinct fields (**Table 6.3**).

   To fix this problem, I'll create separate *first name* and *last name* fields, each of which contains only one value.

   continues on next page

continues on next page

Database Design

3. Turn any repeating column groups into their own table.

The forum database doesn't have this problem currently, so to demonstrate what would be a violation, consider **Table 6.4**. The repeating columns (the multiple actor fields) introduce two problems. First of all, there's no getting around the fact that each movie will be limited to a certain number of actors when stored this way. Even if you add columns *actor 1* through *actor 100*, there will still be that limit (of a hundred). Second, any record that doesn't have the maximum number of actors will have NULL values in those extra columns. You should generally avoid columns with NULL values in your database schema. As another concern, the actor and director columns are not atomic.

To fix the problems in the *movies* table, a second table would be created (**Table 6.5**). This table uses one row for each actor in a movie, which solves the problems mentioned in the last paragraph. The actor names are also broken up to be atomic. Notice as well that a primary-key column should be added to the new table. The notion that each table has a primary key is implicit in the First Normal Form.

4. Double-check that all new columns and tables created in Steps 2 and 3 pass the 1NF test.

✔ Tips

■ The simplest way to think about 1NF is that this rule analyzes a table horizontally. You inspect all of the columns within a single row to guarantee specificity and avoid repetition of similar data.

■ Various resources will describe the normal forms in somewhat different ways, likely with much more technical jargon. What is most important is the spirit—and end result—of the normalization process, not the technical wording of the rules.

Table 6.4 This *movies* table violates the 1NF rule for two reasons. First, it has repeating columns of similar data (*actor 1* etc.). Second, the actor and director columns are not atomic.

Movies Table	
COLUMN	VALUE
movie ID	976
movie title	Casablanca
year released	1943
director	Michael Curtiz
actor 1	Humphrey Bogart
actor 2	Ingrid Bergman
actor 3	Peter Lorre

Table 6.5 To make the *movies* table (Table 6.4) 1NF compliant, the association of actors with a movie would be made in this table.

Movies-Actors Table			
ID	MOVIE	ACTOR FIRST NAME	ACTOR LAST NAME
1	Casablanca	Humphrey	Bogart
2	Casablanca	Ingrid	Bergman
3	Casablanca	Peter	Lorre
4	The Maltese Falcon	Humphrey	Bogart
5	The Maltese Falcon	Peter	Lorre

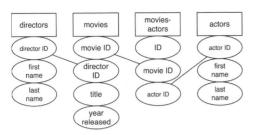

Figure 6.2 To make the *cinema* database 2NF compliant (given the information being represented), four tables are necessary. The directors are represented in the *movies* table through the *director ID* key; the movies are represented in the *movies-actors* table through the *movie ID* key; and the actors are represented in the *movies-actors* table through the *actor ID* key.

Second Normal Form

For a database to be in Second Normal Form (2NF), the database must first already be in 1NF (you must normalize in order). Then, every column in the table that is not a key (i.e., a foreign key) must be dependent upon the primary key. You can normally identify a column that violates this rule when it has non-key values that are the same in multiple rows. Such values should be stored in their own table and related back to the original table through a key.

Going back to the *cinema* example, a *movies* table (Table 6.4) would have the director Martin Scorsese listed twenty-plus times. This violates the 2NF rule as the column(s) that store the directors' names would not be keys and would not be dependent upon the primary key (the movie ID). The fix is to create a separate *directors* table that stores the directors' information and assigns each director a primary key. To tie the director back to the movies, the director's primary key would also be a foreign key in the *movies* table.

Looking at Table 6.5 (for actors in movies), both the movie name and the actor names are also in violation of the 2NF rule (they aren't keys and they aren't dependent on the table's primary key). In the end, the cinema database in this minimal form requires four tables (**Figure 6.2**). Each director's name, movie name, and actor's name will be stored only once, and any non-key column in a table is dependent upon that table's primary key. In fact, normalization could be summarized as the process of creating more and more tables until potential redundancies have been eliminated.

DATABASE DESIGN

To make a database 2NF compliant:

1. Identify any non-key columns that aren't dependent upon the table's primary key.

   Looking at Table 6.3, the username, first name, last name, email, and forum values are all non-keys (message ID is the only key column currently), and none are dependent upon the message ID. Conversely, the message subject, body, and date are also non-keys, but these do depend upon the message ID.

2. Create new tables accordingly (**Figure 6.3**).

   The most logical modification for the forum database is to make three tables: *users*, *forums*, and *messages*.

   In a visual representation of the database, create a box for each table, with the table name as a header and all of its columns (also called its *attributes*) underneath.

3. Assign or create new primary keys (**Figure 6.4**).

   Using the techniques described earlier in the chapter, ensure that each new table has a primary key. Here I've added a *user ID* field to the *users* table and a *forum ID* field to *forums*. These are both surrogate primary keys. Because the *username* field in the *users* table and the *name* field in the *forums* table must be unique for each record and must always have a value, you could have them act as the primary keys for their tables. However, this would mean that these values could never change (per the rules of primary keys) and the database will be a little slower, using text-based keys instead of numeric ones.

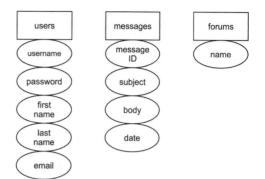

Figure 6.3 To make the *forum* database 2NF compliant, three tables are necessary.

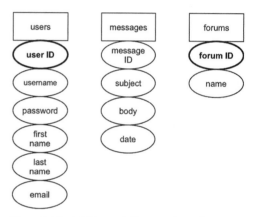

Figure 6.4 Each table needs its own primary key.

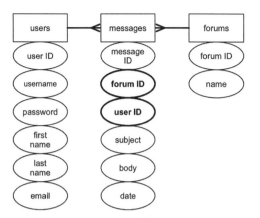

Figure 6.5 To relate the three tables, two foreign keys are added to the *messages* table, each key representing one of the other two tables.

4. Create the requisite foreign keys and indicate the relationships (**Figure 6.5**).

The final step in achieving 2NF compliance is to incorporate foreign keys to link associated tables. Remember that a primary key in one table will most likely be a foreign key in another.

With this example, the *user ID* from the *users* table links to the *user ID* column in the *messages* table. Therefore, *users* has a one-to-many relationship with *messages* (because each user can post multiple messages but each message can only be posted by one user).

Also, the two *forum ID* columns are linked, creating a one-to-many relationship between *messages* and *forums* (each message can only be in one forum but each forum can have multiple messages).

There is no relationship between the *users* and *forums* tables.

✔ Tips

■ Another way to test for 2NF is to look at the relationships between tables. The ideal is to create one-to-many situations. Tables that have a many-to-many relationship may need to be restructured.

■ Looking back at Figure 6.2, the *movies-actors* table is an *intermediary table*, which turns the many-to-many relationship between movies and actors into two one-to-many relationships. You can often tell a table is acting as an intermediary when all of its columns are keys. In fact, in this table, no *ID* column would be required, as the primary key could be the combination of the *movie ID* and the *actor ID*.

■ A properly normalized database should never have duplicate rows in the same table (two or more rows in which the values in every non–primary key column match).

■ To simplify how you conceive of the normalization process, remember that 1NF is a matter of inspecting a table horizontally, and 2NF is a vertical analysis (hunting for repeating values over multiple rows).

Third Normal Form

A database is in Third Normal Form (3NF) if it is in 2NF and every non-key column is mutually independent. If you followed the normalization process properly to this point, you may not have 3NF issues. You would know that you have a 3NF violation if changing the value in one column would require changing the value in another. In the *forum* example (see Figure 6.5), there aren't any 3NF problems, but I'll explain a hypothetical situation where this rule would come into play.

Take, as a common example, a single table that stores the information for a business' clients: first name, last name, phone number, street address, city, state, zip code, and so on. Such a table would not be 3NF compliant because many of the columns would be interdependent: the street would actually be dependent upon the city; the city would be dependent upon the state; and the zip code would be an issue, too. These values are subservient to each other, not to the person whose record it is. To normalize this database, you would have to create one table for the states, another for the cities (with a foreign key linking to the states table), and another for the zip codes. All of these would then be linked back to the clients table.

If you feel that all that may be overkill, you are correct. To be frank, this higher level of normalization is often unnecessary. The point is that you should strive to normalize your databases but that sometimes you'll make concessions to keep things simple (see the sidebar "Overruling Normalization"). The needs of your application and the particulars of your database will help dictate just how far into the normalization process you should go.

As I said, the *forum* example is fine as is, but I'll outline the 3NF steps just the same, showing how to fix the clients example just mentioned.

To make a database 3NF compliant:

1. Identify any fields in any tables that are interdependent.

   As I just stated, what you look for are columns that depend more upon each other (like city and state) than they do on the record as a whole. In the *forum* database, this isn't an issue. Just looking at the *messages* table, each *subject* will be specific to a *message ID*, each *body* will be specific to that *message ID*, and so forth.

2. Create new tables accordingly.

   If you found any problematic columns in Step 1, like city and state in a clients example, you would create separate *cities* and *states* tables.

3. Assign or create new primary keys.

   Every table must have a primary key, so add *city ID* and *state ID* to the new tables.

4. Create the requisite foreign keys that link any of the relationships (**Figure 6.6**).

   Finally, add a *state ID* to the *cities* table and a *city ID* to the *clients* table. This effectively links each client's record to the city and state in which they live.

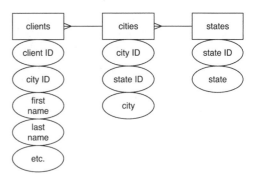

Figure 6.6 Going with a minimal version of a hypothetical *clients* database, two new tables are created for storing the city and state values.

Overruling Normalization

As much as ensuring that a database is in 3NF will help guarantee reliability and viability, you won't fully normalize every database with which you work. Before undermining the proper methods, though, understand that doing so may have devastating long-term consequences.

The two primary reasons to overrule normalization are convenience and performance. Fewer tables are easier to manipulate and comprehend than more. Further, because of their more intricate nature, normalized databases will most likely be slower for updating, retrieving data from, and modifying. Normalization, in short, is a trade-off between data integrity/scalability and simplicity/speed. On the other hand, there are ways to improve your database's performance but few to remedy corrupted data that can result from poor design.

Practice and experience will teach you how best to model your database, but do try to err on the side of abiding by the normal forms, particularly as you are still mastering the concept.

✔ Tips

- As a general rule, I would probably not normalize the clients example to this extent. If I left the city and state fields in the *Clients* table, the worst thing that would happen is that a city would change its name and this fact would need to be updated for all of the users living in that city. But this—cities changing their names—is not a common occurrence.

- Despite there being these set rules for how to normalize a database, two different people could normalize the same example in slightly different ways. Database design does allow for personal preference and interpretations. The important thing is that a database has no clear and obvious NF violations. Any of those will likely lead to problems down the road.

Creating the database

There are three final steps in designing the database:

1. Double-checking that all the requisite information is being stored.

2. Identifying the column types.

3. Naming all database elements.

Table 6.6 shows the final database design. One column has been added to those shown in Figure 6.5. Because one message might be a reply to another, some method of indicating that relationship is required. The solution is to add a *parent_id* column to *messages*. If a message is a reply, its *parent_id* value will be the *message_id* of the original message (so *message_id* is acting as a foreign key in this same table). If a message has a *parent_id* of 0, then it's a new thread, not a reply.

If you make any changes to the tables, you must run through the normal forms one more time to ensure that the database is still normalized.

In terms of choosing the column types and naming the tables and columns, this is covered in Chapter 4.

Once the schema is fully developed, it can be created in MySQL, using the commands shown in Chapter 5, "Introduction to SQL."

To create the database:

1. Access MySQL using whatever client you prefer.

   Like the preceding chapter, this one will also use the mysql client for all of its examples. You are welcome to use phpMyAdmin or other tools as the interface to MySQL.

2. Create the *forum* database (**Figure 6.7**).

   ```
   CREATE DATABASE forum;
   ```
   ```
   USE forum;
   ```

   Depending upon your setup, you may not be allowed to create your own databases. If not, just use the provided database and add the following tables to it.

Table 6.6 The final plan for the *forum* database. Note that every integer column is UNSIGNED, the three primary key columns are also designated as AUTO_INCREMENT, and every column is set as NOT NULL.

The forum Database with Types		
COLUMN NAME	**TABLE**	**COLUMN TYPE**
forum_id	forums	TINYINT
name	forums	VARCHAR(60)
message_id	messages	INT
forum_id	messages	TINYINT
parent_id	messages	INT
user_id	messages	MEDIUMINT
subject	messages	VARCHAR(100)
body	messages	LONGTEXT
date_entered	messages	TIMESTAMP
user_id	users	MEDIUMINT
username	users	VARCHAR(30)
pass	users	CHAR(40)
first_name	users	VARCHAR(20)
last_name	users	VARCHAR(40)
email	users	VARCHAR(80)

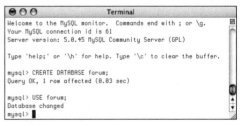

Figure 6.7 The first steps are to create and select the database.

3. Create the *forums* table (**Figure 6.8**).

```
CREATE TABLE forums (

forum_id TINYINT UNSIGNED NOT NULL
→ AUTO_INCREMENT,

name VARCHAR(60) NOT NULL,

PRIMARY KEY (forum_id)

);
```

It does not matter in what order you create your tables, but I'll make the *forums* table first. Remember that you can enter your SQL queries over multiple lines for convenience.

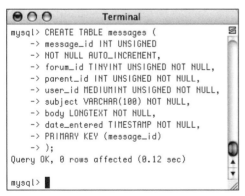

Figure 6.8 Creating the first table.

```
mysql> CREATE TABLE messages (
    -> message_id INT UNSIGNED
    -> NOT NULL AUTO_INCREMENT,
    -> forum_id TINYINT UNSIGNED NOT NULL,
    -> parent_id INT UNSIGNED NOT NULL,
    -> user_id MEDIUMINT UNSIGNED NOT NULL,
    -> subject VARCHAR(100) NOT NULL,
    -> body LONGTEXT NOT NULL,
    -> date_entered TIMESTAMP NOT NULL,
    -> PRIMARY KEY (message_id)
    -> );
Query OK, 0 rows affected (0.12 sec)

mysql>
```

Figure 6.9 Creating the second table.

This table only contains two columns (which will happen frequently in a normalized database). Because I don't expect there to be a lot of forums, the primary key is a really small type (`TINYINT`). If you wanted to add descriptions of each forum, a `VARCHAR(255)` column could be added to this table.

4. Create the *messages* table (**Figure 6.9**).

```
CREATE TABLE messages (

message_id INT UNSIGNED

NOT NULL AUTO_INCREMENT,

forum_id TINYINT UNSIGNED NOT NULL,

parent_id INT UNSIGNED NOT NULL,

user_id MEDIUMINT UNSIGNED NOT NULL,

subject VARCHAR(100) NOT NULL,

body LONGTEXT NOT NULL,

date_entered TIMESTAMP NOT NULL,

PRIMARY KEY (message_id)

);
```

The primary key for this table has to be big, as it could have lots and lots of records. The three foreign key columns—*forum_id*, *parent_id*, and *user_id*—will all be the same size and type as their primary key counterparts. The subject is limited to 100 characters and the body of each message can be a lot of text. The *date_entered* field is a `TIMESTAMP` type. It will store both the date and the time that a record is added, and be automatically updated to the current date and time when the record is inserted (this is how `TIMESTAMP` behaves).

continues on next page

5. Create the *users* table (**Figure 6.10**).

```
CREATE TABLE users (
user_id MEDIUMINT UNSIGNED NOT NULL
›AUTO_INCREMENT,
username VARCHAR(30) NOT NULL,
pass CHAR(40) NOT NULL,
first_name VARCHAR(20) NOT NULL,
last_name VARCHAR(40) NOT NULL,
email VARCHAR(80) NOT NULL,
PRIMARY KEY (user_id)
);
```

Most of the columns here mimic those in the *sitename* database's *users* table, created in the preceding two chapters. The *pass* column is defined as CHAR(40), because the SHA1() function will be used and it always returns a string 40 characters long (see Chapter 5).

6. If desired, confirm the database's structure (**Figure 6.11**).

```
SHOW TABLES;
SHOW COLUMNS FROM forums;
SHOW COLUMNS FROM messages;
SHOW COLUMNS FROM users;
```

This step is optional because MySQL reports on the success of each query as it is entered. But it's always nice to remind yourself of a database's structure.

✔ Tip

- When you have a primary key–foreign key link (like *forum_id* in *forums* to *forum_id* in *messages*), both columns should be of the same type (in this case, TINYINT UNSIGNED NOT NULL).

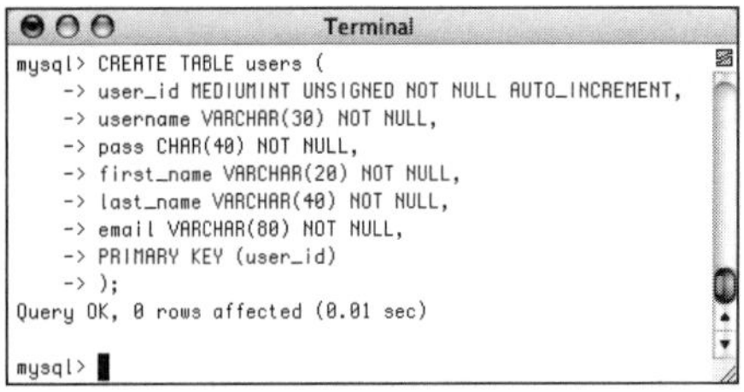

```
mysql> CREATE TABLE users (
    -> user_id MEDIUMINT UNSIGNED NOT NULL AUTO_INCREMENT,
    -> username VARCHAR(30) NOT NULL,
    -> pass CHAR(40) NOT NULL,
    -> first_name VARCHAR(20) NOT NULL,
    -> last_name VARCHAR(40) NOT NULL,
    -> email VARCHAR(80) NOT NULL,
    -> PRIMARY KEY (user_id)
    -> );
Query OK, 0 rows affected (0.01 sec)

mysql>
```

Figure 6.10 The database's third and final table.

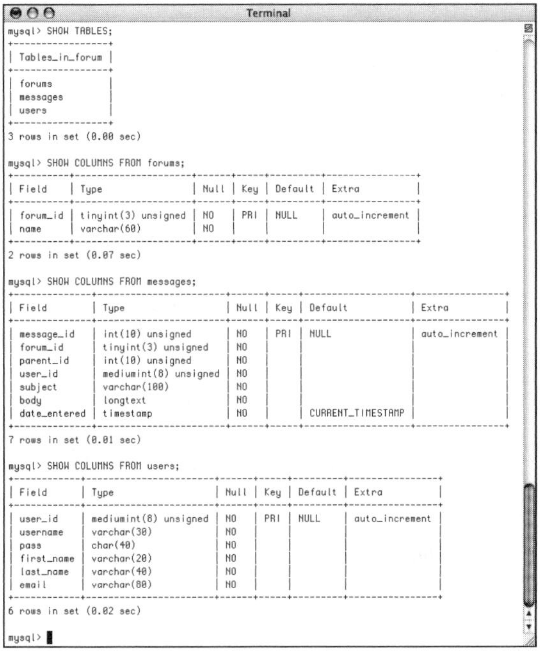

```
mysql> SHOW TABLES;
+-----------------+
| Tables_in_forum |
+-----------------+
| forums          |
| messages        |
| users           |
+-----------------+
3 rows in set (0.00 sec)

mysql> SHOW COLUMNS FROM forums;
+----------+---------------------+------+-----+---------+----------------+
| Field    | Type                | Null | Key | Default | Extra          |
+----------+---------------------+------+-----+---------+----------------+
| forum_id | tinyint(3) unsigned | NO   | PRI | NULL    | auto_increment |
| name     | varchar(60)         | NO   |     |         |                |
+----------+---------------------+------+-----+---------+----------------+
2 rows in set (0.07 sec)

mysql> SHOW COLUMNS FROM messages;
+--------------+-----------------------+------+-----+-------------------+----------------+
| Field        | Type                  | Null | Key | Default           | Extra          |
+--------------+-----------------------+------+-----+-------------------+----------------+
| message_id   | int(10) unsigned      | NO   | PRI | NULL              | auto_increment |
| forum_id     | tinyint(3) unsigned   | NO   |     |                   |                |
| parent_id    | int(10) unsigned      | NO   |     |                   |                |
| user_id      | mediumint(8) unsigned | NO   |     |                   |                |
| subject      | varchar(100)          | NO   |     |                   |                |
| body         | longtext              | NO   |     |                   |                |
| date_entered | timestamp             | NO   |     | CURRENT_TIMESTAMP |                |
+--------------+-----------------------+------+-----+-------------------+----------------+
7 rows in set (0.01 sec)

mysql> SHOW COLUMNS FROM users;
+------------+-----------------------+------+-----+---------+----------------+
| Field      | Type                  | Null | Key | Default | Extra          |
+------------+-----------------------+------+-----+---------+----------------+
| user_id    | mediumint(8) unsigned | NO   | PRI | NULL    | auto_increment |
| username   | varchar(30)           | NO   |     |         |                |
| pass       | char(40)              | NO   |     |         |                |
| first_name | varchar(20)           | NO   |     |         |                |
| last_name  | varchar(40)           | NO   |     |         |                |
| email      | varchar(80)           | NO   |     |         |                |
+------------+-----------------------+------+-----+---------+----------------+
6 rows in set (0.02 sec)

mysql>
```

Figure 6.11 Check the structure of any database or table using SHOW.

Populating the database

In Chapter 15, a Web-based interface to the message board will be written in PHP. That interface will be the standard way to populate the database (i.e., register users and post messages). But there's still a lot to learn to get to that point, so the database has to be populated using a MySQL client application. You can follow these steps or download the SQL commands from the book's corresponding Web site (www.DMCInsights.com/phpmysql3/, click *Downloads*).

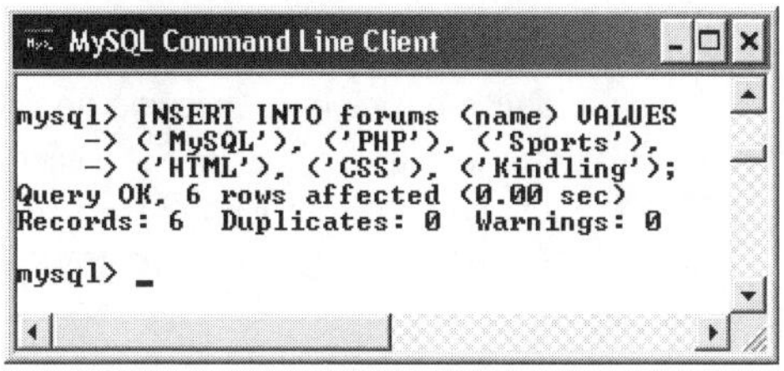

Figure 6.12 Adding records to the *forums* table.

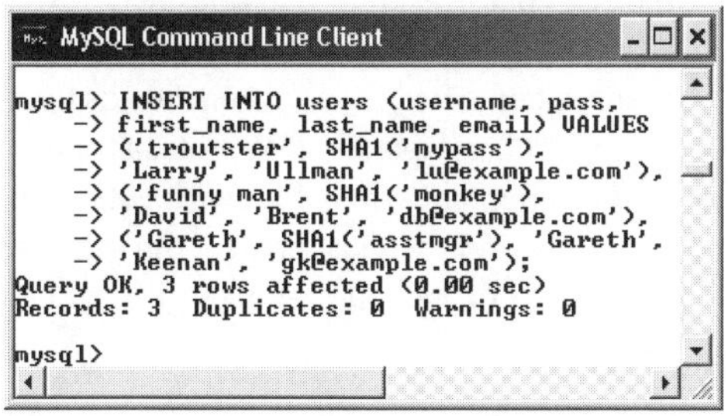

Figure 6.13 Adding records to the *users* table.

To populate the database:

1. Add some new records to the *forums* table (**Figure 6.12**).

   ```
   INSERT INTO forums (name) VALUES
   ('MySQL'), ('PHP'), ('Sports'),
   ('HTML'), ('CSS'), ('Kindling');
   ```

   Since the *messages* table relies on values retrieved from both the *forums* and *users* tables, those two need to be populated first. With this INSERT command, only the *name* column must be provided a value (the table's *forum_id* column will be given an automatically incremented integer by MySQL).

2. Add some records to the *users* table (**Figure 6.13**).

   ```
   INSERT INTO users (username, pass,
   first_name, last_name, email) VALUES
   ('troutster', SHA1('mypass'),
   'Larry', 'Ullman', 'lu@example.com'),
   ('funny man', SHA1('monkey'),
   'David', 'Brent', 'db@example.com'),
   ('Gareth', SHA1('asstmgr'), 'Gareth',
   'Keenan', 'gk@example.com');
   ```

   If you have any questions on the INSERT syntax or use of the SHA1() function here, see Chapter 5.

continues on next page

DATABASE DESIGN

3. Add new records to the *messages* table (**Figure 6.14**).

```
SELECT * FROM forums;

SELECT user_id, username FROM users;

INSERT INTO messages (forum_id,
→ parent_id, user_id, subject, body)
→ VALUES

(1, 0, 1, 'Question about
→ normalization.', 'I\'m confused
→ about normalization. For the second
→ normal form (2NF), I read...'),

(1, 0, 2, 'Database Design', 'I\'m
→ creating a new database and am
→ having problems with the structure.
→ How many tables should I have?...'),

(1, 2, 1, 'Database Design', 'The
→ number of tables your database
→ includes...'),

(1, 3, 2, 'Database Design', 'Okay,
→ thanks!'),

(2, 0, 3, 'PHP Errors', 'I\'m using
→ the scripts from Chapter 3 and I
→ can\'t get the first calculator
→ example to work. When I submit the
→ form...');
```

Because two of the fields in the *messages* table (*forum_id* and *user_id*) relate to values in other tables, you need to know those values before inserting new records into this table. For example, when the *troutocity* user creates a new message in the *MySQL* forum, it will have a *forum_id* of 1 and a *user_id* of 1.

This is further complicated by the *parent_id* column, which should store the *message_id* to which the new message is a reply. The second message added to the database will have a *message_id* of 2, so replies to that message need a *parent_id* of 2.

With your PHP scripts—once you've created an interface for this database, this process will be much easier, but it's important to comprehend the theory in SQL terms first.

You should also notice here that you don't need to enter a value for the `date_entered` field. MySQL will automatically insert the current date and time for this `TIMESTAMP` column.

4. Repeat Steps 1 through 3 to populate the database.

The rest of the examples in this chapter will use the populated database. You'll probably want to download the SQL commands from the book's corresponding Web site, although you can populate the tables with your own examples and then just change the queries in the rest of the chapter accordingly.

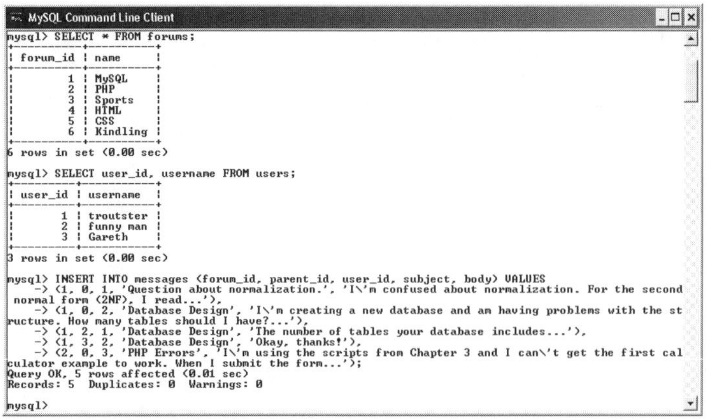

Figure 6.14 Normalized databases will often require you to know values from one table in order to enter records into another. Populating the *messages* table requires knowing foreign key values from *users* and *forums*.

172

Performing Joins

Because relational databases are more complexly structured, they sometimes require special query statements to retrieve the information you need most. For example, if you wanted to know what messages are in the *kindling* forum, you would need to first find the *forum_id* for *kindling*, and then use that number to retrieve all the records from the *messages* table that have that *forum_id*. This one simple (and, in a forum, often necessary) task would require two separate queries. By using a *join,* you can accomplish all of that in one fell swoop.

A join is an SQL query that uses two or more tables, and produces a virtual table of results. The two main types of joins are *inner* and *outer* (there are subtypes within both).

An inner join returns all of the records from the named tables wherever a match is made. For example, to find every message in the *kindling* forum, the inner join would be written as (**Figure 6.15**)

```
SELECT * FROM messages INNER JOIN forums
ON messages.forum_id = forums.forum_id
WHERE forums.name = 'kindling'
```

This join is selecting every column from both tables under two conditions. First, the *forums.name* column must have a value of *kindling* (this will return the *forum_id* of 6). Second, the *forum_id* value in the *forums* table must match the *forum_id* value in the *messages* table. Because of the equality comparison being made across both tables (messages.forum_id = forums.forum_id), this is known as an *equijoin.*

Inner joins can also be written without formally using the term INNER JOIN:

```
SELECT * FROM messages, forums WHERE
messages.forum_id = forums.forum_id
AND forums.name = 'kindling'
```

When selecting from multiple tables, you must use the dot syntax (*table.column*) if the tables named in the query have columns with the same name. This is normally the case when dealing with relational databases because a primary key from one table will have the same name as a foreign key in another. If you are not explicit when referencing your columns, you'll get an error (**Figure 6.16**).

continues on next page

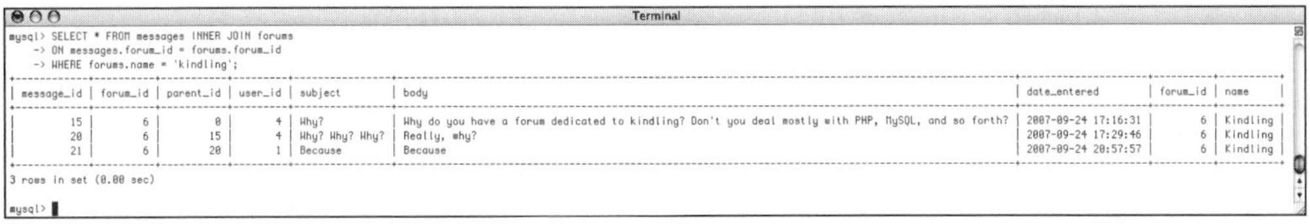

Figure 6.15 This join returns every column from both tables where the *forum_id* values represent the *kindling* forum (6).

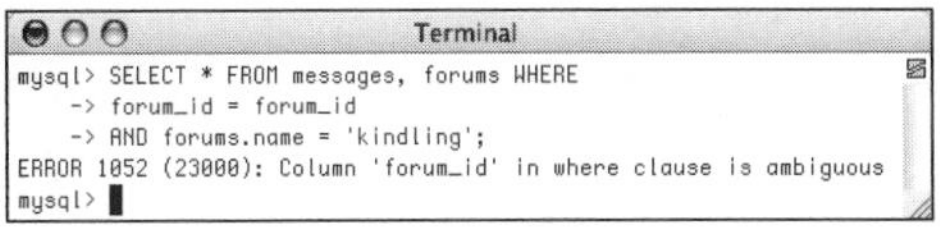

Figure 6.16 Generically referring to a column name present in multiple tables will cause an ambiguity error. In this query, referring to just *name* instead of *forums.name* would be fine, but it's still best to be precise.

An *outer* join differs from an inner join in that an outer join could return records not matched by a conditional. There are three outer join subtypes: *left*, *right*, and *full*. An example of a left join is

```
SELECT * FROM forums LEFT JOIN messages
→ ON forums.forum_id = messages.forum_id
```

The most important consideration with left joins is which table gets named first. In this example, all of the *forums* records will be returned along with all of the *messages* information, if a match is made. If no *messages* records match a *forums* row, then NULL values will be returned instead (**Figure 6.17**).

In both inner and outer joins, if the column in both tables being used in the equality comparison has the same name, you can simplify your query with USING:

```
SELECT * FROM messages INNER JOIN forums
USING (forum_id)
WHERE forums.name = 'kindling'
SELECT * FROM forums LEFT JOIN messages
→ USING (forum_id)
```

Before running through some examples, two last notes. First, because of the complicated syntax with joins, the SQL concept of an alias—introduced in Chapter 5—will come in handy when writing them. Second, because joins often return so much information, it's normally best to specify exactly what columns you want returned, instead of selecting them all (Figure 6.17, in its uncropped form, couldn't even fit within my 22" monitor's screen!).

```
mysql> SELECT * FROM forums LEFT JOIN messages ON forums.forum_id = messages.forum_id;
+----------+-------------+------------+----------+-----------+---------+------------------------------------------+
| forum_id | name        | message_id | forum_id | parent_id | user_id | subject                                  |
+----------+-------------+------------+----------+-----------+---------+------------------------------------------+
|        1 | MySQL       |          1 |        1 |         0 |       1 | Question about normalization.            |
|        1 | MySQL       |          2 |        1 |         0 |       2 | Database Design                          |
|        1 | MySQL       |          3 |        1 |         2 |       2 | Database Design                          |
|        1 | MySQL       |          4 |        1 |         0 |       3 | Database Design                          |
|        2 | PHP         |          5 |        2 |         0 |       3 | PHP Errors                               |
|        2 | PHP         |          6 |        2 |         5 |       1 | PHP Errors                               |
|        2 | PHP         |          7 |        2 |         6 |       3 | PHP Errors                               |
|        2 | PHP         |          8 |        2 |         7 |       1 | PHP Errors                               |
|        2 | PHP         |         16 |        2 |         0 |       3 | Dynamic HTML using PHP                    |
|        2 | PHP         |         17 |        2 |        16 |       1 | Dynamic HTML using PHP                    |
|        2 | PHP         |         18 |        2 |        17 |       3 | Dynamic HTML using PHP, still not clear   |
|        2 | PHP         |         19 |        2 |        18 |       2 | Dynamic HTML using PHP, clearer?          |
|        3 | Sports      |          9 |        3 |         0 |       2 | Rex Grossman                             |
|        3 | Sports      |         10 |        3 |         9 |       1 | Rex Grossman                             |
|        4 | HTML        |         13 |        4 |         0 |       3 | HTML vs. XHTML                            |
|        4 | HTML        |         14 |        4 |        13 |       1 | HTML vs. XHTML                            |
|        5 | CSS         |         11 |        5 |         0 |       3 | CSS Resources                            |
|        5 | CSS         |         12 |        5 |        11 |       1 | CSS Resources                            |
|        6 | Kindling    |         15 |        6 |         0 |       4 | Why?                                     |
|        6 | Kindling    |         20 |        6 |        15 |       4 | Why? Why? Why?                           |
|        6 | Kindling    |         21 |        6 |        20 |       1 | Because                                  |
|        7 | Modern Dance|       NULL |     NULL |      NULL |    NULL | NULL                                     |
+----------+-------------+------------+----------+-----------+---------+------------------------------------------+
22 rows in set (0.00 sec)
```

Figure 6.17 An outer join returns more records than an inner join because all of the first table's records will be returned. This join returns every forum name, even if there are no messages in a forum (like *Modern Dance* at bottom). Also, to make it legible, I've cropped this image, omitting the *body* and *date_entered* columns from the result.

To use joins:

1. Retrieve the forum name and message subject for every record in the *messages* table (**Figure 6.18**).

```
SELECT f.name, m.subject FROM forums
AS f INNER JOIN messages AS m
USING (forum_id) ORDER BY f.name;
```

This query, which contains an inner join, will effectively replace the *forum_id* value in the *messages* table with the corresponding *name* value from the *forums* table for each of the records in the *messages* table. The end result is that it displays the textual version of the forum name for each message subject.

Notice that you can still use ORDER BY clauses in joins.

2. Retrieve the subject and date entered value for every message posted by the user *funny man* (**Figure 6.19**).

```
SELECT m.subject,
→ DATE_FORMAT(m.date_entered, '%M %D,
→ %Y') AS Date FROM users
AS u INNER JOIN messages AS m
USING (user_id)
WHERE u.username = 'funny man';
```

This join also uses two tables, *users* and *messages*. The linking column for the two tables is *user_id*, so that's placed in the USING clause. The WHERE conditional identifies the user being targeted, and the DATE_FORMAT() function will help format the *date_entered* value.

continues on next page

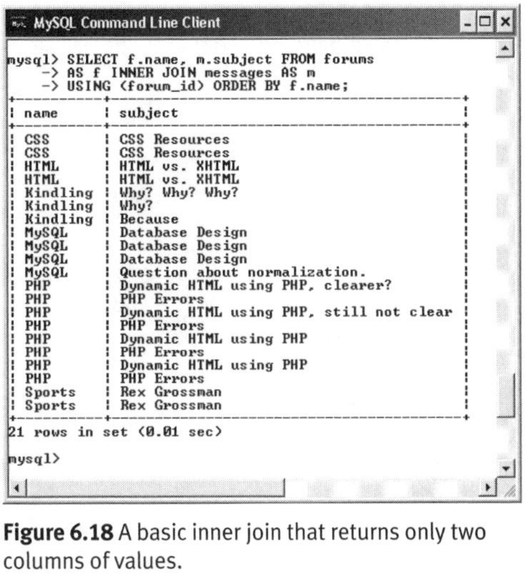

Figure 6.18 A basic inner join that returns only two columns of values.

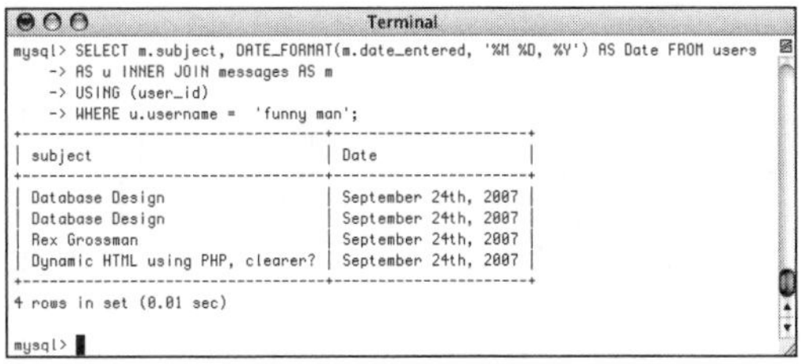

Figure 6.19 A slightly more complicated version of an inner join, using the *users* and *messages* tables.

3. Retrieve the message ID, subject, and forum name for every message posted by the user *troutster* (**Figure 6.20**).

```
SELECT m.message_id, m.subject,
f.name FROM users AS u INNER JOIN
messages AS m USING (user_id)
INNER JOIN forums AS f
USING (forum_id)
WHERE u.username = 'troutster';
```

This join is similar to the one in Step 2, but takes things a step further by incorporating a third table. Take note of how a three-table inner join is written and how the aliases are used for shorthand when referring to the three tables and their columns.

4. Retrieve the username, message subject, and forum name for every user (**Figure 6.21**).

```
SELECT u.username, m.subject,
f.name FROM users AS u LEFT JOIN
messages AS m USING (user_id)
LEFT JOIN forums AS f
USING (forum_id);
```

If you were to run an inner join similar to this, a user who had not yet posted a message would not be listed (**Figure 6.22**). So an outer join is required to be inclusive of all users. Note that the fully included table (here, *users*), must be the first table listed in a left join.

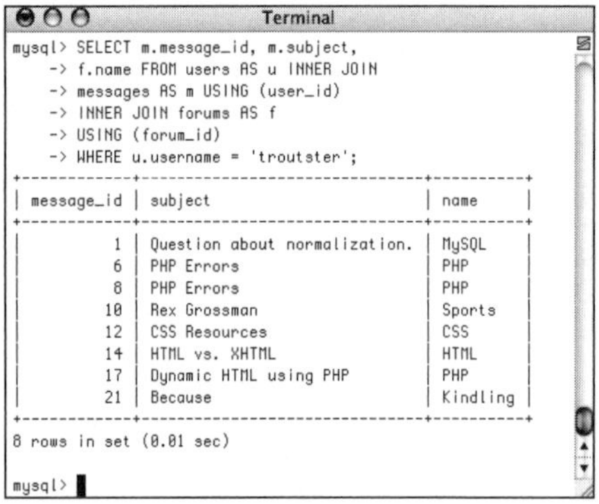

Figure 6.20 An inner join across all three tables.

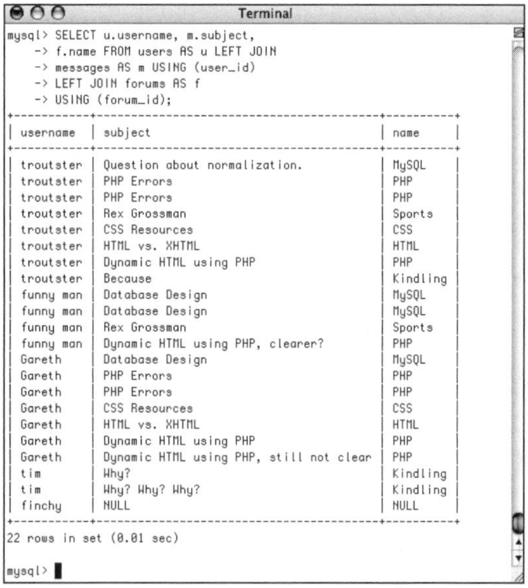

Figure 6.21 This left join returns for every user, every posted message subject, and every forum name. If a user hasn't posted a message (like *finchy* at the bottom), their subject and forum name values will be NULL.

✔ Tips

■ You can even join a table with itself (a *self-join*)!

■ Joins can be created using conditionals involving any columns, not just the primary and foreign keys, although that's most common.

■ You can perform joins across multiple databases using the *database.table.column* syntax, as long as every database is on the same server (you cannot do this across a network) and you're connected as a user with permission to access every database involved.

■ Joins that do not include a WHERE clause (e.g., SELECT * FROM urls, url_associations) are called *full* joins and will return every record from both tables. This construct can have unwieldy results with larger tables.

■ A NULL value in a column referenced in a join will never be returned, because NULL matches no other value, including NULL.

```
● ○ ○                    Terminal
mysql> SELECT u.username, m.subject,
    -> f.name FROM users AS u INNER JOIN
    -> messages AS m USING (user_id)
    -> INNER JOIN forums AS f
    -> USING (forum_id);
+----------+------------------------------------+----------+
| username | subject                            | name     |
+----------+------------------------------------+----------+
| troutster | Question about normalization.     | MySQL    |
| troutster | PHP Errors                        | PHP      |
| troutster | PHP Errors                        | PHP      |
| troutster | Rex Grossman                      | Sports   |
| troutster | CSS Resources                     | CSS      |
| troutster | HTML vs. XHTML                     | HTML     |
| troutster | Dynamic HTML using PHP            | PHP      |
| troutster | Because                           | Kindling |
| funny man | Database Design                   | MySQL    |
| funny man | Database Design                   | MySQL    |
| funny man | Rex Grossman                      | Sports   |
| funny man | Dynamic HTML using PHP, clearer?  | PHP      |
| Gareth   | Database Design                    | MySQL    |
| Gareth   | PHP Errors                         | PHP      |
| Gareth   | PHP Errors                         | PHP      |
| Gareth   | CSS Resources                      | CSS      |
| Gareth   | HTML vs. XHTML                      | HTML     |
| Gareth   | Dynamic HTML using PHP             | PHP      |
| Gareth   | Dynamic HTML using PHP, still not clear | PHP |
| tim      | Why?                               | Kindling |
| tim      | Why? Why? Why?                     | Kindling |
+----------+------------------------------------+----------+
21 rows in set (0.00 sec)

mysql> 
```

Figure 6.22 This inner join will not return any users who haven't yet posted messages (see *finchy* at the bottom of Figure 6.21).

Grouping Selected Results

In the preceding chapter, two different clauses—ORDER BY and LIMIT—were introduced as ways of affecting the returned results. The former dictates the order in which the selected rows are returned; the latter dictates which of the selected rows are actually returned. This next clause, GROUP BY, is different in that it works by grouping the returned data into similar blocks of information. For example, to group all of the messages by forum, you would use

```
SELECT * FROM messages GROUP BY forum_id
```

The returned data is altered in that you've now aggregated the information instead of returned just the specific itemized records. So where you might have lots of messages in each forum, the GROUP BY would return all those messages as one row. That particular example is not particularly useful, but it demonstrates the concept.

You will often use one of several aggregate functions either with a GROUP BY clause or without. **Table 6.7** lists these.

You can apply combinations of WHERE, ORDER BY, and LIMIT conditions to a GROUP BY, normally structuring your query like this:

```
SELECT what_columns FROM table
WHERE condition GROUP BY column
ORDER BY column LIMIT x, y
```

To group data:

1. Count the number of registered users (**Figure 6.23**).

   ```
   SELECT COUNT(user_id) FROM users;
   ```

   COUNT() is perhaps the most popular grouping function. With it, you can quickly count records, like the number of records in the *users* table here. Notice that not all queries using the aggregate functions necessarily have GROUP BY clauses.

Table 6.7 MySQL's grouping functions.

Grouping Functions	
FUNCTION	RETURNS
AVG()	The average of the values in the column.
COUNT()	The number of values in a column.
GROUP_CONCAT()	The concatenation of a column's values.
MAX()	The largest value in a column.
MIN()	The smallest value in a column.
SUM()	The sum of all the values in a column.

Figure 6.23 This grouping query counts the number of *user_id* values in the *users* table.

2. Count the number of times each user has posted a message (**Figure 6.24**).

```
SELECT username,
COUNT(message_id) AS Number
FROM users LEFT JOIN messages AS m
USING (user_id) GROUP BY (m.user_id);
```

This query is an extension of that in Step 1, but instead of counting users, it counts the number of messages associated with each user. A join allows the query to select information from both tables. An inner join is used so that users who have not yet posted will also be represented.

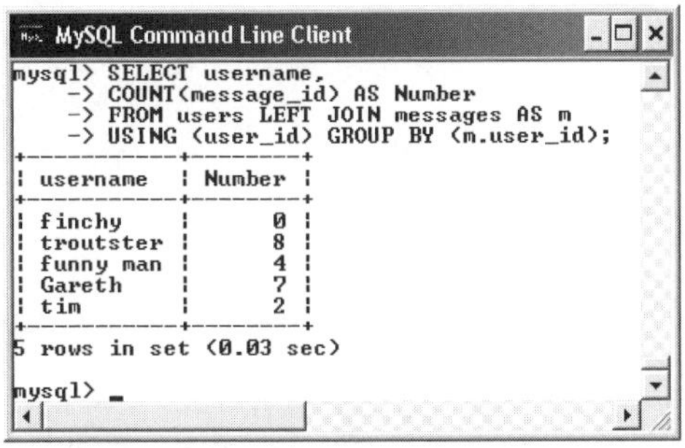

Figure 6.24 This GROUP BY query counts the number of times each user has posted a message.

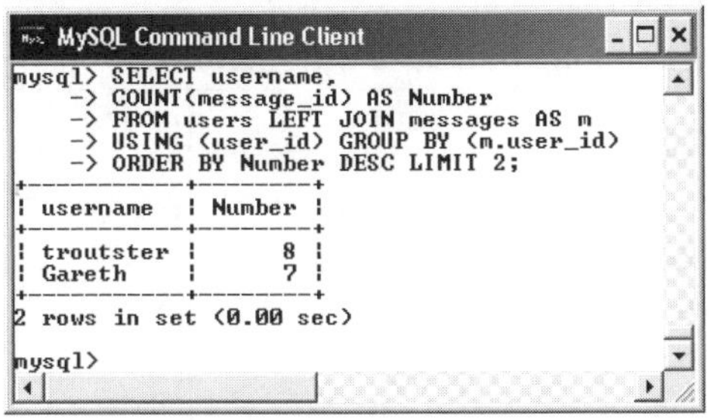

Figure 6.25 An ORDER BY clause is added to sort the most frequent posters by their number of listings. A LIMIT clause cuts the result down to two.

3. Find the top two users that have posted the most (**Figure 6.25**).

```
SELECT username,
COUNT(message_id) AS Number
FROM users LEFT JOIN messages AS m
USING (user_id) GROUP BY (m.user_id)
ORDER BY Number DESC LIMIT 2;
```

With grouping, you can order the results as you would with any other query. Assigning the value of COUNT(*) as the alias *Number* facilitates this process.

✔ Tips

- NULL is a peculiar value, and it's interesting to know that GROUP BY will group NULL values together, since they have the same nonvalue.

- You have to be careful how you apply the COUNT() function, as it only counts non-NULL values. Be certain to use it on either every column (*) or on columns that will not contain NULL values (like the primary key). That being said, if the query in Step 2 and Figure 6.24 applied COUNT() to every column (*) instead of just *message_id*, then users who did not post would erroneously show a COUNT(*) of 1, because the whole query returns one row for that user.

- The GROUP BY clause, and the functions listed here, take some time to figure out, and MySQL will report an error whenever your syntax is inapplicable. Experiment within the mysql client to determine the exact wording of any query you might want to run from a PHP script.

- A related clause is HAVING, which is like a WHERE condition applied to a group.

GROUPING SELECTED RESULTS

179

Creating Indexes

Indexes are a special system that databases use to improve the performance of SELECT queries. Indexes can be placed on one or more columns, of any data type, effectively telling MySQL to pay particular attention to those values.

MySQL allows for a minimum of 16 indexes for each table, and each index can incorporate up to 15 columns. While a multicolumn index may not seem obvious, it will come in handy for searches frequently performed on the same combinations of columns (e.g., first and last name, city and state, etc.).

Although indexes are an integral part of any table, not everything needs to be indexed. While an index does improve the speed of reading from databases, it slows down queries that alter data in a database (because the changes need to be recorded in the index).

Indexes are best used on columns

- That are frequently used in the WHERE part of a query

- That are frequently used in an ORDER BY part of a query

- That are frequently used as the focal point of a join

- That have many different values (columns with numerous repeating values ought not to be indexed)

MySQL has four types of indexes: INDEX (the standard), UNIQUE (which requires each row to have a unique value for that column), FULLTEXT (for performing FULLTEXT searches, discussed later in this chapter), and PRIMARY KEY (which is just a particular UNIQUE index and one you've already been using). Note that a column should only ever have a single index on it, so choose the index type that's most appropriate.

With this in mind, let's modify the *forum* database tables by adding indexes to them. **Table 6.8** lists the indexes to be applied to each column. Adding indexes to existing tables requires use of the ALTER command, as described in the sidebar.

Table 6.8 The indexes to be used in the *forum* database. Not every column will be indexed, and there are two indexes created on a pair of columns: *user.pass* plus *user.username* and *messages.body* plus *messages. subject*.

The forum Database with Indexes

COLUMN NAME	TABLE	INDEX TYPE
forum_id	forums	PRIMARY
name	forums	UNIQUE
message_id	messages	PRIMARY
forum_id	messages	INDEX
parent_id	messages	INDEX
user_id	messages	INDEX
body/subject	messages	FULLTEXT
date_entered	messages	INDEX
user_id	users	PRIMARY
username	users	UNIQUE
pass/username	users	INDEX
email	users	UNIQUE

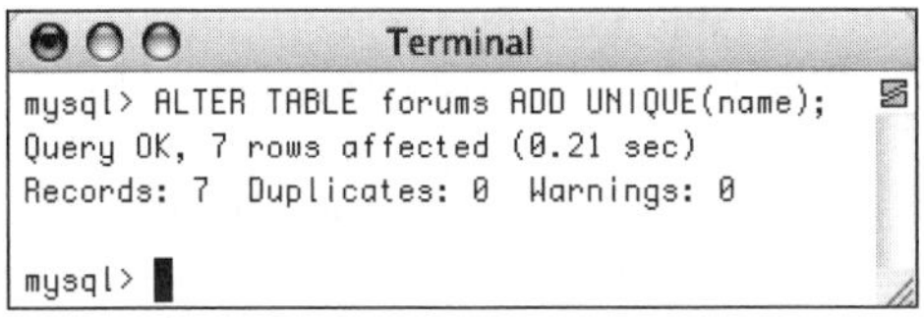

Figure 6.26 A unique index is placed on the *name* column. This will improve the efficiency of certain queries and protect against redundant entries.

To add an index to an existing table:

1. Add an index on the *name* column in the *forums* table (**Figure 6.26**).

```
ALTER TABLE forums ADD UNIQUE(name);
```

The *forums* table already has a primary key index on the *forum_id*. Since the *name* may also be a frequently referenced field and since its value should be unique for every row, add a UNIQUE index to the table.

continues on next page

Altering Tables

The ALTER SQL term is primarily used to modify the structure of an existing table. Commonly this means adding, deleting, or changing the columns therein, but it also includes the addition of indexes. An ALTER statement can even be used for renaming the table as a whole. While proper database design should give you the structure you need, in the real world, making alterations is commonplace. The basic syntax of ALTER is

```
ALTER TABLE tablename CLAUSE
```

There are many possible clauses; **Table 6.9** lists the most common ones. As always, the MySQL manual covers the topic in exhaustive detail.

Table 6.9 Common variants on the ALTER command (where *t* represents the table's name, *c* a column's name, and *i* an index's name). See the MySQL manual for the full specifications.

ALTER TABLE Clauses

CLAUSE	USAGE	MEANING
ADD COLUMN	ALTER TABLE *t* ADD COLUMN *c* TYPE	Adds a new column to the end of the table.
CHANGE COLUMN	ALTER TABLE *t* CHANGE COLUMN *c* *c* TYPE	Allows you to change the data type and properties of a column.
DROP COLUMN	ALTER TABLE *t* DROP COLUMN *c*	Removes a column from a table, including all of its data.
ADD INDEX	ALTER TABLE *t* ADD INDEX *i* (*c*)	Adds a new index on *c*.
DROP INDEX	ALTER TABLE *t* DROP INDEX *i*	Removes an existing index.
RENAME AS	ALTER TABLE *t* RENAME AS *new_t*	Changes the name of a table.

2. Add indexes to the *messages* table
(**Figure 6.27**).

```
ALTER TABLE messages
ADD INDEX(forum_id),
ADD INDEX(parent_id),
ADD INDEX(user_id),
ADD FULLTEXT(body, subject),
ADD INDEX(date_entered);
```

This table contains the most indexes, because it's the most important table and has three foreign keys (*forum_id*, *parent_id*, and *user_id*), all of which should be indexed. The *body* and *subject* columns get a FULLTEXT index, to be used in FULLTEXT searches later in this chapter. The *date_entered* column is indexed, as it will be used in ORDER BY clauses (to sort messages by date).

If you get an error message that the table type doesn't not support FULLTEXT indexes (**Figure 6.28**), omit that one line from this query and then see the next section of the chapter for how to change a table's type.

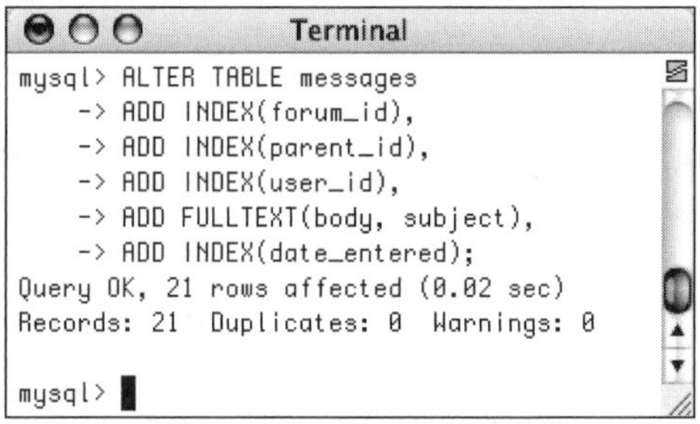

Figure 6.27 Several indexes are added to the *messages* table. MySQL will report on the success of the alteration and how many rows were affected (which should be every row in the table).

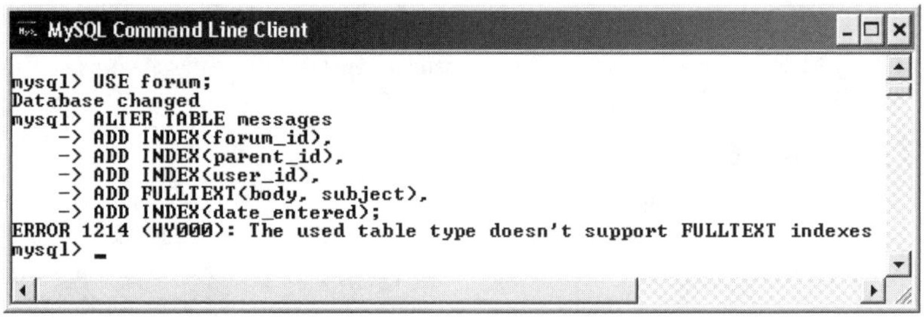

Figure 6.28 FULLTEXT indexes cannot be used on all table types. If you see this error message, read "Using Different Table Types" in this chapter for the solution.

3. Add indexes to the *users* table (**Figure 6.29**).

```
ALTER TABLE users
ADD UNIQUE(username),
ADD INDEX(pass, username),
ADD UNIQUE(email);
```

The *users* table has two UNIQUE indexes and one multicolumn index. UNIQUE indexes are important here because you don't want two people trying to register with the same username (which, among other things, would make it impossible to log in), nor do you want the same user registering multiple times with the same email address.

The index on the combination of the password and username columns will improve the efficiency of login queries, when the combination of those two columns will be used in a WHERE conditional.

4. View the current structure of each table (**Figure 6.30**).

```
DESCRIBE forums;
DESCRIBE messages;
DESCRIBE users;
```

The DESCRIBE SQL term will tell you information about a table's column names and order, column types, and index types (under *Key*). It also indicates whether or not a field can be NULL, what default value has been set (if any), and more.

continues on next page

```
mysql> ALTER TABLE users ADD UNIQUE(username),
    -> ADD INDEX(pass, username),
    -> ADD UNIQUE(email);
Query OK, 5 rows affected (0.07 sec)
Records: 5  Duplicates: 0  Warnings: 0

mysql>
```

Figure 6.29 The requisite indexes are added to the third and final table.

```
mysql> DESCRIBE forums;
+----------+---------------------+------+-----+---------+----------------+
| Field    | Type                | Null | Key | Default | Extra          |
+----------+---------------------+------+-----+---------+----------------+
| forum_id | tinyint(3) unsigned | NO   | PRI | NULL    | auto_increment |
| name     | varchar(60)         | NO   | UNI |         |                |
+----------+---------------------+------+-----+---------+----------------+
2 rows in set (0.06 sec)

mysql> DESCRIBE messages;
+--------------+-----------------------+------+-----+-------------------+----------------+
| Field        | Type                  | Null | Key | Default           | Extra          |
+--------------+-----------------------+------+-----+-------------------+----------------+
| message_id   | int(10) unsigned      | NO   | PRI | NULL              | auto_increment |
| forum_id     | tinyint(3) unsigned   | NO   | MUL |                   |                |
| parent_id    | int(10) unsigned      | NO   | MUL |                   |                |
| user_id      | mediumint(8) unsigned | NO   | MUL |                   |                |
| subject      | varchar(100)          | NO   |     |                   |                |
| body         | longtext              | NO   | MUL |                   |                |
| date_entered | timestamp             | NO   | MUL | CURRENT_TIMESTAMP |                |
+--------------+-----------------------+------+-----+-------------------+----------------+
7 rows in set (0.01 sec)

mysql> DESCRIBE users;
+------------+-----------------------+------+-----+---------+----------------+
| Field      | Type                  | Null | Key | Default | Extra          |
+------------+-----------------------+------+-----+---------+----------------+
| user_id    | mediumint(8) unsigned | NO   | PRI | NULL    | auto_increment |
| username   | varchar(30)           | NO   | UNI |         |                |
| pass       | char(40)              | NO   | MUL |         |                |
| first_name | varchar(20)           | NO   |     |         |                |
| last_name  | varchar(40)           | NO   |     |         |                |
| email      | varchar(80)           | NO   | UNI |         |                |
+------------+-----------------------+------+-----+---------+----------------+
6 rows in set (0.00 sec)

mysql>
```

Figure 6.30 To view the details of a table's structure, use DESCRIBE. The *Key* column indicates the indexes.

✔ Tips

- You'll get an error and the index will not be created if you attempt to add a UNIQUE index to a column that has duplicate values.

- Indexes can be named when they are created:

  ALTER TABLE *tablename*

  ADD INDEX *indexname* (*columnname*)

  If no name is provided, the index will take the name of the column to which it is applied.

- The word COLUMN in most ALTER statements is optional.

- Suppose you define an index on multiple columns, like this:

  ALTER TABLE *tablename*

  ADD INDEX (col1, col2, col3)

  This effectively creates an index for searches on *col1*, on *col1* and *col2* together, or on all three columns together. It does not provide an index for searching just *col2* or *col3* or those two together.

Using Different Table Types

The MySQL database application supports several different types of tables (a table's type is also called its *storage engine*). Each table type supports different features, has its own limits (in terms of how much data it can store), and even performs better or worse under certain situations. Still, how you interact with any table type—in terms of running queries—is generally consistent across them all.

The most important table type is *MyISAM*, which is the default table type on all operating systems except for Windows. MyISAM tables are great for most applications, handling SELECTs and INSERTs very quickly. The MyISAM storage engine cannot handle transactions, though, which is its main drawback.

After MyISAM, the next most common storage engine is *InnoDB*, which is also the default table type for Windows installations of MySQL. InnoDB tables can be used for transactions and perform UPDATEs nicely. But the InnoDB storage engine is generally slower than MyISAM and requires more disk space on the server. Also, an InnoDB table does not support FULLTEXT indexes (which is why, if you're running Windows, you might have seen the error message in Figure 6.28).

To specify the storage engine when you define a table, add a clause to the end of the creation statement:

```
CREATE TABLE tablename (
column1name COLUMNTYPE,
column1name COLUMNTYPE…
) ENGINE = INNODB
```

If you don't specify a storage engine when creating tables, MySQL will use the default type for that MySQL server.

To change the type of an existing table—which is perfectly acceptable—use an ALTER command:

```
ALTER TABLE tablename ENGINE = MYISAM
```

Because the next example in this chapter will require a MyISAM table, let's run through the steps necessary for making sure that the *messages* table is the correct type. The first couple of steps will show you how to see the current storage engine being used (as you may not need to change the *messages* table's type).

To change a table's type:

1. View the current table information (**Figure 6.31**).

   SHOW TABLE STATUS;

   The SHOW TABLE STATUS command returns all sorts of useful information about a database's tables. The returned result will be hard to read, though, as it is a wide table displayed over multiple lines. What you're looking for is this: The first item on each row is the table's name, and the second item is the table's engine, or table type. The engine will most likely be either *MyISAM* (Figure 6.31) or *InnoDB* (**Figure 6.32**).

2. If necessary, change the *messages* table to MyISAM (**Figure 6.33**).

   ALTER TABLE messages ENGINE=MYISAM;

   If the results in Step 1 (Figures 6.31 and 6.32) indicate that the engine is anything other than MyISAM, you'll need to change it over to MyISAM using this command (capitalization doesn't matter). For me, using the default MySQL installation and configuration, changing the table's type wasn't necessary on Mac OS X but was on Windows.

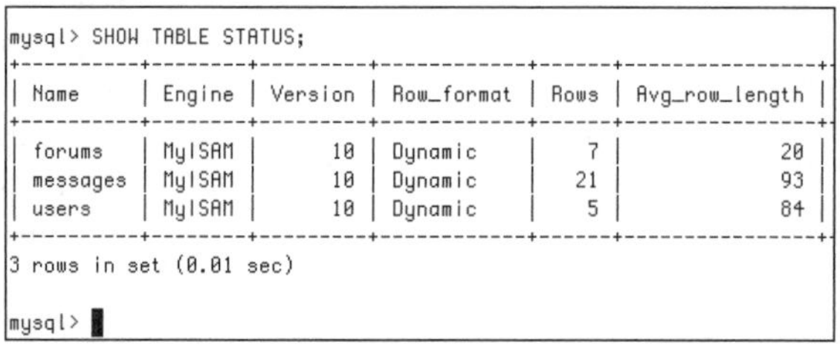

Figure 6.31 Before altering a table's type, view its current type with the SHOW TABLE STATUS command. This is a cropped version of the results using MySQL on Mac OS X.

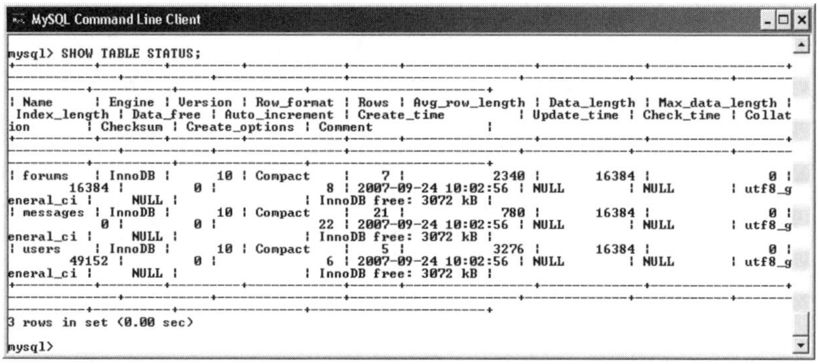

Figure 6.32 The SHOW TABLE STATUS query (using MySQL on Windows) shows that all three tables are, in fact, InnoDB, not MyISAM.

USING DIFFERENT TABLE TYPES

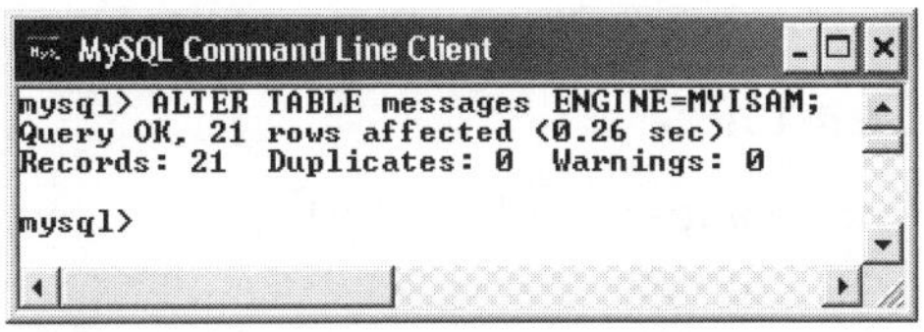

Figure 6.33 Successfully changing a table's type (or storage engine) using an ALTER command.

3. If desired, confirm the engine change by rerunning the SHOW TABLE STATUS command.

✔ Tips

■ To make any query's results easier to view in the mysql client, you can add the \G parameter (**Figure 6.34**):

SHOW TABLE STATUS \G

This flag states that the table of results should be displayed vertically instead of horizontally. Notice that you don't need to use a terminating semicolon now, because the \G ends the command.

■ The same database can have tables of different types. This may be true for your *forum* database now (depending upon your default table type). You may also see this with an e-commerce database that uses MyISAM for customers and products but InnoDB for orders (to allow for transactions).

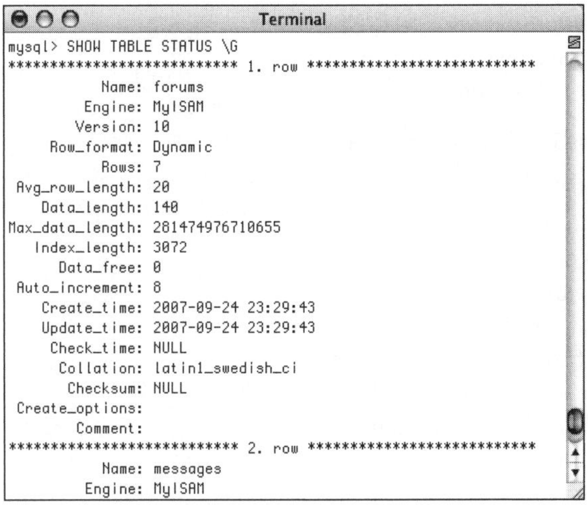

Figure 6.34 For a more legible version of a query's results, add the \G option in the mysql client.

USING DIFFERENT TABLE TYPES

187

Performing FULLTEXT Searches

In Chapter 5, the LIKE keyword was introduced as a way to perform somewhat simple string matches like

```
SELECT * FROM users
```

```
WHERE last_name LIKE 'Smith%'
```

This type of conditional is effective enough but is still very limiting. For example, it would not allow you to do Google-like searches using multiple words. For those kinds of situations, you need FULLTEXT searches.

FULLTEXT searches require a FULLTEXT index, which itself requires a MyISAM table. These next examples will use the *messages* table in the *forum* database. If your *messages* table is not of the MyISAM type and/or does not have a FULLTEXT index on the *body* and *subject* columns, follow the steps in the previous few pages to make that change before proceeding.

✔ Tips

- Inserting records into tables with FULLTEXT indexes can be much slower because of the complex index that's required.

- You can add FULLTEXT indexes on multiple columns, if those columns will all be used in searches.

- FULLTEXT searches can successfully be used in a simple search engine. But a FULLTEXT index can only be applied to a single table at a time, so more elaborate Web sites, with content stored in multiple tables, would benefit from using more formal search engines.

Performing Basic FULLTEXT Searches

Once you've established a FULLTEXT index on a column or columns, you can start querying against it, using MATCH...AGAINST in a WHERE conditional:

```
SELECT * FROM tablename WHERE MATCH
```

```
(columns) AGAINST (terms)
```

MySQL will return matching rows in order of a mathematically calculated relevance, just like a search engine. When doing so, certain rules apply:

- ◆ Strings are broken down into their individual keywords.

- ◆ Keywords less than four characters long are ignored.

- ◆ Very popular words, called *stopwords*, are ignored.

- ◆ If more than fifty percent of the records match the keywords, no records are returned.

This last fact is problematic to many users as they begin with FULLTEXT searches and wonder why no results are retrieved. When you have a sparsely populated table, there just won't be sufficient records for MySQL to return *relevant* results.

To perform FULLTEXT searches:

1. Thoroughly populate the *messages* table, focusing on adding lengthy bodies.

   Once again, SQL INSERT commands can be downloaded from this book's corresponding Web site.

2. Run a simple FULLTEXT search on the word *database* (**Figure 6.35**).

   ```
   SELECT subject, body FROM messages
   WHERE MATCH (body, subject)
   AGAINST('database');
   ```

This is a very simple example that will return some results as long as at least one and less than fifty percent of the records in the *messages* table have the word "database" in their body or subject. Note that the columns referenced in MATCH must be the same as those on which the FULLTEXT index was made. In this case, you could use either body, subject or subject, body, but you could not use just body or just subject (**Figure 6.36**).

continues on next page

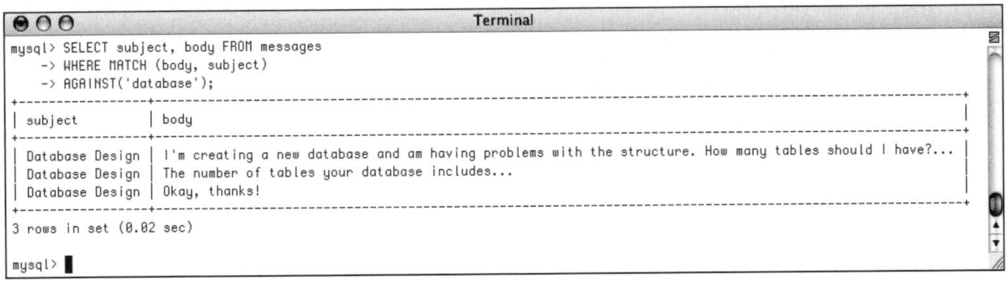

Figure 6.35 A basic FULLTEXT search.

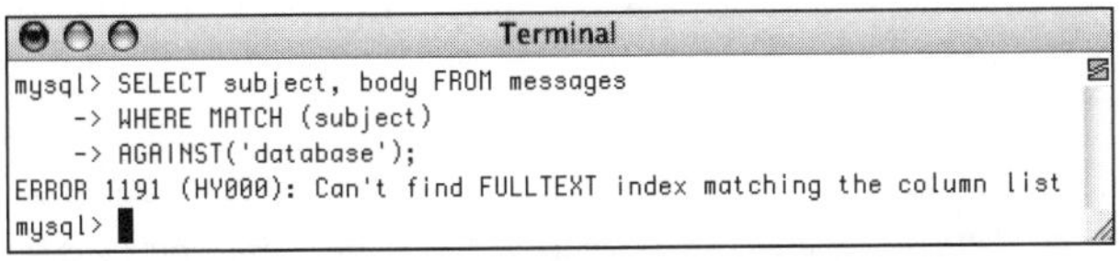

Figure 6.36 A FULLTEXT query can only be run on the same column or combination of columns that the FULLTEXT index was created on. With this query, even though the combination of *body* and *subject* has a FULLTEXT index, attempting to run the match on just *subject* will fail.

3. Run the same FULLTEXT search while also showing the relevance (**Figure 6.37**).

SELECT subject, body, MATCH (body,

subject) AGAINST('database') AS R

FROM messages WHERE MATCH (body,

→ subject) AGAINST('database');

If you use the same MATCH...AGAINST expression as a selected value, the actual relevance will be returned.

4. Run a FULLTEXT search using multiple keywords (**Figure 6.38**).

SELECT subject, body FROM messages

WHERE MATCH (body, subject)

AGAINST('html xhtml');

With this query, a match will be made if the subject or body contains either word. Any record that contains both words will be ranked higher.

✔ Tips

- Remember that if a FULLTEXT search returns no records, this means that either no matches were made or that over half of the records match.

- For sake of simplicity, all of the queries in this section are simple SELECT statements. You can certainly use FULLTEXT searches within joins or more complex queries.

- MySQL comes with several hundred stop-words already defined. These are part of the application's source code.

- The minimum keyword length—four characters by default—is a configuration setting you can change in MySQL.

- FULLTEXT searches are case-insensitive by default.

```
mysql> SELECT subject, body, MATCH (body, subject) AGAINST('database')AS R FROM messages WHERE MATCH (body, subject)
    -> AGAINST('database');
+-----------------+----------------------------------------------------------------------------------------+----------------+
| subject         | body                                                                                   | R              |
+-----------------+----------------------------------------------------------------------------------------+----------------+
| Database Design | I'm creating a new database and am having problems with the structure. How many tables should I have?... | 2.5440027713776 |
| Database Design | The number of tables your database includes...                                         | 2.5194842815399 |
| Database Design | Okay, thanks!                                                                          | 1.7514755725861 |
+-----------------+----------------------------------------------------------------------------------------+----------------+
3 rows in set (0.48 sec)

mysql>
```

Figure 6.37 The relevance of a FULLTEXT search can be selected, too. In this case, you'll see that the two records with the word "database" in both the subject and body have higher relevance than the record that contains the word in just the subject.

```
mysql> SELECT subject, body FROM messages
    -> WHERE MATCH (body, subject)
    -> AGAINST('html xhtml');
+---------------------------------+----------------------------------------------------------------------------------------+
| subject                         | body                                                                                   |
+---------------------------------+----------------------------------------------------------------------------------------+
| HTML vs. XHTML                  | XHTML is a cross between HTML and XML. The differences are largely syntactic. Blah, blah, blah... |
| HTML vs. XHTML                  | What are the differences between HTML and XHTML?                                        |
| Dynamic HTML using PHP          | Can I use PHP to dynamically generate HTML on the fly? Thanks...                        |
| Dynamic HTML using PHP          | You most certainly can.                                                                 |
| Dynamic HTML using PHP, still not clear | Um, how?                                                                        |
| Dynamic HTML using PHP, clearer? | I think what Larry is trying to say is that you should buy and read his book.           |
| CSS Resources                   | Read Elizabeth Castro's excellent book on HTML and CSS. Or search Google on "CSS".      |
+---------------------------------+----------------------------------------------------------------------------------------+
7 rows in set (0.00 sec)

mysql>
```

Figure 6.38 Using the FULLTEXT search, you can easily find messages that contain multiple keywords.

Performing Boolean FULLTEXT Searches

The basic FULLTEXT search is nice, but a more sophisticated FULLTEXT search can be accomplished using its Boolean mode. To do so, add the phrase IN BOOLEAN MODE to the AGAINST clause:

SELECT * FROM *tablename* WHERE

MATCH(*columns*) AGAINST('terms' IN BOOLEAN

MODE)

Boolean mode has a number of operators (**Table 6.10**) to tweak how each keyword is treated:

SELECT * FROM *tablename* WHERE

MATCH(*columns*) AGAINST('+database

-mysql' IN BOOLEAN MODE)

In that example, a match will be made if the word *database* is found and *mysql* is not present. Alternatively, the tilde (~) is used as a milder form of the minus sign, meaning that the keyword can be present in a match, but such matches should be considered less relevant.

Table 6.10 Use these operators to fine-tune your FULLTEXT searches.

Boolean Mode Operators

Operator	Meaning
+	Must be present in every match
-	Must not be present in any match
~	Lowers a ranking if present
*	Wildcard
<	Decrease a word's importance
>	Increase a word's importance
" "	Must match the exact phrase
( )	Create subexpressions

The wildcard character (*) matches variations on a word, so cata* matches *catalog, catalina,* and so on. Two operators explicitly state what keywords are more (>) or less (<) important. Finally, you can use double quotation marks to hunt for exact phrases and parentheses to make subexpressions.

The following query would look for records with the phrase *Web develop* with the word *html* being required and the word *JavaScript* detracting from a match's relevance:

SELECT * FROM *tablename* WHERE

MATCH(*columns*) AGAINST('>"Web develop"

+html ~JavaScript' IN BOOLEAN MODE)

When using Boolean mode, there are several differences as to how FULLTEXT searches work:

◆ If a keyword is not preceded by an operator, the word is optional but a match will be ranked higher if it is present.

◆ Results will be returned even if more than fifty percent of the records match the search.

◆ The results are not automatically sorted by relevance.

Because of this last fact, you'll also want to sort the returned records by their relevance, as demonstrated in the next sequence of steps. One important rule that's the same with Boolean searches is that the minimum word length (four characters by default) still applies. So trying to require a shorter word using a plus sign (+php) still won't work.

To perform FULLTEXT Boolean searches:

1. Run a simple FULLTEXT search that finds *HTML*, *XHTML*, or *(X)HTML* (**Figure 6.39**).

   ```
   SELECT subject, body FROM
   messages WHERE MATCH(body, subject)
   AGAINST('*HTML' IN BOOLEAN MODE)\G
   ```

   The term HTML may appear in messages in many formats, including *HTML*, *XHTML*, or *(X)HTML*. This Boolean mode query will find all of those, thanks to the wildcard character (*).

   To make the results easier to view, I'm using the \G trick mentioned earlier in the chapter, which tells the mysql client to return the results vertically, not horizontally.

2. Find matches involving databases, with an emphasis on normal forms (**Figure 6.40**).

   ```
   SELECT subject, body FROM messages
   WHERE MATCH (body, subject)
   AGAINST('>"normal form"* +database*'
   IN BOOLEAN MODE)\G
   ```

   This query first finds all records that have *database*, *databases*, etc. and *normal form*, *normal forms*, etc. in them. The database* term is required (as indicated by the plus sign), but emphasis is given to the normal form clause (which is preceded by the greater-than sign).

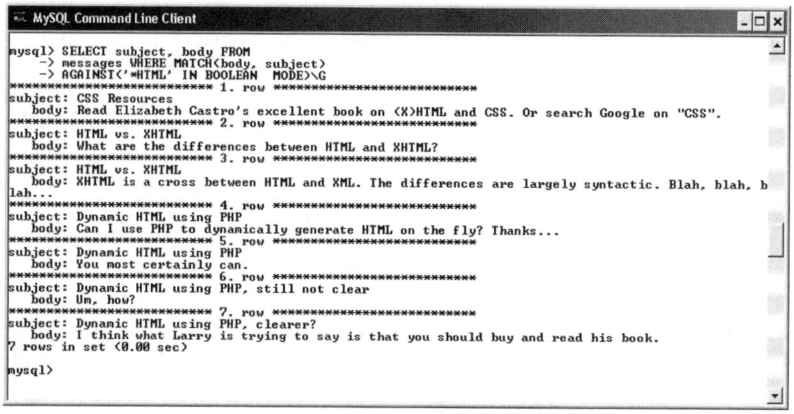

Figure 6.39 A simple Boolean-mode FULLTEXT search.

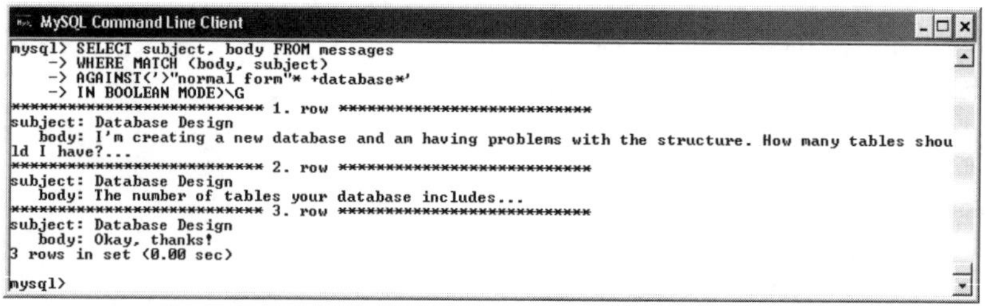

Figure 6.40 This search looks for variations on two different keywords, ranking the one higher than the other.

Database Optimization

The performance of your database is primarily dependent upon its structure and indexes. When creating databases, try to

◆ Choose the best storage engine

◆ Use the smallest data type possible for each column

◆ Define columns as NOT NULL whenever possible

◆ Use integers as primary keys

◆ Judiciously define indexes, selecting the correct type and applying them to the right column or columns

◆ Limit indexes to a certain number of characters, if applicable

Along with these tips, there are two simple techniques for optimizing databases. One way to improve MySQL's performance is to run an OPTIMIZE command on such tables. This query will rid a table of any unnecessary overhead, thereby speeding any interactions with it.

OPTIMIZE TABLE *tablename*

Running this command is particularly beneficial after changing a table via an ALTER command.

To improve a query's efficiency, it helps to understand how exactly MySQL will run that query. This can be accomplished using the EXPLAIN SQL keyword. Explaining queries is a very advanced topic, so see the MySQL manual or search the Web for more information.

✔ Tips

■ MySQL 5.1.7 added another FULLTEXT search mode: natural language. This is the default mode, if no other mode (like Boolean) is specified.

■ The WITH QUERY EXPANSION modifier can increase the number of returned results. Such queries perform two searches and return one result set. It bases a second search on terms found in the most relevant results of the initial search. While a WITH QUERY EXPANSION search can find results that would not otherwise have been returned, it can also return results that aren't at all relevant to the original search terms.

PERFORMING FULLTEXT SEARCHES

Performing Transactions

A *database transaction* is a sequence of queries run during a single session. For example, you might insert a record into one table, insert another record into another table, and maybe run an update. Without using transactions, each individual query takes effect immediately and cannot be undone. With transactions, you can set start and stop points and then enact or retract all of the queries as needed (for example, if one query failed, all of the queries can be undone).

Commercial interactions commonly require transactions, even something as basic as transferring $100 from my bank account to yours. What seems like a simple process is actually several steps:

◆ Confirm that I have $100 in my account.

◆ Decrease my account by $100.

◆ Increase the amount of money in your account by $100.

◆ Verify that the increase worked.

If any of the steps failed, I would want to undo all of them. For example, if the money couldn't be deposited in your account, it should be returned to mine until the entire transaction can go through.

To perform transactions with MySQL, you must use the InnoDB table type (or storage engine). To begin a new transaction in the mysql client, type

START TRANSACTION;

Once your transaction has begun, you can now run your queries. Once you have finished, you can either enter COMMIT to enact all of the queries or ROLLBACK to undo the effect of all of the queries.

After you have either committed or rolled back the queries, the transaction is considered complete, and MySQL returns to an *autocommit* mode. This means that any queries you execute take immediate effect. To start another transaction, just type START TRANSACTION.

It is important to know that certain types of queries cannot be rolled back. Specifically those that create, alter, truncate (empty), or delete tables or that create or delete databases cannot be undone. Furthermore, using such a query has the effect of committing and ending the current transaction.

Finally, you should understand that transactions are particular to each connection. So one user connected through the mysql client has a different transaction than another mysql client user, both of which are different than a connected PHP script.

With this in mind, I'll run through a very trivial use of transactions within the mysql client here. In Chapter 17, "Example—E-Commerce," transactions will be run through a PHP script.

To perform transactions:

1. Connect to the mysql client and select the *test* database.

   Since this is just a demonstration, I'll use the all-purpose *test* database.

2. Create a new *accounts* table (**Figure 6.41**).

   ```
   CREATE TABLE accounts (
   id INT UNSIGNED NOT NULL
   → AUTO_INCREMENT,
   name VARCHAR(40) NOT NULL,
   balance DECIMAL(10,2) NOT NULL
   → DEFAULT 0.0,
   PRIMARY KEY (id)
   ) ENGINE=InnoDB;
   ```

Obviously this isn't a complete table or database design. For starters, normalization would require that the user's name be separated into multiple columns, if not stored in a separate table altogether. But for demonstration purposes, this will be fine.

The most important aspect of the table definition is its engine—InnoDB, which allows for transactions.

3. Populate the table.

   ```
   INSERT INTO accounts (name, balance)
   VALUES ('Sarah Vowell', 5460.23),
   ('David Sedaris', 909325.24),
   ('Kojo Nnamdi', 892.00);
   ```

   You can use whatever names and values here that you want. The important thing to note is that MySQL will automatically commit this query, as no transaction has begun yet.

continues on next page

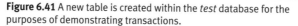

Figure 6.41 A new table is created within the *test* database for the purposes of demonstrating transactions.

PERFORMING TRANSACTIONS

4. Begin a transaction and show the table's current contents (**Figure 6.42**).

```
START TRANSACTION;

SELECT * FROM accounts;
```

5. Subtract $100 from David Sedaris' (or any user's) account.

```
UPDATE accounts

SET balance = (balance-100)

WHERE id=2;
```

Using an UPDATE query, a little math, and a WHERE conditional, I can subtract 100 from a balance. Although MySQL will indicate that one row was affected, the effect is not permanent until the transaction is committed.

6. Add $100 to Sarah Vowell's account.

```
UPDATE accounts

SET balance = (balance+100)

WHERE id=1;
```

This is the opposite of Step 5, as if $100 were being transferred from the one person to the other.

7. Confirm the results (**Figure 6.43**).

```
SELECT * FROM accounts;
```

As you can see in the figure, the one balance is 100 more and the other is 100 less then they originally were (Figure 6.42).

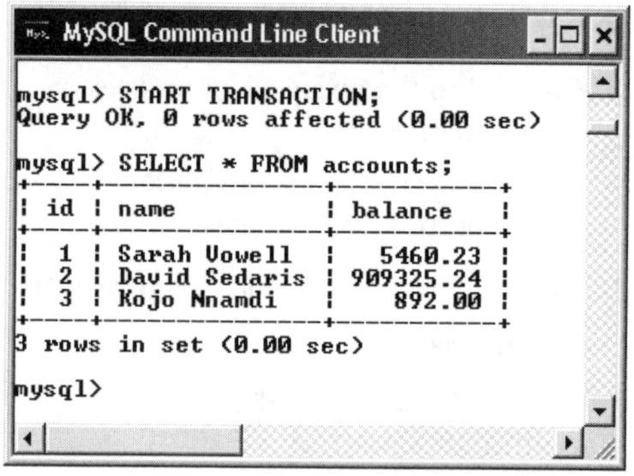

Figure 6.42 A transaction is begun and the existing table records are shown.

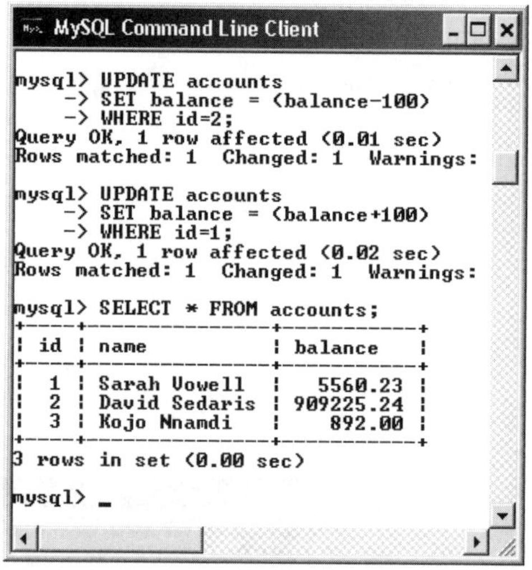

Figure 6.43 Two UPDATE queries are executed and the results are viewed.

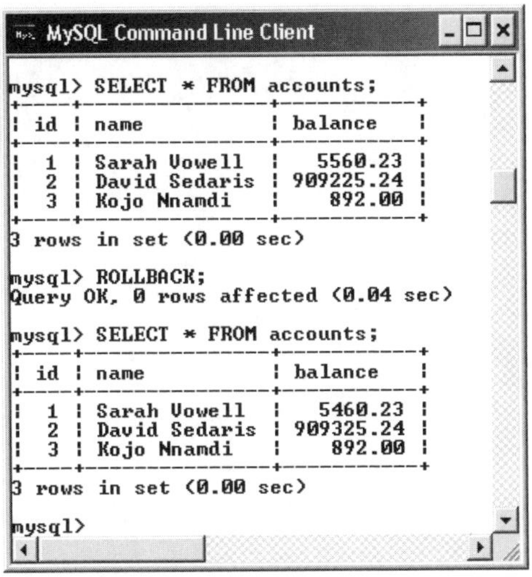

Figure 6.44 Because I used the ROLLBACK command, the potential effects of the UPDATE queries were ignored.

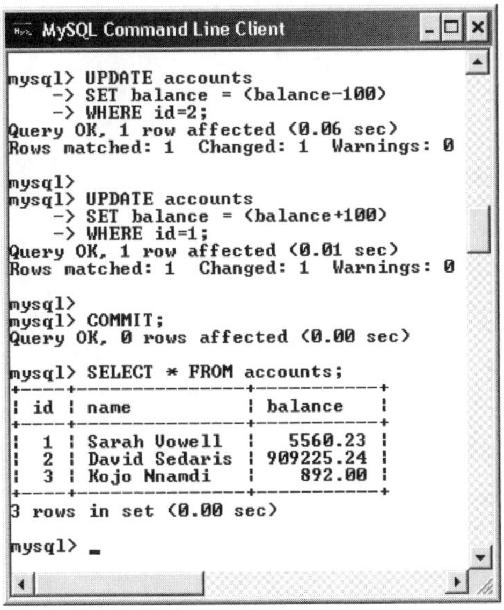

Figure 6.45 Invoking the COMMIT command makes the transaction's effects permanent.

8. Roll back the transaction.

   ```
   ROLLBACK;
   ```

   To demonstrate how transactions can be undone, I'll undo the effects of these queries. The ROLLBACK command returns the database to how it was prior to starting the transaction. The command also terminates the transaction, returning MySQL to its autocommit mode.

9. Confirm the results (**Figure 6.44**).

   ```
   SELECT * FROM accounts;
   ```

   The query should reveal the contents of the table as they original were.

10. Repeat Steps 4 through 6.

    To see what happens when the transaction is committed, the two UPDATE queries will be run again. Be certain to start the transaction first, though, or the queries will automatically take effect!

11. Commit the transaction and confirm the results (**Figure 6.45**).

    ```
    COMMIT;

    SELECT * FROM accounts;
    ```

    Once you enter COMMIT, the entire transaction is permanent, meaning that any changes are now in place. COMMIT also ends the transaction, returning MySQL to autocommit mode.

    continues on next page

✔ Tips

- One of the great features of transactions is that they offer protection should a random event occur, such as a server crash. Either a transaction is executed in its entirety or all of the changes are ignored.

- To alter MySQL's autocommit nature, type

  `SET AUTOCOMMIT=0;`

  Then you do not need to type `START TRANSACTION` and no queries will be permanent until you type `COMMIT` (or use an `ALTER`, `CREATE`, etc., query).

- You can create *savepoints* in transactions:

  `SAVEPOINT savepoint_name;`

  Then you can roll back to that point:

  `ROLLBACK TO SAVEPOINT savepoint_name;`

ERROR HANDLING AND DEBUGGING

7

If you're working through this book sequentially (which would be for the best), the next subject to learn is how to use PHP and MySQL together. However, that process will undoubtedly generate errors, errors that can be tricky to debug. So before moving on to new concepts, these next few pages address the bane of the programmer: errors. As you gain experience, you'll make fewer errors and pick up your own debugging methods, but there are plenty of tools and techniques the beginner can use to help ease the learning process.

This chapter has three main threads. One focus is on learning about the various kinds of errors that can occur when developing dynamic Web sites and what their likely causes are. Second, a multitude of debugging techniques are taught, in a step-by-step format. Finally, you'll see different techniques for handling the errors that occur in the most graceful manner possible.

Before reading on, a word regarding errors: they happen to the best of us. Even the author of this here book sees more than enough errors in his Web development duties (but rest assured that the code in this book should be bug-free). Thinking that you'll get to a skill level where errors never occur is a fool's dream, but there are techniques for minimizing errors, and knowing how to quickly catch, handle, and fix errors is a major skill in its own right. So try not to become frustrated as you make errors; instead, bask in the knowledge that you're becoming a better debugger!

Error Types and Basic Debugging

When developing Web applications with PHP and MySQL, you end up with potential bugs in one of four or more technologies. You could have HTML issues, PHP problems, SQL errors, or MySQL mistakes. To be able to stop the bugs, you must first find the crack they're sneaking in through.

HTML problems are often the least disruptive and the easiest to catch. You normally know there's a problem when your layout is all messed up. Some steps for catching and fixing these, as well as general debugging hints, are discussed in the next section.

PHP errors are the ones you'll see most often, as this language will be at the heart of your applications. PHP errors fall into three general areas:

◆ Syntactical

◆ Run time

◆ Logical

Syntactical errors are the most common and the easiest to fix. You'll see them if you merely omit a semicolon. Such errors stop the script from executing, and if *display_errors* is on in your PHP configuration, PHP will show an error, including the line PHP thinks it's on (**Figure 7.1**). If *display_errors* is off, you'll see a blank page. (You'll learn more about *display_errors* later in this chapter.)

Run-time errors include those things that don't stop a PHP script from executing (like parse errors do) but do stop the script from doing everything it was supposed to do. Examples include calling a function using the wrong number or types of parameters. With these errors, PHP will normally display a message (**Figure 7.2**) indicating the exact problem (again, assuming that *display_errors* is on).

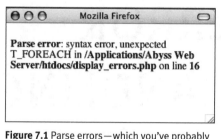

Figure 7.1 Parse errors—which you've probably seen many times over by now—are the most common sort of PHP error, particularly for beginning programmers.

```
● ● ●            Display Errors            ▭

Warning: round() expects at least 1 parameter, 0 given
in /Applications/Abyss Web
Server/htdocs/display_errors.php on line 14
```

Figure 7.2 Misusing a function (calling it with improper parameters) will create errors during the execution of the script.

The final category of error—logical—is actually the worst, because PHP won't necessarily report it to you. These are out-and-out bugs: problems that aren't obvious and don't stop the execution of a script. Tricks for solving all of these PHP errors will be demonstrated in just a few pages.

SQL errors are normally a matter of syntax, and they'll be reported when you try to run the query on MySQL. For example, I've done this many times (**Figure 7.3**):

```
DELETE * FROM tablename
```

The syntax is just wrong, a confusion with the `SELECT` syntax (`SELECT * FROM tablename`). The right syntax is

```
DELETE FROM tablename
```

Again, MySQL will raise a red flag when you have SQL errors, so these aren't that difficult to find and fix. With dynamic Web sites, the catch is that you don't always have static queries, but rather ones dynamically generated by PHP. In such cases, if there's a syntax problem, the issue is probably in your PHP code.

Besides reporting on SQL errors, MySQL has its own errors to consider. An inability to access the database is a common one and a showstopper at that (**Figure 7.4**). You'll also see errors when you misuse a MySQL function or ambiguously refer to a column in a join. Again, MySQL will report any such error in specific detail. Keep in mind that when a query doesn't return the records or otherwise have the result you expect, that's not a MySQL or SQL error, but rather a logical one. Toward the end of this chapter you'll see how to solve SQL and MySQL problems.

But as you have to walk before you can run, the next section covers the fundamentals of debugging dynamic Web sites, starting with the basic checks you should make and how to fix HTML problems.

Basic debugging steps

This first sequence of steps may seem obvious, but when it comes to debugging, missing one of these steps leads to an unproductive and extremely frustrating debugging experience. And while I'm at it, I should mention that the best piece of general debugging advice is this:

When you get frustrated, step away from the computer!

I have solved almost all of the most perplexing issues I've come across by taking a break, clearing my head, and coming back to the

continues on next page

```
MySQL Command Line Client                                          _ □ ×
mysql> DELETE * FROM users;
ERROR 1064 (42000): You have an error in your SQL syntax; check the manual that corresponds to your
MySQL server version for the right syntax to use near '* FROM users' at line 1
mysql>
```

Figure 7.3 MySQL will report any errors found in the syntax of an SQL command.

```
● ● ●                    Terminal
: /usr/local/mysql/bin/mysql -u root -p
Enter password:
ERROR 1045 (28000): Access denied for user 'root'@'localhost'
(using password: YES)
:
```

Figure 7.4 An inability to connect to a MySQL server or a specific database is a common MySQL error.

code with fresh eyes. Readers in the book's supporting forum (www.DMCInsights.com/phorum/) have frequently found this to be true as well. Trying to forge ahead when you're frustrated tends to make things worse.

To begin debugging any problem:

◆ Make sure that you are running the right page.

It's altogether too common that you try to fix a problem and no matter what you do, it never goes away. The reason: you've actually been editing a different page than you thought.

◆ Make sure that you have saved your latest changes.

An unsaved document will continue to have the same problems it had before you edited it (because the edits haven't been enacted).

◆ Make sure that you run all PHP pages through the URL.

Because PHP works through a Web server (Apache, IIS, etc.), running any PHP code requires that you access the page through a URL (http://www.example.com/page.php or http://localhost/page.php). If you double-click a PHP page to open it in a browser (or use the browser's File > Open option), you'll see the PHP code, not the executed result. This also occurs if you load an HTML page without going through a URL (which will work on its own) but then submit the form to a PHP page (**Figure 7.5**).

◆ Know what versions of PHP and MySQL you are running.

Some problems are specific to a certain version of PHP or MySQL. For example, some functions are added in later versions of PHP, and MySQL added significant new features in versions 4, 4.1, and 5. Run a phpinfo() script (**Figure 7.6**, see Appendix A, "Installation," for a script example) and open a mysql client session

```
000                              handle_form.php
<!DOCTYPE html PUBLIC "-//W3C//DTD XHTML 1.0 Transitional//EN" "http://www.w3.org/TR/
xhtml1/DTD/xhtml1-transitional.dtd">
<html xmlns="http://www.w3.org/1999/xhtml" xml:lang="en" lang="en">
<head>
    <meta http-equiv="content-type" content="text/html; charset=iso-8859-1" />
    <title>Form Feedback</title>
    <style type="text/css" title="text/css" media="all">
    .error {
        font-weight: bold;
        color: #C00
    }
    </style>
</head>
<body>
<?php # Script 2.5 - handle_form.php #4

// Print the submitted information:
if ( !empty($_POST['name']) && !empty($_POST['comments']) && !empty($_POST['email']) ) {
    echo "<p>Thank you, <b>{$_POST['name']}</b>, for the following comments:<br />
<tt>{$_POST['comments']}</tt></p>
<p>We will reply to you at <i>{$_POST['email']}</i>.</p>\n";
} else { // Missing form value.
    echo '<p class="error">Please go back and fill out the form again.</p>';
}
?>
</body>
</html>
```

Figure 7.5 PHP code will only be executed if run through a URL. This means that forms that submit to a PHP page must also be loaded through http://.

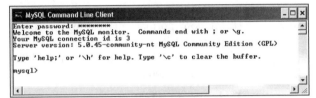

Figure 7.6 A phpinfo() script is one of your best tools for debugging, informing you of the PHP version and how it's configured.

(**Figure 7.7**) to determine this information. phpMyAdmin will often report on the versions involved as well (but don't confuse the version of phpMyAdmin, which will likely be 2.*something* with the versions of PHP or MySQL).

I consider the versions being used to be such an important, fundamental piece of information that I won't normally assist people looking for help until they provide this information!

continues on next page

Figure 7.7 When you connect to a MySQL server, it should let you know the version number.

Book Errors

If you've followed an example in this book and something's not working right, what should you do?

1. Double-check your code or steps against those in the book.

2. Use the index at the back of the book to see if I reference a script or function in an earlier page (you may have missed an important usage rule or tip).

3. View the PHP manual for a specific function to see if it's available in your version of PHP and to verify how the function is used.

4. Check out the book's errata page (through the supporting Web site, www.DMCInsights.com/phpmysql3/) to see if an error in the code does exist and has been reported. Don't post your particular problem there yet, though!

5. Triple-check your code and use all the debugging techniques outlined in this chapter.

6. Search the book's supporting forum to see if others have had this problem and if a solution has already been determined.

7. If all else fails, use the book's supporting forum to ask for assistance. When you do, make sure you include all the pertinent information (version of PHP, version of MySQL, the debugging steps you took and what the results were, etc.).

◆ Know what Web server you are running.

Similarly, some problems and features are unique to your Web serving application—Apache, IIS, or Abyss. You should know which one you are using, and which version, from when you installed the application.

◆ Try executing pages in a different Web browser.

Every Web developer should have and use at least two Web browsers. If you test your pages in different ones, you'll see if the problem has to do with your script or a particular browser.

◆ If possible, try executing the page using a different Web server.

PHP and MySQL errors sometimes stem from particular configurations and versions on one server. If something works on one server but not another, then you'll know that the script isn't inherently at fault. From there it's a matter of using `phpinfo()` scripts to see what server settings may be different.

✔ Tips

■ If taking a break is one thing you should do when you become frustrated, here's what you *shouldn't* do: send off one or multiple panicky and persnickety emails to a writer, to a newsgroup or mailing list, or to anyone else. When it comes to asking for free help from strangers, patience and pleasantries garner much better and faster results.

■ For that matter, I would highly advise against randomly guessing at solutions. I've seen far too many people only complicate matters further by taking stabs at solutions, without a full understanding of what the attempted changes should or should not do.

■ There's another different realm of errors that you could classify as *usage* errors: what goes wrong when the site's user doesn't do what you thought they would. These are very difficult to find on your own because it's hard for the programmer to use an application in a way other than she intended. As a golden rule, write your code so that it doesn't break even if the user doesn't do anything right!

Debugging HTML

Debugging HTML is relatively easy. The source code is very accessible, most problems are overt, and attempts at fixing the HTML don't normally make things worse (as can happen with PHP). Still, there are some basic steps you should follow to find and fix an HTML problem.

To debug an HTML error:

◆ Check the source code.

If you have an HTML problem, you'll almost always need to check the source code of the page to find it. How you view the source code depends upon the browser being used, but normally it's a matter of using something like View > Page Source.

◆ Use a validation tool (**Figure 7.8**).

Validation tools, like the one at `http://validator.w3.org`, are great for finding mismatched tags, broken tables, and other problems.

◆ Add borders to your tables.

Frequently layouts are messed up because tables are incomplete. To confirm this, add a prominent border to your table to make it obvious where the different columns and rows are.

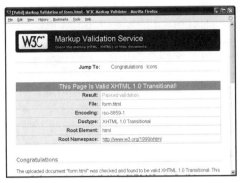

Figure 7.8 Validation tools like the one provided by the W3C (World Wide Web Consortium) are good for finding problems and making sure your HTML conforms to standards.

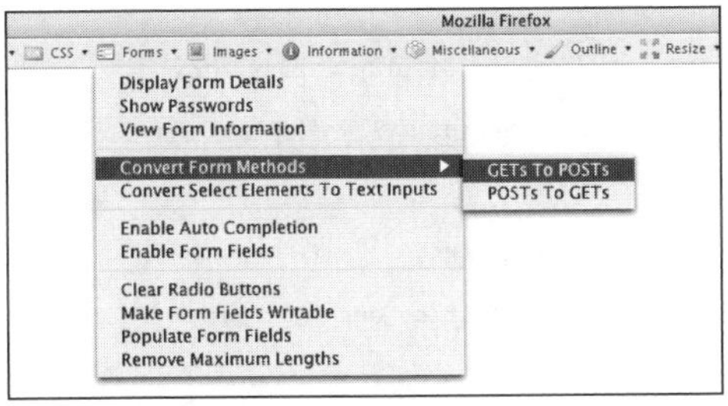

Figure 7.9 Firefox's Web Developer widget provides quick access to lots of useful tools.

✔ Tip

■ The first step toward fixing any kind of problem is understanding what's causing it. Remember the role each technology— HTML, PHP, SQL, and MySQL—plays as you debug. If your page doesn't look right, that's an HTML problem. If your HTML is dynamically generated by PHP, it's still an HTML problem but you'll need to work with the PHP code to make it right.

◆ Use Firefox or Opera.

I'm not trying to start a discussion on which is the best Web browser, and as Internet Explorer is the most used one, you'll need to eventually test using it, but I personally find that Firefox (available for free from www.mozilla.com) and Opera (available for free from www.opera.com) are the best Web browsers for Web developers. They offer reliability and debugging features not available in other browsers. If you want to stick with IE or Safari for your day-to-day browsing, that's up to you, but when doing Web development, start with either Firefox or Opera.

◆ Use Firefox's add-on widgets (**Figure 7.9**).

Besides being just a great Web browser, the very popular Firefox browser has a ton of features that the Web developer will appreciate. Furthermore, you can expand Firefox's functionality by installing any of the free widgets that are available. The Web Developer widget in particular provides quick access to great tools, such as showing a table's borders, revealing the CSS, validating a page, and more. I also frequently use these add-ons: DOM Inspector, Firebug, and HTML Validator, among others.

◆ Test the page in another browser.

PHP code is generally browser-independent, meaning you'll get consistent results regardless of the client. Not so with HTML. Sometimes a particular browser has a quirk that affects the rendered page. Running the same page in another browser is the easiest way to know if it's an HTML problem or a browser quirk.

Displaying PHP Errors

PHP provides remarkably useful and descriptive error messages when things go awry. Unfortunately, PHP doesn't show these errors when running using its default configuration. This policy makes sense for live servers, where you don't want the end users seeing PHP-specific error messages, but it also makes everything that much more confusing for the beginning PHP developer. To be able to see PHP's errors, you must turn on the *display_errors* directive, either in an individual script or for the PHP configuration as a whole.

To turn on *display_errors* in a script, use the ini_set() function. As its arguments, this function takes a directive name and what setting that directive should have:

```
ini_set('display_errors', 1);
```

Including this line in a script will turn on *display_errors* for that script. The only downside is that if your script has a syntax error that prevents it from running at all, then you'll still see a blank page. To have PHP display errors for the entire server, you'll need to edit its configuration, as is discussed in the "Configuring PHP" section of Appendix A.

To turn on display_errors:

1. Create a new PHP document in your text editor or IDE (**Script 7.1**).

```
<!DOCTYPE html PUBLIC "-//W3C//DTD
→ XHTML 1.0 Transitional//EN"

"http://www.w3.org/TR/xhtml1/DTD/
→ xhtml1-transitional.dtd">

<html xmlns="http://www.w3.org/1999/
→ xhtml" xml:lang="en" lang="en">

<head>
```

Script 7.1 The ini_set() function can be used to tell a PHP script to reveal any errors that might occur.

```
1   <!DOCTYPE html PUBLIC "-//W3C//DTD XHTML
    1.0 Transitional//EN"
2       "http://www.w3.org/TR/xhtml1/DTD/
        xhtml1-transitional.dtd">
3   <html xmlns="http://www.w3.org/1999/xhtml"
    xml:lang="en" lang="en">
4   <head>
5     <meta http-equiv="content-type"
      content="text/html; charset=
      iso-8859-1" />
6     <title>Display Errors</title>
7   </head>
8   <body>
9   <h2>Testing Display Errors</h2>
10  <?php # Script 7.1 - display_errors.php
11
12  // Show errors:
13  ini_set('display_errors', 1);
14
15  // Create errors:
16  foreach ($var as $v) {}
17  $result = 1/0;
18
19  ?>
20  </body>
21  </html>
```

```
<meta http-equiv="content-type"
→ content="text/html; charset=
→ iso-8859-1" />

<title>Display Errors</title>
```

`</head>`

`<body>`

```
<?php # Script 7.1 - display_
→ errors.php
```

2. After the initial PHP tags, add

`ini_set('display_errors', 1);`

From this point in this script forward, any errors that occur will be displayed.

3. Create some errors.

`foreach ($var as $v) {}`

`$result = 1/0;`

To test the *display_errors* setting, the script needs to have an error. This first line doesn't even try to do anything, but it's guaranteed to cause an error. There are actually two issues here: first, there's a reference to a variable ($var) that doesn't exist; second, a non-array ($var) is being used as an array in the foreach loop.

The second line is a classic division by zero, which is not allowed in programming languages or in math.

4. Complete the page.

`?>`

`</body>`

`</html>`

5. Save the file as `display_errors.php`, place it in your Web directory, and test it in your Web browser (**Figure 7.10**).

6. If you want, change the first line of PHP code to read

`ini_set('display_errors', 0);`

and then save and retest the script (**Figure 7.11**).

✔ Tips

- There are limits as to what PHP settings the `ini_set()` function can be used to adjust. See the PHP manual for specifics as to what can and cannot be changed using it.

- As a reminder, changing the *display_errors* setting in a script only works so long as that script runs (i.e., it cannot have any parse errors). To be able to *always* see any errors that occur, you'll need to enable *display_errors* in PHP's configuration file (again, see the appendix).

Testing Display Errors

Warning: Invalid argument supplied for foreach() in /Applications/Abyss Web Server/htdocs/display_errors.php on line 16

Warning: Division by zero in /Applications/Abyss Web Server/htdocs/display_errors.php on line 17

Figure 7.10 With *display_errors* turned on (for this script), the page reports the errors when they occur.

Testing Display Errors

Figure 7.11 With *display_errors* turned off (for this page), the same errors (Script 7.1 and Figure 7.10) are no longer reported. Unfortunately, they still exist.

Adjusting Error Reporting in PHP

Once you have PHP set to display the errors that occur, you might want to adjust the level of error reporting. Your PHP installation as a whole, or individual scripts, can be set to report or ignore different types of errors. **Table 7.1** lists most of the levels, but they can generally be one of these three kinds:

- *Notices*, which do not stop the execution of a script and may not necessarily be a problem.

- *Warnings*, which indicate a problem but don't stop a script's execution.

- *Errors*, which stop a script from continuing (including the ever-common parse error, which prevent scripts from running at all).

As a rule of thumb, you'll want PHP to report on any kind of error while you're developing a site but report no specific errors once the site goes live. For security and aesthetic purposes, it's generally unwise for a public user to see PHP's detailed error messages. Frequently, error messages—particularly those dealing with the database—will reveal

Suppressing Errors with @

Individual errors can be suppressed in PHP using the @ operator. For example, if you don't want PHP to report if it couldn't include a file, you would code

```
@include ('config.inc.php');
```

Or if you don't want to see a "division by zero" error:

```
$x = 8;
$y = 0;
$num = @($x/$y);
```

The @ symbol will work only on expressions, like function calls or mathematical operations. You cannot use @ before conditionals, loops, function definitions, and so forth.

As a rule of thumb, I recommend that @ be used on functions whose execution, should they fail, will not affect the functionality of the script as a whole. Or you can suppress PHP's errors when you will handle them more gracefully yourself (a topic discussed later in this chapter).

Table 7.1 PHP's error-reporting settings, to be used with the `error_reporting()` function or in the `php.ini` file. Note that `E_ALL`'s number value was different in earlier versions of PHP and did not include `E_STRICT` (it does in PHP 6).

Error-Reporting Levels

Number	Constant	Report On
1	E_ERROR	Fatal run-time errors (that stop execution of the script)
2	E_WARNING	Run-time warnings (non-fatal errors)
4	E_PARSE	Parse errors
8	E_NOTICE	Notices (things that could or could not be a problem)
256	E_USER_ERROR	User-generated error messages, generated by the `trigger_error()` function
512	E_USER_WARNING	User-generated warnings, generated by the `trigger_error()` function
1024	E_USER_NOTICE	User-generated notices, generated by the `trigger_error()` function
2048	E_STRICT	Recommendations for compatibility and interoperability
8191	E_ALL	All errors, warnings, and recommendations

Script 7.2 This script will demonstrate how error reporting can be manipulated in PHP.

```
⊖ ⊖ ⊖                    Script
1    <!DOCTYPE html PUBLIC "-//W3C//DTD XHTML
     1.0 Transitional//EN"
2        "http://www.w3.org/TR/xhtml1/DTD/
         xhtml1-transitional.dtd">
3    <html xmlns="http://www.w3.org/1999/xhtml"
     xml:lang="en" lang="en">
4    <head>
5      <meta http-equiv="content-type" content=
       "text/html; charset=iso-8859-1" />
6      <title>Report Errors</title>
7    </head>
8    <body>
9    <h2>Testing Error Reporting</h2>
10   <?php # Script 7.2 - report_errors.php
11
12   // Show errors:
13   ini_set('display_errors', 1);
14
15   // Adjust error reporting:
16   error_reporting(E_ALL);
17
18   // Create errors:
19   foreach ($var as $v) {}
20   $result = 1/0;
21
22   ?>
23   </body>
24   </html>
```

certain behind-the-scenes aspects of your Web application that are best not shown. While you hope all of these will be worked out during the development stages, that may not be the case.

You can universally adjust the level of error reporting following the instructions in Appendix A. Or you can adjust this behavior on a script-by-script basis using the error_reporting() function. This function is used to establish what type of errors PHP should report on within a specific page. The function takes either a number or a constant, using the values in Table 7.1 (the PHP manual lists a few others, related to the core of PHP itself).

```
error_reporting(0); // Show no errors.
```

A setting of 0 turns error reporting off entirely (errors will still occur; you just won't see them anymore). Conversely, error_reporting (E_ALL) will tell PHP to report on every error that occurs. The numbers can be added up to customize the level of error reporting, or you could use the bitwise operators—| (or), ~ (not), & (and)—with the constants. With this following setting any non-notice error will be shown:

```
error_reporting (E_ALL & ~E_NOTICE);
```

To adjust error reporting:

1. Open display_errors.php (Script 7.1) in your text editor or IDE.

   To play around with error reporting levels, use display_errors.php as an example.

2. After adjust the *display_errors* setting, add (**Script 7.2**)

   ```
   error_reporting (E_ALL);
   ```

   For development purposes, have PHP notify you of all errors, notices, warnings, and recommendations. This line will

   continues on next page

accomplish that. In short, PHP will let you know about anything that is, or may be, a problem.

Because E_ALL is a constant, it is not enclosed in quotation marks.

3. Save the file as report_errors.php, place it in your Web directory, and run it in your Web browser (**Figure 7.12**).

I also altered the page's title and the heading, but both are immaterial to the point of this exercise.

4. Change the level of error reporting to something different and retest (**Figures 7.13** and **7.14**).

✔ Tips

■ Because you'll often want to adjust the *display_errors* and *error_reporting* for every page in a Web site, you might want to place those lines of code in a separate PHP file that can then be included by other PHP scripts.

■ In case you are curious, the scripts in this book were all written with PHP's error reporting on the highest level (with the intention of catching every possible problem).

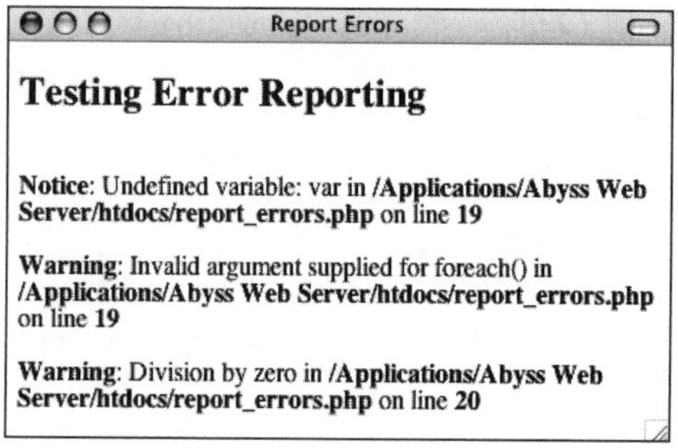

Figure 7.12 On the highest level of error reporting, PHP has two warnings and one notice for this page (Script 7.2).

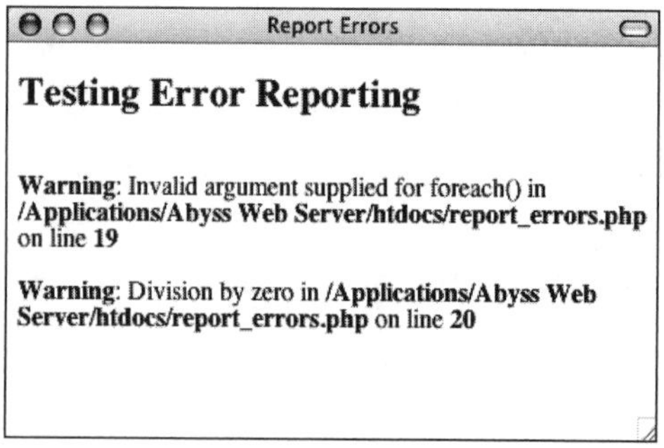

Figure 7.13 The same page (Script 7.2) after disabling the reporting of notices.

Figure 7.14 The same page again (Script 7.2) with error reporting turned off (set to 0). The result is the same as if *display_errors* was disabled. Of course, the errors still occur; they're just not being reported.

Creating Custom Error Handlers

Another option for error management with your sites is to alter how PHP handles errors. By default, if *display_errors* is enabled and an error is caught (that falls under the level of error reporting), PHP will print the error, in a somewhat simplistic form, within some minimal HTML tags (**Figure 7.15**).

You can override how errors are handled by creating your own function that will be called when errors occur. For example,

```
function report_errors (arguments) {

    // Do whatever here.

}
set_error_handler ('report_errors');
```

The set_error_handler() function is used to name the function to be called when an error occurs. The handling function (*report_errors*, in this case) will, at that time, receive several values that can be used in any possible manner.

This function can be written to take up to five arguments. In order, these arguments are: an error number (corresponding to Table 7.1), a textual error message, the name of the file where the error was found, the specific line number on which it occurred, and the variables that existed at the time of the error. Defining a function that accepts all these arguments might look like

```
function report_errors ($num, $msg,
$file, $line, $vars) {…
```

To make use of this concept, the report_errors.php file (Script 7.2) will be rewritten one last time.

```
<br />
<b>Notice</b>:  Undefined variable: var in <b>/Applications/Abyss Web Server/htdocs/report_errors.php</b> on line <b>19</b><br />
<br />
<b>Warning</b>:  Invalid argument supplied for foreach() in <b>/Applications/Abyss Web Server/htdocs/report_errors.php</b> on line <b>19</b><br />
<br />
<b>Warning</b>:  Division by zero in <b>/Applications/Abyss Web Server/htdocs/report_errors.php</b> on line <b>20</b><br />
```

Figure 7.15 The HTML source code for the errors shown in Figure 7.12.

To create your own error handler:

1. Open report_errors.php (Script 7.2) in your text editor or IDE.

2. Remove the ini_set() and error_reporting() lines (**Script 7.3**).

   When you establish your own error handling function, the error reporting levels no longer have any meaning, so that line can be removed. Adjusting the *display_errors* setting is also meaningless, as the error handling function will control whether errors are displayed or not.

3. Before the script creates the errors, add

   define ('LIVE', FALSE);

   This constant will be a flag used to indicate whether or not the site is currently live. It's an important distinction, as how you handle errors and what you reveal in the browser should differ greatly when you're developing a site and when a site is live.

   This constant is being set outside of the function for two reasons. First, I want to treat the function as a black box that does what I need it to do without having to go in and tinker with it. Second, in many sites, there might be other settings (like the database connectivity information) that are also live versus development-specific. Conditionals could, therefore, also refer to this constant to adjust those settings.

4. Begin defining the error handling function.

   function my_error_handler ($e_number,
   → $e_message, $e_file, $e_line,
   → $e_vars) {

   The my_error_handler() function is set to receive the full five arguments that a custom error handler can.

Script 7.3 By defining your own error handling function, you can customize how errors are treated in your PHP scripts.

```
1   <!DOCTYPE html PUBLIC "-//W3C//DTD XHTML
    1.0 Transitional//EN"
2       "http://www.w3.org/TR/xhtml1/DTD/
        xhtml1-transitional.dtd">
3   <html xmlns="http://www.w3.org/1999/xhtml"
    xml:lang="en" lang="en">
4   <head>
5     <meta http-equiv="content-type" content=
      "text/html; charset=iso-8859-1" />
6     <title>Handling Errors</title>
7   </head>
8   <body>
9   <h2>Testing Error Handling</h2>
10  <?php # Script 7.3 - handle_errors.php
11
12  // Flag variable for site status:
13  define('LIVE', FALSE);
14
15  // Create the error handler:
16  function my_error_handler ($e_number,
    $e_message, $e_file, $e_line, $e_vars) {
17
18    // Build the error message:
19    $message = "An error occurred in script
      '$e_file' on line $e_line: $e_message\
      n";
20
21    // Append $e_vars to $message:
22    $message .= print_r ($e_vars, 1);
23
24    if (!LIVE) { // Development (print the
      error).
25      echo '<pre>' . $message . "\n";
26      debug_print_backtrace();
27      echo '</pre><br />';
28    } else { // Don't show the error.
```

(script continues on next page)

Script 7.3 *continued*

```
  ⬤ ⬤ ⬤              📄 Script
29      echo '<div class="error">A system
        error occurred. We apologize for
        the inconvenience.</div><br />';

30      }

31

32  } // End of my_error_handler() definition.

33

34  // Use my error handler:

35  set_error_handler ('my_error_handler');

36

37  // Create errors:

38  foreach ($var as $v) {}

39  $result = 1/0;

40

41  ?>

42  </body>

43  </html>
```

5. Create the error message using the received values.

```
$message = "An error occurred in
→ script '$e_file' on line $e_line:
→ $e_message\n";
```

The error message will begin by referencing the filename and number where the error occurred. Added to this is the actual error message. All of these values are passed to the function when it is called (when an error occurs).

6. Add any existing variables to the error message.

```
$message .= print_r ($e_vars, 1);
```

The $e_vars variable will receive all of the variables that exist, and their values, when the error happens. Because this might contain useful debugging information, it's added to the message.

The print_r() function is normally used to print out a variable's structure and value; it is particularly useful with arrays. If you call the function with a second argument (*1* or TRUE), the result is returned instead of printed. So this line adds all of the variable information to $message.

7. Print a message that will vary, depending upon whether or not the site is live.

```
if (!LIVE) {

    echo '<pre>' . $message . "\n";

    debug_print_backtrace();

    echo '</pre><br />';

} else {

    echo '<div class="error">A
    → system error occurred. We
    → apologize for the
    → inconvenience.</div><br />';

}
```

continues on next page

CREATING CUSTOM ERROR HANDLERS

213

If the site is not live (if LIVE is false), which would be the case while the site is being developed, a detailed error message should be printed (**Figure 7.16**). For ease of viewing, the error message is printed within HTML PRE tags (which aren't XHMTL valid but are very helpful here). Furthermore, a useful debugging function, debug_print_backtrace(), is also called. This function returns a slew of information about what functions have been called, what files have been included, and so forth.

If the site is live, a simple mea culpa will be printed, letting the user know that an error occurred but not what the specific problem is (**Figure 7.17**). Under this situation, you could also use the error_log() function (see the sidebar) to have the detailed error message emailed or written to a log.

8. Complete the function and tell PHP to use it.

```
}
set_error_handler('my_error_handler'
→ );
```

This second line is the important one, telling PHP to use the custom error handler instead of PHP's default handler.

9. Save the file as handle_errors.php, place it in your Web directory, and test it in your Web browser (Figure 7.16).

10. Change the value of LIVE to *TRUE*, save, and retest the script (Figure 7.17).

To see how the error handler behaves with a live site, just change this one value.

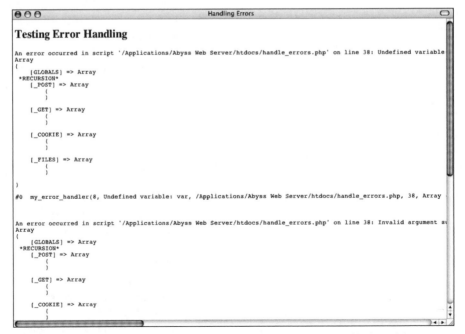

Figure 7.16 During the development phase, detailed error messages are printed in the Web browser. (In a more real-world script, with more code, the messages would be more useful.)

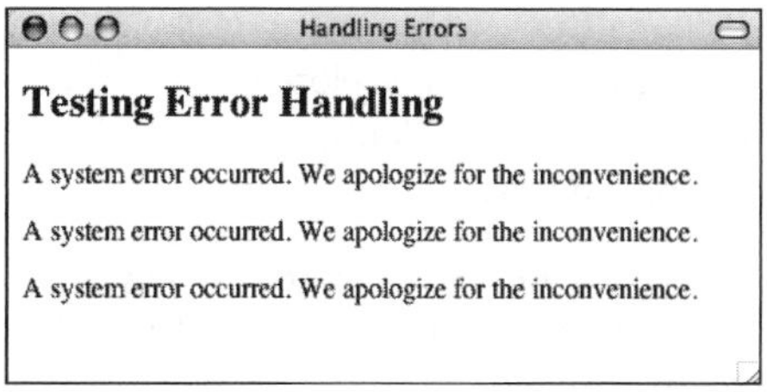

Figure 7.17 Once a site has gone live, more user-friendly (and less revealing) errors are printed. Here, one message is printed for each of the three errors in the script.

Logging PHP Errors

In Script 7.3, errors are handled by simply printing them out in detail or not. Another option is to log the errors: make a permanent note of them somehow. For this purpose, the `error_log()` function instructs PHP how to file an error. It's syntax is

```
error_log (message, type,
→ destination,

extra headers);
```

The *message* value should be the text of the logged error (i.e., `$message` in Script 7.3). The *type* dictates how the error is logged. The options are the numbers 0 through 3: use the computer's default logging method (0), send it in an email (1), send to a remote debugger (2), or write it to a text file (3).

The *destination* parameter can be either the name of a file (for log type 3) or an email address (for log type 1). The *extra headers* argument is used only when sending emails (log type 1). Both the destination and extra headers are optional.

✔ Tips

- If your PHP page uses special HTML formatting—like CSS tags to affect the layout and font treatment—add this information to your error reporting function.

- Obviously in a live site you'll probably need to do more than apologize for the inconvenience (particularly if the error significantly affects the page's functionality). Still, this example demonstrates how you can easily adjust error handling to suit the situation.

- If you don't want the error handling function to report on every notice, error, or warning, you could check the error number value (the first argument sent to the function). For example, to ignore notices when the site is live, you would change the main conditional to

```
if (!LIVE) {
    echo '<pre>' . $message . "\n";
    debug_print_backtrace();
    echo '</pre><br />';
} elseif ($e_number != E_NOTICE) {
    echo '<div class="error">A
    → system error occurred. We
    → apologize for the
    → inconvenience.</div><br />';
}
```

- You can invoke your error handling function using `trigger_error()`.

PHP Debugging Techniques

When it comes to debugging, what you'll best learn from experience are the causes of certain types of errors. Understanding the common causes will shorten the time it takes to fix errors. To expedite the learning process, **Table 7.2** lists the likely reasons for the most common PHP errors.

The first, and most common, type of error that you'll run across is syntactical and will prevent your scripts from executing. An error like this will result in messages like the one in **Figure 7.18**, which every PHP developer has seen too many times. To avoid making this sort of mistake when you program, be sure to:

◆ End every statement (but not language constructs like loops and conditionals) with a semicolon.

◆ Balance all quotation marks, parentheses, curly braces, and square brackets (each opening character must be closed).

◆ Be consistent with your quotation marks (single quotes can be closed only with single quotes and double quotes with double quotes).

◆ Escape, using the backslash, all single- and double-quotation marks within strings, as appropriate.

One thing you should also understand about syntactical errors is that just because the PHP error message says the error is occurring on line 12, that doesn't mean that the mistake is actually on that line. At the very least, it is not uncommon for there to be

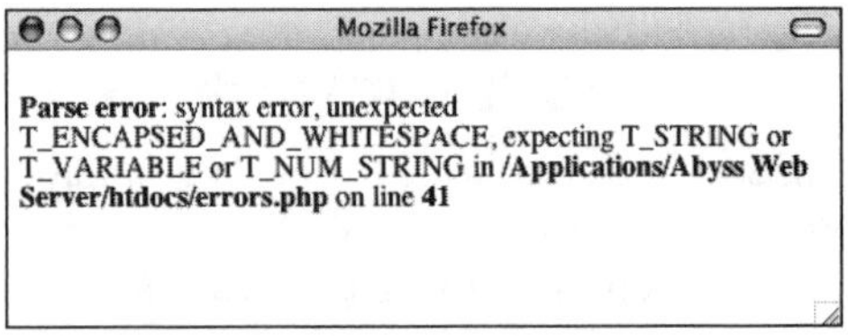

Figure 7.18 The parse error prevents a script from running because of invalid PHP syntax. This one was caused by failing to enclose $array['key'] within curly braces when printing its value.

Table 7.2 These are some of the most common errors you'll see in PHP, along with their most probable causes.

Common PHP Errors	
ERROR	LIKELY CAUSE
Blank Page	HTML problem, or PHP error and *display_errors* or *error_reporting* is off.
Parse error	Missing semicolon; unbalanced curly braces, parentheses, or quotation marks; or use of an unescaped quotation mark in a string.
Empty variable value	Forgot the initial $, misspelled or miscapitalized the variable name, or inappropriate variable scope (with functions).
Undefined variable	Reference made to a variable before it is given a value or an empty variable value (see those potential causes).
Call to undefined function	Misspelled function name, PHP is not configured to use that function (like a MySQL function), or document that contains the function definition was not included.
Cannot redeclare function	Two definitions of your own function exist; check within included files.
Headers already sent	White space exists in the script before the PHP tags, data has already been printed, or a file has been included.

a difference between what PHP thinks is line 12 and what your text editor indicates is line 12. So while PHP's direction is useful in tracking down a problem, treat the line number referenced as more of a starting point than an absolute.

If PHP reports an error on the last line of your document, this is almost always because a mismatched parenthesis, curly brace, or quotation mark was not caught until that moment.

The second type of error you'll encounter results from misusing a function. This error occurs, for example, when a function is called without the proper arguments. This error is discovered by PHP when attempting to execute the code. In later chapters you'll probably see such errors when using the header() function, cookies, or sessions.

To fix errors, you'll need to do a little detective work to see what mistakes were made and where. For starters, though, always thoroughly read and trust the error message PHP offers. Although the referenced line number may not always be correct, a PHP error is very descriptive, normally helpful, and almost always 100 percent correct.

To debug your scripts:

◆ Turn on *display_errors*.

Use the earlier steps to enable *display_errors* for a script, or, if possible, the entire server, as you develop your applications.

◆ Use comments.

Just as you can use comments to document your scripts, you can also use them to rule out problematic lines. If PHP is giving you an error on line 12, then commenting out that line should get rid of the error. If not, then you know the error is elsewhere. Just be careful that you don't introduce more errors by improperly commenting out only a portion of a code block: the syntax of your scripts must be maintained.

◆ Use the print() and echo() functions.

In more complicated scripts, I frequently use echo() statements to leave me notes as to what is happening as the script is executed (**Figure 7.19**). When a script has several steps, it may not be easy to know if the problem is occurring in step 2 or step 5. By using an echo() statement, you can narrow the problem down to the specific juncture.

continues on next page

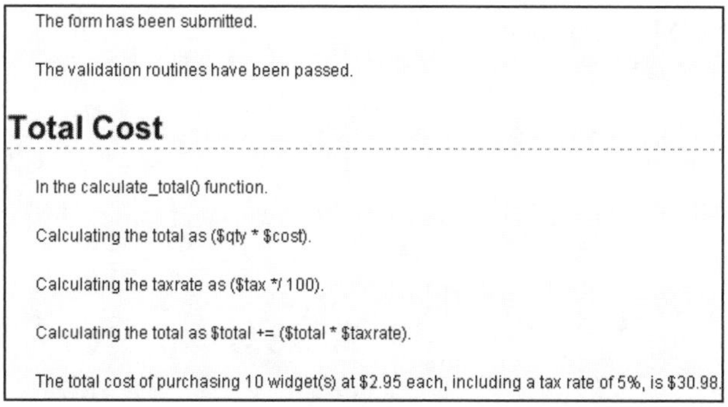

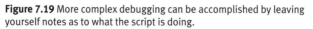

The form has been submitted.

The validation routines have been passed.

Total Cost

In the calculate_total() function.

Calculating the total as ($qty * $cost).

Calculating the taxrate as ($tax */ 100).

Calculating the total as $total += ($total * $taxrate).

The total cost of purchasing 10 widget(s) at $2.95 each, including a tax rate of 5%, is $30.98.

Figure 7.19 More complex debugging can be accomplished by leaving yourself notes as to what the script is doing.

◆ Check what quotation marks are being used for printing variables.

It's not uncommon for programmers to mistakenly use single quotation marks and then wonder why their variables are not printed properly. Remember that single quotation marks treat text literally and that you must use double quotation marks to print out the values of variables.

◆ Track variables (**Figure 7.20**).

It is pretty easy for a script not to work because you referred to the wrong variable or the right variable by the wrong name or because the variable does not have the value you would expect. To check for these possibilities, use the print() or echo() statements to print out the values of variables at important points in your scripts. This is simply a matter of

echo "<p>\$var = $var</p>\n";

The first dollar sign is escaped so that the variable's name is printed. The second reference of the variable will print its value.

◆ Print array values.

For more complicated variable types (arrays and objects), the print_r() and var_dump() functions will print out their values without the need for loops. Both functions accomplish the same task, although var_dump() is more detailed in its reporting than print_r().

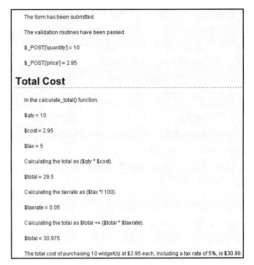

Figure 7.20 Printing the names and values of variables is the easiest way to track them over the course of a script.

Using die() and exit()

Two functions that are often used with error management are die() and exit(), (they're technically language constructs, not functions, but who cares?). When a die() or exit() is called in your script, the entire script is terminated. Both are useful for stopping a script from continuing should something important—like establishing a database connection—fail to happen. You can also pass die() and exit() a string that will be printed out in the browser.

You'll commonly see die() or exit() used in an OR conditional. For example:

```
include('config.inc.php') OR die
→ ('Could not open the file. ');
```

With a line like that, if PHP could not include the configuration file, the die() statement will be executed and the "Could not open the file." message will be printed. You'll see variations on this throughout this book and in the PHP manual, as it's a quick (but potentially excessive) way to handle errors without using a custom error handler.

✔ Tips

- Many text editors include utilities to check for balanced parentheses, brackets, and quotation marks.

- If you cannot find the parse error in a complex script, begin by using the /* */ comments to render the entire PHP code inert. Then continue to uncomment sections at a time (by moving the opening or closing comment characters) and rerun the script until you deduce what lines are causing the error. Watch how you comment out control structures, though, as the curly braces must continue to be matched in order to avoid parse errors. For example:

```
if (condition) {
    /* Start comment.
    Inert code.
    End comment. */
}
```

- To make the results of print_r() more readable in the Web browser, wrap it within HTML <pre> (preformatted) tags. This one line is my absolute favorite debugging tool:

```
echo '<pre>' . print_r ($var, 1) .
→ '</pre>';
```

SQL and MySQL Debugging Techniques

The most common SQL errors are caused by the following issues:

◆ Unbalanced use of quotation marks or parentheses

◆ Unescaped apostrophes in column values

◆ Misspelling a column name, table name, or function

◆ Ambiguously referring to a column in a join

◆ Placing a query's clauses (WHERE, GROUP BY, ORDER BY, LIMIT) in the wrong order

Furthermore, when using MySQL you can also run across the following:

◆ Unpredictable or inappropriate query results

◆ Inability to access the database

Since you'll be running the queries for your dynamic Web sites from PHP, you need a methodology for debugging SQL and MySQL errors within that context (PHP will not report a problem with your SQL).

Debugging SQL problems

To decide if you are experiencing a MySQL (or SQL) problem rather than a PHP one, you need a system for finding and fixing the issue. Fortunately, the steps you should take to debug MySQL and SQL problems are easy to define and should be followed without thinking. If you ever have any MySQL or SQL errors to debug, just abide by this sequence of steps.

To hammer the point home, this next sequence of steps is probably the most useful debugging technique in this chapter and the entire book. You'll likely need to follow these steps in any PHP-MySQL Web application when you're not getting the results you expected.

To debug your SQL queries:

1. Print out any applicable queries in your PHP script (**Figure 7.21**).

   As you'll see in the next chapter, SQL queries will often be assigned to a variable, particularly when you use PHP to dynamically write them. Using the code echo $query (or whatever the query variable is called) in your PHP scripts, you can send to the browser the exact query being run. Sometimes this step alone will help you see what the real problem is.

```
INSERT INTO users (first_name, last_name, email,    Menu
password, registration_date) VALUES ('Larry', 'Ullman',
'email7@example.com', SHA('pass'), NOW() )            Home
                                                     Register
System Error                                        View Users
```

Figure 7.21 Knowing exactly what query a PHP script is attempting to execute is the most useful first step for solving SQL and MySQL problems.

SQL AND MySQL DEBUGGING TECHNIQUES

2. Run the query in the mysql client or other tool (**Figure 7.22**).

The most foolproof method of debugging an SQL or MySQL problem is to run the query used in your PHP scripts through an independent application: the mysql client, phpMyAdmin, or the like. Doing so will give you the same result as the original PHP script receives but without the overhead and hassle.

If the independent application returns the expected result but you are still not getting the proper behavior in your PHP script, then you will know that the problem lies within the script itself, not your SQL or MySQL database.

3. If the problem still isn't evident, rewrite the query in its most basic form, and then keep adding dimensions back in until you discover which clause is causing the problem.

Sometimes it's difficult to debug a query because there's too much going on. Like commenting out most of a PHP script, taking a query down to its bare minimum structure and slowly building it back up can be the easiest way to debug complex SQL commands.

✔ Tips

■ Another common MySQL problem is trying to run queries or connect using the mysql client when the MySQL server isn't even running. Be sure that MySQL is available for querying!

■ As an alternative to printing out the query to the browser, you could print it out as an HTML comment (viewable only in the HTML source), using

```
echo "<!-- $query -->";
```

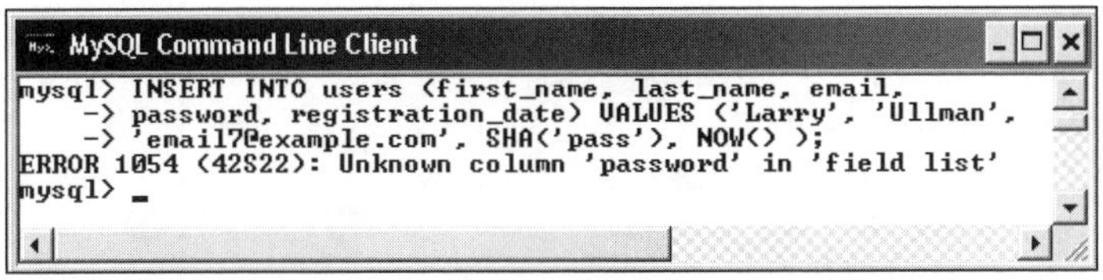

Figure 7.22 To understand what result a PHP script is receiving, run the same query through a separate interface. In this case the problem is the reference to the *password* column, when the table's column is actually called just *pass*.

Debugging access problems

Access denied error messages are the most common problem beginning developers encounter when using PHP to interact with MySQL. These are among the common solutions:

◆ Reload MySQL after altering the privileges so that the changes take effect. Either use the mysqladmin tool or run **FLUSH PRIVILEGES** in the mysql client. You must be logged in as a user with the appropriate permissions to do this (see Appendix A for more).

◆ Double-check the password used. The error message *Access denied for user: 'user@localhost' (Using password: YES)* frequently indicates that the password is wrong or mistyped. (This is not always the cause but is the first thing to check.)

◆ The error message *Can't connect to...* (error number 2002) indicates that MySQL either is not running or is not running on the socket or TCP/IP port tried by the client.

✔ Tips

■ MySQL keeps its own error logs, which are very useful in solving MySQL problems (like why MySQL won't even start). MySQL's error log will be located in the data directory and titled *hostname*.err.

■ The MySQL manual is very detailed, containing SQL examples, function references, and the meanings of error codes. Make the manual your friend and turn to it when confusing errors pop up.

Using PHP with MySQL

Now that you have a sufficient amount of PHP, SQL, and MySQL experience under your belt, it's time to put all of the technologies together. PHP's strong integration with MySQL is just one reason so many programmers have embraced it; it's impressive how easily you can use the two together.

This chapter will use the existing *sitename* database—created in Chapter 5, "Introduction to SQL"—to build a PHP interface for interacting with the *users* table. The knowledge taught and the examples used here will be the basis for all of your PHP-MySQL Web applications, as the principles involved are the same for any PHP-MySQL interaction.

Before heading into this chapter, you should be comfortable with everything covered in the first six chapters. Also, understanding the error debugging and handling techniques covered in Chapter 7 will make the learning process less frustrating, should you encounter snags. Finally, remember that you need a PHP-enabled Web server and access to a running MySQL server in order to test the following examples.

Modifying the Template

Since all of the pages in this chapter and the next will be part of the same Web application, it'll be worthwhile to use a common template system. Instead of creating a new template from scratch, the layout from Chapter 3, "Creating Dynamic Web Sites," will be used again, with only a minor modification to the header file's navigation links.

To make the header file:

1. Open header.html (Script 3.2) in your text editor.

2. Change the list of links to read (**Script 8.1**)

   ```
   <li><a href="index.php">Home
   → Page</a></li>

   <li><a
   → href="register.php">Register</a></li>

   <li><a href="view_users.php">View
   → Users</a></li>

   <li><a href="password.php">Change
   → Password</a></li>

   <li><a href="#">link five</a></li>
   ```

   All of the examples in this chapter will involve the registration, view users, and change password pages. The date form and calculator links from Chapter 3 can be deleted.

3. Save the file as header.html.

4. Place the new header file in your Web directory, within the includes folder along with footer.html (Script 3.3) and style.css (available for download from the book's supporting Web site, www.DMCInsights.com/phpmysql3/).

Script 8.1 The site's header file, used for the pages' template, modified with new navigation links.

```
1   <!DOCTYPE html PUBLIC "-//W3C//DTD XHTML
    1.0 Strict//EN"
    "http://www.w3.org/TR/xhtml1/DTD/xhtml1-
    strict.dtd">
2   <html
    xmlns="http://www.w3.org/1999/xhtml">
3   <head">
4     <title><?php echo $page_title;
      ?></title>
5     <link rel="stylesheet"
      href="includes/style.css"
      type="text/css" media="screen" />
6     <meta http-equiv="content-type"
      content="text/html; charset=utf-8" />
7   </head>
8   <body>
9     <div id="header">
10    <h1>Your Website</h1>
11    <h2>catchy slogan...</h2>
12    </div>
13    <div id="navigation">
14    <ul>
15      <li><a href="index.php">Home
        Page</a></li>
16      <li><a
        href="register.php">Register</a></li>
17      <li><a href="view_users.php">View
        Users</a></li>
18      <li><a href="password.php">Change
        Password</a></li>
19      <li><a href="#">link five</a></li>
20    </ul>
21    </div>
22    <div id="content"><!-- Start of the
      page-specific content. -->
23  <!-- Script 8.1 - header.html -->
```

5. Test the new header file by running `index.php` in your Web browser (**Figure 8.1**).

✔ Tips

■ For a preview of this site's structure, see the sidebar "Organizing Your Documents" in the next section.

■ Remember that you can use any file extension for your template files, including `.inc` or `.php`.

■ To refresh your memory on the template-creation process or the specifics of this layout, see the first few pages of Chapter 3.

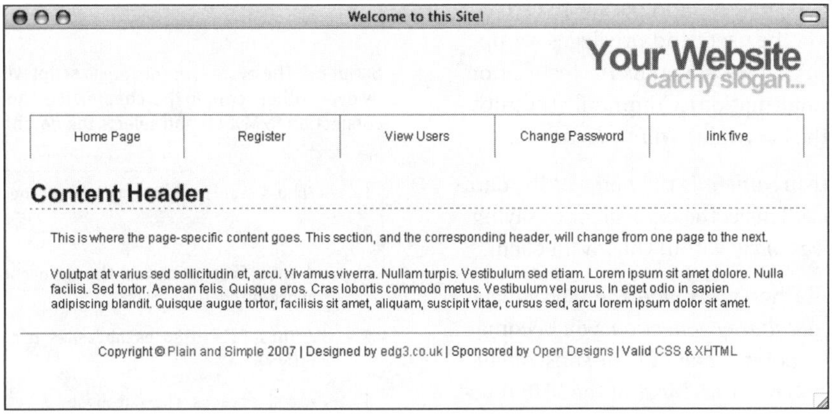

Figure 8.1 The dynamically generated home page with new navigation links.

WARNING: READ THIS!

PHP and MySQL have gone through many changes over the past decade. Of these, the most important for this chapter and one of the most important for the rest of the book involves what PHP functions you use to communicate with MySQL. For years, PHP developers used the standard MySQL functions (called the *mysql* extension). As of PHP 5 and MySQL 4.1, you can use the newer Improved MySQL functions (called the *mysqli* extension). These functions provide improved performance and take advantage of added features (among other benefits).

As this book assumes you're using at least PHP 6 and MySQL 5, all of the examples will only use the Improved MySQL functions. *If your server does not support this extension, you will not be able to run these examples as they are written!* Most of the examples in the rest of the book will also not work for you.

If the server or home computer you're using does not support the Improved MySQL functions, you have three options: upgrade PHP and MySQL, read the second edition of this book (which teaches and primarily uses the older functions), or learn how to use the older functions and modify all the examples accordingly. For questions or problems, see the book's corresponding forum (`www.DMCInsights.com/phorum/`).

Connecting to MySQL

The first step for interacting with MySQL—connecting to the server—requires the appropriately named `mysqli_connect()` function:

```
$dbc = mysqli_connect (hostname,
→ username, password, db_name);
```

The first three arguments sent to the function (host, username, and password) are based upon the users and privileges set up within MySQL (see Appendix A, "Installation," for more information). Commonly (but not always), the host value will be *localhost*.

The fourth argument is the name of the database to use. This is the equivalent of saying USE *databasename* within the mysql client.

If the connection was made, the `$dbc` variable, short for *database connection*, will become a reference point for all of your subsequent database interactions. Most of the PHP functions for working with MySQL will take this variable as its first argument.

Before putting this knowledge to the test, there's one more function to learn about. If a connection problem occurred, you can call `mysqli_connect_error()`, which returns the connection error message. It takes no arguments, so would be called using just

```
mysqli_connect_error();
```

To start using PHP with MySQL, let's create a special script that makes the connection. Other PHP scripts that require a MySQL connection can then include this file.

To connect to and select a database:

1. Create a new PHP document in your text editor or IDE (**Script 8.2**).

   ```
   <?php # Script 8.2 -
   → mysqli_connect.php
   ```

   This file will be included by other PHP scripts, so it doesn't need to contain any HTML.

Script 8.2 The `mysqli_connect.php` script will be used by every other script in this chapter. It establishes a connection to MySQL and selects the database.

```
1   <?php # Script 8.2 - mysqli_connect.php
2
3   // This file contains the database access
    information.
4   // This file also establishes a connection
    to MySQL
5   // and selects the database.
6
7   // Set the database access information as
    constants:
8   DEFINE ('DB_USER', 'username');
9   DEFINE ('DB_PASSWORD', 'password');
10  DEFINE ('DB_HOST', 'localhost');
11  DEFINE ('DB_NAME', 'sitename');
12
13  // Make the connection:
14  $dbc = @mysqli_connect (DB_HOST, DB_USER,
    DB_PASSWORD, DB_NAME) OR die ('Could not
    connect to MySQL: ' .
    mysqli_connect_error() );
15
16  ?>
```

2. Set the MySQL host, username, password, and database name as constants.

```
DEFINE ('DB_USER', 'username');

DEFINE ('DB_PASSWORD', 'password');

DEFINE ('DB_HOST', 'localhost');

DEFINE ('DB_NAME', 'sitename');
```

I prefer to establish these values as constants for security reasons (they cannot be changed this way), but that isn't required. In general, setting these values as some sort of variable or constant makes sense so that you can separate the configuration parameters from the functions that use them, but again, this is not obligatory.

When writing your script, change these values to ones that will work on your setup. If you have been provided with a MySQL username/password combination and a database (like for a hosted site), use that information here. Or, if possible, follow the steps in Appendix A to create a user that has access to the *sitename* database, and insert those values here. Whatever you do, don't just use these values unless you know for certain they will work on your server.

3. Connect to MySQL.

```
$dbc = @mysqli_connect (DB_HOST,
→ DB_USER, DB_PASSWORD, DB_NAME) OR
→ die ('Could not connect to MySQL: ' .
→ mysqli_connect_error() );
```

The `mysqli_connect()` function, if it successfully connects to MySQL, will return a resource link that corresponds to the open connection. This link will be assigned to the `$dbc` variable, so that other functions can make use of this connection.

The function call is preceded by the error suppression operator (@). This prevents the PHP error from being displayed in the Web browser. This is preferable, as the error will be handled by the `OR die()` clause.

If the `mysqli_connect()` function cannot return a valid resource link, then the `OR die()` part of the statement is executed (because the first part of the `OR` will be false, so the second part must be true). As discussed in the preceding chapter, the `die()` function terminates the execution of the script. The function can also take as an argument a string that will be printed to the Web browser. In this case, the string is a combination of *Could not connect to MySQL:* and the specific MySQL error (**Figure 8.2**). Using this blunt error management system makes debugging much easier as you develop your sites.

continues on next page

Figure 8.2 If there were problems connecting to MySQL, an informative message is displayed and the script is halted.

4. Save the file as `mysqli_connect.php`.

   Since this file contains information—the database access data—that must be kept private, it will use a `.php` extension. With a `.php` extension, even if malicious users ran this script in their Web browser, they would not see the page's actual content.

5. Place the file outside of the Web document directory (**Figure 8.3**).

   Because the file contains sensitive MySQL access information, it ought to be stored securely. If you can, place it in the directory immediately above or otherwise outside of the Web directory. This way the file will not be accessible from a Web browser. See the "Organizing Your Documents" sidebar for more.

6. Temporarily place a copy of the script within the Web directory and run it in your Web browser (**Figure 8.4**).

   In order to test the script, you'll want to place a copy on the server so that it's accessible from the Web browser (which means it must be in the Web directory). If the script works properly, the result should be a blank page (see Figure 8.4). If you see an *Access denied...* or similar message (see Figure 8.2), it means that the combination of username, password, and host does not have permission to access the particular database.

7. Remove the temporary copy from the Web directory.

Organizing Your Documents

I introduced the concept of site structure back in Chapter 3 when developing the first Web application. Now that pages will begin using a database connection script, the topic is more important.

Should the database connectivity information (username, password, host, and database) fall into malicious hands, it could be used to steal your information or wreak havoc upon the database as a whole. Therefore, you cannot keep a script like `mysqli_connect.php` too secure.

The best recommendation for securing such a file is to store it outside of the Web documents directory. If, for example, the *htdocs* folder in Figure 8.3 is the root of the Web directory (in other words, the URL www.example.com leads there), then not storing `mysqli_connect.php` anywhere within the *html* directory means it will never be accessible via the Web browser. Granted, the source code of PHP scripts is not viewable from the Web browser (only the data sent to the browser by the script is), but you can never be too careful. If you aren't allowed to place documents outside of the Web directory, placing `mysqli_connect.php` in the Web directory is less secure, but not the end of the world.

Secondarily, I would recommend using a `.php` extension for your connection scripts. A properly configured and working server will execute rather than display code in such a file. Conversely, if you use just `.inc` as your extension, that page's contents would be displayed in the Web browser if accessed directly.

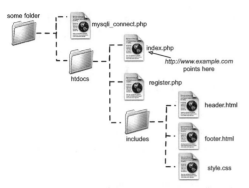

Figure 8.3 A visual representation of a server's Web documents, where mysqli_connect.php is not stored within the main directory (*htdocs*).

```
Mozilla Firefox                        _ □ ✕
File   Edit   View   History   Bookmarks   Tools   Help



```

Figure 8.4 If the MySQL connection script works properly, the end result will be a blank page (no HTML is generated by the script).

```
● ● ●              Mozilla Firefox                  ▭
Could not connect to MySQL: Can't connect to local MySQL server
through socket '/tmp/mysql.sock' (2)




```

Figure 8.5 Another reason why PHP might not be able to connect to MySQL (besides using invalid username/password/hostname/database information) is if MySQL isn't currently running.

```
● ● ●              Mozilla Firefox                  ▭
Warning: mysqli_connect() [function.mysqli-connect]: (28000/1045): Access
denied for user 'username'@'localhost' (using password: YES) in
/Applications/Abyss Web Server/htdocs/mysqli_connect.php on line 14
Could not connect to MySQL: Access denied for user 'username'@'localhost'
(using password: YES)


```

Figure 8.6 If you don't use the error suppression operator (@), you'll see both the PHP error and the custom OR die() error.

✔ Tips

- The same values used in Chapter 5 to log in to the mysql client should work from your PHP scripts.

- If you receive an error that claims mysqli_connect() is an undefined function, it means that PHP has not been compiled with support for the Improved MySQL Extension. See the appendix for installation information.

- If you see a *Can't connect...* error message when running the script (see **Figure 8.5**), it likely means that MySQL isn't running.

- In case you are curious, **Figure 8.6** shows what would happen if you didn't use @ before mysqli_connect() and an error occurred.

- If you don't need to select the database when establishing a connection to MySQL, omit that argument from the mysqli_connect() function:

  $dbc = mysqli_connect (*hostname*,
  → *username*, *password*);

  Then, when appropriate, you can select the database using

  mysqli_select_db($dbc, *db_name*);

CONNECTING TO MySQL

229

Executing Simple Queries

Once you have successfully connected to and selected a database, you can start performing queries. These queries can be as basic as inserts, updates, and deletions or as involved as complex joins returning numerous rows. In any case, the PHP function for executing a query is mysqli_query():

result = mysqli_query(*dbc*, *query*);

The function takes the database connection as its first argument and the query itself as the second. I normally assign the query to another variable, called $query or just $q. So running a query might look like

$r = mysqli_query($dbc, $q);

For simple queries like INSERT, UPDATE, DELETE, etc. (which do not return records), the $r variable—short for *result*—will be either TRUE or FALSE, depending upon whether the query executed successfully. Keep in mind that "executed successfully" means that it ran without error; it doesn't mean it necessarily had the desired result; you'll need to test for that.

For complex queries that return records (SELECT, SHOW, DESCRIBE, and EXPLAIN), $r will be a resource link to the results of the query

if it worked or be FALSE if it did not. Thus, you can use this line of code in a conditional to test if the query successfully ran:

$r = mysqli_query ($dbc, $q);

if ($r) { // Worked!

If the query did not successfully run, some sort of MySQL error must have occurred. To find out what that error was, call the mysqli_error() function:

echo mysqli_error($dbc);

One final, albeit optional, step in your script would be to close the existing MySQL connection once you're finished with it:

mysqli_close($dbc);

This function is not required, because PHP will automatically close the connection at the end of a script, but it does make for good programming form to incorporate it.

To demonstrate this process, let's create a registration script. It will show the form when first accessed (**Figure 8.7**), handle the form submission, and, after validating all the data, insert the registration information into the *users* table of the *sitename* database.

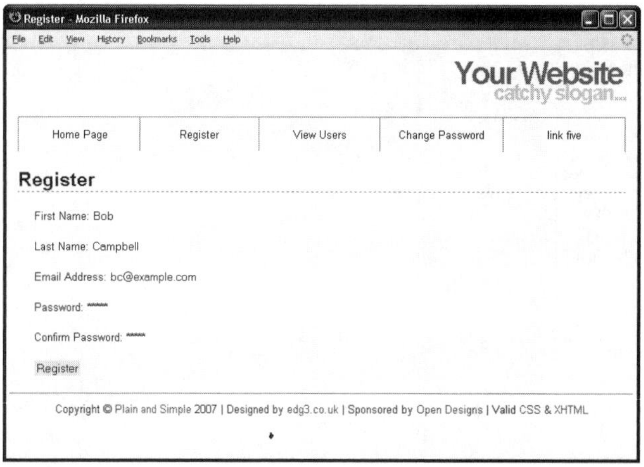

Figure 8.7 The registration form.

Script 8.3 The registration script adds a record to the database by running an INSERT query.

```
1    <?php # Script 8.3 - register.php
2
3    $page_title = 'Register';
4    include ('includes/header.html');
5
6    // Check if the form has been submitted:
7    if (isset($_POST['submitted'])) {
8
9        $errors = array(); // Initialize an
         error array.
10
11       // Check for a first name:
12       if (empty($_POST['first_name'])) {
13           $errors[] = 'You forgot to enter your
             first name.';
14       } else {
15           $fn = trim($_POST['first_name']);
16       }
17
18       // Check for a last name:
19       if (empty($_POST['last_name'])) {
20           $errors[] = 'You forgot to enter your
             last name.';
21       } else {
22           $ln = trim($_POST['last_name']);
23       }
24
25       // Check for an email address:
26       if (empty($_POST['email'])) {
27           $errors[] = 'You forgot to enter your
             email address.';
28       } else {
29           $e = trim($_POST['email']);
30       }
31
32       // Check for a password and match
         against the confirmed password:
33       if (!empty($_POST['pass1'])) {
34           if ($_POST['pass1'] !=
             $_POST['pass2']) {
```

(script continues on next page)

To execute simple queries:

1. Create a new PHP script in your text editor or IDE (**Script 8.3**).

   ```
   <?php # Script 8.3 - register.php
   $page_title = 'Register';
   include ('includes/header.html');
   ```

   The fundamentals of this script—using included files, having the same page both display and handle a form, and creating a sticky form—come from Chapter 3. See that chapter if you're confused about any of these concepts.

2. Create the submission conditional and initialize the $errors array.

   ```
   if (isset($_POST['submitted'])) {
       $errors = array();
   ```

   This script will both display and handle the HTML form. This conditional will check for the presence of a hidden form element to determine whether or not to process the form. The $errors variable will be used to store every error message (one for each form input not properly filled out).

continues on next page

3. Validate the first name.

```
if (empty($_POST['first_name'])) {
    $errors[] = 'You forgot to enter
    → your first name.';
} else {
    $fn =
    → trim($_POST['first_name']);
}
```

As discussed in Chapter 3, the empty() function provides a minimal way of ensuring that a text field was filled out. If the first name field was not filled out, an error message is added to the $errors array. Otherwise, $fn is set to the submitted value, after trimming off any extraneous spaces. By using this new variable—which is obviously short for *first_name*—I make it syntactically easier to write the query later.

4. Validate the last name and email address.

```
if (empty($_POST['last_name'])) {
    $errors[] = 'You forgot to enter
    → your last name.';
} else {
    $ln = trim($_POST['last_name']);
}

if (empty($_POST['email'])) {
    $errors[] = 'You forgot to enter
    → your email address.';
} else {
    $e = trim($_POST['email']);
}
```

These lines are syntactically the same as those validating the first name field. In both cases a new variable will be created, assuming that the minimal validation was passed.

Script 8.3 *continued*

```
35        $errors[] = 'Your password did not
          match the confirmed password.';
36    } else {
37        $p = trim($_POST['pass1']);
38    }
39    } else {
40        $errors[] = 'You forgot to enter your
          password.';
41    }
42
43    if (empty($errors)) { // If everything's
      OK.
44
45        // Register the user in the
          database...
46
47        require_once
          ('../mysqli_connect.php'); // Connect
          to the db.
48
49        // Make the query:
50        $q = "INSERT INTO users (first_name,
          last_name, email, pass,
          registration_date) VALUES ('$fn',
          '$ln', '$e', SHA1('$p'), NOW() )";
51        $r = @mysqli_query ($dbc, $q); // Run
          the query.
52        if ($r) { // If it ran OK.
53
54            // Print a message:
55            echo '<h1>Thank you!</h1>
56            <p>You are now registered. In Chapter
              11 you will actually be able to log
              in!</p><p><br /></p>';
57
58        } else { // If it did not run OK.
59
60            // Public message:
61            echo '<h1>System Error</h1>
62            <p class="error">You could not be
              registered due to a system error.
              We apologize for any
              inconvenience.</p>';
63
```

(script continues on next page)

Script 8.3 *continued*

```
     🔴 🟡 🟢                📄 Script
64          // Debugging message:
65          echo '<p>' . mysqli_error($dbc) .
            '<br /><br />Query: ' . $q .
            '</p>';
66
67          } // End of if ($r) IF.
68
69          mysqli_close($dbc); // Close the
            database connection.
70
71          // Include the footer and quit the
            script:
72          include ('includes/footer.html');
73          exit();
74
75      } else { // Report the errors.
76
77          echo '<h1>Error!</h1>
78          <p class="error">The following
            error(s) occurred:<br />';
79          foreach ($errors as $msg) { // Print
            each error.
80            echo " - $msg<br />\n";
81          }
82          echo '</p><p>Please try
            again.</p><p><br /></p>';
83
84      } // End of if (empty($errors)) IF.
85
86  } // End of the main Submit conditional.
87  ?>
88  <h1>Register</h1>
89  <form action="register.php" method="post">
90      <p>First Name: <input type="text"
        name="first_name" size="15"
        maxlength="20" value="<?php if
        (isset($_POST['first_name'])) echo
        $_POST['first_name']; ?>" /></p>
91      <p>Last Name: <input type="text"
        name="last_name" size="15"
        maxlength="40" value="<?php if
        (isset($_POST['last_name'])) echo
        $_POST['last_name']; ?>" /></p>
```

(script continues on next page)

5. Validate the password.

```
if (!empty($_POST['pass1'])) {

    if ($_POST['pass1'] !=
→ $_POST['pass2']) {

        $errors[] = 'Your password
        → did not match the
        → confirmed password.';

    } else {

        $p = trim($_POST['pass1']);

    }

} else {

    $errors[] = 'You forgot to enter
    → your password.';

}
```

To validate the password, the script needs to check the *pass1* input for a value and then confirm that the *pass1* value matches the *pass2* value (so the password and confirmed password are the same).

6. Check if it's OK to register the user.

```
if (empty($errors)) {
```

If the submitted data passed all of the conditions, the $errors array will have no values in it (it will be empty), so this condition will be TRUE and it's safe to add the record to the database. If the $errors array is not empty, then the appropriate error messages should be printed (see Step 10) and the user given another opportunity to register.

continues on next page

7. Add the user to the database.

```
require_once
→ ('../mysqli_connect.php');

$q = "INSERT INTO users (first_name,
→ last_name, email, pass,
→ registration_date) VALUES ('$fn',
→ '$ln', '$e', SHA1('$p'), NOW() )";

$r = @mysqli_query ($dbc, $q);
```

The first line of code will insert the contents of the `mysqli_connect.php` file into this script, thereby creating a connection to MySQL and selecting the database. You may need to change the reference to the location of the file as it is on your server (as written, this line assumes that `mysqli_connect.php` is in the parent folder of the current folder).

The query itself is similar to those demonstrated in Chapter 5. The `SHA1()` function is used to encrypt the password, and `NOW()` is used to set the registration date as this moment.

After assigning the query to a variable, it is run through the `mysqli_query()` function, which sends the SQL command to the MySQL database. As in the `mysqli_connect.php` script, the `mysqli_query()` call is preceded by @ in order to suppress any ugly errors. If a problem occurs, the error will be handled more directly in the next step.

Script 8.3 *continued*

	Script
92	`<p>Email Address: <input type="text" name="email" size="20" maxlength="80" value="<?php if (isset($_POST['email'])) echo $_POST['email']; ?>" /> </p>`
93	`<p>Password: <input type="password" name="pass1" size="10" maxlength="20" /></p>`
94	`<p>Confirm Password: <input type="password" name="pass2" size="10" maxlength="20" /></p>`
95	`<p><input type="submit" name="submit" value="Register" /></p>`
96	`<input type="hidden" name="submitted" value="TRUE" />`
97	`</form>`
98	`<?php`
99	`include ('includes/footer.html');`
100	`?>`

8. Report on the success of the registration.

```
if ($r) {

    echo '<h1>Thank you!</h1>

    <p>You are now registered. In
    → Chapter 11 you will actually be
    → able to log in!</p><p><br
    → /></p>';

} else {

    echo '<h1>System Error</h1>

    <p class="error">You could not be
    → registered due to a system
    → error. We apologize for any
    → inconvenience.</p>';

    echo '<p>' . mysqli_error($dbc) .
    → '<br /><br />Query: ' . $q .
    → '</p>';

}
```

The $r variable, which is assigned the value returned by mysqli_query(), can be used in a conditional to indicate the successful operation of the query.

If $r is TRUE, then a *Thank you!* message is displayed (**Figure 8.8**). If $r is FALSE, error messages are printed. For debugging purposes, the error messages will include both the error spit out by MySQL (thanks to the mysqli_error() function) and the query that was run (**Figure 8.9**). This information is critical to debugging the problem.

continues on next page

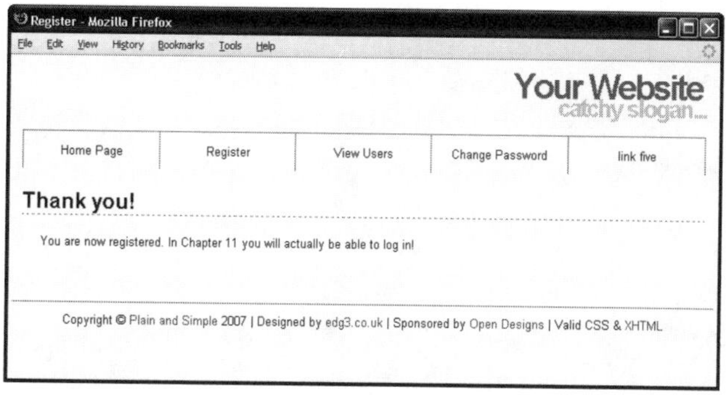

Figure 8.8 If the user could be registered in the database, this message is displayed.

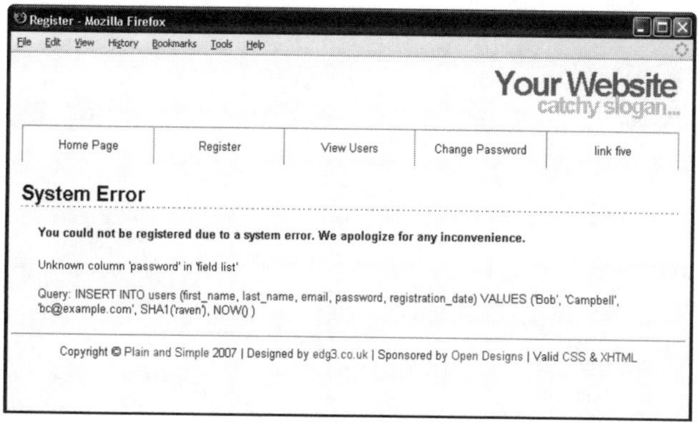

Figure 8.9 Any MySQL errors caused by the query will be printed, as will the query that was being run.

9. Close the database connection and complete the HTML template.

```
mysqli_close();

include ('includes/footer.html');

exit();
```

Closing the connection isn't required but is a good policy. Then the footer is included and the script terminated (thanks to the `exit()` function). If those two lines weren't here, then the registration form would be displayed again (which isn't necessary after a successful registration).

10. Print out any error messages and close the submit conditional.

```
    } else {

        echo '<h1>Error!</h1>

        <p class="error">The
        → following >>error(s)
        → occurred:<br />';

        foreach ($errors as
$msg) {

            echo " - $msg<br
/>\n";

        }

        echo '</p><p>Please try
        → >again.</p><p><br
        /></p>';

    }

}
```

The `else` clause is invoked if there were any errors. In that case, all of the errors are displayed using a `foreach` loop (**Figure 8.10**).

The final closing curly brace closes the main submit conditional. The main conditional is a simple IF, not an `if-else`, so that the form can be made sticky (again, see Chapter 3).

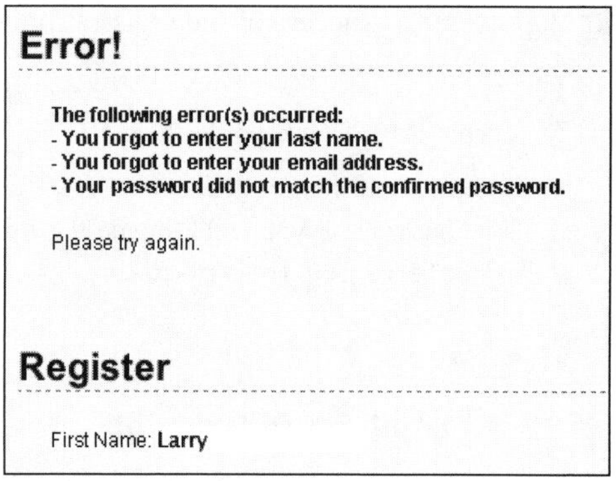

Error!

The following error(s) occurred:
- You forgot to enter your last name.
- You forgot to enter your email address.
- Your password did not match the confirmed password.

Please try again.

Register

First Name: **Larry**

Figure 8.10 Each form validation error is reported to the user so that they may try registering again.

11. Close the PHP section and begin the HTML form.

```
?>

<h1>Register</h1>

<form action="register.php"
→ method="post">

    <p>First Name: <input
    → type="text" name="first_name"
    → size="15" maxlength="20"
    → value="<?php if
    → (isset($_POST['first_name']))
    → echo $_POST['first_name']; ?>"
    → /></p>

    <p>Last Name: <input type="text"
    → name="last_name" size="15"
    → maxlength="40" value="<?php if
    → (isset($_POST['last_name']))
    → echo $_POST['last_name']; ?>"
    → /></p>
```

The form is really simple, with one text input for each field in the *users* table (except for the *user_id* column, which will automatically be populated). Each input is made sticky, using the code

```
value="<?php if
→ (isset($_POST['first_name']))
echo
→ $_POST['first_name']; ?>"
```

Also, I would strongly recommend that you use the same name for your form inputs as the corresponding column in the database where that value will be stored. Further, you should set the maximum input length in the form equal to the maximum column length in the database. Both of these habits help to minimize errors.

12. Complete the HTML form.

```
    <p>Email Address: <input
    → type="text" name="email"
    → size="20" maxlength="80"
    → value="<?php if
    → (isset($_POST['email'])) echo
    → $_POST['email']; ?>" /> </p>

    <p>Password: <input
    → type="password" name="pass1"
    → size="10" maxlength="20" /></p>

    <p>Confirm Password: <input
    → type="password" name="pass2"
    → size="10" maxlength="20" /></p>

    <p><input type="submit"
    → name="submit" value="Register"
    → /></p>

<input type="hidden"
→ name="submitted" value="TRUE"
/>

</form>
```

This is all much like that in Step 11. A submit button and a hidden input are in the form as well. The hidden input trick is discussed in (you guessed it...Chapter 3).

As a side note, I don't need to follow my maxlength recommendation (from Step 11) with the password inputs, because they will be encrypted with SHA1(), which always creates a string 40 characters long. And since there are two of them, they can't both use the same name as the column in the database.

13. Complete the template.

```
<?php

include ('includes/footer.html');

?>
```

continues on next page

14. Save the file as `register.php`, place it in your Web directory, and test it in your Web browser.

Note that if you use an apostrophe in one of the form values, it will likely break the query (**Figure 8.11**). The section "Ensuring Secure SQL" later in this chapter will show how to protect against this.

✔ Tips

■ After running the script, you can always ensure that it worked by using the mysql client or phpMyAdmin to view the values in the *users* table.

■ You should not end your queries with a semicolon in PHP, as you did when using the mysql client. When working with MySQL, this is a common, albeit harmless, mistake to make. When working with other database applications (Oracle, for one), doing so will make your queries unusable.

■ As a reminder, the `mysqli_query()` function returns TRUE if the query could be executed on the database without error. This does not necessarily mean that the result of the query is what you were expecting. Later scripts will demonstrate how to more accurately gauge the success of a query.

■ You are not obligated to create a `$q` variable as I tend to do (you could directly insert your query text into `mysqli_query()`). However, as the construction of your queries becomes more complex, using a variable will be the only option.

■ Practically any query you would run in the mysql client can also be executed using `mysqli_query()`.

■ Another benefit of the Improved MySQL Extension over the standard extension is that the `mysqli_multi_query()` function lets you execute multiple queries at one time. The syntax for doing so, particularly if the queries return results, is a bit more complicated, so see the PHP manual if you have this need.

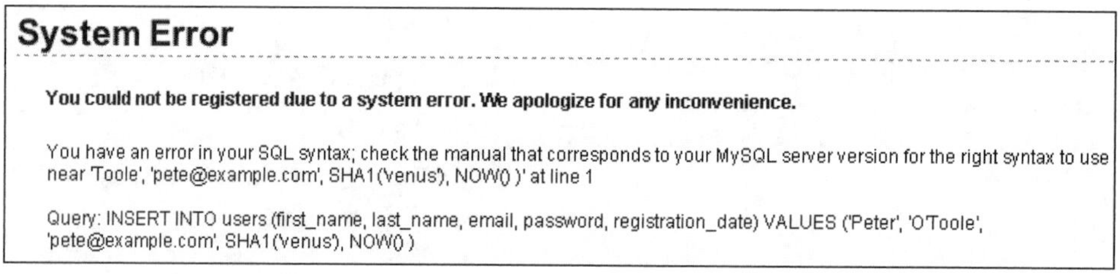

System Error

You could not be registered due to a system error. We apologize for any inconvenience.

You have an error in your SQL syntax; check the manual that corresponds to your MySQL server version for the right syntax to use near 'Toole', 'pete@example.com', SHA1('venus'), NOW())' at line 1

Query: INSERT INTO users (first_name, last_name, email, password, registration_date) VALUES ('Peter', 'O'Toole', 'pete@example.com', SHA1('venus'), NOW())

Figure 8.11 Apostrophes in form values (like the last name here) will conflict with the apostrophes used to delineate values in the query.

Retrieving Query Results

The preceding section of this chapter demonstrates how to execute simple queries on a MySQL database. A *simple query*, as I'm calling it, could be defined as one that begins with INSERT, UPDATE, DELETE, or ALTER. What all four of these have in common is that they return no data, just an indication of their success. Conversely, a SELECT query generates information (i.e., it will return rows of records) that has to be handled by other PHP functions.

The primary tool for handling SELECT query results is mysqli_fetch_array(), which uses the query result variable (that I've been calling $r) and returns one row of data at a time, in an array format. You'll want to use this function within a loop that will continue to access every returned row as long as there are more to be read. The basic construction for reading every record from a query is

```
while ($row = mysqli_fetch_array($r)) {

    // Do something with $row.

}
```

You will almost always want to use a while *loop to fetch the results from a* SELECT *query.*

The mysqli_fetch_array() function takes an optional second parameter specifying what type of array is returned: associative, indexed, or both. An associative array allows you to refer to column values by name, whereas an indexed array requires you to use only numbers (starting at 0 for the first column returned). Each parameter is defined by a constant listed in **Table 8.1**. The MYSQLI_NUM setting is marginally faster (and uses less memory) than the other options. Conversely, MYSQLI_ASSOC is more overt ($row['column'] rather than $row[3]) and may continue to work even if the query changes.

An optional step you can take when using mysqli_fetch_array() would be to free up the query result resources once you are done using them:

```
mysqli_free_result ($r);
```

This line removes the overhead (memory) taken by $r. It's an optional step, since PHP will automatically free up the resources at the end of a script, but—like using mysqli_close()—it does make for good programming form.

To demonstrate how to handle results returned by a query, let's create a script for viewing all of the currently registered users.

Table 8.1 Adding one of these constants as an optional parameter to the mysqli_fetch_array() function dictates how you can access the values returned. The default setting of the function is MYSQLI_BOTH.

mysqli_fetch_array() Constants	
CONSTANT	EXAMPLE
MYSQLI_ASSOC	$row['column']
MYSQLI_NUM	$row[0]
MYSQLI_BOTH	$row[0] or $row['column']

To retrieve query results:

1. Create a new PHP document in your text editor or IDE (**Script 8.4**).

   ```php
   <?php # Script 8.4 - view_users.php
   $page_title = 'View the Current Users';
   include ('includes/header.html');
   echo '<h1>Registered Users</h1>';
   ```

2. Connect to and query the database.

   ```php
   require_once
   → ('../mysqli_connect.php');
   $q = "SELECT CONCAT(last_name, ', ',
   → first_name) AS name,
   → DATE_FORMAT(registration_date, '%M
   → %d, %Y') AS dr FROM users ORDER BY
   → registration_date ASC";
   $r = @mysqli_query ($dbc, $q);
   ```

   The query here will return two columns (**Figure 8.12**): the users' names (formatted as *Last Name, First Name*) and the date they registered (formatted as *Month DD, YYYY*). Because both columns are formatted using MySQL functions, aliases are given to the returned results (*name* and *dr*, accordingly). See Chapter 5 if you are confused by any of this syntax.

3. Display the query results.

   ```php
   if ($r) {
       echo '<table align="center"
   → cellspacing="3"
   cellpadding="3"
   → width="75%">
       <tr><td
   → align="left"><b>Name</b></td><
   td
   → align="left"><b>Date
   → Registered</b></td></tr>
   ';
   ```

Script 8.4 The `view_users.php` script runs a static query on the database and prints all of the returned rows.

```php
1    <?php # Script 8.4 - view_users.php

2    // This script retrieves all the records
     from the users table.

3

4    $page_title = 'View the Current Users';

5    include ('includes/header.html');

6

7    // Page header:

8    echo '<h1>Registered Users</h1>';

9

10   require_once ('../mysqli_connect.php'); //
     Connect to the db.

11

12   // Make the query:

13   $q = "SELECT CONCAT(last_name, ', ',
     first_name) AS name,
     DATE_FORMAT(registration_date, '%M %d,
     %Y') AS dr FROM users ORDER BY
     registration_date ASC";

14   $r = @mysqli_query ($dbc, $q); // Run the
     query.

15

16   if ($r) { // If it ran OK, display the
     records.

17

18   // Table header.

19   echo '<table align="center"
     cellspacing="3" cellpadding="3"
     width="75%">

20   <tr><td align="left"><b>Name</b></td><td
     align="left"><b>Date
     Registered</b></td></tr>

21   ';

22

23   // Fetch and print all the records:

24   while ($row = mysqli_fetch_array($r,
     MYSQL_ASSOC)) {
```

(script continues on next page)

Script 8.4 *continued*

```
000                    Script
25    echo '<tr><td align="left">' .
      $row['name'] . '</td><td align="left">'
      . $row['dr'] . '</td></tr>
26    ';
27    }
28
29    echo '</table>'; // Close the table.
30
31    mysqli_free_result ($r); // Free up the
      resources.
32
33    } else { // If it did not run OK.
34
35    // Public message:
36    echo '<p class="error">The current users
      could not be retrieved. We apologize for
      any inconvenience.</p>';
37
38    // Debugging message:
39    echo '<p>' . mysqli_error($dbc) . '<br
      /><br />Query: ' . $q . '</p>';
40
41    } // End of if ($r) IF.
42
43    mysqli_close($dbc); // Close the database
      connection.
44
45    include ('includes/footer.html');
46    ?>
```

```
while ($row =
→ mysqli_fetch_array($r,
→ MYSQLI_ASSOC)) {

    echo '<tr><td align="left">' .
→ $row['name'] . '</td><td
→ align="left">' . $row['dr'] .
→ '</td></tr>
    ';
}
echo '</table>';
```

To display the results, make a table and a header row in HTML. Then loop through the results using `mysqli_fetch_array()` and print each fetched row. Finally, close the table.

Notice that within the `while` loop, the code refers to each returned value using the proper alias: `$row['name']` and `$row['dr']`. The script could not refer to `$row['first_name']` or `$row['date_registered']` because no such field name was returned (see Figure 8.12).

continues on next page

Figure 8.12 The query results as run within the mysql client.

4. Free up the query resources.

```
mysqli_free_result ($r);
```

Again, this is an optional step but a good one to take.

5. Complete the main conditional.

```
} else {
    echo '<p class="error">The
    → current users could not be
    → retrieved. We apologize for
    any
    → inconvenience.</p>';
    echo '<p>' . mysqli_error($dbc)
    .
    → '<br /><br />Query: ' . $q .
    → '</p>';
}
```

As in the `register.php` example, there are two kinds of error messages here. The first is a generic message, the type you'd show in a live site. The second is much more detailed, printing both the MySQL error and the query, both being critical for debugging purposes.

6. Close the database connection and finish the page.

```
mysqli_close($dbc);

include ('includes/footer.html');

?>
```

7. Save the file as `view_users.php`, place it in your Web directory, and test it in your browser (**Figure 8.13**).

✔ Tips

■ The function `mysqli_fetch_row()`is the equivalent of `mysqli_fetch_array ($r, MYSQLI_NUM);`

■ The function `mysqli_fetch_assoc()` is the equivalent of `mysqli_fetch_array ($r, MYSQLI_ASSOC);`

■ As with any associative array, when you retrieve records from the database, you must refer to the columns exactly as they are defined in the database. This is to say that the keys are case-sensitive.

■ If you are in a situation where you need to run a second query inside of your `while` loop, be certain to use different variable names for that query. For example, the inner query would use `$r2` and `$row2` instead of `$r` and `$row`. If you don't do this, you'll encounter logical errors.

■ I frequently see beginning PHP developers muddle the process of fetching query results. Remember that you must execute the query using `mysqli_query()`, and then use `mysqli_fetch_array()` to retrieve a single row of information. If you have multiple rows to retrieve, use a `while` loop.

Registered Users

Name	Date Registered
Ullman, Larry	September 22, 2007
Isabella, Zoe	September 22, 2007
Starr, Ringo	September 22, 2007
Harrison, George	September 22, 2007
McCartney, Paul	September 22, 2007
Lennon, John	September 22, 2007
Brautigan, Richard	September 22, 2007
Banks, Russell	September 22, 2007
Simpson, Homer	September 22, 2007
Simpson, Marge	September 22, 2007
Simpson, Bart	September 22, 2007
Simpson, Lisa	September 22, 2007
Simpson, Maggie	September 22, 2007
Simpson, Abe	September 22, 2007
Chabon, Michael	September 22, 2007
Greene, Graham	September 22, 2007
DeLillo, Don	September 22, 2007
Jones, David	September 22, 2007
Dolenz, Micky	September 22, 2007
Nesmith, Mike	September 22, 2007
Sedaris, David	September 22, 2007
Hornby, Nick	September 22, 2007
Bank, Melissa	September 22, 2007
Morrison, Toni	September 22, 2007
Franzen, Jonathan	September 22, 2007
Campbell, Bob	September 30, 2007

Figure 8.13 All of the user records are retrieved from the database and displayed in the Web browser.

Ensuring Secure SQL

Database security with respect to PHP comes down to three broad issues:

1. Protecting the MySQL access information

2. Not revealing too much about the database

3. Being cautious when running queries, particularly those involving user-submitted data

You can accomplish the first objective by securing the MySQL connection script outside of the Web directory so that it is never viewable through a Web browser (see Figure 8.3). I discuss this in some detail earlier in the chapter. The second objective is attained by not letting the user see PHP's error messages or your queries (in these scripts, that information is printed out for your debugging purposes; you'd never want to do that on a live site).

For the third objective, there are numerous steps you can and should take, all based upon the premise of never trusting user-supplied data. First, validate that some value has been submitted, or that it is of the proper type (number, string, etc.). Second, use regular expressions to make sure that submitted data matches what you would expect it to be (this topic is covered in Chapter 13, "Perl-Compatible Regular Expressions"). Third, you can typecast some values to guarantee that they're numbers (discussed in Chapter 12, "Security Methods"). A fourth recommendation is to run user-submitted data through the `mysqli_real_escape_string()` function. This function cleans data by escaping what could be problematic characters. It's used like so:

```
$clean = mysqli_real_escape_string($dbc,
→ data);
```

For security purposes, `mysqli_real_escape_string()` should be used on every text input in a form. To demonstrate this, let's revamp `register.php` (Script 8.3).

To use mysqli_real_escape_string():

1. Open register.php (Script 8.3) in your text editor or IDE.

2. Move the inclusion of the mysqli_connect.php file (line 46 in Script 8.3) to just after the main conditional (**Script 8.5**).

   Because the mysqli_real_escape_string() function requires a database connection, the mysqli_connect.php script must be required earlier in the script.

Script 8.5 The register.php script now uses the mysqli_real_escape_string() function to clean the submitted data.

```
1    <?php # Script 8.5 - register.php #2
2
3    $page_title = 'Register';
4    include ('includes/header.html');
5
6    // Check if the form has been submitted:
7    if (isset($_POST['submitted'])) {
8
9        require_once ('../mysqli_connect.php');
         // Connect to the db.
10
11       $errors = array(); // Initialize an
         error array.
12
13       // Check for a first name:
14       if (empty($_POST['first_name'])) {
15           $errors[] = 'You forgot to enter your
             first name.';
16       } else {
17           $fn = mysqli_real_escape_string($dbc,
             trim($_POST['first_name']));
18       }
19
20       // Check for a last name:
21       if (empty($_POST['last_name'])) {
22           $errors[] = 'You forgot to enter your
             last name.';
23       } else {
24           $ln = mysqli_real_escape_string($dbc,
             trim($_POST['last_name']));
25       }
26
27       // Check for an email address:
28       if (empty($_POST['email'])) {
29           $errors[] = 'You forgot to enter your
             email address.';
30       } else {
31           $e = mysqli_real_escape_string($dbc,
             trim($_POST['email']));
```

(script continues on next page)

Script 8.5 *continued*

```
32      }
33
34      // Check for a password and match
        against the confirmed password:
35      if (!empty($_POST['pass1'])) {
36          if ($_POST['pass1'] !=
            $_POST['pass2']) {
37              $errors[] = 'Your password did not
                match the confirmed password.';
38          } else {
39              $p = mysqli_real_escape_string($dbc,
                trim($_POST['pass1']));
40          }
41      } else {
42          $errors[] = 'You forgot to enter your
            password.';
43      }
44
45      if (empty($errors)) { // If everything's
        OK.
46
47          // Register the user in the
            database...
48
49          // Make the query:
50          $q = "INSERT INTO users (first_name,
            last_name, email, pass,
            registration_date) VALUES ('$fn',
            '$ln', '$e', SHA1('$p'), NOW() )";
51          $r = @mysqli_query ($dbc, $q); // Run
            the query.
52          if ($r) { // If it ran OK.
53
54              // Print a message:
55              echo '<h1>Thank you!</h1>
56          <p>You are now registered. In Chapter
            11 you will actually be able to log
            in!</p><p><br /></p>';
57
58          } else { // If it did not run OK.
59
60              // Public message:
```

(script continues on next page)

3. Change the validation routines to use the `mysqli_real_escape_string()` function, replacing each occurrence of *$var* = `trim($_POST['`*var*`'])` with *$var* = `mysqli_real_escape_string($dbc, trim($_POST['`*var*`']))`.

```
$fn = mysqli_real_escape_string($dbc,
→ trim($_POST['first_name']));
```

```
$ln = mysqli_real_escape_string($dbc,
→ trim($_POST['last_name']));
```

```
$e = mysqli_real_escape_string($dbc,
→ trim($_POST['email']));
```

```
$p = mysqli_real_escape_string($dbc,
→ trim($_POST['pass1']));
```

Instead of just assigning the submitted value to each variable (`$fn`, `$ln`, etc.), the values will be run through the `mysqli_real_escape_string()` function first. The `trim()` function is still used to get rid of any unnecessary spaces.

continues on next page

4. Add a second call to `mysqli_close()` before the end of the main conditional.

`mysqli_close($dbc);`

To be consistent, since the database connection is opened as the first step of the main conditional, it should be closed as the last step of this same conditional. It still needs to be closed before including the footer and terminating the script (lines 72 and 73), though.

Script 8.5 *continued*

```
61        echo '<h1>System Error</h1>
62        <p class="error">You could not be
          registered due to a system error.
          We apologize for any
          inconvenience.</p>';
63
64        // Debugging message:
65        echo '<p>' . mysqli_error($dbc) .
          '<br /><br />Query: ' . $q .
          '</p>';
66
67        } // End of if ($r) IF.
68
69        mysqli_close($dbc); // Close the
          database connection.
70
71        // Include the footer and quit the
          script:
72        include ('includes/footer.html');
73        exit();
74
75    } else { // Report the errors.
76
77        echo '<h1>Error!</h1>
78        <p class="error">The following
          error(s) occurred:<br />';
79        foreach ($errors as $msg) { // Print
          each error.
80          echo " - $msg<br />\n";
81        }
82        echo '</p><p>Please try
          again.</p><p><br /></p>';
83
84    } // End of if (empty($errors)) IF.
85
86    mysqli_close($dbc); // Close the
          database connection.
87
88    } // End of the main Submit conditional.
89    ?>
```

(script continues on next page)

Script 8.5 *continued*

```
90    <h1>Register</h1>

91    <form action="register.php" method="post">

92      <p>First Name: <input type="text"
        name="first_name" size="15"
        maxlength="20" value="<?php if
        (isset($_POST['first_name'])) echo
        $_POST['first_name']; ?>" /></p>

93      <p>Last Name: <input type="text"
        name="last_name" size="15"
        maxlength="40" value="<?php if
        (isset($_POST['last_name'])) echo
        $_POST['last_name']; ?>" /></p>

94      <p>Email Address: <input type="text"
        name="email" size="20" maxlength="80"
        value="<?php if (isset($_POST['email']))
        echo $_POST['email']; ?>"  /> </p>

95      <p>Password: <input type="password"
        name="pass1" size="10" maxlength="20"
        /></p>

96      <p>Confirm Password: <input
        type="password" name="pass2" size="10"
        maxlength="20" /></p>

97      <p><input type="submit" name="submit"
        value="Register" /></p>

98      <input type="hidden" name="submitted"
        value="TRUE" />

99    </form>

100   <?php

101   include ('includes/footer.html');

102   ?>
```

5. Save the file as `register.php`, place it in your Web directory, and test it in your Web browser (**Figures 8.14** and **8.15**).

continues on next page

Register

First Name: **Peter**

Last Name: **O'Toole**

Email Address: **pete@example.com**

Password: *****

Confirm Password: *****

Register

Figure 8.14 Values with apostrophes in them, like a person's last name, will no longer break the INSERT query, thanks to the `mysqli_real_escape_string()` function.

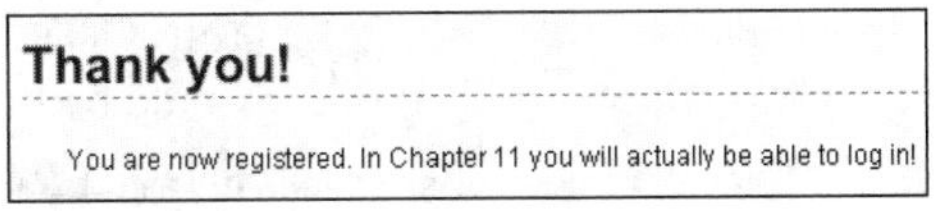

Thank you!

You are now registered. In Chapter 11 you will actually be able to log in!

Figure 8.15 Now the registration process will handle problematic characters and be more secure.

✔ Tips

- The mysqli_real_escape_string() function escapes a string in accordance with the language being used, which is an added advantage over alternative solutions.

- If you see results like those in **Figure 8.16**, it means that the mysqli_real_escape_string() function cannot access the database (because it has no connection, like $dbc).

- If Magic Quotes is enabled on your server (which means you're using a version of PHP prior to 6), you'll need to remove any slashes added by Magic Quotes, prior to using the mysqli_real_escape_string() function. The code (cumbersome as it is) would look like:

```
$fn = mysqli_real_escape_string
→ ($dbc, trim (stripslashes
→ ($_POST['first_name'])));
```

If you don't use stripslashes() and Magic Quotes is enabled, the form values will be doubly escaped.

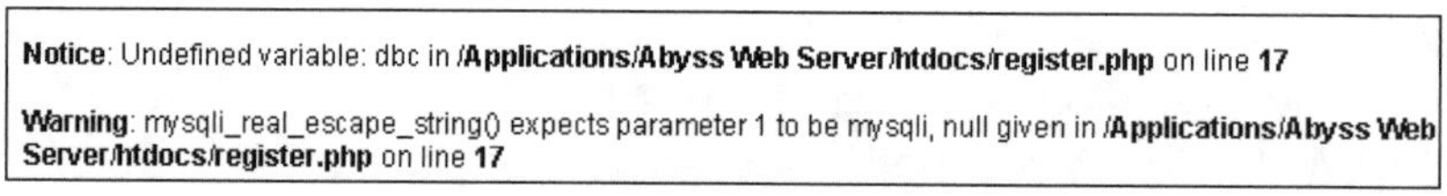

Notice: Undefined variable: dbc in **/Applications/Abyss Web Server/htdocs/register.php** on line **17**

Warning: mysqli_real_escape_string() expects parameter 1 to be mysqli, null given in **/Applications/Abyss Web Server/htdocs/register.php** on line **17**

Figure 8.16 Since the mysqli_real_escape_string() requires a database connection, using it without that connection (e.g., before including the connection script) can lead to other errors.

ENSURING SECURE SQL

Modifying register.php

The mysqli_num_rows() function could be applied to register.php to prevent someone from registering with the same email address multiple times. Although the UNIQUE index on that column in the database will prevent that from happening, such attempts will create a MySQL error. To prevent this using PHP, run a SELECT query to confirm that the email address isn't currently registered. That query would be simply

```
SELECT user_id FROM users WHERE email='$e'
```

You would run this query (using the mysqli_query() function) and then call mysqli_num_rows(). If mysqli_num_rows() returns 0, you know that the email address hasn't already been registered and it's safe to run the INSERT.

Script 8.6 Now the `view_users.php` script will display the total number of registered users, thanks to the `mysqli_num_rows()` function.

```
1    <?php # Script 8.6 - view_users.php #2

2    // This script retrieves all the records
     from the users table.

3

4    $page_title = 'View the Current Users';

5    include ('includes/header.html');

6

7    // Page header:

8    echo '<h1>Registered Users</h1>';

9

10   require_once ('../mysqli_connect.php'); //
     Connect to the db.

11

12   // Make the query:

13   $q = "SELECT CONCAT(last_name, ', ',
     first_name) AS name,
     DATE_FORMAT(registration_date, '%M %d,
     %Y') AS dr FROM users ORDER BY
     registration_date ASC";

14   $r = @mysqli_query ($dbc, $q); // Run the
     query.

15

16   // Count the number of returned rows:

17   $num = mysqli_num_rows($r);

18

19   if ($num > 0) { // If it ran OK, display
     the records.

20

21      // Print how many users there are:

22      echo "<p>There are currently $num
        registered users.</p>\n";

23

24      // Table header.

25      echo '<table align="center"
        cellspacing="3" cellpadding="3"
        width="75%">
```

(script continues on next page)

Counting Returned Records

The next logical function to discuss is `mysqli_num_rows()`. This function returns the number of rows retrieved by a SELECT query. It takes one argument, the query result variable:

`$num = mysqli_num_rows($r);`

Although simple in purpose, this function is very useful. It's necessary if you want to paginate your query results (an example of this can be found in the next chapter). It's also a good idea to use this function before you attempt to fetch any results using a `while` loop (because there's no need to fetch the results if there aren't any, and attempting to do so may cause errors). In this next sequence of steps, let's modify `view_users.php` to list the total number of registered users. For another example of how you might use `mysqli_num_rows()`, see the sidebar.

To modify view_users.php:

1. Open `view_users.php` (refer to Script 8.4) in your text editor or IDE.

2. Before the `if ($r)` conditional, add this line (**Script 8.6**)

   `$num = mysqli_num_rows ($r);`

   This line will assign the number of rows returned by the query to the $num variable.

3. Change the original $r conditional to

   `if ($num > 0) {`

   The conditional as it was written before was based upon whether the query did or did not successfully run, not whether or not any records were returned. Now it will be more accurate.

continues on next page

COUNTING RETURNED RECORDS

4. Before creating the HTML table, print the number of registered users.

```
echo "<p>There are currently $num
→ registered users.</p>\n";
```

5. Change the `else` part of the main conditional to read

```
echo '<p class="error">There are
→ currently no registered users.</p>';
```

The original conditional was based upon whether or not the query worked. Hopefully you've successfully debugged the query so that it is working and the original error messages are no longer needed. Now the error message just indicates if no records were returned.

6. Save the file as `view_users.php`, place it in your Web directory, and test it in your Web browser (**Figure 8.17**).

Script 8.6 *continued*

```
                                    Script
26      <tr><td align="left"><b>Name</b></td><td
        align="left"><b>Date
        Registered</b></td></tr>
27      ';
28
29      // Fetch and print all the records:
30      while ($row = mysqli_fetch_array($r,
        MYSQLI_ASSOC)) {
31          echo '<tr><td align="left">' .
        $row['name'] . '</td><td align="left">' .
        $row['dr'] . '</td></tr>
32          ';
33      }
34
35      echo '</table>'; // Close the table.
36
37      mysqli_free_result ($r); // Free up the
        resources.
38
39  } else { // If no records were returned.
40
41      echo '<p class="error">There are
        currently no registered users.</p>';
42
43  }
44
45  mysqli_close($dbc); // Close the database
        connection.
46
47  include ('includes/footer.html');
48  ?>
```

Registered Users

There are currently 27 registered users.

Name	Date Registered
Ullman, Larry	September 22, 2007
Isabella, Zoe	September 22, 2007
Starr, Ringo	September 22, 2007
Harrison, George	September 22, 2007
McCartney, Paul	September 22, 2007
Lennon, John	September 22, 2007
Chabon, Michael	September 22, 2007
Brautigan, Richard	September 22, 2007
Banks, Russell	September 22, 2007
Simpson, Homer	September 22, 2007

Figure 8.17 The number of registered users is now displayed at the top of the page.

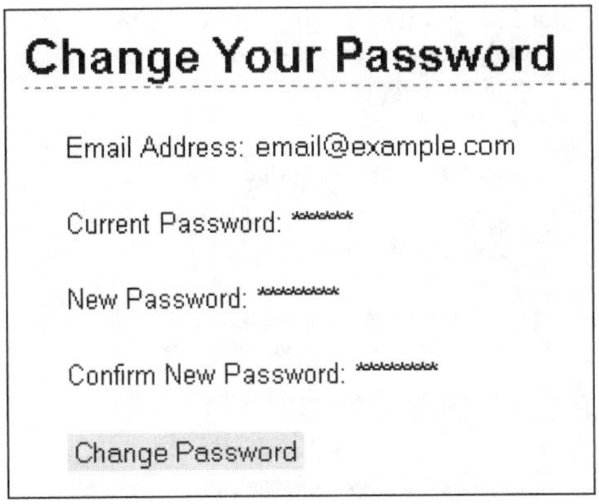

Change Your Password

Email Address: email@example.com

Current Password: ******

New Password: ********

Confirm New Password: ********

Change Password

Figure 8.18 The form for changing a user's password.

Updating Records with PHP

The last technique in this chapter shows how to update database records through a PHP script. Doing so requires an UPDATE query, and its successful execution can be verified with PHP's mysqli_affected_rows() function.

While the mysqli_num_rows() function will return the number of rows generated by a SELECT query, mysqli_affected_rows() returns the number of rows affected by an INSERT, UPDATE, or DELETE query. It's used like so:

```
$num = mysqli_affected_rows($dbc);
```

Unlike mysqli_num_rows(), the one argument the function takes is the database connection ($dbc), not the results of the previous query ($r).

The following example will be a script that allows registered users to change their password. It demonstrates two important ideas:

◆ Checking a submitted username and password against registered values (the key to a login system as well)

◆ Updating database records using the primary key as a reference

As with the registration example, this one PHP script will both display the form (**Figure 8.18**) and handle it.

To update records with PHP:

1. Create a new PHP script in your text editor or IDE (**Script 8.7**).

   ```php
   <?php # Script 8.7 - password.php
   $page_title = 'Change Your Password';
   include ('includes/header.html');
   ```

2. Start the main conditional.

   ```php
   if (isset($_POST['submitted'])) {
   ```

   Since this page both displays and handles the form, it'll use the standard conditional.

3. Include the database connection and create an array for storing errors.

   ```php
   require_once ('../mysqli_connect.php');
   $errors = array();
   ```

   The initial part of this script mimics the registration form.

Script 8.7 The password.php script runs an UPDATE query on the database and uses the mysqli_affected_rows() function to confirm the change.

```
⊖ ⃝ ⃝                    Script
1    <?php # Script 8.7 - password.php
2    // This page lets a user change their
     password.
3
4    $page_title = 'Change Your Password';
5    include ('includes/header.html');
6
7    // Check if the form has been submitted:
8    if (isset($_POST['submitted'])) {
9
10     require_once ('../mysqli_connect.php');
       // Connect to the db.
11
12     $errors = array(); // Initialize an
       error array.
13
14     // Check for an email address:
15     if (empty($_POST['email'])) {
16       $errors[] = 'You forgot to enter your
         email address.';
17     } else {
18       = mysqli_real_escape_string($dbc,
         trim($_POST['email']));
19     }
20
21     // Check for the current password:
22     if (empty($_POST['pass'])) {
23       $errors[] = 'You forgot to enter your
         current password.';
24     } else {
25       $p = mysqli_real_escape_string($dbc,
         trim($_POST['pass']));
26     }
27
28     // Check for a new password and match
29     // against the confirmed password:
```

(script continues on next page)

Script 8.7 *continued*

```
 30    if (!empty($_POST['pass1'])) {

 31        if ($_POST['pass1'] !=
           $_POST['pass2']) {

 32          $errors[] = 'Your new password did
             not match the confirmed password.';

 33        } else {

 34          $np =
             mysqli_real_escape_string($dbc,
             trim($_POST['pass1']));

 35        }

 36    } else {

 37        $errors[] = 'You forgot to enter your
           new password.';

 38    }

 39

 40    if (empty($errors)) { // If everything's
       OK.

 41

 42        // Check that they've entered the
           right email address/password
           combination:

 43        $q = "SELECT user_id FROM users WHERE
           (email='$e' AND pass=SHA1('$p') )";

 44        $r = @mysqli_query($dbc, $q);

 45        $num = @mysqli_num_rows($r);

 46        if ($num == 1) { // Match was made.

 47

 48          // Get the user_id:

 49          $row = mysqli_fetch_array($r,
             MYSQLI_NUM);

 50

 51          // Make the UPDATE query:

 52          $q = "UPDATE users SET
             pass=SHA1('$np') WHERE
             user_id=$row[0]";

 53          $r = @mysqli_query($dbc, $q);

 54

 55          if (mysqli_affected_rows($dbc) ==
             1) { // If it ran OK.

 56
```

(script continues on next page)

4. Validate the email address and current password fields.

```
if (empty($_POST['email'])) {

    $errors[] = 'You forgot to enter
    → your email address.';

} else {

    $e =
    → mysqli_real_escape_string($dbc
    ,
    → trim($_POST['email']));

}

if (empty($_POST['pass'])) {

    $errors[] = 'You forgot to enter
    → your current password.';

} else {

    $p =
    → mysqli_real_escape_string($dbc
    ,
    → trim($_POST['pass']));

}
```

The form (Figure 8.18) has four inputs: the email address, the current password, and two for the new password. The process for validating each of these is the same as it is in register.php. Any data that passes the validation test will be trimmed and run through the mysqli_real_escape_ string() function, so that it is safe to use in a query.

continues on next page

UPDATING RECORDS WITH PHP

253

5. Validate the new password.

```
if (!empty($_POST['pass1'])) {

    if ($_POST['pass1'] !=
    → $_POST['pass2']) {

        $errors[] = 'Your new password
        → did not match the confirmed
        → password.';

    } else {

        $np =
        → mysqli_real_escape_string($
        → dbc, trim($_POST['pass1']));

    }

} else {

    $errors[] = 'You forgot to enter
    → your new password.';

}
```

This code is also exactly like that in the registration script, except that a valid new password is assigned to a variable called $np (because $p represents the current password).

```
⚫ ⚪ ⚪                    📄 Script
57                  // Print a message.
58                  echo '<h1>Thank you!</h1>
59                  <p>Your password has been
                    updated. In Chapter 11 you
                    will actually be able to log
                    in!</p><p><br /></p>';
60
61          } else { // If it did not run OK.
62
63                  // Public message:
64                  echo '<h1>System Error</h1>
65                  <p class="error">Your
                    password could not be
                    changed due to a system
                    error. We apologize for any
                    inconvenience.</p>';
66
67                  // Debugging message:
68                  echo '<p>' .
                    mysqli_error($dbc) . '<br
                    /><br />Query: ' . $q .
                    '</p>';
69
70          }
71
72                  // Include the footer and quit the
                    script (to not show the form).
73                  include ('includes/footer.html');
74                  exit();
75
76          } else { // Invalid email
            address/password combination.
77                  echo '<h1>Error!</h1>
78                  <p class="error">The email address
                    and password do not match those on
                    file.</p>';
79          }
80
81  } else { // Report the errors.
```

(script continues on next page)

Script 8.7 *continued*

```
 82
 83        echo '<h1>Error!</h1>';
 84        <p class="error">The following
           error(s) occurred:<br />';
 85        foreach ($errors as $msg) { // Print
           each error.
 86          echo " - $msg<br />\n";
 87        }
 88        echo '</p><p>Please try
           again.</p><p><br /></p>';
 89
 90      } // End of if (empty($errors)) IF.
 91
 92      mysqli_close($dbc); // Close the
         database connection.
 93
 94    } // End of the main Submit conditional.
 95    ?>
 96    <h1>Change Your Password</h1>
 97    <form action="password.php" method="post">
 98      <p>Email Address: <input type="text"
         name="email" size="20" maxlength="80"
         value="<?php if (isset($_POST['email']))
         echo $_POST['email']; ?>"  /> </p>
 99      <p>Current Password: <input
         type="password" name="pass" size="10"
         maxlength="20" /></p>
100      <p>New Password: <input type="password"
         name="pass1" size="10" maxlength="20"
         /></p>
101      <p>Confirm New Password: <input
         type="password" name="pass2" size="10"
         maxlength="20" /></p>
102      <p><input type="submit" name="submit"
         value="Change Password" /></p>
103      <input type="hidden" name="submitted"
         value="TRUE" />
104    </form>
105    <?php
106    include ('includes/footer.html');
107    ?>
```

6. If all the tests are passed, retrieve the user's ID.

```
if (empty($errors)) {
    $q = "SELECT user_id FROM users
    → WHERE (email='$e' AND
    → pass=SHA1('$p') )";
    $r = @mysqli_query($dbc, $q);
    $num = @mysqli_num_rows($r);
    if ($num == 1) {
        $row = mysqli_fetch_array($r,
        → MYSQLI_NUM);
```

This first query will return just the user_id field for the record that matches the submitted email address and password (**Figure 8.19**). To compare the submitted password against the stored one, encrypt it again with the SHA1() function. If the user is registered and has correctly entered both the email address and password, exactly one row will be selected (since the email value must be unique across all rows). Finally, this one record is assigned as an array (of one element) to the $row variable.

continues on next page

Figure 8.19 The result when running the SELECT query from the script (the first of two queries it has) within the mysql client.

If this part of the script doesn't work for you, apply the standard debugging methods: remove the error suppression operators (@) so that you can see what errors, if any, occur; use the `mysqli_error()` function to report any MySQL errors; and print, then run the query using another interface (as in Figure 8.19).

7. Update the database.

```
$q = "UPDATE users SET
→ pass=SHA1('$np') WHERE
→ user_id=$row[0]";

$r = @mysqli_query($dbc, $q);
```

This query will change the password—using the new submitted value—where the `user_id` column is equal to the number retrieved from the previous query.

8. Check the results of the query.

```
if (mysqli_affected_rows($dbc) == 1) {

    echo '<h1>Thank you!</h1>

    <p>Your password has been
    → updated. In Chapter 11 you
    will
    → actually be able to log
    → in!</p><p><br /></p>';

} else {

    echo '<h1>System Error</h1>

    <p class="error">Your password
    → could not be changed due to a
    → system error. We apologize for
    → any inconvenience.</p>';

    echo '<p>' . mysqli_error($dbc)
    .
    → '<br /><br />Query: ' . $q .
    → '</p>';

}
```

This part of the script again works similar to `register.php`. In this case, if `mysqli_affected_rows()` returns the number *1*, the record has been updated, and a success message will be printed. If not, both a public, generic message and a more useful debugging message will be printed.

9. Include the footer and terminate the script.

```
include ('includes/footer.html');

exit();
```

At this point in the script, the UPDATE query has been run. It either worked or it did not (because of a system error). In both cases, there's no need to show the form again, so the footer is included (to complete the page) and the script is terminated, using the `exit()` function.

10. Complete the if (`$num` == 1) conditional.

```
} else {

    echo '<h1>Error!</h1>

    <p class="error">The email
    → address and password do not
    → match those on file.</p>';

}
```

If `mysqli_num_rows()` does not return a value of *1*, then the submitted email address and password do not match those on file and this error is printed. In this case, the form will be displayed again so that the user can enter the correct information.

11. Print any validation error messages.

```
} else {

    echo '<h1>Error!</h1>

    <p class="error">The following
    → error(s) occurred:<br />';

    foreach ($errors as $msg) {

        echo " - $msg<br />\n";

    }

    echo '</p><p>Please try
    → again.</p><p><br /></p>';

}
```

This **else** clause applies if the **$errors** array is not empty (which means that the form data did not pass all the validation tests). As in the registration page, the errors will be printed.

12. Close the database connection and complete the PHP code.

```
    mysqli_close($dbc);

}

?>
```

13. Display the form.

```
<h1>Change Your Password</h1>

<form action="password.php"
→ method="post">

    <p>Email Address: <input
    → type="text" name="email"
    → size="20" maxlength="80"
    → value="<?php if
    → (isset($_POST['email'])) echo
    → $_POST['email']; ?>" /> </p>

    <p>Current Password: <input
    → type="password" name="pass"
    → size="10" maxlength="20" /></p>

    <p>New Password: <input
    → type="password" name="pass1"
    → size="10" maxlength="20" /></p>

    <p>Confirm New Password: <input
    → type="password" name="pass2"
    → size="10" maxlength="20" /></p>

    <p><input type="submit"
    → name="submit" value="Change
    → Password" /></p>

    <input type="hidden"
    → name="submitted" value="TRUE"
    → />

</form>
```

The form takes three different inputs of type password—the current password, the new one, and a confirmation of the new password—and one text input for the email address. The email address input is sticky (password inputs cannot be).

continues on next page

14. Include the footer file.

```php
<?php

include ('includes/footer.html');

?>
```

15. Save the file as `password.php`, place it in your Web directory, and test it in your Web browser (**Figures 8.20** and **8.21**).

✔ Tips

■ If you delete every record from a table using the command TRUNCATE `tablename`, `mysqli_affected_rows()` will return *0*, even if the query was successful and every row was removed. This is just a quirk.

■ If an UPDATE query runs but does not actually change the value of any column (for example, a password is replaced with the same password), `mysqli_affected_rows()` will return *0*.

■ The `mysqli_affected_rows()` conditional used here could (and maybe should) also be applied to the `register.php` script to confirm that one record was added. That would be a more exacting condition to check than `if ($r)`.

Thank you!

Your password has been updated. In Chapter 11 you will actually be able to log in!

Figure 8.20 The password was changed in the database.

Error!

The email address and password do not match those on file.

Change Your Password

Email Address: email@example.com

Current Password:

New Password:

Confirm New Password:

Change Password

Figure 8.21 If the entered email address and password don't match those on file, the password will not be updated.

COMMON PROGRAMMING TECHNIQUES

Now that you have a little PHP and MySQL interaction under your belt, it's time to take things up a notch. This chapter is similar to Chapter 3, "Creating Dynamic Web Sites," in that it covers myriad independent topics. But what all of these have in common is that they demonstrate common PHP-MySQL programming techniques. You won't learn new functions here; instead, you'll see how to use the knowledge you already possess to create standard Web functionality.

The examples themselves will broaden the Web application started in the preceding chapter by adding new, popular features. You'll see several tricks for managing database information, in particular editing and deleting records using PHP. At that same time a couple new ways of passing data to your PHP pages will be introduced. The final sections of the chapter add features to the `view_users.php` page.

Sending Values to a Script

In the examples so far, all of the data received in the PHP script came from what the user entered in a form. There are, however, two different ways you can pass variables and values to a PHP script, both worth knowing.

The first method is to make use of HTML's hidden input type:

```
<input type="hidden" name="do"
value="this" />
```

As long as this code is anywhere between the form tags, the variable $_POST['do'] will have a value of *this* in the handling PHP script (assuming that the form uses the POST method). You've already been using this technique in the book with a hidden input named *submitted*, used to test when a form should be handled.

The second method for sending values to a PHP script is to append it to the URL:

www.example.com/page.php?do=this

This technique emulates the GET method of an HTML form. With this specific example, page.php receives a variable called $_GET['do'] with a value of *this*.

To demonstrate this GET method trick, a new version of the view_users.php script, first created in the last chapter, will be written. This one will provide links to pages that will allow you to edit or delete an existing user's record. The links will pass the user's ID to the handling pages, both of which will also be written in this chapter.

To manually send values to a PHP script:

1. Open view_users.php (Script 8.6) in your text editor or IDE.

Script 9.1 The view_users.php script, started in Chapter 8, "Using PHP with MySQL," now modified so that it presents *Edit* and *Delete* links, passing the user's ID number along in each URL.

```
1    <?php # Script 9.1 - view_users.php #3
2
3    // This script retrieves all the records
     from the users table.
4    // This new version links to edit and
     delete pages.
5
6    $page_title = 'View the Current Users';
7    include ('includes/header.html');
8
9    echo '<h1>Registered Users</h1>';
10
11   require_once ('../mysqli_connect.php');
12
13   // Make the query:
14   $q = "SELECT last_name, first_name,
     DATE_FORMAT(registration_date, '%M %d,
     %Y') AS dr, user_id FROM users ORDER BY
     registration_date ASC";
15   $r = @mysqli_query ($dbc, $q);
16
17   // Count the number of returned rows:
18   $num = mysqli_num_rows($r);
19
20   if ($num > 0) { // If it ran OK, display
     the records.
21
22      // Print how many users there are:
23      echo "<p>There are currently $num
        registered users.</p>\n";
24
25      // Table header.
26      echo '<table align="center" cellspacing=
        "3" cellpadding="3" width="75%">
27      <tr>
28      <td align="left"><b>Edit</b></td>
29      <td align="left"><b>Delete</b></td>
```

(script continues on next page)

Script 9.1 *continued*

```
┌─────────────────────────────────────────┐
│ ⊖ ⊖ ⊖            📄 Script               │
├─────────────────────────────────────────┤
30   <td align="left"><b>Last Name</b></td>

31   <td align="left"><b>First Name</b></td>

32   <td align="left"><b>Date Registered</b>
     </td>

33   </tr>

34   ';

35

36   // Fetch and print all the records:

37   while ($row = mysqli_fetch_array($r,
     MYSQLI_ASSOC)) {

38   echo '<tr>

39     <td align="left"><a href="edit_user.
       php?id=' . $row['user_id'] . '">Edit
       </a></td>

40     <td align="left"><a href="delete_user.
       php?id=' . $row['user_id'] . '">Delete
       </a></td>

41     <td align="left">' . $row['last_name']
       . '</td>

42     <td align="left">' . $row['first_
       name'] . '</td>

43     <td align="left">' . $row['dr'] .
       '</td>

44   </tr>

45   ';

46   }

47

48   echo '</table>';

49   mysqli_free_result ($r);

50

51   } else { // If no records were returned.

52     echo '<p class="error">There are
       currently no registered users.</p>';

53   }

54

55   mysqli_close($dbc);

56

57   include ('includes/footer.html');

58   ?>
```

2. Change the SQL query to read (**Script 9.1**).

```
$q = "SELECT last_name, first_name,
→ DATE_FORMAT(registration_date, '%M
→ %d, %Y') AS dr, user_id FROM users
→ ORDER BY registration_date ASC";
```

The query has been changed in a couple of ways. First, the first and last names are selected separately, not concatenated together. Second, the *user_id* is also now being selected, as that value will be necessary in creating the links.

3. Add three more columns to the main table.

```
echo '<table align="center"
→ cellspacing="3" cellpadding="3"
→ width="75%">

<tr>

    <td align="left"><b>Edit</b>
    → </td>

    <td align="left"><b>Delete</b>
    → </td>

    <td align="left"><b>Last Name
    → </b></td>

    <td align="left"><b>First Name
    → </b></td>

    <td align="left"><b>Date
    → Registered</b></td>

</tr>

';
```

In the previous version of the script, there were only two columns: one for the name and another for the date the user registered. The name column has been separated into its two parts and two new columns added: one for the *Edit* link and another for the *Delete* link.

continues on next page

4. Change the echo statement within the while loop to match the table's new structure.

```
echo '<tr>
        <td align="left"><a href=
        → "edit_user.php?id=' . $row
        → ['user_id'] . '">Edit</a></td>

        <td align="left"><a href=
        → "delete_user.php?id=' .
        → $row['user_id'] . '">Delete
        → </a></td>

        <td align="left">' . $row
        → ['last_name'] . '</td>

        <td align="left">' . $row
        → ['first_name'] . '</td>

        <td align="left">' . $row['dr']
        → . '</td>

</tr>
';
```

For each record returned from the database, this line will print out a row with five columns. The last three columns are obvious and easy to create: just refer to the returned column name.

For the first two columns, which provide links to edit or delete the user, the syntax is slightly more complicated. The desired end result is HTML code like *<a href= "edit_user.php?id=X">Edit</a>*, where *X* is the user's ID. Knowing this, all the PHP code has to do is print $row['user_id'] for *X*, being mindful of the quotation marks to avoid parse errors.

Because the HTML attributes use a lot of double quotation marks and this echo() statement requires a lot of variables to be printed, I find it easiest to use single quotes for the HTML and then to concatenate the variables to the printed text.

5. Save the file as view_users.php, place it in your Web directory, and run it in your Web browser (**Figure 9.1**).

Registered Users

There are currently 27 registered users.

Edit	Delete	Last Name	First Name	Date Registered
Edit	Delete	Ullman	Larry	September 22, 2007
Edit	Delete	Isabella	Zoe	September 22, 2007
Edit	Delete	Starr	Ringo	September 22, 2007
Edit	Delete	Harrison	George	September 22, 2007
Edit	Delete	McCartney	Paul	September 22, 2007
Edit	Delete	Lennon	John	September 22, 2007
Edit	Delete	Chabon	Michael	September 22, 2007
Edit	Delete	Brautigan	Richard	September 22, 2007
Edit	Delete	Banks	Russell	September 22, 2007
Edit	Delete	Simpson	Homer	September 22, 2007

Figure 9.1 The revised version of the view_users.php page, with new columns and links.

6. If you want, view the HTML source of the page to see each dynamically generated link (**Figure 9.2**).

✔ Tips

- To append multiple variables to a URL, use this syntax: `page.php?name1=value1 &name2=value2&name3=value3`. It's simply a matter of using the ampersand, plus another *name=value* pair.

- One trick to adding variables to URLs is that strings should be encoded to ensure that the value is handled properly. For example, the space in the string *Elliott Smith* would be problematic. The solution then is to use the `urlencode()` function:

  `$url = 'page.php?name=' . urlencode`
  `→ ('Elliott Smith');`

  You only need to do this when programmatically adding values to a URL. When a form uses the `GET` method, it automatically encodes the data.

```
<tr>
        <td align="left"><a href="edit_user.php?id=2">Edit</a></td>
        <td align="left"><a href="delete_user.php?id=2">Delete</a></td>
        <td align="left">Isabella</td>
        <td align="left">Zoe</td>
        <td align="left">September 22, 2007</td>
</tr>
<tr>
        <td align="left"><a href="edit_user.php?id=6">Edit</a></td>
        <td align="left"><a href="delete_user.php?id=6">Delete</a></td>
        <td align="left">Starr</td>
        <td align="left">Ringo</td>
        <td align="left">September 22, 2007</td>
</tr>
<tr>
        <td align="left"><a href="edit_user.php?id=5">Edit</a></td>
        <td align="left"><a href="delete_user.php?id=5">Delete</a></td>
        <td align="left">Harrison</td>
        <td align="left">George</td>
        <td align="left">September 22, 2007</td>
</tr>
```

Figure 9.2 Part of the HTML source of the page (see Figure 9.1) shows how the user's ID is added to each link's URL.

Using Hidden Form Inputs

In the preceding example, a new version of the view_users.php script was written. This one now includes links to the edit_user.php and delete_user.php pages, passing each a user's ID through the URL. This next example, delete_user.php, will take the passed user ID and allow the administrator to delete that user. Although you could have this page simply execute a DELETE query as soon as the page is accessed, for security purposes (and to prevent an inadvertent deletion), there should be multiple steps:

1. The page must check that it received a numeric user ID.

2. A message will confirm that this user should be deleted.

3. The user ID will be stored in a hidden form input.

4. Upon submission of this form, the user will actually be deleted.

To use hidden form inputs:

1. Create a new PHP document in your text editor or IDE (**Script 9.2**).

   ```
   <?php # Script 9.2 - delete_user.php
   ```

2. Include the page header.

   ```
   $page_title = 'Delete a User';
   include ('includes/header.html');
   echo '<h1>Delete a User</h1>';
   ```

   This document will use the same template system as the other pages in the application.

continues on page 266

Script 9.2 This script expects a user ID to be passed to it through the URL. It then presents a confirmation form and deletes the user upon submission.

```
1    <?php # Script 9.2 - delete_user.php
2
3    // This page is for deleting a user
     record.
4    // This page is accessed through view_
     users.php.
5
6    $page_title = 'Delete a User';
7    include ('includes/header.html');
8    echo '<h1>Delete a User</h1>';
9
10   // Check for a valid user ID, through GET
     or POST:
11   if ( (isset($_GET['id'])) && (is_numeric
     ($_GET['id'])) ) { // From view_users.php
12       $id = $_GET['id'];
13   } elseif ( (isset($_POST['id'])) &&
     (is_numeric($_POST['id'])) ) { // Form
     submission.
14       $id = $_POST['id'];
15   } else { // No valid ID, kill the script.
16       echo '<p class="error">This page has
         been accessed in error.</p>';
17       include ('includes/footer.html');
18       exit();
19   }
20
21   require_once ('../mysqli_connect.php');
22
23   // Check if the form has been submitted:
24   if (isset($_POST['submitted'])) {
25
26       if ($_POST['sure'] == 'Yes') { // Delete
         the record.
27
28       // Make the query:
```

(script continues on next page)

Using Hidden Form Inputs

Script 9.2 *continued*

```
29    $q = "DELETE FROM users WHERE
      user_id=$id LIMIT 1";

30    $r = @mysqli_query ($dbc, $q);

31    if (mysqli_affected_rows($dbc) == 1) {
      // If it ran OK.

32

33      // Print a message:

34      echo '<p>The user has been
        deleted.</p>';

35

36    } else { // If the query did not run OK.

37      echo '<p class="error">The user could
        not be deleted due to a system error.
        </p>'; // Public message.

38      echo '<p>' . mysqli_error($dbc) . '<br
        />Query: ' . $q . '</p>'; // Debugging
        message.

39    }

40

41    } else { // No confirmation of deletion.

42    echo '<p>The user has NOT been
      deleted.</p>';

43    }

44

45  } else { // Show the form.

46

47      // Retrieve the user's information:

48      $q = "SELECT CONCAT(last_name, ', ',
        first_name) FROM users WHERE
        user_id=$id";

49      $r = @mysqli_query ($dbc, $q);

50

51      if (mysqli_num_rows($r) == 1) { // Valid
        user ID, show the form.

52

53      // Get the user's information:

54      $row = mysqli_fetch_array ($r,
        MYSQLI_NUM);

55
```

(script continues)

Script 9.2 *continued*

```
56      // Create the form:

57      echo '<form action="delete_user.php"
        method="post">

58      <h3>Name: ' . $row[0] . '</h3>

59      <p>Are you sure you want to delete this
        user?<br />

60      <input type="radio" name="sure"
        value="Yes" /> Yes

61      <input type="radio" name="sure" value=
        "No" checked="checked" /> No</p>

62      <p><input type="submit" name="submit"
        value="Submit" /></p>

63      <input type="hidden" name="submitted"
        value="TRUE" />

64      <input type="hidden" name="id" value="'
        . $id . '" />

65      </form>';

66

67      } else { // Not a valid user ID.

68      echo '<p class="error">This page has
        been accessed in error.</p>';

69      }

70

71  } // End of the main submission
    conditional.

72

73  mysqli_close($dbc);

74

75  include ('includes/footer.html');

76  ?>
```

3. Check for a valid user ID value.

```
if ( (isset($_GET['id'])) && (is_
→ numeric($_GET['id'])) ) {

    $id = $_GET['id'];

} elseif ( (isset($_POST['id'])) &&
→ (is_numeric($_POST['id'])) ) {

    $id = $_POST['id'];

} else {

    echo '<p class="error">This page
    → has been accessed in error.
    → </p>';

    include ('includes/footer.
    → html');

    exit();

}
```

This script relies upon having a valid user ID, which will be used in a DELETE query's WHERE clause. The first time this page is accessed, the user ID should be passed in the URL (the page's URL will end with delete_user.php?id=X), after clicking the *Delete* link in the view_users.php page. The first if condition checks for such a value and that the value is numeric.

As you will see, the script will then store the user ID value in a hidden form input. When the form is submitted (back to

this same page), the page will receive the ID through $_POST. The second condition checks this and, again, that the ID value is numeric.

If neither of these conditions are TRUE, then the page cannot proceed, so an error message is displayed and the script's execution is terminated (**Figure 9.3**).

4. Include the MySQL connection script.

```
require_once ('../mysqli_connect.
→ php');
```

Both of this script's processes—showing the form and handling the form—require a database connection, so this line is outside of the main submit conditional (Step 5).

5. Begin the main submit conditional.

```
if (isset($_POST['submitted'])) {
```

6. Delete the user, if appropriate.

```
if ($_POST['sure'] == 'Yes') {

    $q = "DELETE FROM users WHERE
    → user_id=$id LIMIT 1";

    $r = @mysqli_query ($dbc, $q);
```

The form (**Figure 9.4**) will make the user click a radio button to confirm the deletion. This little step prevents any accidents. Thus, the handling process

---

Edit a User

This page has been accessed in error.

Figure 9.3 If the page does not receive a number ID value, this error is shown.

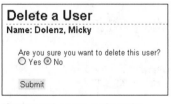

Figure 9.4 The page confirms the user deletion using this simple form.

first checks that the right radio button was selected. If so, a basic DELETE query is defined, using the user's ID in the WHERE clause. A LIMIT clause is added to the query as an extra precaution.

7. Check if the deletion worked and respond accordingly.

```
if (mysqli_affected_rows($dbc) == 1)
→ {

    echo '<p>The user has been
    → deleted.</p>';

} else {

    echo '<p class="error">The user
    → could not be deleted due to a
    → system error.</p>';

    echo '<p>' . mysqli_error($dbc)
    → . '<br />Query: ' . $q .
    → '</p>';

}
```

The mysqli_affected_rows() function checks that exactly one row was affected by the DELETE query. If so, a happy message is displayed (**Figure 9.5**). If not, an error message is sent out.

Keep in mind that it's possible that no rows were affected without a MySQL error occurring. For example, if the query tries to delete the record where the user ID is equal to *42000* (and if that doesn't exist), no rows will be deleted but no MySQL error will occur. Still, because of the checks made when the form is first loaded, it would take a fair amount of hacking by the user to get to that point.

8. Complete the $_POST['sure'] conditional.

```
} else {

    echo '<p>The user has NOT been
    deleted.</p>';

}
```

If the user did not explicitly check the *Yes* box, the user will not be deleted and this message is displayed (**Figure 9.6**).

9. Begin the else clause of the main submit conditional.

```
} else {
```

The page will either handle the form or display it. Most of the code prior to this takes effect if the form has been submitted (if $_POST['submitted'] is set). The code from here on takes effect if the form has not yet been submitted, in which case the form should be displayed.

continues on next page

Delete a User

The user has been deleted.

Figure 9.5 If you select *Yes* in the form (see Figure 9.4) and click Submit, this should be the result.

Delete a User

The user has NOT been deleted.

Figure 9.6 If you do not select *Yes* in the form, no database changes are made.

10. Retrieve the information for the user being deleted.

```
$q = "SELECT CONCAT(last_name, ', ',
→ first_name) FROM users WHERE
→ user_id=$id";

$r = @mysqli_query ($dbc, $q);

if (mysqli_num_rows($r) == 1) {
```

To confirm that the script received a valid user ID and to state exactly who is being deleted (refer back to Figure 9.4), the to-be-deleted user's name is retrieved from the database (**Figure 9.7**).

The conditional—checking that a single row was returned—ensures that a valid user ID was provided.

11. Display the form.

```
$row = mysqli_fetch_array ($r,
→ MYSQLI_NUM);

echo '<form action="delete_user.php"
→ method="post">

<h3>Name: ' . $row[0] . '</h3>

<p>Are you sure you want to delete
→ this user?<br />

<input type="radio" name="sure"
→ value="Yes" /> Yes

<input type="radio" name="sure"
→ value="No" checked="checked" />
→ No</p>

<p><input type="submit" name=
→ "submit" value="Submit" /></p>

<input type="hidden" name=
→ "submitted" value="TRUE" />

<input type="hidden" name="id"
→ value="' . $id . '" />

</form>';
```

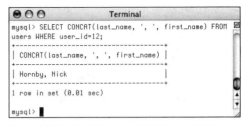

Figure 9.7 Running the same SELECT query in the mysql client.

First, the database record returned by the SELECT query is retrieved using the mysqli_fetch_array() function. Then the form is printed, showing the name value retrieved from the database at the top. An important step here is that the user ID ($id) is stored as a hidden form input so that the handling process can also access this value (**Figure 9.8**).

12. Complete the mysqli_num_rows() conditional.

    ```
    } else {
        echo '<p class="error">This
        → page has been accessed in
        → error.</p>';
    }
    ```

    If no record was returned by the SELECT query (because an invalid user ID was submitted), this message is displayed.

    If you see this message when you test this script but don't understand why, apply the standard debugging steps outlined at the end of Chapter 7, "Error Handling and Debugging."

13. Complete the PHP page.

    ```
    }
    mysqli_close($dbc);
    include ('includes/footer.html');
    ?>
    ```

The closing brace finishes the main submission conditional. Then the MySQL connection is closed and the footer is included.

14. Save the file as delete_user.php and place it in your Web directory (it should be in the same directory as view_users.php).

15. Run the page by first clicking a *Delete* link in the view_users.php page.

✔ Tips

- Another way of writing this script would be to have the form use the GET method. Then the validation conditional (lines 10–19) would only have to validate $_GET['id'], as the ID would be passed in the URL whether the page was first being accessed or the form had been submitted.

- Hidden form elements don't display in the Web browser but are still present in the HTML source code (Figure 9.8). For this reason, never store anything there that must be kept truly secure.

- Using hidden form inputs and appending values to a URL are just two ways to make data available to other PHP pages. Two more methods—cookies and sessions—are thoroughly covered in Chapter 11, "Cookies and Sessions."

```
<h1>Delete a User</h1><form action="delete_user.php" method="post">
    <h3>Name: Hornby, Nick</h3>
    <p>Are you sure you want to delete this user?<br />
    <input type="radio" name="sure" value="Yes" /> Yes
    <input type="radio" name="sure" value="No" checked="checked" /> No</p>
    <p><input type="submit" name="submit" value="Submit" /></p>
    <input type="hidden" name="submitted" value="TRUE" />
    <input type="hidden" name="id" value="12" />
```

Figure 9.8 The user ID is stored as a hidden input so that it's available when the form is submitted.

Editing Existing Records

A common practice with database-driven Web sites is having a system in place so that you can easily edit existing records. This concept seems daunting to many beginning programmers, but the process is surprisingly straightforward. For the following example—editing registered user records—the process combines skills the book has already taught:

◆ Making sticky forms

◆ Using hidden inputs

◆ Validating registration data

◆ Running simple queries

This next example is generally very similar to delete_user.php and will also be linked from the view_users.php script (when a person clicks *Edit*). A form will be displayed with the user's current information, allowing for those values to be changed (**Figure 9.9**). Upon submitting the form, if the data passes all of the validation routines, an UPDATE query will be run to update the database.

Edit a User

First Name: **Lisa**

Last Name: **Simpson**

Email Address: **lisa@simpson.com**

Submit

Figure 9.9 The form for editing a user's record.

To edit an existing database record:

1. Create a new PHP document in your text editor or IDE (**Script 9.3**).

```
<?php # Script 9.3 - edit_user.php
$page_title = 'Edit a User';
include ('includes/header.html');
echo '<h1>Edit a User</h1>';
```

2. Check for a valid user ID value.

```
if ( (isset($_GET['id'])) &&
→ (is_numeric($_GET['id'])) ) {
    $id = $_GET['id'];
} elseif ( (isset($_POST['id'])) &&
→ (is_numeric($_POST['id'])) ) {
    $id = $_POST['id'];
} else {
    echo '<p class="error">This
    → page has been accessed in
    → error.</p>';
    include ('includes/
    → footer.html');
    exit();
}
```

This validation routine is exactly the same as that in delete_user.php, confirming that a numeric user ID has been received, whether the page has first been accessed from view_users.php (the first condition) or upon submission of the form (the second condition).

continues on page 273

EDITING EXISTING RECORDS

Script 9.3 The `edit_user.php` page first displays the user's current information in a form. Upon submission of the form, the record will be updated in the database.

```
1    <?php # Script 9.3 - edit_user.php
2
3    // This page is for editing a user record.
4    // This page is accessed through
     view_users.php.
5
6    $page_title = 'Edit a User';
7    include ('includes/header.html');
8
9    echo '<h1>Edit a User</h1>';
10
11   // Check for a valid user ID, through GET
     or POST:
12   if ( (isset($_GET['id'])) && (is_numeric
     ($_GET['id'])) ) { // From view_users.php
13     $id = $_GET['id'];
14   } elseif ( (isset($_POST['id'])) &&
     (is_numeric($_POST['id'])) ) { // Form
     submission.
15     $id = $_POST['id'];
16   } else { // No valid ID, kill the script.
17     echo '<p class="error">This page has
       been accessed in error.</p>';
18     include ('includes/footer.html');
19     exit();
20   }
21
22   require_once ('../mysqli_connect.php');
23
24   // Check if the form has been submitted:
25   if (isset($_POST['submitted'])) {
26
27     $errors = array();
28
29     // Check for a first name:
30     if (empty($_POST['first_name'])) {
31       $errors[] = 'You forgot to enter
         your first name.';
```

(script continues)

Script 9.3 *continued*

```
32     } else {
33       $fn = mysqli_real_escape_string($dbc,
         trim($_POST['first_name']));
34     }
35
36     // Check for a last name:
37     if (empty($_POST['last_name'])) {
38       $errors[] = 'You forgot to enter your
         last name.';
39     } else {
40       $ln = mysqli_real_escape_string($dbc,
         trim($_POST['last_name']));
41     }
42
43     // Check for an email address:
44     if (empty($_POST['email'])) {
45       $errors[] = 'You forgot to enter your
         email address.';
46     } else {
47       $e = mysqli_real_escape_string($dbc,
         trim($_POST['email']));
48     }
49
50     if (empty($errors)) { // If everything's
       OK.
51
52       // Test for unique email address:
53       $q = "SELECT user_id FROM users WHERE
         email='$e' AND user_id != $id";
54       $r = @mysqli_query($dbc, $q);
55       if (mysqli_num_rows($r) == 0) {
56
57         // Make the query:
58         $q = "UPDATE users SET first_name=
           '$fn', last_name='$ln', email='$e'
           WHERE user_id=$id LIMIT 1";
59         $r = @mysqli_query ($dbc, $q);
60         if (mysqli_affected_rows($dbc) == 1)
           { // If it ran OK.
61
```

(script continues on next page)

Script 9.3 *continued*

```
62      // Print a message:

63      echo '<p>The user has been edited.
        </p>';

64

65      } else { // If it did not run OK.

66      echo '<p class="error">The user could
        not be edited due to a system error.
        We apologize for any inconvenience.
        </p>'; // Public message.

67      echo '<p>' . mysqli_error($dbc) . '<br
        />Query: ' . $q . '</p>'; // Debugging
        message.

68      }

69

70      } else { // Already registered.

71      echo '<p class="error">The email
        address has already been registered.
        </p>';

72      }

73

74      } else { // Report the errors.

75

76      echo '<p class="error">The following
        error(s) occurred:<br />';

77      foreach ($errors as $msg) { // Print
        each error.

78        echo " - $msg<br />\n";

79      }

80      echo '</p><p>Please try again.</p>';

81

82      } // End of if (empty($errors)) IF.

83

84      } // End of submit conditional.

85

86      // Always show the form...

87

88      // Retrieve the user's information:

89      $q = "SELECT first_name, last_name, email
        FROM users WHERE user_id=$id";
```

Script 9.3 *continued*

```
90      $r = @mysqli_query ($dbc, $q);

91

92      if (mysqli_num_rows($r) == 1) { // Valid
        user ID, show the form.

93

94        // Get the user's information:

95        $row = mysqli_fetch_array ($r,
          MYSQL_NUM);

96

97        // Create the form:

98        echo '<form action="edit_user.php"
          method="post">

99      <p>First Name: <input type="text"
        name="first_name" size="15" maxlength="15"
        value="' . $row[0] . '" /></p>

100     <p>Last Name: <input type="text"
        name="last_name" size="15" maxlength="30"
        value="' . $row[1] . '" /></p>

101     <p>Email Address: <input type="text"
        name="email" size="20" maxlength="40"
        value="' . $row[2] . '" /> </p>

102     <p><input type="submit" name="submit"
        value="Submit" /></p>

103     <input type="hidden" name="submitted"
        value="TRUE" />

104     <input type="hidden" name="id" value="' .
        $id . '" />

105     </form>';

106

107     } else { // Not a valid user ID.

108       echo '<p class="error">This page has
          been accessed in error.</p>';

109     }

110

111     mysqli_close($dbc);

112

113     include ('includes/footer.html');

114     ?>
```

(script continues)

3. Include the MySQL connection script and begin the main submit conditional.

```
require_once
('../mysqli_connect.php');

if (isset($_POST['submitted'])) {

    $errors = array();
```

Like the registration examples you have already done, this script makes use of an array to track errors.

4. Validate the first name.

```
if (empty($_POST['first_name'])) {

    $errors[] = 'You forgot to
    → enter your first name.';

} else {

    $fn = mysqli_real_escape_
    → string($dbc, trim($_POST
    → ['first_name']));

}
```

The form (Figure 9.9) is like a registration page but without the password fields. The form data can therefore be validated using the same methods used in the registration scripts. As with the registration examples, the validated data is trimmed and then run through `mysqli_real_escape_string()` for security.

5. Validate the last name and email address.

```
if (empty($_POST['last_name'])) {

    $errors[] = 'You forgot to
    |→ enter your last name.';

} else {

    $ln = mysqli_real_escape_
    → string($dbc, trim($_POST
    → ['last_name']));

}
```

```
if (empty($_POST['email'])) {

    $errors[] = 'You forgot to
    → enter your email address.';

} else {

    $e = mysqli_real_escape_
    → string($dbc, trim($_POST
    → ['email']));

}
```

6. If there were no errors, check that the submitted email address is not already in use.

```
if (empty($errors)) {

    $q = "SELECT user_id FROM users
    → WHERE email='$e' AND user_id
    → != $id";

    $r = @mysqli_query($dbc, $q);

    if (mysqli_num_rows($r) == 0) {
```

The integrity of the database and of the application as a whole partially depends upon having unique email address values in the *users* table. That requirement guarantees that the login system, which uses a combination of the email address and password (to be developed in Chapter 11), works. Because the form allows for altering the user's email address (see Figure 9.9), special steps have to be taken to ensure uniqueness. To understand this query, consider two possibilities....

In the first, the user's email address is being changed. In this case you just need to run a query making sure that that particular email address isn't already registered (i.e., SELECT user_id FROM users WHERE email='$e').

continues on next page

In the second possibility, the user's email address will remain the same. In this case, it's okay if the email address is already in use, because it's already in use *for this user*.

To write one query that will work for both possibilities, don't check to see if the email address is being used, but rather see if it's being used by *anyone else*, hence:

```
SELECT user_id FROM users WHERE
email='$e' AND user_id != $id
```

7. Update the database.

```
$q = "UPDATE users SET first_name=
→ '$fn', last_name='$ln', email='$e'
→ WHERE user_id=$id LIMIT 1";

$r = @mysqli_query ($dbc, $q);
```

The UPDATE query is similar to examples you may have seen in Chapter 5, "Introduction to SQL." The query updates all three fields—first name, last name, and email address—using the values submitted by the form. This system works because the form is preset with the existing values. So, if you edit the first name in the form but nothing else, the first name value in the database is updated using this new value, but the last name and email address values are "updated" using their current values. This system is much easier than trying to determine which form values have changed and updating just those in the database.

8. Report on the results of the update.

```
if (mysqli_affected_rows($dbc) == 1)
→ {

    echo '<p>The user has been
edited.</p>';

} else {
```

```
echo '<p class="error">The user
→ could not be edited due to a
→ system error. We apologize for
→ any inconvenience.</p>';

echo '<p>' . mysqli_error($dbc)
→ . '<br />Query: ' . $q .
→ '</p>';

}
```

The mysqli_affected_rows() function will return the number of rows in the database affected by the most recent query. If any of the three form values was altered, then this function should return the value *1*. This conditional tests for that and prints a message indicating success or failure.

Keep in mind that the mysqli_affected_rows() function will return a value of *0* if an UPDATE command successfully ran but didn't actually affect any records. So if you submit this form without changing any of the form values, a system error is displayed, which may not technically be correct. Once you have this script effectively working, you could change the error message to indicate that no alterations were made if mysqli_affected_rows() returns 0.

9. Complete the email conditional.

```
} else {

    echo '<p class="error">The email
→ address has already been
→ registered.</p>';

}
```

This else completes the conditional that checked if an email address was already being used by another user. If so, that message is printed.

10. Complete the `$errors` and submission conditionals.

```
} else { // Report the errors.
    echo '<p class=
    → "error">The following
    → error(s) occurred:<br
    → />';
    foreach ($errors as
    → $msg) {
        echo " - $msg<br
        → />\n";
    }
    echo '</p><p>Please try
    → again.</p>';
} // End of if (empty($errors))
→ IF.

} // End of submit conditional.
```

The first `else` is used to report any errors in the form (namely, a lack of a first name, last name, or email address). The final closing brace completes the main submit conditional.

In this example, the form will be displayed whenever the page is accessed. So after submitting the form, the database will be updated, and the form will be shown again, now displaying the latest information.

11. Retrieve the information for the user being edited.

```
$q = "SELECT first_name, last_name,
→ email FROM users WHERE user_
→ id=$id";

$r = @mysqli_query ($dbc, $q);

if (mysqli_num_rows($r) == 1) {
```

In order to pre-populate the form elements, the current information for the user must be retrieved from the database. This query is similar to the one in `delete_user.php`. The conditional— checking that a single row was returned—ensures that a valid user ID was provided.

12. Display the form.

```
$row = mysqli_fetch_array ($r,
→ mysqli_NUM);

echo '<form action="edit_user.php"
→ method="post">

<p>First Name: <input type="text"
→ name="first_name" size="15"
→ maxlength="15" value="' . $row[0]
→ . '" /></p>

<p>Last Name: <input type="text"
→ name="last_name" size="15"
→ maxlength="30" value="' . $row[1]
→ . '" /></p>

<p>Email Address: <input type="text"
→ name="email" size="20" maxlength=
→ "40" value="' . $row[2] . '" />
→ </p>

<p><input type="submit" name=
→ "submit" value="Submit" /></p>

<input type="hidden" name=
→ "submitted" value="TRUE" />

<input type="hidden" name="id"
→ value="' . $id . '" />

</form>';
```

The form has but three text inputs, each of which is made sticky using the data retrieved from the database. Again, the user ID (`$id`) is stored as a hidden form input so that the handling process can also access this value.

continues on next page

13. Complete the `mysqli_num_rows()` conditional.

```
} else {
    echo '<p class="error">This
    → page has been accessed in
    → error.</p>';
}
```

If no record was returned from the database, because an invalid user ID was submitted, this message is displayed.

14. Complete the PHP page.

```
mysqli_close($dbc);

include ('includes/footer.html');

?>
```

15. Save the file as `edit_user.php` and place it in your Web directory (in the same folder as `view_users.php`).

16. Run the page by first clicking an *Edit* link in the `view_users.php` page (**Figures 9.10** and **9.11**).

Edit a User

The user has been edited.

First Name: **Lisa**

Last Name: **Van Houten**

Email Address: **lisa@simpson.com**

Submit

Figure 9.10 The new values are displayed in the form after successfully updating the database (compare with the form values in Figure 9.9).

Edit a User

The email address has already been registered.

First Name: **Lisa**

Last Name: **Van Houten**

Email Address: **lisa@simpson.com**

Submit

Figure 9.11 If you try to change a record to an existing email address or if you omit an input, errors are reported.

✔ Tips

■ As written, the sticky form always shows the values retrieved from the database. This means that if an error occurs, the database values will be used, not the ones the user just entered (if those are different). To change this behavior, the sticky form would have to check for the presence of `$_POST` variables, using those if they exist, or the database values if not.

■ This edit page does not include the functionality to change the password. That concept was already demonstrated in `password.php` (Script 8.7). If you would like to incorporate that functionality here, keep in mind that you cannot display the current password, as it is encrypted. Instead, just present two boxes for changing the password (the new password input and a confirmation). If these values are submitted, update the password in the database as well. If these inputs are left blank, do not update the password in the database.

Paginating Query Results

Pagination is a concept you're familiar with even if you don't know the term. When you use a search engine like Google, it displays the results as a series of pages and not as one long list. The `view_users.php` script could benefit from this same feature.

Paginating query results makes extensive use of the `LIMIT` SQL clause introduced in Chapter 5. `LIMIT` restricts which subset of the matched records are actually returned. To paginate the returned results of a query, each page will run the same query using different `LIMIT` parameters. So the first page will request the first *X* records; the second page, the second group of *X* records; and so forth. To make this work, an indicator of

which records the page should display needs to be passed from page to page in the URL, like the user IDs passed from the `view_users.php` page.

Another, more cosmetic technique will be demonstrated here: displaying each row of the table—each returned record—using an alternating background color (**Figure 9.12**). This effect will be achieved with ease, using the ternary operator (see the sidebar "The Ternary Operator").

There's a lot of good, new information here, so be careful as you go through the steps and make sure that your script matches this one exactly. To make it easier to follow along, let's write this version from scratch instead of trying to modify Script 9.1.

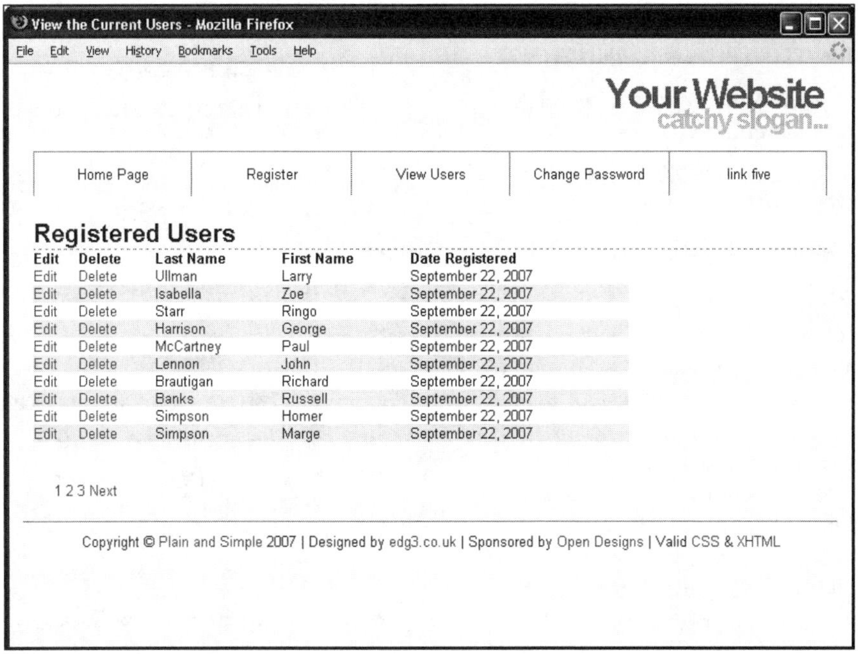

Figure 9.12 Alternating the table row colors makes this list of users more legible (every other row has a light gray background).

To paginate view_users.php:

1. Begin a new PHP document in your text editor or IDE (**Script 9.4**).

```php
<?php # Script 9.4 - #4

$page_title = 'View the Current
→ Users';

include ('includes/header.html');

echo '<h1>Registered Users</h1>';

require_once ('../mysqli_
→ connect.php');
```

2. Set the number of records to display per page.

```php
$display = 10;
```

By establishing this value as a variable here, you'll make it easy to change the number of records displayed on each page at a later date. Also, this value will be used multiple times in this script, so it's best represented as a single variable.

3. Check if the number of required pages has been determined.

```php
if (isset($_GET['p']) && is_numeric
→ ($_GET['p'])) {

    $pages = $_GET['p'];

} else {
```

For this script to display the users over several pages, it will need to determine how many total pages of results will be required. The first time the script is run, this number has to be calculated. For every subsequent call to this page, the total number of pages will be passed to the script in the URL, so it will be available in $_GET['p']. If this variable is set and is numeric, its value will be assigned to the $pages variable. If not, then the number of pages will need to be calculated.

continues on page 280

Script 9.4 This new version of view_users.php incorporates pagination so that the users are listed over multiple Web browser pages.

```php
1   <?php # Script 9.4 - #4
2
3   // This script retrieves all the records
    from the users table.
4   // This version paginates the query
    results.
5
6   $page_title = 'View the Current Users';
7   include ('includes/header.html');
8   echo '<h1>Registered Users</h1>';
9
10  require_once ('../mysqli_connect.php');
11
12  // Number of records to show per page:
13  $display = 10;
14
15  // Determine how many pages there are...
16  if (isset($_GET['p']) && is_numeric($_GET
    ['p'])) { // Already been determined.
17
18      $pages = $_GET['p'];
19
20  } else { // Need to determine.
21
22      // Count the number of records:
23      $q = "SELECT COUNT(user_id) FROM users";
24      $r = @mysqli_query ($dbc, $q);
25      $row = @mysqli_fetch_array ($r,
        MYSQLI_NUM);
26      $records = $row[0];
27
28      // Calculate the number of pages...
29      if ($records > $display) { // More than
        1 page.
30          $pages = ceil ($records/$display);
31      } else {
```

(script continues)

PAGINATING QUERY RESULTS

Script 9.4 *continued*

○ ○ ○	📄 Script

```
32    $pages = 1;

33    }

34

35    } // End of p IF.

36

37    // Determine where in the database to
      start returning results...

38    if (isset($_GET['s']) && is_numeric
      ($_GET['s'])) {

39      $start = $_GET['s'];

40    } else {

41      $start = 0;

42    }

43

44    // Make the query:

45    $q = "SELECT last_name, first_name, DATE_
      FORMAT(registration_date, '%M %d, %Y')
      AS dr, user_id FROM users ORDER BY
      registration_date ASC LIMIT $start,
      $display";

46    $r = @mysqli_query ($dbc, $q);

47

48    // Table header:

49    echo '<table align="center" cellspacing=
      "0" cellpadding="5" width="75%">

50    <tr>

51      <td align="left"><b>Edit</b></td>

52      <td align="left"><b>Delete</b></td>

53      <td align="left"><b>Last Name</b></td>

54      <td align="left"><b>First Name</b></td>

55      <td align="left"><b>Date
      Registered</b></td>

56    </tr>

57    ';

58

59    // Fetch and print all the records....

60

61    $bg = '#eeeeee'; // Set the initial
      background color.
```

(script continues)

Script 9.4 *continued*

○ ○ ○	📄 Script

```
62

63    while ($row = mysqli_fetch_array($r,
      MYSQLI_ASSOC)) {

64

65      $bg = ($bg=='#eeeeee' ? '#ffffff' :
        '#eeeeee'); // Switch the background
        color.

66

67      echo '<tr bgcolor="' . $bg . '">

68      <td align="left"><a
        href="edit_user.php?id=' .
        $row['user_id'] . '">Edit</a></td>

69      <td align="left"><a href="delete_user.
        php?id=' . $row['user_id'] . '">Delete
        </a></td>

70      <td align="left">' . $row['last_name'] .
        '</td>

71      <td align="left">' . $row['first_name']
        . '</td>

72      <td align="left">' . $row['dr'] . '</td>

73      </tr>

74      ';

75

76    } // End of WHILE loop.

77

78    echo '</table>';

79    mysqli_free_result ($r);

80    mysqli_close($dbc);

81

82    // Make the links to other pages, if
      necessary.

83    if ($pages > 1) {

84

85      // Add some spacing and start a
        paragraph:

86      echo '<br /><p>';

87

88      // Determine what page the script is on:

89      $current_page = ($start/$display) + 1;

90
```

(script continues on next page)

4. Count the number of records in the database.

```
$q = "SELECT COUNT(user_id) FROM
→ users";

$r = @mysqli_query ($dbc, $q);

$row = @mysqli_fetch_array ($r,
→ MYSQLI_NUM);

$records = $row[0];
```

Using the COUNT() function, introduced in Chapter 6, "Advanced SQL and MySQL," you can easily see the number of records in the *users* table. This query will return a single row with a single column: the number of records (**Figure 9.13**).

5. Mathematically calculate how many pages are required.

```
if ($records > $display) {

    $pages = ceil ($records/
    → $display);

} else {

    $pages = 1;

}

} // End of np IF.
```

The number of pages required to display all of the records is based upon the total number of records to be shown and the number to display per page (as assigned

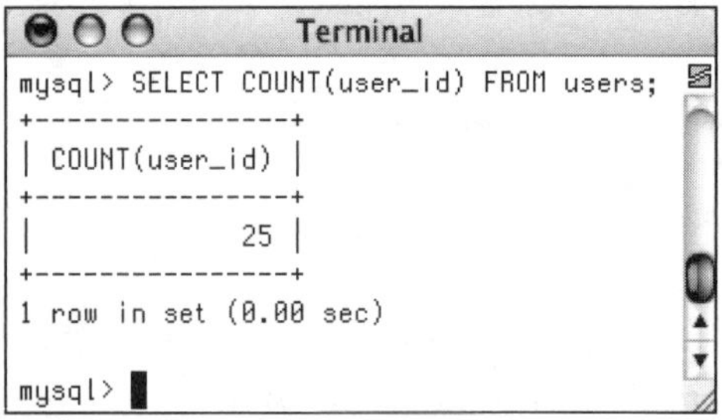

Figure 9.13 The result of running the counting query in the mysql client.

Script 9.4 *continued*

```
91    // If it's not the first page, make a
      Previous button:
92    if ($current_page != 1) {
93      echo '<a href="view_users.php?s=' .
        ($start - $display) . '&p=' . $pages .
        '">Previous</a> ';
94    }
95
96    // Make all the numbered pages:
97    for ($i = 1; $i <= $pages; $i++) {
98      if ($i != $current_page) {
99        echo '<a href="view_users.php?s=' .
          (($display * ($i - 1))) . '&p=' .
          $pages . '">' . $i . '</a> ';
100   } else {
101       echo $i . ' ';
102   }
103   } // End of FOR loop.
104
105   // If it's not the last page, make a
      Next button:
106   if ($current_page != $pages) {
107     echo '<a href="view_users.php?s=' .
        ($start + $display) . '&p=' . $pages .
        '">Next</a>';
108   }
109
110     echo '</p>'; // Close the paragraph.
111
112   } // End of links section.
113
114   include ('includes/footer.html');
115   ?>
```

to the `$display` variable). If there are more rows than there are records to be displayed per page, multiple pages will be required. To calculate exactly how many pages, take the next highest integer from the division of the two (the `ceil()` function returns the next highest integer). For example, if there are 25 records returned and 10 are being displayed per page, then 3 pages are required (the first page will display 10, the second page 10, and the third page 5). If `$records` is not greater than `$display`, only one page is necessary.

6. Determine the starting point in the database.

```
if (isset($_GET['s']) && is_numeric
→ ($_GET['s'])) {
    $start = $_GET['s'];
} else {
    $start = 0;
}
```

The second parameter the script will receive—on subsequent viewings of the page—will be the starting record. This corresponds to the first number in a `LIMIT x, y` clause. Upon initially calling the script, the first ten records should be retrieved (because `$display` has a value of *10*). The second page would show records 10 through 20; the third, 20 through 30; and so forth.

The first time this page is accessed, the `$_GET['s']` variable will not be set, and so `$start` should be *0* (the first record in a `LIMIT` clause is indexed at 0). Subsequent pages will receive the `$_GET['s']` variable from the URL, and it will be assigned to `$start`.

7. Write the query with a `LIMIT` clause.

```
$q = "SELECT last_name, first_name,
→ DATE_FORMAT(registration_date, '%M
→ %d, %Y') AS dr, user_id FROM users
→ ORDER BY registration_date ASC
→ LIMIT $start, $display";

$r = @mysqli_query ($dbc, $q);
```

The `LIMIT` clause dictates which record to begin retrieving (`$start`) and how many to return (`$display`) from that point. The first time the page is run, the query will be `SELECT last_name, first_name … LIMIT 0, 10`. Clicking to the next page will result in `SELECT last_name, first_name … LIMIT 10, 10`.

8. Create the HTML table header.

```
echo '<table align="center"
→ cellspacing="0" cellpadding="5"
→ width="75%">
<tr>
    <td align="left"><b>Edit
→ </b></td>
    <td align="left"><b>Delete
→ </b></td>
    <td align="left"><b>Last Name
→ </b></td>
    <td align="left"><b>First Name
→ </b></td>
    <td align="left"><b>Date
→ Registered</b></td>
</tr>
';
```

In order to simplify this script a little bit, I'm assuming that there are records to be displayed. To be more formal, this script, prior to creating the table, would invoke the `mysqli_num_rows()` function and have a conditional that confirms that some records were returned.

continues on next page

9. Initialize the background color variable.

```
$bg = '#eeeeee';
```

To make each row have its own background color, a variable will be used to store that color. To start, the $bg variable is assigned a value of *#eeeeee*, a light gray. This color will alternate with white (*#ffffff*).

10. Begin the while loop that retrieves every record.

```
while ($row = mysqli_fetch_array($r,
→ MYSQLI_ASSOC)) {

    $bg = ($bg=='#eeeeee' ?
    → '#ffffff' : '#eeeeee');
```

The background color used by each row in the table is assigned to the $bg variable. Because I want this color to alternate, I use this line of code to assign the opposite color to $bg. If it's equal to *#eeeeee*, then it will be assigned the value of *#ffffff* and vice versa (again, see the sidebar for the syntax and explanation of the ternary operator). For the first row, $bg is equal to *#eeeeee* and will therefore be assigned *#ffffff*, making a white background. For the second row, $bg is not equal to *#eeeeee*, so it will be assigned that value, making a gray background.

11. Print the records in a table row.

```
echo '<tr bgcolor="' . $bg . '">
<td align="left"><a href="edit_
→ user.php?id=' . $row['user_id'] .
→ '">Edit</a></td>
<td align="left"><a href="delete_
→ user.php?id=' . $row['user_id'] .
→ '">Delete</a></td>
<td align="left">' . $row['last_
→ name'] . '</td>
```

```
<td align="left">' . $row['first_
→ name'] . '</td>
<td align="left">' . $row['dr'] .
→ '</td>
</tr>

';
```

This code only differs in one way from that in the previous version of this script. The initial TR tag now includes the bgcolor attribute, whose value will be the $bg variable (so *#eeeeee* and *#ffffff*, alternating).

12. Complete the while loop and the table, free up the query result resources, and close the database connection.

```
}
echo '</table>';
mysqli_free_result ($r);
mysqli_close($dbc);
```

13. Begin a section for displaying links to other pages, if necessary.

```
if ($pages > 1) {

    echo '<br /><p>';

    $current_page = ($start/
    → $display) + 1;

    if ($current_page != 1) {

        echo '<a href="view_users.
        → php?s=' . ($start -
        → $display) . '&p=' .
        → $pages . '">Previous
        → </a> ';

    }
```

If the script requires multiple pages to display all of the records, it needs the appropriate links at the bottom of the page (**Figure 9.14**). To make these links, first determine the current page. This can be calculated as the start number divided by the display number, plus 1. For example, on the second instance of this script, $start will be *10* (because on the first instance, $start is *0*), so the current page is *2* (10/10 + 1 = 2).

If the current page is not the first page, it also needs a *Previous* link to the earlier result set (**Figure 9.15**). This isn't strictly necessary, but is nice.

Each link will be made up of the script name, plus the starting point and the number of pages. The starting point for the previous page will be the current starting point minus the number being displayed. These values must be passed in every link, or else the pagination will fail.

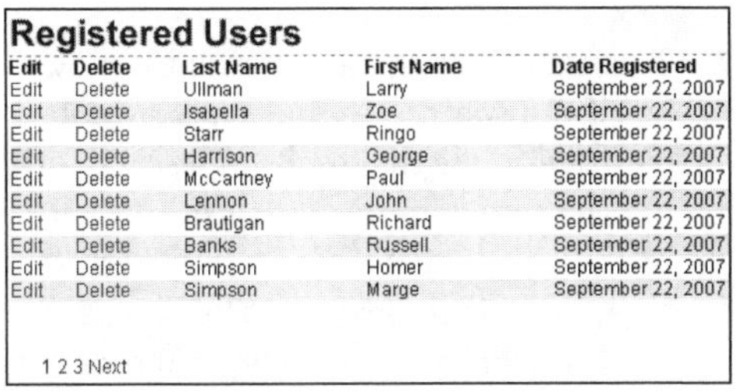

Registered Users

Edit	Delete	Last Name	First Name	Date Registered
Edit	Delete	Ullman	Larry	September 22, 2007
Edit	Delete	Isabella	Zoe	September 22, 2007
Edit	Delete	Starr	Ringo	September 22, 2007
Edit	Delete	Harrison	George	September 22, 2007
Edit	Delete	McCartney	Paul	September 22, 2007
Edit	Delete	Lennon	John	September 22, 2007
Edit	Delete	Brautigan	Richard	September 22, 2007
Edit	Delete	Banks	Russell	September 22, 2007
Edit	Delete	Simpson	Homer	September 22, 2007
Edit	Delete	Simpson	Marge	September 22, 2007

1 2 3 Next

Figure 9.14 After all of the returned records, links are generated to the other result pages.

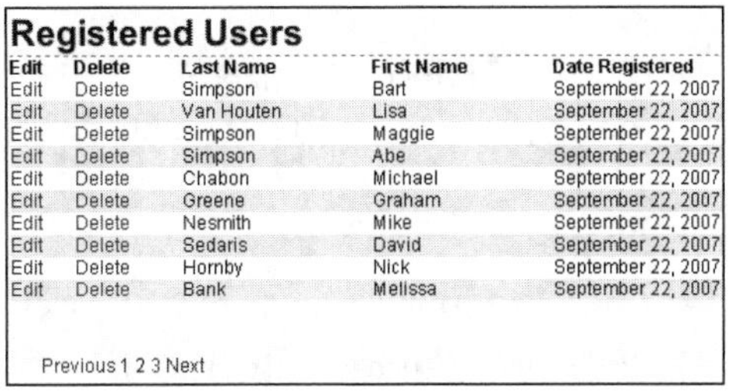

Registered Users

Edit	Delete	Last Name	First Name	Date Registered
Edit	Delete	Simpson	Bart	September 22, 2007
Edit	Delete	Van Houten	Lisa	September 22, 2007
Edit	Delete	Simpson	Maggie	September 22, 2007
Edit	Delete	Simpson	Abe	September 22, 2007
Edit	Delete	Chabon	Michael	September 22, 2007
Edit	Delete	Greene	Graham	September 22, 2007
Edit	Delete	Nesmith	Mike	September 22, 2007
Edit	Delete	Sedaris	David	September 22, 2007
Edit	Delete	Hornby	Nick	September 22, 2007
Edit	Delete	Bank	Melissa	September 22, 2007

Previous 1 2 3 Next

Figure 9.15 The *Previous* link will appear only if the current page is not the first one.

The Ternary Operator

This example uses an operator not introduced before, called the *ternary* operator. Its structure is

```
(condition) ? valueT : valueF
```

The condition in parentheses will be evaluated; if it is TRUE, the first value will be returned (*valueT*). If the condition is FALSE, the second value (*valueF*) will be returned.

Because the ternary operator returns a value, the entire structure is often used to assign a value to a variable or used as an argument for a function. For example, the line

```
echo (isset($var)) ? 'SET' : 'NOT SET';
```

will print out *SET* or *NOT SET*, depending upon the status of the variable $var.

In this version of the view_users.php script, the ternary operator assigns a different value to a variable than its current value. The variable itself will then be used to dictate the background color of each record in the table. There are certainly other ways to set this value, but the ternary operator is the most concise.

PAGINATING QUERY RESULTS

14. Make the numeric links.

```
for ($i = 1; $i <= $pages; $i++) {

    if ($i != $current_page) {

        echo '<a href="view_users.
        → php?s=' . (($display *
        → ($i - 1))) . '&p=' .
        → $pages . '">' . $i .
        → '</a> ';

    } else {

        echo $i . ' ';

    }

}
```

The bulk of the links will be created by looping from 1 to the total number of pages. Each page will be linked except for the current one.

15. Create a *Next* link.

```
if ($current_page != $pages) {

    echo '<a href="view_users.
    → php?s=' . ($start + $display)
    → . '&p=' . $pages . '">Next
    → </a>';

}
```

Finally, a *Next* page link will be displayed, assuming that this is not the final page (**Figure 9.16**).

16. Complete the page.

```
    echo '</p>';

}

include ('includes/footer.html');
?>
```

17. Save the file as view_users.php, place it in your Web directory, and test it in your Web browser.

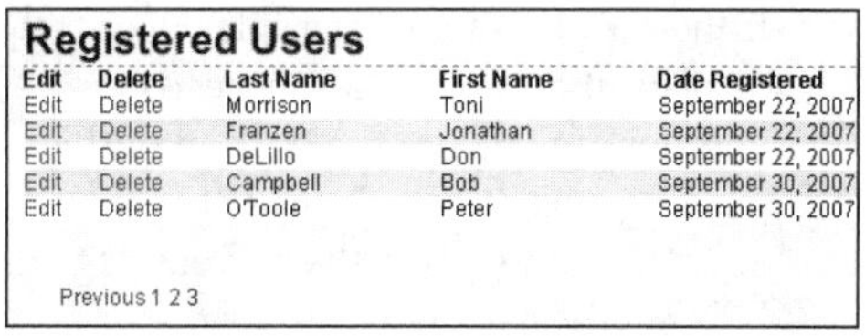

Registered Users

Edit	Delete	Last Name	First Name	Date Registered
Edit	Delete	Morrison	Toni	September 22, 2007
Edit	Delete	Franzen	Jonathan	September 22, 2007
Edit	Delete	DeLillo	Don	September 22, 2007
Edit	Delete	Campbell	Bob	September 30, 2007
Edit	Delete	O'Toole	Peter	September 30, 2007

Previous 1 2 3

Figure 9.16 The final results page will not display a *Next* link.

✔ Tips

■ This example paginates a simple query, but if you want to paginate a more complex query, like the results of a search, it's not that much more complicated. The main difference is that whatever terms are used in the query must be passed from page to page in the links. If the main query is not *exactly the same* from one viewing of the page to the next, the pagination will fail.

■ If you run this example and the pagination doesn't match the number of results that should be returned (for example, the counting query indicates there are 150 records but the pagination only creates 3 pages, with 10 records on each), it's most likely because the main query and the COUNT() query are too different. These two queries will never be the same, but they must perform the same join (if applicable) and have the same WHERE and/or GROUP BY clauses to be accurate.

■ No error handling has been included in this script, as I know the queries function as written. If you have problems, remember your MySQL/SQL debugging steps: print the query, run it using the mysql client or phpMyAdmin to confirm the results, and invoke the mysqli_error() function as needed.

Script 9.5 This latest version of the `view_users.php` script creates clickable links out of the table's column headings.

```php
1    <?php # Script 9.5 - #5
2
3    // This script retrieves all the records
     from the users table.
4    // This new version allows the results to
     be sorted in different ways.
5
6    $page_title = 'View the Current Users';
7    include ('includes/header.html');
8    echo '<h1>Registered Users</h1>';
9
10   require_once ('../mysqli_connect.php');
11
12   // Number of records to show per page:
13   $display = 10;
14
15   // Determine how many pages there are...
16   if (isset($_GET['p']) &&
     is_numeric($_GET['p'])) { // Already been
     determined.
17     $pages = $_GET['p'];
18   } else { // Need to determine.
19      // Count the number of records:
20     $q = "SELECT COUNT(user_id) FROM users";
21     $r = @mysqli_query ($dbc, $q);
22     $row = @mysqli_fetch_array ($r,
       MYSQLI_NUM);
23     $records = $row[0];
24     // Calculate the number of pages...
25     if ($records > $display) { // More than
       1 page.
26       $pages = ceil ($records/$display);
27     } else {
28       $pages = 1;
29     }
30   } // End of p IF.
31
```

(script continues on next page)

Making Sortable Displays

To wrap up this chapter, there's one final feature that could be added to `view_users.php`. In its current state the list of users is displayed in order by the date they registered. It would be nice to be able to view them by name as well.

From a MySQL perspective, accomplishing this task is easy: just change the ORDER BY clause. Therefore, all that needs to be done is to add some functionality in PHP that will change the ORDER BY clause. The logical way to do this is to link the column headings so that clicking them changes the display order. As you hopefully can guess, this involves using the GET method to pass a parameter back to this page indicating the preferred sort order.

To make sortable links:

1. Open `view_users.php` (Script 9.4) in your text editor or IDE.

2. After determining the starting point, define a `$sort` variable (**Script 9.5**).

   ```php
   $sort = (isset($_GET['sort'])) ?
   → $_GET['sort'] : 'rd';
   ```

   The `$sort` variable will be used to determine how the query results are to be ordered. This line uses the ternary operator (see the sidebar earlier in the chapter) to assign a value to `$sort`. If `$_GET['sort']` is set, which will be the case after the user clicks any link, then `$sort` should be assigned that value. If `$_GET['sort']` is not set, then `$sort` is assigned a default value of *rd* (short for *registration date*).

continues on page 287

Script 9.5 *continued*

```
┌─────────────────────────────────────┐
│  ○ ○ ○              📄 Script        │
├─────────────────────────────────────┤
32   // Determine where in the database to
     start returning results...

33   if (isset($_GET['s']) && is_numeric
     ($_GET['s'])) {

34     $start = $_GET['s'];

35   } else {

36     $start = 0;

37   }

38

39   // Determine the sort...

40   // Default is by registration date.

41   $sort = (isset($_GET['sort'])) ? $_GET
     ['sort'] : 'rd';

42

43   // Determine the sorting order:

44   switch ($sort) {

45     case 'ln':

46       $order_by = 'last_name ASC';

47       break;

48     case 'fn':

49       $order_by = 'first_name ASC';

50       break;

51     case 'rd':

52       $order_by = 'registration_date ASC';

53       break;

54     default:

55       $order_by = 'registration_date ASC';

56       $sort = 'rd';

57       break;

58   }

59

60   // Make the query:

61   $q = "SELECT last_name, first_name, DATE_
     FORMAT(registration_date, '%M %d, %Y') AS
     dr, user_id FROM users ORDER BY $order_by
     LIMIT $start, $display";

62   $r = @mysqli_query ($dbc, $q); // Run the
     query.

63
```

(script continues)

Script 9.5 *continued*

```
┌─────────────────────────────────────┐
│  ○ ○ ○              📄 Script        │
├─────────────────────────────────────┤
64   // Table header:

65   echo '<table align="center" cellspacing=
     "0" cellpadding="5" width="75%">

66   <tr>

67     <td align="left"><b>Edit</b></td>

68     <td align="left"><b>Delete</b></td>

69     <td align="left"><b><a href="view_users.
       php?sort=ln">Last Name</a></b></td>

70     <td align="left"><b><a href="view_users.
       php?sort=fn">First Name</a></b></td>

71     <td align="left"><b><a href="view_users.
       php?sort=rd">Date Registered</a></b>
       </td>

72   </tr>

73   ';

74

75   // Fetch and print all the records....

76   $bg = '#eeeeee';

77   while ($row = mysqli_fetch_array($r,
     MYSQLI_ASSOC)) {

78     $bg = ($bg=='#eeeeee' ? '#ffffff' :
       '#eeeeee');

79     echo '<tr bgcolor="' . $bg . '">

80       <td align="left"><a href="edit_user.
         php?id=' . $row['user_id'] . '">Edit</a>
         </td>

81       <td align="left"><a href="delete_user.
         php?id=' . $row['user_id'] . '">Delete
         </a></td>

82       <td align="left">' . $row['last_name'] .
         '</td>

83       <td align="left">' . $row['first_name']
         . '</td>

84       <td align="left">' . $row['dr'] . '</td>

85     </tr>

86     ';

87   } // End of WHILE loop.

88

89   echo '</table>';

90   mysqli_free_result ($r);

91   mysqli_close($dbc);

92
```

(script continues on next page)

Script 9.5 *continued*

```
 93   // Make the links to other pages, if
      necessary.
 94   if ($pages > 1) {
 95
 96     echo '<br /><p>';
 97     $current_page = ($start/$display) + 1;
 98
 99     // If it's not the first page, make a
        Previous button:
100     if ($current_page != 1) {
101     echo '<a href="view_users.php?s=' .
        ($start - $display) . '&p=' . $pages .
        '&sort=' . $sort . '">Previous</a> ';
102     }
103
104     // Make all the numbered pages:
105     for ($i = 1; $i <= $pages; $i++) {
106     if ($i != $current_page) {
107       echo '<a href="view_users.php?s=' .
          (($display * ($i - 1))) . '&p=' .
          $pages . '&sort=' . $sort . '">' . $i
          . '</a> ';
108     } else {
109       echo $i . ' ';
110     }
111     } // End of FOR loop.
112
113     // If it's not the last page, make a
        Next button:
114     if ($current_page != $pages) {
115     echo '<a href="view_users.php?s=' .
        ($start + $display) . '&p=' . $pages .
        '&sort=' . $sort . '">Next</a>';
116     }
117
118     echo '</p>'; // Close the paragraph.
119
120   } // End of links section.
121
122   include ('includes/footer.html');
123   ?>
```

3. Determine how the results should be ordered.

```
switch ($sort) {
    case 'ln':
        $order_by = 'last_name ASC';
        break;
    case 'fn':
        $order_by = 'first_name
        → ASC';
        break;
    case 'rd':
        $order_by = 'registration_
        → date ASC';
        break;
    default:
        $order_by = 'registration_
        → date ASC';
        $sort = 'rd';
        break;
}
```

The switch checks $sort against several expected values. If, for example, it is equal to *ln*, then the results should be ordered by the last name in ascending order. The assigned $order_by variable will be used in the SQL query.

If $sort has a value of *fn*, then the results should be in ascending order by first name. If the value is *rd*, then the results will be in ascending order of registration date. This is also the default case. Having this default case here protects against a malicious user changing the value of $_GET['sort'] to something that could break the query.

continues on next page

MAKING SORTABLE DISPLAYS

4. Modify the query to use the new `$order_by` variable.

```
$q = "SELECT last_name, first_name,
→ DATE_FORMAT(registration_date, '%M
→ %d, %Y') AS dr, user_id FROM users
→ ORDER BY $order_by LIMIT $start,
→ $display";
```

By this point, the `$order_by` variable has a value indicating how the returned results should be ordered (for example, *registration_date ASC)*, so it can be easily added to the query. Remember that the `ORDER BY` clause comes before the `LIMIT` clause. If the resulting query doesn't run properly for you, print it out and inspect its syntax.

5. Modify the table header `echo()` statement to create links out of the column headings.

```
echo '<table align="center"
cellspacing="0" cellpadding="5"
width="75%">

<tr>

    <td align="left"><b>Edit
    → </b></td>

    <td align="left"><b>Delete
    → </b></td>

    <td align="left"><b><a href=
    → "view_users.php?sort=ln">
    → Last Name</a></b></td>

    <td align="left"><b><a href=
    → "view_users.php?sort=fn">
    → First Name</a></b></td>

    <td align="left"><b><a href=
    → "view_users.php?sort=rd">Date
    → Registered</a></b></td>

</tr>

';
```

Registered Users

Edit	Delete	Last Name	First Name	Date Registered
Edit	Delete	Simpson	Abe	September 22, 2007
Edit	Delete	Simpson	Bart	September 22, 2007
Edit	Delete	Campbell	Bob	September 30, 2007
Edit	Delete	Sedaris	David	September 22, 2007
Edit	Delete	DeLillo	Don	September 22, 2007
Edit	Delete	Harrison	George	September 22, 2007
Edit	Delete	Greene	Graham	September 22, 2007
Edit	Delete	Simpson	Homer	September 22, 2007
Edit	Delete	Lennon	John	September 22, 2007
Edit	Delete	Franzen	Jonathan	September 22, 2007

1 2 3 Next

Figure 9.17 The first time viewing the page, the results are shown in ascending order of registration date. After clicking the first name column, the results are shown in ascending order by first name (as seen here).

Registered Users

Edit	Delete	Last Name	First Name	Date Registered
Edit	Delete	Bank	Melissa	September 22, 2007
Edit	Delete	Banks	Russell	September 22, 2007
Edit	Delete	Brautigan	Richard	September 22, 2007
Edit	Delete	Campbell	Bob	September 30, 2007
Edit	Delete	Chabon	Michael	September 22, 2007
Edit	Delete	DeLillo	Don	September 22, 2007
Edit	Delete	Franzen	Jonathan	September 22, 2007
Edit	Delete	Greene	Graham	September 22, 2007
Edit	Delete	Harrison	George	September 22, 2007
Edit	Delete	Hornby	Nick	September 22, 2007

1 2 3 Next

Figure 9.18 Clicking the *Last Name* column displays the results in order by last name ascending.

✔ Tip

■ A very important security concept was also demonstrated in this example. Instead of using the value of $_GET['sort'] directly in the query, it's checked against assumed values in a switch. If, for some reason, $_GET['sort'] has a value other than would be expected, the query uses a default sorting order. The point is this: don't make assumptions about received data, and don't use unvalidated data in an SQL query.

To make the column headings clickable links, just surround them with the <a> tags. The value of the href attribute for each link corresponds to the acceptable values for $_GET['sort'] (see the switch in Step 3).

6. Modify the echo() statement that creates the *Previous* link so that the sort value is also passed.

```
echo '<a href="view_users.php?s=' .
→ ($start - $display) . '&p=' .
→ $pages . '&sort=' . $sort .
→ '">Previous</a> ';
```

Add another *name=value* pair to the *Previous* link so that the sort order is also sent to each page of results. If you don't, then the pagination will fail, as the ORDER BY clause will differ from one page to the next.

7. Repeat Step 6 for the numbered pages and the *Next* link.

```
echo '<a href="view_users.php?s=' .
→ (($display * ($i - 1))) . '&p=' .
→ $pages . '&sort=' . $sort . '">' .
→ $i . '</a> ';

echo '<a href="view_users.php?s=' .
→ ($start + $display) . '&p=' .
→ $pages . '&sort=' . $sort .
→ '">Next</a>';
```

8. Save the file as view_users.php, place it in your Web directory, and run it in your Web browser (**Figures 9.17** and **9.18**).

MAKING SORTABLE DISPLAYS

WEB APPLICATION DEVELOPMENT

The preceding two chapters focus on using PHP and MySQL together (which is, after all, the primary point of this book). But there's still a lot of PHP-centric material to be covered. Taking a quick break from using PHP with MySQL, this chapter covers a handful of techniques that are often used in more complex Web applications.

The first topic covered in this chapter is sending email using PHP. It's a very common thing to do and is surprisingly simple (assuming that the server is properly set up). After that, the chapter touches upon some of the date and time functions present in PHP. The third subject demonstrates how to handle file uploads in an HTML form. This in turn leads to a discussion of using PHP and JavaScript together, then how to use the header() function to manipulate the Web browser.

Sending Email

One of my absolute favorite things about PHP is how easy it is to send an email. On a properly configured server, the process is as simple as using the mail() function:

```
mail (to, subject, body, [headers]);
```

The *to* value should be an email address or a series of addresses, separated by commas. Any of these are allowed:

◆ email@example.com

◆ email1@example.com, email2@example.com

◆ Actual Name <email@example.com>

◆ Actual Name <email@example.com>, This Name <email2@example.com>

The *subject* value will create the email's subject line, and *body* is where you put the contents of the email. To make things more legible, variables are often assigned values and then used in the mail() function call:

```
$to = 'email@example.com';

$subject = 'This is the subject';

$body = 'This is the body.

It goes over multiple lines.';

mail ($to, $subject, $body);
```

As you can see in the assignment to the $body variable, you can create an email message that goes over multiple lines by having the text do exactly that within the quotation marks. You can also use the newline character (\n) within double quotation marks to accomplish this:

```
$body = "This is the body.\nIt goes over
➞ multiple lines.";
```

This is all very straightforward, and there are only a couple of caveats. First, the subject line cannot contain the newline character (\n). Second, each line of the body should be no longer than 70 characters in length. You can accomplish this using the wordwrap() function. It will insert a newline into a string every X number of characters. To wrap text to 70 characters, use

```
$body = wordwrap($body, 70);
```

The mail() function takes a fourth, optional parameter for additional headers. This is where you could set the From, Reply-To, Cc, Bcc, and similar settings. For example,

```
mail ($to, $subject, $body, 'From:
➞ reader@example.com');
```

To use multiple headers of different types in your email, separate each with \r\n:

```
$headers = "From: John@example.com\r\n";

$headers .= "Cc: Jane@example.com,
➞ Joe@example.com\r\n";

mail ($to, $subject, $body, $headers);
```

Although this fourth argument is optional, it is advised that you always include a From value (although that can also be established in PHP's configuration file).

To demonstrate this, let's create a page that shows a contact form (**Figure 10.1**) and then handles the form submission, validating the data and sending it along in an email. This example will also contain a nice variation on the sticky form technique used in this book.

Figure 10.1 A standard (but not very attractive) contact form.

Script 10.1 This page displays a contact form that, upon submission, will send an email with the form data to an email address.

```
1    <!DOCTYPE html PUBLIC "-//W3C//DTD XHTML
     1.0 Transitional//EN"

2        "http://www.w3.org/TR/xhtml1/DTD/
         xhtml1-transitional.dtd">

3    <html xmlns="http://www.w3.org/1999/xhtml"
     xml:lang="en" lang="en">

4    <head>

5      <meta http-equiv="content-type"
       content="text/html; charset=iso-8859-1"
       />

6      <title>Contact Me</title>

7    </head>

8    <body>

9    <h1>Contact Me</h1>

10   <?php # Script 10.1 - email.php

11

12   // Check for form submission:

13   if (isset($_POST['submitted'])) {

14

15       // Minimal form validation:

16       if (!empty($_POST['name']) &&
         !empty($_POST['email']) &&
         !empty($_POST['comments']) ) {

17

18           // Create the body:

19           $body = "Name:
             {$_POST['name']}\n\nComments:
             {$_POST['comments']}";

20

21           // Make it no longer than 70
             characters long:

22           $body = wordwrap($body, 70);

23

24           // Send the email:

25           mail('your_email@example.com',
             'Contact Form Submission', $body,
             "From: {$_POST['email']}");
```

(script continues on next page)

Note two things before running this script: First, for this example to work, the computer on which PHP is running must have a working mail server. If you're using a hosted site, this shouldn't be an issue; on your own computer, you'll likely need to take preparatory steps (see the sidebar). Second, this example, while functional, could be manipulated by bad people, allowing them to send spam through your contact form (not just to you but to anyone). The steps for preventing such attacks are provided in Chapter 12, "Security Methods." Following along and testing this example is just fine; relying upon it as your long-term contact form solution is a bad idea.

To send email:

1. Begin a new PHP script in your text editor or IDE (**Script 10.1**).

   ```
   <!DOCTYPE html PUBLIC "-//W3C//DTD
   → XHTML 1.0 Transitional//EN"

   "http://www.w3.org/TR/xhtml1/DTD/xhtm
   → l1-transitional.dtd">

   <html
   → xmlns="http://www.w3.org/1999/xhtml"
   → xml:lang="en" lang="en">

   <head>
       <meta http-equiv="content-type"
       → content="text/html;
       → charset=iso-8859-1" />

       <title>Contact Me</title>

   </head>

   <body>

   <h1>Contact Me</h1>

   <?php # Script 10.1 - email.php
   ```

   None of the examples in this chapter will use a template, like those in the past two chapters, so it starts with the standard HTML.

continues on next page

2. Create the conditional for checking if the form has been submitted and validate the form data.

```
if (isset($_POST['submitted'])) {

    if (!empty($_POST['name']) &&
    → !empty($_POST['email']) &&
    → !empty($_POST['comments']) ) {
```

The form contains three text inputs (technically one is a textarea). The empty() function will confirm that something was entered into each. In Chapter 13, you'll learn how to use regular expressions to confirm that the supplied email address has a valid format.

3. Create the body of the email.

```
$body = "Name:
→ {$_POST['name']}\n\nComments:
→ {$_POST['comments']}";

$body = wordwrap($body, 70);
```

The email's body will start with the prompt *Name:*, followed by the name entered into the form. Then the same treatment is given to the comments. The wordwrap() function then formats the whole body so that each line is only 70 characters long.

Script 10.1 *continued*

```
                      Script
26
27        // Print a message:
28        echo '<p><em>Thank you for
          contacting me. I will reply some
          day.</em></p>';
29
30        // Clear $_POST (so that the form's
          not sticky):
31        $_POST = array();
32
33    } else {
34        echo '<p style="font-weight: bold;
          color: #C00">Please fill out the
          form completely.</p>';
35    }
36
37 } // End of main isset() IF.
38
39 // Create the HTML form:
40 ?>
41 <p>Please fill out this form to contact
   me.</p>
42 <form action="email.php" method="post">
43    <p>Name: <input type="text" name="name"
      size="30" maxlength="60" value="<?php if
      (isset($_POST['name'])) echo
      $_POST['name']; ?>" /></p>
44    <p>Email Address: <input type="text"
      name="email" size="30" maxlength="80"
      value="<?php if (isset($_POST['email']))
      echo $_POST['email']; ?>" /></p>
45    <p>Comments: <textarea name="comments"
      rows="5" cols="30"><?php if
      (isset($_POST['comments'])) echo
      $_POST['comments']; ?></textarea></p>
46    <p><input type="submit" name="submit"
      value="Send!" /></p>
47    <input type="hidden" name="submitted"
      value="TRUE" />
48 </form>
49 </body>
50 </html>
```

4. Send the email and print a message in the Web browser.

```
mail('your_email@example.com',
→ 'Contact Form Submission', $body,
→ "From: {$_POST['email']}");
```

```
echo '<p><em>Thank you for contacting
→ me. I will reply some day.</em></p>';
```

Assuming the server is properly configured, this one line will send the email. You will need to change the *to* value to your actual email address. The From value will be the email address from the form. The subject will be a literal string.

There's no way of confirming that the email was successfully sent, let alone received, but a generic message is printed.

5. Clear the $_POST array.

```
$_POST = array();
```

In this example, the form will always be shown, even upon successful submission. The form will be sticky in case the user omitted something (**Figure 10.2**). However, if the mail was sent, there's no need to show the values in the form again. To avoid that, the $_POST array can be cleared of its values using the array() function.

Figure 10.2 The contact form will remember the user-supplied values in case it is not completely filled out.

6. Complete the conditionals.

```
} else {
    echo '<p style="font-weight:
    → bold; color: #C00">Please
    → fill out the form
    → completely.</p>';
}
} // End of main isset() IF.
?>
```

The error message contains some inline CSS, so that it's in red and made bold.

7. Begin the form.

```
<p>Please fill out this form to
→ contact me.</p>
<form action="email.php"
→ method="post">
    <p>Name: <input type="text"
    → name="name" size="30"
    → maxlength="60" value="<?php if
    → (isset($_POST['name'])) echo
    → $_POST['name']; ?>" /></p>
    <p>Email Address: <input
    → type="text" name="email"
    → size="30" maxlength="80"
    → value="<?php if
    → (isset($_POST['email'])) echo
    → $_POST['email']; ?>" /></p>
```

The form will submit back to this same page using the POST method. The first two inputs are of type text; both are made sticky by checking if the corresponding $_POST variable has a value. If so, that value is printed as the current value for that input.

continues on next page

8. Complete the form.

```
<p>Comments: <textarea
→ name="comments" rows="5"
→ cols="30"><?php if
→ (isset($_POST['comments']))
→ echo $_POST['comments'];
→ ?></textarea></p>

<p><input type="submit"
→ name="submit" value="Send!"
→ /></p>

<input type="hidden"
→ name="submitted" value="TRUE" />
```

`</form>`

The comments input is a textarea, which does not use a value attribute. Instead, to be made sticky, the value is printed between the opening and closing textarea tags.

9. Complete the HTML page.

`</body>`

`</html>`

10. Save the file as `email.php`, place it in your Web directory, and test it in your Web browser (**Figure 10.3**).

11. Check your email to confirm that you received the message (**Figure 10.4**).

If you don't actually get the email, you'll need to do some debugging work. With this example, you should confirm with your host (if using a hosted site) or yourself (if running PHP on your server), that there's a working mail server installed. You should also test this using different email addresses (for both the *to* and *from* values). Also watch that your spam filter isn't eating up the message.

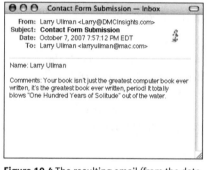

Figure 10.3 Successful completion and submission of the form.

Figure 10.4 The resulting email (from the data in Figure 10.1).

PHP mail() Dependencies

PHP's mail() function doesn't actually send the email itself. Instead, it tells the mail server running on the computer to do so. What this means is that the computer on which PHP is running must have a working mail server in order for this function to work.

If you have a computer running a Unix variant or if you are running your Web site through a professional host, this should not be a problem. But if you are running PHP on your own desktop or laptop computer, you'll probably need to make adjustments.

If you are running Windows and have an Internet service provider (ISP) that provides you with an SMTP server (like *smtp.comcast.net*), this information can be set in the php.ini file (see Appendix A, "Installation," for how to edit this file). Unfortunately, this will only work if your ISP does not require authentication—a username and password combination—to use the SMTP server. Otherwise, you'll need to install an SMTP server on your computer. There are plenty available, and they're not that hard to install and use: just search the Internet for *free windows smtp server* and you'll see some options. There are also threads on this subject in the book's corresponding forum (www.DMCInsights.com/phorum/).

If you are running Mac OS X, you'll need to enable the built-in SMTP server (either sendmail or postfix, depending upon the specific version of Mac OS X you are running). You can find instructions online for doing so (search with *enable sendmail "Mac OS X"*).

✔ Tips

- On some—primarily Unix—systems, the \r\n characters aren't handled properly. If you have problems with them, use just \n instead.

- The mail() function returns a *1* or a *0* indicating the success of the function call. This is not the same thing as the email successfully being sent or received. You cannot easily test for either using PHP.

- While it's easy to send a simple message with the mail() function, sending HTML emails or emails with attachments involves more work. I discuss how you can do both in my book *PHP 5 Advanced: Visual QuickPro Guide* (Peachpit Press, 2007).

- Using a contact form that has PHP send an email is a great way to minimize the spam you receive. With this system, your actual email address is not visible in the Web browser, meaning it can't be harvested by spambots.

SENDING EMAIL

Date and Time Functions

Chapter 5, "Introduction to SQL," demonstrates a handful of great date and time functions that MySQL supports. Naturally, PHP has its own date and time functions. To start, there's `date_default_timezone_set()`. This function is used to establish the default time zone (which can also be set in PHP's configuration file).

```
date_default_timezone_set(tz);
```

The *tz* value is a string like *America/New_York* or *Pacific/Auckland*. There are too many to list here (Africa alone has over 50), but see the PHP manual for them all. Note that as of PHP 5.1, the default time zone must be set prior to calling any of the date and time functions, or else you'll see an error (**Figure 10.5**).

Next up, the `checkdate()` function takes a month, a day, and a year and returns a Boolean value indicating whether that date actually exists (or existed). It even takes into account leap years. This function can be used to ensure that a user supplied a valid date (birth date or other):

```
if (checkdate(month, day, year)) { // OK!
```

Perhaps the most frequently used function is the aptly named `date()`. It returns the date and/or time as a formatted string. It takes two arguments:

```
date (format, [timestamp]);
```

The timestamp is an optional argument representing the number of seconds since the Unix Epoch (midnight on January 1, 1970) for the date in question. It allows you to get

information, like the day of the week, for a particular date. If a timestamp is not specified, PHP will just use the current time on the server.

There are myriad formatting parameters available (**Table 10.1**), and these can be used in conjunction with literal text. For example,

```
echo date('F j, Y'); // January 26, 2008
echo date('H:i'); // 23:14
echo date('D'); // Sat
```

You can find the timestamp for a particular date using the `mktime()` function.

```
$stamp = mktime (hour, minute, second,
→ month, day, year);
```

If called with no arguments, `mktime()` returns the current timestamp, which is the same as calling the `time()` function.

Finally, the `getdate()` function can be used to return an array of values (**Table 10.2**) for a date and time. For example,

```
$today = getdate();
echo $today['month']; // October
```

This function also takes an optional timestamp argument. If that argument is not used, `getdate()` returns information for the current date and time.

These are just a handful of the many date and time functions PHP has. For more, see the PHP manual. To practice working with these functions, let's modify `email.php` (Script 10.1) in an admittedly superfluous way.

Strict Standards: date() [function.date]: It is not safe to rely on the system's timezone settings. Please use the date.timezone setting, the TZ environment variable or the date_default_timezone_set() function. In case you used any of those methods and you are still getting this warning, you most likely misspelled the timezone identifier. We selected 'America/New_York' for 'EDT/-4.0/DST' instead in **/Applications/Abyss Web Server/htdocs/datetime.php** on line 29

Figure 10.5 If running PHP 5.1 and later and *error_reporting* is set on its highest level, PHP will generate a notice when a date or time function is used without the time zone being set.

Table 10.1 The date() function can take any combination of these parameters to format its returned results. A couple more parameters are listed in the PHP manual.

Date Function Formatting

CHARACTER	MEANING	EXAMPLE
Y	year as 4 digits	2008
y	year as 2 digits	05
n	month as 1 or 2 digits	2
m	month as 2 digits	02
F	month	February
M	month as 3 letters	Feb
j	day of the month as 1 or 2 digits	8
d	day of the month as 2 digits	08
l (lowercase L)	day of the week	Monday
D	day of the week as 3 letters	Mon
g	hour, 12-hour format as 1 or 2 digits	6
G	hour, 24-hour format as 1 or 2 digits	18
h	hour, 12-hour format as 2 digits	06
H	hour, 24-hour format as 2 digits	18
i	minutes	45
s	seconds	18
a	am or pm	am
A	AM or PM	PM

Table 10.2 The getdate() function returns this associative array.

The getdate() Array

KEY	VALUE	EXAMPLE
year	year	2007
mon	month	12
month	month name	December
mday	day of the month	25
weekday	day of the week	Tuesday
hours	hours	11
minutes	minutes	56
seconds	seconds	47

To use the date and time functions:

1. Open email.php (Script 10.1) in your text editor or IDE.

2. As the first line of code after the opening PHP tag, establish the time zone (**Script 10.2**).

   ```
   date_default_timezone_set
   → ('America/New_York');
   ```

   Before calling any of the date and time functions (and this script will call two different ones, twice each), the time zone has to be established. To find your time zone, see www.php.net/timezones.

   continues on next page

Script 10.2 This modified version of email.php (Script 10.1) invokes three of PHP's date and time functions in order to report some information (both useful and useless) to the user.

```
1   <!DOCTYPE html PUBLIC "-//W3C//DTD XHTML
    1.0 Transitional//EN"
2      "http://www.w3.org/TR/xhtml1/DTD/
       xhtml1-transitional.dtd">
3   <html xmlns="http://www.w3.org/1999/xhtml"
    xml:lang="en" lang="en">
4   <head>
5     <meta http-equiv="content-type"
      content="text/html; charset=iso-8859-1" />
6     <title>Contact Me</title>
7   </head>
8   <body>
9   <h1>Contact Me</h1>
10  <?php # Script 10.2 - datetime.php
11
12  // Set the default timezone:
13  date_default_timezone_set
    ('America/New_York');
14
15  // Check for form submission:
16  if (isset($_POST['submitted'])) {
```

(script continues on next page)

DATE AND TIME FUNCTIONS

3. In the HTML form, add another hidden input.

```
<input type="hidden" name="start"
→ value="<?php echo time(); ?>" />
```

Just to try something interesting, this script will time how long it takes for the user to receive, fill out, and submit the form. Timing this is just a matter of subtracting the time the form was sent to the Web browser from the time it was submitted back to the server. The time() function will return a timestamp (the number of seconds since the epoch). This value will be stored in the HTML form so that it can be used in the calculation upon submission (**Figure 10.6**).

4. Change the form's action attribute so that it points to this new script.

```
<form action="datetime.php"
→ method="post">
```

This file will be named datetime.php, so the action has to be changed as well.

5. Going back up a few lines in the script to where the form is submitted, change the message so that it includes the current date and time.

```
echo '<p><em>Thank you for contacting
→ me at ' . date('g:i a (T)') . ' on ' .
→ date('l F j, Y') .'. I will reply
→ some day.</em></p>';
```

Two invocations of the date() function are added to this message. The first will return the current time formatted as *HH:MM am/pm (XXX)*, where *XXX* represents the time zone identifier. The second call to date() will return the day of the week, month, day, and year, in the format *Day Month D, YYYY*.

Script 10.2 *continued*

```
                              Script
17
18    // Minimal form validation:
19    if (!empty($_POST['name']) &&
      !empty($_POST['email']) &&
      !empty($_POST['comments']) ) {
20
21        // Create the body:
22        $body = "Name:
          {$_POST['name']}\n\nComments:
          {$_POST['comments']}";
23        $body = wordwrap($body, 70);
24
25        // Send the email:
26        mail('your_email_address@example.com',
          'Contact Form Submission', $body,
          "From: {$_POST['email']}");
27
28        // Print a message:
29        echo '<p><em>Thank you for contacting
          me at ' . date('g:i a (T)') . ' on ' .
          date('l F j, Y') .'. I will reply
          some day.</em></p>';
30
31        // How long did it all take?
32        echo '<p><strong>It took ' .
          (time() - $_POST['start']) . '
          seconds for you to complete and
          submit the form.</strong></p>';
33
34        // Clear $_POST (so that the form's
          not sticky):
35        $_POST = array();
36
37    } else {
38        echo '<p style="font-weight: bold;
          color: #C00">Please fill out the
          form completely.</p>';
39    }
40
41    } // End of main isset() IF.
42
43    // Create the HTML form:
44    ?>
```

(script continues on next page)

Script 10.2 *continued*

```
45    <p>Please fill out this form to contact
      me.</p>

46    <form action="datetime.php" method="post">

47        <p>Name: <input type="text" name="name"
          size="30" maxlength="60" value="<?php if
          (isset($_POST['name'])) echo
          $_POST['name']; ?>" /></p>

48        <p>Email Address: <input type="text"
          name="email" size="30" maxlength="80"
          value="<?php if (isset($_POST['email']))
          echo $_POST['email']; ?>" /></p>

49        <p>Comments: <textarea name="comments"
          rows="5" cols="30"><?php if
          (isset($_POST['comments'])) echo
          $_POST['comments']; ?></textarea></p>

50        <p><input type="submit" name="submit"
          value="Send!" /></p>

51        <input type="hidden" name="start"
          value="<?php echo time(); ?>" />

52        <input type="hidden" name="submitted"
          value="TRUE" />

53    </form>

54    </body>

55    </html>
```

```
<form action="datetime.php" method="post">
    <p>Name: <input type="text" name="name" size="30" maxlength
    <p>Email Address: <input type="text" name="email" size="30"
    <p>Comments: <textarea name="comments" rows="5" cols="30"><
    <p><input type="submit" name="submit" value="Send!" /></p>
    <input type="hidden" name="start" value="1191801778" />
    <input type="hidden" name="submitted" value="TRUE" />
</form>
```

Figure 10.6 The HTML source code of the page reveals the timestamp stored in a hidden input called *start*.

Figure 10.7 The form itself does not seem to be that much different from the original in email.php (see Figure 10.1).

6. Add another message indicating how long the whole process took.

```
echo '<p><strong>It took ' . (time()
→ - $_POST['start']) . ' seconds for
→ you to complete and submit the
→ form.</strong></p>';
```

This message includes the calculation of the current timestamp (returned by time()) minus the timestamp stored in the HTML form.

7. Save the file as datetime.php, place it in your Web directory, and test it in your Web browser (**Figures 10.7** and **10.8**).

✔ Tips

■ The date() function has some parameters that are used for informative purposes, not formatting. For example, date('L') returns *1* or *0* indicating if it's a leap year; date('t') returns the number of days in the current month; and date('I') returns a *1* if it's currently daylight saving time.

■ PHP's date functions reflect the time on the server (because PHP runs on the server); you'll need to use JavaScript if you want to determine the date and time on the user's computer.

Figure 10.8 The response message now uses two date and time functions for a more customized reply.

Handling File Uploads

Chapters 2, "Programming with PHP," and 3, "Creating Dynamic Web Sites," go over the basics of handling HTML forms with PHP. For the most part, every type of form element can be handled the same in PHP, with one exception: file uploads. The process of uploading a file has two dimensions. First the HTML form must be displayed, with the proper code to allow for file uploads. Then upon submission of the form, the PHP script must copy the uploaded file to its final destination.

However, for this process to work, several things must be in place:

◆ PHP must run with the right settings.

◆ A temporary storage directory must exist with the correct permissions.

◆ The final storage directory must exist with the correct permissions.

With this in mind, this next section will cover the server setup to allow for file uploads; then a PHP script will be created that actually does the uploading.

Allowing for file uploads

As I said, certain settings must be established in order for PHP to be able to handle file uploads. I'll first discuss why or when you'd need to make these adjustments before walking you through the steps.

The first issue is PHP itself. There are several settings in PHP's configuration file (`php.ini`) that dictate how PHP handles uploads, specifically stating how large of a file can be uploaded and where the upload should temporarily be stored (**Table 10.3**). Generally speaking, you'll need to edit this file if any of these conditions apply:

◆ *file_uploads* is disabled.

◆ PHP has no temporary directory to use.

◆ You will be uploading very large files (larger than 2 MB).

If you don't have access to your `php.ini` file—like if you're using a hosted site, presumably the host has already configured PHP to allow for file uploads. If you installed PHP on Mac OS X or Unix, you should also be good to go (assuming reasonable-sized files).

The second issue is the location of, and permissions on, the temporary directory. This is where PHP will store the uploaded file until your PHP script moves it to its final destination. If you installed PHP on your own Windows computer, you might need to take steps here (I had no problems with the default PHP 6 installation on Windows XP, but I don't want to assume that'll be the same for everyone). Mac OS X and Unix users need not worry about this, as a temporary directory already exists for such purposes.

Table 10.3 These PHP configuration settings each impact file upload capabilities.

File Upload Configurations

Setting	Value Type	Importance
file_uploads	Boolean	Enables PHP support for file uploads
max_input_time	integer	Indicates how long, in seconds, a PHP script is allowed to run
post_max_size	integer	Size, in bytes, of the total allowed POST data
upload_max_filesize	integer	Size, in bytes, of the largest possible file upload allowed
upload_tmp_dir	string	Indicates where uploaded files should be temporarily stored

Finally, the destination folder must be created and have the proper permissions established on it. This is a step that *everyone* must take for *every* application that handles file uploads. Because there are important security issues involved in this step, please also make sure that you read and understand the sidebar, "Secure Folder Permissions."

With all of this in mind, let's go through the steps.

To prepare the server:

1. Run the `phpinfo()` function to confirm your server settings (**Figure 10.9**).

   The `phpinfo()` function prints out a slew of information about your PHP setup. It's one of the most important functions in PHP, if not the most (in my opinion). Search for the settings listed in Table 10.3 and confirm their values. Make sure that *file_uploads* has a value of *On* and that the limit for *upload_max_filesize* (2MB, by default) and *post_max_size* (8MB) won't be a restriction for you. If running PHP on Windows, see if *upload_tmp_dir* has a value. If it doesn't, that might be a problem (you'll know for certain after running the PHP script that handles the file upload). For non-Windows users, if this value says *no value*, that's perfectly fine.

continues on next page

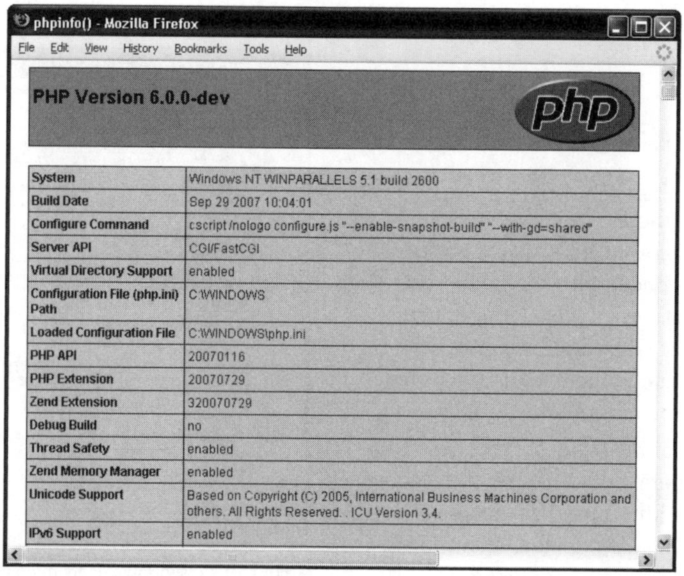

Figure 10.9 A `phpinfo()` script returns all the information regarding your PHP setup, including all the file upload handling stuff.

HANDLING FILE UPLOADS

2. If necessary, open `php.ini` in your text editor.

If there's anything you saw in Step 1 that needs to be changed, or if something happens when you actually go to handle a file upload using PHP, you'll need to edit the `php.ini` file. To find this file, see the *Configuration File (php.ini) path* value in the `phpinfo()` output. This indicates exactly where this file is on your computer (also see Appendix A for more).

If you are not allowed to edit your `php.ini` file (if, for instance, you're using a hosted server), then presumably any necessary edits would have already been made to allow for file uploads. If not, you'll need to request these changes from your hosting company (who may or may not agree to make them).

3. Search the `php.ini` file for the configuration to be changed and make any edits (**Figure 10.10**).

For example, in the File Uploads section, you'll see these three lines:

```
file_uploads = On
```

```
;upload_tmp_dir =
```

```
upload_max_filesize = 2M
```

The first line dictates whether or not uploads are allowed. The second states where the uploaded files should be temporarily stored. On most operating systems, including Mac OS X and Unix, this setting can be left commented out (preceded by a semicolon) without any problem.

If you are running Windows and need to create a temporary directory, set this value to `C:\tmp`, making sure that the line is *not* preceded by a semicolon. Again, using the most recent version of PHP on Windows XP, I did not need to create a temporary directory, so you may be able to get away without one too.

Finally, a maximum upload file size is set (the *M* is shorthand for megabytes in configuration settings).

4. Save the `php.ini` file and restart your Web server.

How you restart your Web server depends upon the operating system and Web serving application being used. See Appendix A for instructions.

```
;;;;;;;;;;;;;;;;
; File Uploads ;
;;;;;;;;;;;;;;;;

; Whether to allow HTTP file uploads.
file_uploads = On

; Temporary directory for HTTP uploaded files (will use system default if not
; specified).
;upload_tmp_dir =

; Maximum allowed size for uploaded files.
upload_max_filesize = 2M
```

Figure 10.10 The File Uploads subsection of the `php.ini` file.

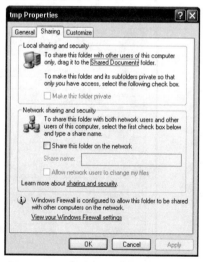

Figure 10.11 Windows users need to make sure that the `C:\tmp` (or whatever directory is used) is writable by PHP. On my Windows XP installation, this just meant that it couldn't be marked private (see the top portion of this image).

HANDLING FILE UPLOADS

5. Confirm the changes by rerunning the `phpinfo()` script.

Before going any further, confirm that the necessary changes have been enacted by repeating Step 1.

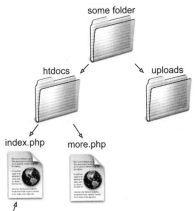

Figure 10.12 Assuming that *htdocs* is the Web root directory (`www.example.com` or `http://localhost` points there), then the *uploads* directory needs to be placed outside of it.

6. If you are running Windows and need to create a temporary directory, add a `tmp` folder within `C:\` and make sure that everyone can write to that directory (**Figure 10.11**).

PHP, through your Web server, will temporarily store the uploaded file in the *upload_tmp_dir*. For this to work, the Web user (if your Web server runs as a particular user) must have permission to write to the folder.

In all likelihood, you may not actually have to change the permissions, but to do so, depending upon what version of Windows you are running, you can normally adjust the permissions by right-clicking the folder and selecting Properties. With the Properties window, there should be a Security tab where permissions are set. It may also be under Sharing. Windows uses a more lax permissions system, so you probably won't have to change anything unless the folder is deliberately restricted. (Note: I haven't tested this on Windows Vista, so I'm unsure what, if anything, might have changed in it.)

Mac OS X and Unix users can skip this step as the temporary directory—/`tmp`— has open permissions already.

7. Create a new directory, called *uploads*, in a directory outside of the Web root directory.

All of the uploaded files will be permanently stored in the *uploads* directory. If you'll be placing your PHP script in the `C:\inetpub\wwwroot\ch10` directory, then create a `C:\inetpub\uploads` directory. Or if the files are going in /Users/~*<username>*/Sites/ch10, make a /Users/~*<username>*/uploads folder. **Figure 10.12** shows the structure you should establish, and the sidebar discusses why this step is necessary.

continues on next page

HANDLING FILE UPLOADS

305

8. Set the permissions on the *uploads* directory so that the Web server can write to it.

Again, Windows users can use the Properties window to make these changes, although it may not be necessary. Mac OS X users can...

A) Select the folder in the Finder.

B) Press Command+I.

C) Allow everyone to Read & Write, under the Ownership & Permissions panel (**Figure 10.13**).

If you're using a hosted site, the host likely provides a control panel through which you can tweak a folder's settings or you might be able to do this within your FTP application.

Depending upon your operating system, you may be able to upload files without first taking this step. You can try the following script before altering the permissions, just to see. If you see messages like those in **Figure 10.14**, then you will need to make some adjustments.

✔ Tips

■ Unix users can use the chmod command to adjust a folder's permissions. The proper permissions in Unix terms will be either 755 or 777.

■ Because of the time it may take to upload a large file, you may also need to change the *max_input_time* value in the php.ini file or temporarily bypass it using the set_time_limit() function in your script.

■ File and directory permissions can be complicated stuff, particularly if you've never dealt with them before. If you have problems with these steps or the next script, search the Web or turn to the book's corresponding forum (www.DMCInsights.com/phorum/).

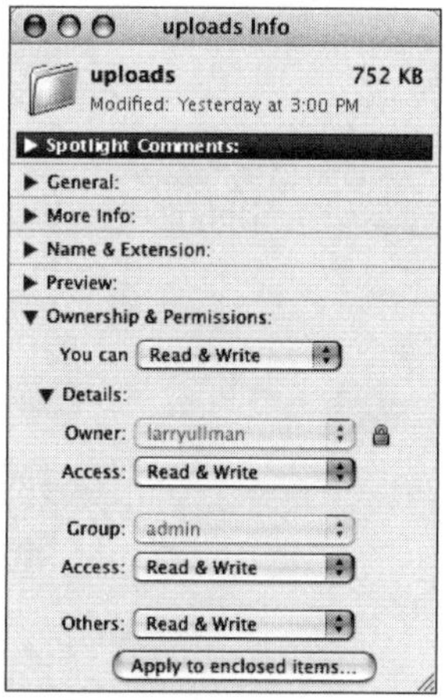

Figure 10.13 Adjusting the properties on the *uploads* folder in Mac OS X.

Warning: move_uploaded_file(../uploads/trout.JPG) [function.move-uploaded-file]: failed to open stream: Permission denied in **/Applications/Abyss Web Server/htdocs/upload_image.php** on line 28

Warning: move_uploaded_file() [function.move-uploaded-file]: Unable to move '/private/var/tmp/phpjhca49' to '../uploads/trout.JPG' in **/Applications/Abyss Web Server/htdocs/upload_image.php** on line 28

Figure 10.14 If PHP could not move the uploaded image over to the *uploads* folder because of a permissions issue, you'll see an error message like this one. Fix the permissions on *uploads* to correct this.

Secure Folder Permissions

There's normally a trade-off between security and convenience. With this example, it'd be more convenient to place the *uploads* folder within the Web document directory (the convenience arises with respect to how easily the uploaded images can be viewed in the Web browser), but doing that is less secure.

For PHP to be able to place files in the *uploads* folder, it needs to have write permissions on that directory. On most servers, PHP is running as the same user as the Web server itself. On a hosted server, this means that all *X* number of sites being hosted are running as the same user. Creating a folder that PHP can write to means creating a folder that everyone can write to. Literally anyone on the server can now move, copy, or write files to the *uploads* folder (assuming that they know it exists). This even means that a malicious user could write a PHP script to your *uploads* directory. However, since the *uploads* directory in this example is not within the Web directory, such a PHP script cannot be run in a Web browser. It's less convenient to do things this way, but more secure.

If you must keep the *uploads* folder publicly accessible, the permissions could be tweaked. For security purposes, you ideally want to allow only the Web server user to read, write, and browse this directory. This means knowing what user the Web server runs as and making that user—and no one else—ruler of the *uploads*. This isn't a perfect solution, but it does help a bit. This change also limits *your* access to that folder, though, as its contents would belong to only the Web server.

Finally, if you're using Apache, you could limit access to the *uploads* folder using an `.htaccess` file. Basically, you would state that only image files in the folder be publicly viewable, meaning that even if a PHP script were to be placed there, it could not be executed. Information on how to use `.htaccess` files can be found online (search on *.htaccess tutorial*).

Sometimes even the most conservative programmer will make security concessions. The important point is that you're aware of the potential concerns and that you do the most you can to minimize the danger.

HANDLING FILE UPLOADS

Uploading files with PHP

Now that the server has (hopefully) been set up to properly allow for file uploads, you can create the PHP script that does the actual file handling. There are two parts to such a script: the HTML form and the PHP code.

The required syntax for a form to handle a file upload has three parts:

```
<form enctype="multipart/form-data"
→ action="script.php" method="post">

<input type="hidden"
→ name="MAX_FILE_SIZE" value="30000" />

File <input type="file" name="upload" />
```

The enctype part of the initial form tag indicates that the form should be able to handle multiple types of data, including files. If you want to accept file uploads, you must include this enctype! Also note that the form *must use* the POST method. The MAX_FILE_SIZE hidden input is a form restriction on how large the chosen file can be, in bytes, and must come before the file input. While it's easy for a user to circumvent this restriction, it should still be used. Finally, the file input type will create the proper button in the form (**Figures 10.15** and **10.16**).

Upon form submission, the uploaded file can be accessed using the $_FILES super-global. The variable will be an array of values, listed in **Table 10.4**.

Once the file has been received by the PHP script, the move_uploaded_file() function can transfer it from the temporary directory to its permanent location.

```
move_uploaded_file (temporary_filename,

/path/to/destination/filename);
```

This next script will let the user select a file on their computer and will then store it in the *uploads* directory. The script will check that the file is of an image type. In the next section of this chapter, another script will list, and create links to, the uploaded images.

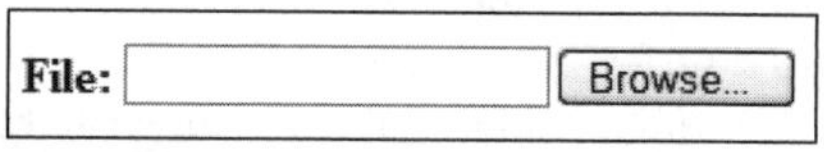

Figure 10.15 The file input as it appears in IE 7 on Windows.

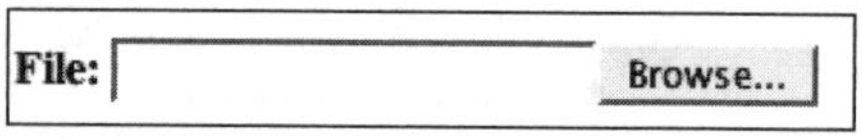

Figure 10.16 The file input as it appears in Firefox on Mac OS X.

Table 10.4 The data for an uploaded file will be available through these array elements.

The $_FILES Array	
INDEX	**MEANING**
name	The original name of the file (as it was on the user's computer).
type	The MIME type of the file, as provided by the browser.
size	The size of the uploaded file in bytes.
tmp_name	The temporary filename of the uploaded file as it was stored on the server.
error	The error code associated with any problem.

Script 10.3 This script allows the user to upload an image file from their computer to the server.

```
 1   <!DOCTYPE html PUBLIC "-//W3C//DTD XHTML
     1.0 Transitional//EN"
 2       "http://www.w3.org/TR/xhtml1/DTD/
         xhtml1-transitional.dtd">
 3   <html xmlns="http://www.w3.org/1999/xhtml"
     xml:lang="en" lang="en">
 4   <head>
 5     <meta http-equiv="content-type"
       content="text/html; charset=iso-8859-1" />
 6     <title>Upload an Image</title>
 7     <style type="text/css" title="text/css"
       media="all">
 8     .error {
 9     font-weight: bold;
10     color: #C00
11     }
12     </style>
13   </head>
14   <body>
15   <?php # Script 10.3 - upload_image.php
16
17   // Check if the form has been submitted:
18   if (isset($_POST['submitted'])) {
19
20     // Check for an uploaded file:
21     if (isset($_FILES['upload'])) {
22
23       // Validate the type. Should be
         JPEG or PNG.
24       $allowed = array ('image/pjpeg',
         'image/jpeg', 'image/jpeg',
         'image/JPG', 'image/X-PNG',
         'image/PNG', 'image/png',
         'image/x-png');
25       if (in_array($_FILES['upload']
         ['type'], $allowed)) {
26
```

(script continues on next page)

To handle file uploads in PHP:

1. Create a new PHP document in your text editor or IDE (**Script 10.3**).

```
<!DOCTYPE html PUBLIC "-//W3C//DTD
→ XHTML 1.0 Transitional//EN"

"http://www.w3.org/TR/xhtml1/DTD/
→ xhtml1-transitional.dtd">

<html
→ xmlns="http://www.w3.org/1999/xhtml"
→ xml:lang="en" lang="en">

<head>

    <meta http-equiv="content-type"
    → content="text/html;
    → charset=iso-8859-1" />

    <title>Upload an Image</title>

    <style type="text/css"
    → title="text/css" media="all">

    .error {

        font-weight: bold;

        color: #C00

    }

    </style>

</head>

<body>

<?php # Script 10.3 - upload_image.php
```

This script will make use of one CSS class to format any errors.

continues on next page

2. Check if the form has been submitted and that a file was selected.

```
if (isset($_POST['submitted'])) {

    if (isset($_FILES['upload'])) {
```

Since this form will have no other fields to be validated (**Figure 10.17**), this is the only conditional required. You could also validate the size of the uploaded file to determine if it fits within the acceptable range (refer to the $_FILES['upload'] ['size'] value).

3. Check that the uploaded file is of the proper type.

```
$allowed = array ('image/pjpeg',
→ 'image/jpeg', 'image/jpeg',
→ 'image/JPG', 'image/X-PNG',
→ 'image/PNG', 'image/png',
→ 'image/x-png');

if
→ (in_array($_FILES['upload']['type'],
→ $allowed)) {
```

The file's type is its *MIME* type, indicating what kind of file it is. The browser can determine and may provide this information, depending upon the properties of the selected file. To validate the file's type, first create an array of allowed options. The list of allowed types is based upon accepting JPEGs and PNGs. Some browsers have variations on the MIME types, so those are included here as well. If the uploaded file's type is in this array, the file is valid and should be handled.

Figure 10.17 This very basic HTML form only takes one input: a file.

Script 10.3 *continued*

```
27    // Move the file over.
28    if (move_uploaded_file
      ($_FILES['upload']['tmp_name'],
      "../uploads/{$_FILES['upload']['name']
      }")) {
29        echo '<p><em>The file has been
          uploaded!</em></p>';
30    } // End of move... IF.
31
32    } else { // Invalid type.
33        echo '<p class="error">Please upload a
          JPEG or PNG image.</p>';
34    }
35
36    } // End of isset($_FILES['upload']) IF.
37
38    // Check for an error:
39
40    if ($_FILES['upload']['error'] > 0) {
41        echo '<p class="error">The file could
          not be uploaded because: <strong>';
42
43        // Print a message based upon the
          error.
44        switch ($_FILES['upload']['error']) {
45          case 1:
46            print 'The file exceeds the
              upload_max_filesize setting in
              php.ini.';
47            break;
48          case 2:
49            print 'The file exceeds the
              MAX_FILE_SIZE setting in the
              HTML form.';
50            break;
51          case 3:
52            print 'The file was only
              partially uploaded.';
```

(script continues on next page)

Script 10.3 *continued*

```
53          break;
54      case 4:
55          print 'No file was uploaded.';
56          break;
57      case 6:
58          print 'No temporary folder was
            available.';
59          break;
60      case 7:
61          print 'Unable to write to the
            disk.';
62          break;
63      case 8:
64          print 'File upload stopped.';
65          break;
66      default:
67          print 'A system error
            occurred.';
68          break;
69      } // End of switch.
70
71      print '</strong></p>';
72
73      } // End of error IF.
74
75      // Delete the file if it still exists:
76      if (file_exists
        ($_FILES['upload']['tmp_name']) &&
        is_file($_FILES['upload']['tmp_name'
        ]) ) {
77          unlink
            ($_FILES['upload']['tmp_name']);
78      }
79
80  } // End of the submitted conditional.
```

(script continues on next page)

4. Copy the file to its new location on the server.

```
if (move_uploaded_file
→ ($_FILES['upload']['tmp_name'],
→ "../uploads/{$_FILES['upload']
→ ['name']}")) {
    echo '<p><em>The file has been
    → uploaded!</em></p>';
}
```

The `move_uploaded_file()` function will move the file from its temporary to its permanent location (in the *uploads* folder). The file will retain its original name. In Chapter 17, "Example—E-Commerce," you'll see how to give the file a new name, which is generally a good idea.

As a rule, you should always use a conditional to confirm that a file was successfully moved, instead of just assuming that the move worked.

5. Complete the image type and `isset($_FILES['upload'])` conditionals.

```
} else { // Invalid type.
    echo '<p class="error">Please
    → upload a JPEG, GIF, or PNG
    → GIF image.</p>';
}
} // End of isset($_FILES['upload'])
→ IF.
```

The first `else` clause completes the `if` begun in Step 3. It applies if a file was uploaded but it wasn't of the right MIME type (**Figure 10.18**).

continues on next page

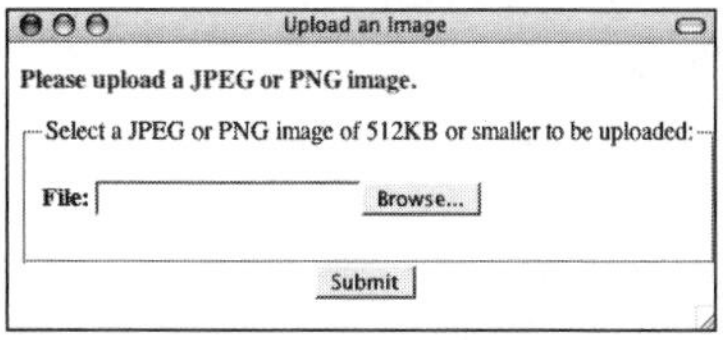

Figure 10.18 If the user uploads a file that's not a JPEG or PNG, this is the result.

6. Check for, and report on, any errors.

```
if ($_FILES['upload']['error'] > 0) {
    echo '<p class="error">The file
    → could not be uploaded because:
    → <strong>';
```

If an error occurred, then `$_FILES['upload']['error']` will have a value greater than *0*. In such cases, this script will report what the error was.

7. Create a `switch` that prints a more detailed error.

```
switch ($_FILES['upload']['error']) {
    case 1:
        print 'The file exceeds the
        → upload_max_filesize setting
        → in php.ini.';
        break;
    case 2:
        print 'The file exceeds the
        → MAX_FILE_SIZE setting in
        → the HTML form.';
        break;
    case 3:
        print 'The file was only
        → partially uploaded.';
        break;
    case 4:
        print 'No file was uploaded.';
        break;
    case 6:
        print 'No temporary folder was
        → available.';
        break;
```

Script 10.3 *continued*

```
81    ?>
82
83    <form enctype="multipart/form-data"
      action="upload_image.php" method="post">
84
85        <input type="hidden"
          name="MAX_FILE_SIZE" value="524288">
86
87        <fieldset><legend>Select a JPEG or PNG
          image of 512KB or smaller to be
          uploaded:</legend>
88
89        <p><b>File:</b> <input type="file"
          name="upload" /></p>
90
91        </fieldset>
92        <div align="center"><input type="submit"
          name="submit" value="Submit" /></div>
93        <input type="hidden" name="submitted"
          value="TRUE" />
94    </form>
95    </body>
96    </html>
```

```
case 7:

    print 'Unable to write to the
    → disk.';

    break;

case 8:

    print 'File upload stopped.';

    break;

default:

    print 'A system error
    → occurred.';

    break;

} // End of switch.
```

There are several possible reasons a file could not be uploaded and moved. The first and most obvious one is if the permissions are not set properly on the destination directory. In such a case, you'll see an appropriate error message (refer back to Figure 10.14). PHP will often also store an error number in the `$_FILES['upload']['error']` variable. The numbers correspond to specific problems, from 0 to 4, plus 6 through 8 (oddly enough, there is no 5). The `switch` conditional here prints out the problem according to the error number. The default case is added for future support (if different numbers are added in later versions of PHP).

For the most part, these errors are useful to you, the developer, and not things you'd indicate to the average user.

8. Complete the error `if` conditional.

```
    print '</strong></p>';

} // End of error IF.
```

9. Delete the temporary file if it still exists and complete the PHP section.

```
if (file_exists
→ ($_FILES['upload']['tmp_name'])
→ &&
→ is_file($_FILES['upload']['tmp_
→ name']) ) {

    unlink
    → ($_FILES['upload']['tmp_
    → name']);

}

} // End of the submitted conditional.

?>
```

If the file was uploaded but it could not be moved to its final destination or some other error occurred, then that file is still sitting on the server in its temporary location. To remove it, use the `unlink()` function. Just to be safe, prior to applying `unlink()`, a conditional checks that the file exists and that it is a file (because the `file_exists()` function will return TRUE if the named item is a directory).

continues on next page

10. Create the HTML form.

```
<form enctype="multipart/form-data"
→ action="upload_image.php"
→ method="post">

    <input type="hidden"
    → name="MAX_FILE_SIZE"
    → value="524288">

    <fieldset><legend>Select a JPEG
    → or PNG image of 512KB or
    → smaller to be uploaded:</legend>

    <p><b>File:</b> <input
    → type="file" name="upload" /></p>

    </fieldset>

<div align="center"><input
→ type="submit" name="submit"
→ value="Submit" /></div>

    <input type="hidden"
    → name="submitted" value="TRUE" />

</form>
```

This form is very simple (Figure 10.17), but it contains the three necessary parts for file uploads: the form's enctype attribute, the MAX_FILE_SIZE hidden input, and the file input.

11. Complete the HTML page.

```
</body>

</html>
```

12. Save the file as upload_image.php, place it in your Web directory, and test it in your Web browser (**Figures 10.19** and **10.20**).

If you want, you can confirm that the script works by checking the contents of the *uploads* directory.

✔ Tips

■ Omitting the enctype form attribute is a common reason for file uploads to mysteriously fail.

■ The existence of an uploaded file can also be validated with the is_uploaded_file() function.

■ Windows users must use forward slashes or double backslashes to refer to directories (so C:\\ or C:/ but not C:\). This is because the backslash is the escape character in PHP.

■ The move_uploaded_file() function will overwrite an existing file without warning if the new and existing files both have the same name.

■ The MAX_FILE_SIZE is a restriction in the browser as to how large a file can be, although not all browsers abide by this restriction. The PHP configuration file has its own restrictions. You can also validate the uploaded file size within the receiving PHP script.

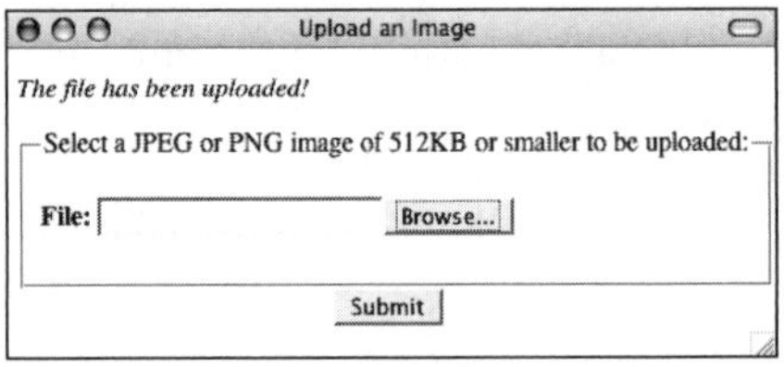

Figure 10.19 The result upon successfully uploading and moving a file.

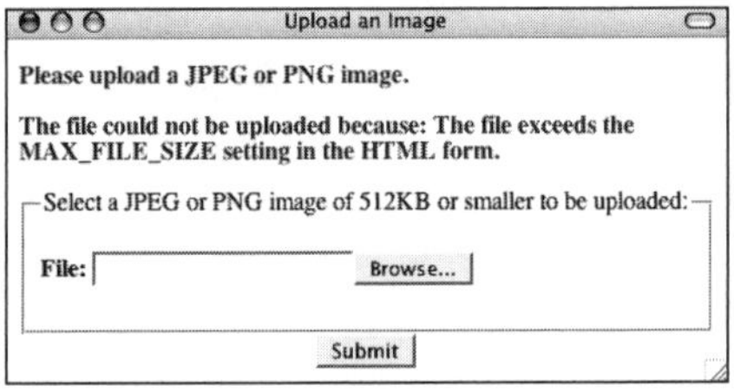

Figure 10.20 The result upon attempting to upload a file that is too large.

HANDLING FILE UPLOADS

PHP and JavaScript

Although PHP and JavaScript are fundamentally different technologies, they can be used together to make better Web sites. The most significant difference between the two languages is that JavaScript is client-side (meaning it runs in the Web browser) and PHP is server-side. Therefore, JavaScript can do such things as detect the size of the browser window, create pop-up windows, and make image mouseovers, whereas PHP can do nothing like these things.

But while PHP cannot do certain things that JavaScript can, PHP can be used to create or work with JavaScript (just as PHP can create HTML). In this example, PHP will list all the images uploaded by the upload_image.php script and make clickable links using their names. The links themselves will call a JavaScript function that creates a pop-up window. This example will in no way be a thorough discussion of JavaScript, but it does adequately demonstrate how the two technologies—PHP and JavaScript—can be used together.

Along with the JavaScript, three new PHP functions are used in this example. The first, getimagesize(), returns an array of information for a given image (**Table 10.5**). The second, scandir(), returns an array listing the files in a given directory (it was added in PHP 5). The third, filesize(), returns the size of a file in bytes.

Table 10.5 The getimagesize() function returns this array of data.

The getimagesize() Array		
ELEMENT	VALUE	EXAMPLE
0	image's width in pixels	423
1	image's height in pixels	368
2	image's type	2 (representing JPG)
3	appropriate HTML img tag data	height="368" width="423"
mime	image's MIME type	image/png

To create JavaScript with PHP:

1. Begin a new PHP document in your text editor or IDE (**Script 10.4**).

   ```
   <!DOCTYPE html PUBLIC "-//W3C//DTD
   → XHTML 1.0 Transitional//EN"

   "http://www.w3.org/TR/xhtml1/DTD/
   → xhtml1-transitional.dtd">

   <html
   → xmlns="http://www.w3.org/1999/xhtml"
   → xml:lang="en" lang="en">

   <head>

       <meta http-equiv="content-type"
   → content="text/html;
   → charset=iso-8859-1" />

       <title>Images</title>

       <script language="JavaScript">
   ```

   This script will display a list of images, along with their file sizes, and create a link to view the actual image itself in a pop-up window. The pop-up window will be created by JavaScript, although PHP will be used to set certain parameters.

Script 10.4 The images.php script uses JavaScript and PHP to create links to images stored on the server. The images will be viewable through show_image.php (Script 10.5).

```
1   «<!DOCTYPE html PUBLIC "-//W3C//DTD XHTML
    1.0 Transitional//EN"

2                   "http://www.w3.org/TR/
                    xhtml1/DTD/
                    xhtml1-transitional.dtd">

3   <html xmlns="http://www.w3.org/1999/xhtml"
    xml:lang="en" lang="en">

4   <head>

5     <meta http-equiv="content-type"
      content="text/html; charset=iso-8859-1"
      />

6     <title>Images</title>

7     <script language="JavaScript">

8     <!-- // Hide from old browsers.

9

10    // Make a pop-up window function:

11    function create_window (image, width,
      height) {

12

13        // Add some pixels to the width and
          height:

14        width = width + 10;

15        height = height + 10;

16

17        // If the window is already open,

18        // resize it to the new dimensions:

19        if (window.popup &&
          !window.popup.closed) {

20          window.popup.resizeTo(width,
            height);

21        }

22

23        // Set the window properties:
```

(script continues on next page)

Script 10.4 *continued*

```
┌─────────────────────────────────────────┐
│  ⊖ ⊖ ⊖              📄 Script             │
├─────────────────────────────────────────┤
24    var specs = "location=no,
      scrollbars=no, menubars=no,
      toolbars=no, resizable=yes, left=0,
      top=0, width=" + width + ", height="
      + height;

25

26    // Set the URL:

27    var url = "show_image.php?image=" +
      image;

28

29    // Create the pop-up window:

30    popup = window.open(url,
      "ImageWindow", specs);

31    popup.focus();

32

33    } // End of function.

34    //--></script>

35    </head>

36    <body>

37    <p>Click on an image to view it in a
      separate window.</p>

38    <table align="center" cellspacing="5"
      cellpadding="5" border="1">

39      <tr>

40        <td align="center"><b>Image
          Name</b></td>

41        <td align="center"><b>Image
          Size</b></td>

42      </tr>

43    <?php # Script 10.4 - images.php

44    // This script lists the images in the
      uploads directory.

45

46    $dir = '../uploads'; // Define the
      directory to view.

47

48    $files = scandir($dir); // Read all the
      images into an array.
```

(script continues on next page)

2. Begin the JavaScript function.

```
<script language="JavaScript">

<!-- // Hide from old browsers.

function create_window (image, width,
→ height) {

    width = width + 10;

    height = height + 10;
```

The JavaScript `create_window()` function will accept three parameters: the image name, its width, and its height. Each of these will be passed to this function when the user clicks a link. The exact values of the image name, width, and height will be determined by PHP.

Some pixels will be added to the width and height values to create a window slightly larger than the image itself.

3. Resize the pop-up window if it is already open.

```
if (window.popup &&
→ !window.popup.closed) {

    window.popup.resizeTo(width,
    → height);

}
```

This code first checks if the pop-up window exists and if it is not closed (`popup` is a user-defined JavaScript variable representing the pop-up window). If it passes both tests (which is to say it's already open), the window will be resized according to the new image dimensions. The purpose of this code is to resize the existing window from one image to another if it was left open.

continues on next page

4. Determine the properties of the pop-up window and the URL, and then create the window.

```
var specs = "location=no,
→ scrollbars=no, menubars=no,
→ toolbars=no, resizable=yes, left=0,
→ top=0, width=" + width + ",
→ height=" + height;

var url = "show_image.php?image=" +
→ image;

popup = window.open(url,
→ "ImageWindow", specs);

popup.focus();
```

The first line sets the properties of the pop-up window (the window will have no location bar, scroll bars, menus, or toolbars; it should be resizable; it will be located in the upper-left corner of the screen; and it will have a width of *width* and a height of *height*). The plus sign is used to perform concatenation in JavaScript, thereby adding the variable's value to a string.

The second line sets the URL of the popup window, which is *show_image. php?image=* plus the name of the image.

Finally, the pop-up window is created using the defined properties and URL, and focus is given to it, meaning it should appear above the current window.

Script 10.4 *continued*

```
49
50   // Display each image caption as a link to
     the JavaScript function:
51   foreach ($files as $image) {
52
53       if (substr($image, 0, 1) != '.') { //
         Ignore anything starting with a period.
54
55           // Get the image's size in pixels:
56           $image_size = getimagesize
             ("$dir/$image");
57
58           // Calculate the image's size in
             kilobytes:
59           $file_size = round ( (filesize
             ("$dir/$image")) / 1024) . "kb";
60
61           // Make the image's name URL-safe:
62           $image = urlencode($image);
63
64           // Print the information:
65           echo "\t<tr>
66   \t\t<td><a href=\"javascript:create_window
     ('$image',$image_size[0],$image_size[1])\"
     >$image</a></td>
67   \t\t<td>$file_size</td>
68   \t</tr>\n";
69
70       } // End of the IF.
71
72   } // End of the foreach loop.
73   ?>
74   </table>
75   </body>
76   </html>
```

5. Conclude the JavaScript function and the HTML head.

```
} // End of function.

//--></script>
```

```
</head>
```

6. Create the introductory text and begin the table.

```
<body>

<p>Click on an image to view it in a
→ separate window.</p>

<table align="center"
→ cellspacing="5" cellpadding="5"
→ border="1">

    <tr>

        <td align="center"><b>Image
        → Name</b></td>

        <td align="center"><b>Image
        → Size</b></td>

    </tr>
```

Not a lot of effort is being put into the appearance of the page. It will be just one table with a caption (**Figure 10.21**).

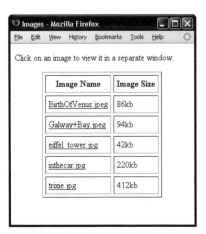

Figure 10.21 This PHP page has a caption and a table that lists all the images, along with their file sizes.

7. Start the PHP code and create an array of images by referring to the *uploads* directory.

```
<?php # Script 10.4 - images.php

$dir = '../uploads';

$files = scandir($dir);
```

This script will automatically list and link all of the images stored in the *uploads* folder (presumably put there by upload_image.php, Script 10.3). The code begins by defining the directory as a variable, so that it's easier to refer to. Then the scandir() function, which returns an array of files and directories found within a folder, assigns that information to an array called $files.

8. Begin looping through the $files array.

```
foreach ($files as $image) {

    if (substr($image, 0, 1) != '.') {
```

This loop will go through every image in the array and create a row in the table for it. Within the loop, there is one conditional that checks if the first character in the file's name is a period. On non-Windows systems, hidden files start with a period, the current directory is referred to using just a single period, and two periods refers to the parent directory. Since all of these might be includes in $files, they need to be weeded out.

continues on next page

PHP AND JAVASCRIPT

9. Get the image information and encode its name.

```
$image_size = getimagesize
→ ("$dir/$image");

$file_size = round ( (filesize
→ ("$dir/$image")) / 1024) . "kb";

$image = urlencode($image);
```

Three PHP functions are used here that haven't been used before (for more information, check the PHP manual). The getimagesize() function returns an array of information about an image (Table 10.5). The values returned by this function will be used to set the width and height sent to the create_window() JavaScript function.

The filesize() function returns the size of a file in bytes. To calculate the kilobytes of a file, divide this number by 1,024 (there are that many bytes in a kilobyte) and round it off.

Lastly, the urlencode() function makes a string safe to pass in a URL. Because the image name may contain characters not allowed in a URL (and it will be passed in the URL when invoking show_image.php), the name should be encoded.

10. Print the table row.

```
echo "\t<tr>

\t\t<td><a
→ href=\"javascript:create_window
→ ('$image',$image_size[0],$image_
→ size[1])\">$image</a></td>

\t\t<td>$file_size</td>

\t</tr>\n";
```

Finally, the loop creates the HTML table row, consisting of the linked image name and the image size. The caption is linked as a call to the JavaScript create_window() function so that when the link is clicked, that function is executed. To make the HTML source more legible, tabs (\t) and newline characters (\n) are printed as well.

11. Complete the PHP code and the HTML page.

```
} // End of the IF.

} // End of the foreach loop.

?>

</table>

</body>

</html>
```

12. Save the file as `images.php`, place it in your Web directory (in the same directory as `upload_image.php`), and test it in your Web browser (Figure 10.21).

13. View the source code to see the dynamically generated links (**Figure 10.22**).

Notice how the parameters to each function call are appropriate to the specific image.

✔ Tips

■ Some versions of Windows create a `Thumbs.db` file in a folder of images. You might want to check for this value in the conditional in Step 8 that weeds out some returned items. That code would be

```
if ( (substr($image, 0, 1) != '.') &&
→ ($image != 'Thumbs.db') ) {
```

■ Not to belabor the point, but most everything Web developers do with JavaScript (for example, resize or move the browser window) cannot be done using the server-side PHP.

■ There is *a little* overlap between the PHP and JavaScript. Both can set and read cookies, create HTML, and do some browser detection.

```
<tr>
        <td><a href="javascript:create_window('eiffel_tower.jpg',822,537)">eiffel_tower.jpg</a></td>
        <td>42kb</td>
</tr>
<tr>
        <td><a href="javascript:create_window('inthecar.jpg',1009,841)">inthecar.jpg</a></td>
        <td>220kb</td>
</tr>
<tr>
        <td><a href="javascript:create_window('trixie.jpg',1280,1024)">trixie.jpg</a></td>
        <td>412kb</td>
</tr>
```

Figure 10.22 Each image's name is linked as a call to a JavaScript function. The function call's parameters were created by PHP.

Understanding HTTP Headers

This chapter will conclude by discussing how you can use HTTP headers with your PHP scripts. HTTP (Hypertext Transfer Protocol) is the technology at the heart of the World Wide Web and defines the way clients and servers communicate (in layman's terms). When a browser requests a Web page, it receives a series of HTTP headers in return. This happens behind the scenes, of course; most users aren't aware of this at all.

PHP's built-in header() function can be used to take advantage of this protocol. The most common example of this will be demonstrated in the next chapter, when the header() function will be used to redirect the Web browser from the current page to another. Here, you'll use it to send files to the Web browser.

In theory, the header() function is easy to use. Its syntax is

```
header(header string);
```

The list of possible header strings is quite long, as headers are used for everything from redirecting the Web browser to sending files to sending cookies to controlling page caching and much, much more. Starting with something simple, to use header() to redirect the Web browser, type

```
header ('Location:
→ http://www.example.com/page.php');
```

That line will send the Web browser from the page it's on over to that URL.

In this next example, which will send a file to the Web browser, three header calls are used. The first is *Content-Type*. This is an indication to the Web browser of what kind of data is about to follow. The *Content-Type* value matches the data's MIME type. This line lets the browser know it's about to receive a PDF file:

```
header("Content-
→ Type:application/pdf\n");
```

Next, you can use *Content-Disposition*, which tells the browser how to treat the data:

```
header ("Content-Disposition: attachment;
→ filename=\"somefile.pdf\"\n");
```

The *attachment* value will prompt the browser to download the file (**Figure 10.23**). An alternative is to use *inline*, which tells the browser to display the data, assuming that the browser can. The filename attribute is just that: it tells the browser the name associated with the data.

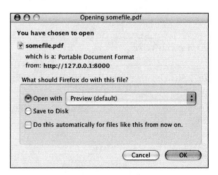

Figure 10.23 Firefox prompts the user to download the file because of the *attachment Content-Disposition* value.

Warning: Cannot modify header information - headers already sent by (output started at /Applications/Abyss Web Server/mysqli_connect.php:20) in **/Applications/Abyss Web Server/htdocs/header.php** on line **12**

Figure 10.24 The *headers already sent* error means that the Web browser was sent something—HTML, plain text, even a space—prior to using the header() function.

Script 10.5 This script retrieves an image from the server and sends it to the browser.

```
1    <?php # Script 10.5 - show_image.php
2    // This page displays an image.
3
4    $name = FALSE; // Flag variable:
5
6    // Check for an image name in the URL:
7    if (isset($_GET['image'])) {
8
9      // Full image path:
10     $image = "../uploads/{$_GET['image']}";
11
12     // Check that the image exists and is a
       file:
13     if (file_exists ($image) &&
       (is_file($image))) {
14
15       // Make sure it has an image's
         extension:
16       $ext = strtolower ( substr
         ($_GET['image'], -4));
17
18       if (($ext == '.jpg') OR ($ext ==
         'jpeg') OR ($ext == '.png')) {
19         // Set the name as this image:
20         $name = $_GET['image'];
21       } // End of $ext IF.
22
23     } // End of file_exists() IF.
24
25   } // End of isset($_GET['image']) IF.
26
27   // If there was a problem, use the default
     image:
28   if (!$name) {
29     $image = 'images/unavailable.png';
```

(script continues on next page)

A third header to use for downloading files is *Content-Length*. This is a value, in bytes, corresponding to the amount of data to be sent.

```
header ("Content-Length: 4096\n");
```

That's the basics with respect to using the header() function. Before getting to the example, note that if a script uses multiple header() calls, each should be terminated by a newline (\n) as in the preceding code snippets. More importantly, the absolutely critical thing to remember about the header() function is that it must be called before *anything* is sent to the Web browser. This includes HTML or even blank spaces. If your code has any echo() or print() statements, has blank lines outside of PHP tags, or includes files that do any of these things before calling header(), you'll see an error message like that in **Figure 10.24**.

To use the header() function:

1. Begin a new PHP document in your text editor or IDE (**Script 10.5**).

```
<?php # Script 10.5 - show_image.php
$name = FALSE;
```

Because this script will use the header() function, nothing, absolutely nothing, can be sent to the Web browser. No HTML, not even a blank line, tab, or space before the opening PHP tag.

The $name variable will be used as a flag, indicating if all of the validation routines have been passed.

2. Check for an image name.

```
if (isset($_GET['image'])) {
```

The script needs to receive a valid image name in the URL. This should be appended to the URL in the JavaScript function that calls this page (see images.php, Script 10.4).

continues on next page

3. Check that the image is a file on the server.

```
$image =
→ "../uploads/{$_GET['image']}";

if (file_exists ($image) &&
→ (is_file($image))) {
```

Before attempting to send the image to the Web browser, make sure that it exists and that it is a file (as opposed to a directory). As a security measure, I hard-code the image's full path as a combination of *../uploads* and the received image name. Even if someone were to attempt to use this page to see */path/to/secret/file*, this script would look for *../uploads//path/to/secret/file* (including the double-slash), which is safe.

4. Validate the image's extension.

```
$ext = strtolower ( substr
→ ($_GET['image'], -4));

if (($ext == '.jpg') OR ($ext ==
→ 'jpeg') OR ($ext == '.png')) {

    $name = $_GET['image'];

} // End of $ext IF.
```

The final check is that the file to be sent to the Web browser has a `.jpeg`, `.jpg`, or `.png` extension. This way the script won't try to send something bad to the user. Even though the `upload_image.php` script also validates the file by type, you can never be too careful.

To validate the extension, the `substr()` function returns the last four characters from the image's name (the `-4` accomplishes this). The extension is also run through the `strtolower()` function so that `.PNG` and `.png` are treated the same. Then a conditional checks to see if `$ext` is equal to any of the three allowed values.

Once the image has passed all of these tests, the `$name` function is assigned the value of the image.

Script 10.5 *continued*

```
 30     $name = 'unavailable.png';

 31   }

 32

 33   // Get the image information:

 34   $info = getimagesize($image);

 35   $fs = filesize($image);

 36

 37   // Send the content information:

 38   header ("Content-Type:
        {$info['mime']}\n");

 39   header ("Content-Disposition: inline;
        filename=\"$name\"\n");

 40   header ("Content-Length: $fs\n");

 41

 42   // Send the file:

 43   readfile ($image);

 44

 45   ?>
```

5. Complete the conditionals begun in Steps 2 and 3.

```
    } // End of file_exists() IF.
} // End of isset($_GET['image']) IF.
```

6. If no valid image was received by this page, use a default image.

```
if (!$name) {
    $image = 'images/unavailable.png';
    $name = 'unavailable.png';
}
```

If the image doesn't exist, if it isn't a file, or if it doesn't have the proper extension, then the $name variable will still have a value of FALSE. In such cases, a default image will be used instead (**Figure 10.25**). The image itself can be downloaded from the book's corresponding Web site (www.DMCInsights.com/phpmysql3/, see the Extras page) and should be placed in an *images* folder. The images folder should be in the same directory as this script, not in the same directory as the uploads folder.

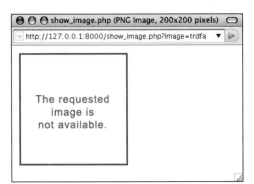

Figure 10.25 This image will be shown any time there's a problem with showing the requested image.

7. Retrieve the image information.

```
$info = getimagesize($image);
$fs = filesize($image);
```

To send the file to the Web browser, the script needs to know the file's type and size. The file's type can be found using getimagesize(). The file's size, in bytes, is found using filesize(). Because the $image variable represents either *../uploads/{$_GET['image']}* or *images/unavailable.png*, these lines will work on both the correct and the unavailable image.

8. Send the file.

```
header ("Content-Type:
→ {$info['mime']}\n");
header ("Content-Disposition: inline;
→ filename=\"$name\"\n");
header ("Content-Length: $fs\n");
readfile ($image);
```

These header() calls will send the file data to the Web browser. The first line uses the image's MIME type for the *Content-Type*. The second line tells the browser the name of the file and that it should be displayed in the browser (*inline*). The last header() function indicates how much data is to be expected. The file data itself is sent using the readfile() function, which reads in a file and immediately sends the content to the Web browser.

9. Complete the page.

```
?>
```

Notice that this page contains no HTML. It only sends an image file to the Web browser.

continues on next page

UNDERSTANDING HTTP HEADERS

10. Save the file as show_image.php, place it in your Web directory, in the same folder as images.php, and test it in your Web browser by clicking a link in images.php (**Figure 10.26**).

✔ Tips

- I cannot stress strongly enough that *nothing* can be sent to the Web browser before using the header() function. Even an included file that has a blank line after the closing PHP tag will make the header() function unusable.

- To avoid problems when using header(), you can call the headers_sent() function first. It returns a Boolean value indicating if something has already been sent to the Web browser:

```
if (!headers_sent()) {
    // Use the header() function.
} else {
    // Do something else.
}
```

Output buffering, demonstrated in Chapter 16, "Example—User Registration," can also prevent problems when using header().

- Debugging scripts like this, where PHP sends data, not text, to the Web browser, can be challenging. For help, use the Live HTTP Headers plug-in for Firefox (**Figure 10.27**).

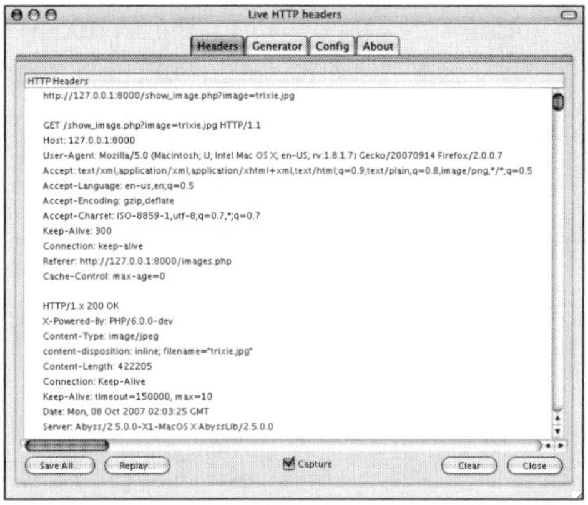

Figure 10.26 This image is displayed by having PHP send the file to the Web browser.

Figure 10.27 The Live HTTP Headers extension for Firefox shows what headers were sent by a page and/or server. This can be useful debugging information.

COOKIES AND SESSIONS

The Hypertext Transfer Protocol (HTTP) is a stateless technology, meaning that each individual HTML page is an unrelated entity. HTTP has no method for tracking users or retaining variables as a person traverses a site. Although your browser tracks the pages you visit, the server keeps no record of who had seen what. Without the server being able to track a user, there can be no shopping carts or custom Web site personalization. Using a server-side technology like PHP, you can overcome the statelessness of the Web. The two best PHP tools for this purpose are cookies and sessions.

As you probably already know, cookies store data in the user's Web browser. When the user accesses a page on the site from which the cookie came, the server can read the data from that cookie. Sessions store data on the server itself. Sessions are generally more secure than cookies and can store much more information. Both technologies are easy to use with PHP and are worth knowing.

In this chapter you'll see uses of both cookies and sessions. The examples for demonstrating this information will be a login system, based upon the existing *users* database.

Making a Login Page

A login process involves just a few components:

◆ A form for submitting the login information

◆ A validation routine that confirms the necessary information was submitted

◆ A database query that compares the submitted information against the stored information

◆ Cookies or sessions to store data that reflects a successful login

Subsequent pages will then contain checks to confirm that the user is logged in (to limit access to that page). There is also, of course, a logging out process, which involves clearing out the cookies or session data representing a logged-in status.

To start all this, let's take some of these common elements and place them into separate files. Then, the pages that require this functionality can include the necessary files. Breaking up the logic this way will make some of the following scripts easier to read and write, plus cut down on their redundancies. I've designed two includable files. This first one will contain the bulk of a login page, including the header, the error reporting, the form, and the footer (**Figure 11.1**).

Figure 11.1 The login form and page.

Script 11.1 The login_page.inc.php script creates the complete login page, including the form, and reports any errors. It will be included by other pages that need to show the login page.

```
1    <?php # Script 11.1 - login_page.inc.php
2
3    // This page prints any errors associated
     with logging in
4    // and it creates the entire login page,
     including the form.
5
6    // Include the header:
7    $page_title = 'Login';
8    include ('includes/header.html');
9
10   // Print any error messages, if they
     exist:
11   if (!empty($errors)) {
12       echo '<h1>Error!</h1>';
13       <p class="error">The following error(s)
         occurred:<br />';
14       foreach ($errors as $msg) {
15       echo " - $msg<br />\n";
16       }
17       echo '</p><p>Please try again.</p>';
18   }
19
20   // Display the form:
21   ?>
22   <h1>Login</h1>
23   <form action="login.php" method="post">
24       <p>Email Address: <input type="text"
         name="email" size="20" maxlength="80" />
         </p>
25       <p>Password: <input type="password"
         name="pass" size="20" maxlength="20"
         /></p>
26       <p><input type="submit" name="submit"
         value="Login" /></p>
```

(script continues on next page)

Script 11.1 *continued*

```
000                    Script
27    <input type="hidden" name="submitted"
      value="TRUE" />

28    </form>

29

30    <?php // Include the footer:

31    include ('includes/footer.html');

32    ?>
```

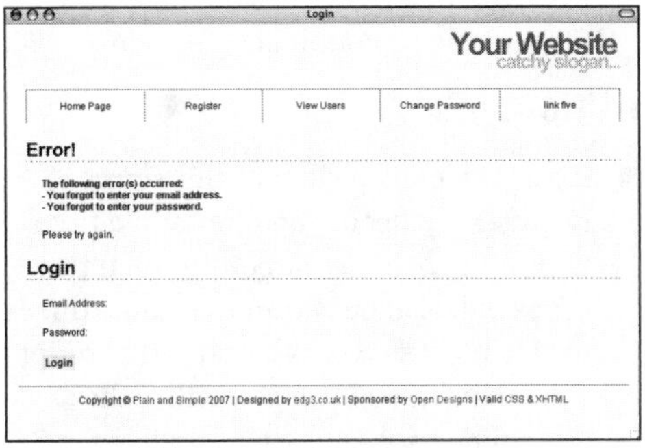

Figure 11.2 The login form and page, with error reporting.

To make a login page:

1. Create a new PHP page in your text editor or IDE (**Script 11.1**).

   ```
   <?php # Script 11.1 - login_
   → page.inc.php
   ```

2. Include the header.

   ```
   $page_title = 'Login';

   include ('includes/header.html');
   ```

   This chapter will make use of the same template system first created in Chapter 3, "Creating Dynamic Web Sites," then modified in Chapter 8, "Using PHP with MySQL."

3. Print any error messages, if they exist.

   ```
   if (!empty($errors)) {

       echo '<h1>Error!</h1>

       <p class="error">The following
       → error(s) occurred:<br />';

       foreach ($errors as $msg) {

           echo " - $msg<br />\n";

       }

       echo '</p><p>Please try again.
       → </p>';

   }
   ```

   This code was also developed back in Chapter 8. If any errors exist (in the $errors array variable), they'll be printed as an unordered list (**Figure 11.2**).

   continues on next page

4. Display the form.

```
?>

<h1>Login</h1>

<form action="login.php" method=
→ "post">

    <p>Email Address: <input type=
    → "text" name="email" size="20"
    → maxlength="80" /> </p>

    <p>Password: <input type=
    → "password" name="pass" size=
    → "20" maxlength="20" /></p>

    <p><input type="submit" name=
    → "submit" value="Login" /></p>

    <input type="hidden" name=
    → "submitted" value="TRUE" />

</form>
```

The HTML form only needs two text inputs: one for an email address and a second for the password. The names of the inputs match those in the *users* table of the *sitename* database (which this login system is based upon).

To make it easier to create the HTML form, the PHP section is closed first. The form is not sticky, but you could easily add code to accomplish that (but only for the email address, as passwords can't be sticky).

5. Complete the page.

```
<?php

include ('includes/footer.html');

?>
```

6. Save the file as login_page.inc.php and place it in your Web directory (in the *includes* folder, along with the files from Chapter 8: header.html, footer.html, and style.css).

The page will use a .inc.php extension to indicate both that it's an includable file and that it contains PHP code.

✔ Tip

- It may seem illogical that this script includes the header and footer file from within the *includes* directory when this script will also be within that same directory. This code works because this script will be included by pages within the main directory; thus the include references are with respect to the parent file, not this one.

Making the Login Functions

Along with the login page that was stored in `login_page.inc.php`, there's a little bit of functionality that will be common to several scripts in this chapter. In this next script, also to be included by other pages in the login/logout system, two functions will be defined.

Many pages will end up redirecting the user from one page to another. For example, upon successfully logging in, the user will be taken to `loggedin.php`. If a user accesses `loggedin.php` and they aren't logged in, they should be taken to `index.php`. Redirection uses the `header()` function, introduced in Chapter 10, "Web Application Development." The syntax for redirection is

```
header ('Location: http://www.example.
→ com/page.php');
```

Script 11.2 The `login_functions.inc.php` script defines two functions that will be used by different scripts in the login/logout process.

```
●●●                    📄 Script
1   <?php # Script 11.2 - login_functions.
    inc.php
2
3   // This page defines two functions used by
    the login/logout process.
4
5   /* This function determines and returns an
    absolute URL.
6    * It takes one argument: the page that
    concludes the URL.
7    * The argument defaults to index.php.
8   */
9   function absolute_url ($page = 'index.
    php') {
10
11    // Start defining the URL...
12    // URL is http:// plus the host name
    plus the current directory:
```

(script continues on next page)

Because this function will send the browser to `page.php`, the current script should be terminated using `exit()` immediately after this:

```
header ('Location: http://www.example.
→ com/page.php');
```

```
exit();
```

If you don't do this, the current script will continue to run (just not in the Web browser).

The location value in the `header()` call should be an absolute URL (`www.example.com/page.php` instead of just `page.php`). You can hard-code this value or, better yet, dynamically determine it. The first function in this next script will do just that.

The other bit of code that will be used by multiple scripts in this chapter validates the login form. This is a three-step process:

1. Confirm that an email address was provided.

2. Confirm that a password was provided.

3. Confirm that the provided email address and password match those stored in the database (during the registration process).

So this next script will define two different functions. The details of how each function works will be explained in the steps that follow.

To create the login functions:

1. Create a new PHP document in your text editor or IDE (**Script 11.2**).

   ```
   <?php # Script 11.2 - login_
   → functions.inc.php
   ```

   As this file will be included by other files, it does not need to contain any HTML.

continues on page 333

Script 11.2 *continued*

```
                        Script
13    $url = 'http://' . $_SERVER['HTTP_HOST']
      . dirname($_SERVER['PHP_SELF']);

14

15    // Remove any trailing slashes:

16    $url = rtrim($url, '/\\');

17

18    // Add the page:

19    $url .= '/' . $page;

20

21    // Return the URL:

22    return $url;

23

24    } // End of absolute_url() function.

25

26

27    /* This function validates the form data
      (the email address and password).

28    * If both are present, the database is
      queried.

29    * The function requires a database
      connection.

30    * The function returns an array of
      information, including:

31    * - a TRUE/FALSE variable indicating
      success

32    * - an array of either errors or the
      database result

33    */

34    function check_login($dbc, $email = '',
      $pass = '') {

35

36    $errors = array(); // Initialize error
      array.

37

38    // Validate the email address:

39    if (empty($email)) {

40    $errors[] = 'You forgot to enter your
      email address.';

41    } else {
```

(script continues)

Script 11.2 *continued*

```
                        Script
42    $e = mysqli_real_escape_string($dbc,
      trim($email));

43    }

44

45    // Validate the password:

46    if (empty($pass)) {

47    $errors[] = 'You forgot to enter your
      password.';

48    } else {

49    $p = mysqli_real_escape_string($dbc,
      trim($pass));

50    }

51

52    if (empty($errors)) { // If everything's
      OK.

53

54    // Retrieve the user_id and first_name
      for that email/password combination:

55    $q = "SELECT user_id, first_name FROM
      users WHERE email='$e' AND
      pass=SHA1('$p')";

56    $r = @mysqli_query ($dbc, $q); // Run
      the query.

57

58    // Check the result:

59    if (mysqli_num_rows($r) == 1) {

60

61    // Fetch the record:

62    $row = mysqli_fetch_array ($r,
      MYSQLI_ASSOC);

63

64    // Return true and the record:

65    return array(true, $row);

66

67    } else { // Not a match!

68    $errors[] = 'The email address and
      password entered do not match those on
      file.';

69    }
```

(script continues on next page)

2. Begin defining a new function.

```
function absolute_url ($page =
→ 'index.php') {
```

The `absolute_url()` function will return an absolute URL that's correct for the site running these scripts. The benefit of doing this dynamically (as opposed to just hard-coding `http://www.example.com/page.php`) is that you can develop your code on one server (like your own computer) and then move it to another server without ever needing to change this code.

The function takes one optional argument: the final destination page name. The default value is *index.php*.

3. Start defining the URL.

```
$url = 'http://' . $_SERVER
→ ['HTTP_HOST'] . dirname($_
→ SERVER['PHP_SELF']);
```

To start, `$url` is assigned the value of *http://* plus the host name (which could be either *localhost* or *www.example.com*). To this is added the name of the current directory using the `dirname()` function, in case the redirection is taking place within

a subfolder. `$_SERVER['PHP_SELF']` refers to the current script (which will be the one calling this function), including the directory name. That whole value might be */somedir/page.php*. The `dirname()` function will return just the directory part from that value (i.e., */somedir/*).

4. Remove any ending slashes from the URL.

```
$url = rtrim($url, '/\\');
```

Because the existence of a subfolder might add an extra slash (/) or backslash (\, for Windows), the function needs to remove that. To do so, use the `rtrim()` function. By default, this function removes spaces from the right side of a string. If provided with a list of characters to remove as the second argument, it'll chop those off instead. With this line of code, the characters to be removed should be either / or \. But since the backslash is the escape character in PHP, you need to use \\ to refer to a single backslash. So, in short, if `$url` concludes with either of these characters, the `rtrim()` function will remove them.

5. Add the specific page to the URL and complete the function.

```
$url .= '/' . $page;

return $url;
```

```
} // End of absolute_url() function.
```

Finally, the specific page name is appended to the `$url`. It's preceded by a slash because any trailing slashes were removed in Step 4 and you can't have `www.example.compage.php` as the URL. The URL is then returned.

This may all seem to be quite complicated, but it's a very effective way to ensure that the redirection works no matter on what server, or from what directory, the

Script 11.2 *continued*

```
70
71    } // End of empty($errors) IF.
72
73    // Return false and the errors:
74    return array(false, $errors);
75
76  } // End of check_login() function.
77
78  ?>
```

continues on next page

script is being run (as long as the redirection is taking place within that directory).

6. Begin a new function.

```
function check_login($dbc, $email =
→ '', $pass = '') {
```

This function will validate the login information. It takes three arguments: the database connection, which is required; the email address, which is optional; and the password, which is also optional.

Although this function could access `$_POST['email']` and `$_POST['pass']` directly, it's better if the function is passed these values, making the function more independent.

7. Validate the email address and password.

```
$errors = array();
if (empty($email)) {
    $errors[] = 'You forgot to enter
    → your email address.';
} else {
    $e = mysqli_real_escape_string
    → ($dbc, trim($email));
}
if (empty($pass)) {
    $errors[] = 'You forgot to enter
    → your password.';
} else {
    $p = mysqli_real_escape_
    → string($dbc, trim($pass));
}
```

This validation routine is similar to that used in the registration page. If any problems occur, they'll be added to the `$errors` array, which will eventually be used on the login page (see Figure 11.2).

8. If no errors occurred, run the database query.

```
if (empty($errors)) {
    $q = "SELECT user_id, first_name
    → FROM users WHERE email='$e'
    → AND pass=SHA1('$p')";
    $r = @mysqli_query ($dbc, $q);
```

The query selects the *user_id* and *first_name* values from the database where the submitted email address (from the form) matches the stored email address and the SHA1() version of the submitted password matches the stored password (**Figure 11.3**).

9. Check the results of the query.

```
if (mysqli_num_rows($r) == 1) {
    $row = mysqli_fetch_array ($r,
    → MYSQLI_ASSOC);
    return array(true, $row);
} else {
    $errors[] = 'The email address
    → and password entered do not
    → match those on file.';
}
```

If the query returned one row, then the login information was correct. The results are then fetched into $row. The final step in a successful login is to return two pieces of information back to the requesting script: the value true, indicating that the login was a success; and the data fetched from MySQL. Using the array() function, both the Boolean value and the $row array can be returned by this function.

If the query did not return one row, then an error message is added to the array. It will end up being displayed on the login page (**Figure 11.4**).

10. Complete the conditional begun in Step 8 and complete the function.

```
    } // End of empty($errors) IF.

    return array(false, $errors);

} // End of check_login() function.
```

The final step is for the function to return a value of `false`, indicating that login failed, and to return the `$errors` array, which stores the reason(s) for failure. This `return` statement can be placed here—at the end of the function instead of within a conditional—because the function will only get to this point if the login failed. If the login succeeded, the `return` line in Step 9 will stop the function from continuing (a function stops as soon as it executes a `return`).

11. Complete the page.

```
?>
```

12. Save the file as `login_functions.inc.php` and place it in your Web directory (in the *includes* folder, along with `header.html`, `footer.html`, and `style.css`).

This page will also use a `.inc.php` extension to indicate both that it's an includable file and that it contains PHP code.

✔ Tips

- The scripts in this chapter include no debugging code (like the MySQL error or query). If you have problems with these scripts, apply the debugging techniques outlined in Chapter 7, "Error Handling and Debugging."

- You can add *name=value* pairs to the URL in a `header()` call to pass values to the target page:

  ```
  $url .= '?name=' . urlencode(value);
  ```

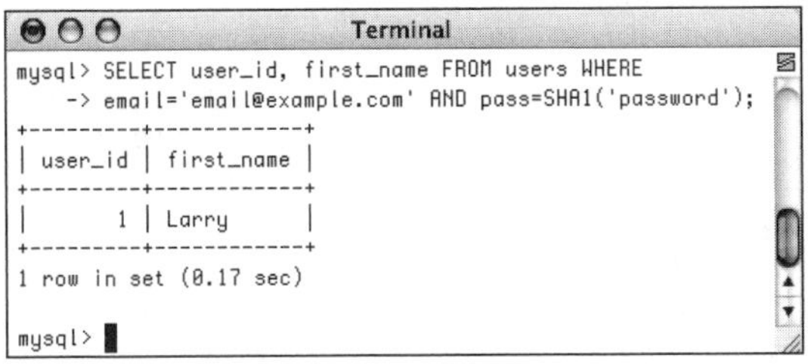

Figure 11.3 The results of the login query if the user submitted the proper email address/password combination.

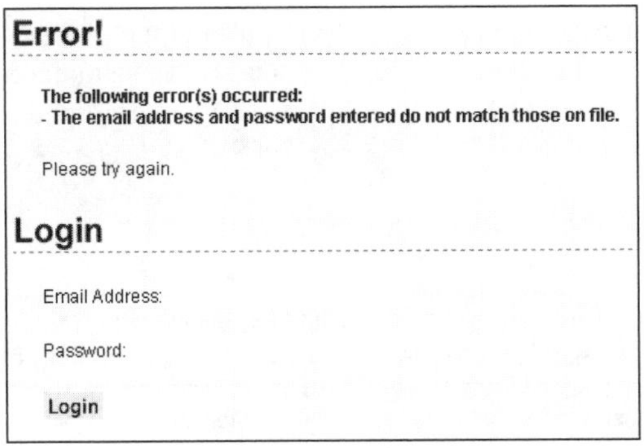

Figure 11.4 If the user entered an email address and password, but they don't match the values stored in the database, this is the result.

Using Cookies

Cookies are a way for a server to store information on the user's machine. This is one way that a site can remember or track a user over the course of a visit. Think of a cookie as being like a name tag: you tell the server your name and it gives you a sticker to wear. Then it can know who you are by referring back to that name tag.

Some people are suspicious of cookies because they believe that cookies allow a server to know too much about them. However, a cookie can only be used to store information that the server is given, so it's no less secure than most anything else online (that saying what it does). Unfortunately, many people still have misconceptions about the technology, which is a problem, as those misconceptions can undermine the functionality of your Web application.

In this section you will learn how to set a cookie, retrieve information from a stored cookie, alter a cookie's settings, and then delete a cookie.

Setting cookies

The most important thing to understand about cookies is that they must be sent from the server to the client prior to *any other information*. Should the server attempt to send a cookie after the Web browser has already received HTML—even an extraneous white space—an error message will result and the cookie will not be sent (**Figure 11.5**). This is by far the most common cookie-related error but is easily fixed.

Testing for Cookies

To effectively program using cookies, you need to be able to accurately test for their presence. The best way to do so is to have your Web browser ask what to do when receiving a cookie. In such a case, the browser will prompt you with the cookie information each time PHP attempts to send a cookie.

Different versions of different browsers on different platforms all define their cookie handling policies in different places. I'll quickly run through a couple of options for popular Web browsers.

To set this up using Internet Explorer on Windows XP, choose Tools > Internet Options. Then click the Privacy tab, followed by the Advanced button under Settings. Click "Override automatic cookie handling" and then choose "Prompt" for both First- and Third-party Cookies.

Using Firefox on Windows, choose Tools > Options > Privacy. In the Cookies section, select "ask me every time" in the "Keep until" drop-down menu. If you are using Firefox on Mac OS X, the steps are the same, but you start by choosing Firefox > Preferences.

Unfortunately, Safari on Mac OS X does not have a cookie prompting option, but it will allow you to view existing cookies, which is still a useful debugging tool. This option can be found under the Security pane of Safari's Preferences panel.

Warning: Cannot modify header information - headers already sent by (output started at /Applications/Abyss Web Server/htdocs/includes/header.html:4) in **/Applications/Abyss Web Server/htdocs/header.php** on line **8**

Figure 11.5 The *headers already sent...* error message is all too common when creating cookies. Pay attention to what the error message says in order to find and fix the problem.

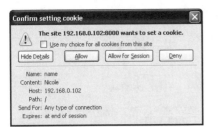

Figure 11.6 If the browser is set to ask for permission when receiving cookies, you'll see a message like this when a site attempts to send one (this is Firefox's version of the prompt).

Script 11.3 The login.php script creates two cookies upon a successful login.

```
1    <?php # Script 11.3 - login.php
2
3    // This page processes the login form
     submission.
4    // Upon successful login, the user is
     redirected.
5    // Two included files are necessary.
6    // Send NOTHING to the Web browser prior
     to the setcookie() lines!
7
8    // Check if the form has been submitted:
9    if (isset($_POST['submitted'])) {
10
11       // For processing the login:
12       require_once ('includes/login_functions.
         inc.php');
13
14       // Need the database connection:
15       require_once ('../mysqli_connect.php');
16
17       // Check the login:
18       list ($check, $data) = check_login($dbc,
         $_POST['email'], $_POST['pass']);
19
```
(script continues on next page)

Cookies are sent via the `setcookie()` function:

```
setcookie (name, value);

setcookie ('name', 'Nicole');
```

The second line of code will send a cookie to the browser with a name of *name* and a value of *Nicole* (**Figure 11.6**).

You can continue to send more cookies to the browser with subsequent uses of the `setcookie()` function:

```
setcookie ('ID', 263);

setcookie ('email', 'email@example.
→ com');
```

As when using any variable in PHP, when naming your cookies, do not use white spaces or punctuation, but do pay attention to the exact case used.

To send a cookie:

1. Create a new PHP document in your text editor (**Script 11.3**).

```
<?php # Script 11.3 - login.php
```

For this example, let's make a `login.php` script that works in conjunction with the scripts from Chapter 8. This script will also require the two files created at the beginning of the chapter.

2. Validate the form.

```
if (isset($_POST['submitted'])) {
    require_once ('includes/login_
    → functions.inc.php');
    require_once ('../mysqli_
    → connect.php');
    list ($check, $data) = check_
    → login($dbc, $_POST['email'],
    → $_POST['pass']);
```

continues on next page

USING COOKIES

This script will do two things: handle the form submission and display the form. This conditional checks for the submission.

Within the conditional, the script must include both `login_functions.inc.php` and `mysqli_connect.php` (which was created in Chapter 8 and should still be in the same location relative to this script).

After including both files, the `check_login()` function can be called. It's passed the database connection (which comes from `mysqli_connect.php`), along with the email address and the password (both of which come from the form).

This function returns an array of two elements: the Boolean value and another array (of user data or errors). To assign those returned values to variables, use the `list()` function. The first value returned by the function (the Boolean) will be assigned to `$check`. The second value returned (either the `$row` or `$errors` array) will be assigned to `$data`.

3. If the user entered the correct information, log them in.

```
if ($check) {
    setcookie ('user_id', $data
    → ['user_id']);
    setcookie ('first_name', $data
    → ['first_name']);
```

The `$check` variable indicates the success of the login attempt. If it's `true`, then `$data` contains the user's ID and first name. These two values can be used in cookies.

Script 11.3 *continued*

```
20    if ($check) { // OK!

21

22        // Set the cookies:
23        setcookie ('user_id', $data
          ['user_id']);
24        setcookie ('first_name', $data
          ['first_name']);

25

26        // Redirect:
27        $url = absolute_url ('loggedin.php');
28        header("Location: $url");
29        exit(); // Quit the script.

30

31    } else { // Unsuccessful!

32

33        // Assign $data to $errors for error
          reporting
34        // in the login_page.inc.php file.
35        $errors = $data;

36

37    }

38

39    mysqli_close($dbc); // Close the database
       connection.

40

41  } // End of the main submit conditional.

42

43  // Create the page:

44  include ('includes/login_page.inc.php');

45  ?>
```

4. Redirect the user to another page.

```
$url = absolute_url ('loggedin.php');
header("Location: $url");
exit();
```

Using the steps outlined earlier in the chapter, the redirection URL is first dynamically generated and returned by the `absolute_url()` function. The specific page to be redirected to is `loggedin.php`. The absolute URL is then used in the `header()` function and the script's execution is terminated with `exit()`.

5. Complete the `$check` conditional (started in Step 3) and then close the database connection.

```
} else {
    $errors = $data;
}
mysqli_close($dbc);
```

If `$check` has a false value, then the `$data` variable is storing the errors generated within the `check_login()` function. If so, they should be assigned to the `$errors` variable, because that's what the code in the script that displays the login page—`login_page.inc.php`—is expecting.

6. Complete the main submit conditional and include the login page.

```
}
include
('includes/login_page.inc.php');
?>
```

This `login.php` script primarily validates the login form by calling the `check_login()` function. The `login_page.inc.php` file contains the login page itself, so it just needs to be included.

7. Save the file as `login.php`, place it in your Web directory (in the same folder as the files from Chapter 8), and load this page in your Web browser (see Figure 11.2).

✔ Tips

■ Cookies are limited to about 4 KB of total data, and each Web browser can remember a limited number of cookies from any one site. This limit is 50 cookies for most of the current Web browsers (but if you're sending out 50 different cookies, you may want to rethink how you do things).

■ The `setcookie()` function is one of the few functions in PHP that could have different results in different browsers, since each browser treats cookies in its own way. Be sure to test your Web sites in multiple browsers on different platforms to ensure consistency.

■ If the first two included files sends anything to the Web browser or even has blank lines or spaces after the closing PHP tag, you'll see a *headers already sent* error. If you see such an error, go to the document and line number referenced in the error (after *output started at*) and fix the problem.

Accessing cookies

To retrieve a value from a cookie, you only need to refer to the $_COOKIE superglobal, using the appropriate cookie name as the key (as you would with any array). For example, to retrieve the value of the cookie established with the line

```
setcookie ('username', 'Trout');
```

you would refer to $_COOKIE['username'].

In the following example, the cookies set by the login.php script will be accessed in two ways. First a check will be made that the user is logged in (otherwise, they shouldn't be accessing this page). Second, the user will be greeted by their first name, which was stored in a cookie.

To access a cookie:

1. Create a new PHP document in your text editor (**Script 11.4**).

   ```
   <?php # Script 11.4 - loggedin.php
   ```

   The user will be redirected to this page after successfully logging in. It will print a user-specific greeting.

2. Check for the presence of a cookie.

   ```
   if (!isset($_COOKIE['user_id'])) {
   ```

   Since a user shouldn't be able to access this page unless they are logged in, check for the cookie that should have been set (in login.php).

3. Redirect the user if they are not logged in.

   ```
   require_once ('includes/login_
   → functions.inc.php');
   $url = absolute_url();
   header("Location: $url");
   exit();
   }
   ```

Script 11.4 The loggedin.php script prints a greeting to a user based upon a stored cookie.

```
1    <?php # Script 11.4 - loggedin.php
2
3    // The user is redirected here from
     login.php.
4
5    // If no cookie is present, redirect the
     user:
6    if (!isset($_COOKIE['user_id'])) {
7
8        // Need the functions to create an
         absolute URL:
9        require_once ('includes/login_
         functions.inc.php');
10       $url = absolute_url();
11       header("Location: $url");
12       exit(); // Quit the script.
13
14   }
15
16   // Set the page title and include the
     HTML header:
17   $page_title = 'Logged In!';
18   include ('includes/header.html');
19
20   // Print a customized message:
21   echo "<h1>Logged In!</h1>
22   <p>You are now logged in, {$_COOKIE
     ['first_name']}!</p>
23   <p><a href=\"logout.php\">Logout</a></p>";
24
25   include ('includes/footer.html');
26   ?>
```

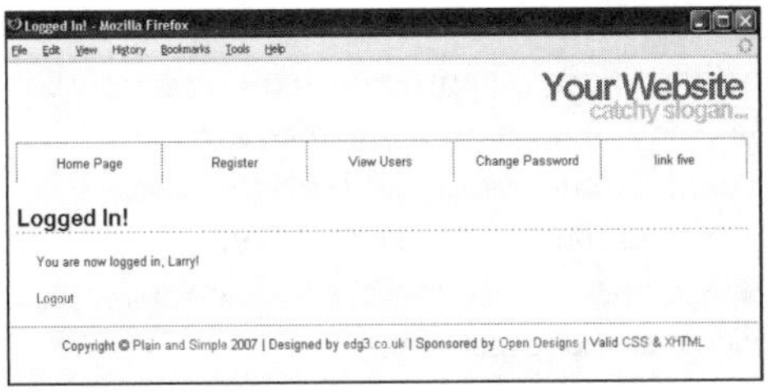

Figure 11.7 If you used the correct email address and password, you'll be redirected here after logging in.

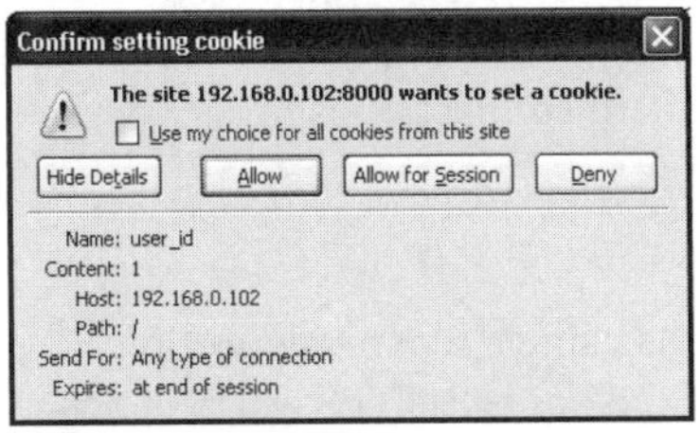

Figure 11.8 The user_id cookie with a value of *1*.

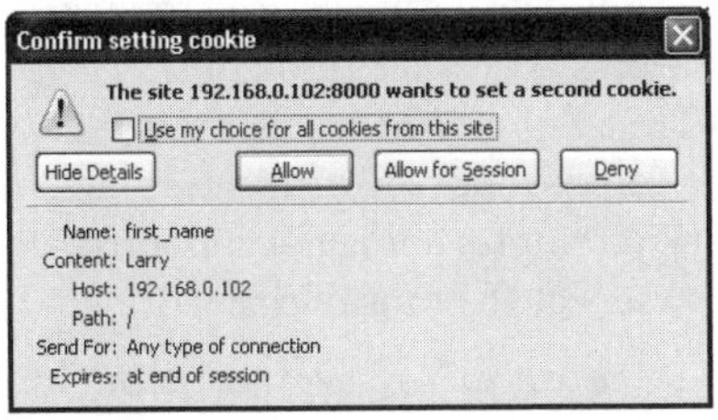

Figure 11.9 The first_name cookie with a value of *Larry* (yours might be different).

✔ Tips

- A cookie is not accessible until the setting page (e.g., login.php) has been reloaded or another page has been accessed (in other words, you cannot set and access a cookie in the same page).

- If users decline a cookie or have their Web browser set not to accept them, they will automatically be redirected to the home page in this example, even if they successfully logged in. For this reason you may want to let the user know that cookies are required.

If the user is not logged in, they will be automatically redirected to the main page. This is a simple way to limit access to content.

4. Include the page header.

```
$page_title = 'Logged In!';

include ('includes/header.html');
```

5. Welcome the user, using the cookie.

```
echo "<h1>Logged In!</h1>

<p>You are now logged in, {$_COOKIE
→ ['first_name']}!</p>

<p><a href=\"logout.php\">
→ Logout</a></p>";
```

To greet the user by name, refer to the $_COOKIE['first_name'] variable (enclosed within curly braces to avoid parse errors). A link to the logout page (to be written later in the chapter) is also printed.

6. Complete the HTML page.

```
include ('includes/footer.html');

?>
```

7. Save the file as loggedin.php, place it in your Web directory (in the same folder as login.php), and test it in your Web browser by logging in through login.php (**Figure 11.7**).

Since these examples use the same database as those in Chapter 8, you should be able to log in using the registered username and password submitted at that time.

8. To see the cookies being set (**Figures 11.8** and **11.9**), change the cookie settings for your browser and test again.

Setting cookie parameters

Although passing just the name and value arguments to the setcookie() function will suffice, you ought to be aware of the other arguments available. The function can take up to five more parameters, each of which will alter the definition of the cookie.

```
setcookie (name, value, expiration,
→ path, host, secure, httponly);
```

The expiration argument is used to set a definitive length of time for a cookie to exist, specified in seconds since the *epoch* (the epoch is midnight on January 1, 1970). If it is not set or if it's set to a value of *0*, the cookie will continue to be functional until the user closes their browser. These cookies are said to last for the browser session (also indicated in Figures 11.8 and 11.9).

To set a specific expiration time, add a number of minutes or hours to the current moment, retrieved using the time() function. The following line will set the expiration time of the cookie to be 30 minutes (60 seconds times 30 minutes) from the current moment:

```
setcookie (name, value, time()+1800);
```

The path and host arguments are used to limit a cookie to a specific folder within a Web site (the path) or to a specific host (www.example.com or *192.168.0.1*). For example, you could restrict a cookie to exist only while a user is within the *admin* folder of a domain (and the *admin* folder's subfolders):

```
setcookie (name, value, expire,
→ '/admin/');
```

Setting the path to / will make the cookie visible within an entire domain (Web site). Setting the domain to .example.com will make the cookie visible within an entire domain and every subdomain (www.example.com, admin.example.com, pages.example.com, etc.).

The secure value dictates that a cookie should only be sent over a secure HTTPS connection. A *1* indicates that a secure connection must be used, and a *0* says that a standard connection is fine.

```
setcookie (name, value, expire, path,
→ host, 1);
```

If your site is using a secure connection, restricting cookies to HTTPS will be much more secure than not doing so.

Finally, added in PHP 5.2 is the *httponly* argument. A Boolean value is used to make the cookie only accessible through HTTP (and HTTPS). Enforcing this restriction will make the cookie more secure (preventing some hack attempts) but is not supported by all browsers at the time of this writing.

```
setcookie (name, value, expire, path,
→ host, secure, TRUE);
```

As with all functions that take arguments, you must pass the setcookie() values in order. To skip any parameter, use NULL, 0, or an empty string (don't use FALSE). The expiration and secure values are both integers and are therefore not quoted.

To demonstrate this information, let's add an expiration setting to the login cookies so that they last for only one hour.

Script 11.5 The login.php script now uses every argument the setcookie() function can take.

```
1    <?php # Script 11.5 - login.php #2

2

3    if (isset($_POST['submitted'])) {

4

5        require_once ('includes/login_
         functions.inc.php');

6        require_once ('../mysqli_connect.php');

7        list ($check, $data) = check_login($dbc,
         $_POST['email'], $_POST['pass']);

8

9        if ($check) { // OK!

10

11           // Set the cookies:

12           setcookie ('user_id', $data['user_id'],
             time()+3600, '/', '', 0, 0);

13           setcookie ('first_name', $data['first_
             name'], time()+3600, '/', '', 0, 0);

14

15           // Redirect:

16           $url = absolute_url ('loggedin.php');

17           header("Location: $url");

18           exit();

19

20       } else { // Unsuccessful!

21           $errors = $data;

22       }

23

24       mysqli_close($dbc);

25

26   } // End of the main submit conditional.

27

28   include ('includes/login_page.inc.php');

29   ?>
```

To set a cookie's parameters:

1. Open login.php in your text editor (refer to Script 11.3).

2. Change the two setcookie() lines to include an expiration date that's 60 minutes away (**Script 11.5**):

   ```
   setcookie ('user_id', $data['user_
   → id'], time()+3600, '/', '', 0, 0);
   ```

   ```
   setcookie ('first_name', $data
   → ['first_name'], time()+3600, '/',
   → '', 0, 0);
   ```

   With the expiration date set to time() + 3600 (60 minutes times 60 seconds), the cookie will continue to exist for an hour after it is set. While making this change, every other parameter is explicitly addressed.

   For the final parameter, which accepts a Boolean value, you can also use *0* to represent false (PHP will handle the conversion for you). Doing so is a good idea, as using false in any of the cookie arguments can cause problems.

continues on next page

3. Save the script, place it in your Web directory, and test it in your Web browser by logging in (**Figure 11.10**).

✔ Tips

■ Some browsers have difficulties with cookies that do not list every argument. Explicitly stating every parameter—even as an empty string—will achieve more reliable results across all browsers.

■ Here are some general guidelines for cookie expirations: If the cookie should last as long as the session, do not set an expiration time; if the cookie should continue to exist after the user has closed and reopened his or her browser, set an expiration time weeks or months ahead; and if the cookie can constitute a security risk, set an expiration time of an hour or fraction thereof so that the cookie does not continue to exist too long after a user has left his or her browser.

■ For security purposes, you could set a five- or ten-minute expiration time on a cookie and have the cookie resent with every new page the user visits (assuming that the cookie exists). This way, the cookie will continue to persist as long as the user is active but will automatically die five or ten minutes after the user's last action.

■ E-commerce and other privacy-related Web applications should use an SSL (Secure Sockets Layer) connection for all transactions, including the cookie.

■ Be careful with cookies created by scripts within a directory. If the path isn't specified, then that cookie will only be available to other scripts within that same directory.

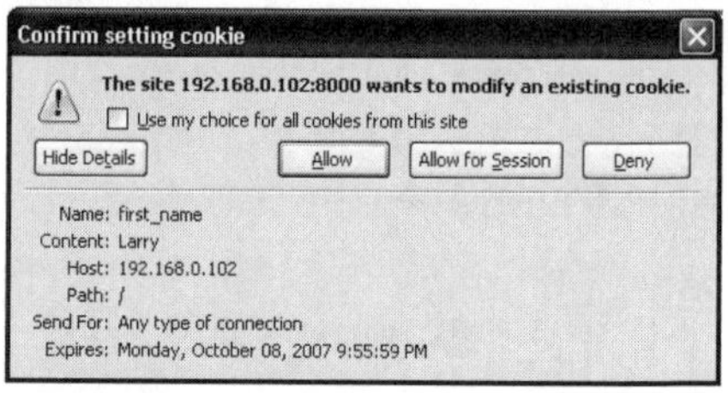

Figure 11.10 Changes to the setcookie() parameters, like an expiration date and time, will be reflected in the cookie sent to the Web browser (compare with Figure 11.9).

Using Cookies

Script 11.6 The `logout.php` script deletes the previously established cookies.

```
1   <?php # Script 11.6 - logout.php
2
3   // This page lets the user logout.
4
5   // If no cookie is present, redirect the
    user:
6   if (!isset($_COOKIE['user_id'])) {
7
8       // Need the functions to create an
        absolute URL:
9       require_once ('includes/login_
        functions.inc.php');
10      $url = absolute_url();
11      header("Location: $url");
12      exit(); // Quit the script.
13
14  } else { // Delete the cookies.
15      setcookie ('user_id', '', time()-3600,
        '/', '', 0, 0);
16      setcookie ('first_name', '', time()-
        3600, '/', '', 0, 0);
17  }
18
19  // Set the page title and include the HTML
    header:
20  $page_title = 'Logged Out!';
21  include ('includes/header.html');
22
23  // Print a customized message:
24  echo "<h1>Logged Out!</h1>
25  <p>You are now logged out,
    {$_COOKIE['first_name']}!</p>";
26
27  include ('includes/footer.html');
28  ?>
```

Deleting cookies

The final thing to understand about using cookies is how to delete one. While a cookie will automatically expire when the user's browser is closed or when the expiration date/time is met, sometimes you'll want to manually delete the cookie instead. For example, in Web sites that have login capabilities, you will want to delete any cookies when the user logs out.

Although the `setcookie()` function can take up to seven arguments, only one is actually required—the cookie name. If you send a cookie that consists of a name without a value, it will have the same effect as deleting the existing cookie of the same name. For example, to create the cookie *first_name*, you use this line:

```
setcookie('first_name', 'Tyler');
```

To delete the *first_name* cookie, you would code:

```
setcookie('first_name');
```

As an added precaution, you can also set an expiration date that's in the past.

```
setcookie('first_name', '', time
→ ()-3600);
```

To demonstrate all of this, let's add a logout capability to the site. The link to the logout page appears on `loggedin.php`. As an added feature, the header file will be altered so that a *Logout* link appears when the user is logged in and a *Login* link appears when the user is logged out.

To delete a cookie:

1. Create a new PHP document in your text editor or IDE (**Script 11.6**).

```
<?php # Script 11.6 - logout.php
```

continues on next page

2. Check for the existence of a *user_id* cookie; if it is not present, redirect the user.

```
if (!isset($_COOKIE['user_id'])) {
    require_once ('includes/login_
    → functions.inc.php');
    $url = absolute_url();
    header("Location: $url");
    exit();
```

As with loggedin.php, if the user is not already logged in, this page should redirect the user to the home page. There's no point in trying to log out a user that isn't logged in!

3. Delete the cookies, if they exist.

```
} else {
    setcookie ('first_name', '',
    → time()-3600, '/', '', 0, 0);
    setcookie ('user_id', '',
→ time()-3600, '/', '', 0, 0);
}
```

If the user is logged in, these two cookies will effectively delete the existing ones. Except for the value and the expiration, the other arguments should have the same values as they do when the cookies were created.

4. Make the remainder of the PHP page.

```
$page_title = 'Logged Out!';
include ('includes/header.html');
echo "<h1>Logged Out!</h1>
<p>You are now logged out, {$_
→ COOKIE['first_name']}!</p>";
include ('includes/footer.html');
?>
```

The page itself is also much like the loggedin.php page. Although it may seem odd that you can still refer to the *first_name* cookie (that you just deleted in this script), it makes perfect sense considering the process:

A) This page is requested by the client.

B) The server reads the available cookies from the client's browser.

C) The page is run and does its thing (including sending new cookies that delete the existing ones).

So, in short, the original *first_name* cookie data is available to this script when it first runs. The set of cookies sent by this page (the delete cookies) aren't available to this page, so the original values are still usable.

5. Save the file as logout.php and place it in your Web directory (in the same folder as login.php).

Script 11.7 The header.html file now displays either a login or a logout link, depending upon the user's current status.

```
○ ○ ○                    Script
1    <!DOCTYPE html PUBLIC "-//W3C//DTD XHTML
     1.0 Strict//EN" "http://www.w3.org/TR/
     xhtml1/DTD/xhtml1-strict.dtd">

2    <html xmlns="http://www.w3.org/
     1999/xhtml">

3    <head">

4      <title><?php echo $page_title;
       ?></title>

5      <link rel="stylesheet" href="includes/
       style.css" type="text/css" media=
       "screen" />

6      <meta http-equiv="content-type"
       content="text/html; charset=utf-8" />

7    </head>

8    <body>

9      <div id="header">

10       <h1>Your Website</h1>

11       <h2>catchy slogan...</h2>

12     </div>

13     <div id="navigation">

14     <ul>

15       <li><a href="index.php">Home
         Page</a></li>

16       <li><a href="register.php">
         Register</a></li>

17       <li><a href="view_users.php">View
         Users</a></li>

18       <li><a href="password.php">Change
         Password</a></li>

19       <li><?php // Create a login/logout
         link:

20       if ( (isset($_COOKIE['user_id'])) &&
         (!strpos($_SERVER['PHP_SELF'],
         'logout.php')) ) {

21         echo '<a href="logout.php">Logout</a>';

22       } else {

23         echo '<a href="login.php">Login</a>';
```

(script continues)

To create the logout link:

1. Open header.html (refer to Script 8.1) in your text editor or IDE.

2. Change the fifth and final link to (**Script 11.7**)

   ```
   <li><?php

   if ( (isset($_COOKIE['user_id'])) &&
   (!strpos($_SERVER['PHP_SELF'],
   'logout.php')) ) {

       echo '<a
   href="logout.php">Logout</a>';

   } else {

       echo '<a
   href="login.php">Login</a>';

   }

   ?></li>
   ```

   Instead of having a permanent login link in the navigation area, it should display a *Logout* link if the user is logged in or a *Login* link if the user is not. The preceding conditional will accomplish just that, depending upon the presence of a cookie.

continues on next page

Script 11.7 *continued*

```
○ ○ ○                    Script
24   }

25   ?></li>

26     </ul>

27   </div>

28   <div id="content"><!-- Start of the
     page-specific content. -->

29   <!-- Script 11.7 - header.html -->
```

Because the `logout.php` script would ordinarily display a logout link (because the cookie exists when the page is first being viewed), the conditional has to check that the current page is not the `logout.php` script. The `strpos()` function, which checks if one string is found within another string, is an easy way to accomplish this.

3. Save the file, place it in your Web directory (within the *includes* folder), and test the login/logout process in your Web browser (**Figures 11.11**, **11.12**, and **11.13**).

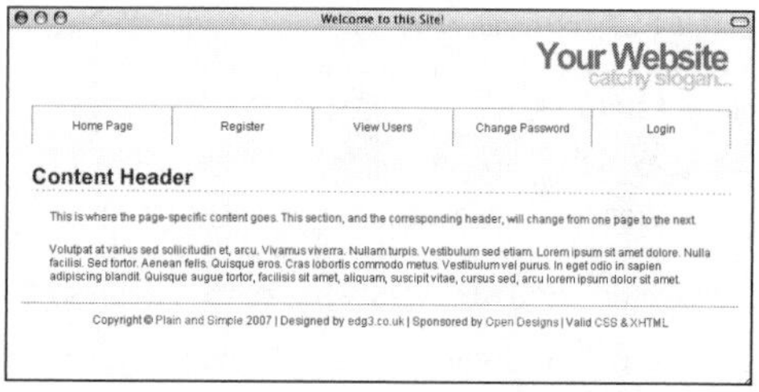

✔ Tips

■ To see the result of the `setcookie()` calls in the `logout.php` script, turn on cookie prompting in your browser (**Figure 11.14**).

■ Due to a bug in how Internet Explorer on Windows handles cookies, you may need to set the *host* parameter to `false` (without quotes) in order to get the logout process to work when developing on your own computer (i.e., through *localhost*).

■ When deleting a cookie, you should always use the same parameters that were used to set the cookie. If you set the host and path in the creation cookie, use them again in the deletion cookie.

■ To hammer the point home, remember that the deletion of a cookie does not take effect until the page has been reloaded or another page has been accessed. In other words, the cookie will still be available to a page after that page has deleted it.

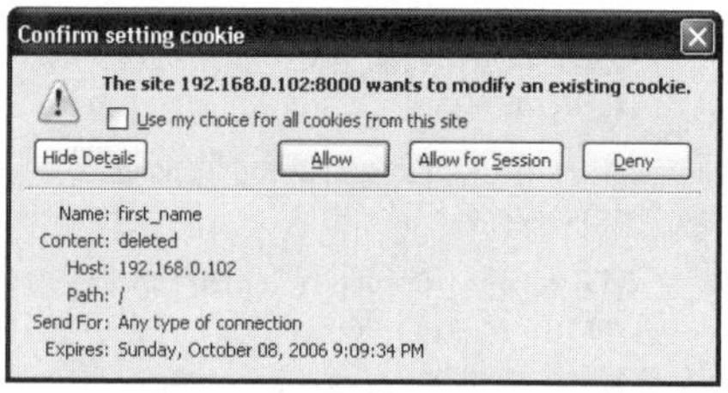

Figure 11.11 The home page with a *Login* link.

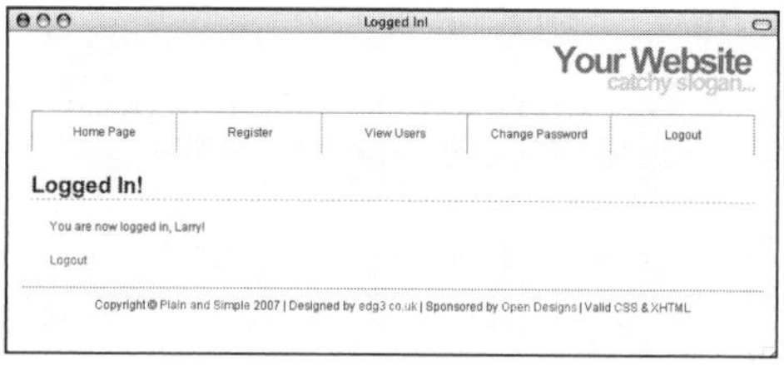

Figure 11.12 After the user logs in, the page now has a *Logout* link.

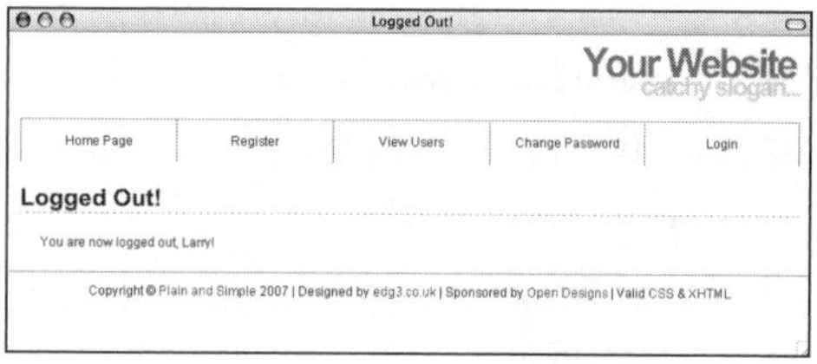

Figure 11.13 The result after logging out.

Figure 11.14 This is how the deletion cookie appears in a Firefox prompt.

Using Sessions

Another method of making data available to multiple pages of a Web site is to use *sessions*. The premise of a session is that data is stored on the server, not in the Web browser, and a session identifier is used to locate a particular user's record (the session data). This session identifier is normally stored in the user's Web browser via a cookie, but the sensitive data itself—like the user's ID, name, and so on—always remains on the server.

The question may arise: why use sessions at all when cookies work just fine? First of all, sessions are likely more secure in that all

---

Sessions vs. Cookies

This chapter has examples accomplishing the same tasks—logging in and logging out—using both cookies and sessions. Obviously, both are easy to use in PHP, but the true question is when to use one or the other.

Sessions have the following advantages over cookies:

◆ They are generally more secure (because the data is being retained on the server).

◆ They allow for more data to be stored.

◆ They can be used without cookies.

Whereas cookies have the following advantages over sessions:

◆ They are easier to program.

◆ They require less of the server.

In general, to store and retrieve just a couple of small pieces of information, use cookies. For most of your Web applications, though, you'll use sessions.

---

of the recorded information is stored on the server and not continually sent back and forth between the server and the client. Second, you can store more data in a session. Third, some users reject cookies or turn them off completely. Sessions, while designed to work with a cookie, can function without them, too.

To demonstrate sessions—and to compare them with cookies—let's rewrite the previous set of scripts.

Setting session variables

The most important rule with respect to sessions is that each page that will use them must begin by calling the `session_start()` function. This function tells PHP to either begin a new session or access an existing one. This function must be called before anything is sent to the Web browser!

The first time this function is used, `session_start()` will attempt to send a cookie with a name of *PHPSESSID* (the session name) and a value of something like *a61f8670baa8e90a30c878df89a2074b* (32 hexadecimal letters, the session ID). Because of this attempt to send a cookie, `session_start()` must be called before any data is sent to the Web browser, as is the case when using the `setcookie()` and `header()` functions.

Once the session has been started, values can be registered to the session using the normal array syntax:

```
$_SESSION['key'] = value;
$_SESSION['name'] = 'Roxanne';
$_SESSION['id'] = 48;
```

Let's update the `login.php` script with this in mind.

continues on next page

continues on next page

To begin a session:

1. Open login.php (refer to Script 11.5) in your text editor or IDE.

2. Replace the setcookie() lines (12–14) with these lines (**Script 11.8**):

   session_start();

   $_SESSION['user_id'] = $data['user_
   → id'];

   $_SESSION['first_name'] = $data
   → ['first_name'];

   The first step is to begin the session. Since there are no echo() statements, inclusions of HTML files, or even blank spaces prior to this point in the script, it will be safe to use session_start() now (although it could be placed at the top of the script as well). Then, two *key-value* pairs are added to the $_SESSION superglobal array to register the user's first name and user ID to the session.

3. Save the page as login.php, place it in your Web directory, and test it in your Web browser (**Figure 11.15**).

   Although loggedin.php and the header and script will need to be rewritten, you can still test the login script and see the resulting cookie (**Figure 11.16**). The loggedin.php page should redirect you back to the home page, though, as it's still checking for the presence of a $_COOKIE variable.

Script 11.8 The login.php script now uses sessions instead of cookies.

```
1    <?php # Script 11.8 - login.php #3
2
3    if (isset($_POST['submitted'])) {
4
5        require_once ('includes/login_
         functions.inc.php');
6        require_once ('../mysqli_connect.php');
7        list ($check, $data) = check_login($dbc,
         $_POST['email'], $_POST['pass']);
8
9        if ($check) { // OK!
10
11           // Set the session data:.
12           session_start();
13           $_SESSION['user_id'] = $data
              ['user_id'];
14           $_SESSION['first_name'] = $data
              ['first_name'];
15
16           // Redirect:
17           $url = absolute_url ('loggedin.php');
18           header("Location: $url");
19           exit();
20
21        } else { // Unsuccessful!
22           $errors = $data;
23        }
24
25        mysqli_close($dbc);
26
27    } // End of the main submit conditional.
28
29    include ('includes/login_page.inc.php');
30    ?>
```

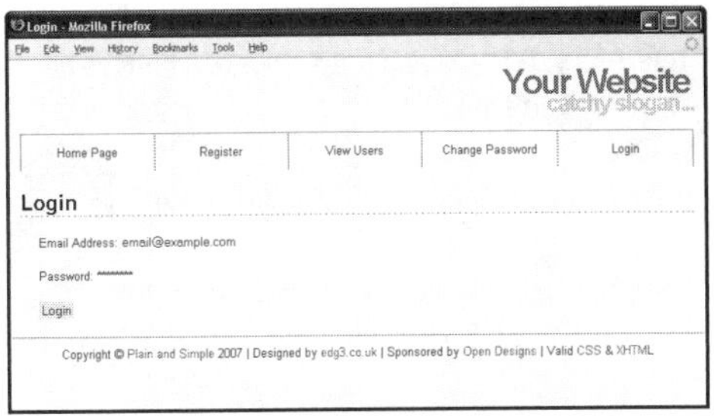

Figure 11.15 The login form remains unchanged to the end user, but the underlying functionality now uses sessions.

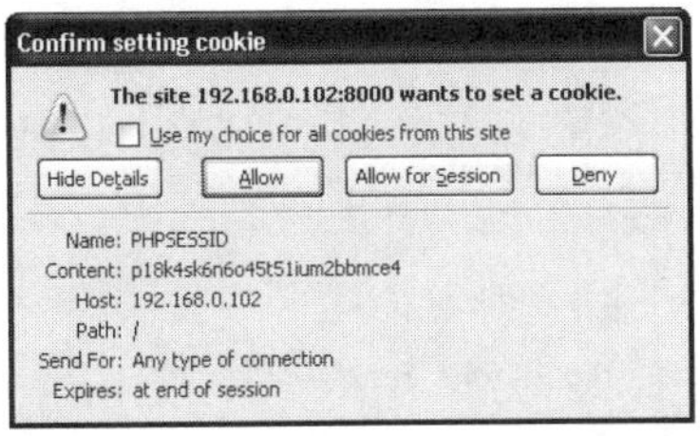

Figure 11.16 This cookie, created by PHP's session_start() function, stores the session ID.

✔ Tips

■ Because sessions will normally send and read cookies, you should always try to begin them as early in the script as possible. Doing so will help you avoid the problem of attempting to send a cookie after the headers (HTML or white space) have already been sent.

■ If you want, you can set *session.auto_start* in the php.ini file to *1*, making it unnecessary to use session_start() on each page. This does put a greater toll on the server and, for that reason, shouldn't be used without some consideration of the circumstances.

■ You can store arrays in sessions (making $_SESSION a multidimensional array), just as you can store strings or numbers.

Accessing session variables

Once a session has been started and variables have been registered to it, you can create other scripts that will access those variables. To do so, each script must first enable sessions, again using session_start().

This function will give the current script access to the previously started session (if it can read the *PHPSESSID* value stored in the cookie) or create a new session if it cannot. Understand that if the current session ID cannot be found and a new session ID is generated, none of the data stored under the old session ID will be available. I mention this here and now because if you're having problems with sessions, checking the session ID value to see if it changes from one page to the next is the first debugging step.

Assuming that there was no problem accessing the current session, to then refer to a session variable, use $_SESSION['var'], as you would refer to any other array.

351

To access session variables:

1. Open loggedin.php (refer to Script 11.4) in your text editor or IDE.

2. Add a call to the session_start() function (**Script 11.9**).

   ```
   session_start();
   ```

   Every PHP script that either sets or accesses session variables must use the session_start() function. This line must be called before the header.html file is included and before anything is sent to the Web browser.

3. Replace the references to $_COOKIE with $_SESSION (lines 6 and 22 of the original file).

   ```
   if (!isset($_SESSION['user_id'])) {
   ```

   and

   ```
   echo "<h1>Logged In!</h1>
   <p>You are now logged in, {$_SESSION
   → ['first_name']}!</p>
   <p><a href=\"logout.php\">Logout
   → </a></p>";
   ```

   Switching a script from cookies to sessions requires only that you change uses of $_COOKIE to $_SESSION (assuming that the same names were used).

4. Save the file as loggedin.php, place it in your Web directory, and test it in your browser (**Figure 11.17**).

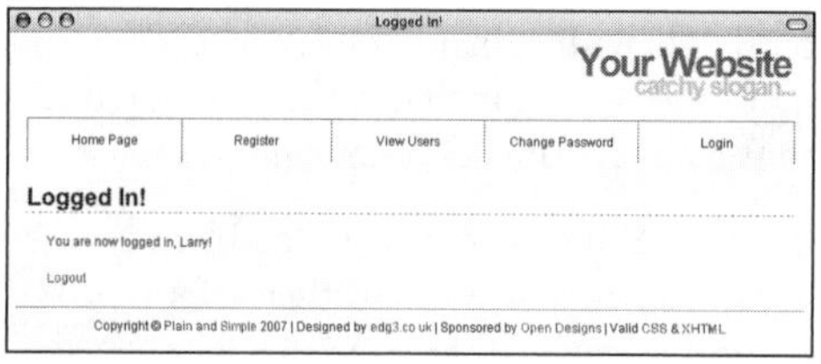

Figure 11.17 After logging in, the user is redirected to loggedin.php, which will welcome the user by name using the stored session value.

Script 11.9 The loggedin.php script is updated so that it refers to $_SESSION and not $_COOKIE (changes are required on two lines).

```
1    <?php # Script 11.9 - loggedin.php #2
2
3    // The user is redirected here from
     login.php.
4
5    session_start(); // Start the session.
6
7    // If no session value is present,
     redirect the user:
8    if (!isset($_SESSION['user_id'])) {
9        require_once ('includes/login_
         functions.inc.php');
10       $url = absolute_url();
11       header("Location: $url");
12       exit();
13   }
14
15   $page_title = 'Logged In!';
16   include ('includes/header.html');
17
18   // Print a customized message:
19   echo "<h1>Logged In!</h1>
20   <p>You are now logged in, {$_SESSION
     ['first_name']}!</p>
21   <p><a href=\"logout.php\">Logout</a></p>";
22
23   include ('includes/footer.html');
24   ?>
```

Script 11.10 The header.html file now also references $_SESSION instead of $_COOKIE.

```
● ● ●                    📄 Script
1    <!DOCTYPE html PUBLIC "-//W3C//DTD XHTML
     1.0 Strict//EN" "http://www.w3.org/TR/
     xhtml1/DTD/xhtml1-strict.dtd">

2    <html xmlns="http://www.w3.org/
     1999/xhtml">

3    <head">

4    <title><?php echo $page_title;
     ?></title>

5    <link rel="stylesheet" href="includes/
     style.css" type="text/css" media=
     "screen" />

6    <meta http-equiv="content-type"
     content="text/html; charset=utf-8" />

7    </head>

8    <body>

9      <div id="header">

10     <h1>Your Website</h1>

11     <h2>catchy slogan...</h2>

12     </div>

13     <div id="navigation">

14     <ul>

15       <li><a href="index.php">Home Page
         </a></li>

16       <li><a href="register.php">
         Register</a></li>

17       <li><a href="view_users.php">View
         Users</a></li>

18       <li><a href="password.php">Change
         Password</a></li>

19       <li><?php // Create a login/logout
         link:

20    if ( (isset($_SESSION['user_id'])) &&
      (!strpos($_SERVER['PHP_SELF'],
      'logout.php')) ) {

21      echo '<a href="logout.php">Logout</a>';

22    } else {

23      echo '<a href="login.php">Login</a>';

24    }
```
(script continues)

5. Replace the reference to $_COOKIE with $_SESSION in header.html (from Script 11.7 to **Script 11.10**).

```
if ( (isset($_SESSION['user_id']))
→ && (!strpos($_SERVER['PHP_SELF'],
→ 'logout.php')) ) {
```

For the *Login/Logout* links to function properly (notice the incorrect link in Figure 11.17), the reference to the cookie variable within the header file must be switched over to sessions. The header file does not need to call the session_start() function, as it'll be included by pages that do.

6. Save the header file, place it in your Web directory (in the includes folder), and test it in your browser (**Figure 11.18**).

continues on next page

Figure 11.18 With the header file altered for sessions, the proper *Login/Logout* links will be displayed (compare with Figure 11.17).

Script 11.10 *continued*

```
● ● ●                    📄 Script
25    ?></li>

26    </ul>

27    </div>

28    <div id="content"><!-- Start of the
      page-specific content. -->

29  <!-- Script 11.10 - header.html -->
```

✔ Tips

- For the *Login/Logout* links to work on the other pages (`register.php`, `index.php`, etc.), you'll need to add the `session_start()` command to each of those.

- As a reminder of what I already said, if you have an application where the session data does not seem to be accessible from one page to the next, it could be because a new session is being created on each page. To check for this, compare the session ID (the last few characters of the value will suffice) to see if it is the same. You can see the session's ID by viewing the session cookie as it is sent or by invoking the `session_id()` function:

  `echo session_id();`

- Session variables are available as soon as you've established them. So, unlike when using cookies, you can assign a value to `$_SESSION['var']` and then refer to `$_SESSION['var']` later in that same script.

Garbage Collection

Garbage collection with respect to sessions is the process of deleting the session files (where the actual data is stored). Creating a logout system that destroys a session is ideal, but there's no guarantee all users will formally log out as they should. For this reason, PHP includes a cleanup process.

Whenever the `session_start()` function is called, PHP's garbage collection kicks in, checking the last modification date of each session (a session is modified whenever variables are set or retrieved). Two settings dictate garbage collection: `session.gc_maxlifetime` and `session.gc_probability`. The first states after how many seconds of inactivity a session is considered idle and will therefore be deleted. The second setting determines the probability that garbage collection is performed, on a scale of 1 to 100. With the default settings, each call to `session_start()` has a 1 percent chance of invoking garbage collection. If PHP does start the cleanup, any sessions that have not been used in more than 1,440 seconds will be deleted.

You can change these settings using the `ini_set()` function, although be careful in doing so. Too frequent or too probable garbage collection can bog down the server and inadvertently end the sessions of slower users.

Script 11.11 Destroying a session, as you would in a logout page, requires special syntax to delete the session cookie and the session data on the server, as well as to clear out the $_SESSION array.

```
1   <?php # Script 11.11 - logout.php #2

2   // This page lets the user logout.

3

4   session_start(); // Access the existing
    session.

5

6   // If no session variable exists, redirect
    the user:

7   if (!isset($_SESSION['user_id'])) {

8

9       require_once ('includes/login_functions.
        inc.php');

10      $url = absolute_url();

11      header("Location: $url");

12      exit();

13

14  } else { // Cancel the session.

15

16      $_SESSION = array(); // Clear the
        variables.

17      session_destroy(); // Destroy the
        session itself.

18      setcookie ('PHPSESSID', '', time()-3600,
        '/', '', 0, 0); // Destroy the cookie.

19

20  }

21

22  // Set the page title and include the HTML
    header:

23  $page_title = 'Logged Out!';

24  include ('includes/header.html');

25

26  // Print a customized message:

27  echo "<h1>Logged Out!</h1>

28  <p>You are now logged out!</p>";

29

30  include ('includes/footer.html');

31  ?>
```

Deleting session variables

When using sessions, you ought to create a method to delete the session data. In the current example, this would be necessary when the user logs out.

Whereas a cookie system only requires that another cookie be sent to destroy the existing cookie, sessions are slightly more demanding, since there are both the cookie on the client and the data on the server to consider.

To delete an individual session variable, you can use the unset() function (which works with any variable in PHP):

unset($_SESSION['var']);

To delete every session variable, reset the entire $_SESSION array:

$_SESSION = array();

Finally, to remove all of the session data from the server, use session_destroy():

session_destroy();

Note that prior to using any of these methods, the page must begin with session_start() so that the existing session is accessed. Let's update the logout.php script to clean out the session data.

To delete a session:

1. Open logout.php (Script 11.6) in your text editor or IDE.

2. Immediately after the opening PHP line, start the session (**Script 11.11**).

    session_start();

    Anytime you are using sessions, you must use the session_start() function, preferably at the very beginning of a page. This is true even if you are deleting a session.

    continues on next page

3. Change the conditional so that it checks for the presence of a session variable.

```
if (!isset($_SESSION['user_id'])) {
```

As with the logout.php script in the cookie examples, if the user is not currently logged in, they will be redirected.

4. Replace the setcookie() lines (that delete the cookies) with

```
$_SESSION = array();

session_destroy();

setcookie ('PHPSESSID', '', time
→ ()-3600, '/', '', 0, 0);
```

The first line here will reset the entire $_SESSION variable as a new array, erasing its existing values. The second line removes the data from the server, and the third sends a cookie to replace the existing session cookie in the browser.

5. Remove the reference to $_COOKIE in the message.

```
echo "<h1>Logged Out!</h1>

<p>You are now logged out!</p>";
```

Unlike when using the cookie version of the logout.php script, you cannot refer to the user by their first name anymore, as all of that data has been deleted.

6. Save the file as logout.php, place it in your Web directory, and test it in your browser (**Figure 11.19**).

✔ Tips

■ Never set $_SESSION equal to NULL and never use unset($_SESSION). Either could cause problems on some servers.

■ In case it's not absolutely clear what's going on, there exists three kinds of information with a session: the session identifier (which is stored in a cookie by default), the session data (which is stored in a text file on the server), and the $_SESSION array (which is how a script accesses the session data in the text file). Just deleting the cookie doesn't remove the text file and vice versa. Clearing out the $_SESSION array would erase the data from the text file, but the file itself would still exist, as would the cookie. The three steps outlined in this logout script effectively remove all traces of the session.

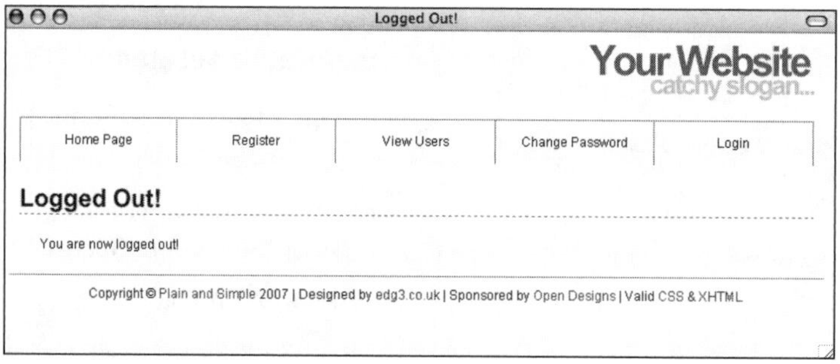

Figure 11.19 The logout page (now featuring sessions).

USING SESSIONS

Changing the Session Behavior

As part of PHP's support for sessions, there are over 20 different configuration options you can set for how PHP handles sessions. For the full list, see the PHP manual, but I'll highlight a few of the most important ones here. Note two rules about changing the session settings:

1. All changes must be made before calling `session_start()`.

2. The same changes must be made on every page that uses sessions.

Most of the settings can be set within a PHP script using the `ini_set()` function (discussed in Chapter 7):

```
ini_set (parameter, new_setting);
```

For example, to require the use of a session cookie (as mentioned, sessions can work without cookies but it's less secure), use

```
ini_set ('session.use_only_cookies', 1);
```

Another change you can make is to the the name of the session (perhaps to use a more user-friendly one). To do so, use the `session_name()` function.

```
session_name('YourSession');
```

The benefits of creating your own session name are twofold: it's marginally more secure and it may be better received by the end user (since the session name is the cookie name the end user will see). The `session_name()` function can also be used when deleting the session cookie:

```
setcookie (session_name(), '', time()-3600);
```

Finally, there's also the `session_set_cookie_params()` function. It's used to tweak the settings of the session cookie.

```
session_set_cookie_params(expire, path, host, secure, httponly);
```

Note that the expiration time of the cookie refers only to the longevity of the cookie in the Web browser, not to how long the session data will be stored on the server.

Improving Session Security

Because important information is normally stored in a session (you should never store sensitive data in a cookie), security becomes more of an issue. With sessions there are two things to pay attention to: the session ID, which is a reference point to the session data, and the session data itself, stored on the server. A malicious person is far more likely to hack into a session through the session ID than the data on the server, so I'll focus on that side of things here (in the tips at the end of this section I mention two ways to protect the session data).

The session ID is the key to the session data. By default, PHP will store this in a cookie, which is preferable from a security standpoint. It is possible in PHP to use sessions without cookies, but that leaves the application vulnerable to *session hijacking*: If I can learn another user's session ID, I can easily trick a server into thinking that their session ID is *my* session ID. At that point I have effectively taken over the original user's entire session and would have access to their data. So storing the session ID in a cookie makes it somewhat harder to steal.

One method of preventing hijacking is to store some sort of user identifier in the session, and then to repeatedly double-check this value. The *HTTP_USER_AGENT*—a combination of the browser and operating system being used—is a likely candidate for this purpose. This adds a layer of security in that one person could only hijack another user's session if they are both running the exact same browser and operating system. As a demonstration of this, let's modify the examples one last time.

Script 11.12 This final version of the login.php script also stores an encrypted form of the user's *HTTP_USER_AGENT* (the browser and operating system of the client) in a session.

```
1    <?php # Script 11.12 - login.php #4
2
3    if (isset($_POST['submitted'])) {
4
5        require_once ('includes/login_functions.
         inc.php');
6        require_once ('../mysqli_connect.php');
7        list ($check, $data) = check_login($dbc,
         $_POST['email'], $_POST['pass']);
8
9        if ($check) { // OK!
10
11           // Set the session data:.
12           session_start();
13           $_SESSION['user_id'] = $data['user_id'];
14           $_SESSION['first_name'] = $data
             ['first_name'];
15
16           // Store the HTTP_USER_AGENT:
17           $_SESSION['agent'] = md5($_SERVER
             ['HTTP_USER_AGENT']);
18
19           // Redirect:
20           $url = absolute_url ('loggedin.php');
21           header("Location: $url");
22           exit();
23
24        } else { // Unsuccessful!
25           $errors = $data;
26        }
27
28        mysqli_close($dbc);
29
30    } // End of the main submit conditional.
31
32    include ('includes/login_page.inc.php');
33    ?>
```

Script 11.13 This `loggedin.php` script now confirms that the user accessing this page has the same *HTTP_USER_AGENT* as they did when they logged in.

```
1    <?php # Script 11.13 - loggedin.php #3
2
3    // The user is redirected here from
     login.php.
4
5    session_start(); // Start the session.
6
7    // If no session value is present,
     redirect the user:
8    // Also validate the HTTP_USER_AGENT!
9    if (!isset($_SESSION['agent']) OR
     ($_SESSION['agent'] != md5($_SERVER
     ['HTTP_USER_AGENT']) ) {
10       require_once ('includes/login_
         functions.inc.php');
11       $url = absolute_url();
12       header("Location: $url");
13       exit();
14   }
15
16   $page_title = 'Logged In!';
17   include ('includes/header.html');
18
19   // Print a customized message:
20   echo "<h1>Logged In!</h1>
21   <p>You are now logged in,
     {$_SESSION['first_name']}!</p>
22   <p><a href=\"logout.php\">Logout
     </a></p>";
23
24   include ('includes/footer.html');
25   ?>
```

To use sessions more securely:

1. Open `login.php` (refer to Script 11.8) in your text editor or IDE.

2. After assigning the other session variables, also store the *HTTP_USER_AGENT* value (**Script 11.12**).

   `$_SESSION['agent'] = md5($_SERVER`
   `→ ['HTTP_USER_AGENT']);`

   The *HTTP_USER_AGENT* is part of the *$_SERVER* array (you may recall using it way back in Chapter 1, "Introduction to PHP"). It will have a value like *Mozilla/4.0 (compatible; MSIE 6.0; Windows NT 5.0; .NET CLR 1.1.4322)*.

   Instead of storing this value in the session as is, it'll be run through the `md5()` function for added security. That function returns a 32-character hexadecimal string (called a *hash*) based upon a value. In theory, no two strings will have the same `md5()` result.

3. Save the file and place it in your Web directory.

4. Open `loggedin.php` (Script 11.9) in your text editor or IDE.

5. Change the `!isset($_SESSION['user_id'])` conditional to (**Script 11.13**)

   `if (!isset($_SESSION['agent']) OR`
   `→ ($_SESSION['agent'] != md5($_SERVER`
   `→ ['HTTP_USER_AGENT']) ) {`

   This conditional checks two things. First, it sees if the *$_SESSION['agent']* variable is not set (this part is just as it was before, although *agent* is being used instead of *user_id*). The second part of the conditional checks if the `md5()` version of *$_SERVER['HTTP_USER_AGENT']* does not equal the value stored in *$_SESSION ['agent']*. If either of these conditions are true, the user will be redirected.

continues on next page

6. Save this file, place in your Web directory, and test in your Web browser by logging in.

✔ Tips

■ For critical uses of sessions, require the use of cookies and transmit them over a secure connection, if at all possible. You can even set PHP to only use cookies by setting *session.use_only_cookies* to *1* (this is the default in PHP 6).

■ If you are using a server shared with other domains, changing the *session. save_path* from its default setting—which is accessible by all users—will be more secure.

■ The session data itself can be stored in a database rather than a text file. This is a more secure, but more programming-intensive, option. I teach how to do this in my book *PHP 5 Advanced: Visual QuickPro Guide*.

■ The user's IP address (the network address from which the user is connecting) is *not* a good unique identifier, for two reasons. First, a user's IP address can, and normally does, change frequently (ISPs dynamically assign them for short periods of time). Second, many users accessing a site from the same network (like a home network or an office) could all have the same IP address.

Preventing Session Fixation

Another specific kind of session attack is known as *session fixation*. This is where one malicious user specifies the session ID that another user should use. This session ID could be randomly generated or legitimately created. In either case, the real user will go into the site using the fixed session ID and do whatever. Then the malicious user can access that session because they know what the session ID is. You can help protect against these types of attacks by changing the session ID after a user logs in. The `session_regenerate_id()` does just that, providing a new session ID to refer to the current session data. You can use this function on sites for which security is paramount (like e-commerce or online banking) or in situations when it'd be particularly bad if certain users (i.e., administrators) had their sessions manipulated.

SECURITY METHODS

The security of your Web applications is such an important topic that it really cannot be overstressed. Although security-related issues have been mentioned throughout this book, this chapter will help to fill in certain gaps and finalize other points.

The most important concept to understand about security is that it's not a binary state: don't think of a Web site or script as being either *secure* or *not secure*. Security isn't a switch that you turn on and off; it's a scale that you can move up and down. When you program, think about what you can do to make your site *more secure* and what you've done that makes it *less secure*. Also, keep in mind that improved security normally comes at a cost of convenience (both to you, the programmer, and to the end user) and performance. Increased security normally means more code, more checks, and more required of the server. When developing Web applications, think about these considerations and make the right decisions—for the particular situation— from the outset.

The topics discussed here include: preventing spam; using typecasting; preventing cross-site scripting (XSS) and SQL injection attacks; and database security. This chapter will use several discrete examples to best demonstrate these concepts. Some other common security issues and best practices will be mentioned in sidebars as well.

Preventing Spam

Spam is nothing short of a plague, cluttering up the Internet and our inboxes. There are steps you can take to avoid receiving spam at your email accounts, but in this book the focus is on preventing spam being sent through your PHP scripts.

Chapter 10, "Web Application Development," shows how easy it is to send email using PHP's `mail()` function. The example there, a contact form, took some information from the user (**Figure 12.1**) and sent it to an email address. Although it may seem like there's no harm in this system, there's actually a big security hole. But first, some background on what an email actually is.

Regardless of how an email is sent, how it's formatted, and what it looks like when it's received, an email contains two parts: a header and a body. The header includes such information as the *to* and *from* addresses, the subject, the date, and more (**Figure 12.2**). Each item in the header is on its own line, in the format *Name: value*. The body of the email is exactly what you think it is: the body of the email.

In looking at PHP's `mail()` function—

`mail (to, subject, body, [headers]);`

—you can see that one of the arguments goes straight to the email's body and the rest appear in its header. To send spam to your address (as in Chapter 10's example), all a person would have to do is enter the spam message into the comments section of the form (Figure 12.1). That's bad enough, but to send spam to anyone else at the same time, all the user would have to do is add *Bcc: poorsap@example.org*, followed by a some sort of line terminator (like a newline or carriage return), to the email's header. With the example as is, this just means entering into the *from* value of the contact form *me@ example.com\nBcc:poorsap@example.org*.

You might think that safeguarding everything that goes into an email's header would be sufficiently safe, but as an email is just one document, bad input in a body can impact the header.

There are a couple of preventive techniques. First, validate any email addresses using regular expressions. Chapter 13, "Perl-Compatible Regular Expressions," covers this subject.

Figure 12.1 A simple, standard HTML contact form.

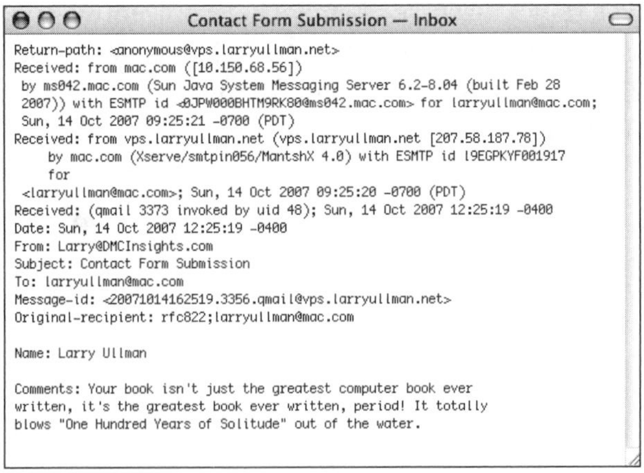

Figure 12.2 The raw source version of the email sent by the contact form (**Figure 12.1**).

Table 12.1 The presence of any of these character strings in a form submission is a likely indicator that someone is trying to send spam through your site. The last four are all different ways of creating newlines.

Spam Tip-offs
CHARACTERS
content-type:
mime-version:
multipart-mixed:
content-transfer-encoding:
bcc:
cc:
to:
\r
\n
%0a
%0d

Script 12.1 This version of the script can now safely send emails without concern for spam. Any problematic characters will be caught by the spam_scrubber() function.

```
1   <!DOCTYPE html PUBLIC "-//W3C//DTD XHTML
    1.0 Transitional//EN"
2       "http://www.w3.org/TR/xhtml1/DTD/
        xhtml1-transitional.dtd">
3   <html xmlns="http://www.w3.org/1999/
    xhtml" xml:lang="en" lang="en">
4   <head>
5     <meta http-equiv="content-type" content=
      "text/html; charset=iso-8859-1" />
6     <title>Contact Me</title>
7   </head>
8   <body>
9   <h1>Contact Me</h1>
10  <?php # Script 12.1 - email.php #2
11
12  // Check for form submission:
13  if (isset($_POST['submitted'])) {
14
15    /* The function takes one argument: a
      string.
16    * The function returns a clean version
      of the string.
```

(script continues on next page)

Second, now that you know what an evildoer must enter to send spam (**Table 12.1**), watch for those characters in form values. If a value contains anything from that list, don't use that value.

In this next example, a modification of the email script from Chapter 10, I'll define a function that scrubs all the potentially dangerous characters from data. Two new PHP functions will be used as well: str_replace() and array_map(). Both will be explained in detail in the steps that follow.

To prevent spam:

1. Open email.php (Script 10.1) in your text editor or IDE.

   To complete this spam-purification, the email script needs to be modified.

2. After checking for the form submission, begin defining a function (**Script 12.1**).

   ```
   function spam_scrubber($value) {
   ```

   This function will take one argument: a string.

3. Create a list of really bad things that wouldn't be in a legitimate contact form submission.

   ```
   $very_bad = array('to:', 'cc:',
   → 'bcc:', 'content-type:', 'mime-
   → version:', 'multipart-mixed:',
   → 'content-transfer-encoding:');
   ```

   Any of these strings should not be present in an honest contact form submission (it's possible someone might legitimately use *to:* in their comments, but unlikely). If any of these strings are present, then this is a spam attempt. To make it easier to test for all these, they're placed in an array, which will be looped through (Step 4).

continues on page 365

Script 12.1 *continued*

```
17    * The clean version may be either an
      empty string or

18    * just the removal of all newline
      characters.

19    */

20    function spam_scrubber($value) {

21

22        // List of very bad values:

23        $very_bad = array('to:', 'cc:', 'bcc:',
          'content-type:', 'mime-version:',
          'multipart-mixed:', 'content-
          transfer-encoding:');

24

25        // If any of the very bad strings are in

26        // the submitted value, return an empty
          string:

27        foreach ($very_bad as $v) {

28          if (stripos($value, $v) !== false)
            return '';

29        }

30

31        // Replace any newline characters with
          spaces:

32        $value = str_replace(array( "\r", "\n",
          "%0a", "%0d"), ' ', $value);

33

34        // Return the value:

35        return trim($value);

36

37    } // End of spam_scrubber() function.

38

39    // Clean the form data:

40    $scrubbed = array_map('spam_scrubber',
      $_POST);

41

42    // Minimal form validation:

43    if (!empty($scrubbed['name']) &&
      !empty($scrubbed['email']) &&
      !empty($scrubbed['comments']) ) {

44

45        // Create the body:

46        $body = "Name: {$scrubbed['name']}
          \n\nComments: {$scrubbed['comments']}";
```

(script continues)

Script 12.1 *continued*

```
47        $body = wordwrap($body, 70);

48

49        // Send the email:

50        mail('your_email@example.com',
          'Contact Form Submission', $body,
          "From: {$scrubbed['email']}");

51

52        // Print a message:

53        echo '<p><em>Thank you for contacting
          me. I will reply some day.</em></p>';

54

55        // Clear $_POST (so that the form's
          not sticky):

56        $_POST = array();

57

58    } else {

59        echo '<p style="font-weight: bold;
          color: #C00">Please fill out the |form
          completely.</p>';

60    }

61

62    } // End of main isset() IF.

63    ?>

64    <p>Please fill out this form to contact
      me.</p>

65    <form action="email.php" method="post">

66        <p>Name: <input type="text" name="name"
          size="30" maxlength="60" value="<?php if
          (isset($_POST['name'])) echo
          $_POST['name']; ?>" /></p>

67        <p>Email Address: <input type="text"
          name="email" size="30" maxlength="80"
          value="<?php if (isset($_POST['email']))
          echo $_POST['email']; ?>" /></p>

68        <p>Comments: <textarea name="comments"
          rows="5" cols="30"><?php if (isset
          ($_POST['comments'])) echo $_POST
          ['comments']; ?></textarea></p>

69        <p><input type="submit" name="submit"
          value="Send!" /></p>

70        <input type="hidden" name="submitted"
          value="TRUE" />

71    </form>

72    </body>

73    </html>
```

4. Loop through the array. If a very bad thing is found, return an empty string.

```
foreach ($very_bad as $v) {
    if (stripos($value, $v) !==
→ false) return '';
}
```

The foreach loop will access each item in $very_bad one at a time. Within the loop, the stripos() function will check if the item is in the string provided to this function as $value. The stripos() function performs a case-insensitive search (so it would match *bcc:*, *Bcc:*, *bCC:*, etc.). The first time that any of these items is found in the submitted value, the function will return an empty string and terminate (functions automatically stop executing once they hit a return).

5. Replace any newline characters with spaces.

```
$value = str_replace(array("\r",
→ "\n", "%0a", "%0d"), ' ', $value);
```

Newline characters, which are represented by \r, \n , %0a, and %0d, may or may not be problematic. A newline character is required to send spam (or else you can't create the proper header) but will also appear if a user just hits Enter while typing in a textarea box. For this reason, any found newlines will just be replaced by a space. This means that the submitted value could lose some of its formatting, but that's a reasonable price to pay to stop spam.

The str_replace() function looks through the value in the third argument and replaces any occurrences of the characters in the first argument with the

character or characters in the second. Or as the PHP manual puts it:

```
mixed str_replace (mixed $search,
→ mixed $replace, mixed $subject)
```

This function is very flexible in that it can take strings or arrays for its three arguments (the *mixed* means it accepts a mix of argument types). So this line of code in the script assigns to the $value variable its original value, with any newline characters replaced by a single space.

There is a case-insensitive version of this function, but it's not necessary, as, for example, \r is a carriage return but \R is not.

6. Return the value and complete the function.

```
    return trim($value);
} // End of spam_scrubber() function.
```

Finally, this function returns the value, trimmed of any leading and ending spaces. Keep in mind that the function will only get to this point if none of the very bad things was found.

7. After the function definition, invoke the spam_scrubber() function.

```
$scrubbed = array_map('spam_
→ scrubber', $_POST);
```

I've demonstrated this technique in the book's supporting forum (www. DMCInsights.com/phorum/), and I think the simplicity of this line confuses many people. The array_map() function has two required arguments. The first is the name of the function to call. In this case, that's *spam_scrubber* (without the parentheses, because you're providing the function's name, not calling the function). The second argument is an array.

continues on next page

PREVENTING SPAM

What `array_map()` does is call the named function, once for each array element, sending each array element's value to that function. In this script, `$_POST` has five elements: *name, email, comments, submit,* and *submitted.* After this line of code, the `$scrubbed` array will end up with five elements: `$scrubbed['name']` will have the value of `$_POST['name']` after running it through `spam_scrubber()`; `$scrubbed['email']` will have the same value as `$_POST['email']` after running it through `spam_scrubber()`; and so forth.

This one line of code then takes an entire array of potentially tainted data (`$_POST`), cleans it using `spam_scrubber()`, and assigns the result to a new variable. Here's the most important thing: from here on out, the script will use the `$scrubbed` array, which is clean, not `$_POST`, which is still potentially dirty.

8. Change the form validation to use this new array.

```
if (!empty($scrubbed['name']) &&
→ !empty($scrubbed['email']) &&
→ !empty($scrubbed['comments']) ) {
```

Each of these elements could have an empty value for two reasons. First, if the user left them empty. Second, if the user entered one of the bad strings in the field, which would be turned into an empty string by the `spam_scrubber()` function.

9. Change the creation of the `$body` variable so that it uses the clean values.

```
$body = "Name: {$scrubbed['name']}
→ \n\nComments: {$scrubbed
→ ['comments']}";
```

Figure 12.3 The presence of *cc:* in the email address field will prevent this submission from being sent in an email (see Figure 12.4).

Figure 12.4 The email was not sent because of the very bad characters used in the email address.

Figure 12.5 Although the comments field contains newline characters (created by pressing Enter or Return), the email will still be sent (Figure 12.6).

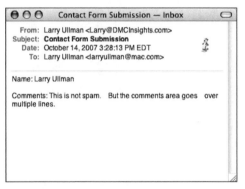

Figure 12.6 The received email, with the newlines in the comments (Figure 12.5) turned into spaces.

10. Change the invocation of the `mail()` function to use the clean email address.

```
mail('your_email@example.com',
→ 'Contact Form Submission', $body,
→ "From: {$scrubbed['email']}");
```

11. Save the script as `email.php`, place it in your Web directory, and test it in your Web browser (**Figures 12.3**, **12.4**, **12.5**, and **12.6**).

✔ Tips

- Using the `array_map()` function as I have in this example is convenient but not without its downsides. First, it blindly applies the `spam_scrubber()` function to the entire `$_POST` array, even to the submit button and hidden form input. This isn't harmful but is unnecessary. Second, any multidimensional arrays within `$_POST` will be lost. In this specific example, that's not a problem but it is something to be aware of.

- To prevent automated submissions to any form, you could use a CAPTCHA test. These are prompts that can only be understood by humans (in theory). While this is commonly accomplished using an image of random characters, the same thing can be achieved using a question like *What is two plus two?* or *On what continent is China?*. Checking for the correct answer to this question would then be part of the validation routine.

- If you wanted, you could change the sticky form so that it refers to the `$scrubbed` values, not the original `$_POST` ones.

PREVENTING SPAM

More Security Recommendations

This chapter covers many specific techniques for improving your Web security. Here are a handful of other recommendations:

◆ Make it your job to study, follow, and abide by security recommendations. Don't just rely upon the advice of one chapter, one book, or one author.

◆ Don't use user-supplied names for uploaded files. You'll see an alternative to doing that in Chapter 17, "Example—E-Commerce."

◆ Watch how database references are used. For example, if a person's user ID is their primary key from the database and this is stored in a cookie (as in Chapter 11, "Cookies and Sessions"), a malicious user just needs to change that cookie value to access another user's account.

◆ Don't show detailed error messages (this point was repeated in Chapter 7, "Error Handling and Debugging").

◆ Use cryptography (this is discussed at the end of the chapter with respect to the database and in my book *PHP 5 Advanced: Visual QuickPro Guide* (Peachpit Press, 2007) with respect to the server).

◆ Don't store credit card numbers, social security numbers, banking information, and the like. The only exception to this would be if you have deep enough pockets to pay for the best security and to cover the lawsuits that arise when this data is stolen from your site (which will inevitably happen).

◆ Use SSL, if appropriate. A secure connection is one of the best protections a server can offer a user.

◆ Reliably and consistently protect every page and directory that needs it. Never assume that people won't find sensitive areas just because there's no link to them. If access to a page or directory should be limited, make sure it is.

My final recommendation is to be aware of your own limitations. As the programmer, you probably approach a script thinking how it *should be* used. This is not the same as to how it *will be* used, either accidentally or on purpose. Try to break your site to see what happens. Do bad things, do the wrong thing. Have other people try to break it, too (it's normally easy to find such volunteers). When you code, if you assume that no one will ever use a page properly, it'll be much more secure than if you assume people always will.

Validating Data by Type

For the most part, the form validation used in this book thus far has been rather minimal, often just checking if a variable has any value at all. In many situations, this really is the best you can do. For example, there's no perfect test for what a valid street address is or what a user might enter into a comments field. Still, much of the data you'll work with can be validated in stricter ways. In the next chapter, the sophisticated concept of regular

Two Validation Approaches

A large part of security is based upon validation: if data comes from outside of the script—from HTML forms, the URL, cookies, sessions, or even form a database, it can't be trusted. There are two types of validation: *whitelist* and *blacklist*. In the calculator example, we know that all values must be positive, that they must all be numbers, and that the quantity must be an integer (the other two numbers could be integers or floats, it makes no difference). Typecasting forces the inputs to be numbers, and a check confirms that they are positive. At this point, the assumption is that the input is valid. This is a whitelist approach: these values are good; anything else is bad.

The preventing spam example uses a blacklist approach. That script knows exactly which characters are bad and invalidates input that contains them. All other input is considered to be good.

Many security experts prefer the whitelist approach, but it can't always be used. The example will dictate which approach will work best, but it's important to use one or the other. Don't just assume that data is safe without some sort of validation.

expressions will demonstrate just that. But here I'll cover the more approachable ways you can validate some data by type.

PHP supports many types of data: strings, numbers (integers and floats), arrays, and so on. For each of these, there's a specific function that checks if a variable is of that type (**Table 12.2**). You've probably already seen the is_numeric() function in action in earlier chapters, and is_array() is great for confirming a variable's type before attempting to use it in a foreach loop.

In PHP, you can even change a variable's type, after it's been assigned a value. Doing so is called *typecasting* and is accomplished by preceding a variable's name by the type in parentheses:

```
$var = 20.2;

echo (int) $var; // 20
```

Depending upon the original and destination types, PHP will convert the variable's value accordingly:

```
$var = 20;

echo (float) $var; // 20.0
```

continues on next page

Table 12.2 These functions return TRUE if the submitted variable is of a certain type and FALSE otherwise.

Type Validation Functions	
FUNCTION	CHECKS FOR
is_array()	Arrays
is_bool()	Booleans (TRUE, FALSE)
is_float()	Floating-point numbers
is_int()	Integers
is_null()	NULLs
is_numeric()	Numeric values, even as a string (e.g., '20')
is_resource()	Resources, like a database connection
is_scalar()	Scalar (single-valued) variables
is_string()	Strings

With numeric values, the conversion is straightforward, but with other variable types, more complex rules apply:

$var = 'trout';

echo (int) $var; // 0

In most circumstances you don't need to cast a variable from one type to another, as PHP will often automatically do so as needed. But forcibly casting a variable's type can be a good security measure in your Web applications. To show how you might use this notion, let's create a calculator script for determining the total purchase price of an item, similar to that defined in earlier chapters.

To use typecasting:

1. Begin a new PHP document in your text editor or IDE (**Script 12.2**).

```
<!DOCTYPE html PUBLIC "-//W3C//DTD
→ XHTML 1.0 Transitional//EN"
"http://www.w3.org/TR/xhtml1/DTD/xhtm
→ l1-transitional.dtd">
<html xmlns="http://www.w3.org/1999/
→ xhtml" xml:lang="en" lang="en">
<head>
    <meta http-equiv="content-type"
    → content="text/html; charset=
    → iso-8859-1" />
    <title>Widget Cost Calculator</
    → title>
</head>
<body>
<?php # Script 12.2 - calculator.php
```

2. Check if the form has been submitted.

```
if (isset($_POST['submitted'])) {
```

Like many previous examples, this one script will both display the HTML form

Script 12.2 By typecasting variables, this script more definitively validates that data is of the correct format.

```
1   <!DOCTYPE html PUBLIC "-//W3C//DTD XHTML
    1.0 Transitional//EN"
2       "http://www.w3.org/TR/xhtml1/DTD/
        xhtml1-transitional.dtd">
3   <html xmlns="http://www.w3.org/1999/xhtml"
    xml:lang="en" lang="en">
4   <head>
5       <meta http-equiv="content-type"
        content="text/html; charset=
        iso-8859-1" />
6       <title>Widget Cost Calculator</title>
7   </head>
8   <body>
9   <?php # Script 12.2 - calculator.php
10
11  // Check if the form has been submitted.:
12  if (isset($_POST['submitted'])) {
13
14      // Cast all the variables to a specific
        type:
15      $quantity = (int) $_POST['quantity'];
16      $price = (float) $_POST['price'];
17      $tax = (float) $_POST['tax'];
18
19      // All variables should be positive!
20      if ( ($quantity > 0) && ($price > 0) &&
        ($tax > 0)) {
21
22          // Calculate the total:
23          $total = ($quantity * $price) *
            (($tax/100) + 1);
24
25          // Print the result:
26          echo '<p>The total cost of purchasing
            ' . $quantity . ' widget(s) at $' .
            number_format ($price, 2) . ' each,
            plus tax, is $' . number_format
            ($total, 2) . '.</p>';
```

(script continues on next page)

Script 12.2 *continued*

```
 27

 28    } else { // Invalid submitted values.

 29       echo '<p style="font-weight: bold;
          color: #C00">Please enter a valid
          quantity, price, and tax rate.</p>';

 30    }

 31

 32  } // End of main isset() IF.

 33

 34  // Leave the PHP section and create the
     HTML form.

 35  ?>

 36  <h2>Widget Cost Calculator</h2>

 37  <form action="calculator.php"
     method="post">

 38    <p>Quantity: <input type="text" name=
       "quantity" size="5" maxlength="10"
       value="<?php if (isset($quantity))
       echo $quantity; ?>" /></p>

 39    <p>Price: <input type="text" name=
       "price" size="5" maxlength="10"
       value="<?php if (isset($price))
       echo $price; ?>" /></p>

 40    <p>Tax (%): <input type="text"
       name="tax" size="5" maxlength="10"
       value="<?php if (isset($tax)) echo
       $tax; ?>" /></p>

 41    <p><input type="submit" name="submit"
       value="Calculate!" /></p>

 42    <input type="hidden" name="submitted"
       value="TRUE" />

 43  </form>

 44  </body>

 45  </html>
```

and handle its submission. By checking for the presence of a specific $_POST element, you can know if the form has been submitted.

3. Cast all the variables to a specific type.

```
$quantity = (int) $_POST['quantity'];

$price = (float) $_POST['price'];

$tax = (float) $_POST['tax'];
```

The form itself has three text boxes (**Figure 12.7**), into which practically anything could be typed (there's no number type of input for HTML forms). But the quantity must be an integer and both price and tax should be floats (they will contain decimal points). To force these issues, cast each one to a specific type.

4. Check if the variables have proper values, and then calculate and print the results.

```
if ( ($quantity > 0) && ($price > 0)
→ && ($tax > 0) ) {

      $total = ($quantity * $price) *
→ (($tax/100) + 1);
```

continues on next page

Figure 12.7 The HTML form takes three inputs: a quantity, a price, and a tax rate.

```
echo '<p>The total cost of
→ purchasing ' . $quantity . '
→ widget(s) at $' . number_
→ format ($price, 2) . ' each,
→ plus tax, is $' . number_
→ format ($total, 2) . '.</p>';
```

For this calculator to work, the three variables must be specific types (see Step 3). More importantly, they must all be positive numbers. This conditional checks for that prior to performing the calculations. Note that, per the rules of typecasting, if the posted values are not numbers, they will be cast to *0* and therefore not pass this conditional.

The calculation itself is accomplished in a single line of code, using parentheses to ensure reliable results (thereby sparing you concern for precedence issues). The quantity is multiplied by the price. This is then multiplied by the tax divided by 100 (so 8% becomes *.08*) plus 1 (*1.08*). The number_format() function is used to print both the price and total values in the proper format.

5. Complete the conditionals.

```
} else {
    echo '<p style="font-weight:
    → bold; color: #C00">Please
    → enter a valid quantity,
    → price, and tax rate.</p>';
}
} // End of main isset() IF.
```

A little CSS is used to create a bold, red error message, should there be a problem (**Figure 12.8**).

6. Begin the HTML form.

```
?>
<h2>Widget Cost Calculator</h2>
<form action="calculator.php" method=
→ "post">
    <p>Quantity: <input type="text"
    → name="quantity" size="5"
    → maxlength="10" value="<?php
    → if (isset($quantity)) echo
    → $quantity; ?>" /></p>
```

The HTML form is really simple and posts back to this same page. The inputs will have a sticky quality, so the user can see what was previously entered. By referring to $quantity etc. instead of $_POST['quantity'] etc., the form will reflect the value for each input *as it was typecast* (see the tax value in Figure 12.8).

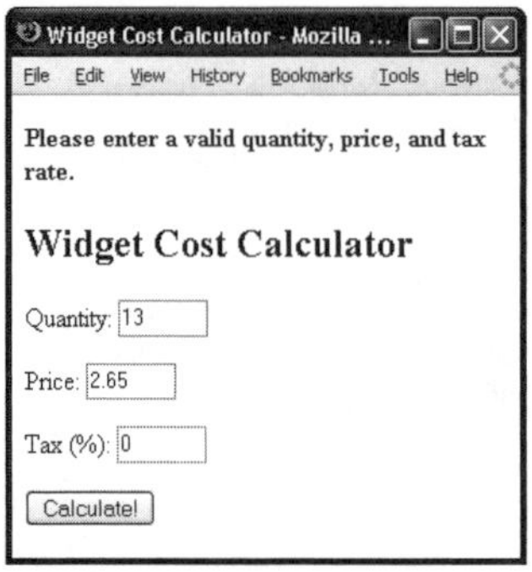

Figure 12.8 An error message is printed in bold, red text if any of the three fields does not contain a positive number.

7. Complete the HTML form.

```
<p>Price: <input type="text"
→ name="price" size="5"
→ maxlength="10" value="<?php if
→ (isset($price)) echo $price;
→ ?>" /></p>

<p>Tax (%): <input type="text"
→ name="tax" size="5" maxlength=
→ "10" value="<?php if (isset
→ ($tax)) echo $tax; ?>" /></p>
```

```
<p><input type="submit" name=
→ "submit" value="Calculate!"
→ /></p>

<input type="hidden" name=
→ "submitted" value="TRUE" />

</form>
```

8. Complete the HTML page.

```
</body>

</html>
```

9. Save the file as `calculator.php`, place it in your Web directory, and test it in your Web browser (**Figures 12.9** and **12.10**).

✔ Tips

- You should definitely use typecasting when working with numbers within SQL queries. Numbers aren't quoted in queries, so if a string is somehow used in a number's place, there will be an SQL syntax error. If you typecast such variables to an integer or float first, the query may not work (in terms of returning a record) but will still be syntactically valid. You'll frequently see this in the book's last three chapters.

- As I implied, regular expressions are a more advanced method of data validation and are sometimes your best bet. But using type-based validation, when feasible, will certainly be faster (in terms of processor speed) and less prone to programmer error (did I mention that regular expressions are complex?).

- To repeat myself, the rules of how values are converted from one data type to another are somewhat complicated. If you want to get into the details, see the PHP manual.

- If you wanted to allow for no tax rate, then change that part of the validation conditional to ... && ($tax >= 0)) { ....

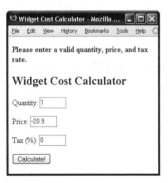

Figure 12.9 If invalid values are entered, such as floats for the quantity or strings for the tax...

Figure 12.10 ...they'll be cast into more appropriate formats. The negative price will also keep this calculation from being made (although the casting won't change that value).

Preventing XSS Attacks

HTML is simply plain text, like <b>, which is given special meaning by Web browsers (as by making text bold). Because of this fact, your Web site's user could easily put HTML in their form data, like in the comments field in the email example. What's wrong with that, you might ask?

Many dynamically driven Web applications take the information submitted by a user, store it in a database, and then redisplay that information on another page. Think of a forum, as just one example. At the very least, if a user enters HTML code in their data, such code could throw off the layout and aesthetic of your site. Taking this a step further, JavaScript is also just plain text, but text that has special meaning—*executable* meaning—within a Web browser. If malicious code entered into a form were re-displayed in a Web browser, it could create pop-up windows (**Figures 12.11** and **12.12**), steal cookies, or redirect the browser to other sites. Such attacks are referred to as *cross-site scripting* (XSS). As in the email example, where you need to look for and nullify bad strings found in data, prevention of XSS attacks is accomplished by addressing any potentially dangerous PHP, HTML, or JavaScript.

PHP includes a handful of functions for handling HTML and other code found within strings. These include:

- htmlspecialchars(), which turns &, ', ", <, and > into an HTML entity format (&, ", etc.)

- htmlentities(), which turns all applicable characters into their HTML entity format

- strip_tags(), which removes all HTML and PHP tags

These three functions are roughly listed in order from least disruptive to most. Which you'll want to use depends upon the application at hand. To demonstrate how these functions work and differ, let's just create a simple PHP page that takes some text (see Figure 12.11) and runs it through these functions, printing the results (**Figure 12.13**).

Figure 12.11 The malicious and savvy user can enter HTML, CSS, and JavaScript into text inputs.

Figure 12.12 The JavaScript entered into the comments field (see Figure 12.11) would create this alert window when the comments were displayed in the Web browser.

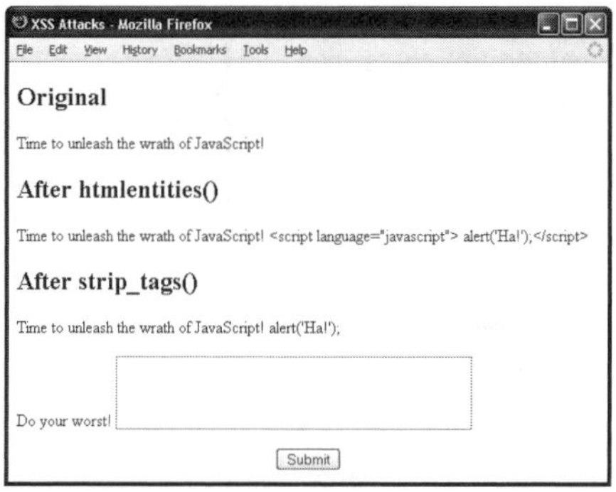

Figure 12.13 Thanks to the htmlentities() and strip_tags() functions, malicious code entered into the a form field (see Figure 12.11) can be rendered inert.

Script 12.3 Applying the `htmlentities()` and `strip_tags()` functions to submitted text can prevent XSS attacks.

```
   ●●●                    Script

1   <!DOCTYPE html PUBLIC "-//W3C//DTD XHTML
    1.0 Transitional//EN"

2
    "http://www.w3.org/TR/xhtml1/DTD/xhtml1-
    transitional.dtd">

3   <html xmlns="http://www.w3.org/1999/xhtml"
    xml:lang="en" lang="en">

4   <head>

5     <meta http-equiv="content-type" content=
    "text/html; charset=iso-8859-1" />

6     <title>XSS Attacks</title>

7   </head>

8   <body>

9   <?php # Script 12.3 - xss.php

10

11  if (isset($_POST['submitted'])) {

12

13    // Apply the different functions,
    printing the results:

14    echo "<h2>Original</h2><p>{$_POST
    ['data']}</p>";

15    echo '<h2>After htmlentities()</h2><p>'
    . htmlentities($_POST['data']). '</p>';

16    echo '<h2>After strip_tags()</h2><p>' .
    strip_tags($_POST['data']). '</p>';

17

18  }

19

20    // Display the form:

21  ?>

22  <form action="xss.php" method="post">

23

24    <p>Do your worst! <textarea name="data"
    rows="3" cols="40"></textarea></p>

25    <div align="center"><input type="submit"
    name="submit" value="Submit" /></div>

26    <input type="hidden" name="submitted"
    value="TRUE" />

27

28  </form>

29  </body>

30  </html>
```

To handle HTML:

1. Create a new PHP document in your text editor or IDE (**Script 12.3**).

   ```
   <!DOCTYPE html PUBLIC "-//W3C//DTD
   → XHTML 1.0 Transitional//EN"

   "http://www.w3.org/TR/xhtml1/DTD/xhtm
   → l1-transitional.dtd">

   <html xmlns="http://www.w3.org/1999/
   → xhtml" xml:lang="en" lang="en">

   <head>

        <meta http-equiv="content-type"
        → content="text/html; charset=
        → iso-8859-1" />

        <title>XSS Attacks</title>

   </head>

   <body>

   <?php # Script 12.3 - xss.php
   ```

2. Check for the form submission and print the received data in its original format.

   ```
   if (isset($_POST['submitted'])) {

        echo "<h2>Original</h2><p>{$_
        → POST['data']}</p>";
   ```

   To compare and contrast what was originally received with the result after applying the functions, the original value must first be printed.

3. Apply the `htmlentities()` function, printing the results.

   ```
   echo '<h2>After htmlentities()
   → </h2><p>' . htmlentities($_POST
   → ['data']). '</p>';
   ```

   To keep submitted information from messing up a page or hacking the Web browser, it's run through the `htmlentities()` function. So, any HTML entity will be translated; for instance, < and > will become < and > respectively.

continues on next page

4. Apply the strip_tags() function, printing the results.

```
echo '<h2>After strip_tags()</h2>
→ <p>' . strip_tags($_POST['data']).
→ '</p>';
```

The strip_tags() function completely takes out any HTML, JavaScript, or PHP tags. It's therefore the most foolproof function to use on submitted data.

5. Complete the PHP section.

```
}
?>
```

6. Display the HTML form.

```
<form action="xss.php" method="post">
    <p>Do your worst! <textarea
    → name="data" rows="3"
    → cols="40"></textarea></p>

    <div align="center"><input
    → type="submit" name="submit"
    → value="Submit" /></div>

    <input type="hidden" name=
    → "submitted" value="TRUE" />
</form>
```

The form (see Figure 12.11) has only one field for the user to complete: a textarea.

7. Complete the page.

```
</body>
</html>
```

8. Save the page as xss.php, place it in your Web directory, and test it in your Web browser.

9. View the source code of the page to see the full effect of these functions (**Figure 12.14**).

✔ Tips

■ Both htmlspecialchars() and htmlentities() take an optional parameter indicating how quotation marks should be handled. See the PHP manual for specifics.

■ The strip_tags() function takes an optional parameter indicating what tags should not be stripped.

```
$var = strip_tags ($var, '<p><br
→ />');
```

■ The strip_tags() function will remove even invalid HTML tags, which may cause problems. For example, strip_tags() will yank out all of the code it thinks is an HTML tag, even if it's improperly formed, like *<b I forgot to close the tag*.

■ Unrelated to security but quite useful is the nl2br() function. It turns every return (such as those entered into a text area) into an HTML <br /> tag.

```
<h2>Original</h2><p>Time to unleash the wrath of JavaScript!
<script language="javascript">
alert('Ha!');</script></p><h2>After htmlentities()</h2><p>Time to unleash the wrath of JavaScript!
&lt;script language=&quot;javascript&quot;&gt;
alert('Ha!');&lt;/script&gt;</p><h2>After strip_tags()</h2><p>Time to unleash the wrath of JavaScript!

alert('Ha!');</p><form action="xss.php" method="post">
```

Figure 12.14 This snippet of the page's HTML source (see Figure 12.13) shows the original, submitted value, the value after using html_entities(), and the value after using strip_tags().

Preventing SQL Injection Attacks

Another type of attack that malicious users can attempt are *SQL injection* attacks. As the name implies, these are endeavors to insert bad code into a site's SQL queries. One aim of such attacks is that they would create a syntactically invalid query, thereby revealing something about the script or database in the resulting error message (**Figure 12.15**). An even bigger aspiration is that the injection attack could alter, destroy, or expose the stored data.

Fortunately SQL injection attacks are rather easy to prevent. Start by validating all data to be used in queries (and perform typecasting, whenever possible). Second, use a function like `mysqli_real_escape_string()`, which makes data safe to use in queries. This function was introduced in Chapter 8, "Using PHP and MySQL." Third, don't show detailed errors on live sites.

An alternative to using `mysqli_real_escape_string()` is to use *prepared statements*. Prepared statements were added to MySQL in version 4.1, and PHP can use them as of version 5 (thanks to the Improved MySQL extension). When not using prepared statements, the entire query, including the SQL syntax and the specific values, is sent to MySQL as one long string. MySQL then parses and executes it. With a prepared query, the SQL syntax is sent to MySQL first, where it is parsed, making sure it's syntactically valid. Then the specific values are sent separately; MySQL assembles the query using those values, then executes it. The benefits of prepared statements are important: greater security and potentially better performance. I'll focus on the security aspect here, but see the sidebar for a discussion of performance.

Prepared statements can be created out of any `INSERT`, `UPDATE`, `DELETE`, or `SELECT` query. Begin by defining your query, marking *placeholders* using question marks. As an example, take the `SELECT` query from `edit_user.php` (Script 9.3):

```
$q = "SELECT first_name, last_name,
→ email FROM users WHERE user_id=$id";
```

As a prepared statement, this query becomes

```
$q = "SELECT first_name, last_name,
→ email FROM users WHERE user_id=?";
```

Next, prepare the statement in MySQL, assigning the results to a PHP variable.

```
$stmt = mysqli_prepare($dbc, $q);
```

At this point, MySQL will parse the query, but it won't execute it.

continues on next page

You could not be registered due to a system error. We apologize for any inconvenience.

You have an error in your SQL syntax; check the manual that corresponds to your MySQL server version for the right syntax to use near ';DELETE TABLE test', 'Ullman', 'email@example.com', SHA1('password'), NOW())' at line 1

Query: INSERT INTO users (first_name, last_name, email, pass, registration_date) VALUES (';DELETE TABLE test', 'Ullman', 'email@example.com', SHA1('password'), NOW())

Figure 12.15 If a site reveals a detailed error message and doesn't properly handle problematic characters in submitted values, hackers can learn a lot about your server.

Next, you *bind* PHP variables to the query's placeholders. In other words, you state that one variable should be used for one question mark, another variable for the other question mark, and so on. Continuing with the same example, you would code

```
mysqli_stmt_bind_param($stmt, 'i', $id);
```

The *i* part of the command indicates what kind of value should be expected, using the characters listed in **Table 12.3**. In this case, the query expects to receive one integer. As another example, here's how the login query from Chapter 11, "Cookies and Sessions," would be handled:

```
$q = "SELECT user_id, first_name FROM
→ users WHERE email=? AND pass=SHA1(?)";

$stmt = mysqli_prepare($dbc, $q);

mysqli_stmt_bind_param($stmt, 'ss', $e,
→ $p);
```

In this example, something interesting is also revealed: even though both the email address and password values are strings, *they are not placed within quotes* in the query. This is another difference between a prepared statement and a standard query.

Once the statement has been bound, you can assign values to the PHP variables (if that hasn't happened already) and then execute the statement. Using the login example, that'd be:

```
$e = 'email@example.com';

$p = 'mypass';

mysqli_stmt_execute($stmt);
```

The values of $e and $p will be used when the prepared statement is executed.

Table 12.3 Use these characters to tell the `mysql_stmt_bind_param()` function what kinds of values to expect.

Bound Value Types	
LETTER	REPRESENTS
d	Decimal
i	Integer
b	Blob (binary data)
s	All other types

Prepared Statement Performance

Prepared statements will always be more secure than running queries in the old-fashioned way, but they may also be faster. If a PHP script sends the same query to MySQL multiple times, using different values each time, prepared statements can really speed things up. In such cases, the query itself is only sent to MySQL and parsed once. Then, the values are sent to MySQL separately.

As a trivial example, the following code would run 100 queries in MySQL:

```
$q = 'INSERT INTO counter (num)
→ VALUES (?)';

$stmt = mysqli_prepare($dbc, $q);

mysqli_stmt_bind_param($stmt, 'i',
→ $n);

for ($n = 1; $n <= 100; $n++) {

    mysqli_stmt_execute($stmt);

}
```

Even though the query is being run 100 times, the full text is only being transferred to, and parsed by, MySQL once. MySQL versions 5.1.17 and later will include a caching mechanism that may also improve the performance of other uses of prepared statements.

Script 12.4 This script, which represents a simplified version of a message posting page, uses prepared statements as a way of preventing SQL injection attacks.

```
●  ○  ○                    📄 Script
1   <!DOCTYPE html PUBLIC "-//W3C//DTD XHTML
    1.0 Transitional//EN"

2       "http://www.w3.org/TR/xhtml1/DTD/
    xhtml1-transitional.dtd">

3   <html xmlns="http://www.w3.org/1999/xhtml"
    xml:lang="en" lang="en">

4   <head>

5     <meta http-equiv="content-type" content=
    "text/html; charset=iso-8859-1" />

6     <title>Post a Message</title>

7   </head>

8   <body>

9   <?php # Script 12.4 - post_message.php

10

11  if (isset($_POST['submitted'])) {

12

13    // Validate the data (omitted)!

14

15    // Connect to the database:

16    $dbc = mysqli_connect ('localhost',
    'username', 'password', 'forum');

17

18    // Make the query:

19    $q = 'INSERT INTO messages (forum_id,
    parent_id, user_id, subject, body,
    date_entered) VALUES (?, ?, ?, ?, ?,
    NOW())';

20

21    // Prepare the statement:

22    $stmt = mysqli_prepare($dbc, $q);

23

24    // Bind the variables:

25    mysqli_stmt_bind_param($stmt, 'iiiss',
    $forum_id, $parent_id, $user_id,
    $subject, $body);

26

27    // Assign the values to variables:

28    $forum_id = (int) $_POST['forum_id'];
```

(script continues on next page)

To see this process in action, let's write a script that adds a message to the *messages* table in the *forum* database (created in Chapter 6, "Advanced SQL and MySQL"). I'll also use the opportunity to demonstrate a couple of the other prepared statement-related functions.

To use prepared statements:

1. Create a new PHP script in your text editor or IDE (**Script 12.4**).

   ```
   <!DOCTYPE html PUBLIC "-//W3C//DTD
   → XHTML 1.0 Transitional//EN"

   "http://www.w3.org/TR/xhtml1/DTD/xhtm
   → l1-transitional.dtd">

   <html xmlns="http://www.w3.org/1999/
   → xhtml" xml:lang="en" lang="en">

   <head>

        <meta http-equiv="content-type"
   → content="text/html; charset=
   → iso-8859-1" />

        <title>Post a Message</title>

   </head>

   <body>

   <?php # Script 12.4 - post_
   → message.php
   ```

2. Check for form submission and connect to the *forum* database.

   ```
   if (isset($_POST['submitted'])) {

        $dbc = mysqli_connect
   → ('localhost', 'username',
   → 'password', 'forum');
   ```

   Note that, for brevity's sake, I'm omitting basic data validation and error reporting. Although a real site (a more realized version of this script can be found in Chapter 15, "Example—Message Board"), would check that the message subject

   continues on next page

and body aren't empty and that the various ID values are positive integers, this script will still be relatively safe, thanks to the security offered by prepared statements.

This example will use the *forum* database, created in Chapter 6.

3. Define and prepare the query.

```
$q = 'INSERT INTO messages (forum_id,
→ parent_id, user_id, subject, body,
→ date_entered) VALUES (?, ?, ?, ?,
→ ?, NOW())';

$stmt = mysqli_prepare($dbc, $q);
```

This syntax has already been explained. The query is defined, using placeholders for values to be assigned later. Then the `mysqli_prepare()` function sends this to MySQL, assigning the result to `$stmt`.

The query itself was first used in Chapter 6. It populates six fields in the *messages* table. The value for the `date_entered` column will be the result of the `NOW()` function, not a bound value.

4. Bind the appropriate variables and create a list of values to be inserted.

```
mysqli_stmt_bind_param($stmt,
→ 'iiiss', $forum_id, $parent_id,
→ $user_id, $subject, $body);

$forum_id = (int) $_POST['forum_id'];

$parent_id = (int) $_POST
→ ['parent_id'];

$user_id = 3;

$subject = strip_tags($_POST
→ ['subject']);

$body = strip_tags($_POST['body']);
```

The first line says that three integers and two strings will be used in the prepared statement. The values will be found in the variables to follow.

Script 12.4 *continued*

```
29    $parent_id = (int) $_POST['parent_id'];

30    $user_id = 3; // The user_id value would
      normally come from the session.

31    $subject = strip_tags($_POST
      ['subject']);

32    $body = strip_tags($_POST['body']);

33

34    // Execute the query:

35    mysqli_stmt_execute($stmt);

36

37    // Print a message based upon the
      result:

38    if (mysqli_stmt_affected_rows($stmt) ==
      1) {

39       echo '<p>Your message has been
         posted.</p>';

40    } else {

41       echo '<p style="font-weight: bold;
         color: #C00">Your message could not
         be posted.</p>';

42       echo '<p>' . mysqli_stmt_error($stmt) .
         '</p>';

43    }

44

45    // Close the statement:

46    mysqli_stmt_close($stmt);

47

48    // Close the connection:

49    mysqli_close($dbc);

50

51    } // End of submission IF.

52

53    // Display the form:

54    ?>

55    <form action="post_message.php"
      method="post">

56

57       <fieldset><legend>Post a message:
         </legend>

58
```

(script continues on next page)

For those variables, the subject and body values come straight from the form, after running them through `strip_tags()` to remove any potentially dangerous code. The forum ID and parent ID (which indicates if the message is a reply to an existing message or not) also come from the form. They'll be typecast to integers (for added security, you would confirm that they're positive numbers after typecasting them).

The user ID value, in a real script, would come from the session, where it would be stored when the user logged in.

5. Execute the query.

```
mysqli_stmt_execute($stmt);
```

Finally, the prepared statement is executed.

Script 12.4 *continued*

```
● ● ●                    📄 Script
59   <p><b>Subject</b>: <input name="subject"
     type="text" size="30" maxlength="100"
     /></p>

60

61   <p><b>Body</b>: <textarea name="body"
     rows="3" cols="40"></textarea></p>

62

63   </fieldset>

64   <div align="center"><input type="submit"
     name="submit" value="Submit" /></div>

65   <input type="hidden" name="submitted"
     value="TRUE" />

66   <input type="hidden" name="forum_id"
     value="1" />

67   <input type="hidden" name="parent_id"
     value="0" />

68

69   </form>

70   </body>

71   </html>
```

6. Print the results of the execution and complete the loop.

```
if (mysqli_stmt_affected_rows
→ ($stmt) == 1) {

    echo '<p>Your message has been
    → posted.</p>';

} else {

    echo '<p style="font-weight:
    → bold; color: #C00">Your
    → message could not be
    → posted.</p>';

    echo '<p>' . mysqli_stmt_
    → error($stmt) . '</p>';

}
```

The successful insertion of a record can be confirmed using the `mysqli_stmt_affected_rows()` function, which works as you expect it would (returning the number of affected rows). If a problem occurred, the `mysqli_stmt_error()` function returns the specific MySQL error message. This is for your debugging purposes, not to be used in a live site.

7. Close the statement and the database connection.

```
mysqli_stmt_close($stmt);

mysqli_close($dbc);
```

The first function closes the prepared statement, freeing up the resources. At this point, `$stmt` no longer has a value. The second function closes the database connection.

8. Complete the PHP section.

```
} // End of submission IF.

?>
```

continues on next page

PREVENTING SQL INJECTION ATTACKS

9. Create the form.

```
<form action="post_message.php"
→ method="post">

<fieldset><legend>Post a message:
→ </legend>

<p><b>Subject</b>: <input name=
→ "subject" type="text" size="30"
→ maxlength="100" /></p>

<p><b>Body</b>: <textarea name="body"
→ rows="3" cols="40"></textarea></p>

</fieldset>

<div align="center"><input type=
→ "submit" name="submit" value=
→ "Submit" /></div>

<input type="hidden" name="submitted"
→  value="TRUE" />

<input type="hidden" name="forum_id"
→ value="1" />

<input type="hidden" name="parent_id"
→ value="0" />

</form>
```

The form contains two fields the user would fill out and two hidden inputs that store values the query needs. In a real version of this script, it would determine the forum_id and parent_id values automatically.

10. Complete the page.

```
</body>

</html>
```

11. Save the file as post_message.php, place it in your Web directory, and test it in your Web browser (**Figures 12.16**, **12.17**, and **12.18**).

✔ Tip

■ There are two kinds of prepared statements. Here I have demonstrated *bound parameters*, where PHP variables are bound to a query. The other type is *bound results*, where the results of a query are bound to PHP variables.

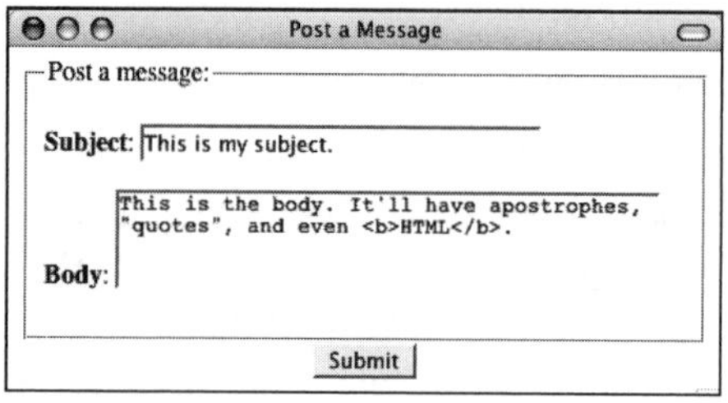

Figure 12.16 The simple HTML form.

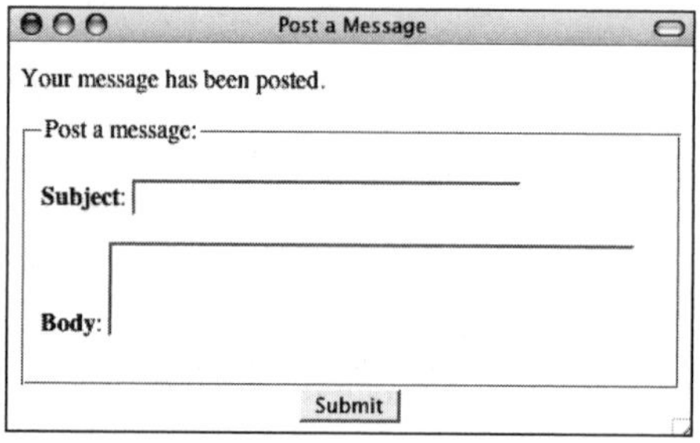

Figure 12.17 If one record in the database was affected by the query, this will be the result.

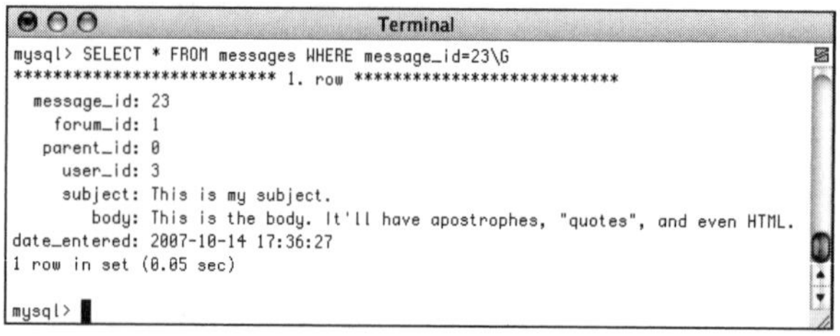

Figure 12.18 Selecting the most recent entry in the *messages* table confirms that the prepared statement (Script 12.4) worked. Notice that the HTML was stripped out of the post but the quotes are still present.

Database Encryption

As a brief conclusion to this chapter, I'll go over true encryption in a MySQL database. Up to this point, pseudo-encryption has been accomplished via the SHA1() function. In the registration and login examples, the user's password has been stored after running it through SHA1(). Although using this function in this way is perfectly fine (and quite common), the function doesn't provide real encryption: the SHA1() function returns a representation of a value. If you need to store data in a protected way while still being able to view the data is its original form at some later point, other MySQL functions are necessary.

Encryption

MySQL has several encryption and decryption functions built into the software. If you require data to be stored in an encrypted form that can be decrypted, you'll want to use AES_ENCRYPT() and AES_DECRYPT(). These functions take two arguments: the string being encrypted or decrypted and a *salt* argument. The salt argument is a string that helps to randomize the encryption. The only trick is that the exact same salt must be used for both encryption and decryption.

To add a record to a table while encrypting the data, the query might look like

```
INSERT INTO tablename (username, pass)
VALUES ('troutster',
AES_ENCRYPT('mypass', 'nacl'))
```

The encrypted data returned by the AES_ENCRYPT() function will be in binary format. To store that data in a table, the column must be defined as one of the binary types (e.g., BLOB).

To run a login query for the record just inserted (matching a submitted username and password against those in the database), you would write

```
SELECT * FROM tablename WHERE
username = 'troutster' AND
AES_DECRYPT(pass, 'nacl') = 'mypass'
```

The AES_ENCRYPT() function is considered to be the most secure encryption option (it's available as of MySQL version 4.0.2). To demonstrate how you'd use it, let's run some queries on the *test* database using a MySQL client.

To encrypt and decrypt data:

1. Access MySQL and select the *test* database (**Figure 12.19**).

   ```
   USE test;
   ```

continues on next page

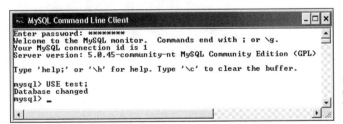

Figure 12.19 The following examples will all be run in the mysql client, on the *test* database.

Follow the steps outlined in Chapter 4, "Introduction to MySQL," to connect to the mysql client. Alternatively, you can use phpMyAdmin or another interface to run the queries in the following steps.

2. Create a new *encode* table (**Figure 12.20**).

```
CREATE TABLE encode (
id INT UNSIGNED NOT NULL
AUTO_INCREMENT,
card_number TINYBLOB,
PRIMARY KEY (id)
);
```

This table, *encode*, will contain fields for just an id and a (credit) card_number. The card_number will be encrypted using AES_ENCRYPT() so that it can be decoded. AES_ENCRYPT() returns a binary value that ought to be stored in a BLOB (or TINYBLOB here) column type.

3. Insert a new record (**Figure 12.21**).

```
INSERT INTO encode (id, card_number)
VALUES (NULL,
AES_ENCRYPT(1234567890123456,
'eLL10tT'));
```

Here I am adding a new record to the table, using the AES_ENCRYPT() function with a salt of *eLL10tT* to encrypt the card number. Always try to use a unique salt with your encryption functions. Also remember that you cannot have spaces between your function names and their opening parentheses.

4. Retrieve the record in an unencrypted form (**Figure 12.22**).

```
SELECT id, AES_DECRYPT(card_number,
'eLL10tT') AS cc FROM encode;
```

This query returns all of the records, decrypting the credit card number in the process. Any value stored using AES_ENCRYPT() can be retrieved (and matched) using AES_DECRYPT(), as long as the same salt is used (here, *eLL10tT*).

5. Check out the table's contents without using decryption (**Figure 12.23**).

```
SELECT * FROM encode;
```

As you can see in the figure, the encrypted version of the credit card number is unreadable. This is exactly the kind of security measure required by e-commerce applications.

Figure 12.20 The *encode* table, consisting of only two columns, is added to the database.

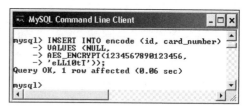

Figure 12.21 A record is inserted, using an encryption function to protect the credit card number.

✔ Tips

- As a rule of thumb, use SHA1() for information that will never need to be viewable, such as passwords and perhaps usernames. Use AES_ENCRYPT() for information that needs to be protected but may need to be viewable at a later date, such as credit card information, Social Security numbers, addresses (perhaps), and so forth.

- As a reminder, it's much more secure to never store credit card numbers and other high-risk data.

Secure salt storage

While the preceding sequence of steps demonstrates how you can add a level of security to your Web applications by encrypting and decrypting sensitive data, there's still room for improvement. The main issue is protecting the encryption salt, which is key to the encryption process.

In order for a PHP script to use a salt in its queries, PHP must have access to it. Most likely, the salt might be placed in the same script that establishes a database connection. But storing this value in a plain text format on the server makes it more vulnerable.

As an alternative, you can store the salt in a database table. Then, when a query needs to use this value, it can be selected. This process can be simplified thanks to user-defined MySQL variables. I discuss this concept in more detail in my book *MySQL: Visual QuickStart Guide, Second Edition* (Peachpit Press, 2006), but I'll provide a quick rundown of that process here.

To just establish a user-defined variable, use this SQL command:

```
SELECT @var:=value
```

So, you could write

```
SELECT @PI:=3.14
```

To define a variable based upon a value stored in a table, the syntax is just an extension of this:

```
SELECT @var:=some_column FROM tablename
```

Once you've established @var, it can be used in other queries:

```
SELECT * FROM tablename WHERE col=@var
```

This next sequence of steps will demonstrate this approach in action, using the mysql client. Doing the same thing in a PHP script is described in the first tip.

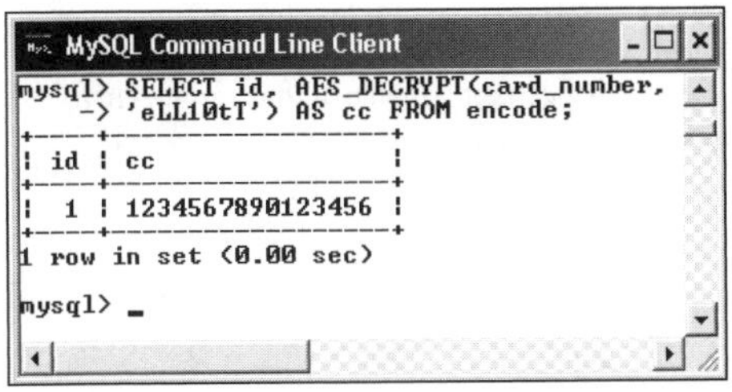

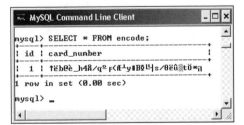

Figure 12.22 The record has been retrieved, decrypting the credit card number in the process.

Figure 12.23 Encrypted data is stored in an unreadable format (here, as a binary string of data).

To use a database-stored salt:

1. Log in to the mysql client and select the *test* database, if you haven't already.

2. Empty the *encode* table (**Figure 12.24**).

   `TRUNCATE TABLE encode;`

   Because I'm going to be using a different encryption function, I'll want to clear out all the existing data before repopulating it. The TRUNCATE command is the best way to do so.

3. Create and populate an *aes_salt* table (**Figure 12.25**).

   ```
   CREATE TABLE aes_salt (

       salt VARCHAR(12) NOT NULL

   );

   INSERT INTO aes_salt (salt)

   VALUES ('0bfuscate');
   ```

   This table, *aes_salt*, will store the encryption salt value in its one column. The INSERT query stores the salt, which will be retrieved and assigned to a user-defined variable as needed.

4. Retrieve the stored salt value and use it to insert a new record into the *encode* table (**Figure 12.26**).

   ```
   SELECT @salt:=salt FROM aes_salt;

   INSERT INTO encode (card_number)

   VALUES (AES_ENCRYPT(1234567890123456,

   @salt));
   ```

   The first line retrieves the stored salt value from the *aes_salt* table and assigns this to @salt (the figure shows the results of the SELECT statement). Then a standard INSERT query is run to add a record to the *encode* table. In this case, @salt is used in the query instead of a hard-coded salt value.

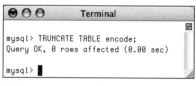

Figure 12.24 Run a TRUNCATE query to empty a table.

```
mysql> CREATE TABLE aes_salt (
    ->    salt VARCHAR(12) NOT NULL
    -> );
Query OK, 0 rows affected (0.01 sec)

mysql> INSERT INTO aes_salt (salt)
    -> VALUES ('0bfuscate');
Query OK, 1 row affected (0.01 sec)

mysql>
```

Figure 12.25 The *aes_salt* table has one column and should only ever have one row of data. The INSERT query stores the salt value in this table.

```
mysql> SELECT @salt:=salt FROM aes_salt;
+-------------+
| @salt:=salt |
+-------------+
| 0bfuscate   |
+-------------+
1 row in set (0.03 sec)

mysql> INSERT INTO encode (card_number)
    -> VALUES (AES_ENCRYPT(1234567890123456,
    -> @salt));
Query OK, 1 row affected (0.01 sec)

mysql>
```

Figure 12.26 These two queries show how you can retrieve a salt value using one query, assigning the value to a variable, then use that variable in a second query.

```
mysql> SELECT @salt:=salt FROM aes_salt;
+-------------+
| @salt:=salt |
+-------------+
| 0bfuscate   |
+-------------+
1 row in set (0.05 sec)

mysql> SELECT id, AES_DECRYPT(card_number,
    -> @salt) AS cc FROM encode;
+----+------------------+
| id | cc               |
+----+------------------+
|  1 | 1234567890123456 |
+----+------------------+
1 row in set (0.05 sec)

mysql>
```

Figure 12.27 A similar query (see Figure 12.22) is used to decrypt stored information using a database-stored salt.

- Prior to version 5.0 of MySQL, user variable names are case-sensitive.

- Never establish and use a user-defined variable within the same SQL statement.

- Storing the salt in the database, as demonstrated in these steps, adds improved security over storing it in a PHP script. Even better security can be had by using unique and random salts for each stored record.

5. Decrypt the stored credit card number (**Figure 12.27**).

SELECT @salt:=salt FROM aes_salt;

SELECT id, AES_DECRYPT(card_number,

@salt) AS cc FROM encode;

The first step retrieves the salt value so that it can be used for decryption purposes. (If you followed these steps without closing the MySQL session, this step wouldn't actually be necessary, as @salt would already be established.) The @salt variable is then used with he AES_DECRYPT() function.

✔ Tips

- The code in these steps (for retrieving and using a salt stored in a table) can easily be used in a PHP script. Run the first query, then run the second query, and then fetch the results:

```
$r = mysqli_query($dbc, 'SELECT
→ @salt:=salt FROM aes_salt');
```

```
$r = mysqli_query($dbc, 'SELECT id,
→ AES_DECRYPT(card_number, @salt)
→ AS cc FROM encode');
```

```
$row = mysqli_fetch_array($r,
→ MYSQLI_ASSOC);
```

You can make this more professional by calling the mysqli_num_rows() function prior to running the second query or fetching the results, of course. But notice that you don't have to fetch the results of the first query into the PHP script. The results of that query will be assigned to the @salt variable, residing in MySQL, associated with this connection.

- User variables are particular to each connection. When one script or one mysql client session connects to MySQL and establishes a variable, only that one script or session has access to that variable.

DATABASE ENCRYPTION

Preventing Brute Force Attacks

A brute force attack is an attempt to log into a secure system by making lots of attempts in the hopes of eventual success. It's not a sophisticated type of attack, hence the name "brute force." For example, if you have a login process that requires a username and password, there is a limit as to the possible number of username/password combinations. That limit may be in the billions or trillions, but still, it's a finite number. Using algorithms and automated processes, a brute force attack repeatedly tries combinations until they succeed.

The best way to prevent brute force attacks from succeeding is requiring users to register with good, hard-to-guess passwords: containing letters, numbers, and punctuation; both upper and lowercase; words not in the dictionary; at least eight characters long, etc. Also, don't give indications as to why a login failed: saying that a username and password combination isn't correct gives away nothing, but saying that a username isn't right or that the password isn't right for that username says too much.

To stop a brute force attack in its tracks, you could also limit the number of incorrect login attempts by a given IP address. IP addresses do change frequently, but in a brute force attack, the same IP address would be trying to login multiple times in a matter of minutes. You would have to track incorrect logins by IP address, and then, after X number of invalid attempts, block that IP address for 24 hours (or something). Or, if you didn't want to go that far, you could use an "incremental delay" defense: each incorrect login from the same IP address creates an added delay in the response (use PHP's `sleep()` function to create the delay). Humans might not notice or be bothered by such delays, but automated attacks most certainly would.

PERL-COMPATIBLE REGULAR EXPRESSIONS

13

Regular expressions are an amazingly powerful (but tedious) tool available in most of today's programming languages and even in many applications. Think of regular expressions as an elaborate system of matching patterns. You first write the pattern and then use one of PHP's built-in functions to apply the pattern to a value (regular expressions are applied to strings, even if that means a string with a numeric value). Whereas a string function could see if the name *John* is in some text, a regular expression could just as easily find *John*, *Jon*, and *Jonathon*.

PHP supports several types of regular expressions, the two most popular being POSIX Extended and Perl-Compatible (PCRE). In previous editions of this book (and in other books), I exclusively use the POSIX version. They are somewhat less powerful and potentially slower than PCRE but are far easier to learn. But PCRE is becoming the preferred type to use in PHP, so I'll provide an introduction to it here instead.

Because the regular expression syntax is so complex, while the functions that use them are simple, the focus in this chapter will be on mastering the syntax in little bites. The PHP code will be very simple; later chapters will better incorporate regular expressions into real-world scripts.

Creating a Test Script

As already stated, regular expressions are a matter of applying patterns to values. The application of the pattern to a value is accomplished using one of a handful of functions, the most important being preg_match(). This function returns a *0* or *1*, indicating whether or not the pattern matched the string. Its basic syntax is

```
preg_match(pattern, subject);
```

The preg_match() function will stop once it finds a single match. If you need to find all the matches, use preg_match_all(). That function will be discussed toward the end of the chapter.

When providing the pattern to preg_match(), it needs to be placed within quotation marks, as it'll be a string. Because many escaped characters within double quotation marks have special meaning (like \n), I advocate using single quotation marks to define your patterns.

Secondarily, within the quotation marks, the pattern needs to be encased within *delimiters*. The delimiter can be any character that's not alphanumeric or the backslash, and the same character must be used to mark the beginning and end of the pattern. Commonly you'll see forward slashes used. So, to see if the word *cat* contains the letter *a*, you would code:

```
if (preg_match('/a/', 'cat')) { …
```

If you need to match a forward slash in the pattern, use a different delimiter, like the pipe (|) or an exclamation mark (!).

The bulk of this chapter covers all the rules for defining patterns. In order to best learn by example, let's start by creating a simple PHP script that takes a pattern and a string (**Figure 13.1**) and returns the regular expression result (**Figure 13.2**).

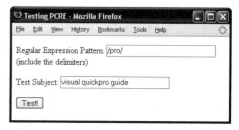

Figure 13.1 The HTML form, which will be used for practicing regular expressions.

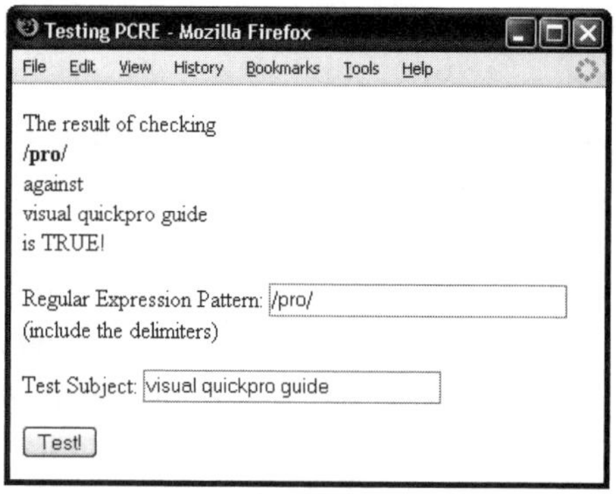

Figure 13.2 The script will print what values were used in the regular expression and what the result was. The form will also be made sticky to remember previously submitted values.

CREATING A TEST SCRIPT

Script 13.1 The complex regular expression syntax will be best taught and demonstrated using this PHP script.

```
                    Script
1   <!DOCTYPE html PUBLIC "-//W3C//DTD XHTML
    1.0 Transitional//EN"

2
    "http://www.w3.org/TR/xhtml1/DTD/xhtml1-
    transitional.dtd">

3   <html xmlns="http://www.w3.org/1999/
    xhtml">

4   <head>

5     <meta http-equiv="content-type" content=
    "text/html; charset=iso-8859-1" />

6     <title>Testing PCRE</title>

7   </head>

8   <body>

9   <?php // Script 13.1 - pcre.php

10

11  // This script takes a submitted string
    and checks it against a submitted pattern.

12

13  if (isset($_POST['submitted'])) {

14

15    // Trim the strings:

16    $pattern = trim($_POST['pattern']);

17    $subject = trim($_POST['subject']);

18

19    // Print a caption:

20    echo "<p>The result of checking<br
    /><b>$pattern</b><br />against<br
    />$subject<br />is ";

21

22    // Test:

23    if (preg_match ($pattern, $subject) ) {

24      echo 'TRUE!</p>';

25    } else {

26      echo 'FALSE!</p>';

27    }

28

29  } // End of submission IF.
```

(script continues)

To match a pattern:

1. Create a new PHP document in your text editor or IDE (**Script 13.1**).

```
<!DOCTYPE html PUBLIC "-//W3C//DTD
→ XHTML 1.0 Transitional//EN"

"http://www.w3.org/TR/xhtml1/DTD/xhtm
→ l1-transitional.dtd">

<html xmlns="http://www.w3.org/
→ 1999/xhtml">

<head>

    <meta http-equiv="content-type"
    → content="text/html; charset=
    → iso-8859-1" />

    <title>Testing PCRE</title>

</head>

<body>

<?php // Script 13.1 - pcre.php
```

continues on next page

Script 13.1 *continued*

```
                    Script
30  // Display the HTML form.

31  ?>

32  <form action="pcre.php" method="post">

33    <p>Regular Expression Pattern: <input
    type="text" name="pattern" value="<?php
    if (isset($pattern)) echo $pattern; ?>"
    size="30" /> (include the
    delimiters)</p>

34    <p>Test Subject: <input type="text"
    name="subject" value="<?php if
    (isset($subject)) echo $subject; ?>"
    size="30" /></p>

35    <input type="submit" name="submit"
    value="Test!" />

36    <input type="hidden" name="submitted"
    value="TRUE" />

37  </form>

38  </body>

39  </html>
```

2. Check for the form submission.

```
if (isset($_POST['submitted'])) {
```

3. Treat the incoming values.

```
$pattern = trim($_POST['pattern']);

$subject = trim($_POST['subject']);
```

The form will submit two values to this same script. Both should be trimmed, just to make sure the presence of any extraneous spaces doesn't skew the results. I've omitted a check that each input isn't empty, but you could include that if you wanted.

4. Print a caption.

```
echo "<p>The result of checking<br
→ /><b>$pattern</b><br />against<br
→ />$subject<br />is ";
```

As you can see in Figure 13.2, the form handling part of this script will start by printing the values used.

5. Run the regular expression.

```
if (preg_match ($pattern, $subject) )
{

  print 'TRUE!</p>';

} else {

  print 'FALSE!</p>';

}
```

To test the pattern against the string, feed both to the preg_match() function. If this function returns *1*, that means a match was made, this condition will be true, and the word *TRUE* will be printed. If no match was made, the condition will be false and that will be stated (**Figure 13.3**).

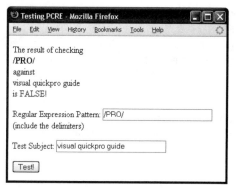

Figure 13.3 If the pattern does not match the string, this will be the result. This image also shows that regular expressions are case-sensitive by default.

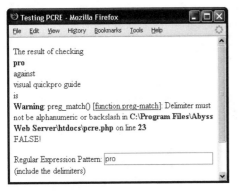

Figure 13.4 If you fail to wrap the pattern in matching delimiters, you'll see an error message.

6. Complete the PHP code and create the HTML form.

```
?>

<form action="pcre.php" method=
→ "post">

    <p>Regular Expression Pattern:
    → <input type="text" name=
    → "pattern" value="<?php if
    → (isset($pattern)) echo
    → $pattern; ?>" size="30" />
    → (include the delimiters)</p>

    <p>Test Subject: <input type=
    → "text" name="subject" value=
    → "<?php if (isset($subject))
    → echo $subject; ?>" size="30"
    → /></p>

    <input type="submit" name=
    → "submit" value="Test!" />

    <input type="hidden" name=
    → "submitted" value="TRUE" />

</form>
```

The form contains two text boxes, both of which are sticky (using the trimmed version of the values).

7. Complete the HTML page.

```
</body>

</html>
```

8. Save the file as `pcre.php`, place it in your Web directory, and test it in your Web browser (Figures 13.1, 13.2, and 13.3).

Although you don't know the rules for creating patterns yet, you could use the literal *a* test (see Figures 13.1 and 13.2) or check any other literal value. Remember to use delimiters around the pattern or else you'll see an error message (**Figure 13.4**).

✔ Tips

■ Some text editors, such as BBEdit and emacs, allow you to use regular expressions to match and replace patterns within and throughout several documents.

■ Another difference between POSIX and PCRE regular expressions is that the latter can be used on binary data while the former cannot.

■ The PCRE functions all use the established locale. A *locale*, discussed more in Chapter 14, "Making Universal Sites," reflects a computer's designated country and language, among other settings.

Defining Simple Patterns

Using one of PHP's regular expression functions is really easy, defining patterns to use is hard. There are lots of rules for creating a pattern. You can use these rules separately or in combination, making your pattern either quite simple or very complex. To start, then, you'll see what characters are used to define a simple pattern. As a formatting rule, I'll define patterns in **bold** and will indicate what the pattern matches in *italics*. The patterns in these explanations won't be placed within delimiters or quotes (both being needed when used within `preg_match()`), just to keep things cleaner.

The first type of character you will use for defining patterns is a *literal*. A literal is a value that is written exactly as it is interpreted. For example, the pattern **a** will match the letter *a*, **ab** will match *ab*, and so forth. Therefore, assuming a case-insensitive search is performed, **rom** will match any of the following strings, since they all contain *rom*:

◆ CD-ROM

◆ Rommel crossed the desert.

◆ I'm writing a roman à clef.

Along with literals, your patterns will use *meta-characters*. These are special symbols that have a meaning beyond their literal value (**Table 13.1**). While **a** simply means *a*, the period (.) will match any single character except for a newline (. matches *a, b, c,* the underscore, a space, etc., just not \n). To match any meta-character, you will need to escape it, much as you escape a quotation mark to print it. Hence \. will match the period itself. So **1.99** matches *1.99* or *1B99* or *1299* (a 1 followed by any character followed by 99) but **1\.99** only matches *1.99*.

Table 13.1 The meta-characters have unique meanings inside of regular expressions.

Meta-Characters	
CHARACTER	MEANING
\	Escape character
^	Indicates the beginning of a string
$	Indicates the end of a string
.	Any single character except newline
|	Alternatives (or)
[	Start of a class
]	End of a class
(	Start of a subpattern
)	End of a subpattern
{	Start of a quantifier
}	End of a quantifier

Two meta-characters specify where certain characters must be found. There is the caret (^), which will match a string that begins with whatever follows the caret. There is also the dollar sign ($), which marks the conclusion of a pattern. Accordingly, **^a** will match any string beginning with an *a*, while **a$** will correspond to any string ending with an *a*. Therefore, **^a$** will only match *a* (a string that both begins and ends with *a*).

These two meta-characters—the caret and the dollar sign—are crucial to validation, as validation normally requires checking the value of an entire string, not just the presence of one string in another. For example, using an email matching pattern without those two characters will match any string containing an email address. Using an email matching pattern that begins with a caret and ends with a dollar sign will match a string that contains only a valid email address.

Regular expressions also make use of the pipe (|) as the equivalent of *or*. Therefore, **a|b** will match strings containing either *a* or *b*. (Using the pipe within patterns is called *alternation* or *branching*). So **yes|no** accepts either of those two words in their entirety (the alternation is *not* just between the two letters surrounding it: *s* and *n*).

Once you comprehend the basic symbols, then you can begin to use parentheses to group characters into more involved patterns. Grouping works as you might expect: **(abc)** will match *abc*, **(trout)** will match *trout*. Think of parentheses as being used to establish a new literal of a larger size. Because of precedence rules in PCRE, **yes|no** and **(yes)|(no)** are equivalent. But **(even|heavy) handed** will match either *even handed* or *heavy handed*.

To use simple patterns:

1. Load `pcre.php` in your Web browser, if it is not already.

2. Check if a string contains the letters *cat* (**Figure 13.5**).

   To do so, use the literal **cat** as the pattern and any number of strings as the subject. Any of the following would be a match: *catalog*, *catastrophe*, *my cat left*, etc. For the time being, use all lowercase letters, as **cat** will not match *Cat* (**Figure 13.6**).

   Remember to use delimiters around the pattern, as well (see the figures).

continues on next page

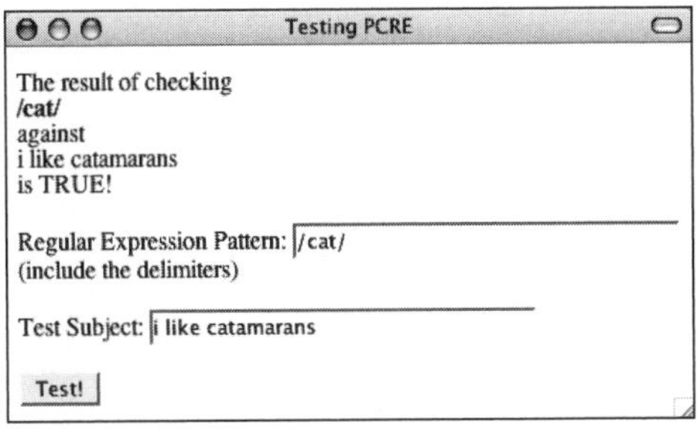

DEFINING **S**IMPLE **P**ATTERNS

Figure 13.5 Looking for a *cat* in a string.

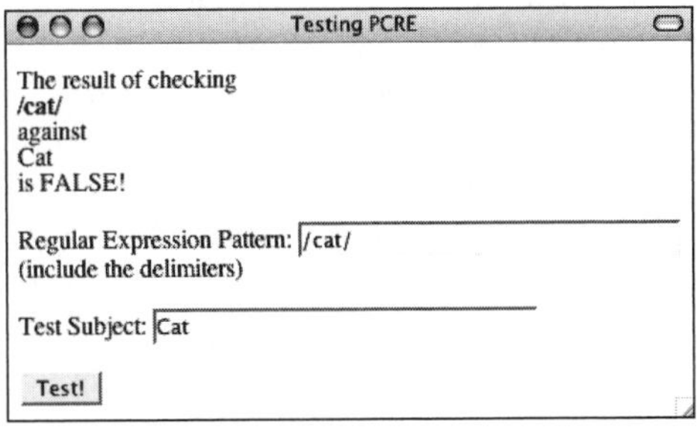

Figure 13.6 Don't forget that PCRE performs a case-sensitive comparison by default.

3. Check if a string starts with *cat* (**Figure 13.7**).

To have a pattern apply to the start of a string, use the caret as the first character (**^cat**). The sentence *my cat left* will not be a match now.

4. Check if a string contains the word *color* or *colour* (**Figure 13.8**).

The pattern to look for the American or British spelling of this word is **col(o|ou)r**. The first three letters —*col*—must be present. This needs to be followed by either an *o* or *ou*. Finally, an *r* is required.

✔ Tips

■ If you are looking to match an exact string within another string, use the `strstr()` function, which is faster than regular expressions. In fact, as a rule of thumb, you should use regular expressions only if the task at hand cannot be accomplished using any other function or technique.

■ You can escape a bunch of characters in a pattern using \Q and \E. Every character within those will be treated literally (so **\Q$2.99?\E** matches *$2.99?*).

■ To match a single backslash, you have to use \\\\. The reason is that matching a backslash in a regular expression requires you to escape the backslash, resulting in \\. Then to use a backslash in a PHP string, it also has to be escaped, so escaping both backslashes means a total of four.

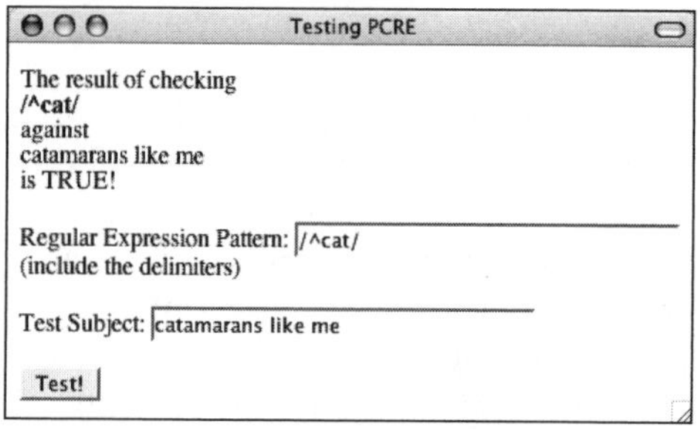

Figure 13.7 The caret in a pattern means that the match has to be found at the start of the string.

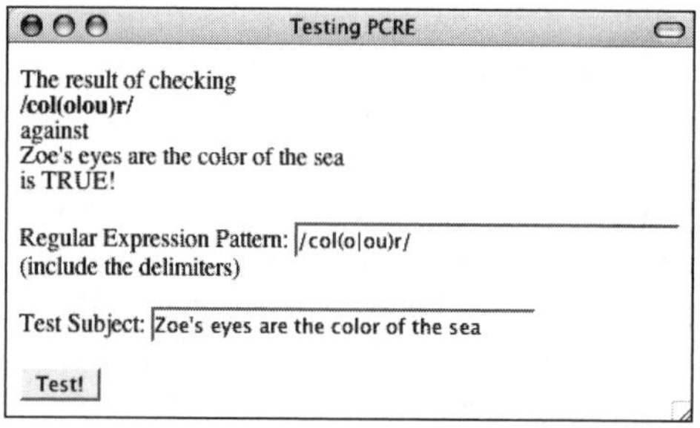

Figure 13.8 By using the pipe meta-character, the performed search can be more flexible.

Table 13.2 The quantifiers allow you to dictate how many times something can or must appear.

Quantifiers	
CHARACTER	MEANING
?	0 or 1
*	0 or more
+	1 or more
{x}	Exactly *x* occurrences
{x, y}	Between *x* and *y* (inclusive)
{x,}	At least *x* occurrences

Using Quantifiers

You've just seen and practiced with a couple of the meta-characters, the most important of which are the caret and the dollar sign. Next, there are three meta-characters that allow for multiple occurrences: **a*** will match zero or more *a*'s (no *a*'s, *a*, *aa*, *aaa*, etc.); **a+** matches one or more *a*'s (*a*, *aa*, *aaa*, etc., but there must be at least one); and **a?** will match up to one *a* (*a* or no *a*'s match). These meta-characters all act as quantifiers in your patterns, as do the curly braces. **Table 13.2** lists all of the quantifiers.

To match a certain quantity of a thing, put the quantity between curly braces ({}), stating a specific number, just a minimum, or both a minimum and a maximum. Thus, **a{3}** will match *aaa*; **a{3,}** will match *aaa*, *aaaa*, etc. (three or more *a*'s); and **a{3,5}** will match just *aaa*, *aaaa*, and *aaaaa* (between three and five).

Note that quantifiers apply to the thing that came before it, so **a?** matches zero or one *a*'s, **ab?** matches an *a* followed by zero or one *b*'s, but **(ab)?** matches zero or one *ab*'s. Therefore, to match *color* or *colour* (see Figure 13.8), you could also use **colou?r** as the pattern.

To use quantifiers:

1. Load pcre.php in your Web browser, if it is not already.

2. Check if a string contains the letters *c* and *t*, with one or more letters in between (**Figure 13.9**).

To do so, use **c.+t** as the pattern and any number of strings as the subject. Remember that the period matches any character (except for the newline). Each of the following would be a match: *cat, count, coefficient,* etc. The word *doctor* would not match, as there are no letters between the *c* and the *t* (although *doctor* would match **c.*t**).

3. Check if a string matches either *cat* or *cats* (**Figure 13.10**).

To start, if you want to make an exact match, use both the caret and the dollar sign. Then you'd have the literal text *cat,* followed by an *s,* followed by a question mark (representing 0 or 1 *s*'s). The final pattern—**^cats?$**—matches *cat* or *cats* but not *my cat left* or *I like cats.*

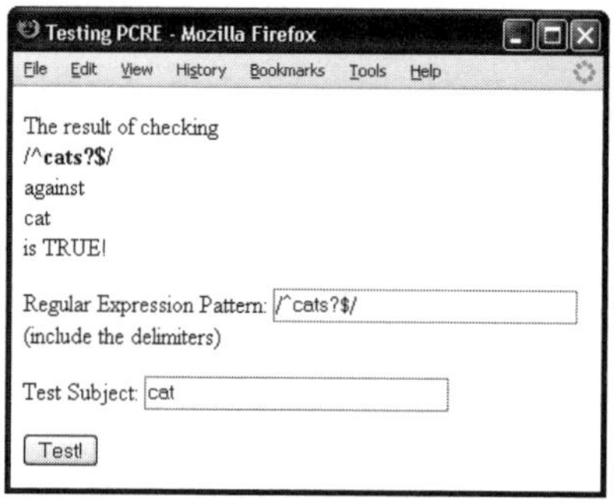

4. Check if a string ends with *.33, .333,* or *.3333* (**Figure 13.11**).

To find a period, escape it with a backslash: \.. To find a three, use a literal **3**. To find a range of 3's, use the curly brackets ({}). Putting this together, the pattern is **\.3{2,4}**. Because the string should end with this (nothing else can follow), conclude the pattern with a dollar sign: **\.3{2,4}$**.

Admittedly, this is kind of a stupid example (not sure when you'd need to do exactly this), but it does demonstrate several things. This pattern will match lots of things—*12.333, varmit.3333, .33, look .33*—but not *12.3* or *12.334.*

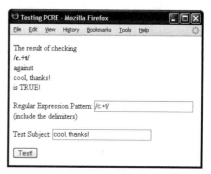

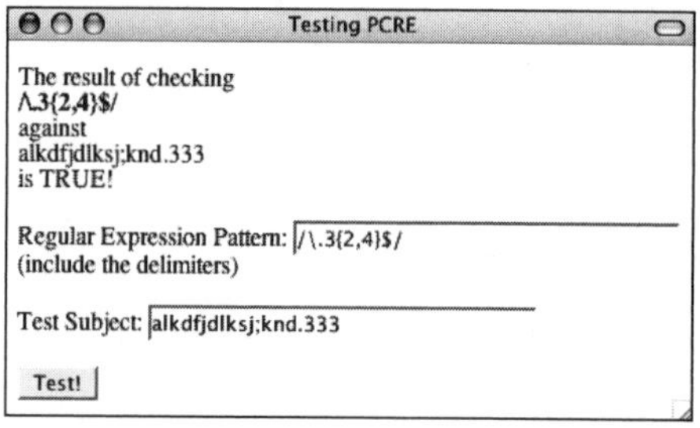

Figure 13.9 The plus sign, when used as a quantifier, requires that one or more of a thing be present.

Figure 13.10 You can check for the plural form of many words by adding *s?* to the pattern.

Figure 13.11 The curly braces let you dictate the acceptable range of quantities present.

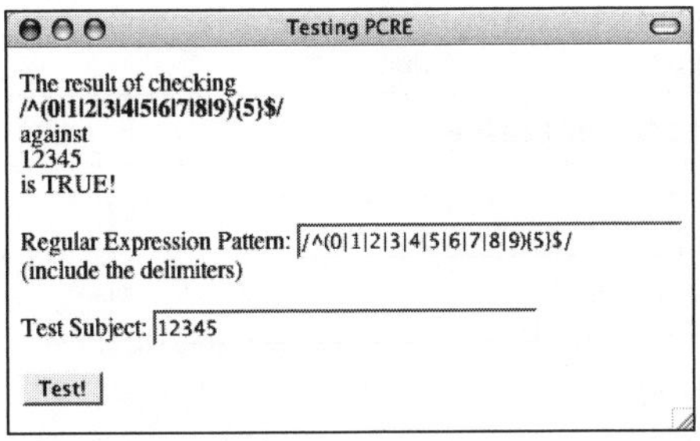

Figure 13.12 The proper test for confirming that a number contains five digits.

5. Match a five-digit number (**Figure 13.12**).

A number can be any one of the numbers 0 through 9, so the heart of the pattern is (**0|1|2|3|4|5|6|7|8|9**). Plainly said, this means: a number is a 0 or a 1 or a 2 or a 3.... To make it a five-digit number, follow this with a quantifier: (**0|1|2|3|4|5|6|7|8|9**){**5**}. Finally, to match this exactly (as opposed to matching a five-digit number within a string), use the caret and the dollar sign: **^(0|1|2|3|4|5|6|7|8|9){5}$**.

This, of course, is one way to match a United States zip code, a very useful pattern.

✔ Tips

■ When using curly braces to specify a number of characters, you must always include the minimum number. The maximum is optional: **a{3}** and **a{3,}** are acceptable, but **a{,3}** is not.

■ Although it demonstrates good dedication to programming to learn how to write and execute your own regular expressions, numerous working examples are available already by searching the Internet.

Using Character Classes

As the last example demonstrated (Figure 13.12), relying solely upon literals in a pattern can be tiresome. Having to write out all those digits to match any number is silly. Imagine if you wanted to match any four-letter word: ^(a|b|c|d...){4}$ (and that doesn't even take into account uppercase letters)! To make these common references easier, you can use *character classes*.

Classes are created by placing characters within square brackets ([]). For example, you can match any one vowel with **[aeiou]**. This is equivalent to **(a|e|i|o|u)**. Or you can use the hyphen to indicate a range of characters: **[a-z]** is any single lowercase letter and **[A-Z]** is any uppercase, **[A-Za-z]** is any letter in general, and **[0-9]** matches any digit. As an example, **[a-z]{3}** would match *abc*, *def*, *oiw*, etc.

Within classes, most of the meta-characters are treated literally, except for four. The backslash is still the escape, but the caret (^) is a negation operator when used as the first character in the class. So **[^aeiou]** will match any non-vowel. The only other meta-character within a class is the dash, which indicates a range. (If the dash is used as the last character in a class, it's a literal dash.) And, of course, the closing bracket (]) still has meaning as the terminator of the class.

Naturally a class can have both ranges and literal characters. A person's first name, which can contain letters, spaces, apostrophes, and periods, could be represented by **[A-z '.]** (again, the period doesn't need to be escaped within the class, as it loses its meta-meaning there).

Along with creating your own classes, there are six already-defined classes that have their own shortcuts (**Table 13.3**). The digit and space classes are easy to understand.

Table 13.3 These character classes are commonly used in regular expressions.

Character Classes		
CLASS	SHORTCUT	MEANING
[0-9]	\d	Any digit
[\f\r\t\n\v]	\s	Any white space
[A-Za-z0-9_]	\w	Any word character
[^0-9]	\D	Not a digit
[^\f\r\t\n\v]	\S	Not white space
[^A-Za-z0-9_]	\W	Not a word character

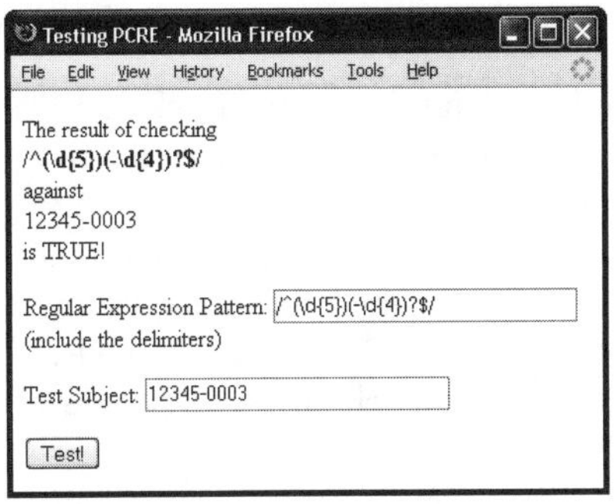

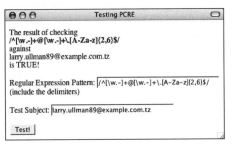

Figure 13.13 The pattern to match a United States zip code, in either the five-digit or five plus four format.

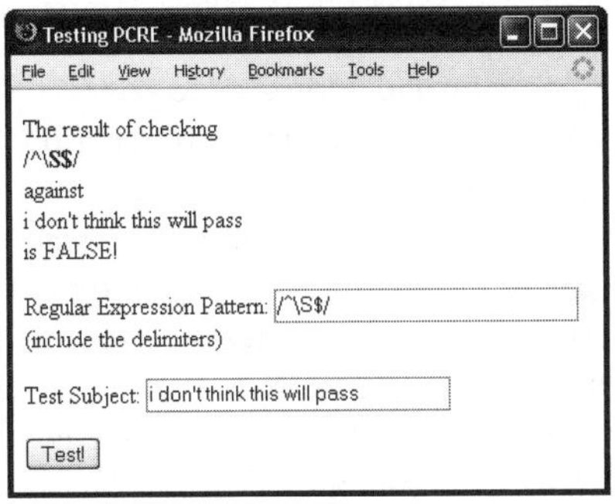

Figure 13.14 The no-white-space shortcut can be used to ensure that a submitting string is contiguous.

Figure 13.15 A pretty good and reliable validation for email addresses.

The word character class doesn't mean "word" in the language sense but rather as in a string unbroken by spaces or punctuation.

Using this information, the five-digit number (aka, zip code) pattern could more easily be written as **^[0-9]{5}$** or **^\d{5}$**. As another example, **can\s?not** will match both *can not* and *cannot* (the word *can*, followed by zero or one space characters, followed by *not*).

To use character classes:

1. Load pcre.php in your Web browser, if it is not already.

2. Check if a string is formatted as a valid United States zip code (**Figure 13.13**).

   A United States zip code always starts with five digits (**^\d{5}**). But a valid zip code could also have a dash followed by another four digits (**-\d{4}$**). To make this last part optional, use the question mark (the 0 or 1 quantifier). This complete pattern is then **^(\d{5})(-\d{4})?$**. To make it all clearer, the first part of the pattern (matching the five digits) is also grouped in parentheses, although this isn't required in this case.

3. Check if a string contains no spaces (**Figure 13.14**).

   The **\S** character class shortcut will match non-space characters. To make sure that the entire string contains no spaces, use the caret and the dollar sign: **^\S$**. If you don't use those, then all the pattern is confirming is that the subject contains at least one non-space character.

4. Validate an email address (**Figure 13.15**).

   The pattern **^[\w.-]+@[\w.-]+\.[A-Za-z]{2,6}$** provides for reasonably good email validation. It's wrapped in the caret and the dollar sign, so the string must be a valid email address and nothing more.

   continues on next page

An email address starts with letters, numbers, and the underscore (represented by \w), plus a period (.) and a dash. This first block will match *larryullman*, *larry77*, *larry.ullman*, *larry-ullman*, and so on. Next, all email addresses include one and only one **@**. After that, there can be any number of letters, numbers, periods, and dashes. This is the domain name: *dmcinsights*, *smith-jones*, *amazon.co* (as in *amazon.co.uk*), etc. Finally, all email addresses conclude with one period and between two and six letters. This accounts for *.com*, *.edu*, *.info*, *.travel*, etc.

✔ Tips

■ I think that the zip code example is a great demonstration as to how complex and useful regular expressions are. One pattern accurately tests for both formats of the zip code, which is fantastic. But when you put this into your PHP code, with quotes and delimiters, it's not easily understood:

```
if (preg_match ('/^(\d{5})(-\d{4})?$/
→ ', $zip)) {…
```

That certainly looks like gibberish, right?

■ This email address validation pattern is pretty good, although not perfect. It will allow some invalid addresses to pass through (like ones starting with a period or containing multiple periods together). However, a 100 percent foolproof validation pattern is ridiculously long, and frequently using regular expressions is really a matter of trying to exclude the bulk of invalid entries without inadvertently excluding any valid ones.

■ Regular expressions, particularly PCRE ones, can be extremely complex. When starting out, it's just as likely that your use of them will break the validation routines instead of improving them. That's why practicing like this is important.

Using Boundaries

Boundaries are shortcuts for helping to find, um, boundaries. In a way, you've already seen this: using the caret and the dollar sign to match the beginning or end of a value. But what if you wanted to match boundaries within a value?

The clearest boundary is between a word and a non-word. A "word" in this case is not *cat*, *month*, or *zeitgeist*, but in the \w shortcut sense: the letters A through Z (both upper- and lowercase), plus the numbers 0 through 9, and the underscore. To use words as boundaries, there's the **\b** shortcut. To use non-word characters as boundaries, there's **\B**. So the pattern **\bfor\b** matches *they've come for you* but doesn't match *force* or *forebode*. Therefore **\bfor\B** would match *force* but not *they've come for you* or *informal*.

Script 13.2 To reveal exactly what values in a string match which patterns, this revised version of the script will print out each match. You can retrieve the matches by naming a variable as the third argument in preg_match() or preg_match_all().

```
              Script
1   <!DOCTYPE html PUBLIC "-//W3C//DTD XHTML
    1.0 Transitional//EN"

2       "http://www.w3.org/TR/xhtml1/DTD/
        xhtml1-transitional.dtd">

3   <html xmlns="http://www.w3.org/1999/
    xhtml">

4   <head>

5     <meta http-equiv="content-type" content=
      "text/html; charset=iso-8859-1" />

6     <title>Testing PCRE</title>

7   </head>

8   <body>

9   <?php // Script 13.2 - matches.php

10

11    // This script takes a submitted string
      and checks it against a submitted pattern.

12    // This version prints every match made.

13

14    if (isset($_POST['submitted'])) {

15

16      // Trim the strings:

17      $pattern = trim($_POST['pattern']);

18      $subject = trim($_POST['subject']);

19

20      // Print a caption:

21      echo "<p>The result of checking<br />
        <b>$pattern</b><br />against<br />
        $subject<br />is ";

22

23      // Test:

24      if (preg_match_all ($pattern, $subject,
        $matches) ) {

25        echo 'TRUE!</p>';

26
```

(script continues on next page)

Finding All Matches

Going back to the PHP functions used with Perl-Compatible regular expressions, preg_match() has been used just to see if a pattern matches a value or not. But the script hasn't been reporting what, exactly, in the value did match the pattern. You can find out this information by using a variable as a third argument to the function:

preg_match(*pattern*, *subject*, $match)

The $match variable will contain the first match found (because this function only returns the first match in a value). To find every match, use preg_match_all(). Its syntax is the same:

preg_match_all(*pattern*, *subject*,
→ $matches)

This function will return the number of matches made, or FALSE if none were found. It will also assign to $matches every match made. Let's update the PHP script to print the returned matches, and then run a couple more tests.

To report all matches:

1. Open pcre.php (Script 13.1) in your text editor or IDE.

2. Change the invocation of preg_match() to (**Script 13.2**)

   if (preg_match_all ($pattern, $subject, $matches)) {

   There are two changes here. First, the actual function being called is different. Second, the third argument is provided a variable name that will be assigned every match.

continues on next page

FINDING ALL MATCHES

3. After printing the value *TRUE*, print the contents of $matches.

```
echo '<pre>' . print_r($matches, 1) .
→ '</pre>';
```

Even though the PRE tags are not XHTML compliant, this is the easiest way to know what's in $matches. As you'll see when you run this script, this variable will be an array whose first element is an array of matches made.

4. Change the form's action attribute to *matches.php*.

```
<form action="matches.php" method=
→ "post">
```

This script will be renamed, so the action attribute must be changed, too.

5. Change the subject input to be a textarea.

```
<p>Test Subject: <textarea name=
→ "subject" rows="5" cols="30"><?php
→ if (isset($subject)) echo $subject;
→ ?></textarea></p>
```

In order to be able to enter in more text for the subject, this element will become a textarea.

Script 13.2 *continued*

```
27      // Print the matches:
28      echo '<pre>' . print_r($matches, 1) .
        '</pre>';
29
30   } else {
31      echo 'FALSE!</p>';
32   }
33
34  } // End of submission IF.
35  // Display the HTML form.
36  ?>
37  <form action="matches.php" method="post">
38      <p>Regular Expression Pattern: <input
        type="text" name="pattern" value="
        <?php if (isset($pattern)) echo
        $pattern; ?>" size="30" /> (include
        the delimiters)</p>
39      <p>Test Subject: <textarea name=
        "subject" rows="5" cols="30"><?php
        if (isset($subject)) echo $subject;
        ?></textarea></p>
40      <input type="submit" name="submit"
        value="Test!" />
41      <input type="hidden" name="submitted"
        value="TRUE" />
42  </form>
43  </body>
44  </html>
```

6. Save the file as `matches.php`, place it in your Web directory, and test it in your Web browser (**Figures 13.16**, **13.17**, **13.18**, and **13.19**).

For the first test, use **for** as the pattern and *This is a formulaic test for informal matches.* as the subject (Figure 13.16). It may not be proper English, but it's a good test subject.

For the second test, change the pattern to **for.*** (Figure 13.17). The result may surprise you, the cause of which is discussed in the sidebar, "Being Less Greedy." To make this search less greedy, the pattern could be changed to **for.*?**, whose results would be the same as those in Figure 13.16.

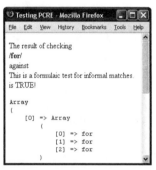

Figure 13.16 This first test returns three matches, as the literal text *for* was found three times.

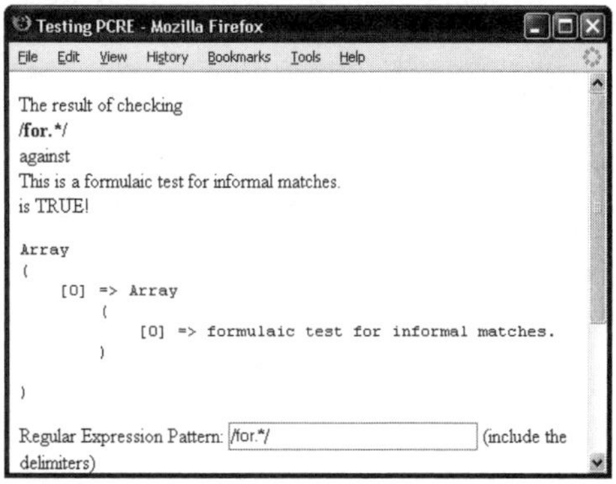

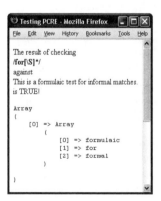

Figure 13.18 This revised pattern matches strings that begin with *for* and end on a word.

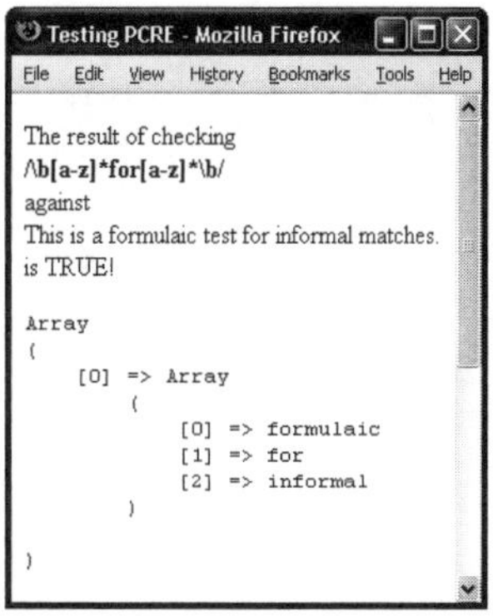

Figure 13.17 Because regular expressions are greedy by default (see the sidebar), this pattern only finds one match in the string. That match happens to start with the first instance of *for* and continue until the end of the string.

Figure 13.19 Unlike the pattern in Figure 13.18, this one matches entire words that contain *for* (*informal* here, *formal* in Figure 13.18).

For the third test, use **for[\S]***, or, more simply **for\S*** (Figure 13.18). This has the effect of making the match stop as soon as a white space character is found (because the pattern wants to match *for* followed by any number of non–white space characters).

For the final test, use **\b[a-z]*for[a-z] *\b** as the pattern (Figure 13.19). This pattern makes use of boundaries, discussed in the sidebar "Using Boundaries," earlier in the chapter.

✔ Tip

- The `preg_split()` function will take a string and break it into an array using a regular expression pattern.

Being Less Greedy

A key component to Perl-Compatible regular expressions, which isn't present in POSIX, is the concept of *greediness*. By default, PCRE will attempt to match as much as possible. For example, the pattern **<.+>** matches any HTML tag. When tested on a string like *<a href="page.php"> Link</a>*, it will actually match that entire string, from the opening < to the closing one. This string contains three possible matches, though: the entire string, the opening tag (from *<a* to *">*), and the closing tag (*</a>*).

To overrule greediness, make the match *lazy*. A lazy match will contain as little data as possible. Any quantifier can be made lazy by following it with the question mark. For example, the pattern **<.+?>** would return two matches in the preceding string: the opening tag and the closing tag. It would not return the whole string as a match. (This is one of the confusing aspects of the regular expression syntax: the same character—here, the question mark—can have different meanings depending on its context.)

Another way to make patterns less greedy is to use negative classes. The pattern **<[^>]+>** matches everything between the opening and closing <> except for a closing >. So using this pattern would have the same result as using **<.+?>**. This pattern would also match strings that contain newline characters, which the period excludes.

Table 13.4 These characters, when placed after the closing delimiter, alter the behavior of a regular expression.

Pattern Modifiers	
CHARACTER	RESULT
A	Anchors the pattern to the beginning of the string
i	Enables case-insensitive mode
m	Enables multiline matching
s	Has the period match every character, including newline
x	Ignores most white space
U	Performs a non-greedy match

Using Modifiers

The majority of the special characters you can use in regular expression patterns are introduced in this chapter. One final type of special character is the pattern modifier. **Table 13.4** lists these. Pattern modifiers are different than the other meta-characters in that they are placed after the closing delimiter.

Of these delimiters, the most important is *i*, which enables case-insensitive searches. All of the examples using variations on *for* (in the previous sequence of steps) would not match the word *For*. However, **/for.*/i** would be a match. Note that I am including the delimiters in that pattern, as the modifier goes after the closing one. Similarly, the last step in that sequence referenced the sidebar "Begin Less Greedy" and stated how **for.*?** would perform a lazy search. So would **/for.*/U**.

The multiline mode is also interesting in that you can make the caret and the dollar sign behave differently. By default, each applies to the entire value. In multiline mode, the caret matches the beginning of any line and the dollar sign matches the end of any line.

USING MODIFIERS

To use modifiers:

1. Load matches.php in your Web browser, if it is not already.

2. Validate a list of email addresses (**Figure 13.20**).

   To do so, use **/^[\w.-]+@[\w.-]+\.[A-Za-z]{2,6}\r?$/m** as the pattern. You'll see that I've added an optional carriage return (**\r?**) before the dollar sign. This is necessary because some of the lines will contain returns and others won't. And in multiline mode, the dollar sign matches the end of a line. (To be more flexible, you could use **\s?** instead.)

3. Validate a list of United States zip codes (**Figure 13.21**).

   Very similar to the example in Step 2, the pattern is now **/^(\d{5})(-\d{4})?\s?$/m**. You'll see that I'm using the more flexible **\s?** instead of **\r?**.

   You'll also notice when you try this yourself (or in Figure 13.21) that the $matches variable contains a lot more information now. This will be explained in the next section of the chapter.

✔ Tip

- To always match the start or end of a pattern, regardless of the multiline setting, there are shortcuts you can use. Within the pattern, the shortcut **\A** will match only the very beginning of the value, **\z** matches the very end, and **\Z** matches any line end, like **$** in single-line mode.

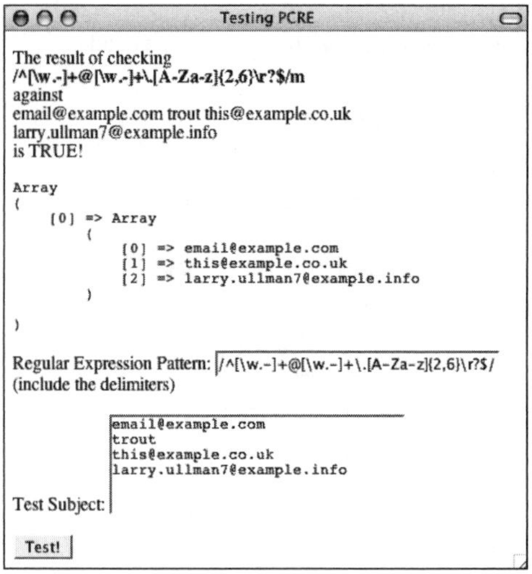

Figure 13.20 A list of email addresses, one per line, can be validated using the multiline mode. Each valid address is stored in $matches.

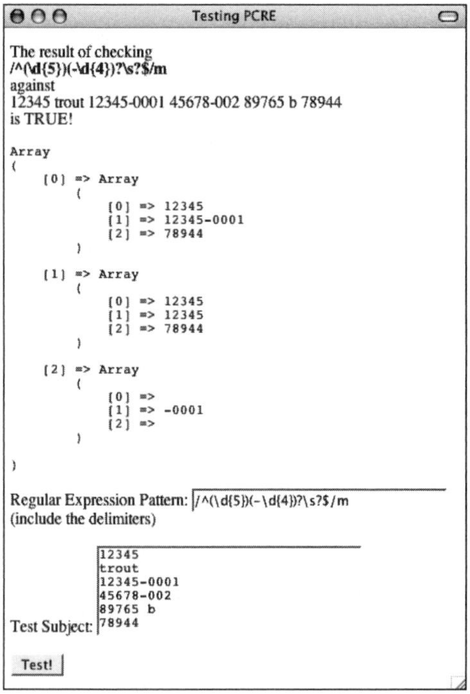

Figure 13.21 Validating a list of zip codes, one per line.

Matching and Replacing Patterns

The last subject to discuss in this chapter is how to match and replace patterns in a value. While `preg_match()` and `preg_match_all()` will find things for you, if you want to do a search and replace, you'll need to use `preg_replace()`. Its syntax is

```
preg_replace(pattern, replacement,
→ subject)
```

This function takes an optional fourth argument limiting the number of replacements made.

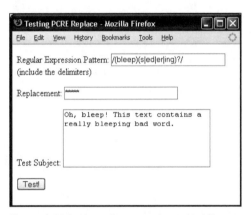

Figure 13.22 One use of `preg_replace()` would be to replace variations on inappropriate words with symbols representing their omission.

To replace all instances of *cat* with *dog*, you would use

```
$str = preg_replace('/cat/', 'dog', 'I
→ like my cat.');
```

This function returns the altered value (or unaltered value if no matches were made), so you'll likely want to assign it to a variable or use it as an argument to another function (like printing it by calling `echo()`). Also, as a reminder, this is just an example: you'd never want to replace one literal string with another using regular expressions, use `str_replace()` instead.

There is a related concept to discuss that is involved with this function: *back referencing*. In a zip code matching pattern—**^(\d{5})(-\d{4})?$**—there are two groups within parentheses: the first five digits and the optional dash plus four-digit extension. Within a regular expression pattern, PHP will automatically number parenthetical groupings beginning at 1. Back referencing allows you to refer to each individual section by using $ plus the corresponding number. For example, if you match the zip code *94710-0001* with this pattern, referring back to **$2** will give you *-0001*. The code **$0** refers to the whole initial string. This is why Figure 13.21 shows entire zip code matches in `$matches[0]`, the matching first five digits in `$matches[1]`, and any matching dash plus four digits in `$matches[2]`.

To practice with this, let's modify Script 13.2 to also take a replacement input (**Figure 13.22**).

To match and replace patterns:

1. Open matches.php (Script 13.2) in your text editor or IDE.

2. Add a reference to a third incoming variable (**Script 13.3**).

   ```
   $replace = trim($_POST['replace']);
   ```

   As you can see in Figure 13.22, the third form input (added between the existing two) takes the replacement value. That value is also trimmed to get rid of any extraneous spaces.

3. Change the caption.

   ```
   echo "<p>The result of replacing<br
   → /><b>$pattern</b><br />with<br
   → />$replace<br />in<br />$subject
   → <br /><br />";
   ```

   The caption will print out all of the incoming values, prior to applying preg_replace().

Script 13.3 To test the preg_replace() function, which replaces a matched pattern in a string with another value, you can use this third version of the PCRE test script.

```
1   <!DOCTYPE html PUBLIC "-//W3C//DTD XHTML
    1.0 Transitional//EN"
2
    "http://www.w3.org/TR/xhtml1/DTD/xhtml1-
    transitional.dtd">
3   <html xmlns="http://www.w3.org/1999/
    xhtml">
4   <head>
5     <meta http-equiv="content-type" content=
      "text/html; charset=iso-8859-1" />
6     <title>Testing PCRE Replace</title>
7   </head>
8   <body>
9   <?php // Script 13.3 - replace.php
10
11  // This script takes a submitted string
    and checks it against a submitted pattern.
12  // This version replaces one value with
    another.
13
14  if (isset($_POST['submitted'])) {
15
16    // Trim the strings:
17    $pattern = trim($_POST['pattern']);
18    $subject = trim($_POST['subject']);
19    $replace = trim($_POST['replace']);
20
21    // Print a caption:
22    echo "<p>The result of replacing<br
      /><b>$pattern</b><br />with<br />
      $replace<br />in<br />$subject<br />
      <br />";
23
24    // Check for a match:
25    if (preg_match ($pattern, $subject) ) {
26      echo preg_replace($pattern, $replace,
        $subject) . '</p>';
27    } else {
```

(script continues on next page)

Script 13.3 *continued*

```
⬤⬤⬤                    📄 Script
28        echo 'The pattern was not found!</p>';

29    }

30

31    } // End of submission IF.

32    // Display the HTML form.

33    ?>

34    <form action="replace.php" method="post">

35        <p>Regular Expression Pattern: <input
          type="text" name="pattern" value="<?php
          if (isset($pattern)) echo $pattern; ?>"
          size="30" /> (include the delimiters)
          </p>

36        <p>Replacement: <input type="text"
          name="replace" value="<?php if
          (isset($replace)) echo $replace; ?>"
          size="30" /></p>

37        <p>Test Subject: <textarea name=
          "subject" rows="5" cols="30"><?php
          if (isset($subject)) echo $subject;
          ?></textarea></p>

38        <input type="submit" name="submit"
          value="Test!" />

39        <input type="hidden" name="submitted"
          value="TRUE" />

40    </form>

41    </body>

42    </html>
```

4. Change the regular expression conditional so that it only calls `preg_replace()` if a match is made.

```
if (preg_match ($pattern, $subject)
→ ) {

    echo preg_replace($pattern,
    → $replace, $subject) . '</p>';

} else {

    echo 'The pattern was not
    → found!</p>';

}
```

You can call `preg_replace()` without running `preg_match()` first. If no match was made, then no replacement will occur. But to make it clear when a match is or is not being made (which is always good to confirm, considering how tricky regular expressions are), the `preg_match()` function will be applied first. If it returns a true value, then `preg_replace()` is called, printing the results (**Figure 13.23**). Otherwise, a message is printed indicating that no match was made (**Figure 13.24**).

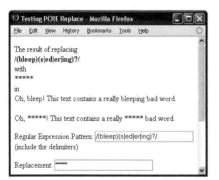

Figure 13.23 The resulting text has uses of *bleep*, *bleeps*, *bleeped*, *bleeper*, and *bleeping* replaced with *****.

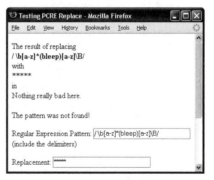

Figure 13.24 If the pattern is not found within the subject, the subject will not be changed. The replacement value is hidden here because it uses HTML tags; see the source code for the full effect.

5. Change the form's action attribute to *replace.php*.

```
<form action="replace.php" method=
→ "post">
```

This file will be renamed, so this value needs to be changed accordingly.

6. Add a text input for the replacement string.

```
<p>Replacement: <input type="text"
→ name="replace" value="<?php if
→ (isset($replace)) echo $replace;
→ ?>" size="30" /></p>
```

7. Save the file as replace.php, place it in your Web directory, and test it in your Web browser (**Figure 13.25**).

As a good example, you can turn an email address found within some text into its HTML link equivalent: <a href="mailto:email@example.com"> email@example.com</a>. The pattern for matching an email address should be familiar by now: **^[\w.-]+@[\w.-]+\.[A-Za-z]{2,6}$**. However, because the email address could be found within some text, the caret and dollar sign need to be replaced by the word boundaries shortcut: **\b**. The final pattern is therefore **/\b[\w.-]+@[\w.-]+\.[A-Za-z]{2,6}\b/**. To refer to this matched email address, you can refer to **$0** (because **$0** refers to the entire match, whether or not parentheses are used). So the replacement value would be *<a href="mailto:$0">$0 </a>*. Because HTML is involved here, look at the HTML source code of the resulting page for the best idea of what happened.

✔ Tips

■ Back references can even be used within the pattern. For example, if a pattern included a grouping (i.e., a subpattern) that would be repeated.

■ I've introduced, somewhat quickly, the bulk of the PCRE syntax here, but there's much more to it. Once you've mastered all this, you can consider moving on to *anchors, named subpatterns, comments, lookarounds, possessive quantifiers,* and more.

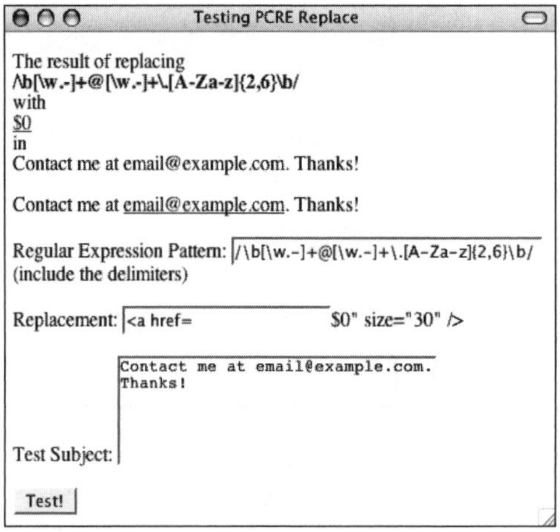

Figure 13.25 Another use of `preg_replace()` is dynamically turning email addresses into clickable links.

MATCHING AND REPLACING PATTERNS

MAKING UNIVERSAL SITES

The biggest change in version 6 of PHP is support for Unicode. But what is Unicode and why should you care? In this chapter, I'll answer those questions, and show you how you might change your Web sites using this new information. But as a preview, if you'd like your Web sites to be usable by people that don't speak the same language as you, or if you don't feel like always programming in your non-native language, keep reading!

This chapter goes over several subjects, all with the goal of making a more global Web site. The bulk of these topics involve text: character sets, encodings, collation, transliteration, and Unicode. These topics apply to PHP, MySQL, HTML, and even the application you create your PHP scripts in. I'll be presenting a book's worth of information in just a few pages, but it'll certainly be enough for you to use in real sites.

The other subjects covered here are time zones and locales. Like the language a user reads and writes, these two ideas reflect the different cultures and regions in the world, and therefore ought to be considered in your Web applications. Understanding all of these subjects, and being able to apply the techniques taught herein, will make your Web sites more reliable, more impressive, and accessible to a larger audience.

Character Sets and Encoding

To understand the concepts of character sets and encoding, you have to first realize that, in your computer, there is no such thing as the letter *A*. The letter *A* is part of a *character set*: the symbols used by a language (also called a *character repertoire*). But the *A* on my screen as I write this, the *A* in the text document itself: these aren't really *A*'s. At their foundation, computers understand numbers, not letters. This works well for computers, but humans like to see letters. The solution is to have numbers represent letters.

ASCII, which you've certainly heard of and is short for American Standard Code for Information Interchange, is a representation of all the letters in the English alphabet—A through Z, both upper- and lowercase—plus the digits 0 through 9, plus all English punctuation. That's a total of 95 characters. Add to this 33 non-printing characters such as the newline (\n) and a tab (\t), and you have 128 characters, associated with the integers 0 through 127 (**Table 14.1**). This is a *coded character set*: each character is represented by a number (the number is also called a *code point*).

When computers store data or transfer it from one computer to another, they don't do so in numbers, they do so in bytes. *Encoding* is how a coded character set is mapped from integers to bytes. Working backward then, by identifying how text is encoded, a computer can recognize its coded character set, and therefore know what characters should be displayed.

Although ASCII represents the entire English character set, it doesn't include all the accented characters in related languages, like French and Spanish. Nor does it include non-Latin characters, like those present in German,

Greek, or Korean. It doesn't even include things like curly quotes. Other encodings have since been defined, lots and lots of them: different encodings for different languages, even different encodings for different computers (e.g., Windows vs. Mac). Making communication difficult, two encodings would commonly use the same number to represent different characters. From this mess, *Unicode* was born.

Unicode provides a unique number representing every symbol in every alphabet for any operating system and program. It's a huge goal and Unicode succeeds rather well. Version 5 of Unicode—the current version at the time of this writing—supports over 99,000 characters, but the upper limit is well over a million. **Table 14.2** lists just a sampling of the scripts supported (a *script* being the collection of symbols used by one or more languages).

Table 14.1 These twelve items are a sampling of the 128 characters defined by the ASCII standard.

Some ASCII Characters	
INTEGER	KEY/CHARACTER
0	NULL
9	\t
10	\n
27	Escape
32	Space
43	+
54	6
64	@
65	A
97	a
126	~
127	Delete

When using Unicode, you still have to choose which encoding to go with. UTF-8 is perhaps the most common, in part because ASCII, used so commonly for years, is a nice little subset of UTF-8. In fact, any ASCII text is also valid UTF-8. There's also UTF-16 and UTF-32, each with larger character sets.

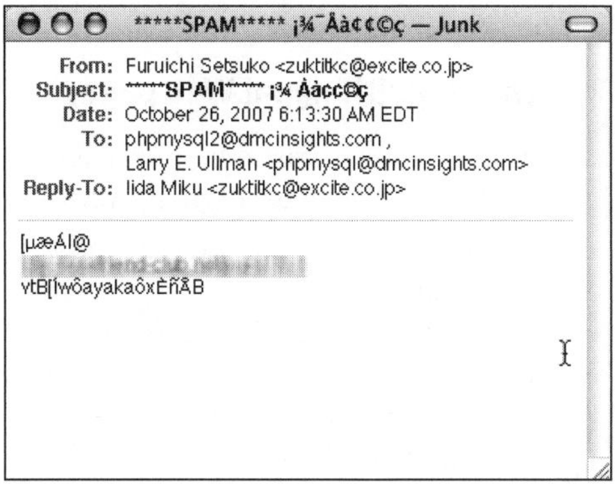

Figure 14.1 This friendly little piece of spam I received didn't use the right encoding, so junk characters appeared instead (thereby denying me the full joy of the message).

Table 14.2 A handful of the scripts represented in Unicode. Some scripts, like Latin, are used in many languages (English, Italian, Portuguese, etc); others, like Hangul, are only used in one (Korean, in this case).

Unicode Supported Scripts
SCRIPT
Arabic
Cherokee
Cyrillic
Greek
Han
Hebrew
Latin
N'Ko
Runic
Tibetan

In these paragraphs I've introduced the key concepts that will help you comprehend the information in the rest of the chapter. Doing so required the distillation of oodles of technical information, the glossing over of many details, and the abbreviation of decades of computer history. If you want to learn more about these subjects, a search online will turn up volumes, but what you most need to understand is this: *the encoding you use dictates what characters can be represented* (and therefore, what languages can be used).

✔ Tips

- Unfortunately, many resources, including HTML and MySQL, use the term *charset* or *character set* to refer to the encoding. The two things are technically different, but the terms are used synonymously.

- Prior to UTF-8, ISO-8859-1 was one of the more commonly used encodings. It represents most Western European languages. It's still the default encoding for many Web browsers and other applications.

- Email messages should (but don't always) indicate the encoding. You can normally see this by viewing the raw source of a message, which will contain a line like

  ```
  Content-Type: text/plain;
  → charset="UTF-8"
  ```

- Any document—email, Web page, or text file—that contains some junk characters probably wasn't encoding properly (**Figure 14.1**).

Creating Multilingual Web Pages

Eventually this chapter will go over how to use multiple languages (i.e., multiple characters) in PHP and MySQL, but doing so mandates that you know how to make an HTML page that can display characters from many languages. Of course, what characters you can display is determined by the encoding, but even that topic comes into play more than once in this process.

Say you want to create a Web page that contains text in both English and Japanese. For starters, your computer must be able to enter characters in both languages (it must have the necessary fonts). Normally you can type in one (native) language, but most operating systems offer tools for inserting characters from other languages, too. If your computer supports both languages, then you need to use an encoding for the Web page that supports both, too. That would be UTF-8, in all likelihood. Therefore, the HTML file needs to be written in an application that supports UTF-8 encoding; not all do.

If you have all that, you can now create a document with both English and Japanese characters. This HTML page will be viewable by others in their Web browsers. The Web browsers, then, need to know what encoding the HTML page uses. One way to convey this information is to use a META tag:

```
<meta http-equiv="Content-Type"
→ content="text/html; charset=utf-8">
```

(To repeat what's said on a previous page, unfortunately the term *charset* is used to mean encoding, not character set.)

The last requirement is that the end user's computer also support both character sets (i.e., they have the necessary fonts). If so, then you've successfully created and shared a multilingual Web page. Before writing another opening PHP tag, let's make sure you can get all this working.

To create a multilingual Web page:

1. Confirm that your text editor or IDE supports UTF-8 encoding (**Figure 14.2**).

   You'll need to check the Web site, help files, or other documentation for your application. Getting this step right is necessary, though, as you can't create a UTF-8-encoded document if your editor doesn't support UTF-8.

   Some applications let you set this in their preferences (as in Figure 14.2). Others set the encoding when you save the file (**Figure 14.3**).

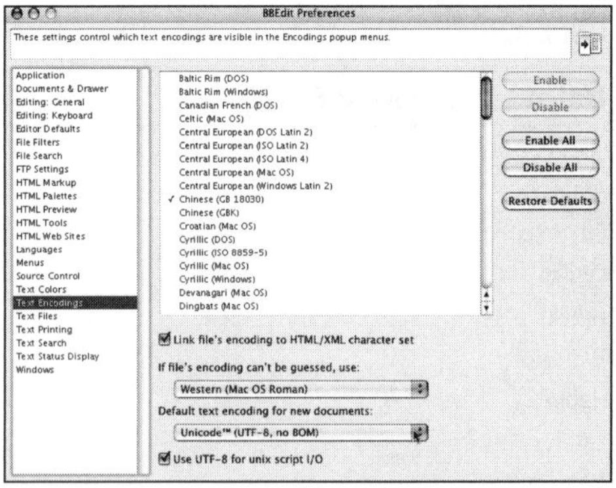

Figure 14.2 My favorite text editor, BBEdit (which sadly only runs on a Mac), has a preferences area where you can set the default encoding for documents.

Script 14.1 This script will be a test to confirm that a UTF-8 Web page can be successfully created and viewed.

```
⊙ ⊙ ⊙                Script
1    <!DOCTYPE html PUBLIC "-//W3C//DTD XHTML
     1.0 Transitional//EN"
2         "http://www.w3.org/TR/xhtml1/DTD/
          xhtml1-transitional.dtd">
3    <html xmlns="http://www.w3.org/1999/
     xhtml" xml:lang="en" lang="en">
4    <head>
5      <meta http-equiv="content-type"
       content="text/html; charset=utf-8" />
6      <title>Testing UTF-8</title>
7    </head>
8    <body style="font-size: 18pt;">
9    <!-- Script 14.1 - utf8.html -->
10   <p>Testing UTF-8 encoding. Here are some
     random words and characters:
11   <ul>
12     <li>Iñtërnâtiônàlizætiøn</li>
13     <li>€</li>
14     <li>ə</li>
15     <li>∞</li>
16     <li>Ħ</li>
17     <li>ċ</li>
18     <li>Ѱ</li>
19     <li>Ẩ</li>
20   </ul>
21   </p>
22   </body>
23   </html>
```

2. Begin a new HTML document (**Script 14.1**).

```
<!DOCTYPE html PUBLIC "-//W3C//DTD
→ XHTML 1.0 Transitional//EN"

"http://www.w3.org/TR/xhtml1/DTD/
→ xhtml1-transitional.dtd">

<html
→ xmlns="http://www.w3.org/1999/
→ xhtml" xml:lang="en" lang="en">

<head>

    <title>Testing UTF-8</title>

</head>

<body style="font-size: 18pt;">

<!-- Script 14.1 - utf8.html -->

</body>

</html>
```

This is mostly standard HTML. To make the resulting page easier to view, an inline CSS style increases the base font size to 18 points.

Note that the language declarations in the opening html tag (the two uses of *lang="en"*) are indications of the document's main language. This is a separate issue from the encoding and the character set.

continues on next page

Figure 14.3 Notepad on Windows, which isn't a great text editor but is usable, lets you define a file's encoding when you save it.

Creating Multilingual Web Pages

3. Add a META tag that indicates the encoding.

```
<meta http-equiv="Content-Type"
→ content="text/html; charset=utf-8">
```

This line should be the first one inside of the HEAD tag, as the browser needs to know this information as soon as possible. It should come before the title tags (see Script 14.1) or any other META tags.

4. Add some characters or text to the body of the page.

```
<p>Testing UTF-8 encoding. Here are
→ some random words and characters:

<ul>

    <li>Iñtërnâtiônàlizætiøn</li>

    <li>€</li>

    <li>ə</li>

    <li>∞</li>

    <li>Ҥ</li>

    <li>ċ</li>

    <li>ѱ</li>

    <li>ᄊᄀ</li>

</ul>

</p>
```

The first word is a good test of encoding, as it contains many different accents and non-Latin characters. You can also throw in symbols or characters from other languages. In a list, I've added the Euro symbol, the schwa, and infinity; then individual characters from the Cyrillic, Arabic, Hebrew, and Hangul scripts (and hopefully I haven't included anything that will offend anyone!).

How you insert characters depends upon your operating system. Windows has the Character Map utility, which lets you choose characters from installed fonts. Mac OS X has the Character Palette, which displays available scripts, and the Keyboard Viewer, which shows characters by font. Both can be accessed in the menu bar, after checking the right boxes in the International System Preferences pane.

5. Save the file as utf.html and test it in your Web browser (**Figures 14.4** and **14.5**).

Because this is just an HTML file, it does not need to be run through a URL, like a PHP script.

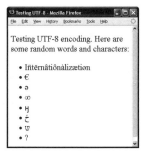

Figure 14.4 A UTF-8 encoded Web page, successfully showing characters and symbols from all over the world.

Figure 14.5 The same HTML page (as in Figure 14.4), viewed in Windows. This browser and operating system didn't support the Korean character (the last one), replacing it with a question mark.

✔ Tips

■ If a page's encoding is different than the encoding it indicates it uses (in the META tag), that will likely lead to problems.

■ Curly quotes often cause problems in improperly encoded documents, as they aren't part of the ASCII standard.

■ Firefox's Page Info window (**Figure 14.6**) will show the document's encoding. This can be a useful debugging tool.

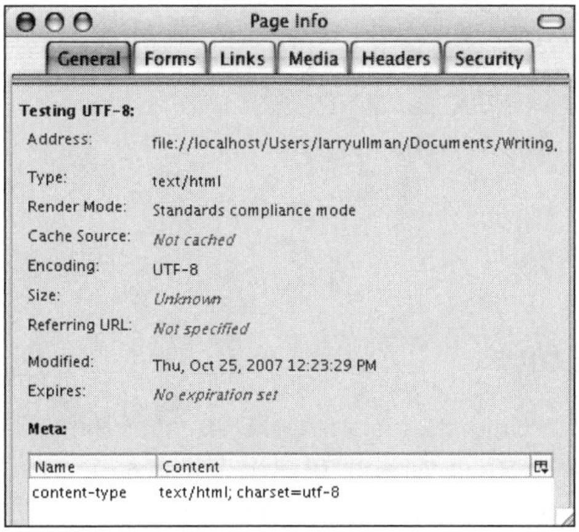

Figure 14.6 The informative Page Info window is yet another reason to use Firefox for your Web development.

■ Because there are so many variables when creating multilingual Web pages, they can be tougher to debug. Make sure that you use the proper encoding in your application that creates the HTML or PHP page, that the encoding is indicated within the file itself, and that you test using as many browsers and operating systems as possible.

■ You can also indicate to the Web browser the page's encoding using PHP and the header() function:

```
<?php header ('Content-Type:
→ text/html; charset=UTF-8'); ?>
```

This can be more effective than using a META tag, but it does require the page to be a PHP script. If using this, it must be the first line in the page, before any HTML.

■ You can specify the encoding to accept in an HTML form tag, too:

```
<form accept-charset="utf-8">
```

By default, a Web page will use the same encoding as the page itself for any submitted data.

■ You can declare the encoding of an external CSS file by adding @charset "utf-8"; as the first line in the file. If you're not using UTF-8, change the line accordingly.

■ Another way to use special characters in an HTML page is by using a numeric character reference (NCR). Any Unicode character can be referenced using the format &#XXXX;. For example, the Latin capital A is A. But ideally you should use your computer to add the character itself instead of using an NCR.

Unicode in PHP

Now that you know what Unicode is and how to create a properly encoded HTML page, how does this affect PHP, which now supports Unicode? Lacking Unicode support, earlier versions of PHP had only one type of string. PHP 6 has three: Unicode, binary (for other encodings and binary data), and native (for backward compatibility). But because PHP is a weakly typed language, you can work with all three types in more or less the same way.

To use Unicode with PHP, it first has to be enabled. Doing so requires modifying PHP's configuration file. The specific setting is *unicode.semantics*, which must be turned on. If you're running your own installation of PHP, see Appendix A, "Installation," for instructions on changing PHP's configuration. If using a hosted server that's running PHP 6, you'll have to ask them to enable Unicode support. You can confirm this setting by calling the phpinfo() function (**Figure 14.7**).

unicode.fallback_encoding	no value	no value
unicode.filesystem_encoding	no value	no value
unicode.http_input_encoding	no value	no value
unicode.output_encoding	utf-8	utf-8
unicode.runtime_encoding	iso-8859-1	iso-8859-1
unicode.script_encoding	utf-8	utf-8
unicode.semantics	On	On
unicode.stream_encoding	UTF-8	UTF-8
unserialize_callback_func	no value	no value

Figure 14.7 In PHP 6, the output generated by calling the phpinfo() function now has a section for Unicode settings.

Unicode and PHP 5

The most important addition to PHP 6 is support for Unicode, including UTF-8, which I'm advocating using in this chapter. What's implied is that earlier versions of PHP did not support Unicode. This isn't just a matter of convenience; it's actually a problem. If you attempt to work with Unicode text in earlier versions of PHP 6, the results can range from being unexpected and unpredictable to insecure.

The reason is that practically every string function in earlier versions of PHP treated each character as a single byte. This was fine when working with English and many other languages, in which each character was, in fact, a single byte. But the characters in other languages sometimes require multiple bytes apiece. Applying even a simple function like substr() to such text would give erroneous results. PHP 5 and earlier has two sets of functions for working with multibyte strings—mb_* and iconv_*—but neither is perfect and you really need to know your stuff to use them.

Simply said, if you need to handle Unicode data, make sure you're using PHP 6. If you're not using PHP 6, don't accept multibyte characters (i.e., use a different encoding).

With Unicode enabled, PHP scripts can properly handle Unicode text that might come from a form, a text file, or a database. Functions like substr() or strlen(), which would not properly work with Unicode data in PHP 5, will now function correctly.

You can also now use non-Latin characters for identifiers: the names of variables, functions, and so forth (keywords in PHP will still be in English). These are possible in PHP 6:

```
// 'student' in French:
$étudiante = 'Christina';
echo "Bonjour, $étudiante!";
// 'date' in Traditional Chinese:
$日期 = getdate();
echo $日期['month'];
// 'to extinguish' in German:
function ablöschen() {…}
$sauber = ablöschen();
```

If you're going to use Unicode characters in identifiers, you need indicate to PHP what encoding you're using (aside from encoding the script itself properly using your application). To do so, use

```
declare (encoding="UTF-8");
```

This must be the first line in the PHP script (after the opening tag, of course). Also, any included file also needs to indicate its encoding (the encoding is not inherited from one script to another).

While I think that being able to use your native language for identifiers is really cool, to demonstrate Unicode in PHP, let's create a script that highlights some differences between PHP 5 and PHP 6.

UNICODE IN PHP

To use Unicode in PHP:

1. Begin a new PHP document in your text editor or IDE (**Script 14.2**).

```
<?php header ('Content-Type:
→ text/html; charset=UTF-8'); ?>

<!DOCTYPE html PUBLIC "-//W3C//DTD
→ XHTML 1.0 Transitional//EN"

"http://www.w3.org/TR/xhtml1/DTD/
→ xhtml1-transitional.dtd">

<html
→ xmlns="http://www.w3.org/1999/xhtml"
→ xml:lang="en" lang="en">

<head>

    <meta http-equiv="content-type"
    → content="text/html;
    → charset=utf-8" />

    <title>Unicode in PHP</title>

</head>

<body style="font-size: 18pt;">

<h1>Names from Around the World</h1>

<?php # Script 14.2 - unicode.php
```

Per a mention in a tip on a previous page, this document will also use a PHP header() call to indicate to the Web browser the encoding.

2. Create a list of names.

```
$names = array('João', 'Γιώργος',
→ 'Anton', 'Tomáš', 'KamilÐ',
‣ 'Frančiška', '愛子', '杰西卡');
```

I've pulled together some names from around the world and placed them into an array for easy access.

Script 14.2 A handful of multilingual names are printed, along with their lengths and their capitalized forms.

```
1    <?php header ('Content-Type: text/html;
     charset=UTF-8'); ?>
2    <!DOCTYPE html PUBLIC "-//W3C//DTD XHTML
     1.0 Transitional//EN"
3        "http://www.w3.org/TR/xhtml1/DTD/
         xhtml1-transitional.dtd">
4    <html xmlns="http://www.w3.org/1999/
     xhtml" xml:lang="en" lang="en">
5    <head>
6      <meta http-equiv="content-type"
       content="text/html; charset=utf-8" />
7      <title>Unicode in PHP</title>
8    </head>
9    <body style="font-size: 18pt;">
10   <em>Names from Around the World</em>
11   <?php # Script 14.2 - unicode.php
12
13   // Create an array of names:
14   $names = array('João', 'Γιώργος',
     'Anton', 'Tomáš', 'KamilÐ', 'Frančiška',
     '愛子', '杰西卡');
15
16   // Loop through the array:
17   foreach ($names as $name) {
18     echo "<p>$name has " . strlen($name) .
       characters<br />\n" . strtoupper($name)
       " in capital letters</p>\n";
19   }
20
21   ?>
22   </body>
23   </html>
```

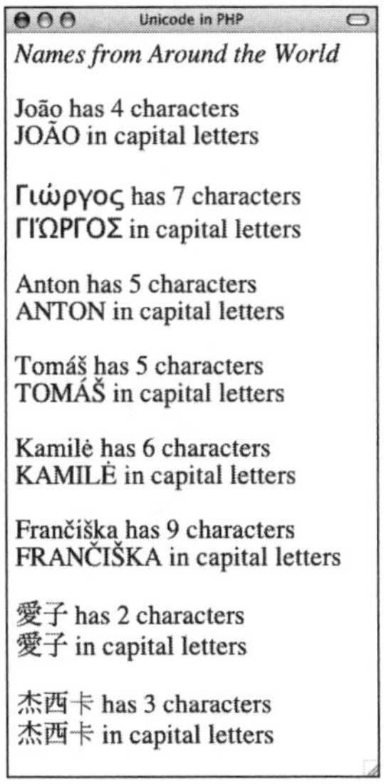

Figure 14.8 The (accurate) results of running the Unicode PHP script using PHP 6.

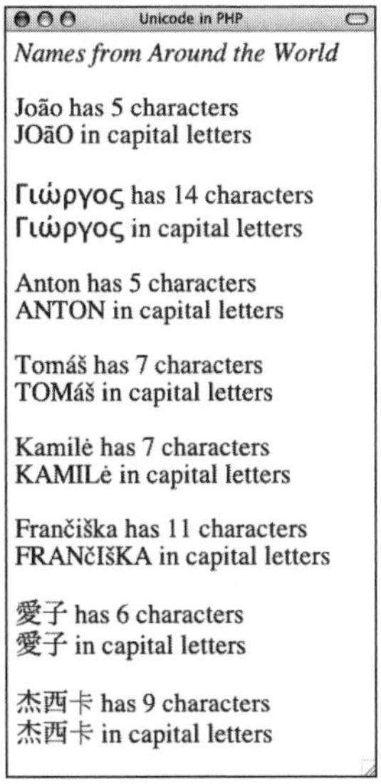

Figure 14.9 The same page (Script 14.2), run under PHP 5.2. Notice how both the character counts and capitalization are incorrect and differ from the results in Figure 14.8.

3. Print each name's length and capitalized version.

```
foreach ($names as $name) {
    echo "<p>$name has " .
    → strlen($name) . "
    → characters<br />\n" .
    → strtoupper($name) . " in
    → capital letters</p>\n";
}
```

This code should be pretty easy to understand, even though it's going to be applied to strings in multiple languages. It loops through the array, printing out each name as it originally is. Then it also prints out the number of characters in the name and the name in all caps.

4. Complete the page.

```
?>
</body>
</html>
```

5. Save the file as unicode.php, place it in your Web directory, and test it in your Web browser (**Figure 14.8**).

6. If possible, run the same script using an older version of PHP (**Figure 14.9**).

✔ Tips

- You can use casting to forcibly convert a string from one encoding type to another (see Chapter 12, "Security Methods," for an introduction to typecasting). The casting keywords are (binary), (unicode), and (string).

- Alternatively, you can use unicode_encode() and unicode_decode() to convert strings from one encoding to another. The unicode_set_error_mode() determines how any conversion problems are handled.

Collation in PHP

Collation refers to the rules used for comparing characters in a set. It's like alphabetization, but takes into account numbers, spaces, and other characters as well. Collation relates to the character set being used, reflecting both the kinds of characters present and cultural habits. How text is sorted in English is not the same as it is in Traditional Spanish or in Arabic. For example, are upper- and a lowercase versions of a character considered to be the same or different (i.e., is it a case-sensitive comparison)? Or, how do accented characters get sorted? Is a space counted or ignored?

The best way to sort Unicode strings in PHP 6 is to use the `Collator` class. This gets into the subject of object-oriented programming (OOP), not otherwise discussed in this book (a solid introduction provided by my book *PHP 5 Advanced: Visual QuickPro Guide* (Peachpit Press, 2007) requires over 100 pages), but the syntax is easy enough to follow.

Start by creating a new object of type `Collator`:

```
$c = new Collator(locale);
```

When doing this, you need to indicate the *locale*. I discuss locales at the end of the chapter, but for now, just know that it'll be a short string indicating a language and geographic reference point. For example, *jp_JP* is Japanese in Japan; *pt_BR* is Portuguese in Brazil.

Next, apply the `sort()` function to an array of strings. Calling functions in a class uses the `$object->function()` syntax:

```
$array = $c->sort($array);
```

Let's run through an example of this.

Script 14.3 The collation.php script sorts several French words using the Collator class. Using that code is demonstrably more effective than using PHP's built-in sort() function.

```
⊝ ⊜ ⊝                    📄 Script
1    <?php header ('Content-Type: text/html;
     charset=UTF-8'); ?>

2    <!DOCTYPE html PUBLIC "-//W3C//DTD XHTML
     1.0 Transitional//EN"

3       "http://www.w3.org/TR/xhtml1/DTD/
        xhtml1-transitional.dtd">

4    <html xmlns="http://www.w3.org/1999/xhtml"
     xml:lang="en" lang="en">

5    <head>

6       <meta http-equiv="content-type"
        content="text/html; charset=utf-8" />

7       <title>Collation in PHP</title>

8    </head>

9    <body style="font-size: 18pt;">

10   <?php # Script 14.3 - collation.php

11

12   // Create an array of words:

13   $words = array('chère', 'côté', 'chaise',
     'château', 'chaînette', 'châle', 'Chère',
     'côte', 'chemise');

14

15   // Sort using the default PHP function:

16   echo '<h3>Using sort()</h3>';

17   sort($words);

18   echo implode('<br />', $words);

19

20   // Sort using the Collator:

21   echo '<h3>Using Collator</h3>';

22   $c = new Collator('fr_FR');

23   $words = $c->sort($words);

24   echo implode('<br />', $words);

25

26   ?>

27   </body>

28   </html>
```

To use collation in PHP:

1. Begin a new PHP document in your text editor or IDE (**Script 14.3**).

   ```
   <?php header ('Content-Type:
   → text/html; charset=UTF-8'); ?>

   <!DOCTYPE html PUBLIC "-//W3C//DTD
   → XHTML 1.0 Transitional//EN"

   "http://www.w3.org/TR/xhtml1/DTD/
   → xhtml1-transitional.dtd">

   <html
   → xmlns="http://www.w3.org/1999/xhtml"
   → xml:lang="en" lang="en">

   <head>

       <meta http-equiv="content-type"
       → content="text/html;
       → charset=utf-8" />

       <title>Collation in PHP</title>

   </head>

   <body style="font-size: 18pt;">

   <?php # Script 14.3 - collation.php
   ```

   Remember that, because this script will use characters in other languages, the file needs to be encoded in your application using UTF-8 and the page itself should indicate to the Web browser this same encoding.

2. Create a list of words.

   ```
   $words = array('chère', 'côté',
   → 'chaise', 'château', 'chaînette',
   → 'châle', 'Chère', 'côte', 'chemise');
   ```

   For this example, I'm using a smattering of French (being about all the French I know). It's a good choice, as it contains lots of accented characters. This example will then be able to demonstrate how accented characters are properly sorted.

   continues on next page

3. Use the sort() function, and then print the results.

```
echo '<h3>Using sort()</h3>';
sort($words);
echo implode('<br />', $words);
```

PHP's sort() function is the default sorting utility and it works just fine...with standard English. Let's see how it does with French!

The third line here uses the implode() function as a quick way of printing each item in the array on its own line. This function turns an array into a string, using the first argument as the glue. The returned string is then printed by echo(). **Figure 14.10** shows the HTML source code resulting from this little shortcut.

4. Use the Collator class, and then print the results.

```
echo '<h3>Using Collator</h3>';
$c = new Collator('fr_FR');
$words = $c->sort($words);
echo implode('<br />', $words);
```

The syntax for using this Collator class is described before these steps. For the locale value, I use *fr_FR*, which means French in France.

5. Complete the page.

```
?>
</body>
</html>
```

6. Save the file as collation.php, place it in your Web directory, and test it in your Web browser (**Figure 14.11**).

✔ Tips

■ Simple comparisons in PHP, using the comparison operators, do not use collation.

■ The Collator class has a setStrength() function that can be used to adjust the collation rules. For example, you can use this to ignore accents or to change the stress placed on case.

```
<body style="font-size: 18pt;">
<h3>Using sort()</h3>Chère<br />chaise<br />chaînette<br />chemise<b
</html>
```

Figure 14.10 To print each item in the array on its own line, I place HTML breaks in between them using implode().

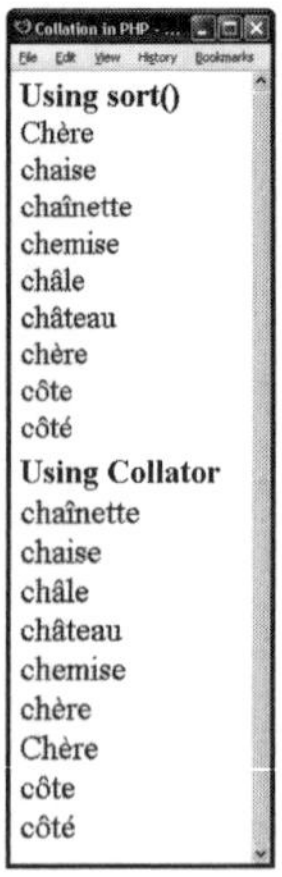

Figure 14.11 The Collator class does a better job sorting accented and capitalized characters than PHP's sort() function.

Transliteration in PHP

Transliteration is the conversion of text from one character set to another. This is not the same thing as *translating*, which involves a certain amount of interpretation. For example, in `unicode.php` (Script 14.2), several names are placed into an array. One of those is Greek: **Γιώργος**. Transliterated into the Latin alphabet, that would be Giórgos. The example also used two Asian names—愛子 and 杰西卡. Those would be turned into Jié Xi Kā and Ài Zi, respectively.

Because Unicode maps all the characters in every language to numbers, it's actually very easy to perform transliteration. To achieve this in PHP, use the `str_transliterate()` function. It takes as its first argument the string to change. The second argument is the *script* of the original string. The third is the destination *script*. For both of these, I'm using "script" in the sense of Table 14.2, which lists the scripts supported by Unicode: Latin, Greek, Cyrillic, Arabic, etc.

To try this out, let's see what my (or your) name looks like in other alphabets.

Unicode Documentation

As I'm currently writing this book, PHP 6 has not yet been officially released. However, using available beta versions of the software, I have been able to test all of the code under PHP 6 with only minor hiccups. Unfortunately, what's not available to me is good, and sometimes any, documentation on many of these new features. In fact, a couple of examples in this chapter use functions that aren't even in the PHP manual yet!

I'm absolutely confident about the examples and content of this book, naturally, but should something change in the official release of PHP 6, you may experience a problem here or there. If so, check out the PHP manual (which will be updated to correspond with the release) and turn to the book's corresponding Web site (`www.DMCInsights.com/phpmysql3/`) or its supporting book forum for assistance.

To use transliteration:

1. Begin a new PHP document in your text editor or IDE (**Script 14.4**).

   ```
   <?php header ('Content-Type:
   → text/html; charset=UTF-8'); ?>

   <!DOCTYPE html PUBLIC "-//W3C//DTD
   → XHTML 1.0 Transitional//EN"

   "http://www.w3.org/TR/xhtml1/DTD/
   → xhtml1-transitional.dtd">

   <html
   → xmlns="http://www.w3.org/1999/xhtml"
   → xml:lang="en" lang="en">

   <head>

       <meta http-equiv="content-type"
       → content="text/html;
       → charset=utf-8" />

       <title>Transliteration</title>

   </head>

   <body style="font-size: 18pt;">

   <em>What's my name?</em>

   <?php # Script 14.4 - trans.php
   ```

   This is all similar to the past two scripts. The PHP header() call indicates the encoding to the Web browser, and some inline CSS increases the font size to make the characters easier to read.

2. Create two variables.

   ```
   $me = 'Larry Ullman';

   $scripts = array('Greek', 'Cyrillic',
   → 'Hebrew', 'Arabic', 'Hangul');
   ```

   The first variable is my name. Feel free to use your own here instead. The second variable is an array of scripts to be used as the third argument in str_transliterate(). These values represent the destination script.

Script 14.4 This script uses the new str_transliteration() function to convert a name from one character set to another.

```
1   <?php header ('Content-Type: text/html;
    charset=UTF-8'); ?>

2   <!DOCTYPE html PUBLIC "-//W3C//DTD XHTML
    1.0 Transitional//EN"

3       "http://www.w3.org/TR/xhtml1/DTD/
        xhtml1-transitional.dtd">

4   <html xmlns="http://www.w3.org/1999/xhtml"
    xml:lang="en" lang="en">

5   <head>

6     <meta http-equiv="content-type"
        content="text/html; charset=utf-8" />

7     <title>Transliteration</title>

8   </head>

9   <body style="font-size: 18pt;">

10  <em>What's my name?</em>

11  <?php # Script 14.4 - trans.php

12

13  // Your name:

14  $me = 'Larry Ullman';

15

16  // Create an array of scripts:

17  $scripts = array('Greek', 'Cyrillic',
    'Hebrew', 'Arabic', 'Hangul');

18

19  // Loop through each script:

20  foreach ($scripts as $script) {

21      echo "<p>$me is " .
        str_transliterate($me, 'Latin', $script) .
        " in $script.</p>\n";

22  }

23

24  ?>

25  </body>

26  </html>
```

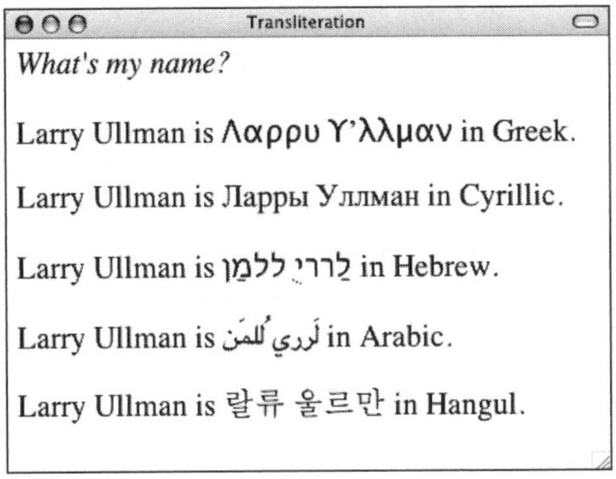

Figure 14.12 My name, transliterated into different alphabets.

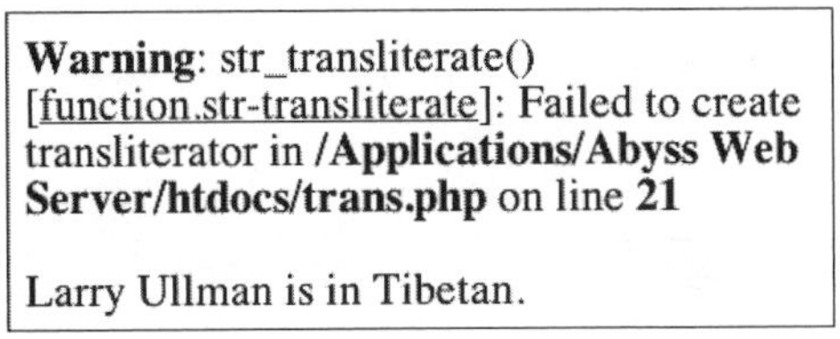

Figure 14.13 The attempted conversion into Tibetan failed, as that script isn't supported by my installation.

3. Print the name in each script.

```
foreach ($scripts as $script) {
    echo "<p>$me is " .
    → str_transliterate($me, 'Latin',
    → $script) . " in $script.</p>\n";
}
```

Within the foreach loop, an echo() statement will print the name as it is originally and then transliterated. It will also print the destination script. For the origination script argument, *Latin* is being used, as the name was written using the Latin alphabet (change this if yours is different).

4. Complete the page.

```
?>

</body>

</html>
```

5. Save the file as trans.php, place it in your Web directory, and test it in your Web browser (**Figure 14.12**).

If you get an error message like the one in **Figure 14.13**, that means that a particular script is not available for transliteration (or you misspelled it).

TRANSLITERATION IN PHP

Languages and MySQL

Just as an HTML page and PHP script can use different encodings, so can MySQL. To see a list of ones supported by your version of MySQL, run a SHOW CHARACTER SET command (**Figure 14.14**). Note that the phrase *character set* is being used in MySQL to mean *encoding* (which I'll generally follow in this section to be consistent with MySQL).

Each character set in MySQL has one or more collations. To view those, run this query, replacing *charset* with the proper value from the result in the last query (**Figure 14.15**):

```
SHOW COLLATION LIKE 'charset%'
```

The results of this query will also indicate the default collation for that character set.

In MySQL, the server as a whole, each database, each table, and even every column can have a character set and collation. To set these values when you create a database, use

```
CREATE DATABASE name CHARACTER SET
→ charset COLLATION collation
```

To set these values when you create a table, use

```
CREATE TABLE name (
column definitions
) CHARACTER SET charset COLLATION
→ collation
```

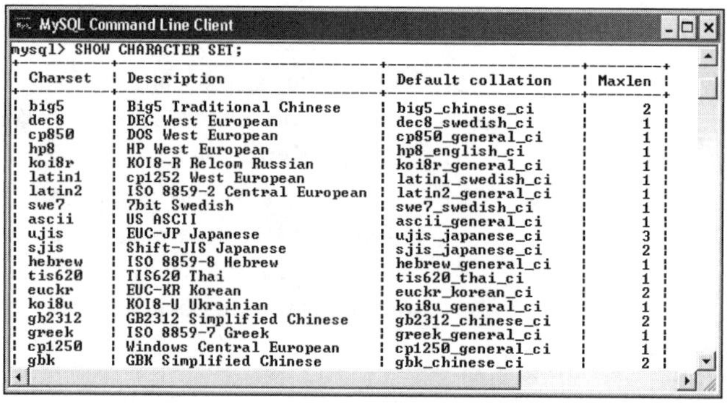

```
mysql> SHOW CHARACTER SET;
```

Charset	Description	Default collation	Maxlen
big5	Big5 Traditional Chinese	big5_chinese_ci	2
dec8	DEC West European	dec8_swedish_ci	1
cp850	DOS West European	cp850_general_ci	1
hp8	HP West European	hp8_english_ci	1
koi8r	KOI8-R Relcom Russian	koi8r_general_ci	1
latin1	cp1252 West European	latin1_swedish_ci	1
latin2	ISO 8859-2 Central European	latin2_general_ci	1
swe7	7bit Swedish	swe7_swedish_ci	1
ascii	US ASCII	ascii_general_ci	1
ujis	EUC-JP Japanese	ujis_japanese_ci	3
sjis	Shift-JIS Japanese	sjis_japanese_ci	2
hebrew	ISO 8859-8 Hebrew	hebrew_general_ci	1
tis620	TIS620 Thai	tis620_thai_ci	1
euckr	EUC-KR Korean	euckr_korean_ci	2
koi8u	KOI8-U Ukrainian	koi8u_general_ci	1
gb2312	GB2312 Simplified Chinese	gb2312_chinese_ci	2
greek	ISO 8859-7 Greek	greek_general_ci	1
cp1250	Windows Central European	cp1250_general_ci	1
gbk	GBK Simplified Chinese	gbk_chinese_ci	2

Figure 14.14 The list of character sets supported by this MySQL installation.

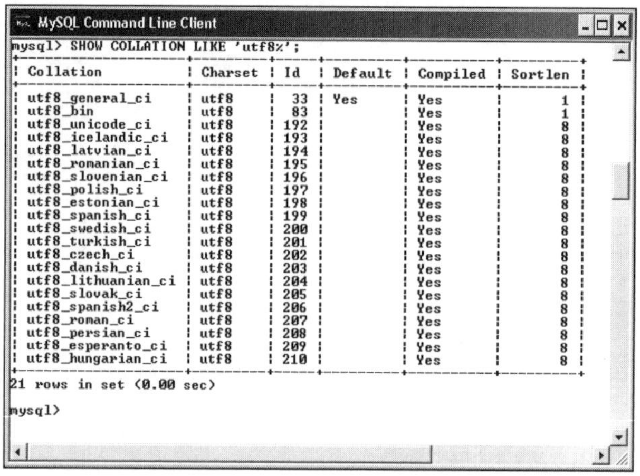

```
mysql> SHOW COLLATION LIKE 'utf8%';
```

Collation	Charset	Id	Default	Compiled	Sortlen
utf8_general_ci	utf8	33	Yes	Yes	1
utf8_bin	utf8	83		Yes	1
utf8_unicode_ci	utf8	192		Yes	8
utf8_icelandic_ci	utf8	193		Yes	8
utf8_latvian_ci	utf8	194		Yes	8
utf8_romanian_ci	utf8	195		Yes	8
utf8_slovenian_ci	utf8	196		Yes	8
utf8_polish_ci	utf8	197		Yes	8
utf8_estonian_ci	utf8	198		Yes	8
utf8_spanish_ci	utf8	199		Yes	8
utf8_swedish_ci	utf8	200		Yes	8
utf8_turkish_ci	utf8	201		Yes	8
utf8_czech_ci	utf8	202		Yes	8
utf8_danish_ci	utf8	203		Yes	8
utf8_lithuanian_ci	utf8	204		Yes	8
utf8_slovak_ci	utf8	205		Yes	8
utf8_spanish2_ci	utf8	206		Yes	8
utf8_roman_ci	utf8	207		Yes	8
utf8_persian_ci	utf8	208		Yes	8
utf8_esperanto_ci	utf8	209		Yes	8
utf8_hungarian_ci	utf8	210		Yes	8

```
21 rows in set (0.00 sec)

mysql>
```

Figure 14.15 The list of collations available in the UTF-8 encoding. The first one, *utf_general_ci*, is the default.

To establish the character set and collation for a column, add the right clause to the column's definition (you'd only use this for text types):

```
CREATE TABLE name (

something TEXT CHARACTER SET charset
→ COLLATION collation

…)
```

In each of these cases, both clauses are optional. If omitted, a default character set or collation will be used.

Collations in MySQL can also be specified within a query, to affect the results:

```
SELECT … ORDER BY column COLLATE collation

SELECT … WHERE column LIKE 'value'
→ COLLATE collation
```

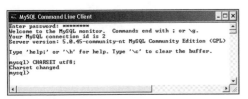

Figure 14.16 When communicating with MySQL, to use a non-default encoding, change it upon connecting to the server.

Establishing the character set and collation when you define a database affects what data can be stored (e.g., you can't store a character in a column if its encoding doesn't support that character). A second issue is the encoding used to communicate with MySQL. If you want to store Chinese characters in a table with a Chinese encoding, those characters will need to be transferred using the same encoding. To do so from a PHP script, execute this query—

```
SET NAMES charset
```

—prior to executing any others. If you fail to do this, all data will be transferred using the default character set, which may or may not cause problems.

Within the mysql client, set the encoding using just

```
CHARSET charset
```

These last two ideas will be revisited in the next chapter.

I've just run through a fair amount of information, so to practice, let's connect to MySQL and run some queries. For the example, I'll use Spanish, which has two collations. Using traditional rules, the letter combinations *ch* and *ll* are each treated as a singular letter. In modern rules, they are not.

To use character sets and collation:

1. Connect to MySQL using the mysql client.

   Recent versions of phpMyAdmin (at the time of this writing) do support setting the character sets and collations, if you'd rather use it.

2. Change the encoding to UTF8 (**Figure 14.16**).

   ```
   CHARSET utf8;
   ```

   continues on next page

3. Select the *test* database and create a new table (**Figure 14.17**).

USE test;

CREATE TABLE test_utf (

id INT UNSIGNED NOT NULL
→ AUTO_INCREMENT,

word VARCHAR(20),

PRIMARY KEY (id)

) CHARSET utf8;

Because this is just practice, create a new table within the *test* database. This table is rather minimally defined, using just two columns. The character set (which is to say the encoding) for the table is UTF-8.

4. Insert some sample records (**Figure 14.18**).

INSERT INTO test_utf (word) VALUES

('Calle'), ('cuchillo'), ('cuchara'),

('castillo'), ('cucaracha'),

('castigo'), ('castizo'),

('cuclillo');

```
mysql> USE test;
Reading table information for completion of table and column names
You can turn off this feature to get a quicker startup with -A

Database changed
mysql> CREATE TABLE test_utf (
    -> id INT UNSIGNED NOT NULL AUTO_INCREMENT,
    -> word VARCHAR(20),
    -> PRIMARY KEY (id)
    -> ) CHARSET utf8;
Query OK, 0 rows affected (0.09 sec)

mysql>
```

Figure 14.17 This table will be used to demonstrate collation and character sets.

```
mysql> INSERT INTO test_utf (word) VALUES
    -> ('Calle'), ('cuchillo'), ('cuchara'),
    -> ('castillo'), ('cucaracha'),
    -> ('castigo'), ('castizo'),
    -> ('cuclillo');
Query OK, 8 rows affected (0.00 sec)
Records: 8  Duplicates: 0  Warnings: 0

mysql>
```

Figure 14.18 Populating the table with some sample data.

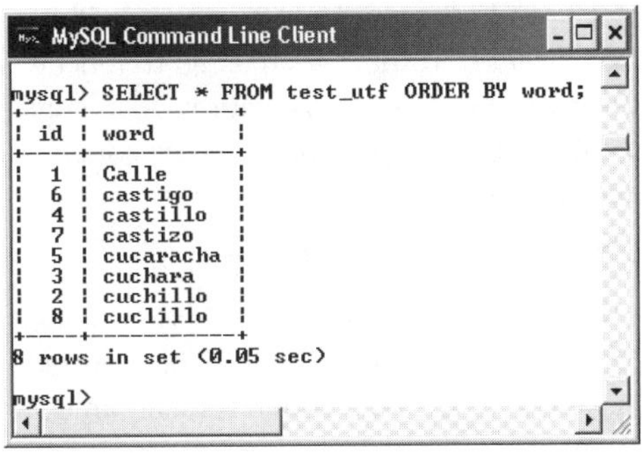

Figure 14.19 The words in order using the default collation.

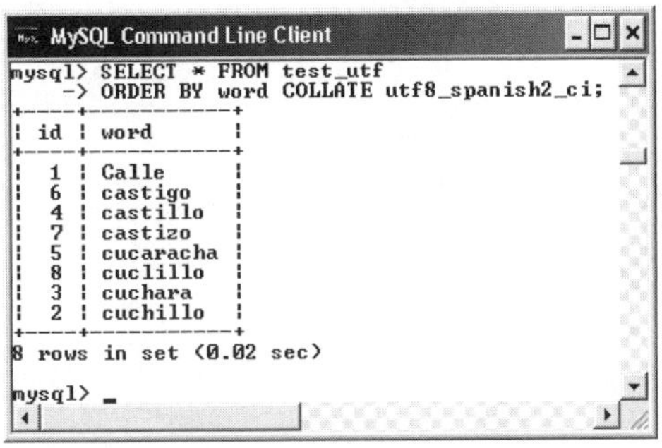

Figure 14.20 The difference in collations is evident in the new location of the word with an ID of 8 (compare with Figure 14.19).

5. Retrieve the records in alphabetical order (**Figure 14.19**).

```
SELECT * FROM test_utf ORDER BY word;
```

This query will use the established collation for the column. With the table definition in Step 3, that would be the default collation for the UTF-8 character set.

6. Retrieve the records in order using Traditional Spanish rules (**Figure 14.20**).

```
SELECT * FROM test_utf

ORDER BY word COLLATE
→ utf8_spanish2_ci;
```

To change the order used in a sort, without making a permanent change in the database, add the COLLATE clause to your query. The *utf8_spanish2_ci* collation uses the Traditional Spanish rules of order.

✔ Tips

- It's recommended that any column using the UTF-8 encoding not be defined as CHAR for performance reasons. Use a text or VARCHAR type instead.

- The CONVERT() function can convert text from one character set to another.

- Because different character sets require more space to represent a string, you will likely need to increase the size of a column for UTF-8 characters. Do this before changing a column's encoding so that no data is lost.

Time Zones and MySQL

Chapter 10, "Web Application Development," introduces a couple of PHP's date and time functions. These include date_default_time-zone_set(), which needs to be called prior to using any other date or time function (as of PHP 5.1). I think there's enough information in that chapter, and in the PHP manual, if you need to work with time zones in PHP. But what about MySQL?

Start by remembering that the date and time in MySQL represents the date and time on the server. Invocations of NOW() and other functions reflect the server's time. Therefore, values stored in a database using these functions are also storing the server's time, reflecting that server's time zone. But say you move your site from one server to another: you export all the data, import it into the other, and everything's fine...unless the two servers are in different time zones, in which case all of the dates are now off. That won't be a big deal for some sites, but what if your site features paid memberships? That means some people's membership might expire a day early and for others, a day late!

The solution is to store dates and times in a time zone–neutral way. Doing so uses something called UTC (Coordinated Universal Time, and, yes, the abbreviation doesn't exactly match the term). UTC, like Greenwich Mean Time (GMT), provides a common point of origin, from which all times in the world can be expressed as UTC plus or minus some hours and minutes (**Table 14.3**).

Fortunately you don't have to perform any calculations in order to determine UTC for your server. Instead, the UTC_DATE() function returns the UTC date; UTC_TIME() returns the current UTC time; and UTC_TIMESTAMP() returns the current date and time.

Once you have stored a UTC time, you'll likely want to retrieve it adjusted to reflect the server's or the user's location. To change a date and time from any one time zone to another, use CONVERT_TZ():

CONVERT_TZ(dt, from, to)

The first argument is a date and time value, like the result of a function or what's stored in a column. The second and third arguments are named time zones (see the sidebar).

Table 14.3 A sampling of cities and how their time would be represented, depending upon daylight saving time. Note that not all time zones use hourly offsets. Some use 30- or 45-minute offsets.

UTC Offsets	
CITY	TIME
New York City, U.S.	UTC−4
Cape Town, South Africa	UTC+2
Mumbai, India	UTC+5:30
Auckland, New Zealand	UTC+13
Kathmandu, Nepal	UTC+5:45
Santiago, Chile	UTC−3
Dublin, Ireland	UTC+1

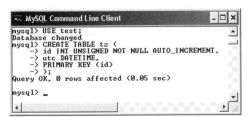

Figure 14.21 Creating another example table.

Using Time Zones in MySQL

MySQL does not install support for time zones by default. In order to use named time zones, there are five tables in the *mysql* database that have to be populated. While MySQL doesn't automatically do this for you, it does provide the tools to do this yourself.

This process is just complicated enough that there's not room to discuss it in this book (not for every possible contingency: operating system etc.). But you can find the instructions by looking up "server time zone support" in the MySQL manual. The manual even has sample queries you can run to confirm that your time zones are accurate.

If you continue to use time zones in MySQL, you also need to keep this information in the *mysql* database updated. The rules for time zones, in particular, when and how they observe daylight saving time, change often. Again, the MySQL manual has instructions for updating your time zones.

To work with UTC:

1. Connect to MySQL.

   You can use the mysql client (as I will in the corresponding figures), phpMyAdmin, or something else.

2. Select the *test* database and create a new table (**Figure 14.21**).

   ```
   USE test;

   CREATE TABLE tz (

   id INT UNSIGNED NOT NULL
   → AUTO_INCREMENT,

   utc DATETIME,

   PRIMARY KEY (id)

   );
   ```

   Because this is just practice, the new table will again be created within the *test* database. This table is also rather minimally defined, using just two columns. The second column, of type DATETIME, will be the important one for this example. I haven't tweaked the character set, as this example won't be working with text.

3. Insert a sample record.

   ```
   INSERT INTO tz (utc) VALUES

   (UTC_TIMESTAMP());
   ```

   Using the UTC_TIMESTAMP() function, the record will store the UTC date and time, not the date and time on the server.

   continues on next page

TIME ZONES AND MySQL

4. View the record as it's stored (**Figure 14.22**).

```
SELECT * FROM tz;
```

As you can see in the figure and the table definition, UTC times are stored just the same as non-UTC times. What's not obvious in the figure is that the record just inserted reflects a time four hours ahead of the server (because the server is in a time zone four hours away).

5. Retrieve the record in your time zone (**Figure 14.23**).

```
SELECT CONVERT_TZ(utc, 'UTC',
→ 'America/New_York') FROM tz;
```

Using the CONVERT_TZ() function, you can format any date and time converted to a different time zone. For the *from* time zone, use *UTC*. For the *to* time zone, use yours. The time zone names match those used by PHP (see Chapter 10 or, more directly, www.php.net/timezones).

If you get a NULL result (**Figure 14.24**), either the name of one of your time zones is wrong or MySQL hasn't had its time zones loaded yet (see the sidebar).

✔ Tips

■ However you decide to handle dates, the key is to be consistent. If you decide to use UTC, then *always* use UTC.

■ UTC is also known as Zulu time, represented by the letter *Z*.

■ Besides being time zone and daylight saving time agnostic, UTC is also more accurate. It has irregular leap seconds that compensate for the inexact movement of the planet.

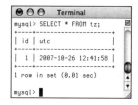

Figure 14.22 The record that was just inserted, which reflects a time four hours ahead (the server is UTC-4).

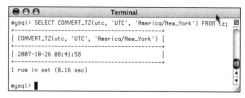

Figure 14.23 The UTC-stored date and time converted to my local time.

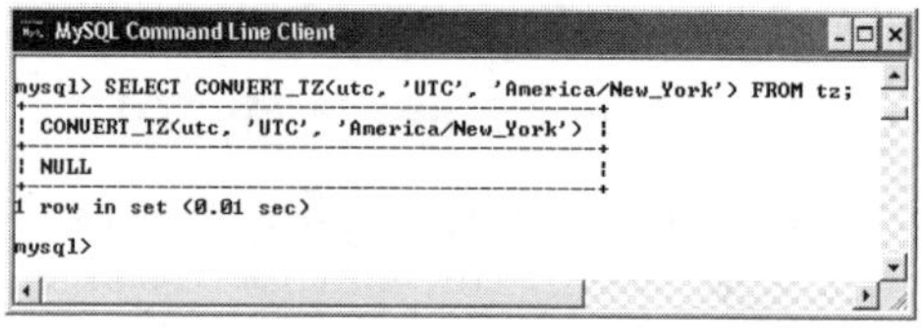

Figure 14.24 The CONVERT_TZ() function will return NULL if it references an invalid time zone or if the time zones haven't been installed in MySQL (which is the case here).

Working with Locales

A *locale* is an interesting concept that most beginner programmers aren't familiar with. It occupies several realms that overlap with some of the other topics in this chapter. A locale represents the language and formatting habits for a culture. Locales describe:

- How dates, times, currencies, and numbers should be written

- What unit of measurement is used

- How text should be sorted or matched

- How characters are capitalized

For example, both the United States and England speak English, but they format dates differently.

Locales in PHP 5

Earlier versions of PHP (prior to 6) use what are called POSIX locales. These are short strings like *en_US* (English, United States), *en_GB* (English, Great Britain), etc. You can establish the locale in PHP using `set_locale()`:

```
set_locale(category, locale);
```

The categories include `LC_ALL`, `LC_MONE-TARY`, `LC_NUMERIC`, and more. So to have numbers formatted as they would be in France, you would use

```
set_locale(LC_NUMERIC, fr_FR);
```

The list of locale abbreviations can be found online. Complicating things, if you're running PHP on Windows, the locale abbreviations differ some.

As of version 6 of PHP, this function and these locales are deprecated (meaning they're still available for backward-compatibility but you should stop using them).

Each computer has a default locale. Using PHP, you can change the locale value. You might want to do this if, for example, your server is located in the United States but you have a site targeting the Swiss population.

To change the locale in version 6 of PHP, use the `locale_set_default()` function (see the sidebar for the PHP 5 alternative). This function takes just one argument, a string in the format

```
<language>[_<script>]_<country>
→ [_<variant>][@<keywords>]
```

Language and country are required; the other values are optional (indicated by the square brackets). A tool for finding all these values is available at `http://demo.icu-project.org/icu-bin/locexp`.

The thing to be aware of is that not all PHP functions are locale-aware. For example, `number_format()` isn't, but `money_format()` is (or should be in the final release of PHP 6; it wasn't at the time of this writing). And the `date()` function won't respect locales, but the new `date_format_locale()` function will. It uses the same formatting parameters as `date()`, but takes a `DateTime` object as its first argument (you'll see what this means in the following script).

Another locale-aware function to be used in this example is `strtotitle()`. It's like `uc_words()`, used to properly capitalize words in a string. Because `strtotitle()` works with locales, it also works on text in languages that are written from right to left or that don't use spaces between words.

As a simple demonstration of this concept, let's create a script that prints the date using different locales.

To use locales:

1. Begin a new PHP document in your text editor or IDE (**Script 14.5**).

```
<?php header ('Content-Type:
→ text/html; charset=UTF-8'); ?>

<!DOCTYPE html PUBLIC "-//W3C//DTD
→ XHTML 1.0 Transitional//EN"

"http://www.w3.org/TR/xhtml1/DTD/
→ xhtml1-transitional.dtd">

<html
→ xmlns="http://www.w3.org/1999/xhtml"
→ xml:lang="en" lang="en">

<head>

    <meta http-equiv="content-type"
    → content="text/html;
    → charset=utf-8" />

    <title>Locales</title>

</head>

<body style="font-size: 18pt;">

<?php # Script 14.5 - locales.php
```

Because some characters to be printed by this script will be in different languages, this page should also use UTF-8 encoding.

2. Set the default time zone.

```
date_default_timezone_set('UTC');
```

Before calling any function that returns a date or a time, you have to set the time zone. I'm setting it to *UTC*, to make it time zone–indifferent.

Script 14.5 In this script, a series of locales are defined, representing languages and countries around the world. Then today's date is printed for each locale.

```
1    <?php header ('Content-Type: text/html;
     charset=UTF-8'); ?>

2    <!DOCTYPE html PUBLIC "-//W3C//DTD XHTML
     1.0 Transitional//EN"

3        "http://www.w3.org/TR/xhtml1/DTD/
         xhtml1-transitional.dtd">

4    <html xmlns="http://www.w3.org/1999/xhtml"
     xml:lang="en" lang="en">

5    <head>

6      <meta http-equiv="content-type"
       content="text/html; charset=utf-8" />

7      <title>Locales</title>

8    </head>

9    <body style="font-size: 18pt;">

10   <?php # Script 14.5 - locales.php

11

12   // Set the default timezone:

13   date_default_timezone_set('UTC');

14

15   // Need a date object:

16   $d = new DateTime();

17

18   // Create a list of locales:

19   $locales = array('en_US', 'fr_FR',
     'es_BO', 'zh_Hans_CN', 'ru_RU', 'el_GR',
     'is_IS');

20

21   // Print the date in each locale:

22   foreach ($locales as $locale) {

23

24     // Set the locale:

25     locale_set_default($locale);

26

27     // Print the date:
```

(script continues on next page)

```
 ⊖ ⊙ ⊖                     📄 Script
28    echo "<p>$locale: " .
      strtotitle(date_format_locale($d, 'l, j
      F Y')) . "</p>\n";

29

30    }

31

32    ?>

33    </body>

34    </html>
```

3. Create a `DateTime` object.

   `$d = new DateTime();`

   As with the collation example earlier in the chapter, this is object-oriented programming, but this one line is all you'll do. The variable $d is now an object of the `DateTime` type. Among other things, it contains the current date and time for the established time zone.

4. Create a list of locales.

   ```
   $locales = array('en_US', 'fr_FR',
   → 'es_BO', 'zh_Hans_CN, 'ru_RU',
   → 'el_GR', 'is_IS');
   ```

   For the locales, I'm using a variety of places and languages around the world. The first is English in the United States, then French in France, Spanish in Bolivia, Chinese (Traditional Han) in China, Russian in Russia, Greek in Greece, and Icelandic in Iceland.

5. Print the date in each locale.

   ```
   foreach ($locales as $locale) {

       locale_set_default($locale);

       echo "<p>$locale: " .
       → strtotitle(date_format_locale
       → ($d, 'l, j F Y')) . "</p>\n";

   }
   ```

   The `foreach` loop will access every locale in the array. Within the loop, the locale is then changed and printed. Then the date for that locale is returned using `date_format_locale()`. Its first argument is $d, the `DateTime` object created in Step 3. Its second argument is the formatting, in this case *Day DD Month YYYY*. This whole returned string will be run though `strtotitle()` to properly capitalize it.

   continues on next page

6. Complete the page.

```
?>
</body>
</html>
```

7. Save the file as locales.php and test it in your Web browser (**Figure 14.25**).

✔ Tips

■ The locale_get_default() function returns the current locale.

■ The topic of locales falls under PHP's support for internationalization (abbreviated *i18n*) and localization (*i10n*).

en_US: Friday, 26 October 2007

fr_FR: Vendredi, 26 Octobre 2007

es_BO: Viernes, 26 Octubre 2007

zh_Hans_CN: 星期五, 26 10 2007

ru_RU: Пятница, 26 Октября 2007

el_GR: Παρασκευή, 26 Οκτωβρίου 2007

is_IS: Föstudagur, 26 Október 2007

Figure 14.25 How the same date would be written in different locales around the world.

EXAMPLE— MESSAGE BOARD

New in this edition of the book is this chapter, in which a message board (aka a forum) is created. I've never before written up such an example because there are so many great forum software packages available already. But readers are clamoring for information on this topic, and I always respect a hardy clamor.

The functionality of a message board is really rather simple: a post can either start a new topic or be in response to an existing one; posts are added to a database and then displayed on a page. That's really about it. Of course, sometimes implementing simple concepts can be quite hard!

To make this example even more exciting and useful, it's not going to be just a message board but rather a multilingual message board. Each language will have its own forum, and all of the key elements—navigation, prompts, introductory text, etc.—will be language-specific. It'll be very cool, really applying the knowledge covered in Chapter 14, "Making Universal Sites."

In order to focus on the most important aspects of this Web application, I'm going to omit some others. The three glaring omissions will be: user management, error handling, and administration. This shouldn't be a problem for you, though, as the next chapter goes over user management and error handling in great detail. Practically all of that chapter's content can be applied to this example. As for the administration, I'll make some recommendations at the chapter's end.

Making the Database

The first step, naturally, is to create the database. A sample message board database is developed in Chapter 6, "Advanced SQL and MySQL." Although that database is perfectly fine, a variation on it will be used here instead. **Figure 15.1** shows the tables and relationships in that database. **Figure 15.2** shows the tables and relationships in this new database. I'll compare and contrast the two to better explain my thinking.

To start, the *forums* table is replaced with a *languages* table. Both serve the same purpose: allowing for multiple forums. In this new database, the topic—*PHP and MySQL for Dynamic Web Sites*—will be the same in every forum, but each forum will use a different language. The posts will differ in each forum (this won't be a translation of the same forum in multiple languages). The *languages* table stores the name of a language in its own alphabet and in English, for the administrator's benefit.

The *threads* table in the new database acts like the *messages* table in the old one, with one major difference. Just as the old *messages* table relates to *forums*, *threads* relates to the *languages* and *users* tables (each message can only be in one forum and by one user; each forum can have multiple messages and each user can post multiple messages). However, this *threads* table will only store the subject, not the message itself. There are a couple of reasons I made this change. First, having a subject repeat multiple times with each reply (replies, in my experience, almost always have the same subject anyway) is unnecessary. The same goes for the *lang_id* association (it doesn't need to be in each reply as long as each reply is associated with a single thread). Third, I'm changing the way a thread's hierarchy will be indicated in this

database (you'll see how in the next paragraph), and changing the table structures helps in that regard. Finally, the *threads* table will be used every time a user looks at the posts in a forum. Removing the message bodies from that table will improve the performance of those queries.

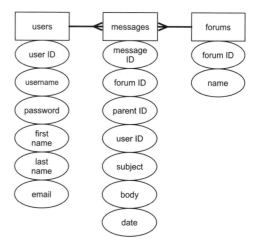

Figure 15.1 The model for the forum database developed in Chapter 6.

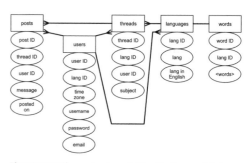

Figure 15.2 The revised model for the forum database to be used in this chapter.

Moving onto the *posts* table, its sole purpose is to store the actual bodies of the messages associated with a thread. In Chapter 6's database, the *messages* table had a *parent_id* column, used to indicate the message to which a new message was a response. It was hierarchical: message 3 might be the starting post; message 18 might be a response to 3, message 20 a response to 18, and so on (**Figure 15.3**). That version of the database more directly indicated the responses; this version will only store the thread that a message goes under. So messages 18 and 20 both use a *thread_id* of 3. This will make showing a thread much more efficient (in terms of the PHP and MySQL required), and the date/time that each message was posted on can still be used to order them.

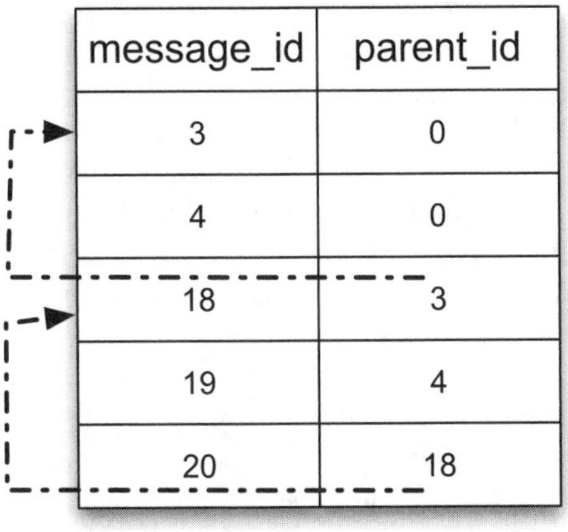

Those three tables provide the bulk of the forum functionality. The database also needs a *users* table. In my version of the forum, only registered users can post messages, which I think is a really, really, really good policy (it cuts way down on spam and hack attempts). Registered users can also indicate their default language (from the *languages* table) and time zone, in order to give them a more personalized experience. A combination of their username and password would be used to log in.

The final table, *words*, is necessary to make the site multilingual. This table will store translations of common elements: navigation links, form prompts, headers, and so forth. Each language in the site will have one record in this table. It'll be a nice and surprisingly easy feature to use. Arguably the words listed in this table could also go in the *languages* table, but then the implication would be that the words are also related to the *threads* table, which would not be the case.

That's the thinking behind this new database design. You'll learn more as you create the tables in the following steps. As with the other examples in this book, you can also download the SQL necessary for this chapter—that in these steps, plus more—from the book's corresponding Web site (www.DMCInsights.com/phpmysql3/, see the Downloads page).

message_id	parent_id
3	0
4	0
18	3
19	4
20	18

Figure 15.3 How the relationship among messages was indicated using the older database schema.

Making the Database

To make the database:

1. Access your MySQL server and set the character set to be used for communicating (**Figure 15.4**).

   CHARSET utf8;

   As always, I'll be using the mysql client in the figures, but you can use whatever you'd like. The first step, though, has to be changing the character set to UTF-8 for the queries to come. If you don't do this, some of the characters in the queries will be stored as gibberish in the database (see the sidebar "Strange Characters").

2. Create a new database (**Figure 15.5**).

   CREATE DATABASE forum2 CHARACTER SET
   → utf8;

   USE forum2;

   So as not to muddle things with the tables created in the original forum database (from Chapter 6), a new database will be created.

   If you're using a hosted site and cannot create your own databases, use the database provided for you and select that. If your existing database has tables with these same names—*words*, *languages*, *threads*, *users*, and *posts*, rename the tables (either the existing or the new ones) and change the code in the rest of the chapter accordingly.

   Whether you create this database from scratch or use a new one, it's very important that the tables use the UTF-8 encoding, in order to be able to support multiple languages (see Chapter 14 for more). If you're using an existing database and don't want to potentially cause problems by changing the character set for all of your tables, just add the CHARACTER SET utf8 clause to each table definition (Steps 3 through 7).

Figure 15.4 In order to use Unicode data in my queries, I need to change the character set used to communicate with MySQL from the mysql client.

Strange Characters

If, when you're implementing this chapter's example, you see strange characters—boxes, numeric codes, or question marks instead of actual language characters, there might be several reasons why. To solve the problem, start by referring to Chapter 14, which goes over Unicode and character sets in detail.

A computer's ability to display a character depends on both the file's encoding and the characters (i.e., fonts) supported by the operating system. This means that every PHP or HTML page must use the proper encoding. Secondarily, the database in MySQL must use the proper encoding (as indicated in the steps for creating the database). Third, and this can be a common cause of problems, the communication between PHP and MySQL must also use the proper encoding. I address this issue in the mysqli_connect.php script (see the first tip). Finally, if you use the mysql client, phpMyAdmin, or another tool to populate the database, that interaction must use the proper encoding, too.

3. Create the *languages* table (**Figure 15.6**).

```
CREATE TABLE languages (

lang_id TINYINT UNSIGNED NOT NULL
→ AUTO_INCREMENT,

lang VARCHAR(60) NOT NULL,

lang_eng VARCHAR(20) NOT NULL,

PRIMARY KEY (lang_id),

UNIQUE (lang)

);
```

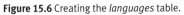

Figure 15.5 Creating and selecting the database for this example. This database uses the UTF-8 character set, so that it can support multiple languages.

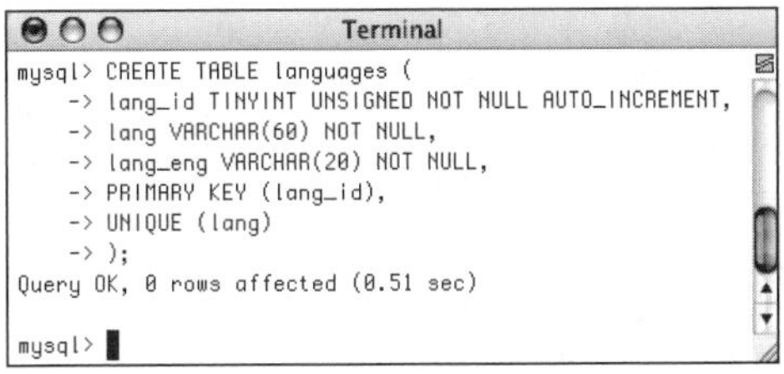

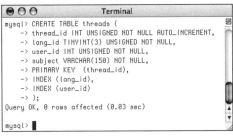

Figure 15.6 Creating the *languages* table.

This is the simplest table of the bunch. There won't be many languages represented, so the primary key (*lang_id*) can be a `TINYINT`. The *lang* column is defined a bit larger, as it'll store characters in other languages, which may require more space. This column must also be unique. Note that I can't call this column "language," as that's a reserved keyword in MySQL (actually, I could still call it that, but I'd need to take extra steps, and it's just not worth it). The *lang_eng* column is the English equivalent of the language so that the administrator can easily see which languages are which.

4. Create the *threads* table (**Figure 15.7**).

```
CREATE TABLE threads (

thread_id INT UNSIGNED NOT NULL
→ AUTO_INCREMENT,

lang_id TINYINT(3) UNSIGNED NOT NULL,

user_id INT UNSIGNED NOT NULL,

subject VARCHAR(150) NOT NULL,

PRIMARY KEY (thread_id),

INDEX (lang_id),

INDEX (user_id)

);
```

The *threads* table contains four columns and relates to both the *languages* and *users* tables (through the *lang_id* and *user_id* foreign keys, respectively). The *subject* here needs to be long enough to store subjects in multiple languages (in other languages the characters take up more space).

The columns that will be used in joins and `WHERE` clauses—*lang_id* and *user_id*— are indexed, as is *thread_id* (as a primary key, it'll be indexed).

continues on next page

Figure 15.7 Creating the *threads* table. This table stores the topic subjects and associates them with a language (i.e., a forum).

5. Create the *posts* table (**Figure 15.8**).

```
CREATE TABLE posts (

post_id INT UNSIGNED NOT NULL
→ AUTO_INCREMENT,

thread_id INT UNSIGNED NOT NULL,

user_id INT UNSIGNED NOT NULL,

message TEXT NOT NULL,

posted_on DATETIME NOT NULL,

PRIMARY KEY (post_id),

INDEX (thread_id),

INDEX (user_id)

);
```

The main column in this table is *message*, which stores each post. Two columns are foreign keys, tying into the *threads* and *users* tables. The *posted_on* column is of type DATETME but will use UTC (Coordinated Universal Time, see Chapter 14). Nothing special needs to be done here for that, though.

6. Create the *users* table (**Figure 15.9**).

```
CREATE TABLE users (

user_id MEDIUMINT UNSIGNED NOT NULL
→ AUTO_INCREMENT,

lang_id TINYINT UNSIGNED NOT NULL,

time_zone VARCHAR(30) NOT NULL,

username VARCHAR(30) NOT NULL,

pass CHAR(40) NOT NULL,

email VARCHAR(60) NOT NULL,

PRIMARY KEY (user_id),

UNIQUE (username),

UNIQUE (email),

INDEX login (username, pass)

);
```

For the sake of brevity, I'm omitting some of the other columns you'd put in this table, such as registration date, first name, and last name. For more on creating and using a table like this, see the next chapter.

In my thinking about this site, I expect users will select their preferred language and time zone when they register, so that they can have a more personalized experience. They can also have a username, which will be displayed in posts (instead of their email address). Both the username and the email address must be unique, which is something you'd need to address in the registration process.

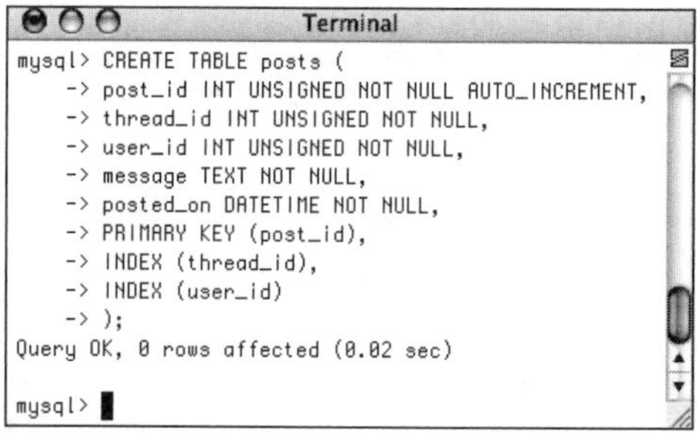

Figure 15.8 Creating the *posts* table, which links to both *threads* and *users*.

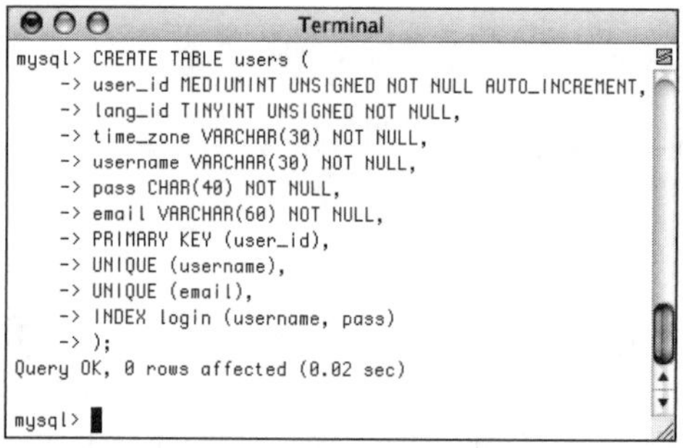

Figure 15.9 Creating a bare-bones version of the *users* table.

7. Create the *words* table (**Figure 15.10**).

```
CREATE TABLE words (

word_id TINYINT UNSIGNED NOT NULL
→ AUTO_INCREMENT,

lang_id TINYINT UNSIGNED NOT NULL,

title VARCHAR(80) NOT NULL,

intro TINYTEXT NOT NULL,

home VARCHAR(30) NOT NULL,

forum_home VARCHAR(40) NOT NULL,

`language` VARCHAR(40) NOT NULL,

register VARCHAR(30) NOT NULL,

login VARCHAR(30) NOT NULL,

logout VARCHAR(30) NOT NULL,

new_thread VARCHAR(40) NOT NULL,

subject VARCHAR(30) NOT NULL,

body VARCHAR(30) NOT NULL,

submit VARCHAR(30) NOT NULL,

posted_on VARCHAR(30) NOT NULL,

posted_by VARCHAR(30) NOT NULL,

replies VARCHAR(30) NOT NULL,

latest_reply VARCHAR(40) NOT NULL,

post_a_reply VARCHAR(40) NOT NULL,

PRIMARY KEY (word_id),

UNIQUE (lang_id)

);
```

This table will store different translations of comment elements used on the site. Some—*home, forum_home, language, register, login, logout,* and *new_thread*— will be the names of links. Others—*subject, body, submit*—are used on the page for posting messages. Another category are those used on the forum's main page: *posted_on, posted_by, replies,* and *latest_reply*.

Some of these will be used multiple times in the site, and yet, this is still an incomplete list. As you implement the site yourself, you'll see other places where word definitions could be used.

Each column is of VARCHAR type, except for *intro*, which is a body of text to be used on the main page. Most of the columns have a limit of 30, allowing for characters in other languages that require more space, except for a handful that might need to be bigger.

For each column, its name implies the value to be stored in that column. For one—*language*—I've used a MySQL keyword to demonstrate how that can be done. The fix is to surround the column's name in backticks so that MySQL doesn't confuse this column's name with the keyword "language".

continues on next page

Figure 15.10 Creating the *words* table, which stores representations of key words in different languages.

8. Populate the *languages* table (**Figure 15.11**).

```
INSERT INTO languages (lang,
▸ lang_eng) VALUES

('English', 'English'),

('Português', 'Portuguese'),

('Français', 'French'),

('Norsk', 'Norwegian'),

('Romanian', 'Romanian'),

('Ελληνικά', 'Greek'),

('Deutsch', 'German'),

('Srpski', 'Serbian'),

('日本語', 'Japanese'),

('Nederlands', 'Dutch');
```

This is just a handful of the languages the site will represent thanks to some assistance provided me (see the sidebar "A Note on Translations"). For each, the native and English word for that language is stored.

```
mysql> SELECT * FROM languages;
+---------+--------------------+------------+
| lang_id | lang               | lang_eng   |
+---------+--------------------+------------+
|       1 | English            | English    |
|       2 | Português          | Portuguese |
|       3 | Français           | French     |
|       4 | Norsk              | Norwegian  |
|       5 | Romanian           | Romanian   |
|       6 | Ελληνικά           | Greek      |
|       7 | Deutsch            | German     |
|       8 | Srpski             | Serbian    |
|       9 | 日本語             | Japanese   |
|      10 | Nederlands         | Dutch      |
+---------+--------------------+------------+
10 rows in set (0.00 sec)

mysql>
```

Figure 15.11 The populated *languages* table, with each language written in its own alphabet.

A Note on Translations

Several readers around the world were kind enough to provide me with translations of key words, names, message subjects, and message bodies. For their help, I'd like to extend my sincerest thanks to (in no particular order): Angelo (Portuguese); Iris (German); Johan (Norwegian); Gabi (Romanian); Darko (Serbian); Emmanuel and Jean-François (French); Andreas and Simeon (Greek); Darius (Filipino/Tagalog); Olaf (Dutch); and Tsutomu (Japanese).

If you know one of these languages, you'll undoubtedly see linguistic mistakes made in this text or in the corresponding images. If so, it's almost certainly my fault, having miscommunicated the words I needed translated or improperly entered the responses into the database. I apologize in advance for any such mistakes but hope you'll focus more on the database, the code, and the functionality. My thanks, again, to those who helped!

9. Populate the *users* table (**Figure 15.12**).

```
INSERT INTO users (lang_id,
→ time_zone, username, pass, email)
→ VALUES
(1, 'America/New_York', 'troutster',
→ SHA1('password'),
→ 'email@example.com'),
(7, 'Europe/Berlin', 'Ute',
→ SHA1('pa24word'),
→ 'email1@example.com'),
(4, 'Europe/Oslo', 'Silje',
→ SHA1('2kll13'),
→ 'email2@example.com'),
(2, 'America/Sao_Paulo', 'João',
→ SHA1('fJDLN34'),
→ 'email3@example.com'),
(1, 'Pacific/Auckland', 'kiwi',
→ SHA1('conchord'),
→ 'kiwi@example.org');
```

Because the PHP scripts will show the users associated with posts, a couple of users are necessary. I've associated a language and a time zone with each (see Chapter 14 for more on time zones in MySQL). Each user's password will be encrypted with the SHA1() function.

continues on next page

MAKING THE DATABASE

```
● ○ ○                              Terminal
mysql> SELECT * FROM users;
+---------+---------+------------------+----------+------------------------------------------+--------------------+
| user_id | lang_id | time_zone        | username | pass                                     | email              |
+---------+---------+------------------+----------+------------------------------------------+--------------------+
|       1 |       1 | America/New_York | troutster | 5baa61e4c9b93f3f0682250b6cf8331b7ee68fd8 | email@example.com  |
|       2 |       7 | Europe/Berlin    | Ute      | a5a7569327c9925049693dbfda8cd1d0106f4550 | email1@example.com |
|       3 |       4 | Europe/Oslo      | Silje    | e408d64f8bcd85ebb7d84bc13540c5683ce1b6c9 | email2@example.com |
|       4 |       2 | America/Sao_Paulo | João    | 2d2553bcdeda4aa9d3b09965e90c6d283a8cfce1 | email3@example.com |
|       5 |       1 | Pacific/Auckland | kiwi     | 9c147500fd397d8f90a2e5005524fee515099760 | kiwi@example.org   |
+---------+---------+------------------+----------+------------------------------------------+--------------------+
5 rows in set (0.01 sec)

mysql>
```

Figure 15.12 A few users were added manually, as there is no registration process in this site (but see Chapter 16, "Example—User Registration," for that).

10. Populate the *words* table.

```
INSERT INTO words VALUES
(NULL, 1, 'PHP and MySQL for Dynamic
→ Web Sites: The Forum!',
→ '<p>Welcome to our site....please
→ use the links above...blah, blah,
→ blah.</p>\r\n<p>Welcome to our
→ site....please use the links
→ above...blah, blah, blah.</p>',
→ 'Home', 'Forum Home', 'Language',
→ 'Register', 'Login', 'Logout',
→ 'New Thread', 'Subject', 'Body',
→ 'Submit', 'Posted on', 'Posted
→ by', 'Replies', 'Latest Reply',
→ 'Post a Reply');
```

These are the words associated with each term in English. The record has a *lang_id* of *1*, which matches the *lang_id* for English in the *languages* table. The SQL to insert words for other languages into this table is available from the book's supporting Web site.

✔ Tips

■ This chapter doesn't go through the steps for creating the mysqli_connect.php page, which connects to the database. Instead, just copy the one from Chapter 8, "Using PHP and MySQL." Then change the parameters in the script to use a valid username/password/hostname combination to connect to the *forum2* database.

This chapter does include one additional requirement: PHP should identify to MySQL the encoding to be used. To do that, add this line after establishing a connection:

```
mysqli_set_charset($dbc, 'utf8');
```

If your installation of PHP or MySQL doesn't support this function (i.e., if you get an error message from it), use this instead:

```
mysqli_query($dbc, 'SET NAMES utf8');
```

With either of those two lines being executed immediately after connecting to MySQL, every interaction should be Unicode-safe.

■ As a reminder, the foreign key in one table should be of the exact same type and size as the matching primary key in another table.

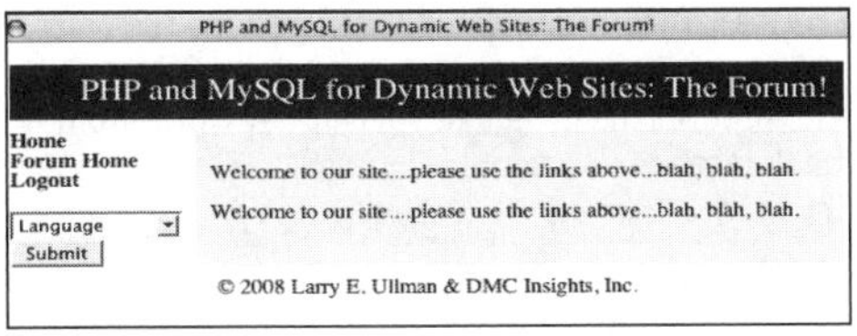

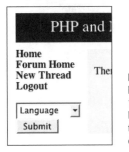

Figure 15.13 The basic layout and appearance of the site.

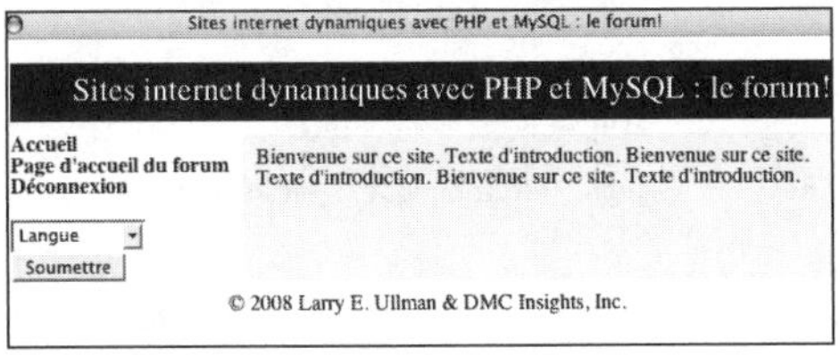

Figure 15.14 The home page viewed in French (compare with Figure 15.13).

Figure 15.15 The same home page as in Figure 15.13, but with different links acknowledging that the user is logged in and on the forum.php page.

Writing the Templates

This example, like any site containing lots of pages, will make use of a template to separate out the bulk of the appearance from the logic. Following the instructions laid out in Chapter 3, "Creating Dynamic Web Sites," a header file and a footer file will store most of the HTML code. Each PHP script will then include these files to make a complete HTML page (**Figure 15.13**). But this example is a little more complicated.

One of the goals of this site is to serve users in many different languages. Accomplishing that involves not just letting them post messages in their native language but making sure they can use the whole site in their native language as well. This means that the page title, the navigation links, the captions, the prompts, and even the menus need to appear in their language (**Figure 15.14**).

The instructions for making the database show how this is accomplished: by storing translations of all key words in a table. The header file, therefore, needs to pull out all these key words so that they can be used as needed. Secondarily, this header file will also show different links based upon whether the user is logged in or not. Adding just one more little twist: if the user is on the forum page, where they view all the threads in a language, they'll also be given the option to post a new thread (**Figure 15.15**).

The template itself uses CSS for some formatting (there's not much to it, really). You can download all these files from the book's supporting Web site (www.DMCInsights.com/phpmysql3/).

To make the template:

1. Begin a new document in your text editor or IDE (**Script 15.1**).

```
<?php # Script 15.1 - header.html
header ('Content-Type: text/html;
→ charset=UTF-8');
```

As this script will need to do a fair amount of data validation and retrieval, it starts with a PHP block. The script also indicates to the Web browser its encoding—UTF-8, using the header() function. See Chapter 14 for more on this.

2. Start a session.

```
session_start();
$_SESSION['user_id'] = 1;
$_SESSION['user_tz'] =
→ 'America/New_York';
// $_SESSION = array();
```

To track users after they log in, the site will use sessions. Since the site doesn't have registration and login functionality in this chapter, two lines can virtually log in the user. Ordinarily both values would come from a database, but they'll be set here for testing purposes. To virtually log the user out, uncomment the third line.

Script 15.1 The header.html file begins the template. It also sets the page's encoding, starts the session, and retrieves the language-specific key words from the database.

```
1    <?php # Script 15.1 - header.html
2    /* This script...
3     * - starts the HTML template.
4     * - indicates the encoding using
         header().
5     * - starts the session.
6     * - gets the language-specific words from
         the database.
7     * - lists the available languages.
8     */
9
10   // Indicate the encoding:
11   header ('Content-Type: text/html;
         charset=UTF-8');
12
13   // Start the session:
14   session_start();
15
16   // For testing purposes:
17   $_SESSION['user_id'] = 1;
18   $_SESSION['user_tz'] = 'America/New_York';
19   // $_SESSION = array();
20
21   // Need the database connection:
22   require_once('../mysqli_connect.php');
23
24   // The language ID is stored in the
         session.
25   // Check for a new language ID...
26   if (isset($_GET['lid']) &&
         is_numeric($_GET['lid'])) {
27     $_SESSION['lid'] = (int) $_GET['lid'];
28   } elseif (!isset($_SESSION['lid'])) {
```

(script continues on next page)

Script 15.1 *continued*

```
29    $_SESSION['lid'] = 1; // Default.

30    }

31

32    // Get the words for this language.

33    $words = FALSE; // Flag variable.

34    if ($_SESSION['lid'] > 0) {

35      $q = "SELECT * FROM words WHERE lang_id
      = {$_SESSION['lid']}";

36      $r = mysqli_query($dbc, $q);

37      if (mysqli_num_rows($r) == 1) {

38      $words = mysqli_fetch_array($r,
      MYSQLI_ASSOC);

39      }

40    }

41

42    // If we still don't have the words, get
      the default language:

43    if (!$words) {

44      $_SESSION['lid'] = 1; // Default.

45      $q = "SELECT * FROM words WHERE lang_id
      = {$_SESSION['lid']}";

46      $r = mysqli_query($dbc, $q);

47      $words = mysqli_fetch_array($r,
      MYSQLI_ASSOC);

48    }

49

50    mysqli_free_result($r);

51    ?>

52    <!DOCTYPE html PUBLIC "-//W3C//DTD XHTML
      1.0 Transitional//EN"

53      "http://www.w3.org/TR/xhtml1/DTD/
      xhtml1-transitional.dtd">

54    <html xmlns="http://www.w3.org/1999/xhtml"
      xml:lang="en" lang="en">

55    <head>

56      <meta http-equiv="content-type"
      content="text/html; charset=utf-8" />
```

(script continues on next page)

3. Include the database connection and validate the language ID, if present.

```
require_once('../mysqli_connect.php');

if (isset($_GET['lid']) &&
→ is_numeric($_GET['lid'])) {
      $_SESSION['lid'] = (int)
      → $_GET['lid'];
} elseif (!isset($_SESSION['lid'])) {
      $_SESSION['lid'] = 1;
}
```

As with many other examples in this book, the assumption is that the mysqli_connect. php script is stored in the directory above the current one, outside of the Web root.

Next, the language ID value (abbreviated *lid*) will be validated, if one was received in the URL. The language ID controls what language is used to show all the site elements, and it also dictates the forum to be viewed. It would be passed to the forum.php page by submitting the language form in the navigation links (see Figure 15.15). In that case, the ID will be stored in the session so that it's always available.

The second clause applies if the page did not receive a language ID in the URL and the language ID has not already been established in the session. In that case, a default language is selected. This value corresponds to English in the *languages* table in the database. You can change it to any ID that matches the default language you'd like to use.

continues on next page

4. Get the key words for this language.

```
$words = FALSE;

if ($_SESSION['lid'] > 0) {

    $q = "SELECT * FROM words WHERE
    → lang_id = {$_SESSION['lid']}";

    $r = mysqli_query($dbc, $q);

    if (mysqli_num_rows($r) == 1) {

        $words = mysqli_fetch_array($r,
        → MYSQLI_ASSOC);

    }

}
```

The next step in the header file is to
retrieve from the database all of the key
words for the given language. A variable
will be used as a flag, indicating whether
this process succeeds or not. Then a
check confirms that the language ID is
positive and the query is run on the
database. If the query returns one record,
those values will be fetched into $words.

5. If a problem occurred, get the default
words.

```
if (!$words) {

    $_SESSION['lid'] = 1;

    $q = "SELECT * FROM words WHERE
    → lang_id = {$_SESSION['lid']}";

    $r = mysqli_query($dbc, $q);

    $words = mysqli_fetch_array($r,
    → MYSQLI_ASSOC);

}
```

If $_SESSION['lid'] is not greater than *0*
or it is but the query in Step 4 did not
return a record, then the words for the
default language need to be retrieved.

Script 15.1 *continued*

```
57    <title><?php echo $words['title'];
      ?></title>

58    <style type="text/css" media="screen">

59    body { background-color: #ffffff; }

60

61    .content {

62      background-color: #f5f5f5;

63      padding-top: 10px; padding-right:
        10px; padding-bottom: 10px; padding-
        left: 10px;

64      margin-top: 10px; margin-right: 10px;
        margin-bottom: 10px; margin-left:
        10px;

65    }

66

67    a.navlink:link { color: #003366; text-
      decoration: none; }

68    a.navlink:visited { color: #003366;
      text-decoration: none; }

69    a.navlink:hover { color: #cccccc; text-
      decoration: none; }

70

71    .title {

72      font-size: 24px; font-weight: normal;
        color: #ffffff;

73      margin-top: 5px; margin-bottom: 5px;
        margin-left: 20px;

74      padding-top: 5px; padding-bottom: 5px;
        padding-left: 20px;

75    }

76    </style>

77    </head>

78    <body>

79

80    <table width="90%" border="0"
      cellspacing="10" cellpadding="0"
      align="center">

81
```

(script continues on next page)

Writing the Templates

Script 15.1 *continued*

```
 ○ ○ ○                 📄 Script

82     <tr>

83     <td colspan="2" bgcolor="#003366"
       align="center"><p class="title"><?php
       echo $words['title']; ?></p></td>

84     </tr>

85

86     <tr>

87     <td valign="top" nowrap="nowrap"
       width="10%"><b>

88     <?php // Display links:

89

90     // Default links:

91     echo '<a href="index.php"
       class="navlink">' . $words['home'] .
       '</a><br />

92     <a href="forum.php" class="navlink">' .
       $words['forum_home'] . '</a><br />';

93

94     // Display links based upon login status:

95     if (isset($_SESSION['user_id'])) {

96

97         // If this is the forum page, add a
           link for posting new threads:

98         if (stripos($_SERVER['PHP_SELF'],
           'forum.php')) {

99             echo '<a href="post.php"
               class="navlink">' .
               $words['new_thread'] .
               '</a><br />';

100        }

101

102        // Add the logout link:

103        echo '<a href="logout.php"
           class="navlink">' . $words['logout'] .
           '</a><br />';

104

105    } else {

106
```

(script continues on next page)

6. Free up the resources and close the PHP section.

```
mysqli_free_result($r);

?>
```

Calling `mysqli_free_result()` isn't necessary, but makes for tidy programming.

7. Begin the HTML page.

```
<!DOCTYPE html PUBLIC "-//W3C//DTD
→ XHTML 1.0 Transitional//EN"

"http://www.w3.org/TR/xhtml1/DTD/
→ xhtml1-transitional.dtd">

<html
→ xmlns="http://www.w3.org/1999/xhtml"
→ xml:lang="en" lang="en">

<head>

    <meta http-equiv="content-type"
    → content="text/html;
    → charset=utf-8" />

    <title><?php echo
    → $words['title']; ?></title>
```

Note that the encoding is also indicated in a META tag, even though the PHP header() call already identifies the encoding. This is just a matter of being thorough.

continues on next page

8. Add the CSS.

```
<style type="text/css"
→ media="screen">
    body { background-color: #ffffff; }
    .content {
    background-color: #f5f5f5;
    padding-top: 10px; padding-right:
→ 10px; padding-bottom: 10px;
→ padding-left: 10px;
    margin-top: 10px; margin-right:
→ 10px; margin-bottom: 10px;
→ margin-left: 10px;
    }
    a.navlink:link { color: #003366;
→ text-decoration: none; }
    a.navlink:visited { color:
→ #003366; text-decoration: none; }
    a.navlink:hover { color: #cccccc;
→ text-decoration: none; }
    .title {
    font-size: 24px; font-weight:
→ normal; color: #ffffff;
    margin-top: 5px; margin-bottom:
→ 5px; margin-left: 20px;
    padding-top: 5px; padding-bottom:
→ 5px; padding-left: 20px;
    }
</style>
```

This is all taken from a template I found somewhere some time ago. It adds a little decoration to the site.

Script 15.1 *continued*

```
000                    📄 Script
107    // Register and login links:
108    echo '<a href="register.php"
       class="navlink">' . $words['register'] .
       '</a><br />
109    <a href="login.php" class="navlink">' .
       $words['login'] . '</a><br />';
110
111    }
112
113    // For choosing a forum/language:
114    echo '</b><p><form action="forum.php"
       method="get">
115    <select name="lid">
116    <option value="0">' . $words['language'] .
       '</option>
117    ';
118
119    // Retrieve all the languages...
120    $q = "SELECT lang_id, lang FROM languages
       ORDER BY lang_eng ASC";
121    $r = mysqli_query($dbc, $q);
122    if (mysqli_num_rows($r) > 0) {
123        while ($menu_row =
           mysqli_fetch_array($r, MYSQLI_NUM)) {
124            echo "<option
               value=\"$menu_row[0]\">$menu_row[1]
               </option>\n";
125        }
126    }
127    mysqli_free_result($r);
128    unset($menu_row);
129
130    echo '</select><br />
131    <input name="submit" type="submit"
       value="' . $words['submit'] . '" />
132    </form></p>
133        </td>
134
135        <td valign="top" class="content">';
136    ?>
```

9. Complete the HTML head and begin the page.

```
</head>

<body>

<table width="90%" border="0"
→ cellspacing="10" cellpadding="0"
→ align="center">

    <tr>

    <td colspan="2" bgcolor="#003366"
    → align="center"><p
    → class="title"><?php echo
    → $words['title']; ?></p></td>

    </tr>

    <tr>

    <td valign="top" nowrap="nowrap"
    → width="10%"><b>
```

The page itself uses a table for the layout, with one row showing the page title, the next row containing the navigation links on the left and the page-specific content on the right, and the final row containing the copyright (**Figure 15.16**). You'll see in this code that the page title will also be language-specific.

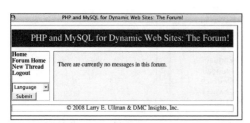

Figure 15.16 The page layout showing the rows and columns of the main HTML table.

10. Start displaying the links.

```
<?php

echo '<a href="index.php"
→ class="navlink">' . $words['home'] .
→ '</a><br />

<a href="forum.php" class="navlink">'
→ . $words['forum_home'] . '</a>
→ <br />';
```

The first two links will always appear, whether the user is logged in or not, and regardless of the page they're currently viewing. For each link, the text of the link itself will be language-specific.

11. If the user is logged in, show "new thread" and logout links.

```
if (isset($_SESSION['user_id'])) {

    if
    → (stripos($_SERVER['PHP_SELF'],
    → 'forum.php')) {

        echo '<a href="post.php"
        → class="navlink">' .
        → $words['new_thread'] .
        → '</a><br />';

    }

    echo '<a href="logout.php"
    → class="navlink">' .
    → $words['logout'] .
    → '</a><br />';
```

Confirmation of the user's logged-in status is achieved by checking for the presence of a $_SESSION['user_id'] variable. If it's set, then the logout link can be created. Before that, a check is made to see if this is the forum.php page. If so, then a link to start a new thread is created (users can only create new threads if they're on the forum page; you wouldn't want them to create a new thread on some of the other pages, like the home page, because it wouldn't be clear to which forum the thread should be posted).

continues on next page

12. Display the links for users not logged in.

```
} else {
    echo '<a href="register.php"
    → class="navlink">' .
    → $words['register'] .
    → '</a><br />

    <a href="login.php"
    → class="navlink">' .
    → $words['login'] . '</a><br />';
}
```

If the user isn't logged in, links are provided for registering and logging in.

13. Begin a form for choosing a language.

```
echo '</b><p><form
→ action="forum.php" method="get">

<select name="lid">

<option value="0">' .
→ $words['language'] . '</option>
';
```

The user can choose a language (which is also a forum), using a pull-down menu (**Figure 15.17**). The first value in the menu will be the word "language," in the user's default language. The select menu's name is *lid*, short for *language ID*, and its action points to forum.php. So when the user submits this simple form, they'll be taken to the forum of their choice.

14. Retrieve every language.

```
$q = "SELECT lang_id, lang FROM
→ languages ORDER BY lang_eng ASC";

$r = mysqli_query($dbc, $q);

if (mysqli_num_rows($r) > 0) {

    while ($menu_row =
    → mysqli_fetch_array($r,
    → MYSQLI_NUM)) {

        echo "<option
        → value=\"$menu_row[0]\">
        → $menu_row[1]</option>\n";

    }

}
```

This query retrieves the languages and the language ID from the *languages* table. Each is added as an option to the select menu.

15. Perform some cleanup.

```
mysqli_free_result($r);

unset($menu_row);
```

Again, these lines aren't required, but they can help limit bugs. In particular, when you have pages that run multiple SELECT queries, mysqli_free_result() can help avoid confusion issues between PHP and MySQL.

Figure 15.17 The language pull-down menu, with each option in its native language.

16. Complete the form and the PHP page.

```
echo '</select><br />

<input name="submit" type="submit"
→ value="' . $words['submit'] . '" />

</form></p>

    </td>

    <td valign="top"
→ class="content">';

?>
```

17. Save the file as `header.html`.

Even though it contains a fair amount of PHP, this script will still use the `.html` extension (which I prefer to use for template files). Make sure that the file is saved using UTF-8 encoding (see Chapter 14).

18. Create a new document in your text editor or IDE (**Script 15.2**).

```
<!-- Script 15.2 - footer.html -->
```

19. Complete the HTML page.

```
        </td>

        </tr>

        <tr>

        <td colspan="2"
→ align="center">&copy; 2008
→ Larry E. Ullman &amp; DMC
→ Insights, Inc.</td>

        </tr>

    </table>

    </body>

</html>
```

20. Save the file as `footer.html`.

Again, make sure that the file is saved using UTF-8 encoding (see Chapter 14).

21. Place both files in your Web directory, within a folder called `includes`.

Script 15.2 The footer file completes the HTML page.

```
1   <!-- Script 15.2 - footer.html -->
2       </td>
3       </tr>
4
5       <tr>
6       <td colspan="2" align="center">&copy;
        2008 Larry E. Ullman &amp; DMC Insights,
        Inc.</td>
7       </tr>
8
9       </table>
10      </body>
11  </html>
```

Creating the Index Page

The index page in this example won't do that much. It'll provide some introductory text and the links for the user to register, log in, choose their language/forum, and so forth. From a programming perspective, it'll show how the template files are to be used.

To make the home page:

1. Create a new PHP document in your text editor or IDE (**Script 15.3**).

   ```
   <?php # Script 15.3 - index.php
   ```

   Because all of the HTML is in the included files, this page can begin with the opening PHP tags.

2. Include the HTML header.

   ```
   include ('includes/header.html');
   ```

   The included file uses the `header()` and `session_start()` functions, so you have to make sure that nothing is sent to the Web browser prior to this line. That shouldn't be a problem as long as there are no spaces before the opening PHP tag.

3. Print the language-specific content.

   ```
   echo $words['intro'];
   ```

   The `$words` array is defined within the header file. It can be referred to here, since the header file was just included. The value indexed at *intro* is some welcoming text in the selected or default language.

4. Complete the page.

   ```
   include ('includes/footer.html');
   ?>
   ```

   That's it for the home page!

5. Save the file as `index.php`, place it in your Web directory, and test it in your Web browser (see Figures 15.13 and 15.14).

   Once again, make sure that the file is saved using UTF-8 encoding (see Chapter 14). This will be the last time I remind you!

Script 15.3 The home page includes the header and footer files to make a complete HTML document. It also prints some introductory text in the chosen language.

```
1   <?php # Script 15.3 - index.php
2   // This is the main page for the site.
3
4   // Include the HTML header:
5   include ('includes/header.html');
6
7   // The content on this page is
       introductory text
8   // pulled from the database, based upon the
9   // selected language:
10  echo $words['intro'];
11
12  // Include the HTML footer file:
13  include ('includes/footer.html');
14  ?>
```

Script 15.4 This script performs one rather complicated query to display five pieces of information—the subject, the original poster, the date the thread was started, the number of replies, and the date of the latest reply—for each thread in a forum.

```
1    <?php # Script 15.4 - forum.php
2    // This page shows the threads in a forum.
3    include ('includes/header.html');
4
5    // Retrieve all the messages in this
     forum...
6
7    // If the user is logged in and has chosen
     a time zone,
8    // use that to convert the dates and
     times:
9    if (isset($_SESSION['user_tz'])) {
10       $first = "CONVERT_TZ(p.posted_on, 'UTC',
         '{$_SESSION['user_tz']}')";
11       $last = "CONVERT_TZ(p.posted_on, 'UTC',
         '{$_SESSION['user_tz']}')";
12   } else {
13       $first = 'p.posted_on';
14       $last = 'p.posted_on';
15   }
16
17   // The query for retrieving all the
     threads in this forum, along with the
     original user,
18   // when the thread was first posted, when
     it was last replied to, and how many
     replies it's had:
```

(script continues on next page)

Creating the Forum Page

The next page in the Web site is the forum page, which displays the threads in a forum (each language being its own forum). The page will use the language ID, passed to this page in a URL and/or stored in a session, to know what threads to display.

The basic functionality of this page—running a query, displaying the results—is simple (**Figure 15.18**). The query this page uses is perhaps the most complex one in the book. It's complicated for three reasons:

1. It performs a join across three tables.

2. It uses three aggregate functions and a GROUP BY clause.

3. It converts the dates to the user's time zone, but only if the person viewing the page is logged in.

So, again, the query is intricate, but I'll go through it in detail in the following steps.

To write the forum page:

1. Create a new PHP document in your text editor or IDE (**Script 15.4**).

```
<?php # Script 15.4 - forum.php
include ('includes/header.html');
```

continues on next page

Figure 15.18 The forum page, which lists information about the threads in a given language. The threads are linked to a page where they can be read.

2. Determine what dates and times to use.

```
if (isset($_SESSION['user_tz'])) {
    $first = "CONVERT_TZ(p.posted_on,
    → 'UTC',
    → '{$_SESSION['user_tz']}')";
    $last = "CONVERT_TZ(p.posted_on,
    → 'UTC',
    → '{$_SESSION['user_tz']}')";
} else {
    $first = 'p.posted_on';
    $last = 'p.posted_on';
}
```

As I already said, the query will format the date and time to the user's time zone (presumably selected during the registration process), but only if the viewer is logged in. This information would be retrieved from the database and stored in the session upon login.

To make the query dynamic, what exact date/time value should be selected will be stored in a variable. If the user is not logged in, which means that $_SESSION['user_tz'] is not set, the two dates—when a thread was started and when the most recent reply was posted—will be unadulterated values from the table. In both cases, the table column being referenced is *posted_on* in the *posts* table (*p* will be an alias to *posts* in the query).

If the user is logged in, the CONVERT_TZ() function will be used to convert the value stored in *posted_on* from UTC to the user's chosen time zone. See Chapter 14 for more on this function.

Script 15.4 *continued*

```
19  $q = "SELECT t.thread_id, t.subject,
    username, COUNT(post_id) - 1 AS responses,
    MAX(DATE_FORMAT($last, '%e-%b-%y %l:%i
    %p')) AS last, MIN(DATE_FORMAT($first,
    '%e-%b-%y %l:%i %p')) AS first FROM
    threads AS t INNER JOIN posts AS p USING
    (thread_id) INNER JOIN users AS u ON
    t.user_id = u.user_id WHERE t.lang_id =
    {$_SESSION['lid']} GROUP BY (p.thread_id)
    ORDER BY last DESC";
20  $r = mysqli_query($dbc, $q);
21  if (mysqli_num_rows($r) > 0) {
22
23      // Create a table:
24      echo '<table width="100%" border="0"
        cellspacing="2" cellpadding="2"
        align="center">
25      <tr>
26          <td align="left" width="50%"><em>' .
        $words['subject'] . '</em>:</td>
27          <td align="left" width="20%"><em>' .
        $words['posted_by'] . '</em>:</td>
28          <td align="center" width="10%"><em>' .
        $words['posted_on'] . '</em>:</td>
29          <td align="center" width="10%"><em>' .
        $words['replies'] . '</em>:</td>
30          <td align="center" width="10%"><em>' .
        $words['latest_reply'] . '</em>:</td>
31      </tr>';
32
33      // Fetch each thread:
34      while ($row = mysqli_fetch_array($r,
        MYSQLI_ASSOC)) {
35
36          echo '<tr>
37              <td align="left"><a
        href="read.php?tid=' . $row['thread_id'] .
        '">' . $row['subject'] . '</a></td>
38              <td align="left">' . $row['username']
        . '</td>
39              <td align="center">' . $row['first'] .
        '</td>
40              <td align="center">' .
        $row['responses'] . '</td>
```

(script continues on next page)

Script 15.4 *continued*

```
◉ ◉ ◉                  📄 Script
41      <td align="center">' . $row['last'] .
    '</td>

42      </tr>';

43

44      }

45

46    echo '</table>'; // Complete the table.

47

48    } else {

49      echo '<p>There are currently no messages
    in this forum.</p>';

50    }

51

52    // Include the HTML footer file:

53    include ('includes/footer.html');

54    ?>
```

3. Define and execute the query.

```
$q = "SELECT t.thread_id, t.subject,
→ username, COUNT(post_id) - 1 AS
→ responses, MAX(DATE_FORMAT($last,
→ '%e-%b-%y %l:%i %p')) AS last,
→ MIN(DATE_FORMAT($first, '%e-%b-%y
→ %l:%i %p')) AS first FROM threads
→ AS t INNER JOIN posts AS p USING
→ (thread_id) INNER JOIN users AS u
→ ON t.user_id = u.user_id WHERE
→ t.lang_id = {$_SESSION['lid']}
→ GROUP BY (p.thread_id) ORDER BY
→ last DESC";

$r = mysqli_query($dbc, $q);

if (mysqli_num_rows($r) > 0) {
```

The query needs to return six things: the ID and subject of each thread (which comes from the *threads* table), the name of the user who posted the thread in the first place (from *users*), the number of replies to each thread, the date the thread was started, and the date the thread last had a reply (all from *posts*).

The overarching structure of this query is a join between *threads* and *posts* using the *thread_id* column (which is the same in both tables). This result is then joined with the *users* table using the *user_id* column.

As for the selected values, three aggregate functions are used (see Chapter 6): COUNT(), MIN(), and MAX(). Each is applied to a column in the *posts* table, so the query has a GROUP BY (p.thread_id) clause. MIN() and MAX() are used to return the earliest (for the original post) and latest dates. Both will be shown on the forum page (see Figure 15.18). The latest date is also used to order the results so that the most recent activity always gets returned first. The COUNT() function is used to count the number of posts in a given thread. Because the original post is also in the *posts* table, it'll be counted as well, so 1 is subtracted from the count.

Finally, aliases are used to make the query shorter to write and to make it easier to use the results in the PHP script. **Figure 15.19** shows this query executed in the mysql client, for a user that's not logged in.

continues on next page

```
◉ ◉ ◉                          Terminal
mysql> SELECT t.thread_id, t.subject, username, COUNT(post_id) - 1 AS responses, MAX(DATE_FORMAT(p.posted_on, '%e-%b-%y %l:%i %p')) AS last,
MIN(DATE_FORMAT(p.posted_on, '%e-%b-%y %l:%i %p')) AS first FROM threads AS t INNER JOIN posts AS p USING (thread_id) INNER JOIN users AS u
ON t.user_id = u.user_id WHERE t.lang_id = 4 GROUP BY (p.thread_id) ORDER BY last DESC;

+-----------+------------------------------------------------------------+-----------+-----------+-------------------+-------------------+
| thread_id | subject                                                    | username  | responses | last              | first             |
+-----------+------------------------------------------------------------+-----------+-----------+-------------------+-------------------+
|         1 | Byttet til PHP 5.0 fra PHP 4.0 - variabler utilgjengelige  | troutster |         4 | 29-Oct-07 6:16 AM | 29-Oct-07 10:26 AM |
|         2 | Automatisk bildekontroll                                   | Ute       |         0 | 29-Oct-07 10:45 PM | 29-Oct-07 10:45 PM |
+-----------+------------------------------------------------------------+-----------+-----------+-------------------+-------------------+
2 rows in set (0.00 sec)

mysql>
```

Figure 15.19 The results of running the complex query in the mysql client.

463

4. Create a table for the results.

```
echo '<table width="100%" border="0"
→ cellspacing="2" cellpadding="2"
→ align="center">

    <tr>

    <td align="left"
→ width="50%"><em>' .
→ $words['subject'] . '</em>:</td>

    <td align="left" width="20%"><em>'
→ . $words['posted_by'] .
→ '</em>:</td>

    <td align="center"
→ width="10%"><em>' .
→ $words['posted_on'] .
'</em>:</td>

    <td align="center"
→ width="10%"><em>' .
→ $words['replies'] . '</em>:</td>

    <td align="center"
→ width="10%"><em>' .
→ $words['latest_reply'] .
→ '</em>:</td>

    </tr>';
```

As with some items in the header file, the captions for the columns in this HTML page will use language-specific terminology.

5. Fetch and print each returned record.

```
while ($row = mysqli_fetch_array($r,
→ MYSQLI_ASSOC)) {

    echo '<tr>

    <td align="left"><a
→ href="read.php?tid=' .
→ $row['thread_id'] . '">' .
→ $row['subject'] . '</a></td>

    <td align="left">' .
→ $row['username'] . '</td>

    <td align="center">' .
→ $row['first'] . '</td>

    <td align="center">' .
→ $row['responses'] . '</td>

    <td align="center">' .
→ $row['last'] . '</td>

    </tr>';

}
```

This code is fairly simple, and there are similar examples many times over in the book. The thread's subject is linked to read.php, passing that page the thread ID in the URL.

6. Complete the page.

```
    echo '</table>';

} else {

    echo '<p>There are currently no
    → messages in this forum.</p>';

}

include ('includes/footer.html');

?>
```

This **else** clause applies if the query returned no results. In actuality, this message should also be in the user's chosen language. I've omitted that for the sake of brevity. To fully implement this feature, create another column in the *words* table and store for each language the translated version of this text.

7. Save the file as **forum.php**, place it in your Web directory, and test it in your Web browser (**Figure 15.20**).

✔ Tips

■ To improve this example, you could add pagination—see Chapter 9, "Common Programming Techniques"—to this script.

■ As noted in the chapter's introduction, I've omitted all error handling in this example. If you have problems with the queries, apply the debugging techniques outlined in Chapter 7, "Error Handling and Debugging."

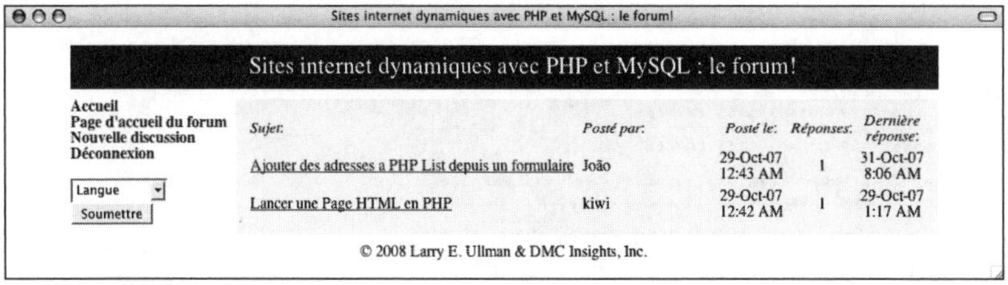

Figure 15.20 The forum.php page, viewed in another language (compare with Figure 15.18).

Creating the Thread Page

Next up is the page for viewing all of the messages in a thread (**Figure 15.21**). This page is accessed by clicking a link in forum.php (**Figure 15.22**). Thanks to a simplified database structure, the query used by this script is not that complicated (with the database design from Chapter 6, this page would have been much more complex). All this page has to do then is make sure it receives a valid thread ID, display every message, and display the form for users to add their own replies.

To make read.php:

1. Create a new PHP document in your text editor or IDE (**Script 15.5**).

   ```
   <?php # Script 15.5 - read.php
   include ('includes/header.html');
   ```

2. Begin validating the thread ID.

   ```
   $tid = FALSE;
   if (isset($_GET['tid']) &&
   → is_numeric($_GET['tid'])) {
       $tid = (int) $_GET['tid'];
       if ($tid > 0) {
   ```

   To start, a flag variable is defined as FALSE, a way of saying: prove that the thread ID is valid. Next, a check confirms that the thread ID was passed in the URL and that it is numeric. Finally, it's typecast as an integer and checked to see if it has a positive value.

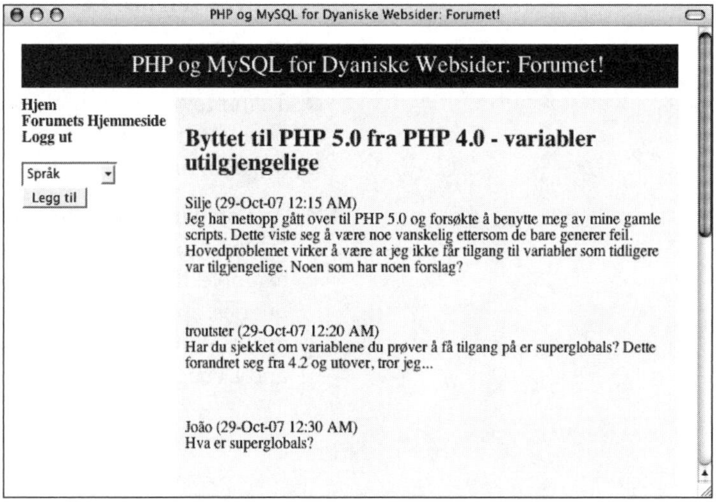

Figure 15.21 The read.php page shows every message in a thread.

```
<td align="left"><a href="read.php?tid=2">Automatisk bildekon
<td align="left">Ute</td>
<td align="center">29-Oct-07 6:45 PM</td>
<td align="center">0</td>
<td align="center">29-Oct-07 6:45 PM</td>
r>
<td align="left"><a href="read.php?tid=1">Byttet til PHP 5.0
<td align="left">troutster</td>
```

Figure 15.22 Part of the source code from forum.php shows how the thread ID is passed to read.php in the URL.

Script 15.5 The read.php page shows all of the messages in a thread, in order of ascending posted date. The page also shows the thread's subject at the top and includes a form for adding a reply at the bottom.

```
⬤ ⬤ ⬤                    📄 Script
1   <?php # Script 15.5 - read.php
2   // This page shows the messages in a
    thread.
3   include ('includes/header.html');
4
5   // Check for a thread ID...
6   $tid = FALSE;
7   if (isset($_GET['tid']) &&
    is_numeric($_GET['tid'])) {
8
9     $tid = (int) $_GET['tid'];
10
11    if ($tid > 0) { // Check against the
      database...
12
13    // Convert the date if the user is
      logged in:
14    if (isset($_SESSION['user_tz'])) {
15      $posted = "CONVERT_TZ(p.posted_on,
        'UTC', '{$_SESSION['user_tz']}')";
16    } else {
17      $posted = 'p.posted_on';
18    }
19
20    // Run the query:
21    $q = "SELECT t.subject, p.message,
      username, DATE_FORMAT($posted, '%e-%b-%y
      %l:%i %p') AS posted FROM threads AS t
      LEFT JOIN posts AS p USING (thread_id)
      INNER JOIN users AS u ON p.user_id =
      u.user_id WHERE t.thread_id = $tid ORDER
      BY p.posted_on ASC";
22    $r = mysqli_query($dbc, $q);
23    if (!(mysqli_num_rows($r) > 0)) {
24      $tid = FALSE; // Invalid thread ID!
25    }
26
```

(script continues on next page)

3. Determine if the dates and times should be adjusted.

```
if (isset($_SESSION['user_tz'])) {
    $posted =
→   "CONVERT_TZ(p.posted_on, 'UTC',
→   '{$_SESSION['user_tz']}')";
} else {
    $posted = 'p.posted_on';
}
```

As in the forum.php page (Script 15.4), the query will format all of the dates and times in the user's time zone, if they are logged in. To be able to adjust the query accordingly, this variable stores either the column's name (*posted_on*, from the *posts* table) or the invocation of MySQL's CONVERT_TZ() function.

continues on next page

4. Run the query.

```
$q = "SELECT t.subject, p.message,
→ username, DATE_FORMAT($posted,
→ '%e-%b-%y %l:%i %p') AS posted FROM
→ threads AS t LEFT JOIN posts AS p
→ USING (thread_id) INNER JOIN users
→ AS u ON p.user_id = u.user_id WHERE
→ t.thread_id = $tid ORDER BY
→ p.posted_on ASC";

$r = mysqli_query($dbc, $q);

if (!(mysqli_num_rows($r) > 0)) {

  $tid = FALSE;

}
```

This query is like the query on the forum page, but it's been simplified in two ways. First, it doesn't use any of the aggregate functions or a GROUP BY clause. Second, it only returns one date/time. The query is still a join across three tables, in order to get the subject, message bodies, and usernames. They are ordered by their posted dates in ascending order (i.e., from the first post to the most recent).

If the query doesn't return any rows, then the thread ID isn't valid and the flag variable is assigned FALSE again.

5. Complete the conditionals and check, again, for a valid thread ID.

```
  } // End of ($tid > 0) IF.

} // End of isset($_GET['tid']) IF.

if ($tid) {
```

Before printing the messages in the thread, one last conditional is used. This conditional would be false if a numeric thread ID greater than 0 was supplied but it didn't return any rows from the database.

Script 15.5 *continued*

```
27     } // End of ($tid > 0) IF.

28

29   } // End of isset($_GET['tid']) IF.

30

31   if ($tid) { // Get the messages in this
     thread...

32

33     $printed = FALSE; // Flag variable.

34

35     // Fetch each:

36     while ($messages =
       mysqli_fetch_array($r, MYSQLI_ASSOC)) {

37

38       // Only need to print the subject once!

39       if (!$printed) {

40         echo
         "<h2>{$messages['subject']}</h2>\n";

41         $printed = TRUE;

42       }

43

44       // Print the message:

45       echo "<p>{$messages['username']}
         ({$messages['posted']})<br />
         {$messages['message']}</p><br />\n";

46

47     } // End of WHILE loop.

48

49     // Show the form to post a message:

50     include ('post_form.php');

51

52   } else { // Invalid thread ID!

53     echo '<p>This page has been accessed in
       error.</p>';

54   }

55

56   include ('includes/footer.html');

57   ?>
```

6. Print each message.

```
$printed = FALSE;

while ($messages =
→ mysqli_fetch_array($r,
→ MYSQLI_ASSOC)) {

    if (!$printed) {

        echo
        → "<h2>{$messages['subject']}
        → </h2>\n";

        $printed = TRUE;

    }

    echo
    → "<p>{$messages['username']}
    → ({$messages['posted']})<br
    → />{$messages['message']}
    → </p><br />\n";

}
```

As you can see in Figure 15.21, the thread subject needs to be printed only once. However, the query will return the subject for each returned message (**Figure 15.23**). To achieve this effect, a flag variable is created. If $printed is false, then the subject needs to be printed. This would be the case for the first row fetched from the database. Once that's been displayed, $printed is set to TRUE so that the subject is not printed again. Then the username, posted date, and message are displayed.

7. Include the form for posting a message.

```
include ('post_form.php');
```

As users could post messages in two ways—as a reply to an existing thread and as the first post in a new thread, I've placed the form itself within a separate file (to be created next).

continues on next page

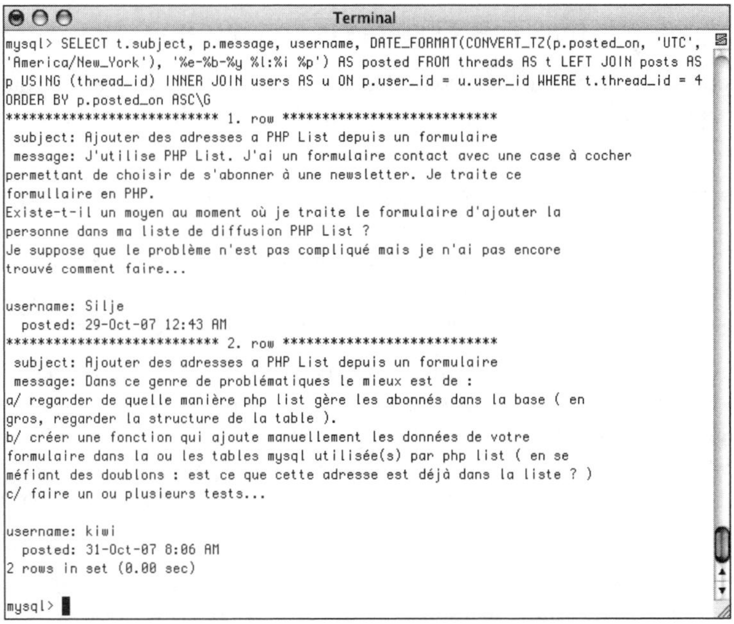

Figure 15.23 The results of the read.php query when run in the mysql client. This version of the query converts the dates to the logged-in user's preferred time zone.

8. Complete the page.

```
} else { // Invalid thread ID!
  echo '<p>This page has been
  → accessed in error.</p>';
}
include ('includes/footer.html');
?>
```

Again, in a complete site, this error message would also be stored in the *words* table in each language. Then you would write here:

```
echo
→ "<p>{$words['access_error']}</p>";
```

9. Save the file as **read.php**, place it in your Web directory, and test it in your Web browser (**Figure 15.24**).

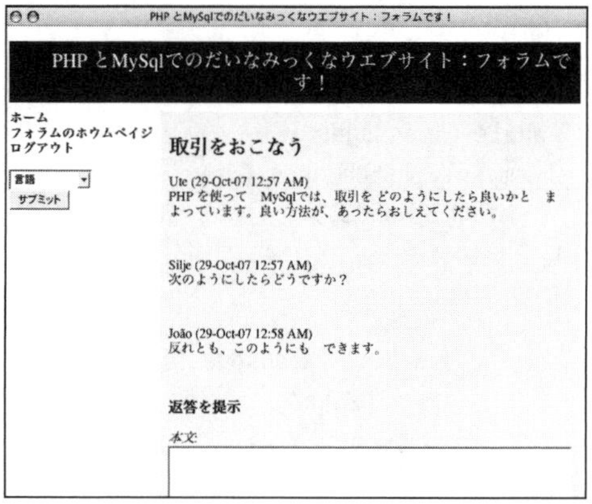

Figure 15.24 The read.php page, viewed in Japanese.

How This Example Is Complicated

In the introduction to this example, I state that it's fundamentally simple, but that sometimes the simple things take some extra effort to do. So how is this example complicated, in my opinion?

First, supporting multiple languages does add a couple of issues. If the encoding isn't handled properly everywhere—when creating the pages in your text editor or IDE, in communicating with MySQL, in the Web browser, etc.—things can go awry. Also, you have to have the proper translations for every language for every bit of text that the site might need. This includes error messages (ones the user should actually see), the bodies of emails, and so forth.

How the PHP files are organized and what they do also complicates things. In particular, variables will be used in one file that are created in another. Doing this can lead to confusion at best and bugs at the worst. To overcome those problems, I recommend adding lots of comments indicating where variables come from or where else they might be used. Also try to use unique variable names within pages so that they are less likely to conflict with variables in included files.

Finally, this example was complicated by the way only one page is used to display the posting form and only one page is used to handle it, despite the fact that messages can be posted in two different ways, with different expectations.

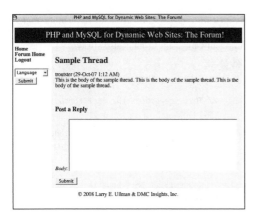

Figure 15.25 The form for posting a message, as shown on the thread-viewing page.

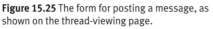

Figure 15.26 The same form for posting a message, if being used to create a new thread.

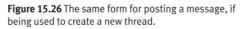

Figure 15.27 The form will recall entered values when not completed correctly.

Posting Messages

The final two pages in this application are the most important, because you won't have threads to read without them. I'm creating two files for posting messages. One will make the form, and the other will handle the form.

Creating the form

The first page required for posting messages is `post_form.php`. It has some contingencies:

1. It can only be included by other files, never accessed directly.

2. It should only be displayed if the user is logged in (which is to say only logged-in users can post messages).

3. If it's being used to add a reply to an existing message, it only needs a message body input (**Figure 15.25**).

4. If it's being used to create a new thread, it needs both subject and body inputs (**Figure 15.26**).

5. It needs to be sticky (**Figure 15.27**).

Still, all of this can be accomplished in just about 60 lines of code and some smart conditionals.

To create post_form.php:

1. Begin a new PHP document in your text editor or IDE (**Script 15.6**).

```
<?php # Script 15.6 - post_form.php
```

2. Redirect the Web browser if this page has been accessed directly.

```
if (!isset($words)) {

    header ("Location:
→ http://www.example.com/index.
→ php");

    exit();

}
```

This script does not include the header and footer and therefore won't make a complete HTML page, so it must be included by a script that does all that. There's no been_included() function that will indicate if this page was included or loaded directly. Instead, since I know that the header file creates a $words variable, if that variable isn't set, then header.html hasn't been included prior to this script and the browser should be redirected.

Change the URL in the header() call to match your site.

3. Confirm that the user is logged in and begin the form.

```
if (isset($_SESSION['user_id'])) {

    echo '<form action="post.php"
→ method="post" accept-
→ charset="utf-8">';
```

Only registered users can post, so check for the presence of $_SESSION['user_id'] before displaying the form. The form itself will be submitted to post.php, to be written next. The accept-charset attribute is added to the form to make it clear that UTF-8 text is acceptable (although this isn't technically required, as each page uses the UTF-8 encoding already).

Script 15.6 This script will be included by other pages (notably, read.php and post.php). It displays a form for posting messages that is also sticky.

```
1    <?php # Script 15.6 - post_form.php

2    // This page shows the form for posting
     messages.

3    // It's included by other pages, never
     called directly.

4

5    // Redirect if this page is called
     directly:

6    if (!isset($words)) {

7        header ("Location:
         http://www.example.com/index.php");

8        exit();

9    }

10

11   // Only display this form if the user is
     logged in:

12   if (isset($_SESSION['user_id'])) {

13

14       // Display the form:

15       echo '<form action="post.php"
         method="post" accept-charset="utf-8">';

16

17       // If on read.php...

18       if (isset($tid) && $tid) {

19

20           // Print a caption:

21           echo '<h3>' .
             $words['post_a_reply'] . '</h3>';

22

23           // Add the thread ID as a hidden
             input:

24           echo '<input name="tid"
             type="hidden" value="' . $tid . '"
             />';

25
```

(script continues on next page)

Script 15.6 *continued*

```
26      } else { // New thread
27
28          // Print a caption:
29          echo '<h3>' . $words['new_thread']
            . '</h3>';
30
31          // Create subject input:
32          echo '<p><em>' . $words['subject']
            . '</em>: <input name="subject"
            type="text" size="60"
            maxlength="100" ';
33
34          // Check for existing value:
35          if (isset($subject)) {
36            echo "value=\"$subject\" ";
37          }
38
39          echo '/></p>';
40
41      } // End of $tid IF.
42
43      // Create the body textarea:
44      echo '<p><em>' . $words['body'] .
        '</em>: <textarea name="body" rows="10"
        cols="60">';
45
46      if (isset($body)) {
47          echo $body;
48      }
49
50      echo '</textarea></p>';
51
52      // Finish the form:
```

(script continues on next page)

4. Check for a thread ID.

```
if (isset($tid) && $tid) {
    echo '<h3>' .
    → $words['post_a_reply'] . '</h3>';
    echo '<input name="tid"
    → type="hidden" value="' . $tid .
    → '" />';
```

This is where things get a little bit tricky. As mentioned earlier, and as shown in Figures 15.25 and 15.26, the form will differ slightly depending upon how it's being used. When included on read.php, it'll be used to provide a reply to an existing thread. To check for this, the script sees if $tid (short for *thread ID*) is set and if it has a TRUE value. That will be the case when this page is included by read.php. When this script is included by post.php, $tid will be set but have a FALSE value.

If this conditional is true, the language-specific version of "Post a Reply" will be printed and the thread ID will be stored in a hidden form input.

continues on next page

POSTING MESSAGES

473

5. Complete the conditional begun in Step 4.

```
} else { // New thread

    echo '<h3>' .
    → $words['new_thread'] . '</h3>';

    echo '<p><em>' .
    → $words['subject'] . '</em>:
    → <input name="subject"
    → type="text" size="60"
    → maxlength="100" ';

    if (isset($subject)) {

        echo "value=\"$subject\" ";

    }

    echo '/></p>';

} // End of $tid IF.
```

If this is not a reply, then the caption should be the language-specific version of "New Thread" and a subject input should be created. That input needs to be sticky. To check for that, look for the existence of a $subject variable. This variable will be created in post.php, and that file will then include this page.

Script 15.6 *continued*

```
53    echo '<input name="submit" type="submit"
      value="' . $words['submit'] . '"
      /><input name="submitted" type="hidden"
      value="TRUE" />

54    </form>';

55

56    } else {

57        echo '<p>You must be logged in to post
          messages.</p>';

58    }

59

60    ?>
```

6. Create the textarea for the message body.

```
echo '<p><em>' . $words['body'] .
→ '</em>: <textarea name="body"
→ rows="10" cols="60">';

if (isset($body)) {

    echo $body;

}

echo '</textarea></p>';
```

Both uses of this page will have this textarea. Like the subject, it will be made sticky if a $body variable (defined in post.php) exists. For both inputs, the prompts will be language-specific.

7. Complete the form.

```
echo '<input name="submit"
→ type="submit" value="' .
→ $words['submit'] . '" /><input
→ name="submitted" type="hidden"
→ value="TRUE" />

</form>';
```

All that's left is a language-specific submit button (**Figure 15.28**) and the hidden input to indicate form submission (the little trick I discuss in Chapter 3).

8. Complete the page.

```
} else {

    echo '<p>You must be logged in to
    → post messages.</p>';

}

?>
```

Once again, you could store this message in the *words* table and use the translated version here. I didn't only for the sake of simplicity.

9. Save the file as post_form.php, place it in your Web directory, and test it in your Web browser by accessing read.php (**Figure 15.29**).

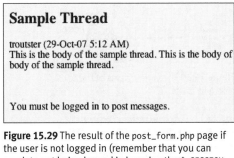

Figure 15.28 The form prompts and even the submit button will be in the user's chosen language (compare with Figures 15.25, 15.26, and 15.27).

Sample Thread

troutster (29-Oct-07 5:12 AM)
This is the body of the sample thread. This is the body of body of the sample thread.

You must be logged in to post messages.

Figure 15.29 The result of the post_form.php page if the user is not logged in (remember that you can emulate not being logged in by using the $_SESSION = array(); line in the header file).

Handling the form

This file, post.php, will primarily be used to handle the form submission from post_form.php. That sounds simple enough, but there's a bit more to it. This page will actually be called in three different ways:

1. To handle the form for a thread reply

2. To display the form for a new thread submission

3. To handle the form for a new thread submission

This means that the page will be accessed using either POST (modes 1 and 3) or GET (mode 2). Also, the data that will be sent to the page, and therefore needs to be validated, will differ between modes 1 and 3. **Figure 15.30** shows a representation of the logic.

Adding to the complications, if a new thread is being created, two queries must be run: one to add the thread to the *threads* table and a second to add the new thread body to the *posts* table. If the submission is a reply to an existing thread, then only one query is required, inserting a record into *posts*.

Of course, successfully pulling this off is just a matter of using the right conditionals, as you'll see. In terms of validation, the subject and body, as text types, will just be checked for a non-empty value. All tags will be stripped from the subject (because why should it have any?) and turned into entities in the body. This will allow for HTML, JavaScript, and PHP code to be used in a post but still not be executed when the thread is shown (because in a forum about Web development, you'll need to show some code).

To create post.php:

1. Begin a new PHP document in your text editor or IDE (**Script 15.7**).

   ```php
   <?php # Script 15.7 - post.php

   include ('includes/header.html');
   ```

   This page will use the header and footer files, unlike post_form.php.

2. Check for the form submission and validate the thread ID.

   ```php
   if (isset($_POST['submitted'])) {

       $tid = FALSE;

       if (isset($_POST['tid']) &&
       is_numeric($_POST['tid']) ) {

           $tid = (int) $_POST['tid'];

           if ($tid <= 0) {

               $tid = FALSE;

           }

       }
   ```

   The thread ID will be present if the form was submitted as a reply to an existing thread (the thread ID is stored as a hidden input, see **Figure 15.31**). The validation process is fairly routine: make sure it's set and is numeric, and then typecast it. If it's not greater than 0, then it's an invalid thread ID.

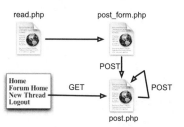

Figure 15.30 The various uses of the post.php page.

```
This is the body of the sample thread. This is the body of the sample thread. This is the body of
I like your thread. It's simple and sweet.</p><br />
accept-charset="utf-8"><h3>Post a Reply</h3><input name="tid" type="hidden" value="7" /><p><em>Bo
er.html -->
```

Figure 15.31 The source code of read.php shows how the thread ID is stored in the form. This indicates to post.php that the submission is a reply, not a new thread.

Script 15.7 The post.php page will process the form submissions when a message is posted. This page will be used to both create new threads and handle replies to existing threads.

```
1   <?php # Script 15.7 - post.php

2   // This page handles the message post.

3   // It also displays the form if creating a
    new thread.

4   include ('includes/header.html');

5

6   if (isset($_POST['submitted'])) { //
    Handle the form.

7

8       // Language ID ($lid) is in the session.

9       // Validate thread ID ($tid), which may
        not be present:

10      $tid = FALSE;

11      if (isset($_POST['tid']) &&
        is_numeric($_POST['tid']) ) {

12          $tid = (int) $_POST['tid'];

13          if ($tid <= 0) {

14              $tid = FALSE;

15          }

16      }

17

18      // If there's no thread ID, a subject
        must be provided:

19      if (!$tid && empty($_POST['subject'])) {

20          $subject = FALSE;

21          echo '<p>Please enter a subject for
            this post.</p>';

22      } elseif (!$tid &&
        !empty($_POST['subject'])) {

23          $subject =
            htmlspecialchars(strip_tags($_POST
            ['subject']));

24      } else { // Thread ID, no need for
        subject.

25          $subject = TRUE;
```

(script continues on next page)

3. Validate the message subject.

```
if (!$tid &&
→ empty($_POST['subject'])) {

    $subject = FALSE;

    echo '<p>Please enter a subject
    → for this post.</p>';

} elseif (!$tid &&
→ !empty($_POST['subject'])) {

    $subject =
    → htmlspecialchars(strip_tags
    → ($_POST['subject']));

} else {

    $subject = TRUE;

}
```

The tricky part about validating the subject is that three scenarios exist. First, if there's no valid thread ID, then this should be a new thread and the subject can't be empty. If it is, then an error occurred and a message is printed. Second, if there's no valid thread ID and the subject isn't empty, then this is a new thread and the subject was entered, so it should be handled. In this case, any tags are removed, using the `strip_tags()` function, and `htmlspecialchars()` will turn any remaining quotation marks into their entity format. Calling this second function will prevent problems should the form be displayed again and the subject placed in the input to make it sticky. To be clear, if the submitted subject contained a double quotation mark but the body wasn't completed, the form will be shown again with the subject placed within `value=""`, and you'll see problems.

The third scenario is when the form has been submitted as a reply to an existing thread. In that case, `$tid` will be valid and no subject is required.

continues on next page

4. Validate the body.

```
if (!empty($_POST['body'])) {
    $body =
    → htmlentities($_POST['body']);
} else {
    $body = FALSE;
    echo '<p>Please enter a body for
    → this post.</p>';
}
```

This is a much easier validation, as the body is always required. If present, it'll be run through htmlentities().

5. Check if the form was properly filled out.

```
if ($subject && $body) {
```

Script 15.7 *continued*

```
26      }
27
28      // Validate the body:
29      if (!empty($_POST['body'])) {
30          $body =
            htmlentities($_POST['body']);
31      } else {
32          $body = FALSE;
33          echo '<p>Please enter a body for
            this post.</p>';
34      }
35
36      if ($subject && $body) { // OK!
37
38      // Add the message to the database...
39
40      if (!$tid) { // Create a new thread.
41          $q = "INSERT INTO threads (lang_id,
            user_id, subject) VALUES ($lid,
            {$_SESSION['user_id']}, '" .
            mysqli_real_escape_string($dbc,
            $subject) . "')";
42          $r = mysqli_query($dbc, $q);
43          if (mysqli_affected_rows($dbc) == 1) {
44              $tid = mysqli_insert_id($dbc);
45          } else {
46              echo '<p>Your post could not be
                handled due to a system
                error.</p>';
47          }
48
49      }
50
51      if ($tid) { // Add this to the replies
        table:
```

(script continues on next page)

Script 15.7 *continued*

```
52
53      $q = "INSERT INTO posts (thread_id,
        user_id, message, posted_on) VALUES
        ($tid, {$_SESSION['user_id']}, '" .
        mysqli_real_escape_string($dbc, $body)
        . "', UTC_TIMESTAMP())";
54      $r = mysqli_query($dbc, $q);
55      if (mysqli_affected_rows($dbc) == 1) {
56          echo '<p>Your post has been
            entered.</p>';
57      } else {
58          echo '<p>Your post could not be
            handled due to a system
            error.</p>';
59      }
60
61      }
62
63      } else { // Include the form:
64          include ('post_form.php');
65      }
66
67  } else { // Display the form:
68
69      include ('post_form.php');
70
71  }
72
73  include ('includes/footer.html');
74  ?>
```

6. Create a new thread, if appropriate.

```
if (!$tid) {
    $q = "INSERT INTO threads
    → (lang_id, user_id, subject)
    → VALUES ($lid,
    → {$_SESSION['user_id']}, '" .
    → mysqli_real_escape_string($dbc,
    → $subject) . "')";
    $r = mysqli_query($dbc, $q);
    if (mysqli_affected_rows($dbc)
    → == 1) {
        $tid = mysqli_insert_id($dbc);
    } else {
        echo '<p>Your post could not
        → be handled due to a system
        → error.</p>';
    }
}
```

If there's no thread ID, then this is a new thread and a query must be run on the *threads* table. That query is simple, populating the three columns. Two of these values come from the session (after the user has logged in). The other is the subject, which is run through mysqli_real_escape_string(). Because the subject already had strip_tags() and htmlspecialchars() applied to it, you could probably get away with not using this function, but there's no need to take that risk.

If the query worked, meaning it affected one row, then the new thread ID is retrieved.

continues on next page

POSTING MESSAGES

7. Add the record to the *posts* table.

```
if ($tid) {

    $q = "INSERT INTO posts
    → (thread_id, user_id, message,
    → posted_on) VALUES ($tid,
    → {$_SESSION['user_id']}, '" .
    → mysqli_real_escape_string($dbc,
    → $body) . "', UTC_TIMESTAMP())";

    $r = mysqli_query($dbc, $q);

    if (mysqli_affected_rows($dbc)

    → == 1) {

        echo '<p>Your post has been
        → entered.</p>';

    } else {

        echo '<p>Your post could not
        → be handled due to a system
        → error.</p>';

    }

}
```

This query should only be run if the thread ID exists. That will be the case if this is a reply to an existing thread or if the new thread was just created in the database (Step 6). If that query failed, then this query won't be run.

The query populates four columns in the table, using the thread ID, the user ID (from the session), the message body, run through `mysqli_real_escape_string()` for security, and the posted date. For this last value, the `UTC_TIMESTAMP()` column is used so that it's not tied to any one time zone (see Chapter 14).

Note that for all of the printed messages in this page, I've just used hard-coded English. To finish rounding out the examples, each of these messages should be stored in the *words* table and printed here instead.

8. Complete the page.

```
    } else { // Include the form:

        include ('post_form.php');

    }

} else { // Display the form:

    include ('post_form.php');

}

include ('includes/footer.html');

?>
```

The first `else` clause applies if the form was submitted but not completed. In that case, the form will be included again and can be sticky, as it'll have access to `$subject` and `$body` created here. The second `else` clause applies if this page was accessed directly (by clinking a link in the navigation) and `$_POST['submitted']` is not set.

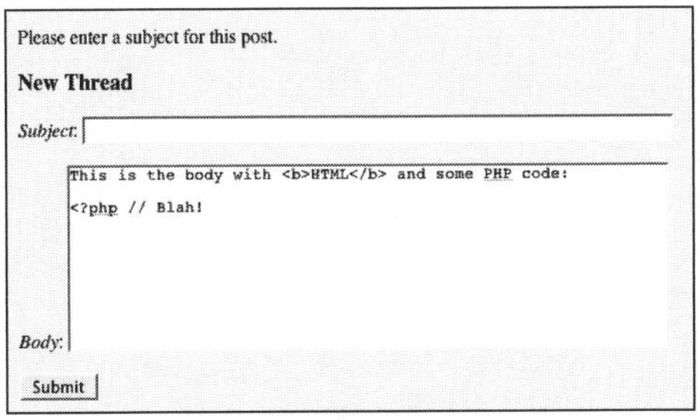

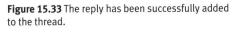

Figure 15.32 The result if no subject was provided while attempting to post a new thread.

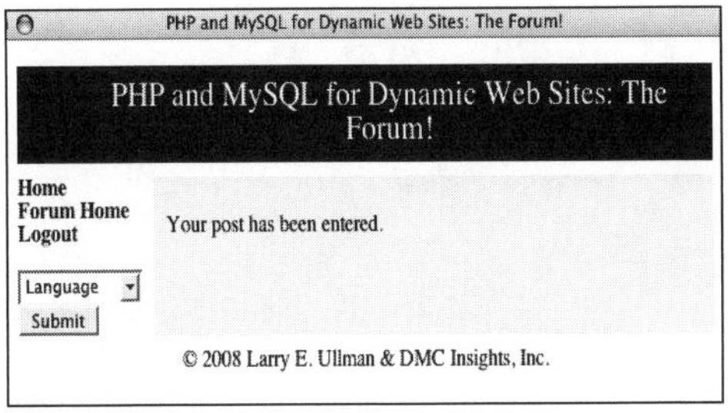

9. Save the file as `post.php`, place it in your Web directory, and test it in your Web browser (**Figures 15.32** and **15.33**).

Figure 15.33 The reply has been successfully added to the thread.

Administering the Forum

Much of the administration of the forum would involve user management, discussed in the next chapter. Depending upon who was administering the forum, you might also create forms for managing the languages and lists of translated words.

Administrators would also likely have the authority to edit and delete posts or threads. To accomplish this, store a user level in the session as well (the next chapter shows you how). If the logged-in user is an administrator, add links to edit and delete threads on `forum.php`. Each link would pass the thread ID to a new page (like `edit_user.php` and `delete_user.php` from Chapter 9). When deleting a thread, you have to make sure you delete all the records in the *posts* table that also have that thread ID.

Finally, an administrator could edit or delete individual posts (the replies to a thread). Again, check for the user level and then add links to `read.php` (a pair of links after each message). The links would pass the post ID to edit and delete pages (different ones than are used on threads).

EXAMPLE— USER REGISTRATION

The second example in the book—a user registration system—is one of the more common uses of PHP and MySQL. Most of the scripts developed here have been introduced and explained in previous chapters, as the registration, login, and logout processes make for good examples of many concepts. But this chapter will place all of that within the same context, using a consistent programming theory.

Users will be able to register, log in, log out, and change their password. One feature not shown elsewhere will be the ability to reset a password, should it be forgotten. Another feature will be the requirement that users activate their account—by clicking a link in an email—before they can log in. Once the user has logged in, sessions will be used to limit access to pages and track the user. New to this edition will be support for different user levels, allowing you to control the available content according to the type of user logged in.

As in the preceding chapter, the focus here will be on the public side of things (never fear: Chapter 17, "Example—E-Commerce," includes some administration). Of course, I'll include notes at the end of the chapter discussing what you might do to add administrative features. Along the way you'll also see recommendations as to how this application could easily be expanded or modified.

Creating the Templates

The application in this chapter will use a new template design (**Figure 16.1**). This template makes extensive use of Cascading Style Sheets (CSS), creating a clean look without the need for images. It has tested well on all current browsers and will appear as unformatted text on browsers that don't support CSS 2 (including text browsers like Lynx). The layout for this site is derived from one freely provided by BlueRobot (`www.bluerobot.com`).

To begin, I'll write two template files: `header.html` and `footer.html`. As in the Chapter 11, "Cookies and Sessions," examples, the footer file will display certain links depending upon whether or not the user is logged in, determined by checking for the existence of a session variable. Taking this concept one step further, additional links will be displayed if the logged-in user is also an administrator (a session value will indicate such).

The header file will begin sessions and output buffering, while the footer file will end output buffering. Output buffering hasn't been formally covered in the book, but it's introduced sufficiently in the sidebar.

To make header.html:

1. Create a new document in your text editor or IDE (**Script 16.1**).

   ```
   <?php # Script 16.1 - header.html
   ```

2. Begin output buffering and start a session.

   ```
   ob_start();
   ```

   ```
   session_start();
   ```

   I'll be using output buffering for this application, so that I need not worry about error messages when I use HTTP headers, redirect the user, or send cookies. Every page will make use of sessions as well. It's safe to place the `session_start()` call after `ob_start()`, since nothing has been sent to the Web browser yet.

   Since every public page will use both of these techniques, placing these lines in the `header.html` file saves me the hassle of placing them in every single page. Secondarily, if you later want to change the session settings, you only need to edit this one file.

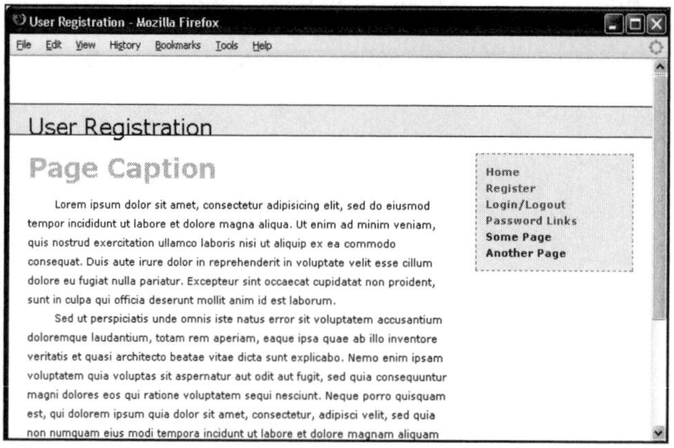

Figure 16.1 The basic appearance of this Web application.

Script 16.1 The header file begins the HTML, starts the session, and turns on output buffering.

```
●●●                Script
1    <?php # Script 16.1 - header.html

2    // This page begins the HTML header for
     the site.

3

4    // Start output buffering:

5    ob_start();

6

7    // Initialize a session:

8    session_start();

9

10   // Check for a $page_title value:

11   if (!isset($page_title)) {

12     $page_title = 'User Registration';

13   }

14   ?><!DOCTYPE html PUBLIC "-//W3C//DTD XHTML
     1.0 Transitional//EN"
```

(script continues)

Script 16.1 *continued*

```
●●●                Script
15       "http://www.w3.org/TR/xhtml1/DTD/
         xhtml1-transitional.dtd">

16   <html xmlns="http://www.w3.org/1999/xhtml"
     xml:lang="en" lang="en">

17   <head>

18     <meta http-equiv="content-type" content=
       "text/html; charset=iso-8859-1" />

19     <title><?php echo $page_title;
       ?></title>

20   <style type="text/css"
     media="screen">@import
     "includes/layout.css";</style>

21   </head>

22   <body>

23   <div id="Header">User Registration</div>

24   <div id="Content">

25   <!-- End of Header -->
```

Using Output Buffering

By default, anything that a PHP script prints or any HTML outside of the PHP tags (even in included files) is immediately sent to the Web browser. *Output buffering* (or *output control*, as the PHP manual calls it) is a PHP feature that overrides this behavior. Instead of immediately sending HTML to the Web browser, that output will be placed in a buffer—temporary memory. Then, when the buffer is *flushed*, it's sent to the Web browser. There can be a performance improvement with output buffering, but the main benefit is that it virtually eradicates those pesky *headers already sent* error messages. Some functions—header(), setcookie(), and session_start()—can only be called if nothing has been sent to the Web browser. With output buffering, nothing will be sent to the Web browser until the end of the page, so you are free to call these functions at any point in a script.

To begin output buffering, use the ob_start() function. Once you call it, every echo(), print(), and similar function will send data to a memory buffer rather than the Web browser. Conversely, HTTP calls (like header() and setcookie()) will not be buffered and will operate as usual.

At the conclusion of the script, call the ob_end_flush() function to send the accumulated buffer to the Web browser. Or, use the ob_end_clean() function to delete the buffered data without sending it. Both functions have the secondary effect of turning off output buffering.

3. Check for a `$page_title` variable and close the PHP section.

```
if (!isset($page_title)) {

    $page_title = 'User
    → Registration';

}
```

As in the other times this book has used a template system, the page's title—which appears at the top of the browser window—will be set on a page-by-page basis. This conditional checks if the `$page_title` variable has a value and, if it doesn't, sets it to a default string. This is a nice, but optional, check to include in the header.

4. Create the HTML head.

```
?><!DOCTYPE html PUBLIC "-//W3C//DTD
→ XHTML 1.0 Transitional//EN"

"http://www.w3.org/TR/xhtml1/DTD/xhtm
→ l1-transitional.dtd">

<html xmlns="http://www.w3.org/1999/
→ xhtml" xml:lang="en" lang="en">

<head>

    <meta http-equiv="content-type"
    → content="text/html; charset=
    → iso-8859-1" />

    <title><?php echo $page_title;
    → ?></title>

<style type="text/css" media="screen"
→ >@import "./includes/layout.css";
→ </style>

</head>
```

The PHP `$page_title` variable is printed out between the title tags here. Then, the CSS document is included. It will be called `layout.css` and stored in a directory called `includes`. You can download the file from the book's supporting Web site (www.DMCInsights.com/phpmysql3/, see the Extras page).

Script 16.2 The footer file concludes the HTML, displaying links based upon the user status (logged in or not, administrator or not), and flushes the output to the Web browser.

```
1   <!-- End of Content -->
2   </div>
3
4   <div id="Menu">
5   <a href="index.php" title="Home
    Page">Home</a><br />
6   <?php # Script 16.2 - footer.html
7   // This page completes the HTML template.
8
9   // Display links based upon the login
    status:
10  if (isset($_SESSION['user_id'])) {
11
12    echo '<a href="logout.php"
      title="Logout">Logout</a><br />
13    <a href="change_password.php" title=
      "Change Your Password">Change
      Password</a><br />
14  ';
15
16    // Add links if the user is an
      administrator:
17    if ($_SESSION['user_level'] == 1) {
18
19      echo '<a href="view_users.php"
        title="View All Users">View Users
        </a><br />
20    <a href="#">Some Admin Page</a><br />
21    ';
22
23    }
24
25  } else { // Not logged in.
26
27    echo '<a href="register.php" title=
      "Register for the Site">Register</a>
      <br />
```

(script continues on next page)

Script 16.2 *continued*

```
 _____
 ●○○              📄 Script
 _____
28   <a href="login.php"
     title="Login">Login</a><br />

29     <a href="forgot_password.php"
       title="Password Retrieval">Retrieve
       Password</a><br />

30   ';

31

32   }

33   ?>

34   <a href="#">Some Page</a><br />

35   <a href="#">Another Page</a><br />

36   </div>

37   </body>

38   </html>

39   <?php // Flush the buffered output.

40   ob_end_flush();

41   ?>
```

```
┌ ─ ─ ─ ─ ─ ─ ─ ─ ─ ─ ─ ─ ─ ─ ─ ─ ┐
│                                  │
│  Home                            │
│  Logout                          │
│  Change Password                 │
│  Some Page                       │
│  Another Page                    │
│                                  │
└ ─ ─ ─ ─ ─ ─ ─ ─ ─ ─ ─ ─ ─ ─ ─ ─ ┘
```

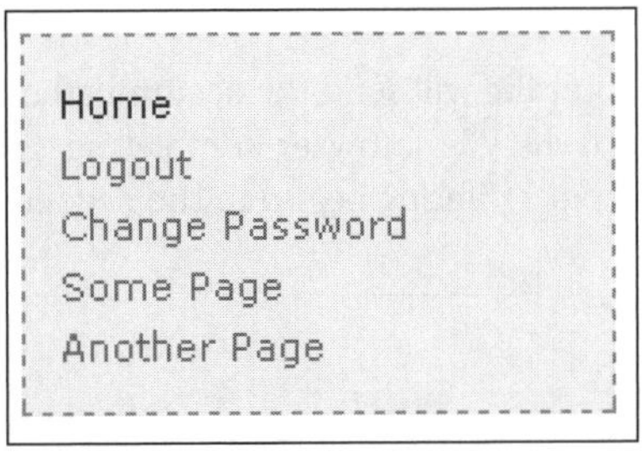

Figure 16.2 The user will see these navigation links while they are logged in.

5. Begin the HTML body.

<body>

<div id="Header">User Registration</div>

<div id="Content">

The body creates the banner across the top of the page and then starts the content part of the Web page (up until *Page Caption* in Figure 16.1).

6. Save the file as header.html.

To make footer.html:

1. Create a new document in your text editor or IDE (**Script 16.2**).

</div>

<div id="Menu">

<a href="index.php" title="Home → Page">Home</a>

<?php # Script 16.2 - footer.html

2. If the user is logged in, show logout and change password links.

if (isset($_SESSION['user_id'])) {

echo '<a href="logout.php" title= → "Logout">Logout</a>

<a href="change_password.php" title= → "Change Your Password">Change → Password</a>

';

If the user is logged in (which means that $_SESSION['user_id'] is set), the user will see links to log out and to change their password (**Figure 16.2**).

continues on next page

3. If the user is also an administrator, show some other links.

```
if ($_SESSION['user_level'] == 1) {
    echo '<a href="view_users.php"
    → title="View All Users">View
    → Users</a><br />
<a href="#">Some Admin Page</a><br />
';
}
```

If the logged-in user also happens to be an administrator, then they should see some extra links (**Figure 16.3**). To test for this, check the user's access level, which will also be stored in a session. A level value of *1* will indicate that the user is an administrator.

4. Show the links for non-logged-in users.

```
} else {
    echo '<a href="register.php"
    → title="Register for the
    → Site">Register</a><br />
<a href="login.php" title="Login">
→ Login</a><br />
<a href="forgot_password.php" title=
→ "Password Retrieval">Retrieve
→ Password</a><br />
```

```
';
}
?>
```

If the user isn't logged in, they will see links to register, log in, and reset a forgotten password (**Figure 16.4**).

5. Complete the HTML.

```
<a href="#">Some Page</a><br />
<a href="#">Another Page</a><br />
</div>
</body>
</html>
```

I've included two dummy links for other pages to be added.

6. Flush the buffer to the Web browser.

```
<?php
ob_end_flush();
?>
```

The footer file will send the accumulated buffer to the Web browser, completing the output buffering begun in the header script.

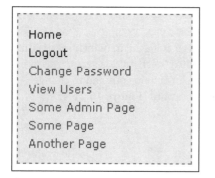

Figure 16.3 A logged-in administrator will see extra links (compare with Figure 16.2).

Figure 16.4 The user will see these links if they are not logged in (including if they just logged out).

7. Save the file as footer.html and place it, along with header.html and layout.css (from the book's supporting Web site), in your Web directory, putting all three in an includes folder (**Figure 16.5**).

✔ Tips

■ If this site has any page that does not make use of the header file but does need to work with sessions, it must call session_start() on its own. If you fail to do so, that script won't be able to access the session.

■ In more recent versions of PHP, output buffering is enabled by default. The buffer size—the maximum number of bytes stored in memory—is 4,096, but this can be changed in PHP's configuration file.

■ The ob_get_contents() function will return the current buffer so that it may be assigned to a variable, should the need arise.

■ The ob_flush() function will send the current contents of the buffer to the Web browser and then discard them, allowing a new buffer to be started. This function allows your scripts to maintain more moderate buffer sizes. Conversely, ob_end_flush() turns off output buffering after sending the buffer to the Web browser.

■ The ob_clean() function deletes the current contents of the buffer without stopping the buffer process.

■ PHP will automatically run ob_end_flush() at the conclusion of a script if it is not otherwise done.

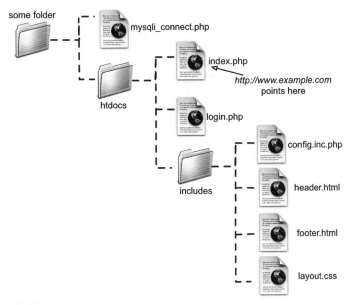

Figure 16.5 The directory structure of the site on the Web server, assuming htdocs is the document root (where www.example.com points).

Writing the Configuration Scripts

This Web site will make use of two configuration-type scripts. One, `config.inc.php`, will really be the most important script in the entire application. It will

◆ Have comments about the site as a whole

◆ Define constants

◆ Establish site settings

◆ Dictate how errors are handled

◆ Define any necessary functions

Because it does all this, the configuration script will be included by every other page in the application.

The second configuration-type script, `mysqli_connect.php`, will store all of the database-related information. It will be included only by those pages that need to interact with the database.

Making a configuration file

The configuration file is going to serve many important purposes. It'll be like a cross between the site's owner's manual and its preferences file. The first purpose of this file will be to document the site overall: who created it, when, why, for whom, etc., etc. The version in the book will omit all that, but you should put it in yours. The second role will be to define all sorts of constants and settings that the various pages will use.

Third, the configuration file will establish the error-management policy for the site. The technique involved—creating your own error handling function—was covered in Chapter 7, "Error Handling and Debugging." As in that chapter, during the development stages, every error will be reported in the most detailed way (**Figure 16.6**). Along with the specific error message, all of the existing variables will be shown, as will the current date and time. This will be formatted so that it fits within the site's template.

```
Welcome, Larry!

An error occurred in script '/Applications/Abyss Web Server/htdocs/ch16/html/index.php' on line 18: Undefined index: nope
Date/Time: 10-21-2007 19:32:09

Array
(
    [GLOBALS] => Array
 *RECURSION*
    [_POST] => Array
        (
        )

    [_GET] => Array
        (
        )

    [_COOKIE] => Array
        (
            [PHPSESSID] => 5bctsej7h9gso8dmrl5ga4dae7
        )

    [_FILES] => Array
        (
        )

    [page_title] => Welcome to this Site!
    [_SESSION] => Array
        (
            [user_id] => 1
            [first_name] => Larry
            [user_level] => 1
        )
)
```

Figure 16.6 During the development stages of the Web site, I want all errors to be made as obvious and as informative as possible.

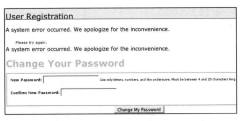

Figure 16.7 If errors occur while a site is live, the user will only see a message like this (but a detailed error message will be emailed to the administrator).

Script 16.3 This configuration script dictates how errors are handled, defines site-wide settings and constants, and could declare any necessary functions.

```
1    <?php # Script 16.3 - config.inc.php
2    /* This script:
3     * - define constants and settings
4     * - dictates how errors are handled
5     * - defines useful functions
6     */
7
8    // Document who created this site, when,
     why, etc.
9
10
11   // ****************************** //
12   // *********** SETTINGS ********** //
13
14   // Flag variable for site status:
15   define('LIVE', FALSE);
16
17   // Admin contact address:
18   define('EMAIL', 'InsertRealAddressHere');
19
20   // Site URL (base for all redirections):
21   define ('BASE_URL',
     'http://www.example.com');
22
23   // Location of the MySQL connection
     script:
```
(script continues on next page)

During the production, or live, stage of the site, errors will be handled more gracefully (**Figure 16.7**). At that time, the detailed error messages will not be printed in the Web browser, but instead sent to an email address.

Finally, this script will define any functions that might be used multiple times in the site. This site won't have any, but I wanted to mention that as another logical use of such a file.

To write the configuration file:

1. Create a new PHP document in your text editor or IDE (**Script 16.3**).

   ```
   <?php # Script 16.3 - config.inc.php
   ```

2. Establish two constants for error reporting.

   ```
   define('LIVE', FALSE);
   define('EMAIL', 'InsertRealAddress
   → Here');
   ```

   The LIVE constant will be used as it was in Chapter 7. If it is FALSE, detailed error messages are sent to the Web browser (Figure 16.6). Once the site goes live, this constant should be set to TRUE so that detailed error messages are never revealed to the Web user (Figure 16.7). The EMAIL constant is where the error messages will be sent when the site is live. You would obviously use your own e-mail address for this value.

   continues on page 493

Script 16.3 *continued*

```
24   define ('MYSQL',
     '/path/to/mysqli_connect.php');

25

26   // Adjust the time zone for PHP 5.1 and
     greater:

27   date_default_timezone_set ('US/Eastern');

28

29   // ************ SETTINGS ************ //

30   // ******************************** //

31

32

33   //
     *****************************************
     //

34   // ************ ERROR MANAGEMENT
     ************ //

35

36   // Create the error handler:

37   function my_error_handler ($e_number,
     $e_message, $e_file, $e_line, $e_vars) {

38

39     // Build the error message.

40     $message = "<p>An error occurred in
       script '$e_file' on line $e_line:
       $e_message\n<br />";

41

42     // Add the date and time:

43     $message .= "Date/Time: " . date('n-j-Y
       H:i:s') . "\n<br />";

44

45     // Append $e_vars to the $message:

46     $message .= "<pre>" . print_r ($e_vars,
       1) . "</pre>\n</p>";

47

48     if (!LIVE) { // Development (print the
       error).

49

50       echo '<div id="Error">' . $message .
         '</div><br />';

51

52     } else { // Don't show the error:

53
```

(script continues)

Script 16.3 *continued*

```
54     // Send an email to the admin:

55     mail(EMAIL, 'Site Error!', $message,
       'From: email@example.com');

56

57     // Only print an error message if the
       error isn't a notice:

58     if ($e_number != E_NOTICE) {

59       echo '<div id="Error">A system error
         occurred. We apologize for the
         inconvenience.</div><br />';

60     }

61   } // End of !LIVE IF.

62

63   } // End of my_error_handler() definition.

64

65   // Use my error handler.

66   set_error_handler ('my_error_handler');

67

68   // ************ ERROR MANAGEMENT
     ************ //

69   // **************************************
     ***** //

70

71   ?>
```

3. Establish two constants for site-wide settings.

```
define ('BASE_URL', 'http://www.
→ example.com/');

define ('MYSQL', '/path/to/mysqli_
→ connect.php');
```

These two constants are defined just to make it easier to redirect the user from one page to another and to include the MySQL connection script. `BASE_URL` refers to the root domain (*http://www.example.com/*), with an ending slash. If developing on your own computer, this might be *http://localhost/*. When a page redirects the browser, it'll now only need to write

```
header('Location: ' . BASE_URL .
→ 'page.php');
```

`MYSQL` is an absolute path to the MySQL connection script (to be written next). By setting this as an absolute path, any file can include the connection script by referring to this constant:

```
include (MYSQL);
```

Change both of these values to correspond with your environment. If you move the site from one server or domain to another, just change these two constants.

4. Establish any other site-wide settings.

```
date_default_timezone_set ('US/
→ Eastern');
```

As mentioned in Chapter 10, "Web Application Development," any use of a PHP date or time function (as of PHP 5.1) requires that the time zone be set. Change this value to match your time zone (see the PHP manual for the list of zones).

5. Begin defining the error-handling function.

```
function my_error_handler ($e_number,
→ $e_message, $e_file, $e_line,
→ $e_vars) {

    $message = "<p>An error occurred
    → in script '$e_file' on line
    → $e_line: $e_message\n<br />";
```

The function definition begins like the one in Chapter 7. It expects to receive five arguments: the error number, the error message, the script in which the error occurred, the line number on which PHP thinks the error occurred, and an array of variables that exist. Then it begins defining the `$message` variable, starting with the information provided to this function.

6. Add the current date and time.

```
$message .= "Date/Time: " . date
→ ('n-j-Y H:i:s') . "\n<br />";
```

To make the error reporting more useful, I'll include the current date and time in the message. A newline character and an HTML `<br />` tag are included to make the resulting display more legible.

7. Append all of the existing variables.

```
$message .= "<pre>" . print_r
→ ($e_vars, 1) . "</pre>\n</p>";
```

The `$e_vars` variable is an array of all variables that exist at the time of the error, along with their values. Calling the `print_r()` function, with a second argument of *1* or *TRUE*, will append the contents of `$e_vars` onto `$message`. To make it easier to read this section of the message in the Web browser, I use the HTML `<pre>` tags (those aren't XHTML-compliant, but that's irrelevant, as they won't be used on the live site).

continues on next page

8. Handle the error according to the value of `LIVE`.

```php
if (!LIVE) {
    echo '<div class="error">' .
    → $message . '</div><br />';
} else {
    mail(EMAIL, 'Site Error!',
    → $message, 'From: email@example.
    → com');
    if ($e_number != E_NOTICE) {
        echo '<div class="error">A
        → system error occurred. We
        → apologize for the
        → inconvenience.</div><br />';
    }
}
```

As I mentioned earlier, if the site isn't live, the entire error message is printed, for any type of error. The message is placed within `<div class="error">`, which will format the message per the rules defined in the site's CSS file.

If the site is live, the detailed message should be sent in an email and the Web user should only see a generic message. To take this one step further, the generic message will not be printed if the error is of a specific type: `E_NOTICE`. Such errors occur for things like referring to a variable that does not exist, which may or may not be a problem. To avoid potentially inundating the user with error messages, only print the error message if `$e_number` is not equal to `E_NOTICE`, which is a constant defined in PHP (see the PHP manual).

9. Complete the function definition and tell PHP to use your error handler.

```php
}
set_error_handler ('my_error_
→ handler');
?>
```

You have to use the `set_error_handler()` function to tell PHP to use your own function for errors.

10. Save the file as `config.inc.php`, and place it in your Web directory, within the `includes` folder (see Figure 16.5)

Making the database script

The second configuration-type script will be `mysqli_connect.php`, the database connection file used multiple times in the book already. Its only purpose is to connect to MySQL and select the database. If a problem occurs, this script will make use of the error-handling tools established in `config.inc.php`. To do so, it'll use the `trigger_error()` function. This function lets you tell PHP that an error occurred. Of course PHP will handle that error using the `my_error_handler()` function, as established in the configuration script.

To connect to the database:

1. Create a new PHP document in your text editor or IDE (**Script 16.4**).

```php
<?php # Script 16.4 - mysqli_
→ connect.php
```

2. Set the database access information.

```php
DEFINE ('DB_USER', 'username');

DEFINE ('DB_PASSWORD', 'password');

DEFINE ('DB_HOST', 'localhost');

DEFINE ('DB_NAME', 'ch16');
```

As always, change these values to those that will work for your MySQL installation.

Script 16.4 This script connects to the *ch16* database. If it can't, then the error handler will be triggered, passing it the MySQL connection error.

```
1   <?php # Script 16.4 - mysqli_connect.php
2
3   // This file contains the database access
    information.
4   // This file also establishes a connection
    to MySQL
5   // and selects the database.
6
7   // Set the database access information as
    constants:
8   DEFINE ('DB_USER', 'username');
9   DEFINE ('DB_PASSWORD', 'password');
10  DEFINE ('DB_HOST', 'localhost');
11  DEFINE ('DB_NAME', 'ch16');
12
13  // Make the connection:
14  $dbc = @mysqli_connect (DB_HOST, DB_USER,
    DB_PASSWORD, DB_NAME);
15
16  if (!$dbc) {
17    trigger_error ('Could not connect to
      MySQL: ' . mysqli_connect_error() );
18  }
19
20  ?>
```

3. Attempt to connect to MySQL and select the database.

```
$dbc = @mysqli_connect (DB_HOST,
→ DB_USER, DB_PASSWORD, DB_NAME);
```

In previous scripts, if the function didn't return the proper result, the die() function was called. Since I will be using my own error-handling function and not simply killing the script, I'll rewrite this process. Any errors raised by this function call will be suppressed (thanks to the @) and handled using the code in the next step.

4. Handle any errors if the database connection was not made.

```
if (!$dbc) {
  trigger_error ('Could not connect
  → to MySQL: ' . mysqli_connect_
  → error() );
}
```

If the script could not connect to the database, I want to send the error message to the my_error_handler() function. By doing so, I can ensure that the error is handled according to the currently set management technique (live stage versus development). Instead of calling my_error_handler() directly, use trigger_error(), whose first argument is the error message. **Figure 16.8** shows the end result if a problem occurs during the development stage.

continues on next page

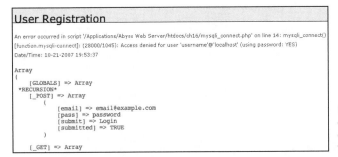

Figure 16.8 A database connection error occurring during the development of the site.

5. Complete the PHP code.

```
?>
```

6. Save the file as `mysqli_connect.php`, and place it in your Web directory, outside of the Web document root (see Figure 16.5).

7. Create the database (**Figure 16.9**).

See the sidebar "Database Scheme" for a discussion of the database and the command required to make the one table. If you cannot create your own database, just add the table to whatever database you have access to. Also make sure that you edit the `mysqli_connect.php` file so that it uses the proper username/password/hostname combination to connect to this database.

```
●●●                  Terminal
mysql> USE ch16;
Database changed
mysql> CREATE TABLE users (
    -> user_id INT UNSIGNED NOT NULL AUTO_INCREMENT,
    -> first_name VARCHAR(20) NOT NULL,
    -> last_name VARCHAR(40) NOT NULL,
    -> email VARCHAR(80) NOT NULL,
    -> pass CHAR(40) NOT NULL,
    -> user_level TINYINT(1) UNSIGNED NOT NULL DEFAULT 0,
    -> active CHAR(32),
    -> registration_date DATETIME NOT NULL,
    -> PRIMARY KEY (user_id),
    -> UNIQUE KEY (email),
    -> INDEX login (email, pass)
    -> );
Query OK, 0 rows affected (0.25 sec)

mysql>
```

Figure 16.9 Creating the database for this chapter.

✔ Tips

■ On the one hand, it might make sense to place the contents of both configuration files in one script for ease of reference. Unfortunately, doing so would add unnecessary overhead (namely, connecting to and selecting the database) to scripts that don't require a database connection (e.g., `index.php`).

■ For the error management file, I used `.inc.php` as the extension, indicating that the script is both an included file but also a PHP script. For the MySQL connection page, I just used `.php`, as it's clear from the file's name what the script does. These are minor, irrelevant distinctions, but I would strongly advocate that both files end with `.php`, for security purposes.

■ In general, I would define common functions in the configuration file. One exception would be any function that required a database connection. If you know that a function will only be used on pages that connect to MySQL, then defining that function within the `mysqli_connect.php` script is only logical.

Database Scheme

The database being used by this application is called *ch16*. The database currently consists of only one table, *users*. To create the table, use this SQL command:

```
CREATE TABLE users (
user_id INT UNSIGNED NOT NULL AUTO_INCREMENT,
first_name VARCHAR(20) NOT NULL,
last_name VARCHAR(40) NOT NULL,
email VARCHAR(80) NOT NULL,
pass CHAR(40) NOT NULL,
user_level TINYINT(1) UNSIGNED NOT NULL DEFAULT 0,
active CHAR(32),
registration_date DATETIME NOT NULL,
PRIMARY KEY (user_id),
UNIQUE KEY (email),
INDEX login (email, pass)
);
```

Most of the table's structure should be familiar to you by now; it's quite similar to the *users* table in the *sitename* database, used in several examples in this book. One new addition is the *active* column, which will be used to indicate whether a user has activated their account (by clicking a link in the registration email) or not. It will either store the 32-character-long activation code or have a NULL value. Because the *active* column may have a NULL value, it cannot be defined as NOT NULL. If you do define *active* as NOT NULL, no one will ever be able to log in (you'll see why later in the chapter). The other new addition is the *user_level* column, which will be used to differentiate the kinds of users the site has.

A unique index is placed on the *email* field, and another index is placed on the combination of the *email* and *pass* fields. These two fields will be used together during the login query, so indexing them as one, which I call *login*, makes sense.

Creating the Home Page

The home page for the site, called index.php, will be a model for the other pages on the public side. It will require the configuration file (for error management) and the header and footer files to create the HTML design. This page will also welcome the user by name, assuming the user is logged in (**Figure 16.10**).

To write index.php:

1. Create a new PHP document in your text editor or IDE (**Script 16.5**).

   ```
   <?php # Script 16.5 - index.php
   ```

2. Include the configuration file, set the page title, and include the HTML header.

   ```
   require_once ('includes/config.
   → inc.php');

   $page_title = 'Welcome to this
   → Site!';

   include ('includes/header.html');
   ```

   The script includes the configuration file first so that everything that happens afterward will be handled using the error-management processes established therein. Then the header.html file is included, which will start output buffering, begin the session, and create the initial part of the HTML layout.

Script 16.5 The script for the site's home page, which will greet a logged-in user by name.

```
1   <?php # Script 16.5 - index.php
2   // This is the main page for the site.
3
4   // Include the configuration file:
5   require_once ('includes/config.inc.php');
6
7   // Set the page title and include the HTML
    header:
8   $page_title = 'Welcome to this Site!';
9   include ('includes/header.html');
10
11  // Welcome the user (by name if they are
    logged in):
12  echo '<h1>Welcome';
13  if (isset($_SESSION['first_name'])) {
14    echo ", {$_SESSION['first_name']}!";
15  }
16  echo '</h1>';
17  ?>
18  <p>Spam spam spam spam spam spam
19  spam spam spam spam spam spam
20  spam spam spam spam spam spam
21  spam spam spam spam spam spam.</p>
22  <p>Spam spam spam spam spam spam
23  spam spam spam spam spam spam
24  spam spam spam spam spam spam
25  spam spam spam spam spam spam.</p>
26
27  <?php // Include the HTML footer file:
28  include ('includes/footer.html');
29  ?>
```

Figure 16.10 If the user is logged in, the index page will greet them by name.

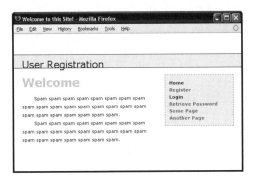

Figure 16.11 If the user is not logged in, this is the home page they will see.

3. Greet the user and complete the PHP code.

```
echo '<h1>Welcome';
if (isset($_SESSION['first_name'])) {
    echo ", {$_SESSION['first_
    → name']}!";
}
echo '</h1>';
?>
```

The *Welcome* message will be printed to all users. If a `$_SESSION['first_name']` variable is set, the user's first name will also be printed. So the end result will be either just *Welcome* (**Figure 16.11**) or *Welcome, <Your Name>!* (Figure 16.10).

4. Create the content for the page.

```
<p>Spam spam...</p>
```

You might want to consider putting something more useful on the home page on a real site. Just a suggestion....

5. Include the HTML footer.

```
<?php
include ('includes/footer.html');
?>
```

The footer file will complete the HTML layout (primarily the menu bar on the right side of the page) and conclude the output buffering.

6. Save the file as `index.php`, place it in your Web directory, and test it in a Web browser.

CREATING THE HOME PAGE

Registration

The registration script was first started in Chapter 8, "Using PHP with MySQL." It has since been improved upon in many ways. This version of register.php will do the following:

◆ Both display and handle the form

◆ Validate the submitted data using regular expressions

◆ Redisplay the form with the values remembered if a problem occurs (the form will be *sticky*)

◆ Process the submitted data using the mysqli_real_escape_string() function for security

◆ Ensure a unique email address

◆ Send an email containing an activation link (users will have to activate their account prior to logging in—see the sidebar)

To write register.php:

1. Create a new PHP document in your text editor or IDE (**Script 16.6**).

```
<?php # Script 16.6 - register.php
```

2. Include the configuration file and the HTML header.

```
require_once ('includes/config.
→ inc.php');
$page_title = 'Register';
include ('includes/header.html');
```

3. Create the conditional that checks for the form submission and then include the database connection script.

```
if (isset($_POST['submitted'])) {
    require_once (MYSQL);
```

continues on page 503

Script 16.6 The registration script uses regular expressions for security and a sticky form for user convenience. It sends an email to the user upon a successful registration.

```
1    <?php # Script 16.6 - register.php
2    // This is the registration page for the
     site.
3
4    require_once ('includes/config.inc.php');
5    $page_title = 'Register';
6    include ('includes/header.html');
7
8    if (isset($_POST['submitted'])) { //
     Handle the form.
9
10     require_once (MYSQL);
11
12     // Trim all the incoming data:
13     $trimmed = array_map('trim', $_POST);
14
15     // Assume invalid values:
16     $fn = $ln = $e = $p = FALSE;
17
18     // Check for a first name:
19     if (preg_match ('/^[A-Z \'.-]{2,20}$/i',
       $trimmed['first_name'])) {
20       $fn = mysqli_real_escape_string ($dbc,
         $trimmed['first_name']);
21     } else {
22       echo '<p class="error">Please enter
         your first name!</p>';
23     }
24
25     // Check for a last name:
26     if (preg_match ('/^[A-Z \'.-]{2,40}$/i',
       $trimmed['last_name'])) {
27       $ln = mysqli_real_escape_string ($dbc,
         $trimmed['last_name']);
28     } else {
29       echo '<p class="error">Please enter
         your last name!</p>';
30     }
```

(script continues on next page)

Script 16.6 *continued*

```
                          Script

31

32    // Check for an email address:

33    if (preg_match ('/^[\w.-]+@[\w.-]+\.[A-
      Za-z]{2,6}$/', $trimmed['email'])) {

34        $e = mysqli_real_escape_string ($dbc,
          $trimmed['email']);

35    } else {

36        echo '<p class="error">Please enter a
          valid email address!</p>';

37    }

38

39    // Check for a password and match
      against the confirmed password:

40    if (preg_match ('/^\w{4,20}$/',
      $trimmed['password1']) ) {

41        if ($trimmed['password1'] ==
          $trimmed['password2']) {

42            $p = mysqli_real_escape_string
              ($dbc, $trimmed['password1']);

43        } else {

44            echo '<p class="error">Your password
              did not match the confirmed
              password!</p>';

45        }

46    } else {

47        echo '<p class="error">Please enter a
          valid password!</p>';

48    }

49

50    if ($fn && $ln && $e && $p) { // If
      everything's OK...

51

52        // Make sure the email address is
          available:

53        $q = "SELECT user_id FROM users WHERE
          email='$e'";

54        $r = mysqli_query ($dbc, $q) or
          trigger_error("Query: $q\n<br />MySQL
          Error: " . mysqli_error($dbc));

55

56        if (mysqli_num_rows($r) == 0) { //
          Available.

57
```

(script continues)

Script 16.6 *continued*

```
                          Script

58        // Create the activation code:

59        $a = md5(uniqid(rand(), true));

60

61        // Add the user to the database:

62        $q = "INSERT INTO users (email,
          pass, first_name, last_name, active,
          registration_date) VALUES ('$e',
          SHA1('$p'), '$fn', '$ln', '$a',
          NOW() )";

63        $r = mysqli_query ($dbc, $q) or
          trigger_error("Query: $q\n<br />MySQL
          Error: " . mysqli_error($dbc));

64

65        if (mysqli_affected_rows($dbc) == 1)
          { // If it ran OK.

66

67            // Send the email:

68            $body = "Thank you for registering
              at <whatever site>. To activate
              your account, please click on this
              link:\n\n";

69            $body .= BASE_URL . 'activate.php?
              x=' . urlencode($e) . "&y=$a";

70            mail($trimmed['email'],
              'Registration Confirmation', $body,
              'From: admin@sitename.com');

71

72            // Finish the page:

73            echo '<h3>Thank you for
              registering! A confirmation email
              has been sent to your address.
              Please click on the link in that
              email in order to activate your
              account.</h3>';

74            include ('includes/footer.html');
              // Include the HTML footer.

75            exit(); // Stop the page.

76

77        } else { // If it did not run OK.

78            echo '<p class="error">You could
              not be registered due to a system
              error. We apologize for any
              inconvenience.</p>';

79        }

80

81    } else { // The email address is not
      available.
```

(script continues on next page)

Script 16.6 *continued*

000	📄 Script

```
82      echo '<p class="error">That email
        address has already been registered.
        If you have forgotten your password,
        use the link at right to have your
        password sent to you.</p>';

83      }

84

85   } else { // If one of the data tests
     failed.

86      echo '<p class="error">Please re-enter
        your passwords and try again.</p>';

87   }

88

89   mysqli_close($dbc);

90

91 } // End of the main Submit conditional.

92 ?>

93

94 <h1>Register</h1>

95 <form action="register.php" method="post">

96   <fieldset>

97

98     <p><b>First Name:</b> <input type="text"
       name="first_name" size="20" maxlength=
       "20" value="<?php if (isset($trimmed
       ['first_name'])) echo $trimmed
       ['first_name']; ?>" /></p>

99

100    <p><b>Last Name:</b> <input type="text"
       name="last_name" size="20" maxlength=
       "40" value="<?php if (isset($trimmed
       ['last_name'])) echo $trimmed
       ['last_name']; ?>" /></p>

101

102    <p><b>Email Address:</b> <input
       type="text" name="email" size="30"
       maxlength="80" value="<?php if
       (isset($trimmed['email'])) echo
       $trimmed['email']; ?>" /> </p>

103

104    <p><b>Password:</b> <input type=
       "password" name="password1" size="20"
       maxlength="20" /> <small>Use only
       letters, numbers, and the underscore.
       Must be between 4 and 20 characters
       long.</small></p>
```

000	📄 Script

```
105

106    <p><b>Confirm Password:</b> <input
       type="password" name="password2"
       size="20" maxlength="20" /></p>

107    </fieldset>

108

109    <div align="center"><input type="submit"
       name="submit" value="Register" /></div>

110    <input type="hidden" name="submitted"
       value="TRUE" />

111

112 </form>

113

114 <?php // Include the HTML footer.

115 include ('includes/footer.html');

116 ?>
```

(script continues)

4. Trim the incoming data and set some flag variables.

```
$trimmed = array_map('trim', $_POST);

$fn = $ln = $e = $p = FALSE;
```

The first line runs every element in $_POST through the trim() function, assigning the returned result to the new $trimmed array. The explanation for this line can be found in Chapter 12, "Security Methods," when array_map() was used with data to be sent in an email. In short, the trim() function will

---

Activation Process

New in this chapter is an activation process, where users have to click a link in an email to confirm their accounts, prior to being able to log in. Using a system like this prevents bogus registrations from being used. If an invalid email address is entered, that account can never be activated. And if someone registered another person's address, hopefully that person would not activate this undesired account.

From a programming perspective, this process requires the creation of a unique activation code for each registered user, to be stored in the *users* table. The code is then sent in the confirmation email to the user (in a link). When the user clicks the link, they'll be taken to a page on the site that activates their account (by removing that code from their record). Using this activation code, instead of just having them go to the activation page without it, keeps people from being able to activate accounts without receiving the confirmation email.

---

be applied to every value in $_POST, saving the hassle of applying trim() to each individually.

The second line initializes four variables as FALSE. This one line is just a shortcut in lieu of

```
$fn = FALSE;

$ln = FALSE;

$e = FALSE;

$p = FALSE;
```

5. Validate the first and last names.

```
if (preg_match ('/^[A-Z \'.-]{2,20}
→ $/i', $trimmed['first_name'])) {

    $fn =
mysqli_real_escape_string($dbc,
→ $trimmed['first_name']);

} else {

    echo '<p class="error">Please
→ enter your first name!</p>';

}

if (preg_match ('/^[A-Z \'.-]{2,40}
→ $/i', $trimmed['last_name'])) {

    $ln = mysqli_real_escape_
→ string($dbc, $trimmed['last_
→ name']);

} else {

    echo '<p class="error">Please
→ enter your last name!</p>';

}
```

The form will be validated using regular expressions, covered in Chapter 13, "Perl-Compatible Regular Expressions." For the first name value, the assumption is that it will contain only letters, a period (as in an initial), an apostrophe, a space, and

continues on next page

the dash. Further, I expect the value to be within the range of 2 to 20 characters long. To guarantee that the value contains only these characters, the caret and the dollar sign are used to match both the beginning and end of the string. While using Perl-Compatible regular expressions, the entire pattern must be placed within delimiters (the forward slashes).

If this condition is met, the $fn variable is assigned the value of the mysqli_real_escape_string() version of the submitted value; otherwise, $fn will still be false and an error message is printed (**Figure 16.12**).

The same process is used to validate the last name, although that regular expression allows for a longer length. Both patterns are also case-insensitive, thanks to the *i* modifier.

6. Validate the email address (**Figure 16.13**).

```
if (preg_match ('/^[\w.-]+@[\w.-]
→ +\.[A-Za-z]{2,6}$/', $trimmed
→ ['email'])) {

    $e = mysqli_real_escape_string
    → ($dbc, $trimmed['email']);

} else {

    echo '<p class="error">Please
    → enter a valid email address
    → !</p>';

}
```

The pattern for the email address was described in Chapter 13. It could be more exacting, of course, but it works well enough, in my opinion.

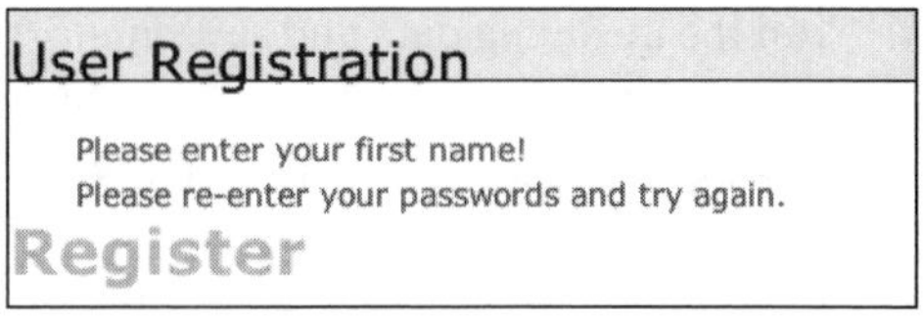

Figure 16.12 If the first name value does not pass the regular expression test, an error message is printed.

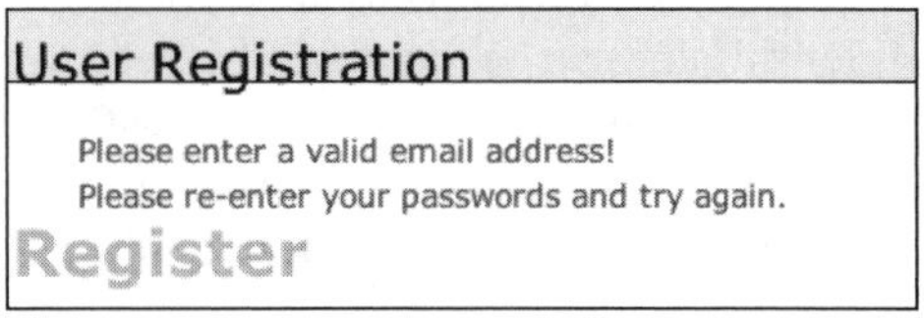

Figure 16.13 The submitted email address must be of the proper format.

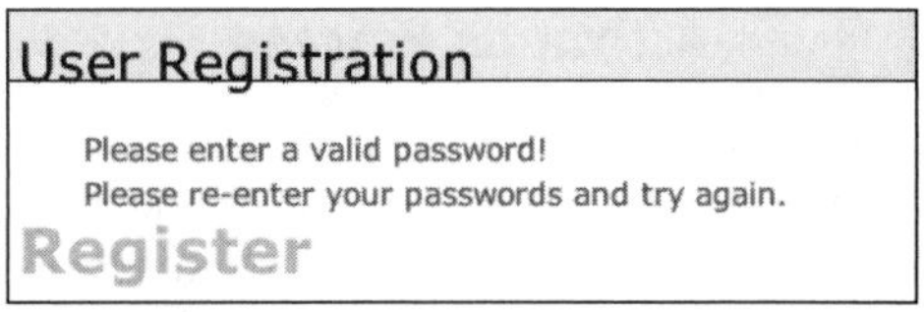

Figure 16.14 The passwords are checked for the proper format, length, and...

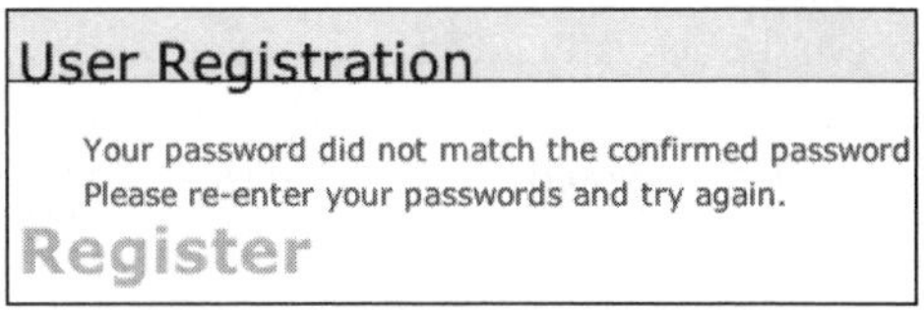

Figure 16.15 ...that the password value matches the confirmed password value.

7. Validate the passwords (**Figures 16.14** and **16.15**).

```
if (preg_match ('/^\w{4,20}$/',
→ $trimmed['password1']) ) {
    if ($trimmed['password1'] ==
    → $trimmed['password2']) {
        $p = mysqli_real_escape_string
        → ($dbc, $trimmed
        ['password1']);
    } else {
        echo '<p class="error">Your
        → password did not match the
        → confirmed password!</p>';
    }
} else {
    echo '<p class="error">Please
    → enter a valid password!</p>';
}
```

The password must be between 4 and 20 characters long and contain only letters, numbers, and the underscore. That exact combination is represented by \w in Perl-Compatible regular expressions. Furthermore, the first password (*password1*) must match the confirmed password (*password2*).

8. If every test was passed, check for a unique email address.

```
if ($fn && $ln && $e && $p) {
    $q = "SELECT user_id FROM users
    → WHERE email='$e'";
    $r = mysqli_query ($dbc, $q) or
    → trigger_error("Query: $q\n<br
    → />MySQL Error: " . mysqli_error
    → ($dbc));
```

If the form passed every test, this conditional will be TRUE. Then the script must search the database to see if the submitted email address is currently being used, since that column's value must be unique across each record. As with the MySQL connection script, if a query doesn't run, call the trigger_error() function to invoke the self-defined error reporting function. The specific error message will include both the query being run and the MySQL error (**Figure 16.16**), so that the problem can easily be debugged.

continues on next page

User Registration

```
An error occurred in script '/Applications/Abyss Web Server/htdocs/ch16/html/register.php' on line 54: Query: SELECT user_id FROM userss
WHERE email='email@example.com'
MySQL Error: Table 'ch16.userss' doesn't exist
Date/Time: 10-21-2007 20:20:44

Array
(
    [GLOBALS] => Array
 *RECURSION*
    [_POST] => Array
        (
            [first_name] => Larry
            [last_name] => Ullman
            [email] => email@example.com
            [password1] => password
            [password2] => password
            [submit] => Register
            [submitted] => TRUE
        )
```

Figure 16.16 If a MySQL query error occurs, it should be easier to debug thanks to this informative error message.

9. If the email address is unused, register the user.

```
if (mysqli_num_rows($r) == 0) {

    $a = md5(uniqid(rand(), true));

    $q = "INSERT INTO users (email,
→ pass, first_name, last_name,
→ active, registration_date)
→ VALUES ('$e', SHA1('$p'),
→ '$fn', '$ln', '$a', NOW() )";

    $r = mysqli_query ($dbc, $q) or
→ trigger_error("Query: $q\n<br
→ />MySQL Error: " . mysqli_error
→ ($dbc));
```

The query itself is rather simple, but it does require the creation of a unique activation code. Generating that uses the `rand()`, `uniqid()`, and `md5()` functions. Of these, `uniqid()` is the most important; it creates a unique identifier. It's fed the `rand()` function to help generate a more random value. Finally, the returned result is *hashed* using `md5()`, which creates a string exactly 32 characters long (a hash is a mathematically calculated representation of a piece of data). You do not need to fully comprehend these three functions, just note that the result will be a unique 32-character string.

As for the query itself, it should be familiar enough to you. Most of the values come from variables in the PHP script, after applying `trim()` and `mysqli_real_escape_string()` to them. The MySQL `SHA1()` function is used to encrypt the password and `NOW()` is used to set the registration date as the current moment. Because the *user_level* column has a default value of *0* (i.e., not an administrator), it does not have to be provided a value in this query. Presumably the site's main administrator would edit a user's record to give them administrative power.

10. Send an email if the query worked.

```
if (mysqli_affected_rows($dbc) ==
→ 1) {

    $body = "Thank you for
→ registering at <whatever
→ site>. To activate your
→ account, please click on
→ this link:\n\n";

    $body .= BASE_URL .
→ 'activate.php?x=' .
→ urlencode($e) . "&y=$a";

    mail($trimmed['email'],
→ 'Registration Confirmation',
→  $body, 'From:
→ admin@sitename.com');

    echo '<h3>Thank you for
→ registering! A confirmation
→ email has been sent to your
→ address. Please click on the
→ link in that email in order to
→ activate your account.</h3>';

    include ('includes/
→ footer.html');

    exit();
```

With this registration process, the important thing is that the confirmation mail gets sent to the user, because they will not be able to log in until after they've activated their account. This email should contain a link to the activation page, `activate.php`. The link to that page starts with `BASE_URL`, which is defined in `config.inc.php`. The link also passes two values along in the URL. The first, generically called *x*, will be the user's email address, encoded so that it's safe to have in a URL. The second, *y*, is the activation code. The URL, then, will be something like *http://www.example.com/ activate.php?x= email%40example.com &y=901e09ef25bf6e3ef95c93088450b008*.

A thank-you message is printed out upon successful registration, along with the activation instructions (**Figure 16.17**).

11. Print errors if the query failed.

```
} else {
    echo '<p class="error">You could
    → not be registered due to a
    → system error. We apologize for
    → any inconvenience.</p>';
}
```

If the query failed for some reason, meaning that mysqli_affected_rows() did not return *1*, an error message is printed to the browser. Because of the security methods implemented in this script, the live version of the site should never have a problem at this juncture.

12. Complete the conditionals and the PHP code.

```
    } else {
        echo '<p class="error">That
        → email address has already
        → been registered. If you
        → have forgotten your
        → password, use the link
        → at right to have your
        → password sent to
        → you.</p>';
    }
} else {
```

```
        echo '<p class="error">Please
        → re-enter your passwords and
        → try again.</p>';
    }
    mysqli_close($dbc);
} // End of the main Submit
→ conditional.
?>
```

The first else is executed if a person attempts to register with an email address that has already been used (**Figure 16.18**). The second else applies when the submitted data fails one of the validation routines (see Figures 16.12 through 16.15).

13. Begin the HTML form (**Figure 16.19**).

```
<h1>Register</h1>
<form action="register.php" method=
→ "post">
```

continues on next page

User Registration

That email address has already been registered. If you have forgotten your password, use the link at right to have your password sent to you.

Register

Figure 16.18 If an email address has already been registered, the user is told as much.

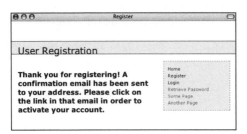

Figure 16.17 The resulting page after a user has been successfully registered.

Figure 16.19 The registration form as it looks when the user first arrives.

REGISTRATION

```
<fieldset>

<p><b>First Name:</b> <input
→ type="text" name="first_name"
→ size="20" maxlength="20"
→ value="<?php if (isset($
→ trimmed['first_name'])) echo
→ $trimmed['first_name']; ?>"
→ /></p>

<p><b>Last Name:</b> <input
→ type="text" name="last_name"
→ size="20" maxlength="40"
→ value="<?php if (isset($
→ trimmed['last_name'])) echo
→ $trimmed['last_name']; ?>"
→ /></p>

<p><b>Email Address:</b> <input
→ type="text" name="email" size=
→ "30" maxlength="80" value=
→ "<?php if (isset($trimmed
→ ['email'])) echo $trimmed
→ ['email']; ?>" /> </p>
```

The HTML form has text inputs for all of the values. Each input has a name and a maximum length that match the corresponding column definition in the *users* table. The form will be sticky, using the trimmed values.

14. Complete the HTML form.

```
<p><b>Password:</b> <input type=
→ "password" name="password1"
→ size="20" maxlength="20" />
→ <small>Use only letters and
→ numbers. Must be between 4 and
→ 20 characters long.</small>
→ </p>

<p><b>Confirm Password:</b>
→ <input type="password" name=
→ "password2" size="20"
→ maxlength="20" /></p>
```

```
</fieldset>

<div align="center"><input
→ type="submit" name="submit"
→ value="Register" /></div>

<input type="hidden" name=
→ "submitted" value="TRUE" />

</form>
```

Requesting the password requires two inputs, so it can be confirmed. Doing this is a good idea, as the user cannot see what they type in a password input. Password inputs cannot be made sticky, though.

15. Include the HTML footer.

```
<?php

include ('includes/footer.html');

?>
```

16. Save the file as `register.php`, place it in your Web directory, and test it in your Web browser.

✔ Tips

■ Because every column in the *users* table cannot be NULL (except for *active*), I require that each input be correctly filled out. If a table has an optional field, you should still confirm that it is of the right type if submitted, but not require it.

■ Except for encrypted fields (such as the password), the maximum length of the form inputs and regular expressions should correspond to the maximum length of the column in the database.

From: admin@larryullman.net
Subject: **Registration Confirmation**
Date: October 21, 2007 8:33:41 PM EDT
To: Larry Ullman <Larry@DMCInsights.com>

Thank you for registering at <whatever site>. To activate your account, please click on this link:

http://larryullman.net/html/activate.php?x=Larry%
40DMCInsights.com&y=fd08331cdc85c6a237007e4b27465cc3

Figure 16.20 The registration confirmation email.

Script 16.7 To activate an account, the user must come to this page, passing it their email address and activation code (all part of the link they received upon registering).

```
1   <?php # Script 16.7 - activate.php
2   // This page activates the user's account.
3
4   require_once ('includes/config.inc.php');
5   $page_title = 'Activate Your Account';
6   include ('includes/header.html');
7
8   // Validate $_GET['x'] and $_GET['y']:
9   $x = $y = FALSE;
10  if (isset($_GET['x']) && preg_match
    ('/^[\w.-]+@[\w.-]+\.[A-Za-z]{2,6}$/',
    $_GET['x']) ) {
11    $x = $_GET['x'];
12  }
13  if (isset($_GET['y']) &&
    (strlen($_GET['y']) == 32 ) {
14    $y = $_GET['y'];
15  }
16
17  // If $x and $y aren't correct, redirect
    the user.
18  if ($x && $y) {
19
20    // Update the database...
21    require_once (MYSQL);
```

(script continues on next page)

Activating an Account

As described in the "Activation Process" sidebar earlier in the chapter, users will have to activate their account prior to being able to log in. Upon successfully registering, users will receive an email containing a link to activate.php (**Figure 16.20**). This link also passes two values to this page: their email address and their unique activation code.

This script needs to first confirm that those two values were received in the URL. Then, if these two values match those in the database, the activation code will be removed from the record, indicating an active account.

To create the activation page:

1. Begin a new PHP script in your text editor or IDE (**Script 16.7**).

```
<?php # Script 16.7 - activate.php
require_once ('includes/config.inc.
→ php');
$page_title = 'Activate Your
→ Account';
include ('includes/header.html');
```

2. Validate the values that should be received by the page.

```
$x = $y = FALSE;
if (isset($_GET['x']) && preg_match
→ ('/^[\w.-]+@[\w.-]+\.[A-Za-z]{2,
→ 6}$/', $_GET['x']) ) {
  $x = $_GET['x'];
}
if (isset($_GET['y']) && (strlen
→ ($_GET['y']) == 32 ) {
  $y = $_GET['y'];
}
```

continues on next page

As I mentioned, if the user clicks the link in the registration confirmation email, they'll pass two values to this page: the email address and the activation code. First check for the presence of *x* (the email address) and that it matches the regular expression pattern for an email address. If both conditions are true, $x is assigned the value of $_GET['x'].

For *y* (the activation code), the code checks for its existence and that its length (how many characters are in it) is exactly 32. The md5() function, which created the activation code, always returns a string 32 characters long.

If *x* or *y* does not pass its corresponding conditional, its value will be FALSE, which is what they were both initialized as (in the first line).

3. If $x and $y have the correct values, activate the user.

```
if ($x && $y) {
    require_once (MYSQL);
    $q = "UPDATE users SET active=
    → NULL WHERE (email='" . mysqli_
    → real_escape_string($dbc, $x) .
    → "' AND active='" . mysqli_real_
    → escape_string($dbc, $y) . "')
    → LIMIT 1";
    $r = mysqli_query ($dbc, $q) or
    → trigger_error("Query: $q\n<br
    → />MySQL Error: " . mysqli_
    → error($dbc));
```

If both conditions are TRUE, an UPDATE query is run. This query removes the activation code from the user's record by setting the *active* column to NULL. Before using the values in the query, both are run through mysqli_real_escape_string() for security.

Script 16.7 *continued*

```
22    $q = "UPDATE users SET active=NULL WHERE
      (email='" . mysqli_real_escape_string
      ($dbc, $x) . "' AND active='" . mysqli_
      real_escape_string($dbc, $y) . "')
      LIMIT 1";
23    $r = mysqli_query ($dbc, $q) or
      trigger_error("Query: $q\n<br />MySQL
      Error: " . mysqli_error($dbc));
24
25    // Print a customized message:
26    if (mysqli_affected_rows($dbc) == 1) {
27        echo "<h3>Your account is now active.
          You may now log in.</h3>";
28    } else {
29        echo '<p class="error">Your account
          could not be activated. Please re-
          check the link or contact the system
          administrator.</font></p>';
30    }
31
32    mysqli_close($dbc);
33
34 } else { // Redirect.
35
36    $url = BASE_URL . 'index.php'; // Define
      the URL:
37    ob_end_clean(); // Delete the buffer.
38    header("Location: $url");
39    exit(); // Quit the script.
40
41 } // End of main IF-ELSE.
42
43 include ('includes/footer.html');
44 ?>
```

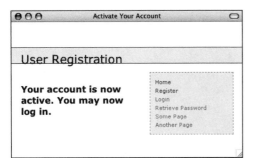

Figure 16.21 If the database could be updated using the provided email address and activation code, the user is notified that their account is now active.

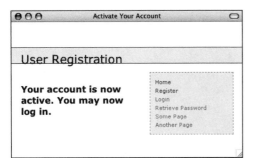

Figure 16.22 If an account is not activated by the query, the user is told of the problem.

4. Report upon the success of the query.

```
if (mysqli_affected_rows($dbc) ==
→ 1) {
    echo "<h3>Your account is now
    → active. You may now log in.
    → </h3>";
} else {
    echo '<p class="error">Your
    → account could not be activated.
    → Please re-check the link
    → or contact the system
    → administrator.</font></p>';
}
```

If one row was affected by the query, then the user's account is now active and a message says as much (**Figure 16.21**). If no rows are affected, the user is notified of the problem (**Figure 16.22**). This would most likely happen if someone tried to fake the *x* and *y* values or if there's a problem in following the link from the email to the Web browser.

5. Complete the main conditional.

```
    mysqli_close($dbc);
} else {
    $url = BASE_URL . 'index.php';
    ob_end_clean();
    header("Location: $url");
    exit();
} // End of main IF-ELSE.
```

The else clause takes effect if $x and $y are not of the proper value and length. In such a case, the user is just redirected to the index page. The ob_end_clean() line here deletes the buffer (whatever was to be sent to the Web browser up to this point, stored in memory), as it won't be used.

continues on next page

6. Complete the page.

```
include ('includes/footer.html');

?>
```

7. Save the file as activate.php, place it in your Web directory, and test it by clicking the link in the registration email.

✔ Tips

- If you wanted to be a little more forgiving, you could have this page print an error similar to that in Figure 16.22, rather than redirect them to the index page (as if they were attempting to hack the site).

- I specifically use the vague *x* and *y* as the names in the URL for security purposes. While someone may figure out that the one is an email address and the other is a code, it's sometimes best not to be explicit about such things.

- An alternative method, which I used in the second edition of this book, was to place the activation code and the user's ID (from the database) in the link. That also works, but from a security perspective, it's really best that users never see, or are even aware of, a user ID that's otherwise not meant to be public.

Script 16.8 The login page will redirect the user to the home page after registering the user ID, first name, and access level in a session.

```
      ┌─────────────────────────────────────┐
      │ ⊖ ⊖ ⊖              📄 Script          │
      ├─────────────────────────────────────┤
1     │ <?php # Script 16.8 - login.php     │
                                              
2     │ // This is the login page for the site.
                                              
3                                             
                                              
4     │ require_once ('includes/config.inc.php');
                                              
5     │ $page_title = 'Login';               
                                              
6     │ include ('includes/header.html');    
                                              
7                                             
                                              
8     │ if (isset($_POST['submitted'])) {    
                                              
9     │   require_once (MYSQL);               
                                              
10                                            
                                              
11    │   // Validate the email address:     
                                              
12    │   if (!empty($_POST['email'])) {      
                                              
13    │     $e = mysqli_real_escape_string ($dbc,
      │     $_POST['email']);                 
                                              
14    │   } else {                            
                                              
15    │     $e = FALSE;                       
                                              
16    │     echo '<p class="error">You forgot to
      │     enter your email address!</p>';   
                                              
17    │   }                                   
                                              
18                                            
                                              
19    │   // Validate the password:          
                                              
20    │   if (!empty($_POST['pass'])) {       
                                              
21    │     $p = mysqli_real_escape_string ($dbc,
      │     $_POST['pass']);                  
                                              
22    │   } else {                            
                                              
23    │     $p = FALSE;                       
                                              
24    │     echo '<p class="error">You forgot to
      │     enter your password!</p>';        
                                              
25    │   }                                   
                                              
26                                            
                                              
27    │   if ($e && $p) { // If everything's OK.
                                              
28                                            
                                              
29    │   // Query the database:             
```

(script continues on next page)

Logging In and Logging Out

In Chapter 11, I wrote many versions of the login.php and logout.php scripts, using variations on cookies and sessions. Here I'll develop standardized versions of both that adhere to the same practices as the whole application. The login query itself is slightly different here in that it also checks that the *active* column has a NULL value, which is the indication that the user has activated their account.

To write login.php:

1. Create a new PHP document in your text editor or IDE (**Script 16.8**).

   ```php
   <?php # Script 16.8 - login.php
   require_once ('includes/config.inc.
   → php');
   $page_title = 'Login';
   include ('includes/header.html');
   ```

2. Check if the form has been submitted, require the database connection, and validate the submitted data.

   ```php
   if (isset($_POST['submitted'])) {
       require_once (MYSQL);
       if (!empty($_POST['email'])) {
           $e = mysqli_real_escape_string
   → ($dbc, $_POST['email']);
       } else {
           $e = FALSE;
       echo '<p class="error">You forgot
   → to enter your email address!
   → </p>';
   }
   ```

continues on page 515

Script 16.8 *continued*

```
Script
30    $q = "SELECT user_id, first_name, user_
      level FROM users WHERE (email='$e' AND
      pass=SHA1('$p')) AND active IS NULL";

31    $r = mysqli_query ($dbc, $q) or
      trigger_error("Query: $q\n<br />MySQL
      Error: " . mysqli_error($dbc));

32

33    if (@mysqli_num_rows($r) == 1) { // A
      match was made.

34

35       // Register the values & redirect:

36       $_SESSION = mysqli_fetch_array ($r,
         MYSQLI_ASSOC);

37       mysqli_free_result($r);

38       mysqli_close($dbc);

39

40       $url = BASE_URL . 'index.php'; //
         Define the URL:

41       ob_end_clean(); // Delete the buffer.

42       header("Location: $url");

43       exit(); // Quit the script.

44

45    } else { // No match was made.

46       echo '<p class="error">Either the
         email address and password entered do
         not match those on file or you have
         not yet activated your account.</p>';

47    }

48

49    } else { // If everything wasn't OK.

50       echo '<p class="error">Please try
         again.</p>';

51    }

52

53    mysqli_close($dbc);

54

55    } // End of SUBMIT conditional.

56    ?>

57
                              (script continues)
```

Script 16.8 *continued*

```
Script
58    <h1>Login</h1>

59    <p>Your browser must allow cookies in
      order to log in.</p>

60    <form action="login.php" method="post">

61      <fieldset>

62      <p><b>Email Address:</b> <input
        type="text" name="email" size="20"
        maxlength="40" /></p>

63      <p><b>Password:</b> <input type=
        "password" name="pass" size="20"
        maxlength="20" /></p>

64      <div align="center"><input type="submit"
        name="submit" value="Login" /></div>

65      <input type="hidden" name="submitted"
        value="TRUE" />

66      </fieldset>

67    </form>

68

69    <?php // Include the HTML footer.

70    include ('includes/footer.html');

71    ?>
```

Figure 16.23 The login form checks only if values were entered, without using regular expressions.

```
if (!empty($_POST['pass'])) {

    $p = mysqli_real_escape_string
    → ($dbc, $_POST['pass']);

} else {

    $p = FALSE;

    echo '<p class="error">You
    → forgot to enter your
    → password!</p>';

}
```

There's two ways of thinking about the validation. On the one hand you could use regular expressions, applying those from `register.php`, to validate these values. On the other hand, the true test of the values will be whether the login query returns a record or not, so one could arguably skip more stringent PHP validation. I'm going with the latter thinking here.

If the user does not enter any values into the form, error messages will be printed (**Figure 16.23**).

3. If both validation routines were passed, retrieve the user information.

```
if ($e && $p) {

    $q = "SELECT user_id, first_name,
    → user_level FROM users WHERE
    → (email='$e' AND pass=SHA1
    → ('$p')) AND active IS NULL";

    $r = mysqli_query ($dbc, $q) or
    → trigger_error("Query: $q\n<br
    → />MySQL Error: " . mysqli_error
    → ($dbc));
```

The query will attempt to retrieve the user ID, first name, and user level for the record whose email address and password match those submitted. The MySQL query uses the SHA1() function on the *pass* column, as the password is encrypted using that function in the first place. The query also checks that the *active* column has a NULL value, meaning that the user has successfully accessed the `activate.php` page. If you know an account has been activated but you still can't log in using the proper values, it's likely because your *active* column was erroneously defined as NOT NULL.

4. If a match was made in the database, log the user in and redirect them.

```
if (@mysqli_num_rows($r) == 1) {

    $_SESSION = mysqli_fetch_array
    → ($r, MYSQLI_ASSOC);

    mysqli_free_result($r);

    mysqli_close($dbc);

    $url = BASE_URL . 'index.php';

    ob_end_clean();

    header("Location: $url");

    exit();
```

The login process consists of storing the retrieved values in the session (which was already started in `header.html`) and then redirecting the user to the home page. Because the query will return an array with three elements—one indexed at *user_id*, one at *first_name*, and the third at *user_level*, they can be fetched right into $_SESSION, resulting in $_SESSION['user_id'], $_SESSION ['first_name'], and $_SESSION['user_level']. If $_SESSION had other values in it already, you would not want to take this shortcut, as you'd wipe out those other elements.

The `ob_end_clean()` function will delete the existing buffer (the output buffering is also begun in `header.html`), since it will not be used.

continues on next page

5. Complete the conditionals and close the database connection.

```
    } else {

        echo '<p class="error">Either
        → the email address and
        → password entered do not match
        → those on file or you have not
        → yet activated your account.
        → </p>';

    }

} else {

    echo '<p class="error">Please try
    → again.</p>';

}

mysqli_close($dbc);

} // End of SUBMIT conditional.

?>
```

The error message (**Figure 16.24**) indicates that the login process could fail for two possible reasons. One is that the submitted email address and password do not match those on file. The other reason is that the user has not yet activated their account.

6. Display the HTML login form (**Figure 16.25**).

```
<h1>Login</h1>

<p>Your browser must allow cookies
→ in order to log in.</p>

<form action="login.php" method=
→ "post">

    <fieldset>

    <p><b>Email Address:</b> <input
    → type="text" name="email" size=
    → "20" maxlength="40" /></p>
```

Figure 16.24 An error message is displayed if the login query does not return a single record.

Figure 16.25 The login form.

Figure 16.26 Upon successfully logging in, the user will be redirected to the home page, where they will be greeted by name.

Script 16.9 The logout page destroys all of the session information, including the cookie.

```
●●●                  Script
1   <?php # Script 16.9 - logout.php

2   // This is the logout page for the site.

3

4   require_once ('includes/config.inc.php');

5   $page_title = 'Logout';

6   include ('includes/header.html');

7

8   // If no first_name session variable
    exists, redirect the user:

9   if (!isset($_SESSION['first_name'])) {

10

11     $url = BASE_URL . 'index.php'; // Define
       the URL.

12     ob_end_clean(); // Delete the buffer.

13     header("Location: $url");

14     exit(); // Quit the script.

15

16  } else { // Log out the user.

17

18     $_SESSION = array(); // Destroy the
       variables.

19     session_destroy(); // Destroy the
       session itself.

20     setcookie (session_name(), '', time()-
       300); // Destroy the cookie.

21

22  }

23

24  // Print a customized message:

25  echo '<h3>You are now logged out.</h3>';

26

27  include ('includes/footer.html');

28  ?>
```

```
<p><b>Password:</b> <input type=
→ "password" name="pass" size=
→ "20" maxlength="20" /></p>

<div align="center"><input type=
→ "submit" name="submit" value=
→ "Login" /></div>

<input type="hidden" name=
→ "submitted" value="TRUE" />

</fieldset>
```

```
</form>
```

The login form, like the registration form, will submit the data back to itself. This one is not sticky, though, as only the one input could be made sticky anyway.

Notice that the page includes a message informing the user that cookies must be enabled to use the site (if a user does not allow cookies, the user will never get access to the logged-in user pages).

7. Include the HTML footer.

```
<?php

include ('includes/footer.html');

?>
```

8. Save the file as login.php, place it in your Web directory, and test it in your Web browser (**Figure 16.26**).

To write logout.php:

1. Create a new PHP document in your text editor or IDE (**Script 16.9**).

```
<?php # Script 16.9 - logout.php

require_once ('includes/config.
→ inc.php');

$page_title = 'Logout';

include ('includes/header.html');
```

continues on next page

LOGGING IN AND LOGGING OUT

517

2. Redirect the user if they are not logged in.

```
if (!isset($_SESSION['first_name']
→ )) {
    $url = BASE_URL . 'index.php';
    ob_end_clean();
    header("Location: $url");
    exit();
```

If the user is not currently logged in (determined by checking for a `$_SESSION['first_name']` variable), the user will be redirected to the home page (because there's no point in trying to log them out).

3. Log out the user if they are currently logged in.

```
} else { // Log out the user.
    $_SESSION = array();
    session_destroy();
    setcookie (session_name(), '',
    → time()-300);
}
```

To log the user out, the session values will be reset, the session data will be destroyed on the server, and the session cookie will be deleted. These lines of code were first used and described in Chapter 11. The cookie name will be the value returned by the `session_name()` function. If you decide to change the session name later, this code will still be accurate.

4. Print a logged-out message and complete the PHP page.

```
echo '<h3>You are now logged out.
→ </h3>';
include ('includes/footer.html');
?>
```

5. Save the file as `logout.php`, place it in your Web directory, and test it in your Web browser (**Figure 16.27**).

✔ Tip

- By adding a `last_login` DATETIME field to the *users* table, you could update it when a user logs in. Then you would know the last time a person accessed the site and have a method for counting how many users are currently logged in (say, everyone that logged in within the past so many minutes).

Figure 16.27 The results of successfully logging out.

Script 16.10 The forgot_password.php script allows users to reset their password without administrative assistance.

```
         ⬤ ⬤ ⬤              📄 Script
1   <?php # Script 16.10 - forgot_password.php

2   // This page allows a user to reset their
    password, if forgotten.

3

4   require_once ('includes/config.inc.php');

5   $page_title = 'Forgot Your Password';

6   include ('includes/header.html');

7

8   if (isset($_POST['submitted'])) {

9     require_once (MYSQL);

10

11    // Assume nothing:

12    $uid = FALSE;

13

14    // Validate the email address...

15    if (!empty($_POST['email'])) {

16

17      // Check for the existence of that
        email address...

18      $q = 'SELECT user_id FROM users WHERE
        email="'. mysqli_real_escape_string
        ($dbc, $_POST['email']) . '"';

19      $r = mysqli_query ($dbc, $q) or
        trigger_error("Query: $q\n<br />MySQL
        Error: " . mysqli_error($dbc));

20

21      if (mysqli_num_rows($r) == 1) { //
        Retrieve the user ID:

22        list($uid) = mysqli_fetch_array ($r,
          MYSQLI_NUM);

23      } else { // No database match made.

24        echo '<p class="error">The submitted
          email address does not match those
          on file!</p>';

25      }

26

27    } else { // No email!

28      echo '<p class="error">You forgot to
        enter your email address!</p>';
```

(script continues on next page)

Password Management

The final aspect of the public side of this site is the management of passwords. There are two processes to consider: resetting a forgotten password and changing an existing one.

Resetting a password

It inevitably happens that people forget their login passwords for Web sites, so having a contingency plan for these occasions is important. One option would be to have the user email the administrator when this occurs, but administering a site is difficult enough without this extra hassle. Instead, let's make a script whose purpose is to reset a forgotten password.

Because the passwords stored in the database are encrypted using MySQL's SHA1() function, there's no way to retrieve an unencrypted version. The alternative is to create a new, random password and change the existing password to this value. Rather than just display the new password in the Web browser (that would be terribly insecure), it will be emailed to the address with which the user registered.

To write forgot_password.php:

1. Create a new PHP document in your text editor or IDE (**Script 16.10**).

```
<?php # Script 16.10 - forgot_
→ password.php

require_once ('includes/config.
→ inc.php');

$page_title = 'Forgot Your Password';

include ('includes/header.html');
```

continues on page 521

Script 16.10 *continued*

```
000                    📄 Script
29    } // End of empty($_POST['email']) IF.

30

31    if ($uid) { // If everything's OK.

32

33        // Create a new, random password:

34        $p = substr ( md5(uniqid(rand(),
          true)), 3, 10);

35

36        // Update the database:

37        $q = "UPDATE users SET pass=SHA1('$p')
          WHERE user_id=$uid LIMIT 1";

38        $r = mysqli_query ($dbc, $q) or
          trigger_error("Query: $q\n<br />MySQL
          Error: " . mysqli_error($dbc));

39

40        if (mysqli_affected_rows($dbc) == 1) {
          // If it ran OK.

41

42            // Send an email:

43            $body = "Your password to log into
              <whatever site> has been temporarily
              changed to '$p'. Please log in using
              this password and this email address.
              Then you may change your password to
              something more familiar.";

44            mail ($_POST['email'], 'Your
              temporary password.', $body, 'From:
              admin@sitename.com');

45

46            // Print a message and wrap up:

47            echo '<h3>Your password has been
              changed. You will receive the new,
              temporary password at the email
              address with which you registered.
              Once you have logged in with this
              password, you may change it by
              clicking on the "Change Password"
              link.</h3>';

48            mysqli_close($dbc);

49            include ('includes/footer.html');

50            exit(); // Stop the script.

51
```

(script continues)

Script 16.10 *continued*

```
000                    📄 Script
52        } else { // If it did not run OK.

53            echo '<p class="error">Your password
              could not be changed due to a system
              error. We apologize for any
              inconvenience.</p>';

54        }

55

56    } else { // Failed the validation test.

57        echo '<p class="error">Please try
          again.</p>';

58    }

59

60    mysqli_close($dbc);

61

62  } // End of the main Submit conditional.

63

64  ?>

65

66  <h1>Reset Your Password</h1>

67  <p>Enter your email address below and your
      password will be reset.</p>

68  <form action="forgot_password.php"
      method="post">

69      <fieldset>

70          <p><b>Email Address:</b> <input
              type="text" name="email" size="20"
              maxlength="40" value="<?php if
              (isset($_POST['email'])) echo
              $_POST['email']; ?>" /></p>

71      </fieldset>

72      <div align="center"><input type="submit"
          name="submit" value="Reset My Password"
          /></div>

73      <input type="hidden" name="submitted"
          value="TRUE" />

74  </form>

75

76  <?php

77  include ('includes/footer.html');

78  ?>
```

2. Check if the form has been submitted and validate the email address.

```
if (isset($_POST['submitted'])) {

  require_once (MYSQL);

  $uid = FALSE;

  if (!empty($_POST['email'])) {

    $q = 'SELECT user_id FROM users
→ WHERE email="'.

    mysqli_real_escape_string
→($dbc, $_POST['email']) . '"';

    $r = mysqli_query ($dbc, $q) or
→ trigger_error("Query: $q\n<br
→ />MySQL Error: " . mysqli_
→ error($dbc));

    if (mysqli_num_rows($r) == 1) {

      list($uid) = mysqli_fetch_array
→ ($r, MYSQLI_NUM);
```

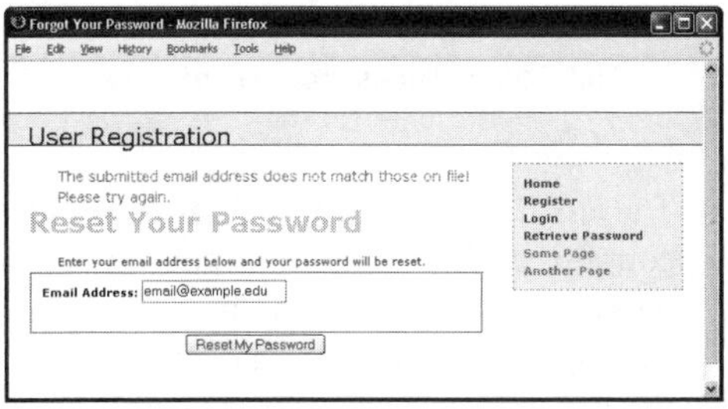

Figure 16.28 If the user entered an email address that is not found in the database, an error message is shown.

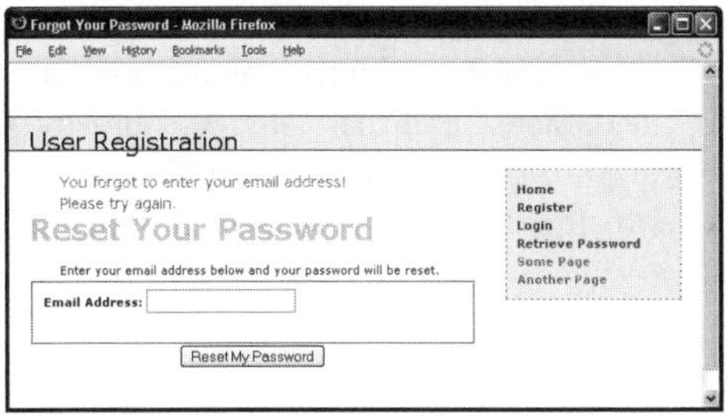

Figure 16.29 Failure to provide an email address also results in an error.

This form will take an email address input and update the password for that record. The first step is to validate that an email address was entered (there's no need for the extra overhead of a regular expression). If so, an attempt is made to retrieve the user ID for that email address in the database. If the query returns one row, it'll be fetched and assigned to $uid (short for *user ID*). This value will be needed to update the database with the new password, and it'll also be used as a flag variable.

The list() function has not been formally discussed in the book, but you may have run across it. It's a shortcut function that allows you to assign array elements to other variables. Since mysqli_fetch_array() will always return an array, even if it's an array of just one element, using list() can save having to write:

```
$row = mysqli_fetch_array($r, MYSQLI_
→ NUM);
```

```
$uid = $row[0];
```

3. Report any errors.

```
      } else {

        echo '<p class="error">The
→ submitted email address does
→ not match those on file!</p>';

      }

    } else {

      echo '<p class="error">You forgot
→ to enter your email address!
→ </p>';

    }
```

If no such record could be found, an error message is displayed (**Figure 16.28**). If no email address was provided, that is also reported (**Figure 16.29**).

continues on next page

PASSWORD MANAGEMENT

4. Create a new, random password.

```
if ($uid) {

    $p = substr ( md5(uniqid(rand(),
    → true)), 3, 10);
```

To create a new, random password, I'll make use of four PHP functions. The first is `uniqid()`, which will return a unique identifier. It is fed the arguments `rand()` and *true*, which makes the returned string more random. This returned value is then sent through the `md5()` function, which calculates the MD5 hash of a string. At this stage, a hashed version of the unique ID is returned, which ends up being a string 32 characters long. This part of the code is similar to that used to create the activation code in `activate.php` (Script 16.7).

From this string, the password is determined by pulling out ten characters starting with the third one, using the `substr()` function. All in all, this code will return a very random and meaningless ten-character string (containing both letters and numbers) to be used as the temporary password.

5. Update the password in the database.

```
$q = "UPDATE users SET pass=SHA1
→ ('$p') WHERE user_id=$uid LIMIT 1";

$r = mysqli_query ($dbc, $q) or
→ trigger_error("Query: $q\n<br
→ />MySQL Error: " . mysqli_error
→ ($dbc));

if (mysqli_affected_rows($dbc) ==
→ 1) {
```

Using the user ID (the primary key for the table) that was retrieved earlier, the password for this particular user is updated to the `SHA1()` version of $p, the random password.

6. Send the password to the user and complete the page.

```
$body = "Your password to log into
→ <whatever site> has been
→ temporarily changed to '$p'. Please
→ log in using this password and this
→ email address. Then you may change
→ your password to something more
→ familiar.";

mail ($_POST['email'], 'Your
→ temporary password.', $body,
→ 'From: admin@sitename.com');

echo '<h3>Your password has been
→ changed. You will receive the new,
→ temporary password at the email
→ address with which you registered.
→ Once you have logged in with this
→ password, you may change it by
→ clicking on the "Change Password"
→ link.</h3>';

mysqli_close($dbc);

include ('includes/footer.html');

exit();
```

The email sent to the user (**Figure 16.30**) contains the new, randomly generated password. Then a message is printed and the page is completed so as not to show the form again (**Figure 16.31**).

You may wonder why the email address is not run through any kind of regular expression prior to using it in `mail()`. To get to this point, the submitted email address must match the value stored in the database and that value was already run through fairly strict validation, guaranteeing that it's safe to use.

Figure 16.30 The email message received after resetting a password.

Figure 16.31 The resulting page after successfully resetting a password.

Figure 16.32 The simple form for resetting a password.

7. Complete the conditionals and the PHP code.

```
    } else {
        echo '<p class="error">Your
        → password could not be
        → changed due to a system
        → error. We apologize for any
        → inconvenience.</p>';
    }
} else {
    echo '<p class="error">Please
    try → again.</p>';
}
mysqli_close($dbc);
}
?>
```

The first `else` clause applies only if the `UPDATE` query doesn't work, which hopefully shouldn't happen on a live site. The second `else` applies if the user didn't submit a password or if the submitted password didn't match any in the database (Figures 16.28 and 16.29).

8. Make the HTML form (**Figure 16.32**).

```
<h1>Reset Your Password</h1>

<p>Enter your email address below and
→ your password will be reset.</p>

<form action="forgot_password.php"
→ method="post">

    <fieldset>

    <p><b>Email Address:</b> <input
    → type="text" name="email"
    → size="20" maxlength="40"
    → value="<?php if (isset($_POST
    → ['email'])) echo $_POST
    → ['email']; ?>" /></p>
```

continues on next page

```
</fieldset>

<div align="center"><input type=
→ "submit" name="submit" value=
→ "Reset My Password" /></div>

<input type="hidden" name=
→ "submitted" value="TRUE" />

</form>
```

The form takes only one input, the email address. If there is a problem when the form has been submitted, the submitted email address value will be shown again.

9. Include the HTML footer.

```
<?php

include ('includes/footer.html');

?>
```

10. Save the file as `forgot_password.php`, place it in your Web directory, and test it in your Web browser.

11. Check your email to see the resulting message after a successful password reset (see Figure 16.30).

Changing a password

The `change_password.php` script was initially written in Chapter 8 (called just `password.php`), as an example of an UDPATE query. The one developed here will be very similar in functionality but will differ in that only users who are logged in will be able to access it. Therefore, the form will only need to accept the new password and a confirmation of it (the user's existing password and email address will have already been confirmed by the login page).

To write change_password.php:

1. Create a new PHP document in your text editor or IDE (**Script 16.11**).

```
<?php # Script 16.11 - change_
→ password.php

require_once ('includes/config.
→ inc.php');

$page_title = 'Change Your Password';

include ('includes/header.html');
```

2. Check that the user is logged in.

```
if (!isset($_SESSION['first_name']
→ )) {

    $url = BASE_URL . 'index.php';

    ob_end_clean();

    header("Location: $url");

    exit();

}
```

The assumption is that this page is accessed only by logged-in users. To enforce this idea, the script checks for the existence of the `$_SESSION['first_name']` variable. If it is not set, then the user will be redirected.

3. Check if the form has been submitted and include the MySQL connection.

```
if (isset($_POST['submitted'])) {

    require_once (MYSQL);
```

The key to understanding how this script functions is remembering that there are three possible scenarios: the user is not logged in (and therefore redirected), the user is logged in and viewing the form, and the user is logged in and has submitted the form.

The user will only get to this point in the script if they are logged in. Otherwise, they would have been redirected. So the script now needs to determine if the form has been submitted or not.

continues page 526

Script 16.11 With this page, users can change an existing password (if they are logged in).

```
1    <?php # Script 16.11 - change_password.php

2    // This page allows a logged-in user to
     change their password.

3

4    require_once ('includes/config.inc.php');

5    $page_title = 'Change Your Password';

6    include ('includes/header.html');

7

8    // If no first_name session variable
     exists, redirect the user:

9    if (!isset($_SESSION['first_name'])) {

10

11       $url = BASE_URL . 'index.php'; // Define
         the URL.

12       ob_end_clean(); // Delete the buffer.

13       header("Location: $url");

14       exit(); // Quit the script.

15

16   }

17

18   if (isset($_POST['submitted'])) {

19       require_once (MYSQL);

20

21       // Check for a new password and match
         against the confirmed password:

22       $p = FALSE;

23       if (preg_match ('/^(\w){4,20}$/', $_POST
         ['password1']) ) {

24           if ($_POST['password1'] ==
             $_POST['password2']) {

25               $p = mysqli_real_escape_string
                 ($dbc, $_POST['password1']);

26           } else {

27               echo '<p class="error">Your password
                 did not match the confirmed
                 password!</p>';

28           }

29       } else {
```

(script continues)

Script 16.11 *continued*

```
30           echo '<p class="error">Please enter a
             valid password!</p>';

31       }

32

33       if ($p) { // If everything's OK.

34

35           // Make the query.

36           $q = "UPDATE users SET pass=SHA1('$p')
             WHERE user_id={$_SESSION['user_id']}
             LIMIT 1";

37           $r = mysqli_query ($dbc, $q) or
             trigger_error("Query: $q\n<br />MySQL
             Error: " . mysqli_error($dbc));

38           if (mysqli_affected_rows($dbc) == 1) {
             // If it ran OK.

39

40               // Send an email, if desired.

41               echo '<h3>Your password has been
                 changed.</h3>';

42               mysqli_close($dbc); // Close the
                 database connection.

43               include ('includes/footer.html'); //
                 Include the HTML footer.

44               exit();

45

46           } else { // If it did not run OK.

47

48               echo '<p class="error">Your password
                 was not changed. Make sure your new
                 password is different than the
                 current password. Contact the system
                 administrator if you think an error
                 occurred.</p>';

49

50           }

51

52       } else { // Failed the validation test.

53           echo '<p class="error">Please try
             again.</p>';

54       }

55
```

(script continues on next page)

4. Validate the submitted password.

```
$p = FALSE;
if (preg_match ('/^(\w){4,20}$/',
→ $_POST['password1']) ) {
    if ($_POST['password1'] ==
    → $_POST['password2']) {
        $p = mysqli_real_escape_string
        → ($dbc, $_POST['password1']);
    } else {
        echo '<p class="error">Your
        → password did not match the
        → confirmed password!</p>';
    }
} else {
    echo '<p class="error">Please
    → enter a valid password!</p>';
}
```

The new password should be validated
using the same tests as those in the
registration process. Error messages
will be displayed if problems are found
(**Figure 16.33**).

5. Update the password in the database.

```
if ($p) {
    $q = "UPDATE users SET pass=
    → SHA1('$p') WHERE user_id=
    → {$_SESSION['user_id']} LIMIT
    → 1";
    $r = mysqli_query ($dbc, $q) or
    → trigger_error("Query: $q\n<br
    → />MySQL Error: " . mysqli_
    → error($dbc));
    if (mysqli_affected_rows($dbc) ==
    → 1) {
        echo '<h3>Your password has
        → been changed.</h3>';
        mysqli_close($dbc);
        include ('includes/footer.html');
        exit();
```

Script 16.11 *continued*

```
56    mysqli_close($dbc); // Close the
      database connection.

57

58    } // End of the main Submit conditional.

59

60    ?>

61

62    <h1>Change Your Password</h1>

63    <form action="change_password.php"
      method="post">

64      <fieldset>

65      <p><b>New Password:</b> <input type=
        "password" name="password1" size="20"
        maxlength="20" /> <small>Use only
        letters, numbers, and the underscore.
        Must be between 4 and 20 characters
        long.</small></p>

66      <p><b>Confirm New Password:</b> <input
        type="password" name="password2"
        size="20" maxlength="20" /></p>

67      </fieldset>

68      <div align="center"><input type="submit"
        name="submit" value="Change My Password"
        /></div>

69      <input type="hidden" name="submitted"
        value="TRUE" />

70    </form>

71

72    <?php

73    include ('includes/footer.html');

74    ?>
```

User Registration

Please enter a valid password!
Please try again.

Change Your Password

Figure 16.33 As in the registration process, the user's
new password must pass the validation routines;
otherwise, they will see error messages.

Using the user's ID—stored in the session when the user logged in—the password field can be updated in the database. The `LIMIT 1` clause isn't strictly necessary but adds extra insurance. If the update worked, a confirmation message is printed to the Web browser (**Figure 16.34**).

6. Complete the conditionals and the PHP code.

```
    } else {
        echo '<p class="error">Your
        → password was not changed.
        → Make sure your new
        → password is different than
        → the current password.
        → Contact the system
        → administrator if you think
        → an error occurred.</p>';

    }
    } else {
    echo '<p class="error">Please try
    → again.</p>';
    }
    mysqli_close($dbc);
} // End of the main Submit
→ conditional.

?>
```

The first `else` clause applies if the `mysqli_affected_rows()` function did not return a value of *1*. This could occur for two reasons. The first is that a query or database error happened. Hopefully that's not likely on a live site, after you've already worked out all the bugs. The second reason is that the user tried to "change" their password but entered the same password again. In that case, the `UPDATE` query wouldn't affect any rows because the password column in the database wouldn't be changed. A message implying such is printed.

7. Create the HTML form (**Figure 16.35**).

```
<h1>Change Your Password</h1>

<form action="change_password.php"
method="post">

    <fieldset>

    <p><b>New Password:</b> <input
    → type="password" name=
    → "password1" size="20"
    → maxlength="20" /> <small>Use
    → only letters, numbers, and the
    → underscore. Must be between 4
    → and 20 characters long.</small>
    → </p>
```

continues on next page

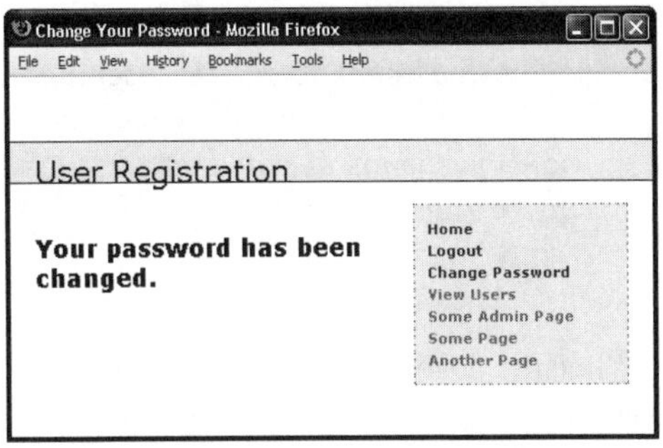

PASSWORD MANAGEMENT

Figure 16.34 The script has successfully changed the user's password.

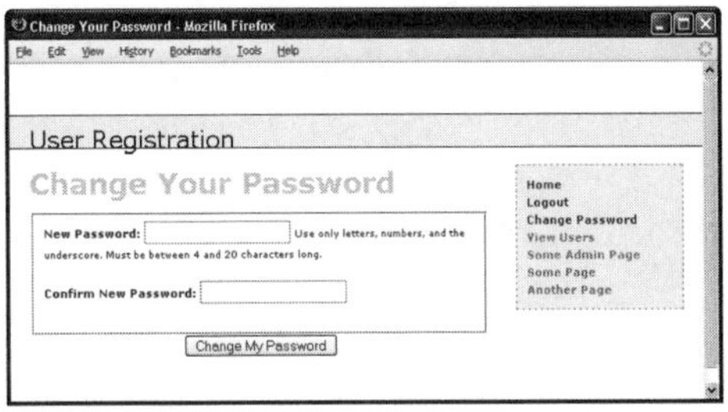

Figure 16.35 The *Change Your Password* form.

```
<p><b>Confirm New Password:</b>
→ <input type="password" name=
→ "password2" size="20"
→ maxlength="20" /></p>

</fieldset>

<div align="center"><input type=
→ "submit" name="submit" value=
→ "Change My Password" /></div>

<input type="hidden" name=
→ "submitted" value="TRUE" />
```

```
</form>
```

This form takes two inputs: the new password and a confirmation of it. A description of the proper format is given as well.

Since password inputs in HTML forms cannot be given preset values, there's no reason to set them using PHP (to make the form sticky).

8. Complete the HTML page.

```
<?php

include ('includes/footer.html');

?>
```

9. Save the file as change_password.php, place it in your Web directory, and test it in your Web browser.

✔ Tips

■ Once this script has been completed, users can reset their password with the previous script and then log in using the temporary, random password. After logging in, users can change their password back to something more memorable with this page.

■ Because the site's authentication does not rely upon the user's password from page to page (in other words, the password is not checked on each subsequent page after logging in), changing a password will not require the user to log back in.

Site Administration

For this application, how the site administration works depends upon what you want it to do. One additional page you would probably want for an administrator would be a view_users.php script, like the one created in Chapter 8 and modified in Chapter 9, "Common Programming Techniques." It's already listed in the administrator's links. You could use this to link to an edit_user.php page, which would allow you to manually activate an account, declare that a user is an administrator, or change a person's password. You could also delete a user using such a page.

While the header file creates links to administrative pages only if the logged-in user is an administrator, every administration page should also include such a check.

EXAMPLE—
E-COMMERCE

In this, the final chapter of the book, I'll develop one last Web application, an e-commerce site. In this example, I'll design a site for the purpose of selling prints of art. Unfortunately, to write and explain the entire application would require a book in itself. Furthermore, some aspects of e-commerce—like how you handle the money— are extremely particular to each individual site. Trying to demonstrate such a process would be a waste of space. With these restrictions in mind, the focus in this chapter is on the core functionality of an e-commerce site: designing the database, populating a catalog as an administrator, displaying products to the public, creating a shopping cart, and storing orders in a database.

This example includes a lot of concepts that have already been covered: using PHP with MySQL (of course) via the MySQL Improved extension, handling file uploads, using PHP to send images to the Web browser, prepared statements, sessions, etc. This chapter will also introduce one new topic: how to perform MySQL transactions from a PHP script. In order to save space in an already extended example, some corners will be cut. However, when that does occur, I'll offer suggestions for improving the scripts.

Creating the Database

The e-commerce site in this example will use the simply named *ecommerce* database. I'll explain each table's role prior to creating the database in MySQL.

With any type of e-commerce application there are three broad kinds of data to be stored: the product information (what is being sold), the customer information (who is making purchases), and the order information (what was purchased and by whom). Going through the normalization process (see Chapter 6, "Advanced SQL and MySQL"), I've come up with five tables (**Figure 17.1**).

The first two tables store all of the products being sold. As already stated, the site will be selling artistic prints. The *artists* table (**Table 17.1**) stores the information for the artists whose work is being sold. This table contains just a minimum of information (the artists' first, middle, and last names), but you could easily add the artists' birth and death dates, biographical data, and so forth. The *prints* table (**Table 17.2**) is the main products table for the site. It stores the print names, prices, and other relevant details. It is linked to the *artists* table using the *artist_id*. This table is arguably the most important, as it provides a unique identifier for each product being sold. That concept is key to any e-commerce site (without unique identifiers, how would you know what a person bought?).

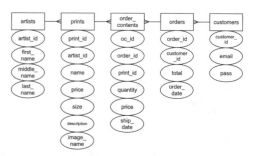

Figure 17.1 This entity-relationship diagram (ERD) shows how the five tables in the *ecommerce* database relate to one another.

Table 17.1 The *artists* table will be used to link artist names to each individual print (see Table 17.2).

The artists Table

COLUMN	TYPE
artist_id	INT(3) UNSIGNED NOT NULL
first_name	VARCHAR(20) DEFAULT NULL
middle_name	VARCHAR(20) DEFAULT NULL
last_name	VARCHAR(40) NOT NULL

Table 17.2 The *prints* table is the equivalent of a products table in other e-commerce applications. Items listed in the *prints* table will be purchased by the customer.

The prints Table

COLUMN	TYPE
print_id	INT(4) UNSIGNED NOT NULL
artist_id	INT(3) UNSIGNED NOT NULL
print_name	VARCHAR(60) NOT NULL
price	DECIMAL(6,2) UNSIGNED NOT NULL
size	VARCHAR(60) DEFAULT NULL
description	VARCHAR(255) DEFAULT NULL
image_name	VARCHAR(60) NOT NULL

Table 17.3 The *customers* table is being defined in the most minimal way for the purposes of this chapter's example. Expand its definition to suit your application's needs.

The customers Table

COLUMN	TYPE
customer_id	INT(5) UNSIGNED NOT NULL
email	VARCHAR(60) NOT NULL
pass	CHAR(40) NOT NULL

Table 17.4 The *orders* table will record the customer's ID, the order total, and the date of the order.

The orders Table

COLUMN	TYPE
order_id	INT(10) UNSIGNED NOT NULL
customer_id	INT(5) UNSIGNED NOT NULL
total	DECIMAL(10,2) UNSIGNED NOT NULL
order_date	TIMESTAMP

Table 17.5 The *order_contents* table stores the specific items in an order.

The order_contents Table

COLUMN	TYPE
oc_id	INT(10) UNSIGNED NOT NULL
order_id	INT(10) UNSIGNED NOT NULL
print_id	INT(4) UNSIGNED NOT NULL
quantity	TINYINT UNSIGNED NOT NULL DEFAULT 1
price	DECIMAL(6,2) UNSIGNED NOT NULL
ship_date	DATETIME DEFAULT NULL

The *customers* table (**Table 17.3**) does exactly what you'd expect: it records the personal information for each client. At the least, it reflects the person's first name, last name, email address, password, and shipping address, as well as the date they registered. Presumably the combination of the email address and password would allow the user to log in, shop, and access their account. Since it's fairly obvious what information this table would store, I'll define it with only the three essential columns for now.

The final two tables store all of the order information. There are any number of ways you could do this, but I've chosen to store general order information—the total, the date, and the customer's ID—in an *orders* table (**Table 17.4**). This table could also have separate columns reflecting the shipping cost, the amount of sales tax, any discounts that applied, and so on. The *order_contents* table (**Table 17.5**) will store the actual items that were sold, including the quantity and price. The *order_contents* table is essentially a middleman, used to intercept the many-to-many relationship between *prints* and *orders* (each print can be in multiple orders, and each order can have multiple prints).

In order to be able to use transactions (in the final script), the two order tables will use the InnoDB storage engine. The others will use the default MyISAM type. See Chapter 6 for more information on the available storage engines (table types).

CREATING THE DATABASE

To create the database:

1. Log in to the mysql client and create the *ecommerce* database, if it doesn't already exist.

```
CREATE DATABASE ecommerce;
```

```
USE ecommerce;
```

For these steps, you can use either the mysql client or another tool like phpMyAdmin.

2. Create the *artists* table (**Figure 17.2**).

```
CREATE TABLE artists (
```

```
artist_id INT(3) UNSIGNED NOT NULL
→ AUTO_INCREMENT,
```

```
first_name VARCHAR(20) DEFAULT NULL,
```

```
middle_name VARCHAR(20) DEFAULT NULL,
```

```
last_name VARCHAR(40) NOT NULL,
```

```
PRIMARY KEY (artist_id),
```

```
INDEX full_name (last_name,
→ first_name)
```

```
) ENGINE=MyISAM;
```

This table stores just four pieces of information for each artist. Of these, only *last_name* is required (is defined as NOT NULL), as there are artists that go by a single name (e.g., Christo). I've added definitions for the indexes as well. The primary key is the *artist_id*, and an index is placed on the combination of the first and last name, which may be used in an ORDER BY clause.

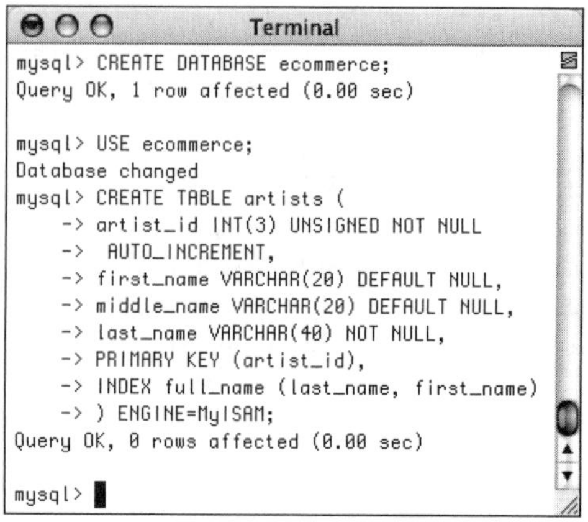

Figure 17.2 Making the first table.

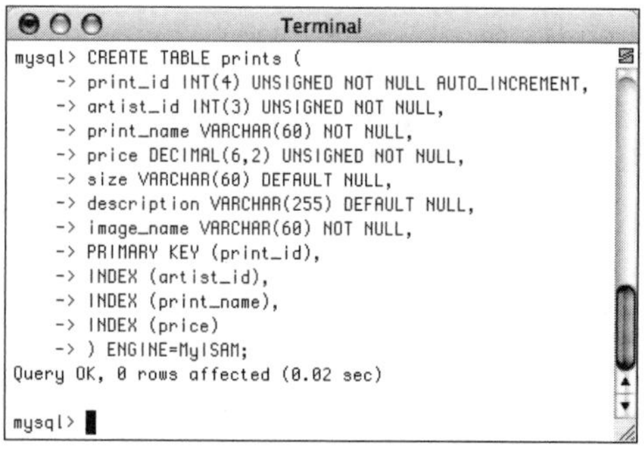

```
mysql> CREATE DATABASE ecommerce;
Query OK, 1 row affected (0.00 sec)

mysql> USE ecommerce;
Database changed
mysql> CREATE TABLE artists (
    -> artist_id INT(3) UNSIGNED NOT NULL
    ->  AUTO_INCREMENT,
    -> first_name VARCHAR(20) DEFAULT NULL,
    -> middle_name VARCHAR(20) DEFAULT NULL,
    -> last_name VARCHAR(40) NOT NULL,
    -> PRIMARY KEY (artist_id),
    -> INDEX full_name (last_name, first_name)
    -> ) ENGINE=MyISAM;
Query OK, 0 rows affected (0.00 sec)

mysql>
```

Figure 17.3 Making the second table.

```
mysql> CREATE TABLE prints (
    -> print_id INT(4) UNSIGNED NOT NULL AUTO_INCREMENT,
    -> artist_id INT(3) UNSIGNED NOT NULL,
    -> print_name VARCHAR(60) NOT NULL,
    -> price DECIMAL(6,2) UNSIGNED NOT NULL,
    -> size VARCHAR(60) DEFAULT NULL,
    -> description VARCHAR(255) DEFAULT NULL,
    -> image_name VARCHAR(60) NOT NULL,
    -> PRIMARY KEY (print_id),
    -> INDEX (artist_id),
    -> INDEX (print_name),
    -> INDEX (price)
    -> ) ENGINE=MyISAM;
Query OK, 0 rows affected (0.02 sec)

mysql>
```

3. Create the *prints* table (**Figure 17.3**).

```
CREATE TABLE prints (

print_id INT(4) UNSIGNED NOT NULL
→ AUTO_INCREMENT,

artist_id INT(3) UNSIGNED NOT NULL,

print_name VARCHAR(60) NOT NULL,

price DECIMAL(6,2) UNSIGNED NOT NULL,

size VARCHAR(60) DEFAULT NULL,

description VARCHAR(255) DEFAULT NULL,

image_name VARCHAR(60) NOT NULL,

PRIMARY KEY (print_id),

INDEX (artist_id),

INDEX (print_name),

INDEX (price)
```
```
) ENGINE=MyISAM;
```

All of the columns in the *prints* table are required except for the *size* and *description*. I've also set indexes on the *artist_id*, *print_name*, and *price* fields, each of which may be used in queries.

Each print will be associated with one image. The image will be stored on the server using the same value as the *print_id*. When displaying the image in the Web browser, its original name will be used, so that needs to be stored in this table.

You could add to this table an *in_stock* or *qty_on_hand* field, to indicate the availability of products.

continues on next page

Security

With respect to an e-commerce site, there are four broad security considerations. The first is how the data is stored on the server. You need to protect the MySQL database itself (by setting appropriate access permissions) and the directory where session information is stored (see Chapter 11, "Cookies and Sessions," for what settings could be changed). With respect to these issues, using a non-shared hosting would definitely improve the security of your site.

The second security consideration has to do with protecting access to sensitive information. The administrative side of the site, which would have the ability to view orders and customer records, must be safeguarded to the highest level. This means requiring authentication to access it, limiting who knows the access information, using a secure connection, and so forth.

The third factor is protecting the data during transmission. By the time the customer gets to the checkout process (where credit card and shipping information comes in), secure transactions must be used. To do so entails establishing a Secure Sockets Layer (SSL) on your server with a valid certificate and then changing to an *https://* URL. Also be aware of what information is being sent via e-mail, since those messages are frequently not transmitted through secure avenues.

The fourth issue has to do with the handling of the payment information. You really, really, really, really (*really!*) don't want to keep this information in any way. Ideally, let a third-party resource handle the payment and keep your site's figurative hands clean. I discuss this a little bit in a sidebar entitled "The Checkout Process," found at the end of the chapter.

CREATING THE DATABASE

4. Create the *customers* table (**Figure 17.4**).

```
CREATE TABLE customers (
customer_id INT(5) UNSIGNED NOT NULL
→ AUTO_INCREMENT,
email VARCHAR(60) NOT NULL,
pass CHAR(40) NOT NULL,
PRIMARY KEY (customer_id),
INDEX email_pass (email, pass)
) ENGINE=MyISAM;
```

This is the code used to create the *customers* table. You could throw in the other appropriate fields (name, address, phone number, the registration date, etc.). As I won't be dealing with those values—or user management at all—in this chapter, I've omitted them.

5. Create the *orders* table (**Figure 17.5**).

```
CREATE TABLE orders (
order_id INT(10) UNSIGNED NOT NULL
→ AUTO_INCREMENT,
customer_id INT(5) UNSIGNED NOT NULL,
total DECIMAL(10,2) UNSIGNED NOT NULL,
order_date TIMESTAMP,
PRIMARY KEY (order_id),
INDEX (customer_id),
INDEX (order_date)
) ENGINE=InnoDB;
```

All of the *orders* fields are required, and three indexes have been created. Notice that a foreign key column here, like *customer_id*, is of the same exact type as its corresponding primary key (*customer_id* in the *customers* table). The *order_date* field will store the date and time an order was entered. Being defined as a TIMESTAMP, it will automatically be given the current value when a record is inserted (for this reason it does not formally need to be declared as NOT NULL).

Finally, because I'll want to use transactions with the *orders* and *order_contents* tables, both will use the InnoDB storage engine.

```
● ○ ○              Terminal
mysql> CREATE TABLE customers (
    -> customer_id INT(5) UNSIGNED NOT NULL
    ->    AUTO_INCREMENT,
    -> email VARCHAR(60) NOT NULL,
    -> pass CHAR(40) NOT NULL,
    -> PRIMARY KEY (customer_id),
    -> INDEX email_pass (email, pass)
    -> ) ENGINE=MyISAM;
Query OK, 0 rows affected (0.01 sec)

mysql>
```

Figure 17.4 Creating a basic version of the *customers* table. In a real e-commerce site, you'd need to expand this table to store more information.

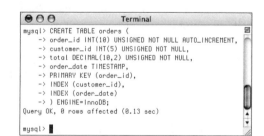

```
● ○ ○              Terminal
mysql> CREATE TABLE orders (
    -> order_id INT(10) UNSIGNED NOT NULL AUTO_INCREMENT,
    -> customer_id INT(5) UNSIGNED NOT NULL,
    -> total DECIMAL(10,2) UNSIGNED NOT NULL,
    -> order_date TIMESTAMP,
    -> PRIMARY KEY (order_id),
    -> INDEX (customer_id),
    -> INDEX (order_date)
    -> ) ENGINE=InnoDB;
Query OK, 0 rows affected (0.13 sec)

mysql>
```

Figure 17.5 Making the *orders* table.

6. Create the *order_contents* table (**Figure 17.6**).

```
CREATE TABLE order_contents (

oc_id INT(10) UNSIGNED NOT NULL
→ AUTO_INCREMENT,

order_id INT(10) UNSIGNED NOT NULL,

print_id INT(4) UNSIGNED NOT NULL,

quantity TINYINT UNSIGNED NOT NULL
→ DEFAULT 1,

price DECIMAL(6,2) UNSIGNED NOT NULL,

ship_date DATETIME default NULL,

PRIMARY KEY (oc_id),

INDEX (order_id),

INDEX (print_id),

INDEX (ship_date)

) ENGINE=InnoDB;
```

```
mysql> CREATE TABLE order_contents (
    -> oc_id INT(10) UNSIGNED NOT NULL
    ->  AUTO_INCREMENT,
    -> order_id INT(10) UNSIGNED NOT NULL,
    -> print_id INT(4) UNSIGNED NOT NULL,
    -> quantity TINYINT UNSIGNED NOT NULL
    ->  DEFAULT 1,
    -> price DECIMAL(6,2) UNSIGNED NOT NULL,
    -> ship_date DATETIME default NULL,
    -> PRIMARY KEY (oc_id),
    -> INDEX (order_id),
    -> INDEX (print_id),
    -> INDEX (ship_date)
    -> ) ENGINE=InnoDB;
Query OK, 0 rows affected (0.06 sec)

mysql>
```

Figure 17.6 Making the final table for the *ecommerce* database.

In order to have a normalized database structure, I've separated out each order into its general information—the customer, the order date, and the total amount—and its specific information—the actual items ordered and in what quantity. The table has foreign keys to the *orders* and *prints* tables. The *quantity* has a set default value of *1*. The *ship_date* is defined as a DATETIME, so that it can have a NULL value, indicating that the item has not yet shipped. Again, this table must use the InnoDB storage engine in order to be part of a transaction.

You may be curious why I'm storing the price in this table when that information is already present in the *prints* table. The reason is simply this: the price of a product may change. The *prints* table indicates the current price of an item; the *order_contents* table indicates the price at which an item was purchased.

✔ Tips

- Depending upon what a site is selling, it would have different tables in place of *artists* and *prints*. The most important attribute of any e-commerce database is that there is a products table that lists the individual items being sold with a product ID associated with each. So a large, red polo shirt would have one ID, which is different than a large, blue polo shirt's ID, which is different than a medium, blue polo shirt's ID. Without unique, individual product identifiers, it would be impossible to track orders and product quantities.

- If you wanted to store multiple addresses for users—home, billing, friends, etc.—create a separate addresses table. In this table store all of that information, including the address type, and link those records back to the customers table using the customer ID as a primary-foreign key.

CREATING THE DATABASE

535

The Administrative Side

The first script I'll write will be for the purpose of adding products (specifically a print) to the database. The page will allow the administrator to select the artist by name or enter a new one, upload an image, and enter the details for the print (**Figure 17.7**). The image will be stored on the server and the print's record inserted into the database. By far, this will be the most complicated script in this chapter, but all of the technology involved has already been covered elsewhere in the book.

This—and pretty much every script in this chapter—will require a connection to the MySQL database. Instead of writing a new one from scratch, just copy `mysqli_connect.php` (Script 8.2) from Chapter 8, "Using PHP with MySQL," to the appropriate directory for this site's files. Then edit the information so that it connects to a database called *ecommerce*, using a username/password/hostname combination that has the proper privileges.

Do note that all of these scripts, like every other PHP and MySQL script in this book, make use of PHP's Improved MySQL extension functions. If you're not using at least version 5 of PHP and version 4.1 of MySQL, with these functions enabled, you'll need to modify these scripts to get them to work (see Chapter 8 for more).

To create add_print.php:

1. Create a new PHP document, beginning with the HTML head (**Script 17.1**).

```
<!DOCTYPE html PUBLIC "-//W3C//DTD
→ XHTML 1.0 Transitional//EN"

"http://www.w3.org/TR/xhtml1/DTD/
→ xhtml1-transitional.dtd">

<html
→ xmlns="http://www.w3.org/1999/xhtml"
→ xml:lang="en" lang="en">

<head>

    <meta http-equiv="content-type"
    content="text/html; charset=iso-
    8859-1" />

    <title>Add a Print</title>

</head>

<body>

<?php # Script 17.1 - add_print.php
```

Normally, I would create a template system for the administrative side, but since I'll be writing only this one administrative script in this chapter, I'll do without.

continues on page 543

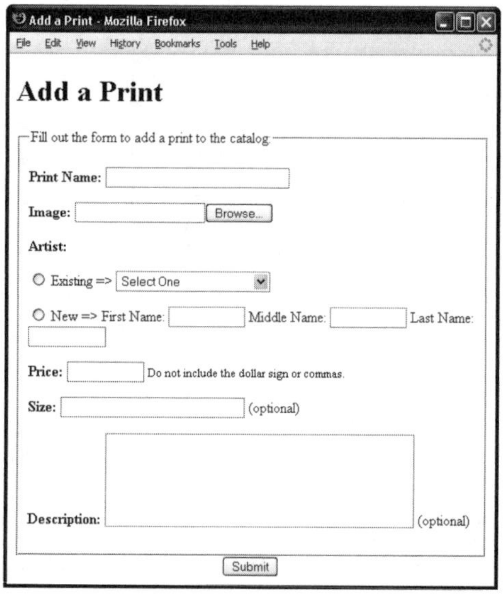

Figure 17.7 The HTML form for adding prints to the catalog.

Script 17.1 This administration page adds products to the database. It handles a file upload, inserts the new print into the *prints* table, and even allows for a new artist to be added at the same time.

```
1    <!DOCTYPE html PUBLIC "-//W3C//DTD XHTML 1.0 Transitional//EN"
2                "http://www.w3.org/TR/xhtml1/DTD/xhtml1-transitional.dtd">
3    <html xmlns="http://www.w3.org/1999/xhtml" xml:lang="en" lang="en">
4    <head>
5      <meta http-equiv="content-type" content="text/html; charset=iso-8859-1" />
6      <title>Add a Print</title>
7    </head>
8    <body>
9    <?php # Script 17.1 - add_print.php
10   // This page allows the administrator to add a print (product).
11
12   require_once ('../../mysqli_connect.php');
13
14   if (isset($_POST['submitted'])) { // Handle the form.
15
16     // Validate the incoming data...
17     $errors = array();
18
19     // Check for a print name:
20     if (!empty($_POST['print_name'])) {
21       $pn = trim($_POST['print_name']);
22     } else {
23       $errors[] = 'Please enter the print\'s name!';
24     }
25
26     // Check for an image:
27     if (is_uploaded_file ($_FILES['image']['tmp_name'])) {
28
29       // Create a temporary file name:
30       $temp = '../../uploads/' . md5($_FILES['image']['name']);
31
32       // Move the file over:
33       if (move_uploaded_file($_FILES['image']['tmp_name'], $temp)) {
34
35         echo '<p>The file has been uploaded!</p>';
36
```

(script continues on next page)

Script 17.1 *continued*

```
37          // Set the $i variable to the image's name:
38          $i = $_FILES['image']['name'];
39
40      } else { // Couldn't move the file over.
41          $errors[] = 'The file could not be moved.';
42          $temp = $_FILES['image']['tmp_name'];
43      }
44
45      } else { // No uploaded file.
46          $errors[] = 'No file was uploaded.';
47          $temp = NULL;
48      }
49
50      // Check for a size (not required):
51      $s = (!empty($_POST['size'])) ? trim($_POST['size']) : NULL;
52
53      // Check for a price:
54      if (is_numeric($_POST['price'])) {
55          $p = (float) $_POST['price'];
56      } else {
57          $errors[] = 'Please enter the print\'s price!';
58      }
59
60      // Check for a description (not required):
61      $d = (!empty($_POST['description'])) ? trim($_POST['description']) : NULL;
62
63      // Validate the artist...
64      if (isset($_POST['artist']) && ($_POST['artist'] == 'new') ) {
65          // If it's a new artist, add the artist to the database...
66
67          // Validate the first and middle names (neither required):
68          $fn = (!empty($_POST['first_name'])) ? trim($_POST['first_name']) : NULL;
69          $mn = (!empty($_POST['middle_name'])) ? trim($_POST['middle_name']) : NULL;
70
71          // Check for a last_name...
72          if (!empty($_POST['last_name'])) {
```

(script continues on next page)

Script 17.1 *continued*

```
73
74          $ln = trim($_POST['last_name']);
75
76          // Add the artist to the database:
77          $q = 'INSERT INTO artists (first_name, middle_name, last_name) VALUES (?, ?, ?)';
78          $stmt = mysqli_prepare($dbc, $q);
79          mysqli_stmt_bind_param($stmt, 'sss', $fn, $mn, $ln);
80          mysqli_stmt_execute($stmt);
81
82          // Check the results....
83          if (mysqli_stmt_affected_rows($stmt) == 1) {
84                  echo '<p>The artist has been added.</p>';
85                  $a = mysqli_stmt_insert_id($stmt); // Get the artist ID.
86          } else { // Error!
87                  $errors[] = 'The new artist could not be added to the database!';
88          }
89
90          // Close this prepared statement:
91          mysqli_stmt_close($stmt);
92
93      } else { // No last name value.
94          $errors[] = 'Please enter the artist\'s name!';
95      }
96
97  } elseif ( isset($_POST['artist']) && ($_POST['artist'] == 'existing') && ($_POST['existing'] >
0) ) { // Existing artist.
98      $a = (int) $_POST['existing'];
99  } else { // No artist selected.
100     $errors[] = 'Please enter or select the print\'s artist!';
101 }
102
103 if (empty($errors)) { // If everything's OK.
104
105     // Add the print to the database:
106     $q = 'INSERT INTO prints (artist_id, print_name, price, size, description, image_name) VALUES
(?, ?, ?, ?, ?, ?)';
107     $stmt = mysqli_prepare($dbc, $q);
```

(script continues on next page)

Script 17.1 *continued*

```
000                                          Script
108      mysqli_stmt_bind_param($stmt, 'isdsss', $a, $pn, $p, $s, $d, $i);
109      mysqli_stmt_execute($stmt);
110
111      // Check the results...
112      if (mysqli_stmt_affected_rows($stmt) == 1) {
113
114        // Print a message:
115        echo '<p>The print has been added.</p>';
116
117        // Rename the image:
118        $id = mysqli_stmt_insert_id($stmt); // Get the print ID.
119        rename ($temp, "../../uploads/$id");
120
121        // Clear $_POST:
122        $_POST = array();
123
124      } else { // Error!
125        echo '<p style="font-weight: bold; color: #C00">Your submission could not be processed due
             to a system error.</p>';
126      }
127
128      mysqli_stmt_close($stmt);
129
130    } // End of $errors IF.
131
132    // Delete the uploaded file if it still exists:
133    if ( isset($temp) && file_exists ($temp) && is_file($temp) ) {
134      unlink ($temp);
135    }
136
137  } // End of the submission IF.
138
139  // Check for any errors and print them:
140  if ( !empty($errors) && is_array($errors) ) {
141    echo '<h1>Error!</h1>
142    <p style="font-weight: bold; color: #C00">The following error(s) occurred:<br />';
143    foreach ($errors as $msg) {
```

(script continues on next page)

Script 17.1 *continued*

```
144        echo " - $msg<br />\n";
145    }
146    echo 'Please reselect the print image and try again.</p>';
147 }
148
149 // Display the form...
150 ?>
151 <h1>Add a Print</h1>
152 <form enctype="multipart/form-data" action="add_print.php" method="post">
153
154    <input type="hidden" name="MAX_FILE_SIZE" value="524288" />
155
156    <fieldset><legend>Fill out the form to add a print to the catalog:</legend>
157
158    <p><b>Print Name:</b> <input type="text" name="print_name" size="30" maxlength="60"
       value="<?php if (isset($_POST['print_name'])) echo htmlspecialchars($_POST['print_name']); ?>"
       /></p>
159
160    <p><b>Image:</b> <input type="file" name="image" /></p>
161
162    <div><b>Artist:</b>
163    <p><input type="radio" name="artist" value="existing" <?php if (isset($_POST['artist'])) &&
       ($_POST['artist'] == 'existing') ) echo ' checked="checked"'; ?>/> Existing =>
164    <select name="existing"><option>Select One</option>
165    <?php // Retrieve all the artists and add to the pull-down menu.
166    $q = "SELECT artist_id, CONCAT_WS(' ', first_name, middle_name, last_name) FROM artists ORDER BY
       last_name, first_name ASC";
167    $r = mysqli_query ($dbc, $q);
168    if (mysqli_num_rows($r) > 0) {
169        while ($row = mysqli_fetch_array ($r, MYSQLI_NUM)) {
170            echo "<option value=\"$row[0]\"";
171            // Check for stickyness:
172            if (isset($_POST['existing']) && ($_POST['existing'] == $row[0]) ) echo '
               selected="selected"';
173            echo ">$row[1]</option>\n";
174        }
175    } else {
176        echo '<option>Please add a new artist.</option>';
```

(script continues on next page)

Script 17.1 *continued*

```
⊖ ○ ○                                    📄 Script
177    }

178    mysqli_close($dbc); // Close the database connection.

179    ?>

180    </select></p>

181

182    <p><input type="radio" name="artist" value="new" <?php if (isset($_POST['artist']) &&
       ($_POST['artist'] == 'new') ) echo ' checked="checked"'; ?>/> New =>

183    First Name: <input type="text" name="first_name" size="10" maxlength="20" value="<?php if
       (isset($_POST['first_name'])) echo $_POST['first_name']; ?>" />

184    Middle Name: <input type="text" name="middle_name" size="10" maxlength="20" value="<?php if
       (isset($_POST['middle_name'])) echo $_POST['middle_name']; ?>" />

185    Last Name: <input type="text" name="last_name" size="10" maxlength="40" value="<?php if
       (isset($_POST['last_name'])) echo $_POST['last_name']; ?>" /></p>

186    </div>

187

188    <p><b>Price:</b> <input type="text" name="price" size="10" maxlength="10" value="<?php if
       (isset($_POST['price'])) echo $_POST['price']; ?>" /> <small>Do not include the dollar sign or
       commas.</small></p>

189

190    <p><b>Size:</b> <input type="text" name="size" size="30" maxlength="60" value="<?php if
       (isset($_POST['size'])) echo htmlspecialchars($_POST['size']); ?>" /> (optional)</p>

191

192    <p><b>Description:</b> <textarea name="description" cols="40" rows="5"><?php if
       (isset($_POST['description'])) echo $_POST['description']; ?></textarea> (optional)</p>

193

194    </fieldset>

195

196    <div align="center"><input type="submit" name="submit" value="Submit" /></div>

197    <input type="hidden" name="submitted" value="TRUE" />

198

199    </form>

200

201    </body>

202    </html>
```

2. Include the database connection script and check if the form has been submitted.

```
require_once
→ ('../../mysqli_connect.php');

if (isset($_POST['submitted'])) {

  $errors = array();
```

The administration folder will be located inside of the main (htdocs) folder and is therefore two directories above the connection script. Keep your directory structure (**Figure 17.8**) in mind when including files.

Any form validation problems will be added to the $errors array, which is initiated here.

3. Validate the print's name.

```
if (!empty($_POST['print_name'])) {

    $pn = trim($_POST['print_name']);

} else {

    $errors[] = 'Please enter the
    → print\'s name!';

}
```

This is one of the required fields in the *prints* table and should be checked for a value. Because this script will use prepared statements, the values to be used in the query don't need to be run through mysqli_real_escape_string(). See Chapter 12, "Security Methods," for more on this subject.

If you wanted to be extra careful, you could apply strip_tags() here (although if a malicious user has gotten into the administrative area, you've got bigger problems).

If no value is entered, an error message is added to the $errors array.

continues on next page

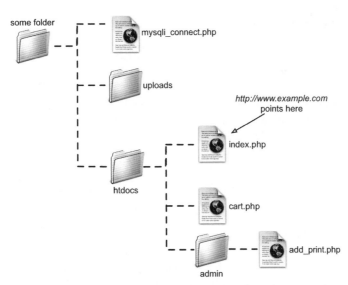

Figure 17.8 The site structure for this Web application. The MySQL connection script and the uploads directory (where images will be stored) are not within the Web directory (they aren't available via *http://*).

4. Handle the image file, if one was selected.

```
if (is_uploaded_file
→ ($_FILES['image']['tmp_name'])) {

    $temp = '../../uploads/' .
    → md5($_FILES['image']['name']);

    if
    → (move_uploaded_file($_FILES
    → ['image']['tmp_name'], $temp)) {

        echo '<p>The file has been
        → uploaded!</p>';

    $i = $_FILES['image']['name'];
```

When I demonstrated the techniques for handling file uploads with PHP (in Chapter 10, "Web Application Development"), I mentioned the is_uploaded_file() function. It returns TRUE if a file was uploaded and FALSE if not. If a file was uploaded, the script will attempt to move the file over to the uploads directory. Messages are printed (**Figure 17.9**) indicating its success in doing so. Finally, the $i variable will be set to the name of the file (for use later on in the script).

There is one other thing happening here: the images will not be stored on the server using their given names (which can be a security concern). Instead the images will be stored using their associated print ID. However, since that value isn't yet known (because the print hasn't been added to the database), a temporary name for this file has to be generated. To do so, the md5() function, which returns a 32-character hash, is applied to the image's original name. At this point in the script, the print image will have been moved to its permanent location (the uploads directory) but given a temporary name (to be renamed later).

There are improvements you could make in this one area. You could also validate that the image is of the right size and type. To keep an already busy script more manageable, I've omitted that here, but see Chapter 10 for the exact code to apply.

5. Complete the image handling section.

```
    } else {

        $errors[] = 'The file could
        → not be moved.';

        $temp =
        → $_FILES['image']['tmp_name'
        → ];

    }

} else { // No uploaded file.

    $errors[] = 'No file was
    → uploaded.';

    $temp = NULL;

}
```

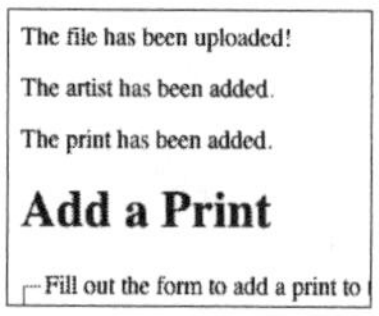

The file has been uploaded!
The artist has been added.
The print has been added.

Add a Print

⌐ Fill out the form to add a print to

Figure 17.9 The result if a file was selected for the print's image and it was successfully uploaded.

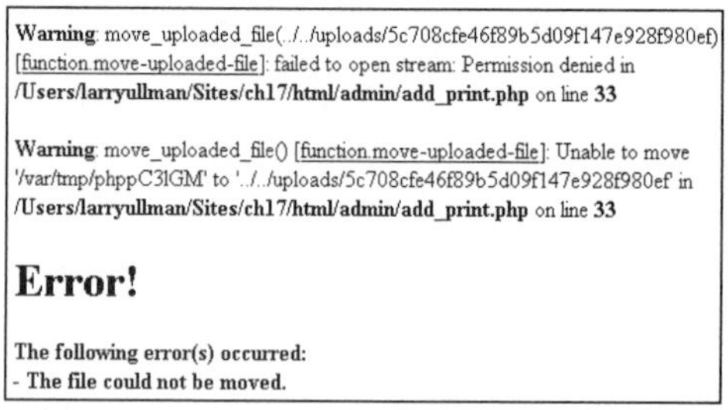

Warning: move_uploaded_file(../../uploads/5c708cfe46f89b5d09f147e928f980ef) [function.move-uploaded-file]: failed to open stream: Permission denied in **/Users/larryullman/Sites/ch17/html/admin/add_print.php** on line **33**

Warning: move_uploaded_file() [function.move-uploaded-file]: Unable to move '/var/tmp/phppC3IGM' to '../../uploads/5c708cfe46f89b5d09f147e928f980ef' in **/Users/larryullman/Sites/ch17/html/admin/add_print.php** on line **33**

Error!

The following error(s) occurred:
- The file could not be moved.

Figure 17.10 If the uploads directory is not writable by PHP, you'll see errors like these.

The first `else` clause applies if the file could not be moved to the destination directory. This should only happen if the path to that directory is not correct or if the proper permissions haven't been set on the directory (**Figure 17.10**). In this case, the `$temp` variable is assigned the value of the upload, which is still residing in its temporary location. This is necessary, as the script will attempt to remove unused files later in the script.

The second `else` clause applies if no file was uploaded. As the purpose of this site is to sell prints, it's rather important to actually display what's being sold. If you wanted, you could add to this error message more details or recommendations as to what type and size of file should be uploaded.

6. Validate the size, price, and description inputs.

```
$s = (!empty($_POST['size'])) ?
→ trim($_POST['size']) : NULL;

if (is_numeric($_POST['price'])) {
    $p = (float) $_POST['price'];
} else {
    $errors[] = 'Please enter the
    → print\'s price!';
}

$d = (!empty($_POST['description']))
→ ? trim($_POST['description']) :
→ NULL;
```

The size and description values are optional, but the price is not. As a basic validity test, I ensure that the submitted price is a number (it should be a decimal) using the `is_numeric()` function. If the value is numeric, I typecast it as a floating-point number just to be safe. An error message will be added to the array if no price or an invalid price is entered.

If the size and description inputs are not used, I'll set the `$s` and `$d` variables to `NULL`. For these two validation routines, I've reduced the amount of code by using the ternary operator (introduced in Chapter 9, "Common Programming Techniques"). The code here is the same as

```
if (!empty($_POST['size'])) {
    $s = trim($_POST['size']);
} else {
    $s = NULL;
}
```

7. Check if a new artist is being entered.

```
if (isset($_POST['artist']) && (
→ $_POST['artist'] == 'new') ) {
```

To enter the print's artist, the administrator will have two choices (**Figure 17.11**): select an existing artist (from the records in the *artists* table) using a pull-down menu or enter the name of a new artist. If a new artist is being entered, the record will have to be inserted into the *artists* table before the print is added to the *prints* table.

continues on next page

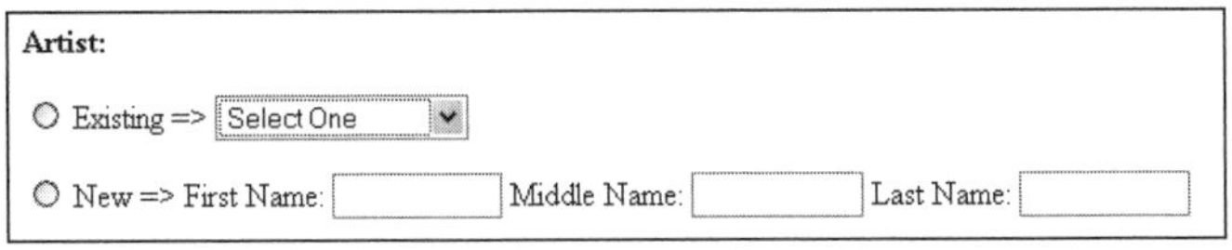

Figure 17.11 The administrator can select an existing artist from the database or choose to submit a new one.

8. Validate the artist's names.

```
$fn = (!empty($_POST['first_name']))
→ ? trim($_POST['first_name']) : NULL;

$mn = (!empty($_POST['middle_name']))
→ ? trim($_POST['middle_name']) : NULL;

if (!empty($_POST['last_name'])) {

    $ln = trim($_POST['last_name']);
```

The artist's first and middle names are optional fields, whereas the last name is not (since there are artists referred to by only one name). To validate the first two name inputs, the same ternary structure as in Step 6 is used.

9. Add the artist to the database.

```
$q = 'INSERT INTO artists
→ (first_name, middle_name,
→ last_name) VALUES (?, ?, ?)';

$stmt = mysqli_prepare($dbc, $q);

mysqli_stmt_bind_param($stmt, 'sss',
→ $fn, $mn, $ln);

mysqli_stmt_execute($stmt);

if (mysqli_stmt_affected_rows($stmt)
→ == 1) {

    echo '<p>The artist has been
    → added.</p>';

    $a = mysqli_stmt_insert_id($stmt);

} else {

    $errors[] = 'The new artist could
    → not be added to the database!';

}

mysqli_stmt_close($stmt);
```

To add the artist to the database, the query will be something like INSERT INTO artists (first_name, middle_name, last_name) VALUES ('John', 'Singer', 'Sargent') or INSERT INTO artists (first_name, middle_name, last_name) VALUES (NULL, NULL, 'Christo'). The query is run using prepared statements, covered in Chapter 12.

If the new artist was added to the database, the artist's ID will be retrieved (for use in the print's INSERT query) using the mysqli_stmt_insert_id() function. Otherwise an error is added to the array (in which case, you'll need to do some debugging).

10. Complete the artist conditional.

```
    } else { // No last name value.

        $errors[] = 'Please enter
        → the artist\'s name!';

    }

} elseif ( isset($_POST['artist'])
→ && ($_POST['artist'] == 'existing')
→ && ($_POST['existing'] > 0) ) {

    $a = (int) $_POST['existing'];

} else { // No artist selected.

    $errors[] = 'Please enter or
    → select the print\'s artist!';

}
```

If the administrator opted to use an existing artist, then a check is made that an artist was selected from the pull-down menu. If this condition fails, then an error message is added to the array.

The Administrative Side

11. Insert the record into the database.

```
if (empty($errors)) {

    $q = 'INSERT INTO prints
    → (artist_id, print_name, price,
    → size, description, image_name)
    → VALUES (?, ?, ?, ?, ?, ?)';

    $stmt = mysqli_prepare($dbc, $q);

    mysqli_stmt_bind_param($stmt,
    → 'isdsss', $a, $pn, $p, $s, $d,
    → $i);

    mysqli_stmt_execute($stmt);
```

If the `$errors` array is empty, then all of the validation tests were passed and the print can be added. Using prepared statements again, the query is something like `INSERT INTO prints (artist_id, print_name, price, size, description, image_name) VALUES (34, 'The Scream', 25.99, NULL, 'This classic…', 'scream.jpg')`.

The `mysqli_stmt_bind_param()` function indicates that the query needs six inputs (one for each question mark) of the type: integer, string, double (aka float), string, string, and string. For questions on any of this, see Chapter 12.

12. Confirm the results of the query.

```
if (mysqli_stmt_affected_rows($stmt)
→ == 1) {

    echo '<p>The print has been
    → added.</p>';

    $id =
    → mysqli_stmt_insert_id($stmt);

    rename ($temp,
    → "../../uploads/$id");

    $_POST = array();

} else {

    echo '<p style="font-weight:
    → bold; color: #C00">Your
    → submission could not be
    → processed due to a system
    → error.</p>';

}
```

If the query affected one row, then a message of success is printed in the Web browser (see Figure 17.9). Next, the print ID has to be retrieved so that the associated image can be renamed (it currently is in the `uploads` folder but under a temporary name). Finally, the `$_POST` array is cleared so that its values are displayed in the sticky form.

If the query did not affect one row, there's probably some MySQL error happening and you'll need to apply the standard debugging techniques to figure out why. See Chapter 7, "Error Handling and Debugging," for specifics.

continues on next page

THE ADMINISTRATIVE SIDE

13. Complete the conditionals.

```
    mysqli_stmt_close($stmt);

} // End of $errors IF.

if ( isset($temp) && file_exists
→ ($temp) && is_file($temp) ) {

    unlink ($temp);

}

} // End of the submission IF.
```

The first closing brace terminates the check for $errors being empty. In this case, the file on the server should be deleted because it hasn't been permanently moved and renamed.

14. Print any errors.

```
    if ( !empty($errors) &&
    → is_array($errors) ) {

        echo '<h1>Error!</h1>

        <p style="font-weight: bold;
        → color: #C00">The following
        → error(s) occurred:<br />';

    foreach ($errors as $msg) {

        echo " - $msg<br />\n";

    }

    echo 'Please reselect the print
    → image and try again.</p>';

}

?>
```

All of the errors that occurred would be in the $errors array. These can be printed using a foreach loop (**Figure 17.12**). The errors are printed within some CSS to make them bold and red. Also, since a sticky form cannot recall a selected file, the user is reminded to reselect the print image.

15. Begin creating the HTML form.

```
<h1>Add a Print</h1>

<form enctype="multipart/form-data"
→ action="add_print.php"
→ method="post">

    <input type="hidden"
    → name="MAX_FILE_SIZE"
    → value="524288" />

    <fieldset><legend>Fill out the
    → form to add a print to the
    → catalog:</legend>

    <p><b>Print Name:</b> <input
    → type="text" name="print_name"
    → size="30" maxlength="60"
    → value="<?php if
    → (isset($_POST['print_name']))
    → echo htmlspecialchars($_POST
    → ['print_name']); ?>" /></p>

    <p><b>Image:</b> <input
    → type="file" name="image" /></p>
```

Because this form will allow a user to upload a file, it must include the enctype in the form tag and the MAX_FILE_SIZE hidden input. The form will be sticky, thanks to the code in the value attribute of its inputs. Note that you cannot make a file input type sticky. In case the print's name, size, or description uses potentially problematic characters, each is run through htmlspecialchars(), so as not to mess up the value (**Figure 17.13**).

Error!

The following error(s) occurred:
- Please enter the print's name!
- No file was uploaded.
- Please enter the print's price!
- Please enter or select the print's artist!
Please reselect the print image and try again.

Add a Print

┌─ Fill out the form to add a print to the catalog: ─

Figure 17.12 An incompletely filled out form will generate several errors.

16. Begin the artist pull-down menu.

```
<div><b>Artist:</b>

<p><input type="radio" name="artist"
→ value="existing" <?php if
→ (isset($_POST['artist']) &&
→ ($_POST['artist'] == 'existing') )
→ echo ' checked="checked"'; ?>/>
→ Existing =>
     <select
     → name="existing"><option>Select
     → One</option>
```

The artist pull-down menu will be dynamically generated (**Figure 17.14**) from the records stored in the *artists* table using this PHP code. It's prefaced by a radio button so that the administrator can select an existing artist or enter a new one (see Step 18).

Complicating things a bit, to make this form sticky, the radio buttons have to check to see if $_POST['artist'] is set (because it won't be the first time the page is loaded) and if its value equals *existing*. If both conditions are true, the code checked="checked" is added to the HTML to pre-check this button.

continues on next page

Figure 17.13 The sticky form uses htmlspecialchars() to encode some characters, like quotation marks, that could be used in form values. If this function wasn't invoked, such characters would otherwise make a mess of things when placed in the input's value attribute.

```
         <div><b>Artist:</b>
         <p><input type="radio" name="artist" value="existing" /> Existing =>
         <select name="existing"><option>Select One</option>
         <option value="1">Sandro Botticelli</option>
<option value="3">Claude Monet</option>
         </select></p>

         <p><input type="radio" name="artist" value="new" /> New =>
         First Name: <input type="text" name="first_name" size="10" maxlength="20" value="" />
         Middle Name: <input type="text" name="middle_name" size="10" maxlength="20" value="" />
         Last Name: <input type="text" name="last_name" size="10" maxlength="40" value="" /></p>
         </div>
```

Figure 17.14 The PHP-generated HTML source code for the artists portion of the form.

17. Retrieve every artist.

```php
<?php

$q = "SELECT artist_id, CONCAT_WS
→ (' ', first_name, middle_name,
→ last_name) FROM artists ORDER BY
→ last_name, first_name ASC";

$r = mysqli_query ($dbc, $q);

if (mysqli_num_rows($r) > 0) {

    while ($row = mysqli_fetch_array
    → ($r, MYSQLI_NUM)) {

        echo "<option
        → value=\"$row[0]\"";

        if (isset($_POST['existing'])
        → && ($_POST['existing'] ==
        → $row[0]) ) echo '
        → selected="selected"';

            echo
            → ">$row[1]</option>\n";

    }

} else {

    echo '<option>Please add a new
    → artist.</option>';

}

mysqli_close($dbc);

?>
```

```
</select></p>
```

This query retrieves every artist's name and ID from the database (it doesn't use prepared statements, as there's really no need). The MySQL CONCAT_WS() function—short for *concatenate with separator*—is used to retrieve the artist's entire name as one value. If you are confused by the query's syntax, run it in the mysql client or other interface to see the results.

The first time the administrator runs this script, there will be no existing artists. In that case, there won't be any options in this pull-down menu, so an indication to add an artist is made (**Figure 17.15**).

This otherwise-basic code is complicated by the desire to make the pull-down menu sticky. To make any select menu sticky, you have to add selected="selected" to the proper option. So the code in the while loop checks if $_POST['existing'] is set and, if so, if its value is the same as the current artist ID being added to the menu.

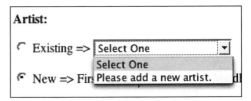

Figure 17.15 Before any artists have been added to the *artists* table, the pull-down menu tells the administrator that they have to add a new artist.

18. Create the inputs for adding a new artist.

```
<p><input type="radio" name="artist"
→ value="new" <?php if
→ (isset($_POST['artist']) &&
→ ($_POST['artist'] == 'new') ) echo '
→ checked="checked"'; ?>/> New =>

First Name: <input type="text"
→ name="first_name" size="10"
→ maxlength="20" value="<?php if
→ (isset($_POST['first_name']))
echo
→ $_POST['first_name']; ?>" />

Middle Name: <input type="text"
→ name="middle_name" size="10"
→ maxlength="20" value="<?php if
→ (isset($_POST['middle_name'])) echo
→ $_POST['middle_name']; ?>" />

Last Name: <input type="text"
→ name="last_name" size="10"
→ maxlength="40" value="<?php if
→ (isset($_POST['last_name'])) echo
→ $_POST['last_name']; ?>" /></p>

</div>
```

Rather than create a separate form for adding artists to the database, the administrator will have the option of doing so directly here. The PHP code that handles the form (described earlier) will create a new database record using the new artist information. Each form element is also made sticky, although not using the htmlspecialchars() function, as these values shouldn't contain problematic characters.

19. Complete the HTML form.

```
<p><b>Price:</b> <input
→ type="text" name="price"
→ size="10" maxlength="10"
→ value="<?php if
→ (isset($_POST['price'])) echo
→ $_POST['price']; ?>" />
→ <small>Do not include the
dollar
→ sign or commas.</small></p>

<p><b>Size:</b> <input
→ type="text" name="size"
→ size="30" maxlength="60"
→ value="<?php if
→ (isset($_POST['size'])) echo
→ htmlspecialchars($_POST['size']
→ ); ?>" /> (optional)</p>

<p><b>Description:</b> <textarea
→ name="description" cols="40"
→ rows="5"><?php if
→ (isset($_POST['description']))
→ echo $_POST['description'];
→ ?></textarea> (optional)</p>

</fieldset>

<div align="center"><input
→ type="submit" name="submit"
→ value="Submit" /></div>

<input type="hidden"
→ name="submitted" value="TRUE" />

</form>
```

20. Complete the HTML page.

```
</body>

</html>
```

21. Save the file as add_print.php.

continues on next page

22. Create the necessary directories on your server.

This administrative page will require the creation of two new directories. One, which I'll call `admin` (see Figure 17.8), will house the administrative files themselves. On a real site, it'd be better to name your administrative directory something less obvious.

The second, `uploads`, should be placed below the Web document directory and have its privileges changed so that PHP can move files into it. See Chapter 10 for more information on this.

23. Place `add_print.php` in your Web directory (in the administration folder) and test it in your Web browser (**Figures 17.16** and **17.17**).

Don't forget that you'll also need to place a `mysqli_connect.php` script, edited to connect to the ecommerce database, in the right directory as well.

✔ Tips

■ This is actually the most complicated script in this entire chapter, if not the book. In part, the complexity arises from the artists option (use an existing one or add a new one). Secondarily, making it a sticky form really adds some code. To simplify this aspect of the application, you could create one form for adding artists to the database and a separate one for adding prints (the separate `add_print.php` page would therefore only allow the selection of an existing artist).

■ Although I did not do so here for the sake of brevity, I would recommend that separate MySQL users be created for the administrative and the public sides. The admin user would need `SELECT`, `INSERT`, `UPDATE`, and `DELETE` privileges, while the public one would need only `SELECT`, `INSERT` and `UPDATE`.

■ The administrative pages should be protected in the most secure way possible. This could entail HTTP authentication using Apache, a login system using sessions or cookies, or even placing the admin pages on another, possibly offline, server (so the site could be managed from just one location).

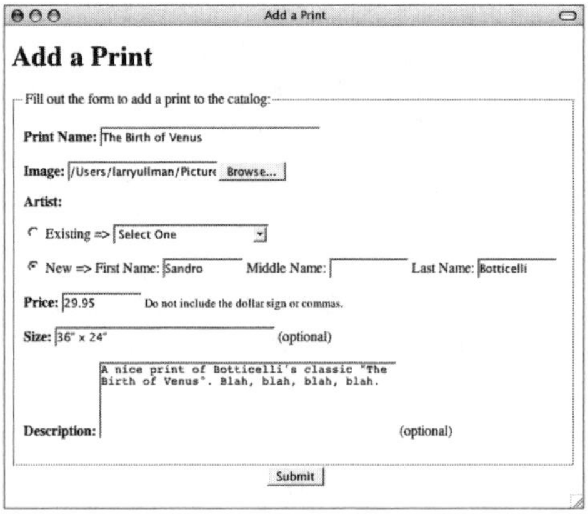

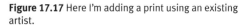

Figure 17.16 In this example, I'm adding a print for a new artist.

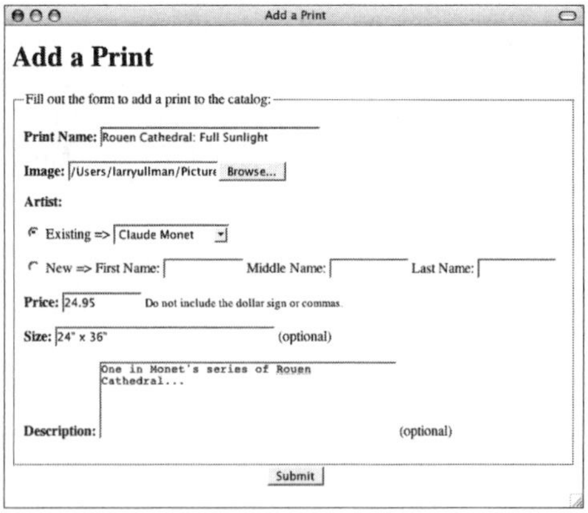

Figure 17.17 Here I'm adding a print using an existing artist.

Creating the Public Template

Before I get into the heart of the public side, I'll need to create the requisite HTML header and footer files. I'll whip through these quickly, since the techniques involved should be familiar territory by this point in the book.

Script 17.2 The header file creates the initial HTML and begins the PHP session.

```
        ⬤ ⬤ ⬤                  📄 Script
1    <?php # Script 17.2 - header.html

2    // This page begins the session, the HTML
     page, and the layout table.

3

4    session_start(); // Start a session.

5    ?><!DOCTYPE html PUBLIC "-//W3C//DTD XHTML
     1.0 Transitional//EN"

6        "http://www.w3.org/TR/xhtml1/DTD/
         xhtml1-transitional.dtd">

7    <html xmlns="http://www.w3.org/1999/xhtml"
     xml:lang="en" lang="en">

8    <head>

9      <meta http-equiv="content-type"
       content="text/html; charset=iso-8859-1" />

10     <title><?php echo (isset($page_title)) ?
       $page_title : 'Welcome!'; ?></title>

11   </head>

12   <body>

13   <table cellspacing="0" cellpadding="0"
     border="0" align="center" width="600">

14     <tr>

15     <td align="center" colspan="3"><img
       src="images/title.jpg" width="600"
       height="61" border="0" alt="title"
       /></td>

16     </tr>

17     <tr>
```

(script continues on next page)

To make header.html:

1. Create a new PHP document in your text editor or IDE (**Script 17.2**).

   ```
   <?php # Script 17.2 - header.html
   ```

2. Begin the session.

   ```
   session_start();
   ```

   It's very important that the user's session be maintained across every page, so I'll start the session in the header file. If the session was lost on a single page, then a new session would begin on subsequent pages, and the user's history—the contents of the shopping cart—would be gone.

3. Create the HTML head.

   ```
   ?><!DOCTYPE html PUBLIC "-//W3C//DTD
   → XHTML 1.0 Transitional//EN"
   "http://www.w3.org/TR/xhtml1/DTD/
   → xhtml1-transitional.dtd">
   <html
   → xmlns="http://www.w3.org/1999/xhtml"
   → xml:lang="en" lang="en">
   <head>
       <meta http-equiv="content-type"
       → content="text/html;
       → charset=iso-8859-1" />
       <title><?php echo
       → (isset($page_title)) ?
       → $page_title : 'Welcome!';
       → ?></title>
   </head>
   ```

   As with all the other versions of this script, the page's title will be set as a PHP variable and printed out within the title tags. In case it's not set before this page is included, a default title is also provided.

continues on next page

4. Create the top row of the table.

```
<body>
<table cellspacing="0"
→ cellpadding="0" border="0"
→ align="center" width="600">

    <tr>

    <td align="center"
    → colspan="3"><img
    → src="images/title.jpg"
    → width="600" height="61"
    → border="0" alt="title" /></td>

    </tr>

    <tr>

    <td><a href="index.php"><img
    → src="images/home.jpg"
    → width="200" height="39"
    → border="0" alt="home page"
    → /></a></td>

    <td><a href="browse_prints.php">
    → <img src="images/prints.jpg"
    → width="200" height="39"
    → border="0" alt="view the
    → prints" /></a></td>

    <td><a href="view_cart.php"><img
    → src="images/cart.jpg"
    → width="200" height="39"
    → border="0" alt="view your cart"
    → /></a></td>

    </tr>

    <tr>

    <td align="left" colspan="3"
    → bgcolor="#ffffcc"><br />
```

This layout will use images to create the links for the public pages (**Figure 17.18**).

Script 17.2 *continued*

```
18    <td><a href="index.php"><img
      src="images/home.jpg" width="200"
      height="39" border="0" alt="home page"
      /></a></td>

19    <td><a href="browse_prints.php"><img
      src="images/prints.jpg" width="200"
      height="39" border="0" alt="view the
      prints" /></a></td>

20    <td><a href="view_cart.php"><img
      src="images/cart.jpg" width="200"
      height="39" border="0" alt="view your
      cart" /></a></td>

21    </tr>

22    <tr>

23    <td align="left" colspan="3"
      bgcolor="#ffffcc"><br />
```

Figure 17.18 The banner created by the header file.

Script 17.3 The footer file closes the HTML, creating a copyright message in the process.

```
         Script
1    <!-- Script 17.3 - footer.html -->

2    <br /></td>

3    </tr>

4    <tr>

5    <td align="center" colspan="3"
     bgcolor="#669966"><font
     color="#ffffff">&copy;
     Copyright...</font></td>

6    </tr>

7    </table>

8    </body>

9    </html>
```

5. Start the middle row.

```
<tr>
    <td align="left" colspan="3"
    → bgcolor="#ffffcc"><br />
```

All of each individual page's content will go in the middle row, so the header file begins this row and the footer file will close it.

6. Save the file as `header.html` and place it in your Web directory (create an `includes` folder in which to store it).

To make footer.html:

1. Create a new HTML document in your text editor or IDE (**Script 17.3**).

```
<!-- Script 17.3 - footer.html -->
```

2. Complete the middle row, create the bottom row, and complete the HTML (**Figure 17.19**).

```
        <br /></td>
    </tr>
    <tr>
    <td align="center" colspan="3"
    → bgcolor="#669966"><font
    → color="#ffffff">&copy;
    → Copyright...</font></td>
    </tr>
</table>
</body>
</html>
```

3. Save the file as `footer.html` and place it in your Web directory (also in the `includes` folder).

Figure 17.19 The copyright row created by the footer file.

To make index.php:

1. Create a new PHP document in your text editor or IDE (**Script 17.4**).

   ```php
   <?php # Script 17.4 - index.php

   $page_title = 'Make an Impression!';

   include ('includes/header.html');

   ?>
   ```

2. Create the page's content.

   ```
   <p>Welcome to our site....please use
   → the links above...blah, blah,
   → blah.</p>
   ```

   ```
   <p>Welcome to our site....please use
   → the links above...blah, blah,
   → blah.</p>
   ```

   Obviously a real e-commerce site would have some actual content on the main page. You could put lists of recently added items here (if you added a *date_entered* column to the *prints* table), highlight specials, or do whatever.

3. Complete the HTML page.

   ```php
   <?php

   include ('includes/footer.html');

   ?>
   ```

4. Save the file as index.php, place it in your Web directory, and test it in your Web browser (**Figure 17.20**).

Figure 17.20 The public home page for the e-commerce site.

✔ Tips

- The images used in this example are available for download through the book's companion Web site: www.DMCInsights.com/phpmysql3/.

  See the Extras page.

- Since sessions are key to the functionality of this application, review the information presented in Chapter 11, "Cookies and Sessions," or in the PHP manual to understand all of the session considerations.

Script 17.4 A minimal script for the site's home page.

```
1    <?php # Script 17.4 - index.php

2    // This is the main page for the site.

3

4    // Set the page title and include the HTML
     header:

5    $page_title = 'Make an Impression!';

6    include ('includes/header.html');

7    ?>

8

9    <p>Welcome to our site....please use the
     links above...blah, blah, blah.</p>

10   <p>Welcome to our site....please use the
     links above...blah, blah, blah.</p>

11

12   <?php // Include the HTML footer file:

13   include ('includes/footer.html');

14   ?>
```

Figure 17.21 The current product listing, created by browse_prints.php.

Figure 17.22 If a particular artist is selected (by clicking on the artist's name), the page displays works only by that artist.

The Product Catalog

For customers to be able to purchase products, they'll need to view them first. To this end, I'll create two scripts for accessing the product catalog. The first, browse_prints.php, will display a list of the available prints (**Figure 17.21**). If a particular artist has been selected, only that artist's work will be shown (**Figure 17.22**); otherwise, every print will be listed.

The second script, view_print.php, will be used to display the information for a single print, including the image (**Figure 17.23**). On this page customers will find an *Add to Cart* link, so that the print may be added to the shopping cart. Because the print's image is stored outside of the Web root directory, view_print.php will use a separate script—nearly identical to show_image.php from Chapter 10—for the purpose of displaying the image.

Figure 17.23 The page that displays an individual product.

To make browse_prints.php:

1. Create a new PHP document in your text editor or IDE (**Script 17.5**).

```
<?php # Script 17.5 -
→ browse_prints.php

$page_title = 'Browse the Prints';

include ('includes/header.html');

require_once
→ ('../mysqli_connect.php');
```

2. Define the query.

```
$q = "SELECT artists.artist_id,
→ CONCAT_WS(' ', first_name,
→ middle_name, last_name) AS artist,
→ print_name, price, description,
→ print_id FROM artists, prints
WHERE
→ artists.artist_id =
→ prints.artist_id ORDER BY
→ artists.last_name ASC,
→ prints.print_name ASC";
```

The query is a standard join across the *artists* and *prints* tables (to retrieve the artist name information with each print's information). The first time the page is viewed, every print by every artist will be returned (**Figure 17.24**).

3. Check for an artist ID in the URL.

```
if (isset($_GET['aid']) &&
→ is_numeric($_GET['aid'])) ) {

    $aid = (int) $_GET['aid'];

    if ($aid > 0) {

        $q = "SELECT artists.artist_id,
        → CONCAT_WS(' ', first_name,
        → middle_name, last_name) AS
        → artist, print_name, price,
        → description, print_id FROM
        → artists, prints WHERE
        → artists.artist_id =
        → prints.artist_id AND
        → prints.artist_id = $aid ORDER
        → BY prints.print_name";
```

Script 17.5 The `browse_prints.php` script displays every print in the catalog or every print for a particular artist, depending upon the presence of `$_GET['aid']`.

```
1    <?php # Script 17.5 - browse_prints.php
2    // This page displays the available prints
     (products).
3
4    // Set the page title and include the HTML
     header:
5    $page_title = 'Browse the Prints';
6    include ('includes/header.html');
7
8    require_once ('../mysqli_connect.php');
9
10   // Default query for this page:
11   $q = "SELECT artists.artist_id,
     CONCAT_WS(' ', first_name, middle_name,
     last_name) AS artist, print_name, price,
     description, print_id FROM artists, prints
     WHERE artists.artist_id = prints.artist_id
     ORDER BY artists.last_name ASC,
     prints.print_name ASC";
12
13   // Are we looking at a particular artist?
14   if (isset($_GET['aid']) &&
     is_numeric($_GET['aid'])) ) {
15       $aid = (int) $_GET['aid'];
16       if ($aid > 0) { // Overwrite the query:
17           $q = "SELECT artists.artist_id,
             CONCAT_WS(' ', first_name,
             middle_name, last_name) AS artist,
             print_name, price, description,
             print_id FROM artists, prints WHERE
             artists.artist_id = prints.artist_id
             AND prints.artist_id = $aid ORDER BY
             prints.print_name";
18       }
19   }
20
21   // Create the table head:
22   echo '<table border="0" width="90%"
     cellspacing="3" cellpadding="3"
     align="center">
```

(script continues on next page)

THE PRODUCT CATALOG

Script 17.5 *continued*

```
23    <tr>

24    <td align="left"
      width="20%"><b>Artist</b></td>

25    <td align="left" width="20%"><b>Print
      Name</b></td>

26    <td align="left"
      width="40%"><b>Description</b></td>

27    <td align="right"
      width="20%"><b>Price</b></td>

28    </tr>';

29

30    // Display all the prints, linked to URLs:

31    $r = mysqli_query ($dbc, $q);

32    while ($row = mysqli_fetch_array ($r,
      MYSQLI_ASSOC)) {

33

34      // Display each record:

35      echo "\t<tr>

36      <td align=\"left\"><a
        href=\"browse_prints.php?aid={$row
        ['artist_id']}\">{$row['artist']}</a></td>

37      <td align=\"left\"><a
        href=\"view_print.php?pid={$row
        ['print_id']}\">{$row['print_name']}</a></td>

38      <td
        align=\"left\">{$row['description']}</td>

39      <td
        align=\"right\">\${$row['price']}</td>

40      </tr>\n";

41

42    } // End of while loop.

43

44    echo '</table>';

45    mysqli_close($dbc);

46    include ('includes/footer.html');

47    ?>
```

```
      }

    }
```

If a user clicks one artist's name, the user will be returned back to this page, but now the URL will be, for example, *browse_prints.php?aid=529*. In that case, the query is redefined, adding the clause `AND prints.artist_id = $aid`, so just that artist's works are displayed (and the `ORDER BY` is slightly modified). So the two different roles of this script—showing every print or just those for an individual artist—are handled by variations on the same query, while the rest of the script works the same in either case.

For security purposes, I use typecasting on the artist ID and make sure that it's a positive integer prior to using it in a query.

continues on next page

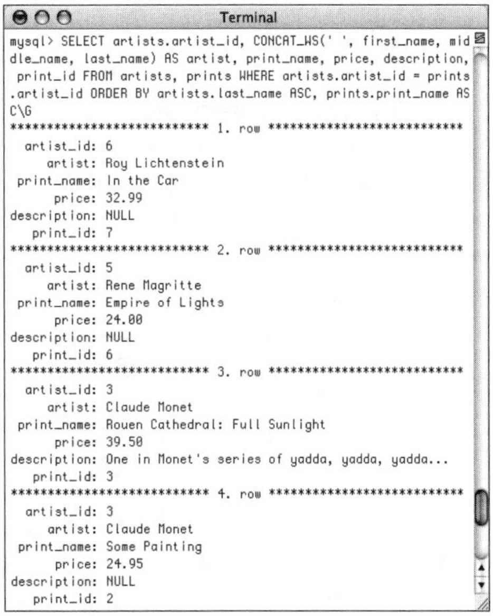

Figure 17.24 The results after running the main `browse_prints.php` query in the mysql client. Remember that running a PHP script's query in another interface is one of the best debugging tools!

4. Create the table head.

```
echo '<table border="0" width="90%"
→ cellspacing="3" cellpadding="3"
→ align="center">

    <tr>

    <td align="left"
→ width="20%"><b>Artist</b></td>

    <td align="left"
→ width="20%"><b>Print
→ Name</b></td>

    <td align="left"
→ width="40%"><b>Description</b>
→ </td>

    <td align="right"
→ width="20%"><b>Price</b></td>

    </tr>';
```

5. Display every returned record.

```
$r = mysqli_query ($dbc, $q);

while ($row = mysqli_fetch_array ($r,
→ MYSQLI_ASSOC)) {

    echo "\t<tr>

    <td align=\"left\"><a
→ href=\"browse_prints.php?aid=
→ {$row['artist_id']}\">{$row
→ ['artist']}</a></td>
```

```
    <td align=\"left\"><a
→ href=\"view_print.php?pid={$row
→ ['print_id']}\">{$row['print_
→ name']}</td>

    <td
→ align=\"left\">{$row
→ ['description']}</td>

    <td
→ align=\"right\">\${$row
→ ['price']}</td>

    </tr>\n";

} // End of while loop.
```

I want the page to display the artist's full name, the print name, the description, and the price for each returned record. Further, the artist's name should be linked back to this page (with the artist's ID appended to the URL), and the print name should be linked to view_print.php (with the print ID appended to the URL).

Figure 17.25 shows some of the resulting HTML source code.

This code doesn't include a call to mysqli_num_rows(), to confirm that some results were returned prior to fetching them, but you could add that in a live version, just to be safe.

```
</tr>   <tr>
        <td align="left"><a href="browse_prints.php?aid=6">Roy Lichtenstein</a></td>
        <td align="left"><a href="view_print.php?pid=7">In the Car</td>
        <td align="left"></td>
        <td align="right">$32.99</td>
</tr>
<tr>
        <td align="left"><a href="browse_prints.php?aid=5">Rene Magritte</a></td>
        <td align="left"><a href="view_print.php?pid=6">Empire of Lights</td>
        <td align="left"></td>
        <td align="right">$24.00</td>
</tr>
<tr>
        <td align="left"><a href="browse_prints.php?aid=3">Claude Monet</a></td>
        <td align="left"><a href="view_print.php?pid=3">Rouen Cathedral: Full Sunlight</td>
        <td align="left">One in Monet's series of yadda, yadda, yadda...</td>
        <td align="right">$39.50</td>
</tr>
```

Figure 17.25 The source code for the page reveals how the artist and print IDs are appended to the links.

Script 17.6 The `view_print.php` script shows the details for a particular print. It also includes a link to add the product to the customer's shopping cart.

```
1    <?php # Script 17.6 - view_print.php
2    // This page displays the details for a
     particular print.
3
4    $row = FALSE; // Assume nothing!
5
6    if (isset($_GET['pid']) &&
     is_numeric($_GET['pid']) ) { // Make sure
     there's a print ID!
7
8        $pid = (int) $_GET['pid'];
9
10       // Get the print info:
11       require_once ('../mysqli_connect.php');
12       $q = "SELECT CONCAT_WS(' ', first_name,
         middle_name, last_name) AS artist,
         print_name, price, description, size,
         image_name FROM artists, prints WHERE
         artists.artist_id = prints.artist_id AND
         prints.print_id = $pid";
13       $r = mysqli_query ($dbc, $q);
14       if (mysqli_num_rows($r) == 1) { // Good
         to go!
15
16           // Fetch the information:
17           $row = mysqli_fetch_array ($r,
             MYSQLI_ASSOC);
18
19           // Start the HTML page:
20           $page_title = $row['print_name'];
21           include ('includes/header.html');
22
23           // Display a header:
24           echo "<div align=\"center\">
25           <b>{$row['print_name']}</b> by
```

(script continues on next page)

6. Close the table, the database connection, and the HTML page.

```
echo '</table>';
mysqli_close($dbc);
include ('includes/footer.html');
?>
```

7. Save the file as `browse_prints.php`, place it in your Web directory, and test it in your Web browser (Figures 17.21 and 17.22).

✔ Tips

- You could easily take the dynamically generated pull-down menu from `add_print.php` and use it as a navigational tool on the public side. Set the form's action attribute to `browse_print.php`, change the name of the pull-down menu to *aid*, use the `get` method, and when users select an artist and click Submit, they'll be taken to, for example, *browse_print.php?aid=5*.

- Although I did not do so here, you could paginate the returned results using the technique described in Chapter 9 (see the `view_users.php` script).

- Another feature you could add to this page is the option to choose how the prints are displayed. By adding links to the column headings (e.g., to *browse_prints.php?order=price*), you could change the `ORDER BY` in the query and therefore the resulting display. Again, this idea was demonstrated in Chapter 9.

To make view_print.php:

1. Create a new PHP document in your text editor or IDE (**Script 17.6**).

```
<?php # Script 17.6 - view_print.php
$row = FALSE;
```

continues on next page

I'll use the $row variable to track whether or not a problem occurred on this page. This variable, if everything went right, will store the print information from the database. If a problem occurred, then, at the end of the script, $row will still be false, and the page should indicate an error.

2. Validate that a print ID has been passed to this page.

```
if (isset($_GET['pid']) &&
→ is_numeric($_GET['pid']) ) {
```

This script won't work if it does not receive a valid print ID, so check for a numeric ID's existence first.

3. Retrieve the information from the database.

```
$pid = (int) $_GET['pid'];

require_once
→ ('../mysqli_connect.php');

$q = "SELECT CONCAT_WS(' ',
→ first_name, middle_name, last_name)
→ AS artist, print_name, price,
→ description, size, image_name FROM
→ artists, prints WHERE
→ artists.artist_id = prints.artist_id
→ AND prints.print_id = $pid";

$r = mysqli_query ($dbc, $q);
```

The query is a join like the one in browse_prints.php, but it selects only the information for a particular print (**Figure 17.26**). The print ID is typecast as an integer prior to using it in the query for security purposes (so that a malicious user doesn't try to break the query using invalid $_GET['pid'] values).

Script 17.6 *continued*

```
26        {$row['artist']}<br />";

27

28        // Print the size or a default
          message:

29        echo (is_null($row['size'])) ? '(No
          size information available)' :
          $row['size'];

30

31        echo "<br />\${$row['price']}

32        <a
          href=\"add_cart.php?pid=$pid\">Add
          to Cart</a>

33        </div><br />";

34

35        // Get the image information and
          display the image:

36        if ($image = @getimagesize
          ("../uploads/$pid")) {

37            echo "<div align=\"center\"><img
              src=\"show_image.php?image=$pid&na
              me=" .
              urlencode($row['image_name']) .
              "\" $image[3]
              alt=\"{$row['print_name']}\"
              /></div>\n";

38        } else {

39            echo "<div align=\"center\">No
              image available.</div>\n";

40        }

41

42        // Add the description or a default
          message:

43        echo '<p align="center">' .
          ((is_null($row['description'])) ?
          '(No description available)' :
          $row['description']) . '</p>';

44

45    } // End of the mysqli_num_rows() IF.

46

47    mysqli_close($dbc);
```

(script continues on next page)

Script 17.6 *continued*

```
48
49   }
50
51   if (!$row) { // Show an error message.
52     $page_title = 'Error';
53     include ('includes/header.html');
54     echo '<div align="center">This page has
         been accessed in error!</div>';
55   }
56
57   // Complete the page:
58   include ('includes/footer.html');
59   ?>
```

4. If a record was returned, retrieve the information, set the page title, and include the HTML header.

```
if (mysqli_num_rows($r) == 1) {
    $row = mysqli_fetch_array ($r,
    → MYSQLI_ASSOC);
    $page_title = $row['print_name'];
    include ('includes/header.html');
```

The browser window's title (**Figure 17.27**) will be the name of the print.

continues on next page

```
● ○ ○                          Terminal
mysql> SELECT CONCAT_WS(' ', first_name, middle_name, last_name) AS artist, print_name, price, description,
size, image_name FROM artists, prints WHERE artists.artist_id = prints.artist_id AND prints.print_id = 4\G
*************************** 1. row ***************************
      artist: Georges-Pierre Seurat
  print_name: Sunday Afternoon on the Island of La Grande Jatte
       price: 37.50
 description: One of the most famous painting's in the world and the best example of pointillism...
        size: 40" by 30"
  image_name: C50741big.jpg
1 row in set (0.01 sec)

mysql>
```

Figure 17.26 The results after running the view_print.php query in the mysql client.

Figure 17.27 The browser page title will be the name of the print being viewed (like *The Birth of Venus* here).

5. Begin displaying the print information.

```
echo "<div align=\"center\">
<b>{$row['print_name']}</b> by
{$row['artist']}<br />";
echo (is_null($row['size'])) ? '(No
→ size information available)' :
→ $row['size'];
echo "<br />\${$row['price']}
<a href=\"add_cart.php?pid=$pid\">Add
→ to Cart</a>
</div><br />";
```

The header for the print will be the print's name (in bold), followed by the artist's name, the size of the print, and its price. Finally, a link is displayed giving the customer the option of adding this print to the shopping cart (**Figure 17.28**). The shopping cart link is to the add_cart.php script, passing it the print ID.

Because the print's size can have a NULL value, the ternary operator is used to print out either the size or a default message.

6. Display the image and description.

```
if ($image = @getimagesize
→ ("../uploads/$pid")) {
    echo "<div align=\"center\"><img
    → src=\"show_image.php?image=
    → $pid&name=" .
    → urlencode($row['image_name']) .
    → "\" $image[3]
    → alt=\"{$row['print_name']}\"
    → /></div>\n";
} else {
```

```
echo "<div align=\"center\">No
→ image available.</div>\n";
}
echo '<p align="center">' .
→ ((is_null($row['description'])) ?
→ '(No description available)' :
→ $row['description']) . '</p>';
```

This section of the script will first attempt to retrieve the image's dimensions by using the getimagesize() function. If it is successful in doing so, the image itself will be displayed. That process is a little unusual in that the source for the image calls the show_image.php page (**Figure 17.29**). This script, to be written next, expects the print ID to be passed in the URL, along with the image's filename (stored in the database when the print is added). This use of a PHP script to display an image is exactly like the use of show_image.php in Chapter 10, only now it's occurring within another page, not in its own window.

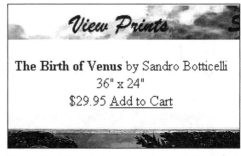

Figure 17.28 The print information and a link to buy it are displayed at the top of the page.

```
<b>The Birth of Venus</b> by
Sandro Botticelli<br />36" x 24"<br />$29.95
<a href="add_cart.php?pid=1">Add to Cart</a>
</div><br /><div align="center"><img src="show_image.php?image=1&name=BirthOfVenus.jpeg" width="366" height="240" alt="The Birth of Venus" />
="center">A nice print of Botticelli's classic "The Birth of Venus". Blah, blah, blah, blah.</p><!-- Script 17.3 - footer.html -->
        <br /></td>
```

Figure 17.29 The HTML source of the view_print.php page shows how the *src* attribute of the img tag calls the show_image.php script, passing it the values it needs.

If the script could not retrieve the image information (because the image is not on the server or no image was uploaded), a message is displayed instead.

Finally, the print's description is added (**Figure 17.30**). A default message will be printed if no print description was stored in the database.

7. Complete the two main conditionals.

```
} // End of the mysqli_num_rows()
→ IF.
mysqli_close($dbc);
}
```

A nice print of Botticelli's classic "The Birth of Venus". Blah, blah, blah, blah.

Figure 17.30 The print's image followed by its description.

Figure 17.31 The view_print.php page, should it not receive a valid print ID in the URL.

8. If a problem occurred, display an error message,

```
if (!$row) {
    $page_title = 'Error';
    include
('includes/header.html');
        echo '<div align="center">This
→ page has been accessed in
→ error!</div>';
}
```

If the print's information could not be retrieved from the database for whatever reason, then $row is still false and an error should be displayed (**Figure 17.31**). Because the HTML header would not have already been included if a problem occurred, it must be included here first.

9. Complete the page.

```
include ('includes/footer.html');
?>
```

10. Save the file as view_print.php and place it in your Web directory.

✔ Tips

- Many e-commerce sites use an image for the *Add to Cart* link. To do so in this example, replace the text *Add to Cart* (within the <a> link tag) with the code for the image to be used. The important consideration is that the add_cart.php page still gets passed the product ID number.

- If you wanted to add *Add to Cart* links on a page that displays multiple products (like browse_prints.php), do exactly what's done here for individual products. Just make sure that each link passes the right print ID to the add_cart.php page.

- If you want to show the availability of a product, add an *in_stock* field to the *prints* table. Then display an *Add to Cart* link or *Product Currently Out of Stock* message according to the value in this column for that print.

To write show_image.php:

1. Create a new PHP document in your text editor or IDE (**Script 17.7**).

   ```php
   <?php # Script 17.7 - show_image.php

   $image = FALSE;

   $name = (!empty($_GET['name'])) ?
   → $_GET['name'] : 'print image';
   ```

   This script will do the same thing as show_image.php from Chapter 10, except that there are two values being passed to this page. The actual image's filename on the server will be a number, corresponding to the print ID. The original image's filename was stored in the database and will be used when sending the image to the Web browser. This page will not contain any HTML, and nothing can be sent to the Web browser prior to this opening PHP tag.

   Two flag variables are initialized here. The first, $image, will refer to the physical image on the server. It's assumed to be false and needs to be proven otherwise. The $name variable, which will be the name of the file provided to the Web browser, should come from the URL. If not, a default value is assigned.

2. Check for an image value in the URL.

   ```php
   if (isset($_GET['image']) &&
   → is_numeric($_GET['image']) ) {
   ```

   Before continuing, ensure that the script received an image value, which should be part of the HTML *src* attribute for each print (see Figure 17.29) in view_print.php.

Script 17.7 This script is called by view_print.php (Script 17.6) and displays the image stored in the uploads directory.

```php
1   <?php # Script 17.7 - show_image.php
2   // This pages retrieves and shows an
    image.
3
4   // Flag variables:
5   $image = FALSE;
6   $name = (!empty($_GET['name'])) ?
    $_GET['name'] : 'print image';
7
8   // Check for an image value in the URL:
9   if (isset($_GET['image']) &&
    is_numeric($_GET['image']) ) {
10
11      // Full image path:
12      $image = '../uploads/' . (int)
        $_GET['image'];
13
14      // Check that the image exists and is a
        file:
15      if (!file_exists ($image) ||
        (!is_file($image))) {
16          $image = FALSE;
17      }
18
19  }
20
21  // If there was a problem, use the default
    image:
22  if (!$image) {
23      $image = 'images/unavailable.png';
24      $name = 'unavailable.png';
25  }
26
```

(script continues on next page)

Script 17.7 *continued*

```
        📄 Script

27    // Get the image information:

28    $info = getimagesize($image);

29    $fs = filesize($image);

30

31    // Send the content information:

32    header ("Content-Type:
      {$info['mime']}\n");

33    header ("Content-Disposition: inline;
      filename=\"$name\"\n");

34    header ("Content-Length: $fs\n");

35

36    // Send the file:

37    readfile ($image);

38

39    ?>
```

Figure 17.32 If show_image.php cannot access a valid print image, this default image will be displayed.

3. Check that the image is a file on the server.

```
$image = '../uploads/' . (int)
→ $_GET['image'];

if (!file_exists ($image) ||
→ (!is_file($image))) {

    $image = FALSE;

}
```

As a security measure, I hard-code the image's full path as a combination of *../uploads* and the received image name. As the name of the file on the server is an integer, it's typecast for extra security. You could also validate the MIME type (*image/jpg, image/gif*) of the file here.

Next, the script checks that the image exists on the server and that it is a file (as opposed to a directory). If either condition is false, then $image is set to FALSE, indicating a problem.

4. Complete the validation conditional and check for a problem.

```
}

if (!$image) {

    $image =
    → 'images/unavailable.png';

    $name = 'unavailable.png';

}
```

If the image doesn't exist or isn't a file, this conditional applies. If no image name was passed to this script, the second else clause applies. In either case, a default image will be used (**Figure 17.32**).

5. Retrieve the image information.

```
$info = getimagesize($image);

$fs = filesize($image);
```

To send the file to the Web browser, the scripts needs to know the file's type and size. This code is the same as in Chapter 10.

continues on next page

THE PRODUCT CATALOG

6. Send the file.

```
header ("Content-Type:
→ {$info['mime']}\n");

header ("Content-Disposition: inline;
→ filename=\"$name\"\n");

header ("Content-Length: $fs\n");

readfile ($image);
```

These `header()` calls will send the file data to the Web browser, exactly as they did in Chapter 10. To revisit the overall syntax, the first line prepares the browser to receive the file, based upon the MIME type. The second line sets the name of the file being sent.

The last `header()` function indicates how much data is to be expected. The file data itself is sent using the `readfile()` function, which reads in a file and immediately sends the content to the Web browser.

7. Complete the page.

```
?>
```

Notice that this page contains no HTML. It only sends an image file to the Web browser.

8. Save the file as `show_image.php`, place it in your Web directory, and test it in your Web browser by viewing any print (**Figure 17.33**).

✔ Tips

- The end user is unlikely to see results like those in Figure 17.32 unless there's a problem with your scripts or they're doing some serious hacking. The `view_print.php` script does some preliminary verification of the image, only calling `show_image.php` if it can access the image.

- If the `view_print.php` page does not show the image for some reason, you'll need to debug the problem by running the `show_image.php` directly in your Web browser. View the HTML source of `view_print.php` and find the value of the `img` tag's *src* attribute. Then use this as your URL (in other words, go to `http://www.example.com/show_image.php?image=23&name=BirthOfVenus.jpeg`). If an error occurred, running `show_image.php` directly is the best way to find it.

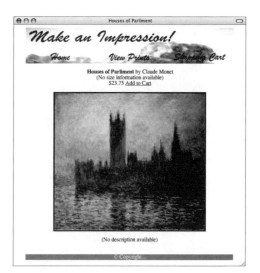

Figure 17.33 The `view_print.php` page, where the print's image is retrieved and shown thanks to `show_image.php`.

Table 17.6 The $_SESSION['cart'] variable will be a multidimensional array. Each array element will use the print ID for its index. Each array value will be another array of two elements: the quantity of that print ordered and the price of that print.

Sample $_SESSION['cart'] Values

(INDEX)	QUANTITY	PRICE
2	1	54.00
568	2	22.95
37	1	33.50

Script 17.8 This script adds products to the shopping cart by referencing the product (or print) ID and manipulating the session data.

```
1    <?php # Script 17.8 - add_cart.php

2    // This page adds prints to the shopping
     cart.

3

4    // Set the page title and include the HTML
     header:

5    $page_title = 'Add to Cart';

6    include ('includes/header.html');

7

8    if (isset ($_GET['pid']) &&
     is_numeric($_GET['pid']) ) { // Check for
     a print ID.

9

10       $pid = (int) $_GET['pid'];

11

12       // Check if the cart already contains
         one of these prints;

13       // If so, increment the quantity:

14       if (isset($_SESSION['cart'][$pid])) {

15

16           $_SESSION['cart'][$pid]['quantity']
             ++; // Add another.

17
```

(script continues on next page)

The Shopping Cart

Once you have created a product catalog, as the preceding pages do, the actual shopping cart itself can be surprisingly simple. The method I've chosen to use in this example is to record the product IDs, prices, and quantities in a session. Knowing these three things will allow the scripts to calculate totals and do everything else required.

These next two examples will provide all the necessary functionality for the shopping cart. The first script, add_cart.php, will add items to the shopping cart. The second, view_cart.php, will both display the contents of the cart and allow the customer to update it.

Adding items

The add_cart.php script will take one argument—the ID of the print being purchased—and will use this to update the cart. The cart itself is stored in a session; it'll be accessed through the $_SESSION['cart'] variable. The cart will be a multidimensional array whose keys will be product IDs. The values of the array elements will themselves be arrays: one element for the quantity and another for the price (**Table 17.6**).

To create add_cart.php:

1. Create a new PHP document in your text editor or IDE (**Script 17.8**).

   ```
   <?php # Script 17.8 - add_cart.php
   ```

2. Include the page header and check that a print was selected.

   ```
   $page_title = 'Add to Cart';

   include ('includes/header.html');

   if (isset ($_GET['pid']) &&
   → is_numeric($_GET['pid']) ) {
   ```

   As with the view_print.php script, I do not want to proceed with this script if no, or a non-numeric, print ID has been received.

continues on next page

3. Determine if a copy of this print had already been added.

```
$pid = (int) $_GET['pid'];

if (isset($_SESSION['cart'][$pid])) {

    $_SESSION['cart'][$pid]
→ ['quantity']++;

    echo '<p>Another copy of the
→ print has been added to your
→ shopping cart.</p>';
```

Before adding the current print to the shopping cart (by setting its quantity to *1*), check if a copy is already in the cart. For example, if the customer selected print #519 and then decided to order another, the cart should now contain two copies of the print. So first check if the cart has a value for the current print ID. If so, the quantity is incremented. The code `$_SESSION['cart'][$pid]` `['quantity']++` is the same as

```
$_SESSION['cart'][$pid]['quantity'] =
→ $_SESSION['cart'][$pid]['quantity']
→ + 1
```

Then, a message is displayed (**Figure 17.34**).

Figure 17.34 The result after clicking an *Add to Cart* link for an item that was already present in the shopping cart.

Script 17.8 *continued*

```
18        // Display a message.
19        echo '<p>Another copy of the
          print has been added to your
          shopping cart.</p>';
20
21   } else { // New product to the cart.
22
23        // Get the print's price from the
          database:
24        require_once
          ('../mysqli_connect.php');
25        $q = "SELECT price FROM prints
          WHERE prints.print_id = $pid";
26        $r = mysqli_query ($dbc, $q);
27        if (mysqli_num_rows($r) == 1) {
          // Valid print ID.
28
29           // Fetch the information.
30           list($price) = mysqli_fetch_array
             ($r, MYSQLI_NUM);
31
32           // Add to the cart:
33           $_SESSION['cart'][$pid] =
             array ('quantity' => 1, 'price'
             => $price);
34
35           // Display a message:
36           echo '<p>The print has been
             added to your shopping
             cart.</p>';
37
38        } else { // Not a valid print ID.
39           echo '<div align="center">This
             page has been accessed in
             error!</div>';
40        }
41
42        mysqli_close($dbc);
```

(script continues on next page)

Script 17.8 *continued*

```
43
44    } // End of
      isset($_SESSION['cart'][$pid]
      conditional.
45
46   } else { // No print ID.
47      echo '<div align="center">This page has
      been accessed in error!</div>';
48   }
49
50   include ('includes/footer.html');
51   ?>
```

Figure 17.35 The result after adding a new item to the shopping cart.

4. Add the new product to the cart.

```
} else { // New product to the cart.

    require_once
→ ('../mysqli_connect.php');

    $q = "SELECT price FROM prints
→ WHERE prints.print_id = $pid";

    $r = mysqli_query ($dbc, $q);

    if (mysqli_num_rows($r) == 1) {

    list($price) = mysqli_fetch_array
→ ($r, MYSQLI_NUM);

    $_SESSION['cart'][$pid] = array
→ ('quantity' => 1, 'price' =>
→ $price);

    echo '<p>The print has been added
→ to your shopping cart.</p>';
```

If the product is not currently in the cart, this else clause comes into play. Here, the print's price is retrieved from the database using the print ID. If the price is successfully retrieved, a new element is added to the $_SESSION['cart'] multidimensional array.

Since each element in $_SESSION['cart'] is itself an array, use the array() function to set the quantity and price. A simple message is then displayed (**Figure 17.35**).

continues on next page

5. Complete the conditionals.

```
    } else {
        echo '<div
        → align="center">This
        → page has been accessed in
        → error!</div>';
    }
    mysqli_close($dbc);

}
} else { // No print ID.
    echo '<div align="center">This
    → page has been accessed in
    → error!</div>';
}
```

The first else applies if no price could be retrieved from the database, meaning that the submitted print ID is invalid. The second else applies if no print ID, or a non-numeric one, is received by this page. In both cases, an error message will be displayed (**Figure 17.36**).

6. Include the HTML footer and complete the PHP page.

```
include ('includes/footer.html');

?>
```

7. Save the file as add_cart.php, place it in your Web directory, and test it in your Web browser (by clicking an *Add to Cart* link).

✔ Tips

■ If you would rather display the contents of the cart after something's been added, you could combine the functionality of this script with that of view_cart.php, written next.

■ Similarly, you could easily copy the technique used in view_print.php to this script so that it would display the details of the product just added. There are any number of variations on this process.

■ The most important thing to store in the cart is the unique product ID and the quantity of that item. Everything else, including the price, can be retrieved from the database. Alternatively, you could retrieve the price, print name, and artist name from the database, and store all that in the cart so that it's easily displayed.

■ The shopping cart is stored in $_SESSION ['cart'], not just $_SESSION. Presumably other information, like the user's ID from the database, would also be stored in $_SESSION.

Figure 17.36 The add_cart.php page will only add an item to the shopping cart if the page received a valid print ID in the URL.

Script 17.9 The `view_cart.php` script both displays the contents of the shopping cart and allows the user to update the cart's contents.

```
Script
1   <?php # Script 17.9 - view_cart.php
2   // This page displays the contents of the
    shopping cart.
3   // This page also lets the user update the
    contents of the cart.
4
5   // Set the page title and include the HTML
    header:
6   $page_title = 'View Your Shopping Cart';
7   include ('./includes/header.html');
8
9   // Check if the form has been submitted
    (to update the cart):
10  if (isset($_POST['submitted'])) {
11
12      // Change any quantities:
13      foreach ($_POST['qty'] as $k => $v) {
14
15          // Must be integers!
16          $pid = (int) $k;
17          $qty = (int) $v;
18
19          if ( $qty == 0 ) { // Delete.
20              unset ($_SESSION['cart'][$pid]);
21          } elseif ( $qty > 0 ) { // Change
            quantity.
22              $_SESSION['cart'][$pid]
                ['quantity'] = $qty;
23          }
24
25      } // End of FOREACH.
26  } // End of SUBMITTED IF.
27
28  // Display the cart if it's not empty...
```

(script continues on next page)

Viewing the shopping cart

The `view_cart.php` script will be more complicated than `add_cart.php` because it serves two purposes. First, it will display the contents of the cart in detail (**Figure 17.37**). Second, it will give the customer the option of updating the cart by changing the quantities of the items therein (or deleting an item by making its quantity 0). To fulfill both roles, I'll display the cart's contents as a form and have the page submit the form back to itself.

Finally, this page will link to a `checkout.php` script, intended as the first step in the checkout process.

To create view_cart.php:

1. Create a new PHP document in your text editor or IDE (**Script 17.9**).

   ```
   <?php # Script 17.9 - view_cart.php
   $page_title = 'View Your Shopping
   → Cart';
   include ('./includes/header.html');
   ```

   continues on next page

Figure 17.37 The shopping cart displayed as a form where the specific quantities can be changed.

2. Update the cart if the form has been submitted.

```
if (isset($_POST['submitted'])) {

    foreach ($_POST['qty'] as $k =>
    → $v) {

    $pid = (int) $k;

    $qty = (int) $v;

    if ( $qty == 0 ) {

        unset
        → ($_SESSION['cart'][$pid]);

    } elseif ( $qty > 0 ) {

        $_SESSION['cart'][$pid]
        → ['quantity'] = $qty;

    }

    } // End of FOREACH.

} // End of SUBMITTED IF.
```

If the form has been submitted, then the script needs to update the shopping cart to reflect the entered quantities. These quantities will come in as an array called $_POST['qty'] whose index is the print ID and whose value is the new quantity (see **Figure 17.38** for the HTML source code of the form). If the new quantity is *0*, then that item should be removed from the cart by unsetting it. If the new quantity is not *0* but is a positive number, then the cart is updated to reflect this.

Script 17.9 *continued*

```
29   if (!empty($_SESSION['cart'])) {

30

31       // Retrieve all of the information for
         the prints in the cart:

32       require_once ('../mysqli_connect.php');

33       $q = "SELECT print_id, CONCAT_WS(' ',
         first_name, middle_name, last_name) AS
         artist, print_name FROM artists, prints
         WHERE artists.artist_id = prints.artist_id
         AND prints.print_id IN (";

34       foreach ($_SESSION['cart'] as $pid =>
         $value) {

35           $q .= $pid . ',';

36       }

37       $q = substr($q, 0, -1) . ') ORDER BY
         artists.last_name ASC';

38       $r = mysqli_query ($dbc, $q);

39

40       // Create a form and a table:

41       echo '<form action="view_cart.php"
         method="post">

42   <table border="0" width="90%"
     cellspacing="3" cellpadding="3"
     align="center">

43       <tr>

44       <td align="left"
         width="30%"><b>Artist</b></td>

45       <td align="left" width="30%"><b>Print
         Name</b></td>
```

(script continues on next page)

```
<tr>
    <td align="left">Sandro Botticelli</td>
    <td align="left">The Birth of Venus</td>
    <td align="right">$29.95</td>
    <td align="center"><input type="text" size="3" name="qty[1]" value="1" /></td>
    <td align="right">$29.95</td>
</tr>
<tr>
    <td align="left">Roy Lichtenstein</td>
    <td align="left">In the Car</td>
    <td align="right">$32.99</td>
    <td align="center"><input type="text" size="3" name="qty[7]" value="2" /></td>
    <td align="right">$65.98</td>
</tr>
<tr>
    <td align="left">Rene Magritte</td>
    <td align="left">Empire of Lights</td>
    <td align="right">$24.00</td>
    <td align="center"><input type="text" size="3" name="qty[6]" value="1" /></td>
    <td align="right">$24.00</td>
</tr>
```

Figure 17.38 The HTML source code of the view shopping cart form shows how the quantity fields reflect both the product ID and the quantity of that print in the cart.

Script 17.9 *continued*

```
46    <td align="right"
      width="10%"><b>Price</b></td>

47    <td align="center"
      width="10%"><b>Qty</b></td>

48    <td align="right" width="10%"><b>Total
      Price</b></td>

49    </tr>

50    ';

51

52    // Print each item...

53    $total = 0; // Total cost of the order.

54    while ($row = mysqli_fetch_array ($r,
      MYSQLI_ASSOC)) {

55

56        // Calculate the total and sub-
          totals.

57        $subtotal =
          $_SESSION['cart'][$row['print_id']]
          ['quantity'] *
          $_SESSION['cart'][$row['print_id']]
          ['price'];

58        $total += $subtotal;

59

60        // Print the row.

61        echo "\t<tr>

62        <td align=\"left\">{$row['artist']}
          </td>

63        <td align=\"left\"
          >{$row['print_name']}</td>

64        <td align=\"right\">\
          ${$_SESSION['cart']
          [$row['print_id']]['price']}</td>

65        <td align=\"center\"><input
          type=\"text\" size=\"3\"
          name=\"qty[{$row['print_id']}]\"
          value=\"{$_SESSION['cart'][$row
          ['print_id']]['quantity']}\" /></td>
```

(script continues on next page)

If the quantity is not a number greater than or equal to *0*, then no change will be made to the cart. This will prevent a user from entering a negative number, creating a negative balance due, and getting a refund.

3. If the cart is not empty, create the query to display its contents.

```
if (!empty($_SESSION['cart'])) {
    require_once
    → ('../mysqli_connect.php');
    $q = "SELECT print_id,
    → CONCAT_WS(' ', first_name,
    → middle_name, last_name) AS
    → artist, print_name FROM
    → artists, prints WHERE
    → artists.artist_id =
    → prints.artist_id AND
    → prints.print_id IN (";
    foreach ($_SESSION['cart'] as
    → $pid => $value) {
        $q .= $pid . ',';
    }
    $q = substr($q, 0, -1) . ') ORDER
    → BY artists.last_name ASC';
    $r = mysqli_query ($dbc, $q);
```

The query is a join similar to one used already in this chapter. It retrieves all the artist and print information for each print in the cart. One addition is the use of the IN SQL clause. Instead of just retrieving the information for one print (as in the view_print.php example), retrieve all the information for every print in the shopping cart. To do so, use a list of print IDs in a query like SELECT… print_id IN (519,42,427)…. I could have also used SELECT… WHERE print_id=519 OR print_id=42 or print_id=427…, but that's unnecessarily long-winded.

continues on next page

575

To generate the IN (519,42,427) part of the query, a for loop adds each print ID plus a comma to $q. To remove the last comma, the substr() function is applied, chopping off the last character.

4. Begin the HTML form and create a table.

```
echo '<form action="view_cart.php"
→ method="post">

<table border="0" width="90%"
→ cellspacing="3" cellpadding="3"
→ align="center">

    <tr>

    <td align="left"
→ width="30%"><b>Artist</b></td>

    <td align="left"
→ width="30%"><b>Print
→ Name</b></td>

    <td align="right"
→ width="10%"><b>Price</b></td>

    <td align="center"
→ width="10%"><b>Qty</b></td>

    <td align="right"
→ width="10%"><b>Total
→ Price</b></td>

    </tr>

';
```

Script 17.9 *continued*

```
000                    Script
66        <td align=\"right\">$" .
          number_format ($subtotal, 2) .
          "</td>

67        </tr>\n";

68

69   } // End of the WHILE loop.

70

71   mysqli_close($dbc); // Close the
     database connection.

72

73   // Print the footer, close the table,
     and the form.

74   echo '<tr>

75   <td colspan="4"
     align="right"><b>Total:</b></td>

76   <td align="right">$' . number_format
     ($total, 2) . '</td>

77   </tr>

78   </table>

79   <div align="center"><input type="submit"
     name="submit" value="Update My Cart"
     /></div>

80   <input type="hidden" name="submitted"
     value="TRUE" />

81   </form><p align="center">Enter a
     quantity of 0 to remove an item.

82   <br /><br /><a
     href="checkout.php">Checkout</a></p>';

83

84   } else {

85      echo '<p>Your cart is currently
        empty.</p>';

86   }

87

88   include ('./includes/footer.html');

89   ?>
```

5. Retrieve the returned records.

```
$total = 0;

while ($row = mysqli_fetch_array ($r,
→ MYSQLI_ASSOC)) {

    $subtotal =
    → $_SESSION['cart'][$row['print_
    → id']]['quantity'] *
    → $_SESSION['cart'][$row['print_
    → id']]['price'];

    $total += $subtotal;
```

When displaying the cart, I will also want to calculate the order total, so I initialize a $total variable first. Then for each returned row (which represents one print), I multiply the price of that item times the quantity to determine the subtotal (the syntax of this is a bit complex because of the multidimensional $_SESSION['cart'] array). This subtotal is added to the $total variable.

6. Print the returned records.

```
echo "\t<tr>

<td
→ align=\"left\">{$row['artist']}
→ </td>

<td align=\"left\">{$row['print_
→ name']}</td>

<td align=\"right\">\${$_SESSION
→ ['cart'][$row['print_id']]
→ ['price']}</td>

<td align=\"center\"><input
→ type=\"text\" size=\"3\"
→ name=\"qty[{$row['print_id']}]\"
→ value=\"{$_SESSION['cart'][$row
→ ['print_id']]['quantity']}\"
→ /></td>

<td align=\"right\">$" .
→ number_format ($subtotal, 2) .
→ "</td>

</tr>\n";

} // End of the WHILE loop.
```

Each record is printed out as a row in the table, with the quantity displayed as a text input type whose value is preset (based upon the quantity value in the session). The subtotal amount (the quantity times the price) for each item is also formatted and printed.

continues on next page

7. Close the database connection, and then complete the table and the form.

```
mysqli_close($dbc);

echo '<tr>
    <td colspan="4"
    → align="right"><b>Total:</b></td
    >
    <td align="right">$' .
    → number_format ($total, 2) .
    → '</td>
</tr>
</table>

<div align="center"><input
→ type="submit" name="submit"
→ value="Update My Cart" /></div>

<input type="hidden" name="submitted"
→ value="TRUE" />

</form><p align="center">Enter a
→ quantity of 0 to remove an item.

<br /><br /><a
→ href="checkout.php">Checkout</a>
→ </p>';
```

The running order total is displayed in the final row of the table, using the `number_format()` function for formatting. The form also provides instructions to the user on how to remove an item, and a link to the checkout page is included.

8. Finish the main conditional and the PHP page.

```
} else {
    echo '<p>Your cart is currently
    → empty.</p>';
}
include ('./includes/footer.html');
?>
```

This `else` clause completes the `if (!empty($_SESSION['cart'])) {` conditional.

9. Save the file as `view_cart.php`, place it in your Web directory, and test it in your Web browser (**Figures 17.39** and **17.40**).

✔ Tips

■ On more complex Web applications, I would be inclined to write a PHP page strictly for the purpose of displaying a cart's contents. Since several pages might want to display that, having that functionality in an includable file would make sense.

■ One aspect of a secure e-commerce application is watching how data is being sent and used. For example, it would be far less secure to place a product's price in the URL, where it could easily be changed.

Figure 17.39 If I make changes to any quantities and click *Update My Cart*, the shopping cart and order total are updated (compare with Figure 17.37).

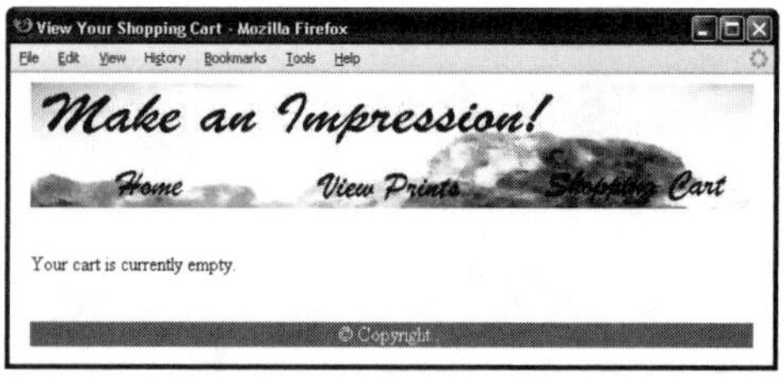

Figure 17.40 I removed everything in the shopping cart by setting the quantities to 0.

Recording the Orders

After displaying all the products as a catalog, and after the user has filled up their shopping cart, there are three final steps:

◆ Checking the user out

◆ Recording the order in the database

◆ Fulfilling the order

Ironically, the most important part—checking out (i.e., taking the customer's money)—could not be adequately demonstrated in a book, as it's so particular to each individual site. So what I've done instead is given an overview of that process in the sidebar.

Similarly, the act of fulfilling the order is beyond the scope of the book. For physical products, this means that the order will need to be packaged and shipped. Then the order in the database would be marked as shipped by indicating the shipping date. This concept shouldn't be too hard for you to implement.

What I can properly show in this chapter is how the order information would be stored in the database. To ensure that the order is completely and correctly entered into both the *orders* and *order_contents* tables, I'll use transactions. This subject was introduced in Chapter 6, using the mysql client. Here the transactions will be performed through a PHP script. For added security and performance, this script will also make use of prepared statements, discussed in Chapter 12.

This script, `checkout.php`, represents the final step the customer would see in the e-commerce process. Because the steps that would precede this script have been skipped in this book, a little doctoring of the process is required.

To create submit_order.php:

1. Create a new PHP document in your text editor or IDE (**Script 17.10**).

   ```
   <?php # Script 17.10 - checkout.php
   $page_title = 'Order Confirmation';
   include ('./includes/header.html');
   ```

2. Create two temporary variables.

   ```
   $customer = 1;
   $total = 178.93;
   ```

   To enter the orders into the database, this page needs two additional pieces of information: the customer's identification number (which is the *customer_id* from the *customers* table) and the total of the order. The first would presumably be determined when the customer logged in (it would probably be stored in the session). The second value may also be stored in a session (after tax and shipping are factored in) or may be received by this page from the billing process. But as I don't have immediate access to either value (having skipped those steps), I'll create these two variables to fake it.

3. Include the database connection and turn off MySQL's autocommit mode.

   ```
   require_once
   → ('../mysqli_connect.php');
   mysqli_autocommit($dbc, FALSE);
   ```

   The mysqli_autocommit() function can turn MySQL's autocommit feature on or off. Since I'll want to use a transaction to ensure that the entire order is entered properly, I'll turn off autocommit first. If you have any questions about transactions, see Chapter 6 or the MySQL manual.

Script 17.10 The final script in the e-commerce application records the order information in the database. It uses transactions to ensure that the whole order gets submitted properly.

```
1    <?php # Script 17.10 - checkout.php
2    // This page inserts the order information
     into the table.
3    // This page would come after the billing
     process.
4    // This page assumes that the billing
     process worked (the money has been taken).
5
6    // Set the page title and include the HTML
     header.
7    $page_title = 'Order Confirmation';
8    include ('includes/header.html');
9
10   // Assume that the customer is logged in
     and that this page has access to the
     customer's ID:
11   $customer = 1; // Temporary.
12
13   // Assume that this page receives the
     order total.
14   $total = 178.93; // Temporary.
15
16   require_once ('../mysqli_connect.php'); //
     Connect to the database.
17
18   // Turn autocommit off.
19   mysqli_autocommit($dbc, FALSE);
20
21   // Add the order to the orders table...
22   $q = "INSERT INTO orders (customer_id,
     total) VALUES ($customer, $total)";
23   $r = mysqli_query($dbc, $q);
24   if (mysqli_affected_rows($dbc) == 1) {
25
26       // Need the order ID:
```

(script continues on next page)

RECORDING THE ORDERS

Script 17.10 *continued*

```
 Script
27    $oid = mysqli_insert_id($dbc);

28

29    // Insert the specific order contents
      into the database...

30

31    // Prepare the query:

32    $q = "INSERT INTO order_contents
      (order_id, print_id, quantity, price)
      VALUES (?, ?, ?, ?)";

33    $stmt = mysqli_prepare($dbc, $q);

34    mysqli_stmt_bind_param($stmt, 'iiid',
      $oid, $pid, $qty, $price);

35

36    // Execute each query, count the total
      affected:

37    $affected = 0;

38    foreach ($_SESSION['cart'] as $pid =>
      $item) {

39        $qty = $item['quantity'];

40        $price = $item['price'];

41        mysqli_stmt_execute($stmt);

42        $affected +=
          mysqli_stmt_affected_rows($stmt);

43    }

44

45    // Close this prepared statement:

46    mysqli_stmt_close($stmt);

47

48    // Report on the success....

49    if ($affected ==
      count($_SESSION['cart'])) { // Whohoo!

50

51        // Commit the transaction:

52        mysqli_commit($dbc);

53

54        // Clear the cart.
```

(script continues on next page)

4. Add the order to the *orders* table.

```
$q = "INSERT INTO orders
→ (customer_id, total) VALUES
→ ($customer, $total)";
```

```
$r = mysqli_query($dbc, $q);
```

```
if (mysqli_affected_rows($dbc) == 1) {
```

This query is very simple, entering only the customer's ID number and the total amount of the order into the *orders* table. The *order_date* field in the table will automatically be set to the current date and time, as it's a TIMESTAMP column.

5. Retrieve the order ID and prepare the query that inserts the order contents into the database.

```
$oid = mysqli_insert_id($dbc);
```

```
$q = "INSERT INTO order_contents
→ (order_id, print_id, quantity,
→ price) VALUES (?, ?, ?, ?)";
```

```
$stmt = mysqli_prepare($dbc, $q);
```

```
mysqli_stmt_bind_param($stmt, 'iiid',
→ $oid, $pid, $qty, $price);
```

The *order_id* value from the *orders* table is needed in the *order_contents* table to relate the two. The query itself inserts four values into the *order_contents* table, where there will be one record for each print purchased in this order. The query is defined, using placeholders for the values, and prepared. The mysqli_stmt_bind_param() function associates four variables to the placeholders. Their types, in order, are: integer, integer, integer, double (aka float).

continues on next page

6. Run through the cart, inserting each print into the database.

```
$affected = 0;

foreach ($_SESSION['cart'] as $pid =>
→ $item) {

    $qty = $item['quantity'];

    $price = $item['price'];

    mysqli_stmt_execute($stmt);

    $affected +=
    → mysqli_stmt_affected_rows($stmt);

}

mysqli_stmt_close($stmt);
```

By looping through the shopping cart, as I did in view_cart.php, I can access each item, one at a time. To be clear about what's happening here: the query has already been prepared—sent to MySQL and parsed—and variables have been assigned to the placeholders. Within the loop, two new variables are assigned values that come from the session. The mysqli_stmt_execute() function is called, which executes the prepared statement, using the variable values at that moment. The $oid value will not change from iteration to iteration, but $pid, $qty, and $price will.

If you have any problems with this or the other queries in this script, use your standard MySQL debugging techniques: print out the query using PHP, print out the MySQL error, and run the query using another interface, like the mysql client.

To confirm the success of all the queries, the number of affected rows must be tracked. A variable, $affected, is initialized to 0 outside of the loop. Within the loop, the number of affected rows is added to this variable after each execution of the prepared statement.

Script 17.10 *continued*

55	`//unset($_SESSION['cart']);`
56	
57	`// Message to the customer:`
58	`echo '<p>Thank you for your order. You will be notified when the items ship.</p>';`
59	
60	`// Send emails and do whatever else.`
61	
62	`} else { // Rollback and report the problem.`
63	
64	`mysqli_rollback($dbc);`
65	
66	`echo '<p>Your order could not be processed due to a system error. You will be contacted in order to have the problem fixed. We apologize for the inconvenience.</p>';`
67	`// Send the order information to the administrator.`
68	
69	`}`
70	
71	`} else { // Rollback and report the problem.`
72	
73	`mysqli_rollback($dbc);`
74	
75	`echo '<p>Your order could not be processed due to a system error. You will be contacted in order to have the problem fixed. We apologize for the inconvenience.</p>';`
76	
77	`// Send the order information to the administrator.`
78	

(script continues on next page)

Script 17.10 *continued*

```
                          Script
79   }

80

81   mysqli_close($dbc);

82

83   include ('./includes/footer.html');

84   ?>
```

7. Report on the success of the transaction.

```
if ($affected ==
→ count($_SESSION['cart'])) {
      mysqli_commit($dbc);
      unset($_SESSION['cart']);
      echo '<p>Thank you for your
      → order. You will be notified
      → when the items ship.</p>';
```

The conditional checks to see if as many records were entered into the database as exist in the shopping cart. In short: did each product get inserted into the *order_contents* table? If so, then the transaction is complete and can be committed. Then the shopping cart is emptied and the user is thanked. Logically you'd want to send a confirmation email to the customer here as well.

continues on next page

RECORDING THE ORDERS

Searching the Product Catalog

The structure of this database makes for a fairly easy search capability, should you desire to add it. As it stands, there are only three logical fields to use for search purposes: the print's name, its description, and the artist's last name. A LIKE query could be run on these using the following syntax:

```
SELECT...WHERE prints.description LIKE
  '%keyword%' OR prints.print_name
  LIKE '%keyword%' …
```

Another option would be to create an advanced search, wherein the user selects whether to search the artist's name or the print's name (similar to what the Internet Movie Database, www.imdb.com, does with people versus movie titles).

8. Handle any MySQL problems.

```
    } else {

        mysqli_rollback($dbc);

        echo '<p>Your order could not
        → be processed due to a
        → system error. You will be
        → contacted in order to have
        → the problem fixed. We
        → apologize for the
        → inconvenience.</p>';

    }

} else {

    mysqli_rollback($dbc);

    echo '<p>Your order could not be
    → processed due to a system
    → error. You will be contacted in
    → order to have the problem
    → fixed. We apologize for the
    → inconvenience.</p>';

}
```

The first else clause applies if the correct number of records were not inserted into the *order_contents* table. The second else clause applies if the original *orders* table query fails. In either case, the entire transaction should be undone, so the mysqli_rollback() function is called.

If a problem occurs at this point of the process, it's rather serious because the customer has been charged but no record of their order has made it into the database. This shouldn't happen, but just in case, you should write all the data to a text file and/or email all of it to the site's administrator or do *something* that will create a record of this order. If you don't, you'll have some very irate customers on your hands.

Figure 17.41 The customer's order is now complete, after entering all of the data into the database.

```
mysql> SELECT * FROM orders;
+----------+-------------+--------+---------------------+
| order_id | customer_id | total  | order_date          |
+----------+-------------+--------+---------------------+
|       10 |           1 | 178.93 | 2007-10-20 21:31:04 |
+----------+-------------+--------+---------------------+
1 row in set (0.00 sec)

mysql> SELECT * FROM order_contents;
+-------+----------+----------+----------+-------+-----------+
| oc_id | order_id | print_id | quantity | price | ship_date |
+-------+----------+----------+----------+-------+-----------+
|     1 |       10 |        1 |        1 | 29.95 | NULL      |
|     2 |       10 |        6 |        1 | 24.00 | NULL      |
|     3 |       10 |        7 |        2 | 32.99 | NULL      |
+-------+----------+----------+----------+-------+-----------+
3 rows in set (0.00 sec)

mysql>
```

Figure 17.42 The order in the MySQL database, as viewed using the mysql client.

9. Complete the page.

   ```
   mysqli_close($dbc);

   include ('./includes/footer.html');

   ?>
   ```

10. Save the file as checkout.php, place it in your Web directory, and test it in your Web browser (**Figure 17.41**).

    You can access this page by clicking the link in view_cart.php.

11. Confirm that the order was properly stored by looking at the database using another interface (**Figure 17.42**).

✔ Tips

- On a live, working site, you should assign the $customer and $total variables real values for this script to work. You would also likely want to make sure that the cart isn't empty prior to trying to store the order in the database.

- Creating an administrative script for viewing orders is rather simple. The first page would function like browse_prints.php, except it would perform a join across the *orders* and *customers* tables. This page could display the order total, the order ID, the order date, and the customer's name. You could link the order ID to a view_order.php script, passing the order ID in the URL. That script would use the order ID to retrieve the details of the order from the *order_contents* table (joining *prints* and *artists* in the process).

- If you'd like to learn more about e-commerce or see variations on this process, a quick search on the Web will turn up various examples and tutorials for making e-commerce applications with PHP.

RECORDING THE ORDERS

585

RECORDING THE ORDERS

The Checkout Process

The checkout process (which I will not discuss in detail) involves three steps:

1. Confirm the order.

2. Confirm/submit the billing and shipping information.

3. Process the billing information.

Steps 1 and 2 should be easy enough for intermediate programmers to complete on their own by now. In all likelihood, most of the data in Step 2 would come from the *customers* table, after the user has registered and logged in.

Step 3 is the trickiest one and could not be adequately addressed in any book. The particulars of this step vary greatly, depending upon how the billing is being handled and by whom. To make it more complex, the laws are different depending upon whether the product being sold is to be shipped later or is immediately delivered (like access to a Web site or a downloadable file).

Most small to medium-sized e-commerce sites use a third party to handle the financial transactions. Normally this involves sending the billing information, the order total, and a store number (a reference to the e-commerce site itself) to another Web site. This site will handle the actual billing process, debiting the customer and crediting the store. Then a result code will be sent back to the e-commerce site, which would be programmed to react accordingly. In such cases, the third-party handling the billing will provide the developer with the appropriate code and instructions to interface with their system.

INSTALLATION

As I mention in the introduction to the book, there are three technical requirements for executing all of the examples: MySQL (the database application), PHP (the scripting language), and the Web serving application (that PHP runs through). In this appendix I will describe the installation of these tools on two different platforms—Windows and Macintosh—which should cover the needs of most readers. (My assumption has always been that if you know enough to be running some version of Unix, you probably already know how to install software like PHP and MySQL.) If you are using a hosted Web site, all of this will already be provided for you, but these products are all free and easy enough to install, so putting them on your own computer still makes sense.

After covering installation, the appendix discusses related issues that will be of importance to almost every user. First, I introduce how to create users in MySQL. Next, I demonstrate how to test your PHP and MySQL installation, showing techniques you'll want to use when you begin working on any server for the first time. Finally, you'll learn how to configure PHP to change how it runs.

Before getting into the particulars, there's one little heads-up: PHP 6 has not been formally released at the time of this writing. I was able to use PHP 6 for all of the examples by building my own installation of PHP 6 for both Windows and Mac. However, in these steps I highly recommend using pre-made installers, so what you'll see in this appendix are installers and images for PHP 5. When PHP 6 is formally released, these installers will undoubtedly be updated and the steps will likely be the same or very nearly so.

Installation on Windows

In previous versions of this book I've advocated that Windows users take advantage of the available, and free, all-in-one installers. These programs will install and configure the Web server (like Apache, Abyss, or IIS), PHP, and MySQL for you. In past editions, after making that recommendation, I have also demonstrated how to install PHP and MySQL individually yourself. But repeated changes in those installation steps and multiple questions from readers having problems have convinced me to cut to the chase and walk through the all-in-one steps instead.

There are several all-in-one installers out there for Windows. The two that I see mentioned most frequently are XAMPP (www.apachefriends.org) and WAMP (www.wampserver.com). For this appendix, I'll use XAMPP, which runs on Windows 98, NT, 2000, 2003, XP.

Along with Apache, PHP, and MySQL, XAMPP also installs:

◆ PEAR, a library of PHP code

◆ Perl, a very popular programming language

◆ phpMyAdmin, the Web-based interface to a MySQL server

◆ A mail server (for sending email)

◆ Several useful extensions

At the time of this writing XAMPP (Version 1.6.4) installs both PHP 5.2.4 and 4.4.7, MySQL 5.0.45, Apache 2.2.6, and phpMyAdmin 2.11.0.

I'll run through the installation process in these next steps. Note that if you have any problems, you can use the book's supporting forum (www.DMCInsights.com/phorum/), but you'll probably have more luck turning to the XAMPP site (it is their product, after all). Also, the installer works really well and isn't that hard to use, so rather than detail every single step in the process, I'll highlight the most important considerations.

To install XAMPP on Windows:

1. Download the latest release of XAMPP for Windows from www.apachefriends.org.

   You'll need to click around a bit to find the download section, but eventually you'll come to an area like that in **Figure A.1**. Then click *Installer*, which is the specific item you want.

2. On your computer, double-click the downloaded file in order to begin the installation process.

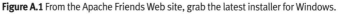

XAMPP for Windows 1.6.4, 2007/10/03		
Version	Size	Content
XAMPP Windows 1.6.4 [Basic package]		Apache HTTPD 2.2.6, MySQL 5.0.45, PHP 5.2.4 + 4.4.7 + PEAR + Switch, MiniPerl 5.8.7, Openssl 0.9.8e, PHPMyAdmin 2.11.1, XAMPP Control Panel 2.5, Webalizer 2.01-10, Mercury Mail Transport System v4.01a, FileZilla FTP Server 0.9.23, SQLite 2.8.15, ADODB 4.94, Zend Optimizer 3.3.0, XAMPP Security, Ming. For Windows 98, 2000, XP. See also ☑ README
☑ Installer	34 MB	Installer MD5 checksum: 34c14906adab7b0436f740bdd423bca7
☑ ZIP	80 MB	ZIP archive MD5 checksum: 202b0d5a81305e6a059158b3d115cd6c
☑ EXE (7-zip)	28 MB	Selfextracting 7-ZIP archive MD5 checksum: f79a7b63733e74b7b695c824d1d0f45c

Figure A.1 From the Apache Friends Web site, grab the latest installer for Windows.

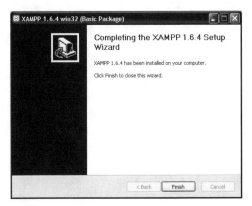

Figure A.2 Select where XAMPP should be installed.

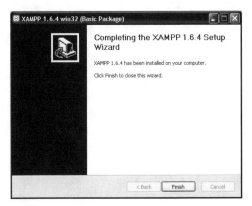

Figure A.3 The XAMPP options I'd recommend using.

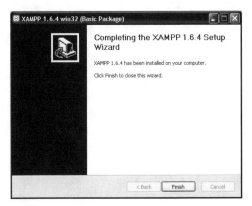

Figure A.4 Installation is complete!

3. Click your way through the installation process.

4. When prompted (**Figure A.2**), install XAMPP somewhere other than in the Program Files directory.

You shouldn't install it in the Program Files directory because of a permissions issue in Windows Vista. I'd recommend installing XAMPP in your root directory (e.g., C:\).

Wherever you decide to install the program, make note of that location, as you'll need to know it several other times as you work through this appendix.

5. If given the option, install both Apache and MySQL as services (**Figure A.3**).

Installing them as services just changes how they can be started and stopped, among other things.

6. After the installation process has done its thing, click Finish (**Figure A.4**).

After you click Finish, a DOS prompt (aka console window) will open up for XAMPP to try a couple of things. If you see a message like that in **Figure A.5**, choose the Unblock option (see the sidebar "On Firewalls" for more on this subject).

continues on next page

Figure A.5 If you're running a firewall of any kind, you'll see some messages like this when Apache, and possibly the other applications, are started. See the sidebar "On Firewalls" for more.

INSTALLATION ON WINDOWS

589

7. To start, stop, and configure XAMPP, open the XAMPP Control Panel (**Figure A.6**).

   A shortcut to the control panel may be created on your Desktop and in your Start menu, if you checked those options in Figure A.3.

8. Using the control panel, start Mercury (see Figure A.6).

   This is the mail server that XAMPP installs. It needs to be running in order to send email using PHP (see Chapter 10, "Web Application Development").

9. Immediately set a password for the root MySQL user.

   How you do this is explained later in the chapter.

✔ Tips

■ See the configuration section at the end of this chapter to learn how to configure PHP by editing the php.ini file.

■ Your Web root directory—where your PHP scripts should be placed in order to test them—is the htdocs folder in the directory where XAMPP was installed. For my installation (see Figure A.2), this would be C:\xampp\htdocs.

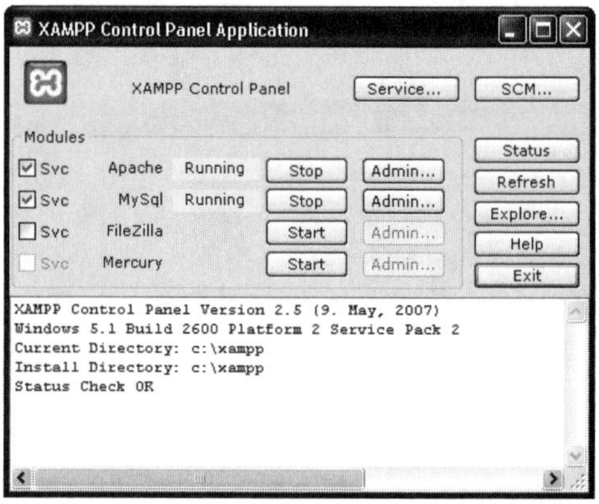

Figure A.6 The XAMPP Control Panel, your gateway to using all of the installed software.

On Firewalls

A firewall prevents communication over ports (a port being an access point to a computer). Versions of Windows starting with Service Pack 2 of XP include a built-in firewall. You can also download and install third-party firewalls, like ZoneAlarm. Firewalls improve the security of your computer, but they will also interfere with your ability to run Apache, MySQL, and some of the other tools used by XAMPP because these all use ports.

If you see a message like that in Figure A.5, choose Unblock. Otherwise, you can configure your firewall manually (for example, on Windows XP, it's done through Control Panel > Security Center). The ports that need to be open are: 80 (for Apache), 3306 (for MySQL), and 25 (for the Mercury mail server). If you have any problems starting or accessing one of these, disable your firewall and see if it works then. If so, you'll know the firewall is the problem and that it needs to be reconfigured.

Just to be clear, firewalls aren't found just on Windows, but in terms of the instructions in this appendix, the presence of a firewall will more likely trip up a Windows user than any other.

Installation on Mac OS X

The Macintosh was always a user-friendly computer, frequently used by Web developers for graphic design and HTML coding. Now, thanks to OS X, the Macintosh is a programmer's computer as well.

OS X, in version 10.5 (aka Leopard) at the time of this writing, has a Unix base with a glorious Macintosh interface. The Unix aspect of the operating system—predicated upon Free BSD—allows the use of standard Unix tools, such as PHP, MySQL, and Apache, with remarkable ease. In fact, Leopard comes with Apache and PHP already installed (but the latter may not be enabled by default).

As with any other Unix technology, you can download the source code for these packages and manually build them (I had to do exactly that for this book, and it's not too strenuous). However, I would recommend you take the easy way out and use Marc Liyanage's precompiled installers, available at www.entropy. ch/software/macosx. Marc—who ought to receive an award for the amount of OS X–specific work he does—provides up-to-date, easy-to-use installers for many different technologies. In this appendix, I'll install MySQL using the package provided by MySQL

and PHP using Marc's precompiled module. The instructions will demonstrate this process using Mac OS X 10.4 (Tiger), but the steps will be similar with Leopard or Panther (10.3).

As an aside, these instructions are particular to the basic version of Mac OS X. The server version of Mac OS X comes with Apache, PHP, and MySQL preinstalled.

To install and start MySQL:

1. Download the latest Generally Available (GA) release of the MySQL Community Server.

   Start at http://dev.mysql.com, and then click the appropriate links until you get to the package format installer for Mac OS X (**Figure A.7**). You'll want to download the one that matches your version of Mac OS X and your processor (if you have an Intel chip, use the x86 link; all others use PowerPC). Note that as I write this, Mac OS X 10.5 (Leopard) has only been out for two days, so MySQL's Web site (Figure A.7) doesn't list it as an option yet.

   After you click Pick a Mirror, you'll go through a couple more quick steps to download the actual file.

   continues on next page

Mac OS X (package format) downloads (platform notes)			
Mac OS X 10.3 (PowerPC, 32-bit)	5.0.45	66.2M	Pick a mirror
MD5: 24aeeb5f992284acb73101d28b0acb7a | Signature			
Mac OS X 10.4 (PowerPC, 32-bit)	5.0.45	62.6M	Pick a mirror
MD5: fbf4b96a0ea03e0b979096c44bc05f89 | Signature			
Mac OS X 10.4, (PowerPC, 64-bit)	5.0.45	60.9M	Pick a mirror
MD5: 8dac0fd7ad7673930cf0fe9931e182e3 | Signature			
Mac OS X 10.4 (x86)	5.0.45	61.0M	Pick a mirror
MD5: ccb1b2221bea3a613d0ddc085ee350d3 | Signature			

Figure A.7 The available downloads of MySQL for Mac OS X.

2. On your computer, double-click the downloaded file to mount it.

The downloaded file is a disk image that must then be mounted. The Disk Utility application will automatically do this once you double-click the `.dmg` file.

3. Open the disk image and double-click the *mysql-<version>...* package (**Figure A.8**) to begin the installation process.

If upgrading MySQL from a previous version, be certain to stop the existing MySQL server before installing the new version.

4. Follow through the installation process.

There are a few, very obvious steps, like agreeing to the license and selecting a destination disk (**Figure A.9**). Behind the scenes, the package will install all of the necessary files into the `/usr/local/mysql-<version>` directory. It will also create a symbolic link from `/usr/local/mysql` to this directory so that the MySQL files can be more easily accessed.

5. Install the MySQL preference pane by double-clicking the `MySQL.prefPane` file in the disk image (see Figure A.8).

After a couple more steps, you'll have installed a System Preferences pane so that you can easily start and stop MySQL.

6. Open System Preferences and click MySQL, under Other.

The new MySQL preferences pane will be available the next time you open the System Preferences. If System Preferences was open when you installed the MySQL pane, you'll need to quit and reopen System Preferences.

7. Use the new pane to start and stop the MySQL server (**Figure A.10**).

8. Immediately set a password for the root MySQL user.

How you do this is explained later in the chapter.

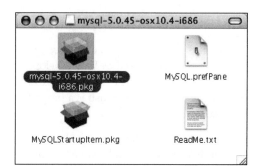

Figure A.8 The mounted disk image contains a few files. I have highlighted the actual installer in this image.

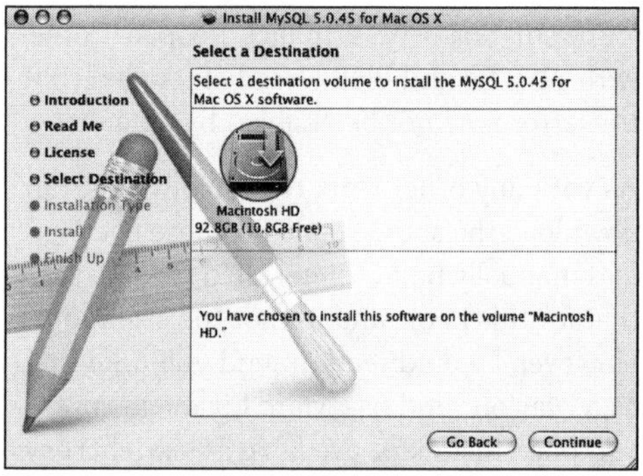

Figure A.9 Choose the disk where MySQL should be installed. If you have multiple hard drives or partitions (which I do not), install MySQL on the one with your operating system.

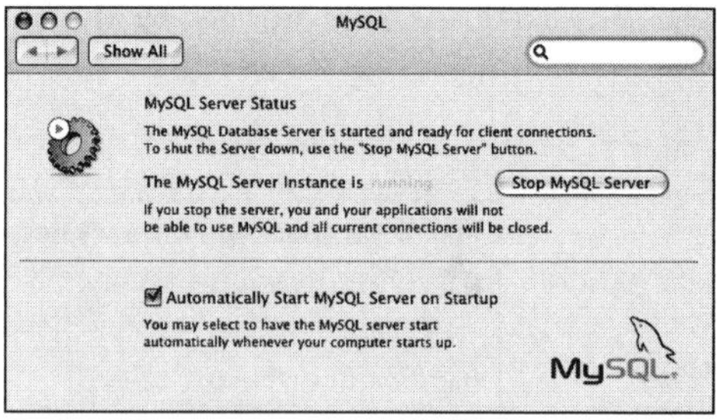

Figure A.10 The MySQL preferences pane can be used to control the MySQL database server.

Figure A.11 The PHP installer for Mac OS X.

entropy–php.mpkg

To install PHP:

1. In your Web browser, head over to www.entropy.ch/software/macosx/php.

2. Download the appropriate version of PHP for your operating system.

   At the time of this writing, the only difference between the two versions the site offers is that one is for Apache 1.3 and the other for Apache 2.4. Every version of Mac OS X I've used includes the 1.*x* version of Apache. I expect this will be the same in Leopard, too.

3. On your computer, double-click the downloaded file in order to access its contents.

4. Double-click the PHP package (**Figure A.11**) to begin the installation process.

5. Follow through the installer.

   The installer is really easy to use. You'll need to click Continue a couple of times, select a destination disk (this should be the same hard disk or partition that also has your operating system), and enter the administrative password.

✔ Tips

- See the section "Testing Your Installation" later in this appendix for guidelines on confirming the results of installing PHP and MySQL.

- See the configuration section at the end of this chapter to learn how to configure PHP by editing the php.ini file.

- Your Web root directory—where your PHP scripts should be placed in order to test them—is the Sites folder in your home directory. The URL you would use to access those files is http://localhost/~*<user>*, replacing *<user>* with the short version of your actual username (see the Accounts System Preferences pane to find this value if you don't know it).

INSTALLATION ON MAC OS X

593

MySQL Permissions

Once MySQL has been successfully installed, you should immediately set a password for the root user. Until you have done so, anyone can access your databases and have administrative-level privileges.

Once you've established the root user's password, you can begin establishing the users who will regularly access the database (for example, from PHP scripts). It is very insecure to use the root user for general purposes, so everyone should create some new MySQL users for regular use.

I'll walk you through both of these processes over the next couple of pages. Note that if you're using a hosted server, they'll likely create the MySQL users for you.

Setting the root user password

The mysqladmin utility, as the name might imply, is used to perform administrative-level tasks on your database. These include stopping MySQL, setting the root user's password, and more. (Some of the things you can do with mysqladmin can also be accomplished more directly within the mysql client, though.)

One of the first uses of mysqladmin is to assign a password to the root user. When MySQL is installed, there is no such value established. This is certainly a security risk that ought to be remedied before you begin to use the server. Just to clarify, your databases can have several users, just as your operating system might. The MySQL users are different from the operating system users, even if they share a common name. Therefore, the MySQL root user is a different entity than the operating system's root user, having different powers and even different passwords (preferably but not necessarily).

Most important, understand that the MySQL server must be running for you to use mysqladmin.

To assign a password to the root user:

1. Log in to your system from a command-line interface.

   For Mac OS X and Linux users, this is just a matter of opening the Terminal application. For Windows users, you'll need to choose Start > Run, then enter cmd in the prompt, and click OK.

2. Move to the mysql/bin directory.

   The proper command will be something like

   ```
   cd /usr/local/mysql/bin (Unix or Mac
   → OS X)
   ```

   or

   ```
   cd C:\xampp\mysql\bin (Windows)
   ```

   You'll need to change the values you use here to match where MySQL was installed (the bin directory will be found within it).

3. Enter the following, replacing *thepassword* with the password you want to use (**Figure A.12**):

   On Windows, you can just type

   ```
   mysqladmin -u root password
   → thepassword
   ```

   On Mac OS X and Unix you'll need to use

   ```
   ./mysqladmin -u root password
   → thepassword
   ```

Figure A.12 Establishing a password for the root MySQL user.

Keep in mind that passwords within MySQL are case-sensitive, so *Kazan* and *kazan* are not interchangeable. The term *password* that precedes the actual quoted password tells MySQL to encrypt that string.

✔ Tips

- Accessing the MySQL utilities from the command line can be daunting. If you have any problems with these steps, consult the MySQL manual, search the Web, or turn to the book's supporting forum for help.

- If you installed XAMPP on Windows, you'll need to change the phpMyAdmin configuration file after changing the MySQL root user password. Head to the directory where you installed XAMPP and open a file called `config.inc.php` in the `phpMyAdmin` folder. Find the line that says

Table A.1 The list of privileges that can be assigned to MySQL users.

MySQL Privileges	
PRIVILEGE	ALLOWS
SELECT	Read rows from tables.
INSERT	Add new rows of data to tables.
UPDATE	Alter existing data in tables.
DELETE	Remove existing data from tables.
INDEX	Create and drop indexes in tables.
ALTER	Modify the structure of a table.
CREATE	Create new tables or databases.
DROP	Delete existing tables or databases.
RELOAD	Reload the grant tables (and therefore enact user changes).
SHUTDOWN	Stop the MySQL server.
PROCESS	View and stop existing MySQL processes.
FILE	Import data into tables from text files.
GRANT	Create new users.
REVOKE	Remove the permissions of users.

```
$cfg['Servers'][$i]['password']
→ = '';
```

and change it to

```
$cfg['Servers'][$i]['password']
→ = 'the new password';
```

Creating users and privileges

After you have MySQL successfully up and running, and after you've established a password for the root user, it's time to begin adding other users. To improve the security of your applications, you should always create new users for accessing your databases, rather than continue to use the root user at all times.

The MySQL privileges system was designed to restrict access to only certain commands on specific databases by individual users. This technology is how a Web host, for example, can securely have several users accessing several databases, without concern. Each user within the MySQL system can have specific capabilities on specific databases from specific hosts (computers). The root user—the MySQL root user, not the system's—has the most power and is used for creating subusers, although subusers can be given rootlike powers (inadvisably so).

When a user attempts to do something with the MySQL server, MySQL will first check to see if the user has the permission to connect to the server at all (based upon the username, the user's password, and the information in the *user* table of the *mysql* database). Second, MySQL will check to see if the user has the permission to run the specific SQL statement on the specific databases—for example, to select data, insert data, or create a new table. To determine this, MySQL uses the *db*, *host*, *user*, *tables_priv*, and *columns_priv* tables, again from the *mysql* database. **Table A.1** lists the various privileges that can be set on a user-by-user basis.

continues on next page

MySQL PERMISSIONS

There are a handful of ways to set users and privileges within MySQL. One way is to use the mysql client to execute a `GRANT` command. The syntax goes like this:

```
GRANT privileges ON database.*
TO username IDENTIFIED BY 'password'
```

For the *privileges* aspect of this statement, you can list specific privileges from the list in Table A.1, or you can allow for all of them using `ALL` (which is not prudent). The *database.** part of the statement specifies which database and tables the user can work on. You can name specific tables using the *database. tablename* syntax or allow for every database with `*.*` (again, not prudent). Finally, you can specify the username and a password.

The username has a maximum length of 16 characters. When creating a username, be sure to avoid spaces (use the underscore instead) and note that usernames are case-sensitive. The password has no length limit but is also case-sensitive. The passwords will be encrypted within the *mysql* database, meaning they cannot be recovered in a plain text format. Omitting the `IDENTIFIED BY 'password'` clause results in that user not being required to enter a password (which, once again, should be avoided).

Finally, there is the option of limiting users to particular hostnames. The hostname is either the name of the computer on which the MySQL server is running (*localhost* being the most common value here) or the name of the computer from which the user will be accessing the server. This can even be an IP address, should you choose. To specify a particular host, change your statement to

```
GRANT privileges ON database.*
TO username@hostname
IDENTIFIED BY 'password'
```

To allow for any host, use the hostname wildcard character (`%`).

```
GRANT privileges ON database.*

TO username@'%' IDENTIFIED BY 'password'
```

As an example of this process, I will create a new user with specific privileges for a database called *sitename*. The following instructions will require using the mysql client or a similar interface to MySQL. I discuss how to access this tool in detail in Chapter 4, "Introduction to SQL and MySQL."

To create new users:

1. Log in to your system from a command-line interface.

   For Mac OS X and Linux users, this is just a matter of opening the Terminal application. For Windows users, you'll need to choose Start > Run, then enter cmd in the prompt, and click OK.

2. Log in to the mysql client.

   If you are using Windows, the command would be

   `C:\xampp\mysql\bin\mysql -u root -p`

   If you are using Mac OS X or Unix, you'll need to type

   `/usr/local/mysql/bin/mysql -u root -p`

   In both cases, if MySQL was not installed in that directory, you'll need to change your pathname accordingly.

   At the prompt, enter the root user's password.

   If you don't feel like messing with all of this, you can use phpMyAdmin to create the users instead. It's installed by XAMPP but also freely available to download and install yourself.

3. Create the *example* database.

   `CREATE DATABASE example;`

   Creating a database is quite easy, using the preceding syntax. This command will work as long as you're connected as a user with the proper privileges.

4. Create a user that has basic-level privileges on the *example* database (**Figure A.13**).

   `GRANT SELECT, INSERT, UPDATE, DELETE`

   `ON example.* TO`

   `'someuser'@'localhost'`

   `IDENTIFIED BY 'somepass';`

   The generic *someuser* user can browse through records (SELECT from tables) and add (INSERT), modify (UPDATE), or DELETE them. The user can only connect from *localhost* (from the same computer) and can only access the *example* database.

5. Apply the changes.

   `FLUSH PRIVILEGES;`

   The changes just made will not take effect until you have told MySQL to reset the list of acceptable users and privileges, which is what this command will do. Forgetting this step and then being unable to access the database using the newly created users is a common mistake.

✔ Tip

- Any database whose name begins with *test_* can be accessed by any user who has permission to connect to MySQL. Therefore, be careful not to create databases named this way unless it truly is experimental.

Figure A.13 Creating a user that can perform basic tasks on one database.

Testing Your Installation

Now that you've installed everything and created the necessary MySQL users, you should test the installation. I'll create two quick PHP scripts for this purpose. In all likelihood, if an error occurred, you would already know it by now, but these steps will allow you to perform tests on your (or any other) server before getting into complicated PHP programming.

The first script being run is `phpinfo.php`. It both tests if PHP is enabled and shows a ton of information about the PHP installation. As simple as this script is, it is one of the most important scripts PHP developers ever write because it provides so much valuable knowledge.

The second script will serve two purposes. It will first see if support for MySQL has been enabled. If not, you'll need to see the next section of this chapter to change that. The script will also test if the MySQL user has permission to connect to a specific MySQL database.

To test PHP:

1. Create the following PHP document in a text editor (**Script A.1**).

```
<?php
phpinfo();
?>
```

The `phpinfo()` function returns the configuration information for a PHP installation in a table. It's the perfect tool to test that PHP is working properly.

You can use almost any application to create your PHP script as long as it can save the file in a plain text format.

2. Save the file as `phpinfo.php`.

You need to be certain that the file's extension is just `.php`. Be careful when using Notepad on Windows, as it will secretly append `.txt`. Similarly, TextEdit on Mac OS X wants to save everything as `.rtf`.

3. Place the file in the proper directory on your server.

What the proper directory is depends upon your operating system and your Web server. If you are using a hosted site, check with the hosting company. For Windows users who installed XAMPP, the directory is called `htdocs` and is within the XAMPP directory. For Mac OS X users, the proper directory is called `Sites`, found within your home folder.

Script A.1 The `phpinfo.php` script tests and reports upon the PHP installation.

```
1   <?php
2   phpinfo();
3   ?>
```

Figure A.14 The information for this server's PHP configuration.

4. Test the PHP script by accessing it in your Web browser (**Figure A.14**).

Run this script in your Web browser by going to http://*your.url.here*/phpinfo.php. On your own computer, this may be something like http://localhost/phpinfo.php (Windows with XAMPP) or http://localhost/~*<user>*/phpinfo.php, where *<user>* is your short username (Mac OS X).

Script A.2 The mysqli_test.php script tests for MySQL support in PHP and if the proper MySQL user privileges have been set.

```
1   <?php

2   mysqli_connect ('localhost', 'someuser',
    'somepass', 'example');

3   ?>
```

To test PHP and MySQL:

1. Create a new PHP document in your text editor (**Script A.2**).

```
<?php

mysqli_connect ('localhost',
→ 'someuser', 'somepass', 'example');

?>
```

This script will attempt to connect to the MySQL server using the username and password just established in this appendix.

2. Save the file as mysqli_test.php, place it in the proper directory for your Web server, and test it in your Web browser (**Figure A.15**).

If the script was able to connect, the result will be a blank page. If it could not connect, you should see an error message like that in **Figure A.16**. Most likely this indicates a problem with the MySQL user's privileges (see the preceding section of this chapter).

If you see an error like in **Figure A.17**, this means that PHP does not have MySQL support enabled. See the next section of this chapter for the solution.

continues on next page

Figure A.15 The PHP script was able to connect to the MySQL server as indicated by this blank page. Any errors would have been revealed (as in Figure A.16).

Warning: mysqli_connect() [function.mysqli-connect]: (28000/1045): Access denied for user 'someuser'@'localhost' (using password: YES) in /Applications/Abyss Web Server/htdocs/mysqli_test.php on line 3

Figure A.16 The script was not able to connect to the MySQL server.

Fatal error: Call to undefined function mysqli_connect() in C:\xampp\htdocs\mysqli_test.php on line 2

Figure A.17 The script was not able to connect to the MySQL server because PHP does not have MySQL support enabled.

✔ Tips

- For security reasons, you should not leave the `phpinfo.php` script on a live server because it gives away too much information.

- If you run a PHP script in your Web browser and it attempts to download the file, then your Web server is not recognizing that file extension as PHP. Check your Apache (or other Web server) configuration to correct this.

- PHP scripts must always be run from a URL starting with *http://*. They cannot be run directly off a hard drive (as if you had opened it in your browser).

- If a PHP script cannot connect to a MySQL server, it is normally because of a permissions issue. Double-check the username, password, and host being used, and be absolutely certain to flush the MySQL privileges.

Enabling Extension Support

Many PHP configuration options can be altered by just editing the `php.ini` file. But enabling (or disabling) an extension—in other words, adding support for extended functionality—requires more effort. To enable support for an extension for just a single PHP page, you can use the `dl()` function. To enable support for an extension for all PHP scripts requires a bit of work. Unfortunately, for Unix and Mac OS X users, you'll need to rebuild PHP with support for this new extension. Windows users have it easier:

First, edit the `php.ini` file (see the steps in this section), removing the semicolon before the extension you want to enable. For example, to enable Improved MySQL Extension support, you'll need to find the line that says

```
;extension=php_mysqli.dll
```

and remove that semicolon.

Next, find the line that sets the *extension_dir* and adjust this for your PHP installation. Assuming you installed PHP into `C:\php`, then your `php.ini` file should say

```
extension_dir = "C:/php/ext"
```

This tells PHP where to find the extension.

Next, make sure that the actual extension file, `php_mysqli.dll` in this example, exists in the extension directory.

Save the `php.ini` file and restart your Web server. If the restart process indicates an error finding the extension, double-check to make sure that the extension exists in the *extension_dir* and that your pathnames are correct. If you continue to have problems, search the Web or use the book's corresponding forum for assistance.

Configuring PHP

If you have installed PHP on your own computer, then you also have the ability to configure how PHP runs. Changing PHP's behavior is very simple and will most likely be required at some point in time. Just a few of the things you'll want to consider adjusting are

♦ Whether or not *display_errors* is on

♦ The default level of error reporting

♦ The Unicode settings

♦ Support for the Improved MySQL Extension functions

♦ SMTP values for sending emails

What each of these means—if you don't already know—is covered in the book's chapters and in the PHP manual. But for starters, I would highly recommend that you make sure that *display_errors* is on.

Changing PHP's configuration is really simple. The short version is: edit the php.ini file and then restart the Web server. But because many different problems can arise, I'll cover configuration in more detail. If you are looking to enable support for an extension, like the MySQL functions, the configuration is more complicated (see the sidebar).

To configure PHP:

1. Run a phpinfo() script (see the preceding section) in your Web browser.

2. In the resulting page, look for the line that says "Configuration File (php.ini) Path" (see Figure A.14).

   It should be about six rows down in the table.

3. Note the location of your php.ini file.

   This will be the value listed on the line mentioned in Step 2 (it'll be found in the right-hand column).

   This is the active configuration file PHP is using. Your server may have multiple php.ini files on it, but this is the one that counts.

4. Open the php.ini file in any text editor.

   If you are using Mac OS X, you do not have easy access to the php.ini directory. You can either use the Terminal to access the file, open it using BBEdit's *Open Hidden* option, or use something like TinkerTool to show hidden files in the Finder.

   If you go to the directory listed and there's no php.ini file there, you'll need to download this file from the PHP Web site (it's part of the PHP source code).

continues on next page

CONFIGURING PHP

5. Make any changes you want, keeping in mind the following:

▲ Comments are marked using a semicolon. Anything after the semicolon is ignored.

▲ Instructions on what most of the settings mean are included in the file.

▲ The top of the file lists general information with examples. Do not change these values! Change the settings where they appear later in the file.

▲ For safety purposes, don't change any original settings. Just comment them out (by preceding the line with a semicolon) and then add the new, modified line afterward.

▲ Add a comment (using the semicolon) to mark what changes you made and when. For example:

```
; unicode.semantics = Off
; Next line added by LEU
→ 10/28/2007
unicode.semantics = On
```

6. Save the file.

7. Restart the Web server (Apache, IIS, Xitami, etc.).

You do not have to restart the entire computer, just the Web serving application (Apache, IIS, etc.). How you do this depends upon the application being used, the operating system, and the installation method. Windows users can use the XAMPP Control Panel (see Figure A.6). Mac OS X users can stop and then start Personal Web Sharing (under System Preferences > Sharing). Unix users can normally just enter `apachectl graceful` in a Terminal window.

8. Rerun the `phpinfo.php` script to make sure the changes took effect.

✔ Tips

■ Any changes to PHP's (or Apache's) configuration file do not take effect until you restart Apache. Always make sure that you restart the Web server to enact changes!

■ Editing the wrong `php.ini` file is a common mistake. This is why I recommend that you run a `phpinfo.php` script to see which `php.ini` file PHP is using.

INDEX

F

G